LANGUAGE AS SYMBOLIC ACTION

· LANGUAGE AS ·

SYMBOLIC ACTION

Essays on Life, Literature, and Method

■ *by* KENNETH BURKE ■

UNIVERSITY OF CALIFORNIA PRESS/BERKELEY & LOS ANGELES 1966

UNIVERSITY OF CALIFORNIA PRESS
BERKELEY AND LOS ANGELES, CALIFORNIA
CAMBRIDGE UNIVERSITY PRESS
LONDON, ENGLAND
© 1966 by The Regents of the University of California
Library of Congress Catalog Card Number: 66-27655
Designed by Hans Wehrli
Printed in the United States of America

To J. Sibling W.

Preface

The title for this collection was the title of a course in literary criticism that I gave for many years at Bennington College. And much of the material presented here was used in that course. The title should serve well to convey the gist of these various pieces. For all of them are explicitly concerned with the attempt to define and track down the implications of the term "symbolic action," and to show how the marvels of literature and language look when considered from that point of view. (I take it for granted that any selection of terms used for explanatory purposes is, in effect, a "point of view.")

As for the subtitle: Much good criticism has been written in keeping with some such pair of terms as "Literature and Life," or "Art and Nature." And perhaps a critic should always confine himself to an alignment of that sort if he aims at maximum sales to the general public.

But what of the great difference between "Poetry" and "Poetics"? When posing that problem, don't we encounter a "scholastic" dimension, involving a concern with critical *method* that requires consideration in its own right? There is "Life"; there is "Literature" in the sense of stories, poems, plays, and the like; and there is the criticism of "Life" or "Literature" or of criticism itself.

The third term in my subtitle reflects the fact that the ways of education as an institution are not reducible to terms of either "Literature" or "Life," but involve (however unsystematically) a concern with systematic inquiries into the nature of both.

The third term has the advantage that even readers who do not share one's judgments on "Literature" and "Life" might find something of use in one's methods and talk of method. In any case these essays are intended to exemplify: A theory of language, a philosophy of language based on that theory, and methods of analysis developed in accordance with the theory and the philosophy. The term for the lot, as one will be reminded often, is "Dramatism."

Since each of these chapters was originally meant to stand alone (either as an article or as a public talk or both), at times some basic tenets of our position had to be restated. And the attempt to make the first five essays serve as a summation of the book as a whole imposed the same requirement somewhat. But I have retained the overlaps on the assumption that their recurrence in varying contexts can help indicate the range of their relevance, while their retention in different spots along the way should help preserve for each piece its original measure of self-sufficiency. And when he encounters recurrences, may the reader please think of us as mulling over something, forever hanging on, so that, if we mention B when talking about A, we're likely to mention A when talking about B. And why not, in the effort, to bring out as clearly as possible the basic pattern of one's thinking?

When in these pieces I speak of "prophesying after the event" (as I shall on several occasions), please note that the expression is used somewhat *figuratively*. I do not mean "prophecy" as when announcing the assassination of some important public figure before the event actually takes place. I merely have in mind a systematic analysis of the implications inherent in terms. For instance, one need not be clairvoyant to "anticipate" a work's structure through observations of this sort: "It stands to reason that, if there is to be an assassination, there must be an assassin; there must be a victim; there must be the kind of circumstances that make the assassination possible," etc. "Prophecy" as so conceived is hardly other than a study in tautology (as with the "tautological dog" of my fourth chapter, or my "Cycle of Terms Implicit in the Idea of 'Order' " in *The Rhetoric of Religion*).

Being designed to help reveal the logic of a given symbol system, "prophecy" in this sense should help correct the current cult of the irrational which often makes critics fail to discern and properly evaluate the resources of internal consistency whereby the terms of a symbol system imply one another. And in the piously fearful study of ourselves through the methodic or haphazard study of ingenious texts, we keep peering into such possibilities.

The "methodism" inherent in the nature of formal education is preparatory for students but consummatory for educators—and the humanist might be redefined as a person who, carrying the principle of study beyond the stage of mere preparation, transforms it into a permanent aspect of his personality. In effect he asks himself, not just "How can I most effectively do such-and-such?" but "How can I *methodically meditate* on our involvement in kinds of action not wholly reducible to terms of motion?"

We are the instruments of our instruments. And we are necessarily susceptible to the particular ills that result from our prowess in the ways of symbolicity. Yet, too, we are equipped in principle to join in the enjoying of all such quandaries, until the last time.

Men's modes of symbolic action are simultaneously untanglings and entanglements. And these pieces are offered in that spirit.

Who can know how much I must be indebted to masters, students, colleagues, correspondents, enemies, and audiences generally for many of the statements here made without acknowledgement? I certainly can't, though much is unquestionably developed from interchange of one sort or another. Meanwhile, I can at least explicitly thank those kindly editors who printed the substance of these essays in the following magazines and who concurred in the republication here.

Perhaps the most methodic way to give credit for official permission to reprint items that have appeared elsewhere is by making a division between my own articles and quotations from other sources.

As regards the articles themselves, in the order of their appearance, I am indebted to the following persons or sources, listed as follows:

"Definition of Man" is reprinted from *Hudson Review*, Vol. XVI, no. 4 (Winter, 1963–1964). Copyright © by The Hudson Review, Inc.

My essay "Poetics in Particular, Language in General" contains portions of an article built around Poe, and originally published in the October, 1961, issue of *Poetry*.

"Terministic Screens." In *Proceedings of the American Catholic Philosophical Association*, Vol. XXXIX (1965).

"*Coriolanus*—and the Delights of Faction." Reprinted from *Hudson Review*, Vol. XIX, no. 2 (Summer, 1966). Copyright © 1966 by The Hudson Review, Inc.

"Shakespearean Persuasion—*Antony and Cleopatra*." *Antioch Review* (Spring, 1964). Copyright 1964 by The Antioch Press, Yellow Springs, Ohio.

"*Timon of Athens* and Misanthropic Gold." The Laurel Shakespeare; Francis Fergusson, General Editor. Copyright 1963 by Dell Publishing Company, Inc.

"Form and Persecution in the *Oresteia*." *Sewanee Review*, Vol. LX (Summer, 1952).

"Goethe's *Faust, Part I*." *Chicago Review* (Fall, 1954). This piece was originally prepared for the Faculty Seminar of the Institute for Religious and Social Studies of the Jewish Theological Seminary of America, March 19, 1953, and is used with permission of the Institute.

"*Faust II*—The Ideas Behind the Imagery." *Centennial Review*, Vol. IX, no. 4 (Fall, 1965).

"I, Eye, Ay—Concerning Emerson's Early Essay on 'Nature' and the Machinery of Transcendence." *Sewanee Review*, Vol. LXXIV, no. 4 (Fall, 1966). The University of Michigan Press is publishing the same essay in the volume *Transcendentalism and Its Legacy*, edited by Myron Simon and Thornton H. Parsons.

" 'Kubla Khan,' Proto-Surrealist Poem." *Master Poems of the English Language*, edited by Oscar Williams. Trident Press, 1966.

"Social and Cosmic Mystery: *A Passage to India.*" *Lugano Review.* Vol. I/ 5–6 (Summer, 1966).

"Version, Con-, Per-, and In- (Thoughts on Djuna Barnes's *Nightwood*)." *Southern Review*, Vol. II, no. 2, n. s. (Spring, 1966).

"The Vegetal Radicalism of Theodore Roethke." *Sewanee Review*, Vol. LVIII (1950).

"William Carlos Williams, 1883–1963." Reprinted from *New York Review of Books*, Vol. I, no. 2. Copyright © 1963 by The New York Review.

"Rhetoric and Poetics." Copy of a talk presented at a Symposium on the History and Significance of Rhetoric, held in May, 1965, under the auspices of the Department of Classics at the University of California, Los Angeles.

"The Thinking of the Body (Comments on the Imagery of Catharsis in Literature)." Reprinted from *Psychoanalytic Review*, vol. 50, no. 3 (Fall, 1963), through the courtesy of the editors of *Psychoanalytic Review* and the publisher, National Association for Psychoanalysis, New York, New York.

"*Somnia ad Urinandum*: More Thoughts on Motion and Action." *Limbo*, Vol. I, no. 12 (February, 1965).

"What Are the Signs of What? (A Theory of 'Entitlement')." *Anthropological Linguistics* (June, 1962).

"Myth, Poetry, and Philosophy." *Journal of American Folklore*, Vol. LXXIII (October-December, 1960).

"A Dramatistic View of the Origins of Language." *Quarterly Journal of Speech*, Vol. XXXVIII, nos. 3, 4 (October, December, 1952); Vol. XXXIX, nos. 1, 2 (February, April, 1963).

"Formalist Criticism: Its Principles and Limits." *Texas Quarterly* (Summer, 1966).

For permission to quote from other authors, I would state my indebtedness to:

The author and to Harcourt, Brace and World, Inc., for quotations from E. M. Forster's *A Passage to India* and Cleanth Brooks's *The Well-Wrought Urn* (Harvest Books: Copyright 1947 by Cleanth Brooks).

Farrar, Straus & Giroux, Inc., for quotations from *Knowledge and Experience in the Philosophy of F. H. Bradley.* (Copyright © 1964 by T. S. Eliot.)

Butterworths and the Colston Research Society, for quotations from *Metaphor and Symbol*, edited by L. C. Knights and Basil Cottle. Proceedings of the Twelfth Symposium of the Colston Research Society held in the University of Bristol, March, 1960.

Susan Sontag, Farrar, Straus & Giroux, Inc., and Eyre and Spottiswoode, for quotation from *The Benefactor*, by Susan Sontag (Farrar, Straus and Company: Copyright © 1963 by Susan Sontag).

Wallace Fowlie, the University of Chicago Press, and Dennis Dobson, for quotations from *Mallarmé, With Ten Line Drawings by Henri Matisse*, by Wallace Fowlie (published, 1953; First Phoenix edition, 1962).

Mrs. Beatrice Roethke and Doubleday & Company, Inc., for quotations from *The Lost Son and Other Poems*, by Theodore Roethke (Doubleday & Company, Inc.: Copyright 1948 by Theodore Roethke).

Mrs. William Carlos Williams and New Directions, for quotations from *Collected Earlier Poems*, by William Carlos Williams (New Directions: Copyright 1938, 1951 by William Carlos Williams) and *Collected Later Poems*, by William Carlos Williams (New Directions: Copyright 1944, 1948, 1950, © 1963 by William Carlos Williams).

Yale University Press, for quotations from Cleanth Brooks's *William Faulkner: the Yoknapatawpha Country* (published, 1963).

To the author and the *Kenyon Review* for quotations from Cleanth Brooks, "The Formalist Critic," the *Kenyon Review* (1951).

Of my own work, my essay "Rhetoric and Poetics" ends on an excerpt from a declamatory poem, "Introduction to What," that was originally published in *Location*, Vol. I, no. 1 (Spring, 1963). The recipe for tragedy at the end of my essay on *Coriolanus* originally appeared in *Arts In Society*, Vol. 2, no. 3 (1963). The clauses in my "Definition of Man" (minus the "codicil") were discussed more briefly in my book *The Rhetoric of Religion* (Beacon Press, 1961). And the poem on which that essay ends was originally published in the Duquesne University Festival issue of *Overture* (1959).

K. B.

Contents

PART I

FIVE SUMMARIZING ESSAYS

Note

The first five of these chapters have been set apart from the rest because I think that, taken as a group, they best convey the gist of the collection as a whole. The remainder could be viewed as developing one or another aspect of the same position, with more arguments or evidence, and wider application.

Since a definition of man is at least *implicit* in any writer's comments on cultural matters, the book begins with an essay on that subject. But the definition's concern with "symbolic action" involves a distinction between the limiting of this concept to the specifically artistic and a broader application to symbol systems in general; so the second essay deals with that problem. Since all definitions involve the use of terminology, and many kinds of terminology are available, the third essay attempts to argue for a "Dramatistic" solution. But, dialectic being what it is, any formal concern with the realm of the symbolic also prods us to inquire about the relation between the symbolic and its nonsymbolic or extrasymbolic context; and in dealing with the relation between these two realms of the symbolic and nonsymbolic, the fourth chapter considers ambiguities inherent in the range of meanings that complicate the concept of the "Unconscious." The fifth piece ties things down by focusing on a single work.

Further, since the third essay had closed on an admittedly ideal (Platonistic) view of a Dramatistic terminology, the fifth essay, in studying one Shakespearean tragedy, emphasizes the drastic nature of a troublesome motive that had been considered, but not fully developed, in the opening definition. For a Dramatistic definition of man requires an admonitory stress upon *victimage* as the major temptation in the symbol systems by which men build up their ideas, concepts, and images of identity and community (with correspondingly troublesome attitudes that prod to correspondingly turbulent acts).

Chapter One

Definition of Man

I

First, a few words on definition in general. Let's admit it: I see in a definition the critic's equivalent of a lyric, or of an aria in opera. Also, we might note that, when used in an essay, as with Aristotle's definition of tragedy in his *Poetics*, a definition so sums things up that all the properties attributed to the thing defined can be as though "derived" from the definition. In actual development, the definition may be the last thing a writer hits upon. Or it may be formulated somewhere along the line. But logically it is prior to the observations that it summarizes. Thus, insofar as all the attributes of the thing defined fit the definition, the definition should be viewed as "prior" in this purely nontemporal sense of priority.

Definitions are also the critic's equivalent of the lyric (though a poet might not think so!) in that the writer usually "hits on them." They are "breakthroughs," and thus are somewhat hard to come by. We should always keep trying for them—but they don't always seem to "click."

A definition should have just enough clauses, and no more. However, each clause should be like a chapter head, under which appropriate observations might be assembled, as though derived from it.

I am offering my Definition of Man in the hope of either persuading the reader that it fills the bill, or of prompting him to decide what should be added, or subtracted, or in some way modified.

II

Man is the symbol-using animal.

Granted, it doesn't come as much of a surprise. But our definition is being offered not for any possible paradoxical value. The aim is to get as essential a set of clauses as possible, and to meditate on each of them.

I remember one day at college when, on entering my philosophy class, I found all blinds up and the windows open from the top, while a bird kept flying nervously about the ceiling. The windows were high, they extended almost to the ceiling; yet the bird kept trying to escape by batting against the ceiling rather than dipping down and flying out one of the open windows. While it kept circling thus helplessly over our heads, the instructor explained that this was an example of a "tropism." This particular bird's instinct was to escape by flying *up*, he said; hence it ignored the easy exit through the windows.

But how different things would be if the bird could speak and we could speak his language. What a simple statement would have served to solve his problem. "Fly down just a foot or so, and out one of those windows."

Later, I ran across another example that I cite because it has further implications, with regard to a later clause in our definition. I witnessed the behavior of a wren that was unquestionably a genius within the terms of its species. The parents had succeeded in getting all of a brood off the nest except one particularly stubborn or backward fellow who still remained for a couple of days after the others had flown. Despite all kinds of threats and cajolery, he still lingered, demanding and getting the rations which all concerned seem to consider his rightful lot. Then came the moment of genius. One of the parent wrens came to the nest with a morsel of food. But instead of simply giving it to the noisy youngster, the parent bird held it at a distance. The fledgling in the nest kept stretching its neck out farther and farther with its beak gaping until, of a sudden, instead of merely putting the morsel of food into the bird's mouth, the parent wren clamped its beak shut on the young one's lower mandible, and with a slight jerk caused the youngster, with his outstretched neck, to lose balance and tumble out of the nest.

Surely this was an "act" of genius. This wren had discovered how to use the principle of leverage as a way of getting a young bird off the nest. Had that exceptionally brilliant wren been able to conceptualize this discovery in such terms as come easy to symbol systems, we can imagine him giving a dissertation on "The Use of the Principle of Leverage as an Improved Method for Unnesting Birds or Debirding a Nest." And within a few years the invention would spread throughout all birddom, with an incalculable saving in bird-hours as compared with the traditional turbulent and inefficient method still in general practice.

There are three things to note about this incident:

1) The ability to describe this method in words would have readily made it possible for all other birds to take over this same "act" of genius, though they themselves might never have hit upon it.

2) The likelihood is that even this one wren never used the method again. For the ability to conceptualize implies a kind of *attention* without which this innovation could probably not advance beyond the condition of a mere accident to the condition of an invention.

3) On the happier side, there is the thought that at least, through lack of such ability, birds are spared our many susceptibilities to the ways

of demagogic spellbinders. They cannot be filled with fantastic hatreds for alien populations they know about mainly by mere hearsay, or with all sorts of unsettling new expectations, most of which could not possibly turn out as promised.

The "symbol-using animal," yes, obviously. But can we bring ourselves to realize just what that formula implies, just how overwhelmingly much of what we mean by "reality" has been built up for us through nothing but our symbol systems? Take away our books, and what little do we know about history, biography, even something so "down to earth" as the relative position of seas and continents? What is our "reality" for today (beyond the paper-thin line of our own particular lives) but all this clutter of symbols about the past combined with whatever things we know mainly through maps, magazines, newspapers, and the like about the present? In school, as they go from class to class, students turn from one idiom to another. The various courses in the curriculum are in effect but so many different terminologies. And however important to us is the tiny sliver of reality each of us has experienced firsthand, the whole overall "picture" is but a construct of our symbol systems. To meditate on this fact until one sees its full implications is much like peering over the edge of things into an ultimate abyss. And doubtless that's one reason why, though man is typically the symbol-using animal, he clings to a kind of naïve verbal realism that refuses to realize the full extent of the role played by symbolicity in his notions of reality.

In responding to words, with their overt and covert modes of persuasion ("progress" is a typical one that usually sets expectations to vibrating), we like to forget the kind of relation that really prevails between the verbal and the nonverbal. In being a link between us and the nonverbal, words are by the same token a screen separating us from the nonverbal—though the statement gets tangled in its own traces, since so much of the "we" that is separated from the nonverbal by the verbal would not even exist were it not for the verbal (or for our symbolicity in general, since the same applies to the symbol systems of dance, music, painting, and the like).

A road map that helps us easily find our way from one side of the continent to the other owes its great utility to its exceptional existential poverty. It tells us absurdly little about the trip that is to be experienced in a welter of detail. Indeed, its value for us is in the very fact that it is so essentially inane.

Language referring to the realm of the nonverbal is necessarily talk about things in terms of what they are not—and in this sense we start out beset by a paradox. Such language is but a set of labels, signs for helping us find our way about. Indeed, they can even be so useful that they help us to invent ingenious ways of threatening to destroy ourselves. But even accuracy of this powerful sort does not get around the fact that such terms are sheer emptiness, as compared with the substance of the things they name. Nor is such abstractness confined to the language of scientific prose. Despite the concrete richness of the imagery in Keats's poems, his letters repeatedly refer to his art as "abstract." And the same kind of considerations would apply to the symbol systems of all other arts. Even so bodily a form of expression as the dance is abstract in this sense. (Indeed, in this regard it is so abstract that, when asking students to sum up the gist of a plot, I usually got the best results from dance majors, with music students a close second. Students specializing in literature or the social sciences tended to get bogged down in details. They were less apt at "abstracting.")

When a bit of talking takes place, just what is doing the talking? Just where are the words coming from? Some of the motivation must derive from our animality, and some from our symbolicity. We hear of "brainwashing," of schemes whereby an "ideology" is imposed upon people. But should we stop at that? Should we not also see the situation the other way around? For was not the "brainwasher" also similarly motivated? Do we simply use words, or do they not also use us? An "ideology" is like a god coming down to earth, where it will inhabit a place pervaded by its presence. An "ideology" is like a spirit taking up its abode in a body: it makes that body hop around in certain ways; and that same body would have hopped around in different ways had a different ideology happened to inhabit it.

I am saying in one way what Paul said in another when he told his listeners that "Faith comes from hearing." He had a doctrine which, if his hearers were persuaded to accept it, would direct a body somewhat differently from the way it would have moved and been moved in its daily rounds under the earlier pagan dispensation. Consider the kind of German boys and girls, for instance, who became burghers in the old days, who during the period of inflation and U.S.-financed reparation payments after World War I wanted but to be Wandering Birds, and who with the rise of the Third Reich were got to functioning as Hitlerite fiends.

With regard to this first clause in our definition (man as the "symbol-using" animal) it has often been suggested that "symbol-making" would be a better term. I can go along with that emendation. But I'd want to add one further step. Then, for the whole formula we'd have: the "symbol-using, symbol-making, and symbol-misusing animal."

In referring to the misuse of symbols, I have in mind not only such demagogic tricks as I have already mentioned. I also think of "psychogenic illnesses," violent dislocations of bodily motion due to the improperly criticized action of symbolicity. A certain kind of food may be perfectly wholesome, so far as its sheer material nature is concerned. And people in some areas may particularly prize it. But our habits may be such that it seems to us loathsome; and under those conditions, the very thought of eating it may be nauseating to us. (The most drastic instance is, of course, provided by the ideal diets of cannibals.) When the body rebels at such thoughts, we have a clear instance of the ways whereby the realm of symbolicity may affect the sheerly biologic motions of animality. Instances of "hexing" are of the same sort (as when a tribesman, on entering his tent, finds there the sign that for some reason those in authority have decreed his death by magic, and he promptly begins to waste away and die under the burden of this sheer thought).

A merely funny example concerns an anecdote told by the anthropologist, Franz Boas. He had gone to a feast being given by Esquimaux. As a good anthropologist, he would establish rapport by eating what they ate. But there was a pot full of what he took to be blubber. He dutifully took some, and felt sick. He went outside the igloo to recover. There he met an Esquimau woman, who was scandalized when she heard that they were serving blubber. For they hadn't told her! She rushed in—but came out soon after in great disgust. It wasn't blubber at all, it was simply dumplings. Had the good savant only known, he could have taken dumplings in his stride. But it was a battle indeed for him to hold them down when he thought of them as blubber!

So, in defining man as the symbol-using animal, we thereby set the conditions for asking: Which motives derive from man's animality, which from his symbolicity, and which from the combination of the two? Physicality is, of course, subsumed in animality. And though the *principles* of symbolism are not reducible to sheerly physical terms (quite as the rules of football are not so reducible despite the physicality of the players' hulks and motions as such), the meanings cannot be conceived by empirical organisms except by the aid of a sheerly physical dimension.

One further point, and we shall have finished with our first clause. In his analysis of dream symbolism, Freud laid great stress upon the two processes of "condensation" and "displacement." His observations are well taken. But, since we are here using the term "symbolism" in a much wider sense, we might remind ourselves that the processes of "condensation" and "displacement" are not confined merely to the symbolism of dreams and neuroses, but are also an aspect of normal symbol systems. A fundamental resource "natural" to symbolism is *substitution*. For instance, we can paraphrase a statement; if you don't get it one way, we can try another way. We translate English into French, Fahrenheit into Centigrade, or use the Greek letter *pi* to designate the ratio of the circumference of a circle to its diameter, otherwise stated as 3.14159. . . . In this sense, substitution is a quite rational resource of symbolism. Yet it is but a more general aspect of what Freud meant by "displacement" (which is a confused kind of substitution).

Or, as Horne Tooke pointed out a century and a half ago, a typical resource of language is abbreviation. And obviously, abbreviation is also a

kind of substitution, hence a kind of "displacement," while it is also necessarily a kind of "condensation." And language is an abbreviation radically.
If I refer to Mr. Jones by name, I have cut countless corners, as regards the
particularities of that particular person. Or if I say, "Let's make a fire,"
think of what all I have left out, as regards the specific doing. Or if I give a
book a title, I thereby refer to, while leaving unsaid, all that is subsumed
under that title. Thus, condensation also can be viewed as a species of substitution. And a quite "rational" kind of "condensation" has taken place if,
instead of referring to "tables," "chairs," and "rugs," I refer to "furniture,"
or if we put "parents" for "mother and father," and "siblings" for "brothers
or sisters."

To say as much is to realize how many muddles such as Freud is
concerned with may also be implicit in the symbols of "condensation" in
his particular sense of the term. For my remarks are not intended as a
"refutation" of Freud's terminology. By all means, my haggling about "condensation" and "displacement" as aspects of *all* symbolizing is not meant to
question his line of investigation. All I am saying is that there still are some
dividing lines to be drawn between the two realms (of symbolism in his
sense and symbolism in general).

In any case, Freud (like Frazer) gives us ample grounds for trying
never to forget that, once emotional involvement is added to symbolism's
resources of substitution (which included the invitations to both condensation and displacement) the conditions are set for the symbol-using animal,
with its ailments both physically and symbolically engendered, to tinker
with such varying kinds of substitution as we encounter in men's modes of
penance, expiation, compensation, paying of fines in lieu of bodily punishment, and cult of the scapegoat.

Obviously, to illustrate this point, there is an embarrassment of riches
everywhere we choose to look, in the history of mankind. But, almost by
accident, let us pick one, from a book, *Realm of the Incas*, by Victor W.
Von Hagen. I refer to the picture of a

> propitiatory cairn, called *apacheta*, found in all of the high places of
> Peru on the ancient road. As heavily laden travelers passed along the
> road, they placed a stone on the *apacheta* as a symbol of the burden,
> "and so left their tiredness behind."

We are further told that "The Persians, the Chinese, and the Greeks
adopted more or less the same custom."

Substitution sets the condition for "transcendence," since there is a
technical sense in which the name for a thing can be said to "transcend"
the thing named (by making for a kind of "ascent" from the realm of
motion and matter to the realm of essence and spirit). The subterfuges of

euphemism can carry this process still further, culminating in the resources of idealization that Plato perfected through his dialectic of the Upward Way and Downward Way.

The designation of man as the symbol-using animal parallels the traditional formulas, "rational animal" and *Homo sapiens*—but with one notable difference. These earlier versions are honorific, whereas the idea of symbolicity implies no such temptation to self-flattery, and to this extent is more admonitory. Such definitions as "two-footed land-animal" (referred to in Aristotle's *Topics*) or "featherless biped" (referred to in Spinoza's *Ethics*) would be inadequate because they would confine the horizon to the realm of motion.

So much for our first clause.

III

The second clause is: *Inventor of the negative*. I am not wholly happy with the word, "inventor." For we could not properly say that man "invented" the negative unless we can also say that man is the "inventor" of language itself. So far as sheerly empirical development is concerned, it might be more accurate to say that language and the negative "invented" man. In any case, we are here concerned with the fact that there are no negatives in nature, and that this ingenious addition to the universe is solely a product of human symbol systems. In an age when we are told, even in song, to "accentuate the positive," and when some experts in verbalization make big money writing inspirational works that praise "the power of positive thinking," the second clause of my definition must take on the difficult and thankless task of celebrating that peculiarly human marvel, the negative.

I have discussed elsewhere what an eye-opener the chapter, "The Idea of Nothing," was to me, in Bergson's *Creative Evolution*. It jolted me into realizing that there are no negatives in nature, where everything simply is what it is and as it is. To look for negatives in nature would be as absurd as though you were to go out hunting for the square root of minus-one. The negative is a function peculiar to symbol systems, quite as the square root of minus-one is an implication of a certain mathematical symbol system.

The quickest way to demonstrate the sheer symbolicity of the negative is to look at any object, say, a table, and to remind yourself that, though it is exactly what it is, you could go on for the rest of your life saying all the things that it is not. "It is not a book, it is not a house, it is not Times Square," etc., etc.

One of the negative's prime uses, as Bergson points out, involves its role with regard to unfulfilled expectations. If I am expecting a certain situation, and a different situation occurs, I can say that the expected situation did *not* occur. But so far as the actual state of affairs is concerned, some situation positively prevails, and that's that. If you are here but someone is expecting to meet you elsewhere, he will *not* meet you elsewhere because you positively *are* here. I can ask, "Does the thermometer read 54?" And if it registers anything in the world but 54, your proper answer can be "It is not 54." Yet there's no such thing as it's simply *not* being 54; it *is* 53, or 55, or whatever.

However, I would make one change of emphasis with regard to Bergson's fertile chapter. His stress is a bit too "Scientistic" for specifically "Dramatistic" purposes. Thus, in keeping with the stress upon matters of knowledge, he stresses the propositional negative, "It *is* not." Dramatistically, the stress should be upon the hortatory negative, "Thou *shalt* not." The negative begins not as a resource of definition or information, but as a command, as "Don't." Its more "Scientistic" potentialities develop later. And whereas Bergson is right in observing that we can't have an "idea of nothing" (that we must imagine a black spot, or something being annihilated, or an abyss, or some such), I submit that we *can* have an "idea of No," an "idea of don't." The Existentialists may amuse themselves and bewilder us with paradoxes about *le Néant*, by the sheer linguistic trick of treating no-thing as an abstruse kind of something. It's good showmanship. But there's no paradox about the idea of "don't," and a child can learn its meaning early.

No, I must revise that statement somewhat. In one sense, there is a paradox about "don't." For the negative is but a *principle*, an *idea*, not a name for a *thing*. And thus, whereas an injunction such as "thou shalt not kill" is understandable enough as a negative *idea*, it also has about its edges the positive *image* of killing. But the main point is: Though a child may not always obey the "thou shalt not," and though there may inevitably be, in the offing, an image positively inviting disobedience, the child "gets the idea."

In this sense, though we can't have an "idea of nothing," we can have an "idea of no." When first working on the negative, I thought of looking through the documents on the training of Helen Keller and Laura Bridgeman, whose physical privations made it so difficult to teach them language. And in both cases the records showed that the hortatory negative was taught first, and it was later applied for use as propositional negative, without explicit recognition of the change in application.

There is a superbly relevant passage in Emerson's early long essay, *Nature*, in the chapter "Discipline," a paragraph ending thus: All things "shall hint or thunder to man the laws of right and wrong, and echo the ten commandments." In our scheme, this could be presented thus: "Reverse the statement, start with the principle of negation as in the Mosaic Decalogue, and everything encountered along your way will be negatively infused."

In other words, if our character is built of our responses (positive or negative) to the thou-shalt-not's of morality, and if we necessarily approach life from the standpoint of our personalities, will not all experience reflect the genius of this negativity? Laws are essentially negative; "mine" equals "not thine"; insofar as property is not protected by the thou-shalt-not's of either moral or civil law, it is not protected at all.

The negative principle in morals is often hidden behind a realm of quasi-positives. One can appreciate this situation most readily by thinking of monastic discipline. The day may be filled with a constant succession of positive acts. Yet they are ultimately guided or regulated by proscriptive principles, involving acquiescence to vows consciously and conscientiously taken, while such vows come to fulfillment formally in such admonitions as are embodied in the Decalogue. Next, bearing in mind such clear evidence of the moralistic negativity that underlies the "quasi-positives" of the monastic rituals and routines, look at sheerly secular ambitions, with their countless ways of "justifying" oneself—and all such efforts too will be seen for what they are, not simply positives, but "quasi-positives," countless improvised ways of responding to the negativity so basic to man as moral agent.

Thus, all definitions stressing man as moral agent would tie in with this clause (if I may quote a relevant passage from a recent book of mine, *The Rhetoric of Religion*):

> *Action* involves *character*, which involves *choice*—and the *form* of choice attains its perfection in the distinction between Yes and No (shall and shall-not, will and will-not). Though the concept of sheer *motion* is non-ethical, *action* implies the ethical, the human personality. Hence the obvious close connection between the ethical and negativity, as indicated in the Decalogue.[1]

Is more needed on this point? We might say a few words about the role of antithesis in what are often called "polar" terms, not just Yes-No, but such similarly constructed pairs as: true-false, order-disorder, cosmos-chaos, success-failure, peace-war, pleasure-pain, clean-unclean, life-death, love-hate. These are to be distinguished from sheerly positive terms. The word "table," for instance, involves no thought of counter-table, anti-table, non-table, or un-table (except perhaps in the inventions of our quite positively negative-minded poet, E. E. Cummings).

We need not now decide whether, in such paired opposites, the posi-

---

[1] It suggests the thought that our second clause might be rephrased: "Moralized by the negative."

tive or the negative member of the pair is to be considered as essentially prior. We can settle for the indubitable fact that all *moral* terms are of this polar sort. And we can settle merely for the fact that such positives and negatives imply each other. However, in a hit-and-run sort of way, before hurrying on, I might avow that I personally would treat the negative as in principle prior, for this reason: (1) Yes and No imply each other; (2) in their role as opposites, they *limit* each other; (3) but limitation itself is the "negation of part of a divisible quantum." (I am quoting from the article on Fichte in the *Encyclopaedia Britannica*, eleventh edition.)

There is an implied sense of negativity in the ability to use words at all. For to use them properly, we must know that they are *not* the things they stand for. Next, since language is extended by metaphor which gradually becomes the kind of dead metaphor we call abstraction, we must know that metaphor is *not* literal. Further, we cannot use language maturely until we are spontaneously at home in irony. (That is, if the weather is bad, and someone says, "What a beautiful day!" we spontaneously know that he does *not* mean what the words say on their face. Children, before reaching "the age of reason," usually find this twist quite disturbing, and are likely to object that it is *not* a good day. Dramatic irony, of course, carries such a principle of negativity to its most complicated perfection.)

Our tendency to write works on such topics as "The Spirit of Christianity," or "The Soul of Islam," or "The Meaning of Judaism," or "Buddha and Eternity," or "Hinduism and Metempsychosis," leads us to overlook a strongly negativistic aspect of religions. I refer here not just to the principle of moral negativity already discussed, but also to the fact that religions are so often built *antithetically* to other persuasions. Negative motivation of this sort is attested by such steps as the formation of Christianity in opposition to paganism, the formation of Protestant offshoots in opposition to Catholicism, and the current reinvigoration of churchgoing, if not exactly of religion, in opposition to communism. So goes the dialectic!

Only one more consideration, and we are through with thoughts on this clause in our definition:

In an advertising world that is so strong on the glorification of the positive (as a way of selling either goods or bads), how make the negative enticing? At times the job has been done negatively, yet effectively, by the threat of hell. But what sanctions can we best build on now?

What a notable irony we here confront! For some of man's greatest acts of genius are in danger of transforming millions and millions of human agents into positive particles of sheer motion that go on somehow, but that are negative indeed as regards even the minimum expectations to which we might feel entitled.

And what is this new astounding irony? Precisely the fact that all these new positive powers developed by the new technology have introduced a vast new era of negativity. For they are deadly indeed, unless we make haste to develop the controls (the negatives, the thou-shalt-not's) that become necessary, if these great powers are to be kept from getting out of hand.

Somewhat ironically, even as the possibilities of ultimate man-made suicide beset us, we also face an opposite kind of positive technologic threat to the resources of our moral negativity. I refer to the current "population explosion." In earlier days, the problem was solved automatically by plagues, famines, high rate of infant mortality, and such. But now the positive resources of technology have undone much of those natural "adjustments," so that new burdens are placed upon the Muscles of Negativity as the need arises for greater deliberate limitation of offspring.

However, ironically again, we should not end our discussion of this clause until we have reminded ourselves: There is a kind of aesthetic negativity whereby any moralistic thou-shalt-not provides material for our entertainment, as we pay to follow imaginary accounts of "deviants" who, in all sorts of ingenious ways, are represented as violating these very Don'ts.

IV

Third clause: *Separated from his natural condition by instruments of his own making.* It concerns the fact that even the most primitive of tribes are led by inventions to depart somewhat from the needs of food, shelter, sex as defined by the survival standards of sheer animality. The implements of hunting and husbandry, with corresponding implements of war, make for a set of habits that become a kind of "second nature," as a special set of expectations, shaped by custom, comes to seem "natural." (I recall once when there was a breakdown of the lighting equipment in New York City. As the newspapers the next day told of the event, one got almost a sense of mystical terror from the description of the darkened streets. Yet but fifty miles away, that same evening, we had been walking on an unlit road by our house in the country, in a darkness wholly "natural." In the "second nature" of the city, something so natural as dark roadways at night was weirdly "unnatural.")

This clause is designed to take care of those who would define man as the "tool-using animal" (*homo faber, homo economicus,* and such). In adding this clause, we are immediately reminded of the close tie-up between tools and language. Imagine trying to run a modern factory, for instance, without the vast and often ungainly nomenclatures of the various technological specialties, without instructions, education, specifications, filing systems, accountancy (including mathematics and money or some similar counters). And I already referred to the likelihood that the development of tools requires a kind of attention not possible without symbolic means of conceptualization. The connection between tools and language is also observable in what we might call the "second level" aspect of both. I refer to the fact that, whereas one might think of other animals as using certain rudiments of symbolism and rudimentary tools (for instance, when an ape learns to use a stick as a means of raking in a banana that the experimenter has purposely put beyond arm's length), in both cases the "reflexive" dimension is missing. Animals do not use words about words (as with the definitions of a dictionary)—and though an ape may even learn to put two sticks together as a way of extending his reach in case the sticks are so made that one can be fitted into the other, he would not take a knife and deliberately hollow out the end of one stick to make possible the insertion of the other stick. This is what we mean by the reflexive or second-level aspect of human symbolism. And it would presumably apply also to such complex sign systems as bees apparently have, to spread information about the distance and direction of a newly discovered food supply. Apparently investigators really have "cracked" such a code in certain dancelike motions of bees—but we should hardly expect ever to find that student bees are taught the language by teacher bees, or that there are apiaries where bees formulate the grammar and syntax of such signaling. "Information" in the sense of sheer motion is not thus "reflexive," but rather is like that of an electric circuit where, if a car is on a certain stretch of track, it automatically turns off the current on the adjoining piece of track, so that any car on that other piece of track would stop through lack of power. The car could be said to behave in accordance with this "information."

However, in saying that the human powers of symbolicity are interwoven with the capacity for making tools (and particularly for making tools that make tools), we still haven't answered one objection. If the two powers involve each other, if the same reflexive trait is characteristic of both, why start with symbol-using rather than with toolmaking? I'd propose an answer of this sort:

Formally, is not the choice implicit in the very act of definition itself? If we defined man first of all as the tool-using animal (or, old style, as *homo faber* rather than as *homo sapiens*), our definition would not be taking into account the "priority" of its very own nature as a definition. Inasmuch as definition is a symbolic act, it must begin by explicitly recognizing its formal grounding in the *principle* of definition as an act. In choosing *any definition at all*, one implicitly represents man as the kind of animal that is capable of definition (that is to say, capable of symbolic action). Thus, even if one views the powers of speech and mechanical invention as mutually involving each other, in a technical or formal sense one should make the implications explicit by treating the gifts of symbolicity as the "prior" member of the pair.

Also, we should note that one especially good result follows from this choice. Those who begin with the stress upon *tools* proceed to define language itself as a species of tool. But though instrumentality is an important aspect of language, we could not properly treat it as the *essence* of language. To define language simply as a species of tool would be like defining metals merely as species of tools. Or like defining sticks and stones simply as primitive weapons. Edward Sapir's view of language as "a collective means of expression" points in a more appropriate direction. The instrumental value of language certainly accounts for much of its development, and this instrumental value of language may even have been responsible for the survival of language itself (by helping the language-using animal to survive), quite as the instrumental value of language in developing atomic power now threatens the survival of the language-using animal; but to say as much is not by any means to say that language is in its essence a tool. Language is a species of action, symbolic action—and its nature is such that it can be used as a tool.

In any case, the toolmaking propensities envisioned in our third clause result in the complex network of material operations and properties, public or private, that arise through men's ways of livelihood, with the different *classes* of society that arise through the division of labor and the varying relationships to the property structure. And that brings us to our fourth clause.

V

Fourth clause: *Goaded by the spirit of hierarchy*. But if that sounds too weighted, we could settle for, "Moved by a sense of order." Under this clause, of course, would fall the incentives of organization and status. In my *Rhetoric of Motives*, I tried to trace the relation between social hierarchy and mystery, or guilt. And I carried such speculations further in my *Rhetoric of Religion*. Here we encounter secular analogues of "original sin." For, despite any cult of good manners and humility, to the extent that a social structure becomes differentiated, with privileges to some that are denied to others, there are the conditions for a kind of "built in" pride. King and peasant are "mysteries" to each other. Those "Up" are guilty of not being "Down," those "Down" are certainly guilty of not being "Up."

Here man's skill with symbols combines with his negativity and with the tendencies towards different modes of livelihood implicit in the inventions that make for division of labor, the result being definitions and differentiations and allocations of property protected by the negativities of the law. I particularly like E. M. Forster's novel, *A Passage to India*, for its ingenious ways of showing how social mystery can become interwoven with ideas of cosmic mystery. The grotesque fictions of Franz Kafka are marvelous in this regard. The use of the word "Lord," to designate sometimes the Deity and sometimes an aristocrat, in itself indicates the shift between the two kinds of "worship." In *Book of the Courtier* Castiglione brings out the relationship nicely when he writes of kneeling on one knee to the sovereign, on both knees to God. Or, in ancient Rome, the application of the term *pontifex maximus* to the Emperor specifically recognized his "bridging" relationship as both a god and the head of the social hierarchy. Milton's use of terms such as Cherubim, Seraphim, Thrones, Dominations, Powers, reflects the conceiving of supernatural relations after the analogy of a social ladder. The religious vision of the city on a hill is similarly infused—making in all a ziggurat-like structure without skyscrapers. (Recall a related image, El Greco's painting of Toledo.) And, of course, the principles of such hierarchal order are worked out with imaginative and intellectual fullness in Dante's *Divine Comedy*. The medieval pageant probably represents the perfection of this design. All the various "mysteries" were represented, each distinct from all the others, yet all parts of the same overarching order.

VI

By now we should also have taken care of such definitions as man the "political animal" or the "culture-bearing animal." And for a while, I felt that these clauses sufficiently covered the ground. However, for reasons yet to be explained, I decided that a final codicil was still needed, thus making in all:

> *Man is*
> *the symbol-using (symbol-making, symbol-misusing) animal*
> *inventor of the negative (or moralized by the negative)*
> *separated from his natural condition by instruments of his own making*
> *goaded by the spirit of hierarchy (or moved by the sense of order)*
> *and rotten with perfection.*

I must hurry to explain and justify this wry codicil.

The principle of perfection is central to the nature of language as motive. The mere desire to name something by its "proper" name, or to speak a language in its distinctive ways is intrinsically "perfectionist." What is more "perfectionist" in essence than the impulse, when one is in dire need of something, to so state this need that one in effect "defines" the situation? And even a poet who works out cunning ways of distorting language does so with perfectionist principles in mind, though his ideas of improvement involve recondite stylistic twists that may not disclose their true nature as judged by less perverse tests.

Thoughts on this subject induce us to attempt adapting, for sheerly logological purposes, the Aristotelian concept of the "entelechy," the notion that each being aims at the perfection natural to its kind (or, etymologically, is marked by a "possession of telos within"). The stone would be all that is needed to make it a stone; the tree would be all that is needed to make it a tree; and man would (or should!) be all that is needed to make him the perfectly "rational" being (presumably a harder entelechial job to accomplish than lower kinds of entities confront). Our point is: Whereas Aristotle seems to have thought of all beings in terms of the entelechy (in keeping with the ambiguities of his term, *kinesis*, which includes something of both "action" and "motion"), we are confining our use of the principle to the realm of symbolic action. And in keeping with this view, we would state merely: There is a principle of perfection implicit in the nature of symbol systems; and in keeping with his nature as symbol-using animal, man is moved by this principle.

At this point we must pause to answer an objection. In *Beyond the Pleasure Principle* (near the end of Chapter V) Freud explicitly calls upon us "to abandon our belief that in man there dwells an impulse towards perfection, which has brought him to his present heights of intellectual prowess and sublimation." Yet a few sentences later in that same closing paragraph, we find him saying, "The repressive instinct never ceases to strive after its complete satisfaction." But are not these two sentences mutually contradictory? For what could more clearly represent an "impulse to perfection" than a "striving" after "complete satisfaction"?

The alternative that Freud proposes to the striving after perfection is what he calls a "repetition compulsion." And near the end of Chapter III he has described it thus:

> One knows people with whom every human relationship ends in the same way: benefactors whose protégés, however different they may otherwise have been, invariably after a time desert them in ill-will, so that they are apparently condemned to drain to the dregs all the bitterness of ingratitude; men with whom every friendship ends in the friend's treachery; others who indefinitely often in their lives invest some other person with authority either in their own eyes or generally, and themselves overthrow such authority after a given time, only to replace it by a new one; lovers whose tender relationships with women each and all run through the same phases and come to the same end, and so on. We are less astonished at this "endless repetition of the same" if there is involved a question of active behaviour on the part of the person concerned, and if we detect in his character an unalterable trait which must always manifest itself in the repetition of identical experiences. Far more striking are those cases where the person seems to be experiencing something passively, without exerting any influence of his own, and yet always meets with the same fate over and over again.

Freud next mentions in Tasso's *Gerusalemme Liberata* the story of the hero Tancred who, having unwittingly slain his beloved Clorinda, later in an enchanted wood hews down a tall tree with his sword, and when blood streams from the gash in the tree, he hears the voice of Clorinda whose soul was imprisoned in the tree, and who reproaches him for having again "wrought" the same "baleful deed."

Freud sees in all such instances the workings of what he calls the neurotic attempt to so shape one's later life that some earlier unresolved problem is lived over and over again. Freud also calls it a "destiny compulsion," to bring out the thought that the sufferer unconsciously strives to form his destiny in accordance with this earlier pattern.

My point is: Why should such a "destiny compulsion" or "repetition compulsion" be viewed as antithetical to the "principle of perfection"? Is not the sufferer exerting almost superhuman efforts in the attempt to give his life a certain *form*, so shaping his relations to people in later years that they will conform perfectly to an emotional or psychological pattern already established in some earlier formative situation? What more thorough illustrations could one want, of a drive to make one's life "perfect," despite the fact that such efforts at perfection might cause the unconscious striver great suffering?

To get the point, we need simply widen the concept of perfection to the point where we can also use the term *ironically*, as when we speak of a "perfect fool" or a "perfect villain." And, of course, I had precisely such possibilities in mind when in my codicil I refer to man as being "rotten" with perfection.

The ironic aspect of the principle is itself revealed most perfectly in our tendency to conceive of a "perfect" enemy. (See on " 'Perfection' as a Motive," in *Permanence and Change*, Hermes edition, pp. 292-294.) The Nazi version of the Jew, as developed in Hitler's *Mein Kampf*, is the most thoroughgoing instance of such ironic "perfection" in recent times, though strongly similar trends keep manifesting themselves in current controversies between "East" and "West." I suppose the most "perfect" definition of man along these lines is the formula derived from Plautus: *homo homini lupus*, or one to suit the sort of imaginary herding animal that would fit Hobbes's notion of the *bellum omnium contra omnes*.

The principle of perfection in this dangerous sense derives sustenance from other primary aspects of symbolicity. Thus, the principle of drama is implicit in the idea of action, and the principle of victimage is implicit in the nature of drama. The negative helps radically to define the elements to be victimized. And inasmuch as substitution is a prime resource of symbol systems, the conditions are set for catharsis by scapegoat (including the "natural" invitation to "project" upon the enemy any troublesome traits of our own that we would negate). And the unresolved problems of "pride" that are intrinsic to privilege also bring the motive of hierarchy to bear here; for many kinds of guilt, resentment, and fear tend to cluster about the hierarchal psychosis, with its corresponding search for a sacrificial principle such as can become embodied in a political scapegoat.

Similar ominous invitations along these lines derive from the terministic fact that, as Aristotle observes in his *Rhetoric*, antithesis is an exceptionally effective rhetorical device. There is its sheerly *formal* lure, in giving dramatic saliency and at least apparent clarity to any issue. One may find himself hard put to define a policy purely in its own terms, but one can advocate it persuasively by an urgent assurance that it is decidedly *against* such-and-such other policy with which people may be disgruntled. For this reason also, the use of antithesis helps deflect embarrassing criticism (as when rulers silence domestic controversy by turning public attention to animosity against some foreign country's policies). And in this way, of course, antithesis helps reinforce unification by scapegoat.

The principle of perfection (the "entelechial" principle) figures in other notable ways as regards the genius of symbolism. A given terminology contains various *implications*, and there is a corresponding "perfectionist" tendency for men to attempt carrying out those implications. Thus, each of our scientific nomenclatures suggests its own special range of possible developments, with specialists vowed to carry out these terministic possibilities to the extent of their personal ability and technical resources. Each such specialty is like the situation of an author who has an idea for a novel, and who will never rest until he has completely embodied it in a book. Insofar as any of these terminologies happen also to contain the risks of destroying the world, that's just too bad; but the fact remains that, so far as the sheer principles of the investigation are concerned, they are no different from those of the writer who strives to complete his novel. There is a kind of "terministic compulsion" to carry out the implications of one's terminology, quite as, if an astronomer discovered by his observations and computations that a certain wandering body was likely to hit the earth and destroy us, he would nonetheless feel compelled to *argue for the correctness of his computations*, despite the ominousness of the outcome. Similarly, of course, men will so draw out the implications of their terminologies that new expectations are aroused (promises that are now largely interwoven with the state of Big Technology, and that may prove to be true or false, but that can have revolutionary effects upon persons who agree with such terministic "extrapolations").

Whereas there seems to be no principle of control intrinsic to the ideal of carrying out any such set of possibilities to its "perfect" conclusion, and whereas all sorts of people are variously goaded to track down their particular sets of terministically directed insights, there is at least the fact that the schemes get in one another's way, thus being to some extent checked by rivalry with one another. And such is especially the case where *allocation of funds* is concerned.

To round out the subject of "perfection," in both honorific and ironic senses, we might end by observing that, without regard for the ontological truth or falsity of the case, there are sheerly technical reasons, intrinsic to the nature of language, for belief in God and the Devil. Insofar as language is intrinsically hortatory (a medium by which men can obtain the cooperation of one another), God perfectly embodies the petition. Similarly, insofar as vituperation is a "natural" resource of speech, the Devil provides a perfect butt for invective. Heaven and Hell together provide the ultimate, or perfect, grounding for sanctions. God is also the perfect audience for praise and lamentation (two primary modes of symbolic action, with lamentation perhaps the "first" of all, as regards tests of biological priority). Such considerations would provide a strictly logological treatment of Martin Buber's "I-Thou Relation."

VII

So much for the clauses of our Definition, a definition which most people would probably want to characterize as "descriptive" rather than "normative," yet which is surely normative in the sense that its implications are strongly admonitory, suggesting the kind of foibles and crotchets which a "comic" theory of education[2] would feature, in asking man to center his attention on the understanding of his "natural temptations" towards kinds of turbulence that, when reinforced with the powers of the new weapons, threaten to undo us.

I'm not too sure that, in the present state of Big Technology's confusions, any educational policy, even if it were itself perfect and were adopted throughout the world, would be able to help much, when the world is so ardently beset by so much distress and malice. The dreary likelihood is that, if we do avoid the holocaust, we shall do so mainly by bits of political patchwork here and there, with alliances falling sufficiently on the bias across one another, and thus getting sufficiently in one another's road, so that there's not enough "symmetrical perfection" among the contestants to set up the "right" alignment and touch it off.

---

[2] In his *Parts of Animals*, Chapter X, Aristotle mentions the definition of man as the "laughing animal," but he does not consider it adequate. Though I would hasten to agree, I obviously have a big investment in it, owing to my conviction that mankind's only hope is a cult of comedy. (The cult of tragedy is too eager to help out with the holocaust. And in the last analysis, it is too pretentious to allow for the proper recognition of our animality.) Also, I'd file "risibility" under "symbolicity." Insofar as man's laughter is to be distinguished from that of the Hyena, the difference derives from ideas of *incongruity* that are in turn derived from principles of *congruity* necessarily implicit in any given symbol system.

Perhaps because of my special liking for the sympathetically ironic point of view in E. M. Forster's novel, *A Passage to India*, I place a wan hope in the sheer muddle of current international relations. That is, there is the chance that the problem, in its very insolubility, also contains enough elements of self-cancellation to keep things from coming to a perfect fulfillment in a perfect Apocalyptic holocaust. Meanwhile, the most that one can do, when speculating on a definition, is to ask oneself whether it is turned somewhat in the right direction.

But what of an ending for this discussion? After so much talk about "perfection," I feel quite self-conscious. For obviously, my discussion should itself have a perfect ending.

A perfect ending should promise something. In this regard, I guess the most perfect ending is provided by a sermon in which, after a threat of total loss unless we mend our ways, we are promised the hope of total salvation if we do mend our ways. But even though, today, we stand as close as mankind ever has stood, in secular regards, to a choice precisely as radical as that, I can build up no such perfectly urgent pattern (partly because, as we generally recognize now, it is impossible for us truly to imagine that next day, no matter how earnestly some writers try to help us by inventing imaginary accounts of it, accounts which even they can't believe, despite the enterprise of their imaginings).

The best I can do is state my belief that things might be improved somewhat if enough people began thinking along the lines of this definition; my belief that, if such an approach could be perfected by many kinds of critics and educators and self-admonishers in general, things might be a little less ominous than otherwise.

However, at this point I hit upon a kind of *Ersatz* promise for an ending. As you will see, it is concerned with perfection on a grand scale. And it has in its favor the further fact that it involves the modernizing, or perfecting, of a traditional vision, one even so primal as to be expressed in a nursery jingle. I shall give the traditional jingle first, and then my proposed modernized perfecting of it. The older form ran thus:

> If all the trees were one tree
> What a great tree that would be
>
> If all the axes were one axe
> What a great axe that would be.
>
> If all the men were one man
> What a great man he would be.
>
> And if all the seas were one sea
> What a great sea that would be.

> And if the great man
> Took the great axe
> And chopped down the great tree
> And let it fall into the great sea
>
> What a Splish-Splash that would be!

Modernized, perfected, the form runs thus:

> If all the thermo-nuclear warheads
> Were one thermo-nuclear warhead
> What a great thermo-nuclear warhead that would be.
>
> If all the intercontinental ballistic missiles
> Were one intercontinental ballistic missile
> What a great intercontinental ballistic missile that would be.
>
> If all the military men
> Were one military man
> What a great military man he would be.
>
> And if all the land masses
> Were one land mass
> What a great land mass that would be.
>
> And if the great military man
> Took the great thermo-nuclear warhead
> And put it into the great intercontinental ballistic missile
> And dropped it on the great land mass,
>
> What great PROGRESS that would be!

Comments

One might ask the question: "What does it mean, to approach reality through one language rather than another?" Or one might ask: "What does it mean to be the kind of animal that uses *any* language (to view reality through *any* kind of highly developed symbol system)?" Benjamin Lee Whorf's ingenious speculations (many of them collected in his volume, *Language, Thought, and Reality*) suggest answers to the first question. The present "Definition" has been concerned rather with answers to the second.

Men can be studied as individuals, as members of groups (tribes, classes, organizations, and the like), or as generically "human." The present essay has been concerned with the most "universal" of such classifications. But elsewhere we deal with the fact that the analysis of particular idioms can be methodically narrowed even to the study of one particular writer's terminology (with its own unique set of "personal equations").

Given the range of meanings in the ancient Greeks' concept of "politics," the anthropologists' definition of man as the "culture-bearing animal" is not far from Aristotle's view of man as the "political animal." Both imply the ability to develop and transmit conventions and institutions. Just as Aristotle's definition serves most directly for his book on politics, so the anthropologists' definition serves most directly for their studies of tribal cultures. "Social animal" might most directly suit sociologists. Our point is simply that for our purposes a still more general starting point is necessary, analogous to *homo sapiens,* but minus the "built-in" honorific connotations of that formula (though perhaps it did perform a notable rhetorical function in prodding many of the perverse to cherish after the manner of Flaubert the lore of *la bêtise humaine*). For the psychologist, man is a "psychological" animal; for the psychoanalyst a mentally sick animal (a psychopathology being a natural part of even the average or "normal" Everyman's everyday life); for the chemist man should be a congeries of chemicals; and so on. But since man can't be called any of these various things except insofar as, encompassing the lot, he is the kind of animal that can haggle about the definition of himself, in this sense he is what Ernst Cassirer has called the *animal symbolicum;* yet I feel that the post-Kantian way of understanding such a formula tends to get epistemologically ("Scientistically") sidetracked from the more ontological ("Dramatistic") approach grounded in the older scholastic tradition.

The idealizing of man as a species of machine has again gained considerable popularity, owing to the great advances in automation and "sophisticated" computers. But such things are obviously inadequate as models since, not being biological organisms, machines lack the capacity for pleasure or pain (to say nothing of such subtler affective states as malice, envy, amusement, condescension, friendliness, sentimentality, embarrassment, etc., *ad nauseam*). One might so construct a computer that, if its signals got into a traffic jam, it would give forth a cry like a child in agony. And this "information" might make you impulsively, despite yourself, feel compassion for it. Yet, not being an organism, the ingenious artificial construct would all the while be as impassive as a Stoic's ideal of the perfect philosopher. For though the contraption might be so designed that it could *record* its own outcry, it could not "hear" that cry in the sense in which you, as an organism of pleasure and pain, would hear it. Until, like the robots in Capek's *R.U.R.,* men's contrivances can be made actually to ache, they cannot possibly serve as adequate models for the total human condition (that is, for a definition of "man in general").

When two machines get cruelly smashed in an accident, it's all the same to them, so far as pain goes. Hence a definition of man without reference to the animality of pain is, on its face, as inadequate as a definition would be that reduced man to the sheer kinetics of chemistry. Unquestionably, such a reduction could tell us much about the realm of motions that underlies our modes of action, and without which we could not act. But we *intuitively* recognize that such terms alone cannot deal with the qualities of experience as we necessarily suffer and enact it. (Awareness itself, by the way, is ambiguously on the dividing line between "action" and "knowledge"; or, otherwise put, intuitive knowledge is a spontaneous activity much like what we call an "act of faith," as per Santayana's ingenious concept of "animal faith.")

Insofar as the concept of "action" gets reduced to terms of "work," conditions are set for an antithetical stress upon play, as with Huizinga's formula, *homo ludens.* While obviously not general enough to cover all cases, it serves well as an instrument to warn us against an overly instrumentalist view of man's ways with symbols. Here would belong also a related view of man, as the "laughing animal." While laughter, like tears, is grounded in the motions of animality, it also depends upon principles of congruity that are due to conventions or proprieties developed through the resources of symbolicity. It embodies these norms of congruity in reverse, by their violation within limits, a kind of "planned incongruity" (as discussed in my *Permanence and Change.*) Thus the incongruously perfect definition of man as a wolf (in keeping with man's traditional attitude towards that much maligned, but highly social-minded animal) comes down to us through comedy.

The reference to proprieties suggests the observation that the definition of man as a "moral being" centers in that mighty symbolic invention, the negative, involving the "thou-shalt-not's" (and corresponding "thou shalt's") of law and conscience, and the saying yes or no to such proscriptions and prescriptions. Here would belong Whitman's celebration of the "Answerer," and Nietzsche's paradoxical, negativity-saturated idea of the "Yea-sayer." I remember having heard that William Blackstone somewhere defines man as a being endowed with the capacity for all kinds of crime. Though I have not been able to verify the reference, such a definition would be the most direct fit for commentaries on the law; yet "crime" is but a reflex of human prowess in the making of laws, that is, man's "symbolicity." And Goethe has offered us an attenuated variant of the same notion when confessing an ability to *imagine* all kinds of crime.

The third essay will illustrate the basic symbolic devices under which one should class man as a being typically endowed with the powers of "transcendence." And many subsequent chapters will provide other instances of such resourcefulness (for instance, the piece on Emersonian transcendentalism) including its relation to the hierarchal motive, as embodied in the social order.

Man's "time-binding" propensities would be a subdivision of his traffic with symbols, though the fourth chapter will also consider a sense in which the past is preserved "unconsciously" in the animal tissues.

All told, we should by now have reviewed a sufficient range of cases to indicate why we feel that any possible definition of man will necessarily fall somewhere within the five clauses in our "Definition." Basically, these involve concepts of motion and action (or otherwise put, physicality, animality, and symbolicity). And above all, we would want to emphasize: Whereas many other animals seem sensitive in a rudimentary way to the motivating force of symbols, they seem to lack the "second-level" aspect of symbolicity that is characteristically human, the "reflexive" capacity to develop highly complex symbol systems about symbol systems, the pattern of which is indicated in Aristotle's definition of God as "thought of thought," or in Hegel's dialectics of "self-consciousness."

As we proceed, there will be other chances to consider these matters.

Chapter Two

Poetics in Particular; Language in General

I

The primary text for this talk will be from Poe's essay, "The Principle of Composition." This essay has not fared well with critics, or with readers generally. Though it purports to be an account of how Poe went about the writing of his poem, "The Raven," and though he might be expected to know more about his procedures than any one else, the general tendency has been to feel that he is making the genesis of the poem look much more deliberate than could possibly have been the case, and to assume that he did so either for purposes of showmanship or to compensate for his own personal shortcomings by representing himself as a paragon of rational control (a sheerly designing craftsman, who worked out the methods and contents of the poem by sheer theory, deducing every detail from poetic principles with the precision of a demonstation in Euclid).

He would try to show, he said, "that the work proceeded, step by step, to its completion with the precision and rigid consequences of a mathematical problem."

The passage which I shall use as our text occurs just after Poe has "explained" how he decided on the figure of the Raven, after having discarded the much less appropriate notion of having the fatal refrain "Nevermore" repeated by a parrot, "in a poem of melancholy tone, and in length about one hundred lines." (He decides that this would be about the ideal length for such a lyric—and lo! his own poem turns out to have 108 lines, a pretty close hit as such things go.) He had already arrived at the "conclusion" that the ideal lyric should aim at *Beauty*, an "intense elevation of the *soul*," with an effect best got by a "tone" of "sadness," since Melancholy is "the most legitimate of the poetic tones." He continues (and this is the quotation which best suits our present purposes):

> Never losing sight of the object *supremeness*, or perfection, at all points, [and for later use in this chapter, I would also emphasize those words, *"supremeness*, or perfection"] I asked myself—"Of all melancholy topics, what, according to the *universal* understanding of mankind, is the *most* melancholy?" Death—was the obvious reply. "And when," I said, "is this most melancholy of topics most poeti-

cal?" From what I have already explained at some length, the answer, here also, is obvious—"When it most closely allies itself to *Beauty*: the death, then, of a beautiful woman is, unquestionably the most poetical topic in the world—and equally is it beyond doubt that the lips best suited for such a topic are those of a bereaved lover."

For our purposes, the important question with regard to this passage involves the fact that two quite different lines of comment suggest themselves. The assertion, "the most poetical topic in the world" is that of a *beautiful woman dead*, suggests answers in either the Poetics department or the Psychiatry department. Our main task here is to consider it in terms of Poetics. Yet one can hardly overlook the necrophile connotations of Poe's formula, particularly in view of the fact that such themes were somewhat of an *idée fixe* with him, recurring with the persistence of what psychologists call a "tic" (as with people who, for instance, impulsively blink their eyes when certain topics are mentioned). If a writer keeps returning to a certain morbid theme, we incline to think of his work not merely as a professional accomplishment, but also as the revelation, however enigmatic, of some personal, emotional disorder affecting him outside the orbit of his aptitude as an artist. And we can feel all the more justified in doing so, when the subject is a writer like Poe, whose personal disturbances were notorious.

· Be that as it may, there are many things to be said about the choice, purely from the standpoint of Poetics. For instance, when Poe calls Beauty the "province" of his poem, and says that it is best got by a tone of sadness, or Melancholy, we might say: He is calling for a kind of *attitude* or *sentiment* that will be the lyric equivalent of the appeal to the *passions* in tragic drama proper. Similarly, insofar as tragedy excites to pity, and pity eventuates in tears, we could say that Poe's idea of Beauty in the lyric hovers about this same motive, as when he says: "Beauty of whatever kind, in its supreme development, invariably excites the sensitive soul to tears. Melancholy is thus the most legitimate of all the poetic tones." Thus, before narrowing down to the particular topic of the beautiful woman dead, we might say that Poe is aiming, *mutatis mutandis*, to get the equivalent of dramatic tragic *action* in lyric tragic *attitude*, which he would equate with an attitude of tearful melancholy.

As for the subject of Death in general: this choice would be justified poetically (or should we say rhetorically?) in the sense that an idea of tragic lyric beauty would surely require a topic endowed with solemn, or "elevated" connotations. And the topic of Death, so treated, has traditionally served as a means of tragic dignification.

Still more specifically, recall that for Poe the object of his ideal, beautifully solemn poem would be *"supremeness*, perfection." We can't go into this matter at sufficient length now, but note that "perfection" means *literally* a *finishedness*. The "perfect" is the *completely done*. In this sense, Death provides a quite relevant source of imagery for the idea of perfection.

Next, if you are to use the topic of Death for poetic purposes, you'd certainly want the general topic tied down to *particulars,* and you'd want those particulars *personalized.* The topic of at least *someone* dead would fill this part of the recipe.

Another notion of perfection is associated with the idea of a person in full bloom. And could any topic more fully meet this test than the theme of persons in love? Thus, if the dead person were associated with the height of love, another requirement of Poetics would be met.

Poe's idea of Beauty, being aesthetic, was integrally interwoven with the idea of extreme sensibility. And traditionally the role of a sensitive woman could fill the bill here. Thereby the category of the personal could be narrowed more specifically to thoughts of a feminine object.

Thus, all told, considerations sheerly of Poetics seem adequate to account for the choice of subject matter: a beautiful woman dead, being lamented by her lover, while a solemn deathy Raven croaks a fatal refrain.

Yet the psychiatrically inclined might tend to question whether this "derivation" purely in terms of Poetics does dispose of all the important motivational possibilities involved here; and I admit that I personally am inclined to agree with such reservations, particularly in view of the necrophile theme that saturates Poe's work, and in view of the fact that his writings were entangled with so much personal disorder. I do not by any means subscribe to the blunt notion that his writings may be a mere "compensation" for personal difficulties. One could with as much justice turn the situation around, and say that his personal difficulties happen to be practical reflections of his literary methods. For though it is true that artists use art, sometimes successfully, sometimes unsuccessfully, to get themselves out of trouble, the practice of art just as often gets artists into trouble. Yet I would go along with anyone who felt that the "derivation" of Poe's topic in terms of Poetics alone would probably not be sufficient to handle the entire motivational problem.

Or, to state the matter in terms of the title for this discussion: What we might say about the poem specifically *as a poem* might not adequately cover the wider motivational problem of what we might say about the poem (and Poe's essay on the poem) as aspects of *language in general.*

II

We are now ready for our next step: From Poetics in particular to Language in general. For the best way-in here, let's begin by moving a bit farther off. First, note a distinction between "animality" and what we might (for want of a better word) call "symbolicity." If you say something, or read something, or write something, or think something, or hear something being said, etc., the grammar, syntax, ideas, meanings connected with such operations would be in the realm of "symbolicity." "Animality" is the realm for our sheer bodily processes: growth, respiration, digestion, and the like. Beneath "animality" in turn there is sheer "physicality": the animal's nature as chemicals, and such.

There are certain kinds of purpose that arise out of our sheer animality: the desires for food, shelter, mates, rest, and the like, reduced to the most rudimentary forms. Then there are the complex, alembicated purposes that arise out of our "symbolicity." These are the aims developed by custom, education, political systems, moral codes, religions, commerce, money, and so on. They require a terrific lot of verbalization. Think of the elaborate terminology required, for instance, to make possible the productive and distributive operations involved in the availability of the items listed in a mail order catalogue. All that naming would fall under the head of "symbolicity," as I would here use the term. However, besides such verbalization, or talk, "symbolicity" would also include all other human symbol systems, such as mathematics, music, sculpture, painting, dance, architectural styles, and so on.

Viewed from the standpoint of "symbolicity" in general, Poetics is but one of the four primary linquistic dimensions. The others are: logic, or grammar; rhetoric, the *hortatory* use of language, to induce cooperation by persuasion and dissuasion; and ethics.

By the ethical dimension, I have in mind the ways in which, through language, we express our characters, whether or not we intend to do so. In his *Biographia Literaria*, Coleridge makes an observation perfect for our purposes: "Every man's language has, first, its *individualities*; secondly, the common properties of the *class* to which he belongs; and thirdly, words and phrases of *universal* use."

Applying that statement for present purposes (as regards the "ethical dimension" in language), we could say that language reflects the "personal equations" by which each person is different from any one else, a unique combination of experiences and judgments. Thus there is a sense in which each poet speaks his own dialect. Or, at the very opposite extreme, there are respects in which we use language "universally." That is, we are the kind of animal that approaches everything through modes of thought developed by the use of symbol systems; what we don't have names for, we at least think of as "nameable"—and in this respect we differ categorically from animals whose relation to their environment eliminates this roundabout, midway stage. (My next chapter, on "Terministic Screens," will deal more fully with this matter. In the meantime, I might offer an illustrative reminder: though an institution like the United Nations is beset by disputes, it represents a *kind* of organization, the parliamentary, that in some form or other is *natural* to human beings as a species. In this respect, all institutions designed for the methodic *discussion* of human quandaries represent the *universal* aspects of our nature as a species.)

As for that middle realm, between the individual and the universal: We necessarily represent ourselves as members of classes, to varying degrees, whether we know it or not, and though no one particular set of classifications need be agreed upon by all. The disclosure of a man's nature in this respect depends largely upon the particular terministic screen in terms of which he is being observed. Coleridge had in mind *social* classes, but many other kinds of classification are possible. For instance, we began this discussion by asking, in effect, whether the language of Poe's poem and of his corresponding poetics would justify our including him not only in the class of poets and critics as such, but also in a class of poets and critics whose work properly lends itself to psychiatric analysis.

As for poetics pure and simple: I would take this motivational dimension to involve the sheer exercise of "symbolicity" (or "symbolic action") for its own sake, purely for love of the art. If man is characteristically the symbol-using animal, then he should take pleasure in the use of his powers as a symbolizer, just as a bird presumably likes to fly or a fish to swim. Thus, on some occasions, in connection with aesthetic activities, we humans might like to exercise our prowess with symbol systems, just because that's the kind of animal we are. I would view the poetic motive in that light.

However, complications arise secondarily. Even if you would write a drama, for instance, simply for the satisfaction of writing a drama, you must write your drama about *something*. And you or your potential audience will be more interested in some subjects than others. These subjects involve tensions, or problems—and since you can't make a drama without the use of some situation marked by *conflict*, even though you hypothetically began through a sheer love of dramatic exercise, in the course of so exercising you tend to use as your subject matter such tensions or problems as exercise yourself, or your potential audience, or mankind in general. Thereby you become variously involved in ways of "resolving" such tensions or problems. And even though your drama is still motivated poetically by the love of the exercising for its own sake, it becomes so interwoven with the problems you symbolically resolve, people tend to see these problems as the motivating source of your activity. The extreme psychological approach to art from this point of view may thus see it as merely "compensatory," a muddled way of trying to solve on paper various difficulties that should be confronted practically, in life itself. And the issue is too complicated for anyone to say with certainty that such motives do not figure with writers, in varying degrees.

In sum, then, there are certain things to be said about a poem *as poem*; and there are certain things to be said about it as an example of *language in general*. From the standpoint of Poetics, one should try ideally to work out explanations in terms of the poem as poem. But such a puristic attempt should in itself be enough to admonish us that a wider range of derivations may be necessary. This wider range may sometimes be necessary as the only available explanation. Sometimes it may be advisable because, whereas an answer to the problems in terms of Poetics is sufficient, there is evidence of "perturbations" which require explanations in other terms as well.

In the case of T. S. Eliot's poetry, an interesting shift took place, as regards questions of this sort. In his early "Prufrock" days, when Mr. Eliot insisted that even quite personal lyrics were to be viewed not as in any sense self-portraits but as dramatic postures adopted professionally by the poet, the critics in the quarterlies generally abided by these rules. But later, when he began writing such poems of religious devotion as the *Quartets*, the rules somehow became altered; and the attitudes in these later poems were treated not simply as dramatic postures adopted by a professional for poetic effects, but as a sincere personal interchange between Mr. Eliot and his God, though under conditions that permitted the public at large to take a sympathetic peek at this poignant private drama.

Similarly, critics will often refer to the profoundly religious sense of fatality that overhangs classic Greek drama. Here would be a dimension involving motives far wider than Poetics alone. Yet in Section IX of his *Poetics*, Aristotle offers an explanation which is reducible to the realm of Poetics specifically. I refer to a passage where he is discussing the dramatic effectiveness that results when the dramatist makes the course of his plot appear inevitable. "In that way," he says, "the incidents will seem much more wonderful than if they happened of themselves or accidentally; for such things most cause wonder if they seem to have occurred by design." And he cites as an example: When the man who had killed Mitys was looking at a statue of Mitys, the statue fell upon him and killed him. Such a pattern seems not merely coincidental, but fatal. In sum, a belief in fate involves dimensions that extend far beyond a man's trade as playwright. But approaching the matter from the standpoint of Poetics alone, Aristotle seems to be here considering the use of fatality as little more than a dramaturgic device whereby the audience is induced to feel the imitation, not as the ingenious contrivance of a showman, but as an actual manifestation of a supernatural cause. He seems to be saying in effect: The way to make a plot effective is to make it seem inevitable, and the way to make it seem wonderful is to make its imitation of inevitability seem fate-driven.

Or, again, consider the Freudian concept of the Oedipus complex. A psychologist would assign this to a realm of symbolism far wider than Poetics. And he would incline to say that it operates in poetry because it permeates the human psyche in general. But note how differently the subject is approached in Aristotle's *Poetics*. Having laid great stress upon the arousing of pity as a major aspect of the appeal in tragedy, Aristotle next observes that the most effective way to arouse pity in an audience is not through the imitating of struggles between enemies or between persons indifferent to each other, "but by situations in which conflicts occur among intimates—for example, when brother kills brother, or son father, or mother son, or son mother—or starts to do so." Note that where Freud, approaching Greek tragedy in terms of psychoanalysis, features one of these themes, Aristotle simply lists fratricide, patricide, infanticide, and matricide as four effective situations for the arousing of pity (the feeling which he considers indispensable if the audience is to experience the "tragic pleasure").

I have never found in Freud any reference to this passage of Aristotle's. But obviously, as regards the whole range of plots that are used in Greek tragedies, Aristotle's formula is the only one that meets the situation. However,. one might still concede special grounds, beyond the range of Poetics, for giving the Oedipus myth precedence over the others. It might be worth noting on the side that, whereas Aristotle's list omits a father's killing or near-killing of his son, the important Old Testament story concerning Abraham's near-sacrifice of Isaac and the basic New Testament doctrine concerning the Father's sacrifice of the Son involve eulogistic variants of precisely this pattern. I say "eulogistic," to distinguish the stories of Isaac and Christ from the kind of situations with which Aristotle is concerned.

In any case, our central point here is this: Even though Freud bases his theory of the Oedipus complex on the myth embodied in Sophocles' play, his kind of speculations would necessarily move us beyond the realm of Poetics to the realm of language (or symbolicity) in general. I intend to say more, in a later chapter, about Freudian terminology since, whatever its services in its field, the particular Freudian concept of symbolic action has a different range of reference from that needed for our purposes.

III

We have discussed Poe's text primarily from the standpoint of Poetics. We have discussed the distinction between Poetics in particular and language in general. We are now ready for our next step. Note that, even when we do confine ourselves to Poetics, another kind of problem arises. As the term "Poetics" is here being used, poem is to poet as Poetics is to critic. Often, literary criticism is merely advice to customers, as with book reviewing; or it is like the academic grading of examination papers, in the distribution of praise and blame; or it can be a substitute for the reading of the book itself (as with surveys and impressionistic criticism, or with treatment of a work purely as a symptom—frequently the method of psychological or sociological analysis—or with treatment of books in terms of cultural history in general). All such approaches serve their purposes, and there is no good reason for outlawing any of them; but none of them meets the tests peculiar to Poetics.

An approach to the poem in terms of Poetics is an approach in terms of the poem's nature as a kind (a literary species, or mode). True, there are Croce's vigorous attacks upon such an approach to the study of literature (by defining comedy, tragedy, epic, tragicomedy, romance, pastoral, and the like, each with a particular set of principles and proprieties which the critic would forbid the poet to violate). The history of the use and misuse of such procedures would fill many shelves. We might mention in particular two remarkable scholarly volumes, *A History of Literary Criticism in the Italian Renaissance*, by Bernard Weinberg (University of Chicago Press). The work both attests to the great vitality of such theorizing in sixteenth century Italy and provides ample evidence of such excesses as Croce doubtless had in mind, when he proposed to supplant traditional Poetics by Aesthetics. For much theorizing about poetic principles and proprieties was done by inferior critics who attempted legislating to poets very much their betters.

But I'd like to present the issue in a slightly different way whereby the role of the critic in such a situation would avoid this invidious policy. Indeed, rather than arrogating to himself a position as legislator to the poet, or even as judge, by this proposal the critic's role primarily (as viewed from the standpoint of Poetics) would be to formulate the critical precepts implicit in the poet's practices.

For instance, imagine that Wordsworth had never published, or even written, the preface which he added to the second edition of the *Lyrical Ballads* (1800). Imagine, therefore, that he had never published, or written, or even thought, a paragraph such as this:

> The principal object, then, which I proposed to myself in these Poems was to chuse incidents and situations from common life, and to relate or describe them, throughout, as far as was possible, in a selection of language really used by men, and, at the same time, to throw over them a certain coloring of imagination, whereby ordinary things should be presented to the mind in an unusual way; and, further, and above all, to make these incidents and situations interesting by tracing in them, truly though not ostentatiously, the primary laws of our nature: chiefly, as far as regards the manner in which we associate ideas in a state of excitement.

Imagine that this statement had been written not by Wordsworth, but by some critic. And to make the case as sharp as possible, imagine that this critic had arrived at the paragraph purely from an examination of the poems themselves. And in any case, bear it in mind that Wordsworth himself is writing here, not as a poet, but as a critic. That should serve to illustrate how a critical stress upon questions of Poetics might work to the advantage of both poetry and criticism.

Nor will it be necessarily true that the critic would, for good and all, propound a set of principles adequate to cover a given case. As a matter of fact, much of Coleridge's *Biographia Literaria* is taken up with the contention that Wordsworth as critic did not adequately state the principles which, as poet, he exemplified in the "greater number" of his own poems. (In particular, Coleridge was much exercised about Wordsworth's formula, "a selection of language really used by men." And Coleridge objected when Wordsworth, in his role as critical spokesman for his own work, "was understood to contend for the extension of this style to poetry of all kinds.")

As I see this issue, the statement I have quoted from Wordsworth's preface is in effect a *critic's* attempt to formulate some of the practices which the *poems* exemplify. We erroneously tend to think that Wordsworth is here speaking as a *poet*, whereas actually he is speaking as a *critic*. And Coleridge is in the role of another critic who objects that the first critic did not find a wholly adequate formula for Wordsworth's kind of poetry—whereupon the second critic modifies the first critic's formulations, and explains why he does so.

All told, by this emphasis, "value judgments" would not be eliminated; but they would be subordinated to the problem of systematically translating poetic practices into a corresponding set of critical precepts.

Poets tend to resent any such efforts on the critic's part, since they feel that a similar kind of effort is being demanded of them. Yet the situation is exactly the contrary. The poet's job is simply to write his poem as best he knows how. He may actually do some theorizing of a sort. At the very least, he is likely to have some rules of thumb that he goes by; and often he will be quite vocal as to the kind of poem he does *not* want to write. But he needs make no mention of any such notions, and can treat them in as flimsy or haphazard a fashion as he likes. They're not his business. Yet they *are* the critic's business. And to the extent that the critic carries out such a task, he contributes simultaneously to the vitality of criticism as an autonomous activity with its own principles, and to the glory of poetry by showing that the poems are "principled" (insofar as the critic's formulations bring out the modes of judgment implicit in the decisions which the poet's work exemplifies, regardless of whether the poet explicitly told himself that he was making such decisions).

In sum, the poet as poet makes a poem; and his ways of making the poem are practices which implicitly involve principles, or precepts. The critic, in matching the poetry with a poetics, seeks to make these implicit principles explicit. But he may not be wholly equal to the task—whereupon other critics may arise who offer solutions somewhat different from his.

In itself, such a plea for the propounding of principles is as old as criticism itself, however greatly it may sometimes be neglected or resented. But we would stress the point primarily because we need it as a basis for the *next* step in our argument, which concerns a qualified defense of Poe's essay on the writing of "The Raven."

IV

There is a remarkable paradox in the notion of "principles." The principles embodied in a given kind of poetry might happen never to be adequately formulated at all, by any critic, or any poet acting in the role of critic (just as many a primitive language has lived and died without ever having been explicitly reduced to the rules of grammar implicit in it). And whenever a critic *does* formulate the principles of a poetic species, he necessarily cannot do so with reference to *examples*, unless the poetry has already been produced. (Every once in a while a critical fantasy or *tour de force* turns up, such as a literary manifesto—but such prophetic gestures are merely a critic's way of writing a poem.) The great classic example of the relation between poetry and poetics is, of course, Aristotle's analysis of Greek Tragedy, made after the form had attained its perfection (or "finish"), and thus had ceased to develop.

Yet there is a sense in which, though such principles of poetics were formulated *after* the poetry had been produced, these principles can be treated as "prior" to the poems in which they are embodied. Principles are "prior" in the sense of the "logically prior." We should keep it in mind that the very word "principles" stems from a Latin word meaning "firsts." In the Latin version of the Bible, for instance, the first words of Genesis, "in the beginning," are *in principio*. In this ambiguous sense, insofar as a poet's practices involve decisions, and decisions imply principles, the principles implicitly guiding his procedures are "logically prior" to the poems in which they are embodied. In this sense the principles of a poetics could be treated as *logically* prior to the poems that exemplify them, *though they are formulated afterwards in time*, as with Aristotle's reduction of Greek tragedy to Poetics, or the codifying of the grammar implicit in a language.

Such considerations give us another slant on Poe's essay, "The Principle of Composition." To make our case as complete as possible, let's assume that, as regards the actual way in which Poe went about it to write "The Raven," the account in his essay is an absolute lie. Actually, insofar as any poet does follow the deductive method which Poe describes, Poe should be among those most likely to do so. For as regards his "stories of ratiocination" (such as "The Gold Bug") many were obviously constructed in this way. For there's no other way to proceed with the planning of such stories. The author must plan them in reverse, beginning with the solution, and deducing from the preordained solution the kind of problem with which to begin the actual story, and for which the solution would serve as the proper ending. In an article on this subject, published in *Poetry*, October 1961, I suggested an analogy of this sort:

> Houdini didn't let the public set the conditions from which he should escape. Rather, having hit upon the device that would permit him to escape, he next figured out the exact conditions of confinement that would make such a means of escape possible. In brief, from his idea of the *dénouement* he deduced his ideas of the prior complications.

With models of that sort in mind, let's assume that Poe didn't, for instance, think first of a parrot, and then later replace "parrot" with the obviously much better word, "raven," so far as the norms of his particular poem are concerned. And let's assume that he didn't arrive at his choice of the refrain "Nevermore" by the theories of sound effects he gives as the reason in his essay. Let's assume that, as things actually happened, Poe started to work on the poem because several things had already clicked into a relationship: say, the idea of a poem about a lover lamenting a dead beloved in a room invaded by a sinister Raven, the incident to be narrated in a generally trochaic and dactylic rhythm of this sort:

> Dumpty Dumpty Dumpty Dumpty—Dumpty Dumpty Dumpty
>   Dumpty
> Dumpty Dumptitty Dumpty Dumptitty—Dumpty Dumpty Dum

that is:

> Once upon a midnight dreary, while I pondered, weak and weary,
> Over many a quaint and curious volume of forgotten lore—
> While I nodded, nearly napping, suddenly there came a tapping,
> As of some one gently rapping, rapping at my chamber door—
>   Only this and nothing more.

It's quite conceivable that some such bundle of notions suggested themselves to him, already somewhat merged with one another, at the very start. At least, as a general thing, it's most likely that a poet goes to work on a theme precisely because several things have already fallen together— and he sees, or vaguely feels, a way to unfold, to make progressively manifest, the set of timeless relationships that prevails among them.

Be that as it may, even if we hypothetically assume that Poe's account of the *poet's* procedure was an absolute lie, I submit that his essay came quite close to the ideal procedure for *critics* to follow, in relating a poem to the principles of its composition. The only trouble was that he didn't formulate the case quite correctly, as regards the overall nature of language.

The century in which Poe lived, with its excessively historicist emphasis (it was par excellence the century of Darwin) was most prone to his temptation, in his way of stating his case. In the nineteenth century (and today insofar as we are still in the remains of that century) the spontaneous thing to do always was to treat questions of *essence*, or *logical* priority, in terms of *temporal* priority. Thus the historicist style of expression led him into a quasi-temporal or quasi-narrative way of stating a relation between poetry and poetic principles, though this relation actually is not temporal at all. The principles of composition "come first" in the sense of *logical* priority. Their formulation may or may not, and most often decidedly does not, come first in the sense of *temporal* priority. Yielding to the terministic temptations most typical of his century, Poe went out of his way to present every one of his guiding principles in terms of *temporal* priority. *First* he is supposed to have made this decision, *then* that, *then* the next *in time*. It's much as though, when confronting a syllogism such as "All men are mortal, Socrates is a man, therefore Socrates is mortal," we were to situate the first premise yesterday, the second premise today, and the conclusion tomorrow.

Perhaps I had best pause here to remind that there is nothing invidious in my attitude towards history. So far as I am concerned, to deny the reality and importance of history is on its face absurd. And I strongly subscribe to Croce's admonition that, unless we sometimes interpret a text in terms of the times in which it arose, we'll necessarily miss many considerations that contribute vitally to the meaning of some particular passage. I subscribe eagerly to Croce's ingenious notion that, in many instances, if we don't know the history of the times from which certain passages emerged, in effect we make a "palimpsest." That is, we build a later text atop an earlier text, and are thereby prevented even from perceiving the significance of the earlier text. There is nothing invidious in the theories I would here uphold. All kinds of approaches are needed, to throw full light upon the objects of our study. So my critique of "historicism" in this particular application has nothing to do with the principle of historiography as such. All I am asserting is that a temporal, or narrative account of derivations is the wrong one for this particular problem.

But if we discount Poe's procedure properly, it does make clear the obligations of critics (as viewed in terms of Poetics). For a critic might well build up a set of principles after studying a particular school of poetry, and then might point up the relevance of these principles by viewing the poetry *as though it had been written in response to the explicit formulating of these specifications*.

I can cite an excellent illustration, though I have time only for a bit of it. I refer to a section in J. W. Mackail's volume, *The Meaning of Vergil for our World of Today*. Here the author accentuates the nature of the *Aeneid* by saying not what the poem *is* but what it *ought to be* (as though the poem were still to be written, in accordance with the critic's specifications). Yet he is "putting in an order" for precisely the kind of poem that the *Aeneid* actually is. To pick a few details that most quickly illustrate the method:

> The work must be a national poem. . . . It must establish and vindicate the vital interconnection of Rome and Italy. . . . It must link up Rome and the new nation to the Greek civilization. . . . It must bring well into the foreground of the picture the historic conflict between Rome and Carthage. . . . It must celebrate the feats of heroes. . . . It must find expression for the romantic spirit, in its two principal fields of love and adventure. . . . It must exalt the new regime.

There are twelve sets of such "specifications," written long after the poem, yet presented as though they had been formulated *prior* to the poem, and as though the poem were still to be supplied, as a way of filling the critic's order. By this method the critic clearly points up the quality of the poem; yet he could certainly not be accused of making his formulations in a way that "legislated" to the poet. And it is, I submit, a kind of "priority" that Poe's essay nearly got, but that it lost through an unnecessarily temporal mode of presentation.

V

As regards this problem of the relation between poet and critic (the problem underlying the relation between poetry and poetics), I had originally thought of beginning this essay by a quotation from a quite different source, Boethius on music. (The reference is in E. K. Rand's *Founders of the Middle Ages*.) Boethius excludes performers from the number of real musicians, since they are merely slaves, obeying orders. The composers are also excluded, since they are merely inspired, and the Muses are responsible for their contribution. Then there are the critics. "They alone are the real musicians, since their function consists entirely in reason and philosophy, in a knowledge of modes and rhythms, of the varieties of melodies and their combinations, in short, of all matters that I shall treat in Volume II."

I thought it might be a good bargaining point to start from, for I am sure that any contemporary critic would be willing to settle for much less. Insofar as Poetics is concerned, I'd simply ask that the original poem be treated as the authoritative intuition which the critic then translates into terms of its nature as a *kind* of poetry, with its corresponding kind of *principles* and *proprieties*. And such a procedure might be profitably pursued, even though it led eventually to the discovery that each poem, like a Thomistic angel, is the only one of its kind. From inspection of the poem, the critic will formulate its principles. Then reversing the process, and prophesying after the event, he will test his formulations by "deducing" or "deriving" the poem from the principles. Insofar as feasible, the critic's formulations will be in terms of Poetics. That is, ideally, the entire work should be ex-

plainable in such terms unless, for some reason or other, the critic is unequal
to the task.

But at this point we are brought back to our first consideration in this
talk: The very thoroughness of the critic's attempt to discuss the poem exclusively in terms of Poetics should help us realize the points at which the
poem requires analysis not just in terms of Poetics, but also as an example
of language in general, a piece of "symbolicity" in the large. Otherwise put:
At such points the very attempt to discuss the poem purely as the *product
of a poet* should eventually help sharpen our perception of the respects in
which the poem must be analyzed rather as the product of a citizen and taxpayer, subject to various social embarrassments, physical ills, and mental
aberrations.

The scheme thus leaves room for everybody. Yet methodically so.

All told, then, where are we? Using as our point of departure a passage from Poe's essay on the writing of "The Raven," particularly his statement that "the most poetic topic" for a lyric would be a beautiful woman
dead, we considered tentatively the fact that it might be "derived" either in
terms of Poetics or in terms of psychiatry. This led to the first statement of
our problem, involving the fact that a poem can be analyzed *either as a poem
or as an example of language in general.* This led to a discussion of the
relation between poet and critic, and to suggestions for a critical program
whereby the critic's formulation of poetic principles could avoid the charge
of *legislating* to the poet. This concept of the critic's role led to a concern with
the ways in which the *logical* priority of principles can become erroneously
stated in terms of *temporal* priority. And this distinction was utilized as a
way of reinterpreting Poe's essay, and of showing how, with but a slight
shift of emphasis, it could be treated as an ideal procedure for critics. Furthermore, the very rigors of an approach to the poem strictly in terms of
Poetics should serve to make clear the kinds of "perturbation" which require
placement in different or wider terms.

VI

But in closing, perhaps I should admonish against one possible misunderstanding of this position. In referring to four realms of language (logical or
grammatical, rhetorical, poetic, and ethical) I may unintentionally suggest
to some people the notion that the realm of the poetic motive is somewhat
aside from the main pressures of motivation.

On the contrary. As I see the situation, the very essence of the poetic
motive is suggested in the opening quotation, where Poe refers to the
"object" of the poem as "*supremeness*, or perfection." The poetic motive
does indeed come to a head in the principle of perfection, as exemplified

most obviously in the aim to produce a work in which the parts are in perfect relationship to one another.

But the principle of perfection should not be viewed in too simple a sense. We should also use the expression ironically, as when we speak of perfect fools and perfect villains. In this sense, insofar as the world falls into disarray, the motive of perfection may extend to areas far beyond the confines of poetry and poetics. On the one hand, it shows in visions of Utopian promise, ideal expectations of varying scope. On the other hand, it shows in the tendency to search out people who, for one reason or another, can be viewed as perfect villains, perfect enemies, and thus, if possible, can become perfect victims of retaliation. Where the poetic motive thus ties in with perfection in its ironically manifold manifestations, it lies at the very roots of symbolicity.

Later in this series, I plan to consider, among other things, how man's special prowess in the use of symbol systems drives towards the search for ideal victims, perfect scapegoats under one form or another. In my fifth chapter, "*Coriolanus*, and the Delights of Faction," I shall analyze, from this point of view, Shakespeare's grotesque drama of sacrifice, and what I take to be the curative (purgative, cathartic) effect of this sacrifice, as an imitation, or symbolic enactment, sympathetically participated in by the audience.

In Greek tragedy, as well as in Shakespeare's kind, the principle of perfect victimage (a victim perfect for the given dramatic situation) was enacted purely by imitation. We see similar lineaments in Poe's tragic lyric attitude built around an ideal of poetic "perfection" or "supremeness" that attains its most succinct expression in the dictum: "The death, then, of a beautiful woman is, unquestionably, the most poetical topic in the world." The Roman circus embodied the principle in the *literal* sacrifice of victims. Our news media work in a somewhat intermediate stage, entertaining us not by the deliberate sacrifice of real victims, as with the Roman circus, yet at least by documents designed to assure us that the calamities actually did happen to real victims. And Christianity is built, of course, about the story of a perfect sacrificial king.

However, it would be an error to assume that the principle of victimage is confined to strictly personal forms. Not only animals, but even inanimate nature can serve as "perfect victim" in one situation or another. Some engineers, for instance, seem to have a "bulldozer mentality," and are never quite happy unless plotting roads through areas that require the destruction of great trees, as solemn as cathedrals. And words, too, can be "victimized" after a fashion, as with the later works of James Joyce, or the verbal mayhem perpetrated in Lewis Carroll's Wonderland.

I end on a "report" of "objective" victimage in Santa Barbara, California:

Ejaculations Anent a Flaming Catastrophe
(to view things simply yes, just as what is)

Strike up the band—let's all be doing the same
But what?

Flames lick up and down the adjoining canyons
with apocalyptic glows and spurts at night—
and a dust settles about us, as though spewed from a volcano

The sky is aglow
there is a rain of parched Vesuvius-ash all about us

You should see what can be done
To make the sky red with mountainsides

The dry slopes are tender with tinder
and at the slightest touch they yield
—flaring

Among the more recondite problems
count bordering areas invaded
by snakes and burned deer

If the blaze was set by an arsonist,
as one thing led to another
his whimper must have ended with a bang
Or what does happen to such odd creatures
when finding themselves thus expressed by proxy?

My sense of simple parsimony was outraged (stop)
Yet, granted, there was a grandeur
In the sweep of calamity all across the sky (stop)
To that extent was I, then,
Kindred with the kindler?!

Gnaw!
I fear it all started
Not from some morbid baystard in need of reassurance
slinkingly
Rather it got here
through sheer lack of imagination,
the inability to glimpse beforehand
what leads to what
under circumstances in which a match was dropped
by such a one of us who
except for what a moron can buy boxes of in a supermarket

couldn't strike up a fire
no matter how ardently he tried (stop)

Mankind's worst enemy
just good old normal human *Dummheit*
and always with us
(stop, if possible)

> (Thoughts on a costly fire that spread through
> the mountains like wildfire)

Comments

A later essay, "Myth, Poetry, and Philosophy," approaches this subject from another angle: There a treatment of the ancient Greek "combat myth" in terms of its possible temporal and geographic origins is contrasted with its "derivation" purely in terms of Poetic "principles." For the fullest treatment of the distinction between "logical" priority and "temporal" priority (with the Platonic archetype as a midway stage between the two), see in particular my section on "The First Three Chapters of Genesis," in *The Rhetoric of Religion.*

As regards "considerations methodological," our tactics should be:

Make the rules of Poetics as strict as theories of method would allow. Thereby, two good results should follow. First, the study of a poem *qua* poem would be made as exacting as possible. (For instance, much close analysis now classed as literary *explication de texte* does not wholly meet the demands of Poetics, since it is weak on explicit definition of the work as a literary species.) And second, the very severity of such rules would help admonish us that the study of a work in terms of Poetics alone is not nearly enough, if we are also inquiring *humanistically* into the poem's full nature as a symbolic act.

In the cause of method, one must not confuse these three quite different procedures: (1) Saying *only* what could be said about a work, considered in itself; (2) saying all that might be said about the work in terms of its relation to the author, his times, etc.; (3) while meeting tests of the first sort (discussing the work intrinsically, as a poem) also making observations of the second sort (concerning its possible relation to nonpoetic elements, such as author or background). In practice, much that would pass purely as the first sort of criticism does smuggle in quite a bit of the second sort; but often the "outlaw" elements are sporadic and unsystematic enough to escape detection; or their nature can be concealed from both author and reader by the mere denial of their presence (a device not alien to the Brooks book on Faulkner). I would contend that truly humanistic meditations on a text are possible only if both kinds of analysis are welcomed, as systematically as the subject matter permits.

In failing to size up this terministic situation correctly, courses in literature and literary criticism can be as though guided by a deliberate vow to make sure that great texts teach us much less than they could. I incline to suspect that often the error is aggravated by an attempt to get a kind of criticism as different as possible from Marxism. Thus, since Marxism is much concerned with the relationship between a literary work and the nonliterary context from which it arose, Formalism sets up antithetical demands not only that such considerations be excluded from the special field of Poetics (or, more commonly Aesthetics), but also that such speculations about texts be ruled out entirely, as questions unfit for discussion under any circumstances.

Marxism has many faults, the most obvious being that it is a poor critique of Marxism. But, like the German philosophy, English economics and French politics from which it sprang, it also has many virtues. And it can be wholly rejected only at a great sacrifice of intelligence (a sacrifice which many of our colleagues seem quite willing to make).

Whereas I would subscribe to the notion that the study of a text in terms of *Poetics* should treat the work wholly as though it were anonymous (so far as references to the personality of the author are concerned), I would also contend that questions about symbolic action in general should be asked, and that the answers to such questions do involve the relation of the work to the author and his environment, insofar as such information is available.

Incidentally, in saying that Poetics should consider a work without regard to the personality of the author, we do *not* mean that the work could not be discussed as manifesting *in itself* a certain kind of "personal" identity.

Granted: One may become impatient with attempts to categorize works, by trying to decide whether they should be classed as essays, stories, odes, ballads, etc. Such labeling is not worth much unless backed by a full definition, with corresponding rules—and the demands of such critical exactness can be quite vexing, particularly under contemporary conditions, when so many kinds of formal (or informal!) experiment are welcomed, at least in principle. (Presumably the experimentalist attitude or "methodism" in the arts is largely an aesthetic reflex of present-day science and its characteristic technological psychosis.)

Yet it is an ironic fact that, in *failing* to define a form, one may *actually* fall into critical errors much like those committed by post-Aristotelian pedants who deliberately applied Aristotle's rules for Greek tragedy and epic to forms that should not have been judged by such tests. For instance, a failure to make precise all the distinctions between epic and mock-epic could result in applying to Joyce's *Ulysses* criteria proper only to *The Iliad*. In this respect, the failure to consider a work in terms of its kind and of the rules proper to its kind can be in effect as Procrustean as the programmatic application of Aristotle's *Poetics* to forms for which it was not designed. (One encounters the same fallacy in arguments whether a play such as *Death of a Salesman* is "really" tragedy, whereas it definitely is *not* tragedy if we use the term *only* as it applies to the plays of ancient Athens.)

Hence, though good definitions of modern forms are usually hard to get (and one can expect criticism to continue skimping on that score), there's a notable difference between a critic's willingness to admit that he had fallen short of the ideal and his insistence that we should not even bother to make such efforts. There's a notable difference between a true believer who cries *peccavi* and a hardened sinner proudly proclaiming, like Stephen Dedalus in another connection, *non serviam*.

Much good contemporary criticism is under the sign of Crocean Aesthetics which refused to serve in the defining of poetic categories. Yet, in the last analysis, a critic cannot get at the very core of a work except by specifying *exactly what kind* of work it is. To be sure, often a critic's observations can be *implicitly* right even without reference to definitions. But even so, to that extent the critic has cheated; for his job above all is to be *explicit*.

At the end of our essay the "news" of violence, as "reported" in my closing verses, concerns a disastrous brush fire directly known to the audience at the University of California, Santa Barbara, before whom my paper was first presented, in the fall of 1964.

Terministic Screens

I
Directing the Attention

We might begin by stressing the distinction between a "scientistic" and a "dramatistic" approach to the nature of language. A "scientistic" approach begins with questions of *naming*, or *definition*. Or the power of language to define and describe may be viewed as derivative; and its essential function may be treated as attitudinal or hortatory: attitudinal as with expressions of complaint, fear, gratitude, and such; hortatory as with commands or requests, or, in general, an instrument developed through its use in the social processes of cooperation and competition. I say "developed"; I do *not* say "originating." The ultimate *origins* of language seem to me as mysterious as the origins of the universe itself. One must view it, I feel, simply as the "given." But once an animal comes into being that does happen to have this particular aptitude, the various tribal idioms are unquestionably *developed* by their use as instruments in the tribe's way of living (the practical role of symbolism in what the anthropologist, Malinowski, has called "context of situation"). Such considerations are involved in what I mean by the "dramatistic," stressing language as an aspect of "action," that is, as "symbolic action."

The two approaches, the "scientistic" and the "dramatistic" (language as definition, and language as act) are by no means mutually exclusive. Since both approaches have their proper uses, the distinction is not being introduced invidiously. Definition itself is a symbolic act, just as my proposing of this very distinction is a symbolic act. But though at this moment of beginning, the overlap is considerable, later the two roads diverge considerably, and direct our attention to quite different kinds of observation. The quickest way to indicate the differences of direction might be by this formula: The "scientistic" approach builds the edifice of language with primary stress upon a proposition such as "It *is*, or it *is not*." The "dramatistic" approach puts the primary stress upon such hortatory expressions as "thou *shalt*, or thou *shalt not*." And at the other extreme the distinction be-

comes quite obvious, since the scientistic approach culminates in the kinds
of speculation we associate with symbolic logic, while the dramatistic culminates in the kinds of speculation that find their handiest material in stories,
plays, poems, the rhetoric of oratory and advertising, mythologies, theol-
ogies, and philosophies after the classic model.

The dramatistic view of language, in terms of "symbolic action," is
exercised about the necessarily *suasive* nature of even the most unemotional
scientific nomenclatures. And we shall proceed along those lines; thus:

Even if any given terminology is a *reflection* of reality, by its very
nature as a terminology it must be a *selection* of reality; and to this extent
it must function also as a *deflection* of reality.

In his seventh *Provincial Letter*, Pascal satirizes a device which the
Jesuits of his day called "directing the intention." For instance, to illustrate
satirically how one should "direct the intention," he used a burlesque example of this sort: Dueling was forbidden by the Church. Yet it was still a
prevalent practice. Pascal satirically demonstrated how, by "directing the
intention," one could both take part in a duel and not violate the Church
injunctions against it. Thus, instead of intentionally going to take part in a
duel, the duelists would merely go for a walk to the place where the duel
was to be held. And they would carry guns merely as a precautionary means
of self-protection in case they happened to meet an armed enemy. By so
"directing the intention," they could have their duel without having trans-
gressed the Church's thou-shalt-not's against dueling. For it was perfectly
proper to go for a walk; and in case one encountered an enemy bent on
murder, it was perfectly proper to protect oneself by shooting in self-defense.

I bring up this satirically excessive account of directing the *in*tention,
in the hopes that I can thereby settle for less when discussing the ways in
which "terministic screens" direct the *at*tention. Here the kind of deflection
I have in mind concerns simply the fact that any nomenclature necessarily
directs the attention into some channels rather than others. In one sense,
this likelihood is painfully obvious. A textbook on physics, for instance,
turns the *at*tention in a different direction from a textbook on law or psychology. But some implications of this terministic incentive are not so obvious.

When I speak of "terministic screens," I have particularly in mind
some photographs I once saw. They were *different* photographs of the
same objects, the difference being that they were made with different color
filters. Here something so "factual" as a photograph revealed notable distinctions in texture, and even in form, depending upon which color filter was
used for the documentary description of the event being recorded.

Similarly, a man has a dream. He reports his dream to a Freudian
analyst, or a Jungian, or an Adlerian, or to a practitioner of some other

school. In each case, we might say, the "same" dream will be subjected to a different color filter, with corresponding differences in the nature of the event as perceived, recorded, and interpreted. (It is a commonplace that patients soon learn to have the kind of dreams best suited to the terms favored by their analysts.)

II
Observations Implicit in Terms

We have now moved things one step further along. Not only does the nature of our terms affect the nature of our observations, in the sense that the terms direct the *attention* to one field rather than to another. Also, *many of the "observations" are but implications of the particular terminology in terms of which the observations are made.* In brief, much that we take as observations about "reality" may be but the spinning out of possibilities implicit in our particular choice of terms.

Perhaps the simplest illustration of this point is to be got by contrasting secular and theological terminologies of motives. If you want to operate, like a theologian, with a terminology that includes "God" as its key term, the only sure way to do so is to put in the term, and that's that. The Bible solves the problem by putting "God" into the first sentence—and from this initial move, many implications "necessarily" follow. A naturalistic, Darwinian terminology flatly omits the term, with a corresponding set of implications— and that's that. I have called metaphysics "coy theology" because the metaphysician often introduces the term "God" not outright, as with the Bible, but by beginning with a term that *ambiguously* contains such implications; then he gradually makes these implications explicit. If the term is not introduced thus ambiguously, it can be introduced only by fiat, either outright at the beginning (like the Bible) or as a *non sequitur* (a break in the argument somewhere along the way). In Platonic dialogues, myth sometimes serves this purpose of a leap en route, a step prepared for by the fact that, in the Platonic dialectic, the methodic progress towards *higher levels of generalization* was in itself thought of as progress towards *the divine.*

But such a terministic situation is not by any means confined to matters of theology or metaphysics. As Jeremy Bentham aptly pointed out, all terms for mental states, sociopolitical relationships, and the like are necessarily "fictions," in the sense that we must express such concepts by the use of terms borrowed from the realm of the physical. Thus, what Emerson said in the accents of transcendental enthusiasm, Bentham said in the accents of "tough-mindedness." In Emerson's "tender-minded" scheme, "nature" exists to provide us with terms for the physical realm that are transferable to the moral realm, as the sight of a straight line gives us our word for "right," and of a crooked or twisted line our word for "wrong"; or as we derived our word for "spirit" from a word for "breath," or as "superciliousness" means literally a raising of the eyebrow. But Bentham would state the same relationship "tough-mindedly" by noting that our words for "right," "wrong," "spirit," etc. are "fictions" carried over from their strictly literal use in the realm of physical sensation. Bentham does not hope that such "fictions" can be avoided. He but asks that we recognize their nature as fictions. So he worked out a technique for helping to disclose the imagery in such ideas, and to discount accordingly. (See C. K. Ogden's book, *Bentham's Theory of Fictions.*)

But though this situation is by no means confined to the terminologies of theology and metaphysics, or even to such sciences as psychology (with terms for the out-going as vs. the in-turning, for dispositions, tendencies, drives, for the workings of the "it" in the Unconscious, and so on), by its very thoroughness theology does have a formula that we can adapt, for purely secular purposes of analysis. I have in mind the injunction, at once pious and methodological, "Believe, that you may understand (*crede, ut intelligas*)." In its theological application, this formula served to define the relation between faith and reason. That is, if one begins with "faith," which must be taken on authority, one can work out a rationale based on this faith. But the faith must "precede" the rationale. (We here impinge upon considerations of logical and temporal priority that were approached from another angle in the previous chapter.)

In my book, *The Rhetoric of Religion*, I have proposed that the word "logology" might be applied in a special way to this issue. By "logology," as so conceived, I would mean the systematic study of theological terms, not from the standpoint of their truth or falsity as statements about the supernatural, but purely for the light they might throw upon the *forms* of language. That is, the tactics involved in the theologian's "words about God" might be studied as "words about words" (by using as a methodological bridge the opening sentence in the Gospel of John: "In the beginning was the Word, and the Word was with God, and the Word was God").

"Logology" would be a purely empirical study of symbolic action. Not being a theologian, I would have no grounds to discuss the truth or falsity of theological doctrines as such. But I do feel entitled to discuss them with regard to their nature merely as language. And it is my claim that the injunction, "Believe, that you may understand," has a fundamental application to the purely secular problem of "terministic screens."

The "logological," or "terministic" counterpart of "Believe" in the formula would be: *Pick some particular nomenclature, some one terministic screen.* And for "That you may understand," the counterpart would be: *"That you may proceed to track down the kinds of observation implicit in the terminology you have chosen, whether your choice of terms was deliberate or spontaneous."*

III
Examples

I can best state the case by giving some illustrations. But first let me ask you
to reconsider a passage from Chapter One which presents the matter in the
most general sense:[1]

> . . . can we bring ourselves to realize just how overwhelmingly
> much of what we mean by "reality" has been built up for us through
> nothing but our symbol systems? Take away our books, and what
> little do we know about history, biography, even something so "down
> to earth" as the relative position of seas and continents? What is our
> "reality" for today (beyond the paper-thin line of our own particular
> lives) but all this clutter of symbols about the past, combined with
> whatever things we know mainly through maps, magazines, news-
> papers, and the like about the present? In school, as they go from
> class to class, students turn from one idiom to another. The various
> courses in the curriculum are in effect but so many different termi-
> nologies. And however important to us is the tiny sliver of reality
> each of us has experienced firsthand, the whole overall "picture" is
> but a construct of our symbol systems. To meditate on this fact until
> one sees its full implications is much like peering over the edge of
> things into an ultimate abyss. And doubtless that's one reason why,
> though man is typically the symbol-using animal, he clings to a kind
> of naïve verbal realism that refuses to let him realize the full extent
> of the role played by symbolicity in his notions of reality.

I hope the passage can serve at least somewhat to suggest how fantastically much of our "Reality" could not exist for us, were it not for our profound and inveterate involvement in symbol systems. Our presence in a room
is immediate, but the room's relation to our country as a nation, and beyond
that, to international relations and cosmic relations, dissolves into a web of
ideas and images that reach through our senses only insofar as the symbol
systems that report on them are heard or seen. To mistake this vast tangle
of ideas for immediate experience is much more fallacious than to accept a
dream as an immediate experience. For a dream really is an immediate experience, but the information that we receive about today's events throughout the world most decidedly is *not*.

But let us consider some examples of terministic screens, in a more
specific sense. The child psychologist, John Bowlby, writes a subtle and per-
ceptive paper on "The Nature of the Child's Ties to Its Mother." He observes what he calls "five instinctual responses" of infants, which he lists as:
crying, smiling, sucking, clinging, following. Surely no one would deny that

---

[1] See p. 5.

such responses are there to see. But at the same time, we might recall the observations of the behaviorist, John B. Watson. He, too, found things that were there to see. For instance, by careful scientific study, he discovered sure ways to make babies cry in fright or shriek with rage.

In contrast with Watson's terminology of observation regarding the nature of infantile reflexes, note that Bowlby adopted a much more *social* point of view. His terms were explicitly designed to study infantile responses that involved the mother in a reciprocal relationship to the child.

At the time I read Bowlby's paper, I happened to be doing a monograph on "Verbal Action in St. Augustine's *Confessions.*" I was struck by the fact that Augustine's terms for the behavior of infants closely paralleled Bowlby's. Three were definitely the same: crying, smiling, sucking. Although he doesn't mention clinging as a particularly notable term with regard to infancy, as the result of Bowlby's list I noticed, as I might otherwise not have, that he frequently used the corresponding Latin term (*inhaerere*) regarding his attachment to the Lord. "Following" was not explicitly worked out, as an infantile response, though Augustine does refer to God as his leader. And I began wondering what might be done with Spinoza's *Ethics* in this connection, whether his persistent concern with what necessarily "follows" what in Nature could have been in part a metaphysician's transformation of a personal motive strong in childhood. Be that as it may, I was struck by the fact that Augustine made one strategically important addition to Bowlby's list: rest. Once you mention it, you realize that it is very definitely an instinctual response of the sort that Bowlby was concerned with, since it involves a social relation between mother and child. In Augustine's scheme, of course, it also allowed for a transformation from resting as an infant to hopes of ultimately "resting in God."

Our point is: All three terminologies (Watson's, Bowlby's, Augustine's) directed the attention differently, and thus led to a correspondingly different quality of observations. In brief, "behavior" isn't something that you need but observe; even something so "objectively there" as behavior must be observed through one or another kind of *terministic screen*, that directs the attention in keeping with its nature.

Basically, there are two kinds of terms: terms that put things together, and terms that take things apart. Otherwise put, A can feel himself identified with B, or he can think of himself as disassociated from B. Carried into mathematics, some systems stress the principle of continuity, some the principle of discontinuity, or particles. And since all laboratory instruments of measurement and observation are devices invented by the symbol-using animal, they too necessarily give interpretations in terms of either continuity or discontinuity. Hence, physicists forever keep finding that some sub-sub-sub-sub-aspect of nature can be again subdivided; whereupon it's only a question of time until they discover that some new cut merges moments previously considered distinct—and so on. Knowing nothing much about physics ex-

cept the terministic fact that any observation of a physicist must necessarily
be stated within the resources and embarrassments of man-made terminologies, I would still dare risk the proposition that Socrates' basic point about
dialectic will continue to prevail; namely, there is composition, and there
is division.

Often this shows up as a distinction between terministic screens posit-
ing differences of *degree* and those based on differences of *kind*. For instance,
Darwin sees only a difference of degree between man and other animals. But
the theologian sees a difference in kind. That is, where Darwin views man
as *continuous* with other animals, the theologian would stress the principle
of *discontinuity* in this regard. But the theologian's screen also posits a certain kind of *continuity* between man and God that is not ascribed to the relation between God and other animals.

The logological screen finds itself in a peculiar position here. It holds
that, even on the purely secular level, Darwin overstated his case. And as a
consequence, in his stress upon the principle of *continuity* between man and
the other animals, he unduly slighted the evidence for *discontinuity* here. For
he assumed that the principle of discontinuity between man and other animals was necessarily identical with a theological view of man.

Such need not be the case at all. Darwin says astonishingly little about
man's special aptitudes as a symbol-user. His terministic screen so stressed
the principle of continuity here that he could view the principle of discontinuity only as a case of human self-flattery. Yet, logology would point out:
We can distinguish man from other animals without necessarily being over-
haughty. For what other animals have yellow journalism, corrupt politics,
pornography, stock market manipulators, plans for waging thermonuclear,
chemical, and bacteriological war? I think we can consider ourselves different in kind from the other animals, without necessarily being overproud of
our distinction. We don't need theology, but merely the evidence of our
characteristic sociopolitical disorders, to make it apparent that man, the
typically symbol-using animal, is alas! something special.

IV
Further Examples

Where are we, then?

We *must* use terministic screens, since we can't say anything without
the use of terms; whatever terms we use, they necessarily constitute a corresponding kind of screen; and any such screen necessarily directs the attention to one field rather than another. Within that field there can be different screens, each with its ways of directing the attention and shaping the
range of observations implicit in the given terminology. All terminologies
must implicitly or explicitly embody choices between the principle of continuity and the principle of discontinuity.

Two other variants of this point about continuity and discontinuity should be mentioned. First, note how it operates in political affairs: During a national election, the situation places great stress upon a *division* between the citizens. But often such divisiveness (or discontinuity) can be healed when the warring factions join in a common cause against an alien enemy (the division elsewhere thus serving to reestablish the principle of continuity at home). It should be apparent how either situation sets up the conditions for its particular kind of scapegoat, as a device that unifies all those who share the same enemy.

For a subtler variant (and here I am somewhat anticipating the specific subject matter of the next chapter) we might cite an observation by D. W. Harding, printed in *Metaphor and Symbol*, a collection of essays by various writers on literary and psychological symbolism. The author concedes that the Freudian terminology is highly serviceable in calling attention to ideas that are not given full conscious recognition because they are *repressed*. But he asks: Why can there not also be ideas that are unclear simply because we have not yet become familiar enough with a situation to take them adequately into account? Thus, when we see an object at a distance, we do not ordinarily "repress" the knowledge of its identity. We don't recognize it simply because we must come closer, or use an instrument, before we can see it clearly enough to know precisely what it is. Would not a terminology that features the unconscious *repression* of ideas automatically deflect our attention from symbols that are not *repressed* but merely *remote*? (At this point, of course, a Jungian terministic screen would ascribe the remoteness of many dream-symbols to their misty survival from an earlier stage in man's development—a terministic device that I have called the "temporizing of essence," since the nature of conditions *now* is stated quasi-narratively in terms of *temporal priority*, a vestigial derivation from "prehistory.")

One more point will end this part of our discussion. Recently I read a paper in which one sociologist accused other sociologists of "oversocializing" their terms for the discussion of human motives. (The article, "The Oversocialized Conception of Man in Modern Sociology," by Dennis H. Wrong, appears in the April 1961 issue of the *American Sociological Review*.)

This controversy brings us to a variant of the terministic situation I discussed in distinguishing between terms for Poetics in particular and terms for Language in General. But the author's thesis really has a much wider application than he claims for it. To the extent that all scientific terminologies, by their very role in specialized disciplines, are designed to focus attention upon one or another particular field of observation, would it not be technically impossible for any such specialized terminology to supply an adequate definition for the discussion of *man in general*? Each might serve to throw light upon one or another aspect of human motives. But the definition of man in general would be formally possible only to a *philosophic* terminology of motives (insofar as philosophy is the proper field for thoughts on man in general). Any definition of man in terms of specialized scientific nomenclatures would necessarily be "over-socialized," or "over-biologized," or "over-psychologized," or "over-physicized," or "over-poetized," and so on, depending upon which specialized terministic screen was being stretched to cover not just its own special field but a more comprehensive area. Or, if we try to correct the excesses of *one terminology*, by borrowing from several, what strictly *scientific* canon (in the modern sense of scientific specialization) could we adduce as sanction? Would not such an eclectic recipe itself involve a generalized philosophy of some sort?

V
Our Attempt to Avoid Mere Relativism

And now where are we? Must we merely resign ourselves to an endless catalogue of terministic screens, each of which can be valued for the light it throws upon the human animal, yet none of which can be considered central? In one sense, yes. For, strictly speaking, there will be as many different world views in human history as there are people. (*Tot homines, tot sententiae.*) We can safely take it for granted that no one's "personal equations" are quite identical with anyone else's. In the unwritten cosmic constitution that lies behind all man-made Constitutions, it is decreed by the nature of things that each man is "necessarily free" to be his own tyrant, inexorably imposing upon himself the peculiar combination of insights associated with his peculiar combination of experiences.

At the other extreme, each of us shares with all other members of our kind (the often-inhuman human species) the fatal fact that, however the situation came to be, all members of our species conceive of reality somewhat roundabout, through various *media* of symbolism. Any such medium will be, as you prefer, either a way of "dividing" us from the "immediate" (thereby setting up a kind of "alienation" at the very start of our emergence from infancy into that state of articulacy somewhat misleadingly called the "age of reason"); or it can be viewed as a paradoxical way of "uniting" us with things on a "higher level of awareness," or some such. (Here again, we encounter our principles of continuity and discontinuity.)

Whether such proneness to symbolic activity be viewed as a privilege or a calamity (or as something of both), it is a distinguishing characteristic of the human animal in general. Hence it can properly serve as the basis of a general, or philosophic definition of this animal. From this terministic beginning, this intuitive grounding of a position, many observations "necessarily follow." But are we not here "necessarily" caught in our own net? Must we not concede that a screen built on this basis is just one more screen;

and that it can at best be permitted to take its place along with all the others? Can we claim for it special favors?

If I, or any one person, or even one particular philosophic school, had invented it, such doubts would be quite justified. But if we pause to look at it quizzically, I think we shall see that it is grounded in a kind of "collective revelation," from away back. This "collective revelation" involves the pragmatic recognition of a distinction between persons and things. I say "pragmatic" recognition, because often the distinction has not been *formally* recognized. And all the more so because, if an object is closely associated with some person whom we know intimately, it can readily become infused with the identity of that person.

Reverting now to our original term, "dramatistic," I would offer this basic proposition for your consideration: Despite the evidences of primitive animism (that endows many sheer things with "souls") and the opposite modes of contemporary behaviorism (designed to study people as mere things), we do make a pragmatic distinction between the "actions" of "persons" and the sheer "motions" of "things." The slashing of the waves against the beach, or the endless cycle of births and deaths in biologic organisms would be examples of sheer motion. Yet we, the typically symbol-using animal, cannot relate to one another sheerly as things in motion. Even the behaviorist, who studies man in terms of his laboratory experiments, must treat his colleagues as *persons*, rather than purely and simply as automata responding to stimuli.

I should make it clear: I am not pronouncing on the metaphysics of this controversy. Maybe we are but things in motion. I don't have to haggle about that possibility. I need but point out that, whether or not we are just things in motion, we think of one another (and especially of those with whom we are intimate) as *persons*. And the difference between a thing and a person is that the one merely *moves* whereas the other *acts*. For the sake of the argument, I'm even willing to grant that the distinction between *things moving* and *persons acting* is but an illusion. All I would claim is that, illusion or not, the human race cannot possibly get along with itself on the basis of any other intuition. The human animal, as we know it, *emerges into personality* by first mastering whatever tribal speech happens to be its particular symbolic environment.

We could not here list even summarily the main aspects of the Dramatistic screen without launching into a whole new project. For present purposes, I must only say enough to indicate my grounds for contending that a Dramatistic screen does possess the philosophic character adapted to the discussion of man in general, as distinct from the kinds of insight afforded by the application of special scientific terminologies.

In behalf of my claim that the "dramatistic screen" is sanctioned by a "collective revelation" of long standing, suffice it to recall such key terms as *tao, karma, dike, energeia, hodos, actus*—all of them words for *action* (to which we might well add *Islam*, as the name for a submissive *attitude* with its obviously active possibilities). The Bible starts with God's act, by creative fiat. Contemporary sociological theories of "role-taking" fit into the same general scheme. Terms like "transactions," "exchange," "competition," "cooperation," are but more specific terms for "action." And there are countless words for specific acts: give, take, run, think, etc. The contemporary concern with "game theories" is obviously a subdivision of the same term. Add the gloomy thought that such speculative playfulness now is usually concerned with "war games." But in any case, the concept of such games must involve, in however fragmentary a fashion, the picture of persons acting under stress. And even when the "game" hypothetically reduces most of the players to terms of mere pawns, we can feel sure in advance that, if the "game" does not make proper allowance for the "human equation," the conclusions when tested will prove wrong.

But the thought should admonish us. Often it is true that people can be feasibly reduced to terms of sheer motion. About fifty years ago, I was suddenly *startled* into thinking when (encountering experience purely "symbolwise," purely via the news) I read of the first German attacks against a Belgian fortress in World War I. The point was simply this: The approach to the fortress was known to be mined. And the mines had to be exploded. So wave after wave of human flesh was sent forward, as conditioned cattle, to get blown up, until all the mines had been touched off. Then the next wave, or the next two or three waves thereafter, could take the fort. Granted, that comes pretty close to sheer motion, doubtless conceived in the best war-game tradition.

Basically, the Dramatistic screen involves a methodic tracking down of the implications in the idea of symbolic action, and of man as the kind of being that is particularly distinguished by an aptitude for such action. To quote from Webster's *Third New International Dictionary*, which has officially recognized "Dramatism" in my sense of the term, as treated schematically in my *Grammar of Motives*, it is "A technique of analysis of language and thought as basically modes of action rather than as means of conveying information." I would but note that such an "Ism" can also function as a philosophy of human relations. The main consideration to keep in mind, for present purposes, is that two quite different but equally justifiable positions are implicit in this approach to specifically human motivation.

There is a gloomy route, of this sort: If *action* is to be our key term, then *drama*; for drama is the culminative form of action (this is a variant of the "perfection" principle discussed in the previous chapter). But if *drama,* then *conflict.* And if *conflict,* then *victimage.* Dramatism is always on the edge of this vexing problem, that comes to a culmination in tragedy, the song of the scapegoat.

There is also a happy route, along the lines of a Platonic dialectic. For the present, I would close on some lines that proclaim this happier route, in a style that, I must admit, states the *problem* in the accents of an *ideal solution.*

This "idealization" ends on two weighty words. One, "synecdoche," is used in the sense of "part for the whole." The other, "tautology," refers to the fact that, insofar as an entire structure is infused by a single generating principle, this principle will be tautologically or repetitively implicit in all the parts. The lines are meant to suggest that, insofar as man is the symbol-using animal, his world is necessarily inspirited with the quality of the Symbol, the Word, the Logos, through which he conceives it. (The lines are from my volume of poems, *Book of Moments.*)

Dialectician's Hymn

Hail to Thee, Logos,
Thou Vast Almighty Title,
In Whose name we conjure—
Our acts the partial representatives
Of Thy whole act.

May we be Thy delegates
In parliament assembled.
Parts of Thy wholeness.
And in our conflicts
Correcting one another.
By study of our errors
Gaining Revelation.

May we give true voice
To the statements of Thy creatures.
May our spoken words speak for them,
With accuracy,
That we know precisely their rejoinders
To our utterances,
And so may correct our utterances
In the light of those rejoinders.

Thus may we help Thine objects
To say their say—
Not suppressing by dictatorial lie,
Not giving false reports
That misrepresent their saying.

If the soil is carried off by flood,
May we help the soil to say so.
If our ways of living
Violate the needs of nerve and muscle,
May we find speech for nerve and muscle,
To frame objections
Whereat we, listening,
Can remake our habits.
May we not bear false witness to ourselves
About our neighbors,
Prophesying falsely
Why they did as they did.

May we compete with one another,
To speak for Thy Creation with more justice—
Cooperating in this competition
Until our naming
Gives voice correctly,
And how things are
And how we say things are
Are one.

Let the Word be dialectic with the Way—
Whichever the print
The other the imprint.

Above the single speeches
Of things,
Of animals,
Of people
Erecting a speech-of-speeches—
And above this
A Speech-of-speech-of-speeches,
And so on,
Comprehensively,
Until all is headed
In Thy Vast Almighty Title,
Containing implicitly
What in Thy work is drawn out explicitly—
In its plentitude.

And may we have neither the mania of the One
Nor the delirium of the Many—
But both the Union and the Diversity—
The Title and the manifold details that arise
As that Title is restated
In the narrative of History.

Not forgetting that the Title represents the story's Sequence,
And that the Sequence represents the Power entitled.

For us
Thy name a Great Synecdoche
Thy works a Grand Tautology.

Comments

As regards philosophic formulas defining the nature of man in general, poems symbolically acting or "attitudinizing," and scientific tracts: Whatever their differences they all are classifiable together in one critical respect: They all operate by the use of symbol systems; thus all in their various ways manifest the resources and limitations of symbol systems.

But though any symbol system explicitly and implicitly turns our attention in one direction rather than in other directions, there is a striking difference within symbol systems. True, poets feud with philosophers, and many modern philosophers except the rare ones like Santayana feud with poets. But we are here concerned with a distinction that puts poetry quite close to philosophy (as in Aristotle, though his statement of the case did not concern precisely the issue now being considered).

No matter how limited any particular philosopher's definition of man may be (owing to his limitations as a person), if he speaks as a philosopher he necessarily speaks "in terms of" the *whole* man. For his statement is philosophically complete only insofar as it involves a concept of *man in general*. In contrast, a specialized scientific nomenclature (no matter how comprehensive it may be) necessarily involves *fragmentation*. For no special discipline could be special except insofar as it defined man in terms of its specialty.

Let us now turn to the *poet's* limitations. (And by "poet" I here refer broadly to all symbolizers who attitudinize not only in poems, but also in stories and plays, along with the many tentative alembications, deviations, perversions now often encountered.)

The poet may happen to be an extremely "odd" creature, quite limited as an artist. And even if he isn't very inventive, any unusual modes of experience, in deviating from the average, can in effect endow him with the equivalent of exceptional inventiveness. In such cases, accidents of history become attributes of the poem's very essence.

But no matter how limited a poetic production may be, it is *not* reducible to terms of any specialized scientific nomenclature (such as the terms of physics, chemistry, economics, politics, and so on). Nor can it even be adequately described as a combination of the lot. And though any specialized nomenclature may throw light upon the work, there is an obvious sense in which the work necessarily contains elements not only beyond the limits of *each* specialty but also beyond the aggregate of them *all*.

Sometimes, apologists of literature have grown challenging and edified when they touch upon this state of affairs. So far as universities are concerned, it involves such brutal extra-aesthetic considerations as interdepartmental rivalries.

But for present purposes, I would propose to consider it simply as a fact about the nature of terminologies.

A poet's language need not confront the problem of specialized scientific nomenclature. That is to say: The poet's language does not subject Humpty Dumpty to the great fall whereby he can't be put together again. For poetic language is saved by the technical fact that it never quite confronted this problem in the first place. Terministically tied to its uterine beginnings, no poet's terminology need "resynthesize" its picture of man; however limited may be a poet's terms for man's actions, passions, agencies, scenes, purposes, and attitudes, they never quite take Humpty Dumpty, that fatal cultural egg, apart. For even as the poet works with *particulars*, he brings to them the *unification* of an attitude. Otherwise, his work itself would fall apart. And quite as Aristotle, when discussing the principle of poetic consistency, admonished that even an inconsistent character must be consistently so, I would dare contend: Any poetic attitude (like being jaunty today, as distinct from being dismal tomorrow) has a kind of summarizing wholeness that is technically alien to the specialized terminologies of our essentially technology-tinged sciences.

Approaching the question from another angle, but having in mind the previous chapter on Poetics in Particular, as we proceed we should keep asking whether the test for poetry might be "verisimilitude" rather than "truth." And though truth is often the best grounding for verisimilitude, it is not always so.

Viewing the situation in terms of "symbolic action," we might stress a distinction between the "statistically" or "factually" true and a marksman's "true" aim.

In the *Journal of Social Issues* for October 1962 there is an article which, by its very shortcomings, helps illustrate the resources and obligations of a Dramatistic nomenclature. Essentially, this article ("The Image of Man," by Isidor Chein) contends that the story of Creation in the book of Genesis provides a better model, even for a purely secular terminology of human motives, than is to be found in much contemporary psychology. For, according to Dr. Chein, the Biblical model presents "Man" as an "active" being, whereas many current views (in line with behaviorist theories of conditioning) falsely "presuppose a passive image of Man."

I have discussed Dr. Chein's essay at some length in a paper, "Order, Action, Victimage," presented at Grinnell College in January 1964, and to be published with papers by other participants in a series of articles on the general subject of "Order." Here I want to stress only a few of the major dialectical principles considered in that article. Above all, I would point out that Spinoza's *Ethics* (particularly Book IV) clearly indicates why Dr. Chein's statement of the case would not be adequate. A grammatical stress upon the "active" involves a reciprocal stress upon the "passive." And in systematically considering *both* active and passive sides of the human motivational ledger, Spinoza makes it clear how prone man is to the temptations of *passivity*. (Surely, for instance, he would consider as a drastic instance of human bondage our susceptibility to "inadequate ideas" whereby propaganda mills can condition us to acquiesce in the cause of militaristic adventures abroad.) But Dr. Chein maneuvers himself into a position whereby, to glorify the "active" nature of "Man," he must present his cause *antithetically* to deterministic theories that, even if they are not the whole story, could well serve *at least as admonitions* and that are needed to help complete a grammar of "action."

I here omit the third function, the "reflexive," in current cant "feedback." But it will turn up in many forms throughout these pieces. Its "symbolicity" centers in the "second-level" situation whereby there can be words-about-words. But I do want to make it clear that not only Spinoza, but also the Biblical account of Adam's "fall," directly treats of the "passive" element as inherent in the grammar of human action.

However, despite my objections to Dr. Chein's oversimplified use of the Dramatistic grammar, I found myself (uneasily) on his side when Richard E. Carney, of Indiana University, grew wrathful at the thought of Dr. Chein's monograph proclaiming the glory of "Man" as an "active" being. I was uneasy because I consider it a drastic kind of vandalism when one maneuvers oneself into a state of mind whereby one must slight any admonition as regards human susceptibility to the passivities of conditioning. Though Book V of Spinoza's *Ethics* makes it clear enough why any reduction to terms of conditioning alone would be an "inadequate idea," we must not let Dr. Chein's sales talk on "Man" make us forget Book IV and its talk of "human bondage."

Dr. Carney's attack was based on the principle of continuity (between man and other animals) that has been questioned in my foregoing article. His statement could have appropriately quoted Darwin's shrewd remark, "If man had not been his own classifier, he would never have thought of founding a separate order for his own reception." And it could wholly subscribe to Darwin's approval of Huxley's statement that there "is no justification for placing man in a distinct order." Thus, Dr. Carney sloganizes his position visually by opting for a model of "man" rather than an image of "Man." My position would necessarily be that, in the very act of developing a structure of classifications, the human classifier (be he "man" or "Man"!) by the same token does establish his nature as a special class of being. For one cannot be the kind of animal that can study biology except by having a distinctive way with symbol systems. Hence, to that extent we should be on Dr. Chein's side (in his decision to prefer a secular analogue of "Man's" image as presented in the Biblical story of Creation and Ordination). But, once that choice is made, the example of Spinoza reminds us that, even if Dr. Carney's view of "man" does make us out to be as "passive" as Dr. Chein says he does, even so, the most limited studies of Stimulus and Response, involving the narrowest of experiments with animals weak in the ways of human symbolic action, can serve to admonish us: We are constantly beset by *temptation* to become sheer automata.

But there's one further step. It involves an article on "The Personality and Career of Satan," by Henry A. Murray. This appeared appropriately as a companion piece in the same journal with Dr. Chein on "The Image of Man." Possibly because Satan can be such a charmer, it is charming, a much better-natured statement than the one on the grandeur of Man as active being. In any case, our present concerns with a Dramatistic grammar indicate why the two papers so neatly complement each other. For whereas the story in Genesis gives an account of *both the Creation and the Fall* (the *active* and the *passive*), here we find a division of labor. Dr. Chein builds his model by specializing in motives associated solely with the Creation; and Dr. Murray (in his monograph on the Tempter) specializes in motives associated with the Fall.

Neither is concerned explicitly with the ways in which the "mythic" account of motives in Genesis *unites* these motivational lines, a problem I have tried to resolve (cf. *The Rhetoric of Religion*) in terms of Order and the disobeying of orders. And a Dramatistic grammar of motives also makes us aware of a notable lacuna in Dr. Murray's delightful survey concerned with the *personalizing* of problematical inducements that got slighted in Dr. Chein's truncated and overly honorific terminology of "action." When listing the functions of religious myths, Dr. Murray says that "they should comfort the distressed, and, by presenting visions of a realizable future, engender hope, and encourage effort to achieve this." But surely, religion has functioned not only as a means of *solace* or *encouragement*, but also as a system of *controls*. The slighting of *controls* in his list is all the more surprising since he is specializing in Satan, whose Hell was surely designed to scare the devil out of us.

At one point Dr. Chein observes, "Grammar is, of course, indifferent to truth." And there certainly is a sense in which this statement is irrefutable. Yet, Dramatism would contend: Whatever the complications and paradoxes, we must keep asking always about actives, passives, and middles (reflexives)—or, if you will, effectors, receptors, and feedback (for argument's sake, I here concede to the lowest kind of reduction). So I have sought to describe at least enough of the Chein-Carney-Murray papers to indicate why (when we think of symbolicity as existing in its own right though variously modified by animality) the Dramatistic grammar possesses at least a kind of *moral* absolute (and precisely the kind that would admonish us against Dr. Chein's o'ersimplified version of "Man" simply as "active"). "Man" is "active" except when he is "passive" (suffering, in bondage even to his own stupidities). And the more I puzzle over the reflexive, the more convinced I become that all of us, in pious terror, should be on guard regarding the role of the reflexive in our ideas of identity.

We might sum up our point here by saying that the emphasis upon Creation necessarily overstresses "action," the emphasis upon the Fall necessarily overstresses "passion," and the methodic attempt to avoid a Dramatistic grammar as far as possible reaches its fulfillment in a terminology of sheer "motion." However, where the discussion of human motives is at all comprehensive, no statement of the case can exemplify any one of these emphases with complete consistency. Man's involvement in the natural order makes him in many respects analyzable in terms of sheer motion; but his powers of symbolicity give rise to kinds of symbolic action that, by the same token, make him susceptible to corresponding kinds of servitude. (My *Grammar of Motives, Rhetoric of Motives*, and *Rhetoric of Religion* seek, in "Neo-Stoic resignation," to chart a course through this motivational tangle and its terministic paradoxes.)

A few parting remarks about man (or Man!) and symbol systems in general:

In Santayana's *Scepticism and Animal Faith* (Chapter X, second paragraph), we are told that the realm of essence is "the sum of mentionable objects, of terms about which, or in which, something might be said." That one word, "mentionable," has kept vibrating in me incessantly ever since the first time I encountered it (or explicitly recognized that I had encountered it, some two decades or so ago). The word seemed to spin itself along these lines:

The world is doubtless infinitely full of entities, relationships and developments, actual or potential, for which we do not have names, and never shall. Yet for the human animal the nameless is always at least in principle the nameable (or, "mentionable"). "Mentionable" has the advantage that even with persons who would postulate an essential distinction between words and other kinds of symbolic action (such as dance, sculpture, painting, or music) all such modalities could at least be thought of as ways of "mentioning" aspects of experience. And in this sense, the human animal confronts even the nameless and unnameable within the perspective or "psychosis" of symbolicity.

In T. S. Eliot's doctoral thesis, *Knowledge and Experience in the Philosophy of F. H. Bradley* (completed in 1916, but not published until 1964), there is one astonishing puzzle. I quote a passage that got omitted from a review I did of the book:

> I refer to a sudden flurry on pages 132-135, proclaiming the all-importance of *words* or *names* in shaping the objects of attention. "Without words, no objects," he asseverates. Thus he questions whether "the explicit recognition of an object as such" can occur "without the beginnings of speech." The bundle of things that we call an object "would not be a bundle unless it were held together by the moment of objectivity which is realized in the name." After three pages that develop this line of thought vigorously, he breaks off: "This, however, is a digression." And the subject, which had thus of a sudden flared up, is dropped, except for this one later sentence that seems like a sort of retraction: "We may easily be overawed by language, and attribute to it more philosophic prestige than it deserves." Yet what is a philosophy if not the systematic development of such *attention* as depends at every step upon language? What is a philosopher necessarily doing if not attempting to translate the more-than-linguistic, less-than-linguistic, and other-than-linguistic into terms of the linguistic? So I was struck by that sudden "breakthrough," and puzzled by its disappearance promptly thereafter.

Other relevant sentences in the thesis are: "In any knowledge prior to speech the object is not so much an identity recognized as such as it is a similar way of acting; the identity is rather lived out than known. What we are here concerned with is the explicit recognition of an object as such, and I do not believe that this occurs without the beginnings of speech. . . . Our only way of showing that we are attending to an object is to show that it and ourself are independent entities, and to do this we must have names. . . . We have no objects without language."

These remarks could also have been cited when, in "Definition of Man," I was discussing the relationship between symbolism and the kind of attention needed for the development and transmitting of techniques and inventions.

In any case, we must posit a sheerly physiological set of "terms," the mere *motions* of sensation, as the body translates certain kinds of event "into terms of" sight, sound, taste, etc., while the experiencing of pleasure and pain constitutes a rudimentary physiological analogue of the Yes-No pair. Behaviorist experiments help us see how even these primary conditions of awareness can become infused with the rudiments of learning (which, so far as tests of symbolicity are concerned, attains its completion in the "reflexive" or "self-conscious" or "second-level" possibilities of symbol systems that can reflect on the problems and principles of symbol systems).

Insofar as there can be cycles of terms that imply one another, and all such terms can be variously translated into terms of either images or ideas, and any such image or idea can serve as a point of departure, providing a perspective peculiar to its particular point of view, the sheer range of such possibilities sets up the conditions for an ingredient of improvisational "freedom" in men's powers of symbolic action.

The slant of our articles on the "Definition of Man" and "Terministic Screens" might well suggest, to some readers, questions concerning the related but quite different views put forward by Marshall McLuhan, particularly in his volume *Understanding Media.* (He works in an area indeterminately midway between the *homo faber* of Technologism and the concepts of symbolic action inherent in the explicit, systematic application of a Dramatistic perspective.)

Whatever the readers sympathies with regard to McLuhan's thesis, there is the formal fact that the stating of his position necessarily involves the manipulation of his particular terminology. Hence, a Dramatistic analysis of that terminology might help clarify the nature of such projects in general. To this end we have included (pp. 410–418) a discussion of his terms, as viewed in terms of our terms.

Chapter Four

Mind, Body, and the Unconscious

I

The issue: If man is the symbol-using animal, some motives must derive from his animality, some from his symbolicity, and some from mixtures of the two. The computer can't serve as our model (or "terministic screen"). For it is not an animal, but an artifact. And it can't truly be said to "act." Its operations are but a complex set of sheerly physical *motions*. Thus, we must if possible distinguish between the symbolic action of a *person* and the behavior of such a mere *thing*.

On the other hand, psychoanalysis has a concept of "symbolic action" that does distinctly apply to *persons*. But it is not identical with such eventfulness in the sheerly "Dramatistic" sense. By "symbolic action" in the Dramatistic sense is meant any use of symbol systems in general; I am acting symbolically, in the Dramatistic sense, when I speak these sentences to you, and you are acting symbolically insofar as you "follow" them, and thus size up their "drift" or "meaning." True, there are some "Unconscious" processes involved in my speaking and your interpreting what I say. But as we shall see, this is not what Freud had in mind with *his* concept of the "Unconscious" and its relation to what *he* calls "symbolic action." For he specifically says that the "concept of unconscious psychic activity which is peculiar to psychoanalysis" is to be sharply distinguished "from philosophical speculations about the unconscious." (The point is made near the beginning of his essay "History of the Psychoanalytic Movement.")

In the discussion of "terministic screens" we offered reasons why a definition of man must be a general "philosophic" problem rather than a specifically "scientific" one. Each specific science could not be its characteristic self except insofar as it abided by its particular terminology. And each such terminology is designed for a specific set of observations rather than for meditations on the nature of man in general.

A Dramatistic terminology (built around a definition of man as the symbol-using, symbol-misusing, symbol-making, and symbol-made animal) must steer midway between the computer on one side (when taken as a model of the mind) and the neurotic on the other. For instance, while greatly admiring and subscribing to much that Freud discussed so ingeniously and imaginatively in his *Psychopathology of Everyday Life,* Dramatism cannot reduce symbolic action in *general* to the *specific* sense of symbolic action that Freud is dealing with in his studies of neuroses and the unconscious.

As regards our basic Dramatistic distinction, "Things move, persons act," the person who designs a computing device would be *acting,* whereas the device itself would but be going through whatever sheer *motions* its design makes possible. These motions could also be so utilized as to function like a voice in a dialogue. For instance, when you weigh something, it is as though you asked the scales, "How much does this weigh?" and they "answered," though they would have given the same "answer" if something of the same weight had happened to fall upon the scales, and no one happened to be "asking" any question at all. The fact that a machine can be made to function *like* a participant in a human dialogue does not require us to treat the two kinds of behavior as identical. And in one notable respect a *conditioned animal* would be a better model than a computer for the reductive interpretation of man, since it suffers the pains and pleasures of hunger and satiety, along with other manifest forms of distress and gratification, though it's weak in the ways of smiling and laughing.

In brief, man differs qualitatively from other animals since they are too poor in symbolicity, just as man differs qualitatively from his machines, since these man-made caricatures of man are too poor in animality. So our main concern in this talk will be not with the Charybdis of the computer but with the Scylla of "symbolic action" in the specifically psychoanalytic sense of the term. In Freud's sense an action is "symbolic" when, as interpreted in terms of his particular "terministic screen," it reveals the presence of a neurotic motive involving "repressions" due to the particular kind of "Unconscious" which he postulates as a locus of motives. Freud also offers as a synonym for "symbolic action" in this specific psychoanalytic sense the term "symptomatic action." For instance, if a person found it almost impossible to cross streets even when there was no apparent objective danger (as from traffic), the situation might be neurotically symbolic or symptomatic of an inability to arrive at a decision in some other matter that was of great importance to the sufferer, but was not consciously or rationally associated with the crossing of streets.

So this chapter will be concerned primarily with thoughts on the nature of the "Unconscious," in both Freudian and other senses. But first, we must consider some vexing matters having to do with the negative. The question is vexing because, just as the negative has a major place in the Dramatistic view of symbolicity, it is likewise of great moment with regard to the two realms that Dramatism must somehow steer between.

Some years ago, a bit uneasily, I proposed this notion:[1]

> The binary system in mathematics may be no more nor less nega-
> tively infused than, say, the decimal system. But this much seems
> clear: In the application of the binary system to the "electronic
> brains" of the new calculating devices, the genius of the negative is
> uppermost, as it is in the stop-go signals of traffic regulation. For
> the binary system lends itself well to technological devices whereby
> every number is stated as a succession of choices between the closing
> of an electrical current and the leaving of the contact open. In effect,
> then, the number is expressed by a series of yeses and noes, given
> in one particular order.

I am always uneasy when venturing into such areas. But now I can
quote for authority from an interesting, and at times even charming little
book, by D. S. Halacy, Jr., *Computers, the Machines We Think With*, which
on several occasions refers to the "on-off, yes-no nature" of the digital
computer. The author thus views the brain as being constructed like a digital
computer, "composed of billions of neurons, each capable of being on or
off," though he concedes that "many philosophers build a strong case for
the yes-no-maybe approach with its large areas of gray." Neurons or no
neurons, I have myself subscribed to the yes-no-maybe approach, where
human symbolicity is concerned. See, for instance, in the symposium,
Freedom and Authority in Our Time (pp. 371-372) my discussion of the
problem that arises when the public demands "simple yes-no solutions for
yes-no-maybe situations." At least language certainly has plenty of *words*
(for ideas or images) that, like "maybe" itself, fall under the heading of
attitudes midway between yes and no, whether or not the sheer motions
of the brain operate on a flat yes-no basis (like traffic signals that would
not allow for right, left, or U turns). And one possible lure of imagery
resides in the fact that it so readily transcends strict logical distinctions or
clear-cut decisions. The main thing for our purposes is to note Mr. Halacy's
point about the "power of the digital, yes-no approach," due to the fact
that, in such computers, "a single switch can only be on or off," the amazing
results being obtained by the complex interconnections among such switches
(plus the speed of the operations).

Freud's concept of "repression" in the "Unconscious" is on its face
doubly saturated with the negative. Thus we might sum up by saying:
According to the Freudian nomenclature, the "unconscious" process of
"repression" involves the fact that the thou-shalt-not's of the "superego"
would negate the desires of the "id," that portion of the "unconscious"
which knows no Negation (or, more resonantly, "knows no No"). And

[1] From "Postscripts on the Negative," *Quarterly Journal of Speech*, April, 1953.

"symbolic" or "symptomatic" kinds of action are said to result from unconscious attempts to elude the repressions imposed by the tyranny of the "superego."

Though the role of the negative in the Dramatistic concept of "symbolic action" covers a wider area than Freud's usage, the two realms are by no means mutually exclusive. Each in its way stresses the importance of the moralistic negative. But whereas the Freudian negative is identified solely with the process of *repression* in the *Unconscious*, the Dramatistic negative must focus attention upon the negative as a peculiar resource of *symbol systems*. Simplest example: If A explicitly says to B, "Don't do that," the message could hardly be reduced simply to terms of "unconscious repression." The order is clear enough on its face. And far from being "repressive," the remark may even be quite helpful advice, as when an expert is telling a learner how to avoid a mistake. Or when a mathematician's equations introduce a minus sign, we could hardly put such operations in the same class with the "negativism" of a disobedient child.

Or consider the two closely related terms in the Freudian nomenclature, "condensation" and "displacement." In Freudian usage, they refer specifically to an aspect of symbolism characteristic of dreams and neuroses. And Freud has done well by them in that connection. For instance, an "unconscious" resentment against A might be so displaced that it reveals itself as a resentment against B. And "condensation" can take place when, if A is associated in your Unconscious with B, you might have a dream in which various traits of both A and B are combined in a single image. Here would be instances of "symbolic action" in the specifically psychoanalytic sense.

Yet as regards "symbolic action" in general, there are such "displacements" as when a mathematician substitutes a symbol for an equation, or when a translator substitutes terms in one language for terms in another. And a kind of "condensation" results in every case where one moves to a higher order of generalization, as when one goes from "mother and father" to "parents," or from "brothers and sisters" to "siblings." Or, if we may revert to the discussion of poetics in particular and language in general, whereas the logic of symbolism in general might induce a poet to use imagery of death as a surrogate for "perfection" (or "finishedness"), or as a way of dignifying his theme, the implications of a specifically psychoanalytic terminology might suggest rather that a "death wish" was involved. Such instances, I hope, will serve as first rough approximate to indicate the difference between "symbolic action" in the specifically psychoanalytic sense and its more general Dramatistic meaning.

But another problem arises:

Since we began this talk by a reference to Freud's explicit admonition that psychoanalysis applies the concept of the "Unconscious" in a way to be differentiated from the "philosophic" uses of the term, just how might the two realms of meaning diverge, as regards the requirements of Dramatism in general?

Otherwise put: If man is the symbol-using animal, and if his animality is by definition categorically distinguishable from symbolicity (as our bodies differ in essence from the words we utter, or as nobody can live by the sheer *words* for "bread" alone), and as we build around the distinction between "motion" and "action" (which is motion-plus), then how about this realm of the "Unconscious"? How many categories might we need, when discussing the problem of the relation between our bodies, as sheer physical objects, and their emergence into articulacy (that is, symbolicity)? All that has been said up to now has been but a necessary introduction to the list I shall tentatively propose (under the sign of yes-no-maybe).

II
Varieties of "Unconscious"

1) There is the unconscious aspect of sheerly bodily processes (growth, metabolism, digestion, peristaltic "action," respiration, functions of the various organs, secretions of the endocrine glands, ways in which elements in the bloodstream reinforce or check one another, and so on). One may observe the healing of a wound: but there is a sense in which, even under strict observation, the processes of healing proceed *outside* one's consciousness. Possibly we have "repressed" our awareness of all such processes. At least, it is certain that, if we were specifically aware of them all (as some neurotics are sometimes aware of some visceral processes), we'd be in a condition that, as judged by our present norms, would be little short of horrible. Maybe our transcending of all such happenings (except for the "feeling tone" that may strike our "consciousness" as an overall "attitude" or "state of mind"), is to be treated as a kind of "repression." But it seems to differ from the *moralistic* kind of repression with which Freud was concerned. When we read a sentence, we are wholly "unconscious" of all the neural processes involved in our hearing and understanding of that sentence. Indeed, we must even find it hard to understand how the simplest sentence "makes sense." Here also might be included processes of training, or habit, whereby conscious effort becomes spontaneous (as with learning to walk or talk).

2) Freudian nomenclature is partial to what we might call an "archaizing principle," an explanation in terms of the *temporally* prior. Thus, adult disturbances are analyzed as vestiges of experiences undergone in childhood, infancy, and even farther back, in conditions that might possibly have prevailed during "prehistory." Similarly, even "normal" dreams

are considered from this "vestigial" point of view. And the thinking of "primitive" peoples is studied in the same light. Hence, many aspects of expression that once might have been studied in terms of *rhetorical* resources *natural* to language at *all* stages of history are treated rather as *survivals* from eras of primitive magic, ritual, and myth. There is a sense in which this "archaizing principle" can be given a more general, "philosophic" application. I have in mind the thought that *any* present moment is the "Unconscious" repository of the past, not just as regards some possible "primal" scene or "Oedipal" crime, but in terms of *all* the evolutionary unfoldings that are somehow summed up in each of us, at his given moment in history. Viewed thus, even our most mature and conscious functions are but "survivals" from conditions in the remote past. And though one may by a methodic analysis of "free associations" restore the "repressed" memory of a few supposedly "forgotten" details in a particular patient's past, all such conscious recoveries are but *infinitesimal*, as compared with the totality of the past that is somehow unconsciously implicit in us. We shall consider this matter from another standpoint in a later category.

2a) As a kind of "aside" here, we might note that even the specifically Freudian concept of unconscious repression implies at least two kinds of unconsciousness. For instance, in his essay "On the Transformation of Instincts with Special Reference to Anal Eroticism," besides noting that certain symbols "are seldom distinguished and are easily interchangeable," Freud admonishes that he is speaking "figuratively," since some of the terms to which he is referring do not properly belong to the realm of the Unconscious. He then charts some "processes of development" involving different ways in which sheer *equivalence* among terms is replaced by different *sequences* (with corresponding differences in the formation of character). That is, an unconscious *equating* of terms A and B would allow for another kind of unconscious process, the step *from A to B* in *contrast with* the step *from B to A*.

2b) A further "aside" is in order here. The Freudian concept of the "id" envisions an inborn cauldron of desires that "know no No," so that each desire is experienced without regard to the claims of any other desire ("repressions" being presumably due to the unconscious workings of the "superego"). Extending such a concept Dramatistically, one discovers that the same terministic design is involved in the Constitution of the United States. The various "principles" embodied in our Constitution are, in effect, a set of *wishes*, each proclaimed in its own right, without regard to the others. Thus, there are the principles, or "wishes," proclaiming the rights of the individual, of the States, of police powers, of national emergency, of public welfare, and so on. Each is there as a Constitutionally asserted wish, without explicit reference to the other wishes. But legal conflicts arise because, in particular cases, this "id"-like wishing on the part of the Constitution confronts problems of *denial*. In gratifying one Constitutional wish, the courts must frustrate or "repress" another. At such times, the Supreme Court is called upon to decide which wish shall be deemed *primus inter pares* in the given situation. And, necessarily, the history of the Supreme Court has been a history of changing choices as regards the *hierarchy* of such wishes (decisions as to which of the wishes should be given preferential rating), since for better or worse there is nothing in our egalitarian Constitution itself that establishes such a scale once and for all.

In my *Grammar of Motives* I had treated the Constitution's principles thus, as a set of "sovereign wishes" confronting one another like sovereign states, but I had not explicitly noted their analogy to the Freudian "id."

3) There are many kinds of unconscious memories which, though not explicitly recalled, are recallable on demand. Many of the "facts" we learn are of this sort. Thus there are variations in our ability to recall, as some trains of thought contain associations that help us recall certain otherwise "forgotten" bits of knowledge, while other trains of thought throw us off the track, by directing our attention into other associative channels. For instance, if one forgot a language that one had not spoken since childhood, surely this would not be a prime example of repression in Freud's moralistic sense. However, Freud might offer invaluable cues as to why, of a sudden, the "lost" words began turning up again.

4) The above category suggests the possibility of different sub-personalities variously at odds with one another, and to that extent in a corresponding Unconscious relationship. Thus, while writing, an author might embody a different order of motives from those he responds to, in his life outside his study. Or there can be a discontinuity between one's character under alcohol and one's character when sober, with each of them, over the years, coming to have its own character, or order of associations (so that things remembered or given primary importance under one of these dispensations are neglected in the other). Owing to the great dissociation between sleeping and waking, this thought of an Unconscious relation, or disrelation, between sub-personalities brings up another likelihood: That the symbolic consummations in forgotten or vaguely remembered dreams might serve as motivational incentives (as sources of guilt, and the like). The dreams might secretly have the effect of profoundly experienced actualities (as children who watch the brutalities on television may, as it were, "actually" participate in such behavior). But for more on this point, we must consider the next category.

5) Freud's overwhelming tendency to treat of motives in terms of the *temporally* prior (as per Rule Two, the "archaizing" principle) might deflect our attention from the possibility of refurbishing the Aristotelian concept of the "entelechy" for use in naming a species of Unconscious. By the Unconscious in this sense, I have in mind the implications of a symbol system, its "*future* possibilities" in a purely *formal* sense. Surely, in this sense,

the relation between Conscious and Unconscious is not to be considered as a matter of "repression" in the specifically Freudian sense of the term. For instance, one can hardly be said to have "repressed" one's understanding of the propositions that Euclid deduced from the definitions and axioms of his geometry. Rather, we must look upon Euclid as having *developed with thoroughness* the implications of his position. If I discover a body wandering in outer space, and if by my computations I conclude that it will strike the earth at a certain time, thereby destroying all life on this planet, I might well argue for the justice of my computations even though I didn't want the calamity to take place. True, my prophecy might happen to be reinforced by a neurotic yearning for absolute suicide. Or I may even prophesy (out of my hat) a similar calamity. But there is also the sheerly technical fact, as regards the nature of symbolism in general, that the thoroughness of my devotion to my work with a given symbol system may lead me to this "perfect" conclusion. This I call the "entelechial" motive, a motive intrinsic sheerly to symbol systems. And in this connection, the "Unconscious" implications may not be "made conscious" until one has *methodically* devoted oneself to the task of inquiring into the *fulfillment* of a given symbol system as such.

When emerging from infancy into linguistic articulacy, a child "unconsciously learns the rules" of his language's particular grammar and syntax, though these "rules" may never have been systematically formulated. If the rules were never formulated, when speaking his language he will necessarily exemplify these rules while being "unconscious" of them, as regards the *grammarian's* particular kind of explicit consciousness. Plato was much exercised about our unconscious knowledge in this sense (a kind of sheerly formal awareness that is not reducible to terms of the "repressed" in the specifically Freudian sense). Similarly, as was considered in an earlier chapter, a poet may make revisions simply because they "feel right." But *implicit* in such revisions there is a set of judgments, or aesthetic norms, which some critic might translate into an explicit set of poetic principles.

6) Quite closely related to our sixth category there is the sheerly terministic situation whereby *any* "conscious" nomenclature gives rise to a corresponding realm of the "unconscious." This kind of consideration turns up in an interesting way with regard to Marx's adaptation of Hegel's views on "consciousness" and "false consciousness." In Marx's scheme, "class consciousness" greatly overlaps upon what we might well call "class unconsciousness." For instance: By Marx's scheme, if the bourgeois conceives of all mankind in terms of the bourgeois, said bourgeois has *unconsciously* represented (or revealed) his bourgeois *consciousness*. And any concept of "development" or "progress" gives rise to corresponding concepts of "regression" (though we resist the thought that, when breathing naturally, the

body is "regressing" to processes that evolved millions of years ago; and we reserve the term for the partial regression that occurs in psychogenic asthma).

So, necessarily, we must here concern ourselves with many aspects of the Unconscious that are not wholly understandable in Freudian terms of repression. We here confront kinds of *attention* that often are not reducible to terms of *repression*. But any terminology for *directing the attention* is ultimately reducible to terms of a *principle*. That is, in its hypothetical *perfection* it can be called a kind of "Ism." Yet, any examples of the given motive that occurred prior to the formula or without knowledge of it may be said to exemplify that motive "unconsciously." In this sense, there is a kind of "unconsciousness" that is sheerly a reflection of whatever terminology one happens to be using.

7) By the Unconscious we often mean the "intuitive" or "instinctive," the weather eye of the weather prophet, the ability to be a "good judge of character," the mathematical physicist's ability to "idealize" a problem in a way that affords a solution, the expert player's ability to make exactly the right adjustments needed for his play, the ability to so "size up a situation" that one knows *uno intuitu* whether a certain thing should or should not be done, the wit to see a joke, the area of "taste," "tact," "propriety," what the Greeks called *to prepon* and the Latins *decorum*, and the eighteenth century the *je ne sais quoi*—in sum, the recognition that something is as it is, without pausing to ask exactly how one arrived at precisely that decision.

If B is greater than A, and C is greater than B, then "obviously" C is greater than A—but who can say how he "consciously" arrived at this result?! The process involved in such a judgment is as far beyond our "consciousness" as the operation of a miracle. It "just is." Yet surely our bepuzzlements here are not instances of "repression" in the strictly Freudian sense. Someday we might have some more terms for "consciously" charting this process; but we don't have them now. And even if we do, such consciousness is most likely to be "from without," as with our possibly "conscious" ways of describing how a wound heals. One may be wholly conscious of the "feeling tone" that sums up, in a kind of attitude, the diseased or healthy condition of his body. But even if the medical study of symptoms were advanced vastly beyond its present state of knowledge, such conscious "feeling tone" would but correspond to a practically infinite number of relationships about which one is almost as "unconscious" as a book's title is "unconscious" of the book's specific contents.

8) We might add a catchall category, labeled "Error, Ignorance, Uncertainty." One may eat a certain contaminated food through sheer ignorance, not owing to any psychological "repression" of such knowledge. One just happens to be "unconscious" of its true nature. And this category shades

off into many kinds of inadequately criticized responsiveness. Thus, we might make this decision rather than that, not because we have "repressed" a knowledge of the results, but because such adequate knowledge is not available to us. (For instance, what voter can possibly have adequate fore-knowledge of exactly how his candidate will behave under conditions that the candidate himself has not yet confronted?)

All told, then, we have tentatively listed these kinds of "unconscious" (many of which are obviously not reducible to the specifically Freudian concept of repression), our idea being that the very genius of the Freudian terminology leads beyond the specifically psychiatric analysis of symbolic action (the symptoms of sick souls) to thoughts on symbolic action in general.

To sum up, as possible kinds of Unconscious we have listed:

1) The sheerly physiological processes of the body.

2) The universal incorporation of the past within the present.

2a) A possible distinction between the mere unconscious equivalence of terms and unconscious ways of proceeding from one to another.

2b) Comments on the respects in which the Constitution's set of sovereign wishes (each propounded in its own right) is analogous to the Freudian concept of the "Id."

3) The recallable but not explicitly recalled. Here also might be included knowledge which one has, but which does not happen to be associated with the given topic under discussion. My concept of "perspective by incongruity" (as discussed especially in *Permanence and Change*) is concerned with the way in which poets enliven language by metaphors that leap like lightning across such gaps, and thereby bring together terms which we had unconsciously classed as mutually exclusive.

4) The closely related category of dissociation among "sub-personalities."

5) The "entelechial" kind of "futurity" (as certain kinds of observations or conclusions may be *implicit* in a given terminology, quite in the sense that a grammar and syntax are implicit in a given language). One can be moved by a "terministic compulsion" to track down such possibilities.

6) The "Ismic" paradox whereby any terminology that systematically calls attention to a hitherto unnoticed area of speculation by the same token creates a corresponding kind of "unconscious."

7) The "intuitive" recognition that something is as it is.

8) A catchall category. Error, confusion, or uncertainty, due simply to the fact that the conditions for making an accurate judgment are not present (as when trying to identify an object too far off to be seen clearly, or when voting for a candidate when nobody in the world, including the candidate himself, knows how he will act if the unforeseen pressures of history build up this way rather than that).

III
The Five Dogs

So much for our tentative categories of the Unconscious. But where problems of terminology are concerned, we must always keep on the move. So, for a windup, let's try a different slant, having in mind both the psychoanalytic and the Dramatistic concepts of "symbolic action."

Animalistically, there are many species of dogs. But Dramatistically, these reduce to five (not a single one of which might meet the requirements of a dog-fancier—or should we say, a dog-man?).

For a finish, I would propose this other cut across our subject:

First, along psychoanalytic lines, there is the "primal" dog, the first dog you knew, or loved, or were frightened by, or lost. It secretly ties in with what the anthropologist Malinowski would call "context of situation." For though many or all of the details that are associated with that dog may have been forgotten (and thus become "unconscious"), we now know that they are still there within you somehow (and can be disclosed by drugs, hypnosis or psychoanalysis).

Next, there's the "jingle" dog. It concerns the sheerly accidental nature of the *word* "dog," what it rhymes with in English as distinct from what the corresponding word rhymes with in other languages, and above all, in English, we might well keep in mind Cummings' undeniable observation that the jingle dog is "God spelled backwards." (Or did he say it the other way round?)

Third comes the "lexical" dog. This is the one defined in the dictionary, "by genus and differentia." It is the most public, normal, and rational of all dogs—and the emptiest of all, as regards the attitude of either poets or neurotics. If that great, good, sound, healthy, public meaning for "dog" were all we had, I can confidently assure you that the world would be completely clear of poetry. This is the only definition that wholly makes sense, if the world is to be kept going. But along with the fact that this definition of "dog" is tremendously necessary, there's also the fact that "dog" as so conceived is totally inane. You know what I mean. But if you want documentation besides, just track down all the references to dogs in Aeschylus' *Oresteia* (or see the pages on "dog" in William Empson's *The Structure of Complex Words*).

Fourth, there's an "entelechial dog." This is the "perfect" dog *towards which* one might aspire. I might give a roundabout example of this sort: Beginning with the material substance, *bread*, let us next move to the *word* "bread." Once we have that *word*, through sheerly verbal manipulations we can arrive at a term for "perfect bread." Having got to that point, we find two quite different kinds of resources open to us. (1) We may feel disillusioned about "reality" because the *thing* bread falls so tragically short of the ideal that flits about our *word* for "perfect" bread. Or (2) we might be graced with the opportunity to discern, all around us, evidences of ways whereby even the worst of bread embodies, however finitely, the *principle* of an infinitely and absolutely "perfect" bread. Dogs endowed with "personalities" in animal stories would be a fictional variant of such an "entelechial" motive. In their way, they are "perfect" embodiments of certain traits. Lassie has been the Machinery's prime exhibit, as regards the entelechial dog.

Finally, there is the "tautological" dog. We here have in mind the fact that a dog involves a particular set of associations which, in a sense, reproduce his "spirit." For instance: kennel, dog food, master, the hunt, cat, protection, loyalty, slavishness, the place where the dog was killed, and so on. When I was young, I always had a dog, and I always thought of lions as big dogs. It was quite a blow to me when I first learned that lions are really big cats. Looking back, I incline to believe that I had a "cycle" or "ladder" of terms, running from dog, to boy, to father, to lion, to king (or generally, ruler or authority), to God. Here would be a "tautological" terminology in the sense I now have in mind.

Our five dogs overlap considerably, I concede. But there are terministic situations when each is most directly to be considered in its own right, though we should always keep the whole lot in mind, when inquiring into the relations between the overt symbol and its possible dissolvings into the "Where is it?" of the Unconscious.

Comments

As regards category 2a): Note that there is an ever-fluctuant line between conscious and unconscious "equations." A rhetorician ("propagandist") may deliberately identify certain acts with courage, cowardice, negligence, and so on. Or such equations may be but implicit in a work (as when the poet, or the neurotic, spontaneously attitudinizes towards persons and things, thereby in effect pronouncing them admirable, despicable, consoling, fearsome, and the like). And however unconscious such equations may happen to be, the critic or the analyst can make all such associations as explicit as though they had been deliberately intended. The more "unconscious" such equations are (in the minds of an audience), the greater their effectiveness is likely to be as "stimuli" that provoke "responses."

It would seem that both "primal" and "lexical" dogs involve the *forgetting* of specific contexts which figured in the origins of the term's meaning. The "primal" dog is peculiarly *mine*. It can be *thine* only insofar as we both got the "meaning" of "dog" burned into us under the same impressive or traumatic conditions; and it is "symbolic" (in the special psychoanalytic sense) insofar as I "unconsciously" feel that it *implies* these conditions (conditions that, in one sense have been "forgotten," but in another sense are inexorably "unforgettable").

The "lexical" dog can also derive its meaning from forgotten contexts. I heard it used often enough for me to "get the idea" (an outcome which is pragmatically indicated by my ability to use the word "properly" in a sentence and which may occur even after a single "nontraumatic" encounter with the term). Such usage is necessarily public; and as regards hidden emotional contexts, it is essentially so inane that I can "learn the meaning" by merely asking "What does that word mean?" or by looking it up in a dictionary. Here, the necessary context would be "symbolic" in the most general sense of the term—but it probably does involve the "forgetting" of countless contexts, the remembering of which (either explicitly or via the "unconscious" equations inherent in our "primal" dog) would be quite irrelevant to the minimal lexical meaning. Thus, if I asked, "What does that word mean?" prominent among the forgotten contexts of my encounter with the term would necessarily be whatever "punishments" I underwent or whatever "apocalypses" I experienced when learning how to couch that question.

In sum, it would seem that we learn language "rationally" only by much forgetting (which necessarily involves an "unconscious" of *some* sort).

Note also that the "jingle" dog might fit in well with the "primal" dog, as when the name for a person of one's adult acquaintanceship took on furtive connotations by reason of its tonal association (close or remote) with the name for one's primal dog. (We might call this "the Mother Goose principle" in psychiatry.)

The chapter as presented here is part of a paper that was cut considerably, to meet the restrictions of a fifty-minute lecture. The omitted portion, originally presented as a basis of discussion at the October 1959 meeting of the Columbia University Seminar on Problems of Interpretation (Hermeneutics), involves an attempt to "prophesy" the nature of the Freudian terminology, viewed as a dialectical structure spun from its own internal principles of organization. Since Freud is so thoroughly Dramatistic, I thought that I could best reveal the muscularity of the Freudian nomenclature by methodologically "prophesying" after the event.

But though such a terministic inspection of psychoanalysis testifies to my great admiration for Freud's dialectic, I admit that such an inquiry implies a more tentative attitude towards the Freudian "screen" than might serve best in the business of cure. Since it is often the case that a sick soul needs to have implicit faith in the analyst, perhaps a concern, no matter how appreciative, with the terministic deployments of the Freudian nomenclature as such threatens to impair the effectiveness of the analyst's role, with regard to his patient (or customer). In any case, the preparatory summing up of our position in these essays would not be complete unless I here gave the substance of my pages on the approach to the Freudian perspective, viewed purely as a terminology, derivable in accordance with grammatical resources implicit in its key terms.

In *Life Against Death*, Norman O. Brown begins, "There is one word which, if we only understand it, is the key to Freud's thought. That word is 'repression.'" And he quotes from Freud, "The theory of repression is the pillar upon which the edifice of psychoanalysis rests." But Freud also refers to "that concept of unconscious psychic activity which is peculiar to psychoanalysis, and distinguishes it markedly from philosophical speculations about the unconscious." Freud also refers to the major importance of "transference" and "resistance," terms which concern the patient's relation to the analyst.

I would here propose to situate the generating principle of the Freudian nomenclature not, like Norman O. Brown, in one term, but in a *pair* of terms. Just as Berkeley spins his philosophy from the equation, "*esse* is *percipi*," and Spinoza's *Ethics* centers in the equation, "*Deus sive Natura*," so I'd propose to situate the roots of Freud's terminology in the *combining* of two terms; namely: his view of "repression" as an "unconscious" process. In brief, I'd start with a notably altered formula in *Life Against Death*: To put it another way, the unconscious *is* "the dynamically unconscious repressed." Or recall the book's quotation from Freud's *Collected Papers*: "The essence of repression lies simply in the function of rejecting or keeping something out of consciousness." Thus, we should begin with the generative equating of "repression" and "unconscious"—thus the nature of "transference" and "resistance" would have to be "derived" from this primal equation.

But even if we do begin with the repression-unconscious pair, we immediately confront two sets of terms, each of which suggests possibilities not necessarily suggested by the other. For instance, by dwelling on the term "repression," we encounter implications of this sort: If repression (as a process, or verb), then there must be something that acts as a repressive agent. If an agent is in the process of repressing, then there must be something that is repressed. Also, the repressing of the repressed by a represser must take place in some kind of situation. But the concept of repression also implies the concept of resistance. And if there is resistance, then any manifestation of it must involve some kind of deflection, or "sublimation," or transference. Other possibilities suggest themselves (still in line with sheerly grammatical speculations on the kinds of terministic functions inherent in the repression-unconscious pair). From the success or failure or modification of a process we may infer various eventualities of pleasure or pain (reward or punishment). Further: If repression, then certainly *pressure* (hence, possible speculations on degrees of intensity or psychic energy involved in repression and the release from repression). Or we might look for secondary elements that variously assist the repression or the resistance to the repression. Or repression might fold back on itself, allowing for attempts to repress the repression.

One might continue, thus tentatively spinning out a set of functions implicit in the sheer grammar of the term "repression." Thus, there can be *actives* and *passives*, represse*r* and represse*d*. Also, since the idea of *purpose* is implicit in the idea of an act, "repression" takes on teleological possibilities. If A hurts B unintentionally, the incident is not an *act* in the full sense of the term, but an *accident*. However, though we have here been considering only one member of the generative pair, it is obvious that, once the element of the "unconscious" is introduced, a terministic situation is then set up whereby we might look for a kind of "accident" that is "unconsciously" an *act*, in "unconsciously" possessing a kind of *purpose*.

But before turning directly to the second member of our parental pair, we should note one further important grammatical possibility, as viewed from the "pressure" side. If repression (in being active) somehow involves a teleological element (a *purposive* repressing of the repressed), then the standard resources of grammar suggest a further likelihood. Besides a concept of the "re-pressed" (a perfect passive participle), we might propose a blank belonging in the *gerundive* category; namely: not just the "repressed," but the "to-be-re-pressed."

Next, dwelling on the term "unconscious," we note first of all that it implies a direct counterterm, the "conscious." But any such pair of antithetical terms suggests the possibility of an intermediate term (as the terms "God" and "man" set up the terministic conditions for the intermediate idea of a "God-man"). For a reason to be discussed more fully later, "preconscious" is an ideal Freudian choice of intermediate term here, owing to the strongly *temporal* con-notations of the prefix.

But once you have these three terms, there arises the possibility, or rather terministic inevitability, of *metaphor*. Insofar as repression is some kind of *act*, it must take place in some kind of *scene*. Thus, instead of saying merely that the process of repression *is* unconscious, you can figuratively place the process *in* "the" unconscious. (Bentham's study of the "fictions" that are necessary to a psychological nomenclature is of major importance here.) Or, by another ex-tension of such a topological figure, suggestiveness of the figure can invite us to ask how the awareness of unconscious processes can be brought "*into*" the realm of consciousness. Further, insofar as all such processes are rooted in the organic nature of the living, you may (or must) conclude that their elements are in some way related, or *associated*. (And from there we are prodded to ask about pos-sibilities of *dissociation*.) And just as no two leaves are exactly alike, so the systematic study of *associations* should provide a route into inquiries about the unique nature of an *individual* (regardless of the respects in which the same terministic grammar is applied to all men).

Next, insofar as the unconscious is by definition the realm of the unex-pressed (as tested by the norms of consciousness), we encounter a likely pro-portion of this sort: Unconscious is to *re*pression as conscious is to *ex*pression (or as latent is to patent). And to say as much is to bring up questions about placement in terms of the intermediate stage, the preconscious.

We now have further material for consideration of the gerundive (the "to-be-repressed" as vs. the "to-be-expressed"). For, though the *process* takes place "in" the Unconscious, the *associations* involved in such repression come by a roundabout route. Another way to proclaim the *purposive* nature of the Unconscious (and its involvement in the act of repression) is to say simply that it *wishes*. (Freud's stress upon the ubiquity of wishing makes his psychology, in its way, as "teleological" as Aristotelian metaphysics. At the same time, as re-gards the principle of terministic fulfillment in all its resources, one should keep in mind the fact that there is a purely *technical* kind of gratification not reducible to wish fulfillment in the strictly psychoanalytic sense, as one may strive to be "proved right" in a prophecy even though the outcome prophesied is not at all to one's liking.)

Our conscious life introduces associative material for the kind of uncriti-cized expressions that the unconscious seeks to transform. And the manifesta-tions of this material will reveal the pressure of the moralistic "thou-shalt-not's" that the problem-laden "reality" of the individual's *conscious* life in society (and, more directly, the family) imposes upon him. That is, in deriving from the Un-conscious the content for the "to-be-repressed" and the "to-be-expressed how-ever deviously," we do well to realize that such unconscious processes derive an essential aspect of their content from the realm of experience (with its associations) that we encounter in the conscious (and its norms of "Conscience").

It should now be apparent why the Freudian terminology must build atop *two* originating terms rather than *one*. "Repression" suggests a set of terms implicit in the idea of a *process*; the "Unconscious," by reason of its dialectical relation to the Conscious, provides the particular *content* (the realm of *associations*) that is to be "processed" (the *gerundive*). And the two terministic lines, in conjunction, set up the conditions for a dialectical relation between a "pleasure principle" (on the "Unconscious" side) and a "reality principle" (on the Conscious side). Also, by keeping this double genesis in mind, we can more easily understand why Freud never yielded to Utopian hopes for the ultimate elimination of repression. The repression-unconscious-preconscious-conscious relationships are intrinsic to the terminology. Hence, though the ravages of such relationships may be thought of as capable of modification or mitigation, the very nature of the initial equation implies, or "foretells," that conflict is *permanently* "built into" the system. (Incidentally, our previous remarks on the shortcomings of Isidor Chein's Dramatistic grammar should explain why we'd subscribe to Freud's ultimate qualified resignation, as distinct from Norman O. Brown's project for an ultimate Utopianism.)

But in the methodological attempt to reveal the genius of the Freudian terminology by "prophesying after the event," certain contributory rules were found necessary. Let us consider four major ones, without necessarily concluding that we have exhausted the lot.

Rule I: When seeking to define the etiology of a psychic symptom, where possible one should consider the formative situation in terms of the *temporally* prior. Thus, adult disturbances are to be studied as vestiges of experiences undergone in childhood, infancy, and even "prehistory." Similarly, even "normal" dreams are to be considered from this "vestigial" point of view. And the thinking of "primitive" peoples is to be viewed in the same light. Hence, many aspects of expression that might otherwise be treated in terms of resources natural to language *qua* language at any stage in history, will be treated rather as *survivals* from eras of primitive magic and myth. Freud's term, the "preconscious," also reflects this slant. In the previous essay we called this the "archaizing" principle.

Rule II: The principle of "dramatic thoroughness." This rule refers to the ways whereby: Friendship can be viewed in terms of homosexuality; family affection in terms of incest; disagreement (or even agreement) in terms of hostility; resistance to the father (or to authority in general) in terms of a desire to kill. *However*, this "thoroughness" should be strategically modified by the resources of "unconscious repression" (with corresponding allowance for "sublimations," and the like). In sum, any reduction of a motive to its ideally extreme manifestation is to be modified by the advice to look in actuality for *attenuations* of any such extremes.

The rule of "dramatic thoroughness" also ties in with the "archaizing principle" via the concept of the infantile "polymorphous-perverse," and the use of this concept with regard to socially sanctioned variants (such as the "exhibitionism" of actors).

Also, the sexual emphasis in general would belong here. For any translation of sociopolitical situations into terms of personal motives, and any translation of these into terms of sexuality, is in the direction of dramatic saliency. (Freud here even went along with the traditional tendency to "sexualize" the sheer *grammar* of "active" and "passive" motives, by classing them with "masculine" and "feminine" respectively.)

Rule III: The treatment of action in general should retreat behind the study of symbolic action in the specific sense of the *neurotic* or *symptomatic*. For instance, "condensation" and "displacement" are defined from the standpoint of their role in the symbolism of dreams and neurosis. But there are also forms of condensation and displacement natural to symbol systems in general, and so on. This point was sufficiently developed in the article on which we are now commenting.

At least one more rule is needed. Rule IV would concern the animus or spirit of the Freudian nomenclature, viewed as a *Weltanschauung*, an overall working attitude, or "philosophy of life." We might call it the "principle of individualistic libertarianism." The quickest way to suggest the all-importance of this principle is to contrast it with John Bunyan's Calvinistic view of guilt. Bunyan looked upon the sense of guilt as a sign of one's "election," an indication that God had included the sinner among those he had chosen to *call* for *salvation* (unlike the reprobates, whose happy-go-lucky attitude showed that they were among the damned, since they would choose the easy path to perdition). Contrast this view of *guilt as promissory* with the Freudian view of *guilt as a disease* (a kind of "moral masochism") which psychoanalysis would attempt to cure, or at least to greatly remedy. (This is a perfect example of what we mean by "equations.")

Surely, at every turn in the Freudian corpus we encounter the implications of a libertarian and individualistic policy. And though the *familial* nature of the associations with which psychoanalytic therapy is concerned provide interpretative bridges for the study of the ways in which the individual's relation to his family merge into relations with the tribe, the essence of "individualistic libertarianism" is symbolized even in the sheer design of the typical Freudian therapeutic situation. I refer to the individual patient, on a couch, joining with the analyst in a search for the patient's emancipation by tracking down his own particular "equations," as revealed by the methodic study of his "free associations." And characteristically, when the old *metaphysical* (Fichtean) distinction between an "I" and a "Not-I" becomes transformed by Freud into a triadic *psychological* analogue, here a possible grammar of first, second, and third persons becomes instead a *third* person (the "id") set against two kinds of first person ("ego" and "superego"). Contrast this pronominal design (and its corresponding notions of identity) with that of Martin Buber's "I-thou" pair. However, the second person could be considered *implicitly* present, in the sense that the *superego is in effect addressing the ego of the patient*, via the principle of parentage in particular and of authority in general.

The all-important principle of the negative figures here is a big way. Whereas the id knows no negative, the superego is rife with the negativity of moralistic admonition (the principle of the "thou-shalt-not's"). And the ego must scheme somehow to wend its dues-paying way between these antagonistic limits. A kind of grammatical duplication results. For if the id by definition desires and the superego by definition admonishes and the ego by definition selects, we are but saying in effect that the desirer desires, the admonisher admonishes, and the selector selects.

In one notable respect our formula "individualistic libertarianism" is a misnomer. Though the Freudian terminology, viewed as a "philosophy of life," does lay major stress upon emancipating the patient, this very featuring of *Freedom* deflects attention from the notably *Authoritarian* aspects of psychotherapy, in the patient's subjection (however roundabout) to the analyst's role as priest of the confessional couch. But the element of authority is doubly concealed by the fact that the overtly libertarian style of the terminology contrasts so greatly with the authoritarian element explicitly indicated in Fascist, Communist, and theological doctrine (a kind of unconscious deception found also in much contemporary science, that continually appeals to the testimony of the "authorities" in a given field).

Another paradoxical situation might also be worth at least a tentative glance. Whereas the parental connotations of the Freudian "Superego" lend themselves well to a stress upon the vagaries of symbolic *parricide*, there are indications that the terminology of psychoanalysis was actually developed under the sign of symbolic *fratricide*. I refer to the fact that Freud's basic position took form through intimate correspondence with a close friend, Wilhelm Fliess, with whom Freud later broke off all relations. Freud's letters were preserved, but Fliess's were destroyed. Destroyed by whom, the Nazis? No, by Freud himself. We might look upon this moment as the sacrifice upon which the theory of psychoanalysis was founded, a secular analogue of the role played by the symbol of the Crucifix in the incunabula of Christian culture.

Reverting to wider concepts of the "unconscious," we should note that there is also a kind of purely physiological "awareness," or "implicit perception," by which the body responds to situations "unconsciously." For instance, though certain kinds of radiation may not register in terms of *immediate* sensation (being "intangible" and "invisible") they may be producing in the body various deleterious changes ("motions") that will *eventually* be manifested in an altered "feeling tone," with related symptoms. Such processes would be "unconscious" in the sense that (unlike the *explicit* registering of motions in terms of colors, sounds, etc.) they do not show up as "essences." (I here use the term as Santayana might, when referring to a sensory quality purely as an intuition, regardless of its possible nature as a pragmatic sign. For instance, red *qua* red would be an essence, but red as a traffic signal would add a pragmatic dimension to such an essence.) Yet the body somehow "knows" the "unconsciously" recorded motions insofar as its intrinsic nature is altered in the course of being inundated by them.

Chapter Five

Coriolanus—and the Delights of Faction

I

This chapter is to involve one of my experiments with the safest and surest kind of prophecy; namely: prophecy after the event. Our job will be to ask how Shakespeare's grotesque tragedy, *Coriolanus*, "ought to be." And we can check on the correctness of our prophecies by consulting the text.

We begin with these assumptions: Since the work is a tragedy, it will require some kind of symbolic action in which some notable form of victimage is imitated, for the purgation, or edification of an audience. The character that is to be sacrificed must be fit for his role as victim; and everything must so fit together that the audience will find the sacrifice plausible and acceptable (thereby furtively participating in the judgment against the victim, and thus even willing the victimage). The expectations and desires of the audience will be shaped by conditions within the play. But the topics exploited for persuasive purposes *within* the play will also have strategic relevance to kinds of "values" and "tensions" that prevail *outside* the play.

There is a benign perversity operating here. In one sense, the aesthetic and the ethical coincide, since a way of life gives rise to a moral code, and the dramatist can exploit this moral code for poetic effects by building up characters that variously exemplify the system of vices and virtues to which the code explicitly or implicitly subscribes. But in another sense the aesthetic and the ethical are at odds, since the dramatist can transform our moral problems into sources of poetic entertainment. Any ethical "thou shalt not" sets up the conditions for an author to engage an audience by depicting characters that variously violate or threaten to violate the "thou shalt not." And many motivational conflicts that might distress us in real life can be transformed into kinds of poetic imitation that engross us. Thus in the realm of the aesthetic we may be delighted by accounts of distress and corruption that would make the moralist quite miserable.

The moral problem, or social tension, that is here to be exploited for the production of the "tragic pleasure" is purely and simply a kind of discord intrinsic to the distinction between upper classes and lower classes. However, a certain "distance" could be got in Shakespeare's day by treating the problem in terms not of contemporary London but of ancient Rome. A somewhat analogous situation is to be seen in Euripides' tragedy of *The Trojan Women*, which appeared some months after the Athenians had destroyed the little island of Melos, though on its face the play was concerned with the Trojan war, the theme of *The Iliad*. When *Coriolanus* appeared there had been considerable rioting due to the Enclosure Acts by which many tenants had been dispossessed of their traditional rights to the land, and were suffering great hardships. Both of these plays may, in their way, have gained strictly contemporary relevance from the allusive exploiting of a "timely topic." But in any case, each was dealing with a distress of much longer duration, in Euripides' case the horrors of war, and in Shakespeare's case the *malaise* of the conflict between the privileged and the underprivileged, as stated in terms of a struggle between the patricians and plebeians of old Rome.

If we are going to "dramatize" such a tension, we shall want first of all a kind of character who in some way helps *intensify* the tension. Where there are any marked differences in social status, in the situation itself there is a kind of "built-in pride," no matter how carefully one might try to mitigate such contrasts. And despite polite attempts to gloss things over, the unresolved situation is intrinsically there. By the nature of the case, it involves *exclusions*.

But for our purposes the main consideration is this: Whereas a hostess, or a diplomat, or an ingratiating politician, or a public relations counsel might go as far as possible towards *toning down* such situations, the dramatist must work his cures by a quite different method. He must find ways to *play them up*. In some respects, therefore, this play will require a kind of character who is designed to help aggravate the uneasiness of the relationship between nobles and commoners.

For this aspect of his role, our chosen victim is obviously a perfect fit. In contrast with the suave Menenius, who has been addressing the mutinous citizens with such a cautious mixture of gravity and humor, our chosen victim's first words to the people are: "What's the matter, you dissentious rogues, / That, rubbing the poor itch of your opinion, / Make yourselves scabs?" Thereafter, again and again, his gruff (or if you will, arrogant) manner of speaking is designed to point up (for the audience) the conflict intrinsic to the class distinctions with which the play is "drastically" concerned. (It's well to recall here that, in earlier medical usage, a "drastic" was the name for the strongest kind of "cathartic." Also, the word derives etymologically from the same root as "drama.")

The Greek word *hubris* sometimes translates best as "pride," sometimes as "excess." And in Athenian law *hubris* was also used to designate a civil offense, an insulting air of superiority, deemed punishable by death. When you note how neatly all three meanings come together in the role of

Coriolanus, I think you will realize at least one reason why I find the play so fascinating. The grotesque hero is *excessively* downright, forthright, outright (and even, after his fashion upright), in his unquestioned assumption that the common people are intrinsically inferior to the nobility. Indeed, though the word "noble" suggests to most of us *either* moral *or* social connotations, Coriolanus takes it for granted that only the *socially* noble can have nobility of any sort. (The word appears about 76 times in the play. In half of these contexts it is applied to Coriolanus himself. And, to my knowledge, it is never used ironically, as with Mark Antony's transformations of the word "honourable.") Coriolanus is excessive in ways that prepare the audience to relinquish him for his role as scapegoat, in accentuating a trait that the audience also shares with him, though seldom so avowedly.

More "prophesying after the event" is still to be done. But first, perhaps we should pause to give a generalized outline of the plot, having in mind the kind of tension (or factional malaise) that the drama would transform into terms of purgative appeal:

> After having gained popular acclaim through prowess in war, a courageous but arrogant patrician, who had been left fatherless when young and was raised by his mother, is persuaded by his mother to sue for high political office. In campaigning, he alienates the plebeians who, goaded by his political rivals, condemn him to exile. When in exile, making an alliance with the commander of the armies he had conquered, he leads a force against his own country. But before the decisive battle, during a visit by his closest relatives, his mother persuades him not to attack. In so doing, she unintentionally sets in motion the conditions whereby the allied commander, whom he had formerly vanquished and who envies his fame, successfully plots his assassination.

It is impressive how perfectly the chosen victim's virtues and vices work together, in fitting him for his sacrificial function. The several scenes in the first act that build up his prowess as a soldier not only endow him with a sufficient measure of the heroics necessary for tragic dignification. They also serve to make it clear why, when he returns to Rome and, against his will, consents to seek the office of consul, he is bound to be a misfit. Shakespeare himself usually gives us the formula for such matters. It is stated by the Tribune, Brutus, in Act III, scene iii: Get him angry, for

> . . . He hath been us'd
> Ever to conquer, and to have his worth
> Of contradiction. Being once chaf'd, he cannot
> Be rein'd again to temperance; then he speaks
> What's in his heart, and that is there which looks
> With us to break his neck.

He is not the "war games" kind of military man, not the "computer mentality"; thus we spontaneously accept it that his valiant though somewhat swashbuckling ways as a warrior will make him incompetent in the wiles of peaceful persuasion, which the wily Shakespeare so persuasively puts in a bad light, *within* the conditions of the play, by his treatment of the Tribunes. Though Shakespeare's theater is, from start to finish, a masterful enterprise in the arts of persuasion, high among his resources is the building of characters who are weak in such devices. Indeed, considered from this point of view, Coriolanus' bluntness is in the same class with Cordelia's fatal inability to flatter Lear. Later we shall find other reasons to think of Lear in connection with Coriolanus' railings. Meanwhile, note how the Tribunes' skill at petition is portrayed as not much better than mere cunning, even though somewhat justified by our highborn goat's arrogance in his dealings with the commoners. He finds it impossible even to simulate an attitude of deference. And once we have his number, when he sets out to supplicate, armed with the slogan "The word is 'mildly,' " the resources of dramatic irony have already prepared us for the furious outbursts that will get the impetuous war-hero banished from Rome, a climax capped perfectly by his quick rejoinder, "I banish you!" As a fearless fighter, he is trained to give commands and to risk his life, not to supplicate. And the better to build him up, in the role of the Tribunes Shakespeare makes the art of political supplication seem quite unsavory.

All told, Coriolanus' courage and outspokenness make him a sufficiently "noble" character to dignify a play by the sacrificing of him. And excessive ways of constantly reaffirming his assumption that only the *social* nobility can be *morally* noble indicts him for sacrifice. But more than this is needed to make him effectively yieldable.

For one thing, always in drama we encounter a variation on the theme of what I would call the "paradox of substance." A character cannot "be himself" unless many others among the dramatis personae contribute to this end, so that the very essence of a character's nature is in a large measure defined, or determined, by the other characters who variously assist or oppose him. The most obvious instance of what I mean is the role of Aufidius. If it is an integral part of Coriolanus' role to be slain, there must be a slayer. And in this sense Aufidius is "derived from" the character of Coriolanus. The conditions of the play set up Coriolanus as a gerundive, a "to be killed," and Aufidius is to be the primary instrument in the killing. As is typical of a Shakespearean play, just before the close of the first act Aufidius points the arrows of the audience's expectations by announcing to a soldier (and thus to the audience) that he will destroy Coriolanus in whatever way possible. Even so, it's always good if a man speaks with high respect of a slain rival; accordingly, though Aufidius must be plotter enough to fulfill his role in Coriolanus' death, he must be of sufficient dignity so that his final tribute to the "noble memory" of Coriolanus will serve to give the audience a parting reassurance that they have participated in the symbolic sacrifice of a victim worth the killing. The assurance was made doubly necessary by the fact that, just before the slaying, there had been a kind of last-moment revelation, when Aufidius called the bold warrior a "boy of tears," thus propounding a final formula for Coriolanus' relationship to his mother. Aufidius' claims as a worthy opponent (despite his unsavory traits) are established in Coriolanus' first references to him, such as, "I sin in envying his nobility," and "He is a lion / That I am proud to hunt."

This relationship we should dwell on. For it best illustrates just what we mean by "prophesying after the event" in order to "derive" the play in terms of poetics. If the characters are viewed simply as "people," we should treat the relationship between Coriolanus and Volumnia much as Plutarch did, in the "Life" from which Shakespeare borrowed so much of his plot. Coriolanus would thus be interpreted as the offspring of a bellicose, overbearing mother, who sought to compensate for the death of his father by being both mother and father to him. There is one change worth noting. Whereas Plutarch attributes Coriolanus' resultant irritability to womanishness, Shakespeare seems to have settled for a mere failure to outgrow boyishness. But our main point is this: Along the lines of poetic principles, the derivation should be reversed; and instead of viewing Coriolanus as an offspring of his mother, we view her role as a function contributory to his.

Thus, in an early scene, she is portrayed as a pugnacious virago of whom the son became a responsive masculine copy. This portrait of her prepares us to accept it as "natural" that, when he returns from the battlefields, *she* can persuade him, against his wishes, to stand for consul. And thus, later in the play, we will accept it that *she* can persuade him not to attack Rome—and (quite unintentionally on her part) this decision sets up the conditions responsible for his death. In brief, when using her to account for Coriolanus' character in the first place, Shakespeare is preparing her to serve as plausible explanation for two crucial moments in the *plot*: a nonpolitical man's ventures into politics, and a fighting man's failure to join in battle when success was certain. In brief, her relation to Coriolanus motivates for us two decisions of his that are basically necessary, to make the *turns* in the tragedy seem plausible.

I say "turns," having in mind the Aristotelian word, "peripety," to name the striking moment, near the center of a complex plot, when some significant reversal takes place. But I might here pause to note that this is a play of many such reversals. In Act I, there are the many scenes that might in general be entitled the "Tides of Battle," including the one where Coriolanus—or at that time, Caius Marcius, since he has not yet received his new name from the city he conquered—is thought to be lost, through having single-handedly pursued the enemy within the gate of Corioli, fighting alone where Plutarch less theatrically had reported him as but leader of a small band. At the end of Act II, the commoners are persuaded by the Tribunes to retract their intention of voting for Coriolanus as consul. The big peripety is, as one might expect, in Act III, the hero's fatal bursts of rage having been prepared for ironically by his decision to be mild. In this act, there is a kind of peripety-atop-peripety, when Coriolanus retorts to his banishers, "I banish you!"

In Act IV, scene v, there is a neat turn when Aufidius' servingmen, who would treat Coriolanus shabbily when he first appears, abruptly change their tune after he has talked with Aufidius, and the compact against Rome has been agreed on. Besides being one of the few comic spots in the play, this scene is also useful in preparing for the last fatal reversal, since it brings out the fact that, even if Coriolanus and Aufidius are to become allies, Coriolanus' reputation is a threat to Aufidius. Another reversal, in scene vi, occurs when, just after the Tribunes and citizens have been congratulating themselves on the conditions of peace resulting form Coriolanus' banishment, they are startled by the news that Coriolanus is marching on Rome.

In Act V, there is a fatal peripety, when Coriolanus is persuaded by his mother to give up his intention of attacking Rome. This leads to another peripety, the ironic twist whereby, soon after Menenius has explained to one of the Tribunes that Coriolanus will never yield ("There is no more mercy in him than there is milk in a male tiger"), they learn that Coriolanus has begun to withdraw. And even though the arrows of our expectations were clearly pointing in this direction, there is a final peripety in the hero's slaying.

Coriolanus' wife, Virgilia, is quickly "derivable." In contrast with his continual bluster, she is his "gracious silence." Contrasting with his bloodthirsty mother, she faints at the very mention of blood. In her sensitiveness and devotion, she is by implication a vote for Coriolanus. There's a skillful touch, in Act IV, scene ii, where she flares up for a moment against the Tribunes, and boasts her husband as a fighter: "He'ld make an end of thy posterity." There's a different twist, but surely conceived in the spirit of the same theater, when the young son (who is a chip off the old block, and loved to rip apart a butterfly) flares up at his father. The most notable thing about Valeria, from the standpoint of Shakespearean dramaturgy, is the fact that, though this friend of the family serves well for handling the relation between mother-in-law and daughter, she has a much less active role in the play than she does in Plutarch. For in Plutarch, *she* suggests that the women go to plead with Coriolanus and dissuade him from attacking Rome, whereas the whole musculature of Shakespeare's play requires maximum stress upon his mother's role in this development. The two Generals (Titus Lartius and Cominius) are "derivable" from

Coriolanus in the sense that, both being men of high repute, their constant respect for him speaks for him. Also, his loyalty to them serves to establish that he is not avid for dictatorial power, but geniunely represents an integral conflict between patricians and plebeians. (Shakespeare's formula for Coriolanus' treatment of the commoners had been summed up by a minor character thus: "He seeks their hate with greater devotion than they can render it him.") The citizens have the mixture of distress, resentment, and instability that enables them to help Coriolanus get into the kind of quandaries necessary for him to enact his role. As for the Tribunes, besides their function in making Coriolanus' bluster look admirable in comparison with their scheming, they serve to carry the play forward by goading him into the rage that leads to his banishment, and thus eventually (as one thing leads to another) to his death. All told, in being the kind of characters they are, the other figures help Coriolanus be the kind of character he is; and by their actions at precisely the times when they do act, they help lead the appointed (or stylistically anointed) victim to the decision required, by the logic of the plot, for his downfall. He must turn the army away from Rome, and under conditions that lead step by step to the sacrifice that will permit the purging of the audience.

But we have not yet considered the remarkable function of Menenius. At first glance, one could "derive" him from Coriolanus only in the sense that he serves as the ideal link between the patrician and plebeian factions. In this role, along with his loyalty to Coriolanus, he serves particularly well for shaping the audience's sympathies. For though he is a patrician, and frankly shares the prejudices of his class, the commoners (and the audience) like him. His use in this regard is of crucial importance to the play when, in Act IV, scene vi, a messenger brings the news that Coriolanus is leading an army against Rome. To the extent that Rome allusively stood for England, it was not easy to keep the audience sympathetic with a man whose conduct at this point was so close to out-and-out treason (particularly since at so many points in the play he irritates us). But Menenius picks up Cominius' line, placing the blame upon the Tribunes and the people ("O, you have made good work!")—and when two characters of such high repute take this stand, it helps crowd the audience a bit by shifting the emphasis from the *hero's treason* to his *enemies' provocation* (with the bad effects of the provocation being stressed, while the considerations that would justify it were here left unmentioned). The trick was to show the Tribunes and the people regretting their decision to banish Coriolanus rather than to let them review their grounds for the banishment. This is excellent dramaturgic maneuvering—for Shakespeare, as is typical of him, is here working with more complex motives than an audience's simplest responses to patriot and traitor.

But Menenius' "derivation" as a function of Coriolanus' sacrifice contains other notable ingredients. Despite the great contrast between the diplomatic eloquence of the self-styled "humorous patrician" (who is Coriolanus' godfather) and the heavy-footed, grotesquely heroic mouthings of the formally inevitable victim (for one is mellow where the other is raw), Menenius applies almost the same formula to them both. Of himself he says, "What I think, I utter, and spend my malice in my breath." The same readiness with the word he attributes to Coriolanus thus: "His heart's his mouth. / What his breast forges, that his tongue must vent." (War itself, elsewhere in the play, is called "sprightly, waking, audible, and full of vent," an expression that could serve also to describe Coriolanus' invective.)

But whereas Menenius shares Coriolanus' belief in the intrinsic superiority of the patricians, and makes no secret of the fact even when addressing the commoners, his function will be to uphold circumspectly, "reasonably," much the same position that Coriolanus must represent exorbitantly. (I say "must" because his excessiveness is a formal requirement of his role as victim.) Menenius is the only character in the play (except Aufidius' servants) charged with the responsibilities of putting some aspects of this solemn bluster in a comical light.

His early speech likening the body politic to the human body (one of the many themes Shakespeare found in Plutarch, though it was also a standard notion of the times) serves not only to present the attitude of the patricians in the best light (as Coriolanus must present it in the worst). It also sets the conditions for much body imagery throughout the play, particularly images of bodily disease, such as go well with the fact that the body politic is in great disarray. What more relevant than an imagery of bodily diseases in a play dealing with disorders of the body politic? Similarly, since the people are starving, images to do with devouring serve to keep thought of such conditions hovering about the edges of our consciousness. And the many references to animals are so treated as to reinforce the vigorous animality of the underlying situation.

The question of imagery, I submit, should be "derived" thus late in the enterprise. With works of a preponderantly imagistic cast (as in much modern poetry), one might properly *begin* with questions of imagery. But in a drama of this sort, one can most profitably begin with considerations of action and character, afterwards deducing the logic of the imagery from these prior considerations, rather than using imagery as the "way-in."

II

Fundamentally, then, the play exploits to the ends of dramatic entertainment, with corresponding catharsis, the tension intrinsic to a kind of social division, or divisiveness, particularly characteristic of complex societies, but present to some degree in even the simplest modes of living. (I take it that the presence of a priesthood or similar functionaries dealing with things of this world in terms of a "beyond," is on its face evidence that a society is marked by some degree of social differentiation, with corresponding conflicts of interest. And at the very least, even tribes that come closest to a homogeneous way of life are marked by differentiation between the work of men and women or between youth and age.)

This malaise, which affects us all but which in varying degrees and under varying circumstances we attempt to mitigate, is here made insultingly unforgettable. Coriolanus' *hubris* (whether you choose to translate it as "pride" or as "excessiveness") aggravates the situation constantly. And when he dies (after a change of heart that enables us to pity him even while we resent his exaggerated ways of representing our own less admirable susceptibilities, with their corresponding "bad conscience"), he dies as one who has taken on the responsibility and has been appropriately punished. Thereby we are cleansed, thanks to his overstating of our case.

Along with this tension, which is of long duration in societies, we considered the likelihood that, when the play originally appeared, it also exploited a "timely topic," the unrest caused by the Enclosure Acts, when new men of means took over for sheepraising, much land that had traditionally been available to small farmers, and these "legally" dispossessed tenants were in a state of great frustration. Many were starving while the monopolists were being made into patricians. It was a time when many *nouveaux-riches* were being knighted—and as Aristotle points out, it is *new* fortunes that people particularly resent.

An ironic turn of history has endowed this play with a new kind of "timely topic," owing to the vagaries of current dictatorships. But I would incline to contend that this "new immediacy" is more apparent than real. In the first place, Coriolanus isn't a good fit for the contemporary pattern because the frankness of his dislike for the common people would make him wholly incompetent as a rabble-rouser. A modern demagogue might secretly share Coriolanus' prejudices—but he certainly would not advertise the fact as Coriolanus did. His public heart would bleed for the poor, even while he was secretly shipping state funds to a Swiss bank, against the day when his empire would collapse, and he would flee the country, hoping to spend his last years in luxurious retirement on the Riviera. Presumably our nation is always in danger of pouring considerable funds down such ratholes. Thus, I feel that the attempt to present *Coriolanus* in the light of modern conditions can never quite succeed, since these conditions tend rather to conceal than to point up the cultural trends underlying its purgative use of the tension between upper and lower classes. Or should we call it a "tension behind the tension"? I have in mind a situation of this sort:

The Renaissance was particularly exercised by Machiavelli because he so accurately represented the transvaluation of values involved in the rise of nationalism. A transvaluation was called for, because *religion* aimed at *universal* virtues, whereas the virtues of *nationalism* would necessarily be *factional*, insofar as they pitted nation against nation. Conduct viewed as vice from the standpoint of universal religious values might readily be viewed as admirable if it helped some interests prevail over others. This twist greatly exercised Machiavelli. But though (from the universal point of view) nations confront one another as factions, from the standpoint of any one nation factionalism is conceived in a narrower sense, with nationalism itself taking over the role of the universal.

In Shakespeare's day, as so many of his plays indicate, the kind of *family* factionalism that went with feudal relationships was being transformed into the kind of *class* factionalism that would attain its "perfection" (if we may apply that term to so turbulent a development) in the rise of nationalism, with its drive towards the building of the British Empire. And here Shakespeare tackled this particular tangle of motives in a remarkably direct manner, except of course for the kind of "distance" (with corresponding protection) the play got by treating the subject in terms of ancient Rome rather than his contemporary London.

All told, the motivation split into four overlapping loci: nation, class, family, individual. And in *Coriolanus* we witness a remarkably complex simplification of these issues, dramatically translated into terms of action and character.

Individualism may come and go, but there is a compelling sense in which the individual is always basic. The centrality of the nervous system is such that each of us is unique (each man's steak and his particular toothache being his own and no one else's). And even those who are killed *en masse* nonetheless die one by one. Symbolicity (by assigning proper names and attesting to the rights of private ownership) strongly punctuates this physical kind of individuality. And Shakespeare adds his momentous contribution by building so many plays on the "star" system, with a titular role. I think it is safe to say that *Coriolanus* most thoroughly meets this description. Think of such lines as: "O, me alone! Make you a sword of me?" (I, vi); "Alone I fought in your Corioles walls" (I, vii); "Alone I did it." (V, vi)—or his resolve to stand "As if a man were author of himself" (V, iii)— or a Tribune's grudging tribute to him: "He has no equal" (I, i) —or his own mother's formula: "You are too absolute" (III, ii). And the play backs up such statements by incessantly making him the center of our attention whether he is on the stage or off.

Yet even his name is not his own, but derives from the sacking of a city. And when he is threatening to lead an army against Rome, he does not know himself; and the sympathetic Cominius tells us (V, i) that he "forbade all names. / He was a kind of nothing, titleless, / Till he had forged himself a name o' th' fire / of burning Rome"—and that's precisely what, in obedience to his mother's pleadings he did not do.[1] Incidentally, the longer one works with this text, the more ingenious Shakespeare's invention seems when, just before Coriolanus is killed, he *apologizes* because he had fallen into a rage: "Pardon me, lords, 'tis the first time ever / I was forced to scold." But he is addressing the *lords* of Antium, not the commoners. Shortly thereafter the Conspirators will shout, "Kill, kill, kill, kill, kill him!" thereby as they slay modifying poor impotent Lear's line, "Then, kill, kill, kill, kill, kill, kill!" (IV, vi, 192).

But such considerations bring us to the next locus of motives, the *familial*, which the play brings to a focus in the "mother, wife, child" formula, used variously by Menenius (V, i, 28-29), himself (V, ii, 78), and Volumnia (V, iii, 101), hers being the most effective, when she bewails the sight of him for "Making the mother, wife, and child to see / The son, the husband, and the father tearing / His country's bowels out." Yet to say as much is to move us almost as quickly into the realm of *class* and *nation*, since his family identity was so intensely that of a *patrician*, and his individualistic ways of being a patrician had brought him into conflict with all Rome.

Here you confront the true poignancy of his predicament, the formula being: individualistic prowess, made haughty towards the people by mother's training, and naturally unfit for the ways of peaceful persuasion with regard to the citizenry as a whole. The *class* motive comes to a focus terministically in the manipulations that have to do with the key word, "noble." But the *nation* as motive gets its forceful poignancy when the play so sets things up that Coriolanus maneuvers himself and is maneuvered into a situation whereby this individualistic mother-motivated patrician patriot is all set to attack his own country, which at the beginning of the play he had defended with such signal valor, despite his invective against the commoners. As Granville-Barker has well said: "Play and character become truly tragic only when Marcius, to be traitor to Rome, must turn traitor to himself."

Yet, so far as I can see, the treatment of this motivational tangle (individual-family-class-nation) is not in itself "cathartic," unless one uses the term in the Crocean sense rather than the Aristotelian. (That is, I have in mind the kind of relief that results purely from the well-ordered presentation of an entanglement. Such a complexity just *is*. But Shakespeare transforms this motionless knot into terms of an irreversible narrative sequence, the "cure" here residing not in a sacrifice as such, but rather in the feeling of "getting somewhere" by the sheer act of expression, even though the scene centered in conditions when Coriolanus was totally immobilized, a quite unusual state for so outgoing a character.) My soundest evidence for

---

[1] If he had got a new name from the destruction of Rome as he got the name of "Coriolanus" from his victory over Corioli, the preservation of the pattern would have ironically required that in his new identity he be called "Romanus."

catharsis of this sort (whereby the sheer unfolding of expression can impart a kind of relief to our kind of animal, that lives by locomotion) is the nursery rhyme:

> The grand old Duke of York
> He had ten thousand men
> He marched them up to the top of the hill
> Then he marched them down again.
> And when they were up they were up
> And when they were down they were down
> And when they were only halfway up
> They were neither up nor down.

III

I'm among the company of those who would call *Coriolanus* a "grotesque" tragedy. So our final problem is to make clear just wherein its grotesqueness resides, and how this quality might also contribute to its nature as medicinal.

Obviously, in contrast with the typical sacrificial victims of Greek tragedy, Coriolanus rather resembles a character in a satyr play. He is almost like a throwback to the kind of scurrilities that Aristotle associates with the origins of the tragic iamb, in relation to the traditional meter of lampoons. (See Poetics IV) So some critics have called it a "satiric" tragedy. But "grotesque" seems closer, since Coriolanus is *not* being satirized. The clearest evidence that he is being presented as a *bona fide* hero is the fact that *every* person of good standing in the play admires him or loves him and is loyal to him, despite his excesses. What does all this mean?

Still considering the problem from the standpoint of *tensions* and their exploitation for dramatic effects (that is to say, poetic delight), can we not find another kind of tension exploited here for medicinal purposes? It concerns the function of Coriolanus as a "railer," a master of vituperation. Dramaturgically, such a figure is, at the very least, of service in the sense that, by keeping things stirred up, he enables the dramatist to fish in troubled waters. When a cantankerous character like Coriolanus is on the stage (and Shakespeare turns up many such), there is a categorical guaranty that things will keep on the move. Yet, beyond that sheerly technical convenience (whereby Coriolanus does in one way what Iago does in another, towards keeping a play in motion), there is the possibility that such a role in itself may be curative, as a symbolic remedy for one particular kind of repression typical of most societies.

I might best make my point by quoting some remarks I made elsewhere about another scurrilous tragic victim, Shakespeare's Timon of Athens. There, however, the cut is different. Coriolanus throughout is respectful to the patricians and directs his insults only to the plebeians. But Timon, beginning as a great lover of mankind, ends as a total misanthrope. These paragraphs from my essay on *Timon of Athens* bear upon Timon's possible appeal as vilifier in the absolute:[2]

> *Invective*, I submit, is a primary "freedom of speech," rooted extra-linguistically in the helpless rage of an infant that states its attitude by utterances wholly unbridled. In this sense, no mode of expression could be more "radical," unless it be the closely allied motive of sheer *lamentation*, undirected wailing. And perhaps the sounds of contentment which an infant makes, when nursing or when being bedded or fondled, mark the pre-articulate origins of a third basic "freedom," *praise*.
>
> Among these three, if rage is the infantile prototype of invective, it is a kind of "freedom" that must soon be subjected to control, once articulacy develops. For though even praise can get one into trouble (for instance, when one happens to praise A's enemy in the presence of A, who happens also to be both powerful and rancorous); and though lamentation can on occasion be equally embarrassing (if one is heard to lament a situation among persons who favor it), invective most directly invites pugnacity, since it is itself a species of pugnacity.
>
> Obviously, the Shakespearean theater lends itself perfectly to the effects of invective. Coriolanus is an excellent case in point. Even a reader who might loathe his politics cannot but be engrossed by this man's mouthings. Lear also has a strong measure of such appeal, with his impotent senile maledictions that come quite close to the state of man's equally powerless infantile beginnings. . . . And that delightfully run-down aristocrat, Falstaff, delights us by making a game of such exercises.

Though one has heard much about the repression of sexual motives, in our average dealings invective is the mode of expression most thoroughly repressed. This state of affairs probably contributes considerably to such "cultural" manifestations as the excessive violence on television, and the popular consumption of crude political oratory. Some primitive tribes set aside a special place where an aggrieved party can go and curse the king without fear of punishment (though if our society had such an accommodation, I'm sure there'd be a secret agent hiding behind every bush). In earlier days the gifted railer was considered invaluable by reason of his expert skill at cursing the forces deemed dangerous to the welfare of the tribe (see on this point some interesting data in Robert C. Elliott's book, *The Power of Satire: Magic, Ritual, Art,* and above all his suggestive and entertaining Appendix

---

[2] For complete text, see Part Two, Chap. 2, pp. 115–124.

on "The Curse"). At the very least, in figures such as Coriolanus we get much of such expressiveness, without the rationale of magic, but under the "controlled conditions" of a drama about political unrest. And if he dies of being so forthright, downright and outright (if not exactly upright), it's what he "deserved." For as regards the *categorical* appeal of invective, it resides not so much in the particular objects inveighed against, but in the sheer process of inveighing. And Coriolanus, like Timon, has given vent with fatal overthoroughness to untoward tendencies which, in our "second nature," we have "naturally" learned to repress.

IV

In conclusion, then, where are we? We have been considering Coriolanus' qualifications as a scapegoat, whose symbolic sacrifice is designed to afford an audience pleasure. We have suggested: (1) His primary role as a cathartic vessel resides in the excessiveness with which he forces us to confront the discriminatory motives intrinsic to society as we know it. (2) There is a sheerly "expressive" kind of catharsis in his way of giving form to the complexities of *family, class,* and *national* motives as they come to a focus in the self-conflicts of an *individual.* (3) There is the "curative" function of invective as such, when thus released under controlled conditions that transform the repressed into the expressed, yet do us no damage. (4) The attempt has been made to consider the "paradox of substance" whereby the chosen scapegoat can "be himself" and arrive at the end "proper to his nature" only if many events and other persons "conspire" to this end, the persons by being exactly the kind of persons they are, and the events by developing in the exact order in which they do develop. To sum it all up, then, in a final formula for tragic catharsis: (a formula I wrote with such a play as *Coriolanus* in mind, though it could be applied *mutatis mutandis* to other texts):

> Take some pervasive unresolved tension typical of a given social order (or of life in general). While maintaining the "thought" of it in its overall importance, reduce it to terms of personal conflict (conflict between friends, or members of the same family). Feature some prominent figure who, in keeping with his character, though possessing admirable qualities, carries this conflict to excess. Put him in a situation that points up the conflict. Surround him with a cluster of characters whose relations to him and to one another help motivate and accentuate his excesses. So arrange the plot that, after a logically motivated turn, his excesses lead necessarily to his downfall. Finally, suggest that his misfortune will be followed by a promise of general peace.

Comments

Our reference to the Enclosure Acts requires a glass. Though the private enclosing of public lands ("commons") had begun in the thirteenth century, its effects were still being felt at the time when Shakespeare wrote, and indeed much later (as cf. Goldsmith). Indeed, when we read of one churchman's lament, "Where there have been many householders and inhabitants, there is now but a shepherd and his dog," we suddenly get a closer glimpse into the aristocratic connotations of pastoral poetry. It is the shepherd who, among the lowly, would be identified with the big new landowners (who made their money by "legally" dispossessing small farmers of their traditional rights and turning over the land to sheepgrazing, connected with the higher profits in wool).

Professor William Frost, at the University of California, Santa Barbara, has suggested that the tension should be located rather as anticipatory of the later Civil Wars than as reminiscent of earlier disturbances (that had their epitomizing in the Wars of the Roses). Thus he would see a symbol of crown vs. parliament rather than of landowners vs. peasants. I think that both interpretations would fit here. In its possible relation to a "timely topic" (recent rioting) it could be reflecting the result of enclosures that were still "progressively" driving dispossessed peasants to the towns. It would also be reflecting emergent disorders that would come to a focus in Cromwell's time. But essentially, over the long stretch, it would be exploiting the tension intrinsic to differences of status.

As for the food imagery (talk of devouring, etc.): Though its relation to the theme of starving rioters obviously accounts for its presence, students who approach the play from an overly psychoanalytic point of view are likely to become so interested in food imagery as the possible deflection of a sexual motive they completely neglect the primary rational explanation, in terms of the people's economic distress.

Most often, perhaps, the tragic principle operates as follows: The hero acts; in the course of acting, he organizes an opposition; then, in the course of suffering the opposition (or seeing "in terms of" it) he transcends his earlier position—and the audience, by identification with him, undergoes a similar "cathartic" transformation.

But in the case of *Coriolanus* the process seems somewhat different. The hero never really matures. His killer formulates the victim's plight in the formula, "thou boy of tears" (a summarizing "revelation," we might say, which the audience is prepared to receive just before the end of the play). And the ultimate insight is in the audience's own developments rather than in their sympathetic duplication of a higher vision on the part of the sacrificed hero.

Many kinds of works involve variants of this process. In the case of Richard Wright's *Native Son*, for instance, Bigger was not the sort of character who could (while remaining in character) arrive at a conceptually mature statement of his difficulties. But such a statement could properly be made by a lawyer who, in defending him, could present the sheer *theory* of the case. This is probably one reason why, where plots hinge about characters of limited insight, the device of a concluding court trial is especially serviceable. Another resource is the use of an emotionally imagistic solution, as in James Baldwin's *Go Tell It On the Mountain*, where the Negro problem is merged with a religious conversion that ambiguously suggests homosexual connotations.

Coriolanus is to Menenius as raw adolescence is to ripe old age. Lear is sick old age that falls into infantile tantrums, a Coriolanus without the physical power. And I dare repeat: It is tremendously interesting to see how, for all their superficial differences, Cordelia and Coriolanus both exemplify variants of a forthrightness that is essential to the advancing of the plot. If Lear, Cordelia, and Coriolanus were like Menenius, neither of these tragedies would be possible.

Though the names are taken over literally from Plutarch, it is remarkable how tonally suggestive some of them are, from the standpoint of their roles in this English play. "Volumnia" suggests the voluminous—and often, on students' papers, I have seen the name spelled "Volumina." "Virgilia" suggests "virginal." "Aufidius" suggests "perfidious." And in the light of Freudian theories concerning the fecal nature of invective, the last two syllables of the hero's name are so "right," people now often seek to dodge the issue by altering the traditional pronunciation (making the *a* broad instead of long).

This article should be a summing-up in three ways:
First, its stress upon the Dramatistic principle of victimage (the "sacrificial" motive) provides a logological analogue of the issue at which Friedrich Nietzsche grew wroth in his *Birth of Tragedy*. Its concern with dramatic catharsis modifies the version of dialectical (Platonic) transcendence featured in the third of these essays.

Second, it is designed to show by specific example how our theory of symbolic action in general can be tied down to considerations of poetics in particular.

Third, it should serve to point up the difference between an approach to a text in terms of poetics ("intrinsically") and an approach to it ("extrinsically") from the sociological point of view. And above all, the distinction should be made in a *noninvidious* way, both approaches being needed for the full treatment of symbolic action. Besides using beliefs (what Aristotle's *Rhetoric* would call "topics," or "places") to give characters and situations the appeal of verisimilitude (to make an imitation seem "natural" or "lifelike" even while we remain aware that it is an artifact), a work uses beliefs to arouse states of tension, by pitting some beliefs (or "equations") against others. Or, to put the case in sociological terms, we could say that a given society is characterized by a scheme of "values" that variously reinforce one another or conflict with one another in given situations and that authors variously embody such "values" in constructing characters and plots. In this sense, the *Rhetoric* can serve as a bridge between sociology and literary criticism (except insofar as sociologists and literary critics fail to ask how the *Rhetoric* can be applied even to their own field).

Thinking along such lines, in lectures I have at times placed more emphasis upon this area of overlap. For instance, Talcott Parsons' collection of essays, *Social Structure and Personality*, serves as a convenient point of entry for a treatment of the play in terms of "Social Structure and Poetics." But his concern with the interweaving of sociological and psychological coordinates is paralleled by a different but analogous interweaving of poetics and the sociological-psychological.

After noting the recurrence of the term "expectation" in the Parsons volume, one can discuss the similarity between the role of expectation in classical form and the place of expectations in men's notions of current reality and in threats and promises regarding the future. The kind of "values" and "expectations" that a sociologist deals with can be shown to figure also in the structure of a literary work, as enjoyed for its own sake (so that practical problems are transcended by being transformed into sources of artistic enjoyment). And by the same token, the role of "values" can be shown to figure prominently in the "equations" that are either implicit or explicit in a given work. But, of course, the reverse kind of "derivation" which we would consider central to Poetics (as when "deriving" Volumnia from Coriolanus) would be wholly alien to either sociology or psychology. And whereas Plutarch, viewed as biography, would be judged by tests of "truth," or "factuality," the play should be judged by tests of "verisimilitude," or "plausibility." However, the symmetry of the case is impaired by the fact that Plutarch was not by any means a biographer in the sheerly "factual" sense; and his method of writing encouraged kinds of "identification" that go with poetic appeal.

Finally, though I dare hope that one can distinguish between dialectical transcendence and dramatic catharsis at their extremes (as illustrated by my third and fifth essays), I must admit that the realms covered by the two terms considerably overlap. And both in previous works and later in essays included here, I have sometimes used one of the terms where I might as well have used the other.

We might discern the rudiments of transcendence when an individual dons a uniform. For now he is seen in terms of this "more inclusive whole" (that can also be called *less* inclusive, insofar as it eliminates many of the individual's personal possibilities); and it could be called "cathartic" in the sense that the identification indicated by the uniform is in effect the "sacrifice," or symbolic "slaying," of the individual's nonuniformed identity. In story, as in history, a situation can undergo a rudimentary kind of transcendence by the sheer process of moving on to other matters.

The rudiments of catharsis are present in that most readily available resource of symbolism: substitution. For implicit in the possibilities of substitution there is the possibility of vicarious victimage.

There is a further process not reducible to terms of either "transcendence" or "catharsis," as considered in the third and fifth chapters respectively. It involves analogues of unburdening or cleansing, in the sheerly physiological sense (as with the *explicit* use of fecal imagery in Aristophanic comedy or Swiftian satire, and the "dignified" devices for *implicitly* transforming bathos into pathos).

The relation to victimage is revealed in the "fecal" nature of invective. But this "problematic" element can also impinge upon a realm of motives that, while honorifically related in one respect to the hierarchal mysteries of courtliness, in another respect would seem to be rooted in infantile "equations" that *precede* the notions of "propriety" inculcated by toilet training. In his *Psychology of the Unconscious,* Jung offers some excellent instances of "reverence" as so conceived. For related stylistic "miracles," see my chapter on "The Thinking of the Body," or the comments on *"scoriae,"* (p. 198) in my discussion of Emerson's "Nature."

PART II

PARTICULAR WORKS AND AUTHORS

Chapter One

Shakespearean Persuasion: *Antony and Cleopatra*

I

Every writer has some fixed ideas, favorite images, or recurrent manifestations of one sort or another, that are analogous to a psychological tic. They are like a tic because they keep turning up in various situations that must somehow be classifiable under the same head, since in some devious or subtle way they all have this same attribute in common. With most writers, it is not hard to spot the frequent recurrence of such moments—hence analysts try taking the writer's tic apart, to see what makes it tick.

But Shakespeare is so ample and is such a professional schemer, where he is concerned enterprises of that sort encounter their greatest difficulty. So I had first thought of offering a ragbag selection from among notes I had taken on Shakespeare and not yet published.

But I just happened to have been developing further some of the thoughts on "Order" I considered in my book, *The Rhetoric of Religion*. And the closing words of Caesar's final speech in *Antony and Cleopatra* are:

> Our army shall,
> In solemn show, attend this funeral,
> And then to Rome. Come, Dolabella, see
> High order in this great solemnity.

Similarly, I seemed to find special significance in Caesar's words (III, vi) to his sister, Octavia, who had journeyed without her retinue:

> But you are come
> A market-maid to Rome, and have prevented
> The ostentation of our love, which, left unshown,
> Is often left unlov'd.

"The ostentation of our love"—what an excellent formula for the sweeping poetic devices whereby, in this play, the naked physiology of sex is grandly adorned. And such speculation probably led me to begin with *Antony and Cleopatra*. But having so begun, I couldn't get loose. So except for occasional asides, I shall confine myself to thoughts on that one play.

Plus one complication! Since traditional rhetoric lays great stress upon persuasion, there has too often been a tendency (particularly in English departments) to assume that the rhetoric of persuasion has no place in poetics. There is a sense in which this assumption is correct, and a sense in which it is incorrect. For it must be persuasion with a difference. Accordingly, these notes will be designed to show how thoughts on persuasion would shape up, with regard to questions of poetics.

For convenience' sake, let's note these major developments in the plot:

Act I. Antony has been neglecting affairs of state, because of his engrossment with Cleopatra. Learning of his wife's death, he returns to Rome. "I must from this enchanting queen break off."

Act II. At Rome, he is prevailed upon to marry Octavius Caesar's sister. The act gives a good portrait of Cleopatra and establishes the fact that, despite Antony's marriage, "He will to his Egyptian dish again."

Act III. The fatal battle at sea. "O! whither hast thou led me, Egypt?" Or: "We have kiss'd away / Kingdoms and provinces."

Act IV. Antony's suicide, on having been misled by Cleopatra into thinking that she had killed herself. "I am dying, Egypt, dying." But only after her fright at his fury ("She has robb'd me of my sword").

Act V. Cleopatra's suicide, to avoid capture by Caesar. "She levell'd at our purposes, and, being royal, / Took her own way."

At which point, an aside is in order:

> Or were I monarch o' the globe,
> Wi' thee to reign, wi' thee to reign,
> The only jewel in my crown,
> Wad be my queen, wad be my queen.

If it took Burns, who fraternized with dispossessed field mice, only twelve lines to get from a pathetic beloved (needing his shelter in a "cauld blast") to her enthronement as queen of all the world, it "necessarily" follows that Love is in essence an Empire. In *Antony and Cleopatra* Shakespeare works with that motivational trend, grandly.

The plot, adapted from Plutarch, enabled him to write a play in which this old theme is *consummated*. That's the important point: *consummated*. In even the meanest love the lover, however deviously or unconsciously, feels in some way "ennobled." The dramatist had this standard proclivity to work on, in his audience. The basic "tension" he exploits for his effects is as simple as that. He aims to perfect a plot that will translate the theme of love into terms of imperial "ostentation." Hence, insofar as the audience is composed of customers who own some shares in love, he will aggrandize their holdings, however modest, by running up the value of the stock in general. To this extent, they will gladly go along with him, in a benign conspiracy of self-admiration.

Thus, whereas politicians customarily build up their faction by demeaning rivals, Shakespeare builds up Antony by sympathetically portraying the administrative competence of his rival, Octavius Caesar. Caesar, we might say, is shown to possess, in a favorable sense, the kind of "political realism" that the Tribunes in *Coriolanus* exemplified repugnantly, just as the dramatist's "ostentation" of love in the story of Antony and his "Egyptian dish" is a favorable variant of the vice that Regan and Goneril were so handy with, in flattering senile Lear. ("What shall Cordelia do? Love, and be silent.")

However, though all set to solemnize love's empire, Shakespeare's terministic prowess was so complex it could attain a profounder appeal than the sort that can be got by a sheerly grandiloquent "build-up." He would not simply "extrapolate" the innate imperiousness of love by a treatment designed to embody the principle of pomp. That is, his dramaturgy did not require him merely to attempt making his play as pompous as poetically possible. In brief, he was not confined to the kind of show that fits Enobarbus' elaborate description of Cleopatra's barge, "like a burnish'd throne" (II, ii).

Thus, although Antony was much given to revelry, the drama lets us witness not Antony but Lepidus made lax with too much wine, while Antony, in good-natured disdain, is mock-seriously making fun of him. The design gets its trimmest formulation (III, ii) when Agrippa and Enobarbus are ridiculing Lepidus' incompetent attempts to be on good terms with both the rivals at once: "he loves Caesar . . ." "he adores Mark Antony"; Caesar is "the Jupiter of men . . ." Antony is "the god of Jupiter." The third member of the triumvirate is here being sacrificed for the glory of the other two powers, whose natures will be enlisted, each in its way, to further the plot that glorifies romantic love in terms of politics.

In the Cornelian "theater of admiration," only political themes were deemed wholly worthy of the style. Love could be introduced but secondarily, as a motive that helps complicate the plot. (*Cinna* is a perfect example.) In this play, Shakespeare reverses the order and uses politics (with what we now call "global" aspects, its treatment in terms of the *orbis terrarum*) as a means of amplification.

Here's what I'd take to be the underlying situation. Insofar as Elizabethan England was an empire on the make, the motives "natural" to such conditions would be reflected in writers' and audiences' "consciousness" (a term not always easy to distinguish from what is now often called the "unconscious"). Thus, personal relations should be expected to contain a motivational element that we might characterize as "innately" or "implicitly" imperial, a theme especially available to Shakespeare's "Roman plays."

One dramatic way of pointing up personal relations is in terms of love. Thus, if love relationships are already tinctured by the dyes of emergent empire, a perfect fulfillment of this motivational coloration could be obtained by the use of a plot in which the lovers were identified with political empires. (Quite a step from backward-glancing *Romeo and Juliet*, where the lovers were entangled in family feuds. But it's interesting to note that something of the same pattern is employed to wind things up, as the hero kills himself under the mistaken impression that the heroine is already dead. And, as in *Coriolanus*, family motives significantly complicate the political ones, owing to the fact that Antony marries Caesar's sister.)

If an erotic woman could be called by the name of an empire, not just "Cleopatra" but "Egypt," here would be a "breakthrough." "Rome" was divided into a dispute between two men, rivals for empire, not love. So Antony couldn't so simply be called just "Rome." But his fleet is referred to as an "Antoniad."

All told, the plot would be a dramatic way of "acting out" the proposition: "Implicit in human relations under conditions of emergent empire there are the *forms* of empire as such." Here would be a magnificent amplification of the not very gleaming proverb: "A man's house is his castle." But instead of saying, as a problem play might have done, "Everybody is a bit of an imperialist, as indicated to perfection in his dreams of love," the play *fulfills* the pattern, gives us its entelechial completion, in terms of a thoroughness that would apply to no one specifically but to all in principle.

But if we stopped there (with either the problem play or the direct fulfillment in principle), we'd not have the whole of the peculiarly Shakespearean dramaturgy, which has an astonishing additional twist. This twist is difficult enough to explain. But it becomes still more wonderful when we stop to realize that Shakespeare could write so many lines ascribed to characters who lacked it, and whose vigor of statement owed much to that very lack. The twist is of this sort:

Once the "grandeur" has been established (once the audience has come to feel that this is not just a woman and a man having an affair, but a mighty Mediterranean conjunction, an Egyptian empire in relation to a divided Rome), the conditions are set for a further possibility. The Shakespearean theater is now ready for its *ultimate* "breakthrough." Reversing the direction, the playwright now shows us these two people in something of the nonimperial humbleness they were born with.

The playwright began with an appeal to the meanest member of the audience. Assisted, or prodded, by emergent imperialism, he found in Plutarch's account of Antony and Cleopatra the makings of a plot that flatters each customer's sense of the aggrandizement associated with court-ship. To do as much as eloquently, as grandiloquently, as Shakespeare does in this play, would be a plenty.

Yet with him the job is still but half done. And to complete it, he must annihilate nothing less than the grand illusion which he has built up. So Cleopatra ends on the imagery of a simple, irreducibly natural person whose death is presented without "ostentation," in terms of a woman nursing a child, facing death defined euphemistically in terms of sleep.

At that point, we are through? Nothing of the sort. For there is this further twist: The very resimplification of the royal victim is contrived *in terms of* the magnificent nomenclature built up along the way. Here is a "non-Heisenberg principle of determinacy" for you. The vision cannot be obliterated, because its very destruction depends upon the vitality of the terms by which it is being questioned. Its undoing cannot undo the splendor of its having been done. Its denial depends on its affirmation.

What follows from this? Obviously, we are building our analysis of the play on the assumption that it was written not for an Antony or a Cleopatra, but for an audience most of whose members could hardly be expected to think of themselves as Antonies and Cleopatras, though they might be wheedled into some sort of "identification" with these simulated figures' simulated destinies. That is, they might be willing to participate sympathetically in a story told *in terms of* Plutarch's Antony and Cleopatra, as adapted by the playwright in accordance with the laws implicit in his particular dramaturgy.

One such device is to be seen in Shakespeare's many references to eunuchs. Whereas the term appears in Plutarch only incidentally (being used as one might now incidentally refer to someone as a mechanic, or a lawyer, or an advertising man), the play exploits it. At first glance, one might assume that the lines on eunuchs belong in the play sheerly because of their "entertainment" value, since they allow for the kind of "dirty" wisecracks that many people regret in Shakespeare. But are not subtler kinds of persuasion involved here?

At the very least, such references serve (and are explicitly used) to emphasize by contrast the virility of the hero. But is there not a still subtler operation? Without the eunuchs, there would be a much greater risk in the mighty buildup of Antony's sexual prowess, including Cleopatra's envy of his "inches." Add the many telling references to eunuchs' shortcomings, and the drama sets up a terministic situation implying that practically all the men in the audience were *in the same class* with Antony. Such classification-by-contrast enabled Shakespeare to accentuate Antony's exceptional amative prowess without risk that persons of more moderate resources in this regard might lose their sense of "identification" with him.

Similarly, Cleopatra's frailties were the frailties attributed to Everywoman. Hence, though the nature of the plot made it possible to reveal these frailties in terms of situations to do with the exceptional grandeurs of rule, the frailties themselves were of a kind that one could encounter in the lowliest of relationships. Identification is quite easy here, since anyone can "understand" the capriciousness of rulers, insofar as everyone has experienced the capriciousness of either children with regard to parents or parents with regard to children, the infantile and the absolute being enough alike for one to seem like the other. And *a fortiori*, all in the audience knew what it meant to flout the authorities with their powers over life and death (that matched the heavenly powers of binding and loosing proclaimed in the Gospels). Here again were the conditions for such affinity as favors identification.

Only on such grounds, I am compelled to believe, could we explain how the audience could be expected to retain an identification with Antony when, having ordered that an emissary sent by Caesar be beaten, after the beating he sent back to Caesar this sinister message (III, xi):

> If he mislike
> My speech and what is done, tell him he has
> Hipparchus, my enfranched bondman, whom
> He may at pleasure whip, or hang, or torture,
> As he shall like, to quit me.

I would suggest that, along with the many twists possible to the sacrificial motives necessarily involved in rule, the dramatist could here draw on the arbitrariness of parents and on the capriciousness of children. For all of his customers were sure of having experienced both modes at first hand, though in ways unique to each.

But we should note the operation of a much subtler terministic principle. I think in particular of those tremendously moving lines when Cleopatra has poisoned herself with the serpent, Charmian has exclaimed in fright, and Cleopatra remonstrates:

> Peace, peace!
> Dost thou not see my baby at my breast,
> That sucks the nurse asleep?

Here all the Mediterranean grandeurs are swept away in a flash. Here is a sudden return to the simplest bodily image, that unites the dying woman not just with human humbleness but with the humbleness even of dumb animals. What then do we have? We have, simultaneously, the sudden annihilation of the lovely lie which the play has been gloriously built on. It is almost as though Shakespeare had said to himself:

In this narrative by Plutarch, there are the makings of a love story that can exploit the illusion of imperiousness implicit in the nature of courtship (the *social* motives that radically modify the *sexual* motives in the sheerly animal sense, though the two realms of sociality and sexuality are so interwoven that they become indistinguishable, and the social motives can be readily mistaken for "natural" sexual ones). Using this material, I can trick out the love interest with all the pageantry of state, so that the hero, at the moment of his death, can address his woman by the name of a great empire: "I am dying, Egypt, dying." And his ships, I can call an "Antoniad." Then, at the last, I'll let the audience glimpse the fact that the whole pretentious structure is but a mirage. In a flash I'll bring them back to where they started from, in humble animality. Yet, they will have seen this lowly vision *in terms of* a vast pretentiousness. And there it still is, a mirage to be sure, but a mirage of much beauty—and a mirage that has its own kind of irrefutable reality. This will constitute the audience's culminative part in the action. They will get this sense of arriving at an end that, while it "annihilates" what went before, also retains it, since the annihilation will be sympathetically enacted *in terms of* this particular *mythos*, this particular exercise in "ostentation."

The two titular figures illustrate to perfection the "paradox of substance." Though Antony necessarily depends upon the armies that serve under him (and though Plutarch says that he characteristically owed his victories to the ability of others), Shakespeare conveys the feeling that the powers associated with this "triple pillar of the world" are intrinsic to him and prevail except for the fatal weakness that transforms this "plated Mars" into a fan "to cool a gipsy's lust." Similarly the description of Cleopatra approaching in her barge contrives to make us feel that the setting is an aspect of her substance, not defining her but reflecting her. This is, of course, the puzzle at the basis of all drama, as it is in life. The major figures can "be themselves" only because the roles of all the characters are related to this end. I call this the "paradox of substance" (as per my *Grammar of Motives*) because one cannot separate the intrinsic properties of a character from the situation that enables him to be what he is.

The way in which Shakespeare uses references to world order for the amplifying of the lovers' roles may also be indicated by contrast, if we think of Matthew Arnold's lines "To Marguerite," lamenting that "in the sea of life enisl'd / . . . We mortal millions live *alone*." Once "we were / Parts of a single continent. / Now round about us spreads the watery plain— / Oh might our marges meet again!" And in the last stanza we are told that "a God" has decreed such "severance,"

> And bade betwixt their shores to be
> The unplumb'd, salt, estranging sea.

Contrast this natural image (plus a not very determined reference to God) with Shakespeare's way of presenting love in terms of world empire (a "rhetorical radiance" which, in my *Rhetoric of Motives*, I treat as a kind of "social divinity," analyzable by a method I call "socio-anagogic," to parallel and transform the "anagogic" method of medieval theory). How different from Agrippa's formula (II, ii): "Royal wench! / She made great Caesar lay his sword to bed; He plough'd her, and she cropp'd."

The paradox of substance in Cleopatra's case might be summed up thus:

> from the erogenous zones
> radiating to an entire bodily context
> duplicated by a sumptuous setting
> with a personality to fit
> its status amplified by a sovereign role
> involving momentous relations to all the "world"—
>
> then collapse
> to terms of "the worm"

The catharsis? Along these lines, probably: Inasmuch as the vigorous terministic exercising has given us a "world," we are to that extent made ample. In this respect, the tragedy becomes an aesthetic equivalent of the royal *cortège*, using "world politics" as a means to amplify the story of a love affair. Here the self-flattery implicit in courtship (the lovers' secret assumption of "nobility," a kind of appropriation, or climbing-in-principle) is "translated" into terms of the grandest "ostentation." (Recall how Bottom was "translated.")

However, the translation is excessive, "hubristic." Hence, those guilty of gratifying the audience's furtive vanity by being *consummate* lovers must be punished for the very immoderation that allows the audience's timid vanity to wax wanton in principle, through the contemplating of consummations in a fiction. So, along with sympathetic involvement in the two grandiloquent suicides (each by definition an act of *self*-abuse), there are the conditions for a purge. The humble and moderate can thank God that they personally are not driven by this excessiveness, the imitation of which is designed for their gratification.

In this regard, the dramaturgic principle of excess (drama's purely technical need of characters that overdo what all members of the audience do somewhat) automatically sets up a situation whereby we could see in Shakespearean tragedy an "incipiently Puritan" outlook. That is, one could ask what "moral" the play teaches. And it's not a bad question to ask, if one hedges it in with the kind of post-Nietzchean qualifications we have been considering (the ironical view of virtue that Nietzsche himself exemplifies to tragic excess in his *Genealogy of Morals*). A tragedy can entertain us by flattery, if it imitates a weakness in us; but by imitating this weakness "consummately," the tragedy can enable us simultaneously to "identify ourselves" with the imitation and to disclaim it. The process involves redemption by vicarious victimage, since we acquiesce to the sacrifice of the persons who were entrusted with the role of imitating our weakness in an amplified form. However sympathetically, we can renounce our representatives, since they represented us only too thoroughly, though this very thoroughness was itself a necessary ingredient in the recipe for a tragic character. Not all the characters in the tragedy must be similarly excessive. For one constant resource of Shakespearean tragedy is the secondary use of figures who are quite simple, but are dragged into turmoil as it were "by redundancy." The nature of the plot causes them to be like unpretentious people who get slaughtered because persons of great ambition and power involve their nation in adventures abroad.

Should we, in line with the Freudian stress, see things in terms of "Love and Death" (Eros and Thanatos)? To what extent, if any, would that differ from "Love and War" (Venus and Mars)? And about the edges of the Love-Death pair, we should recall that Sleep was the twin brother of Death, an association particularly worth remembering in the light of Cleopatra's dying lines (and in Book XIV of *The Iliad*, Hera having borrowed the charms of Aphrodite, and scheming with the god Sleep, affects the course of the war through mastering Zeus "by love and sleep"). Love, War, Sleep, Death—they're a complex readily merging by many routes into one another. But in any case, one should certainly not let the Love-Death pair detract attention from the logic of the Love-War pair, for the role of Antony as *warrior* is what imparts the political dimension to the love relationship, giving pretexts for the ambiguous treatment of love in terms of Antony's great swordsmanship.

Comparisons between Plutarch and Shakespeare help greatly to throw light upon Shakespeare's approaches to his subject, which differ greatly from Plutarch's, despite the strongly dramatistic nature of Plutarch's thinking. Plutarch's extensive account of military campaigns becomes almost formless, as viewed from the standpoint of drama, since they dissolve into a clutter of minor vicissitudes. So Shakespeare cut many corners here. But he did take over some picturesque details of hardship, which he embellished in ways of his own, and in keeping with the effective tragic formula whereby the hero is at his best in times of greatest adversity.

Whereas Plutarch frequently suggests that Antony was influenced by Cleopatra as a *ruler*, Shakespeare so changes the stress that her influence upon him is solely through her nature as a capricious *woman*. Antony is a *warrior* who is *languishing* as the result of a sexual infatuation with an exotic "serpent of the Nile" who eventually kills herself with the sting of a serpent.

Where matters of manly decision are concerned, Antony decides, except insofar as he is enslaved by his sheerly sexual aberration. Thus Plutarch ascribes to Cleopatra the decision to fight by sea although Antony's best chances were with his army; but Shakespeare treats the decision sheerly as an instance of headstrong bravado on Antony's part (III, vii).

Shakespeare's dramaturgy accommodates itself without the slightest strain to a set of observations in Plutarch that a theater with narrower rules would have almost inevitably ruled out. I refer to the many bits of political shrewdness scattered through Plutarch's text. In more thoroughly ritualistic drama, these might tend to undo the very effect of imperial glory that Shakespeare uses for the adornment of his love story. But his way of introducing them episodically has the effect of silencing objections of any in the audience who might tend to rebel against the overly heroic buildup. Besides their use in simply rounding out the picture, they are variants of a device that every astute author resorts to if he can.

If an audience is likely to feel that it is being crowded into a position, if there is any likelihood that the requirements of dramatic "efficiency" would lead to the blunt ignoring of a possible protest from at least some significant portion of the onlookers, the author must *get this objection stated in the work itself*. But the objection should be voiced in a way that in the same breath disposes of it.

A perfect example of this stratagem is the role of Thersites in *The Iliad*. For any Greeks who were likely to resent the stupidity of the Trojan War, the text itself provided a spokesman who voiced their resistance. And he was none other than the abominable Thersites, for whom no "right-minded" member of the Greek audience was likely to feel sympathy. As early as Hegel, however, his standard role was beginning to be questioned. Consider, for instance, these remarks in the introduction to Hegel's *Philosophy of History*:

> The Thersites of Homer who abuses the kings is a standing figure for all times. He does not get in every age . . . the blows that he gets in Homer. But his envy, his egotism, is the thorn which he has to carry in his flesh. And the undying worm that gnaws him is the tormenting consideration that his excellent views and vituperations remain absolutely without result in the world. But our satisfaction at the fate of Thersitism may also have its sinister side.

Having in mind this passage, I once wrote some lines (*Book of Moments*, p. 25) that run thus:

> And what of Thersites,
> Despised of all his tribe
> (Whipped by power, wisdom, and heroic love, all three:
> By Agamemnon, Ulysses, and Achilles),

Loathed by the bard that made him,
Ultimate filth, speaking against epic war?
What of Thersites?

Salute—
To Saint Thersites.

Here I deliberately ignored his persuasive (or rather, dissuasive) function in the work, his use as a narrator's device for bringing to the fore a possible unconscious protest on the part of the audience (in this case, a protest against the very heroics that formed the stock in trade of the epic), but having it expressed by a figure with whom one decidedly did not want to be associated. Another (though much less subtle) variant of the same device occurs in current political controversy, when some objection to a domestic policy is attacked by the citing of evidence that the same objection has been raised by a foreign "enemy."

Shakespeare's theater allows for a maximum of such reservations. He can introduce them episodically, in the words of minor characters who are not at all as self-defeating as poor "St. Thersites," who was nauseous to look upon, and who was set up to defend his cause *with planned inadequacy* on the part of his creator. But Shakespeare can allow even a strong charge against Antony's heroics to get stated. Thus, following a lead in Plutarch, he lets the wholly reputable Ventidius say: "Caesar and Antony have ever won / More in their officer than person." And he explains that he wants to avoid a triumph lest Antony resent it. For "Who does i' the wars more than his captain / Becomes his captain's captain" (III, i). True, Plutarch presents the charge in terms of an outright indictment, whereas here it is interwoven with the officer's attitude of willing subordination to Antony. But it does get stated, and without recourse to "Thersitism." And opportunities are found to register several more of Plutarch's complaints against Antony despite their tendency to weaken the basic picture of him as a great warrior except for his susceptibility to the "wrangling queen."

It is remarkable how many detracting observations can be included without disaster, once your kind of theater allows for such complexity. Shakespeare knew that you could voice these bits of tearing-down, even while you went blandly about the business of the buildup. As with a department store, you could put in a counter here and there to gratify some particular set of customers—and if you weren't too emphatic about it, with those who wanted other goods it simply would not register. One can easily imagine that a habit of this sort would also fit in well with the piecing together of an empire.

Let's end on a quick *omnium gatherum* of further topics that we'd particularly have liked to dwell on:

How Antony's "masculine" attitude towards a messenger who says that he brings bad news (I, ii) serves as a foil to point up Cleopatra's "feminine" capriciousness in a like situation (II, v). But keep in mind the further development we have already discussed, when Antony has Thyreus beaten (III, xi). . . . What all was there already, when Cleopatra had truck with "joy of the worm" (V, ii). I have in mind at least these prior scatterings that are here brought together: When Cleopatra was addressed (IV, xiii) as "Royal Egypt! Empress!" she replied: "No more, but e'en a woman, and commanded / By such poor passion as the maid that milks / And does the meanest chares." As early as I, v, she had said: " 'Where's my serpent of old Nile?' for so he calls me." The serpent motif had figured also in a speech by Lepidus (II, vii), "Your serpent of Egypt is bred now of your mud by the operation of your sun." And but a few lines previously, Antony had given the subject of the Nile's inundations an explicitly agricultural and implicitly sexual significance when saying that, as the Nile ebbs, "the seedsman / Upon the slime and ooze scatters his grain, / And shortly comes to harvest."

We might also note that all dramatists like cantankerous characters, since they help the dramatist to fish in muddy waters. Thus, Cleopatra's capriciousness is as useful in its way as Lear's or Coriolanus' or Iago's or Falstaff's or Hamlet's, etc., are in theirs. She has the kind of character that keeps things unsettled. Thereby she helps out with the tentatives of storytelling, which are requirement No. 1. If prophets-after-the-event can eventually prove that every last one of her caprices is intrinsic to her nature, that's all to the good. (And, I admit, I am much in favor of methods undertaken in the spirit of *vaticinium post eventum*. If the critic believes that the writer under discussion is in some notable respect a noteworthy writer, his *ideal* task is to show why things "necessarily" turned out as they did.)

Act IV, being the "pity" act in a tragedy, the first scene ends with even Caesar, who plots our hero's downfall, exclaiming "Poor Antony!" In the next scene, where Antony is talking to his servants on the subject of a last supper, Enobarbus says, "To make his followers weep"—and he weeps. The mysterious music that, according to Plutarch, was taken to indicate the forsaking of Antony by Bacchus, is in Shakespeare's translation interpreted thus: " 'Tis the god Hercules, whom Antony lov'd, / Now leaves him." . . . The states of Enobarbus' relationship to Antony are like an indicator that shows you at what floor the elevator is, along its course. Here is perfect *poetic* "reduction" of a theme. And when Enobarbus dies of remorse (as he approximately did also in Plutarch's version) don't forget that this is being done *for you*. His end, too, takes place in the "pity act" (ix).

Plutarch tells of a soldier who, after being rewarded by Antony for bravery in his behalf, deserted to Caesar. Shakespeare retains the reward (even to the extent of asking that the soldier kiss Cleopatra's hand, an act that had infuriated Antony when done by Thyreus); but he passes up the desertion. . . . Cleopatra's dream of Antony (V, ii). This is splendid as an *imperial* use of *natural* imagery. ("His legs bestrid the ocean," etc.) To get the feel of how much is working here, think of those lines as saying in effect: "To sum up what has gone before, we have seen . . ." etc.

As for her lines, "his delights / Were dolphin-like, they show'd his back above / The element they liv'd in," I wonder whether I am being accurate, or merely making an unintended personal confession, when the passage suggests to me not only the transcending of an element (as when dolphins, that hunt in the water, bulge up into the air) but also the same kind of double meaning that was obviously intended when Cleopatra had exclaimed (I, v): "O happy horse, to bear the weight of Antony!" . . . The resources of the Shakespearean metaphor in this connection are well indicated when Cleopatra formulatively exclaims to the messenger (II, v): "Ram thou thy fruitful tidings in mine ears, / That long time have been barren." Here Shakespeare can reinforce a major motive of his story where, in strictly literal speech, Cleopatra could have said only something like, "Let me hear your report." (A novelist of Freudian cast might have struck an eruditely sly compromise: " 'Overwhelm me with some penetrating news of Antony,' she said, while absentmindedly opening her jewel box.")

Act V, scene i. "The death of Antony / Is not a single doom; in the name lay / A moiety of the world." . . . V, ii. Cleopatra's message *to* Caesar: "Pray you, tell him, / I am his fortune's vassal." Earlier she had said *of* Caesar: "Not being Fortune, he's but Fortune's knave, / A minister of her will." But in either case, note that the playwright here astutely deflects our attention towards thoughts of destiny and away from thoughts to do with the fact that "Fortune" is none other than the form given by the playwright to the play (though there was the fatal fact that he could not have done what he did had he not happened by the fates of emergent imperial England to be so endowed—so fate gets back in after all).

In these several instances, one can sense their general tenor, as modes of persuasion. But I shall end on a puzzle. I refer to the *reflexive* pattern that is so intrinsic to the play. It attains its most obvious fulfillment in the fact that both the hero and the heroine are suicides. But it has many other manifestations, some equally clear, some peripheral, some hardly more than traces of the pattern.

An incipient form shows up (I, ii) at the very moment when Antony receives news of his wife's death: "the present pleasure, / By revolution lowering, does become / The opposite of itself." In I, iii, Cleopatra brings out the same design when she says (on the subject of Antony's response to news of Fulvia's death), "Look, prithee, Charmian, / How this Herculean Roman does become / The carriage of his chafe." In I, v, in a standard device of dramatic foreshadowing, Cleopatra sums up: "Now I feed myself / With most delicious poison." . . . Antony's good-naturedly disdainful guying of Lepidus, who is drunk (II, vii), builds comedy out of the pattern: "It is shaped, sir, like itself, and is as broad as it hath breadth; it is just so high as it is," etc. . . . Scarus (referring to Antony's flight in the naval battle, III, viii) states things reflexively thus: "Experience, manhood, honour, ne'er before / Did violate so itself." . . . Act III ends with Enobarbus' diagnosis, "When valour preys on reason / It eats the sword it fights with." . . . Caesar (IV, vi) orders that troops who had deserted Antony should be placed in the van, "That Antony may seem to spend his fury / Upon himself." . . . Enobarbus' remorseful death (IV, ix) after he had gone over to Caesar and Antony had sent his "treasure" after him, is presented as a kind of self-willed end (a similar ambiguity being involved in the death of Cleopatra's servant, Iras). . . . IV, xii: after complaining "She has robb'd me of my sword," Antony says that in Cleopatra's supposed death she has told Caesar, "I am conqueror of myself." In the same scene, Antony's servant Eros kills himself rather than obey Antony's orders to kill Antony. . . . More remote was Ventidius' fear of becoming "a captain's captain." . . . Cleopatra's servant Charmian dies by self-inflicted sting of the asp. . . . And Cleopatra's death is in effect a kind of double reflexive. For in addition to the pattern of her suicide, there is the imaginal fact that here a "serpent" dies by the sting of a serpent.

This symmetry may transcend the ends of persuasion, or may be its ultimate development. In any case, as regards the culminative aspect of this "spectacular" plot, we might appropriately recall that Plutarch, discussing a period when Antony had gone into misanthropic retirement near Pharos, says that Antony had wanted to imitate Timon of Athens. Plutarch also introduces here the characters of both Apemantus and Alcibiades, roles that Shakespeare uses to such good effect in his *Timon of Athens* (in some respects the most "culminative" play Shakespeare ever wrote; for whereas Coriolanus reviles only the plebeians, Timon reviles the whole human race, except for some tricky reservations as regards Alcibiades). In Plutarch, Alcibiades is paired with Coriolanus, who provides Shakespeare with his best *factionally* cantankerous character. The fecal connotations of gold (that are brought out so clearly in *Timon of Athens*, as I have discussed in the Laurel Edition of this play) are nowhere a *theme* in *Antony and Cleopatra* (though in III, ii, as regards Lepidus' toadying to both Caesar and Antony, we learn that "They are his shards, and he their beetle"). But the traces of Shakespeare's play about Timon are visible (in III, vi): "Contemning Rome, he has done all this and more / In Alexandria" (Pharos was in the Bay of Alexandria); "Cleopatra and himself in chairs of gold / Were publicly enthron'd." We are told that Cleopatra was here made "absolute queen," surely a "culminative" attribute.

Chapter Two

Timon of Athens and Misanthropic Gold

I

How best approach this sturdy display of golden misanthropy, this corrupt text on the subject of absolute corruption? First, let's force ourselves to decide exactly what *Timon of Athens* is about.

A man of wealth, generous to a fault, dispenses largesse to the point where he finds himself hopelessly in debt. When he turns for help to those whom he has befriended, they leave him in the lurch. As a result, he becomes embittered not just with them, but with all mankind, whom he reviles constantly, fleeing human society and dying a relentless misanthrope.

Such a reduction of the plot to its simplest and most highly generalized outlines has at least the merit of helping us see why, from the sheerly dramaturgic point of view, Timon's character and situation should have struck the playwright as likely material for a tragedy.

Here would be a role that lent itself well to the kind of rhetorical resonance to which the Shakespearean theater was particularly well suited. It would provide the pretext for as intense and far-ranging an exercise in invective as the poet was capable of. But the very sparseness of our outline suggests the need for at least one major addition. As in Plutarch, the story of Timon crosses with the story of Alcibiades. And though some readers may agree with those critics who feel that the two plots were not quite satisfactorily merged, the fact remains that we cannot adequately list even the minimum developments of this play without also including the banishment of Alcibiades in Act III and his victory over Athens in Act V.

Thus, to suggest the overall course of the unfolding by the use of subtitles and corresponding "arguments," some such designations as these would be necessary:

Act I. "Timon the Bountiful." Here Alcibiades figures in a few scattered bits of dialogue. In one brief, two-line speech he exemplifies a benign variant of a theme that is generally treated malignly in this play, the theme of eating: "Sir, you have saved my longing, and I feed / Most hungerly on your sight." Apemantus has just been railing about "small love 'mongst these sweet knaves, / And all this courtesy!" when Alcibiades directs this courteous greeting to Timon.

Act II. "The Reckoning." This is the act in which Timon is finally brought by his servant, Flavius, to realize his desperate financial straits. In this act, too, Alcibiades figures but incidentally.

Act III. "Timon Transformed and Alcibiades Banished." The scene of Alcibiades' banishment immediately precedes the scene in which Timon invites his guests to the mock feast (at which Alcibiades' banishment is also mentioned). The scene of his banishment begins ambiguously in the suggestion that the Senators may be debating the death penalty for Timon. For when the First Senator says " 'tis necessary he should die," the audience has no reason at all for assuming that Alcibiades is meant. The suggestion is that some further piece of information about Timon is now to be divulged. Even after Alcibiades enters, the ambiguity is kept up for some time. Admittedly, this is not a very rationalistic way of welding the two characters, but it seems to me a kind of magic not at all alien to Shakespeare, though his authorship of both these scenes has been questioned.

Act IV. "The New Life as *Misanthropos*." Even those critics who question whether some parts of the play are Shakespeare's, attribute to Shakespeare this episode in which Timon so renames himself, when rejecting with insults the friendly overtures of Alcibiades.

Act V. "Timon's Death and Alcibiades' Victory." Here Alcibiades, addressing his troops, serves to leave the audience with the parting assurance that the scurrilous Timon was "noble."

Now, having combined the stories of both Timon and Alcibiades as indispensable elements of the total action, what do we have? An inordinately generous man has become a misanthrope and died. He was an enemy of Athens because he was an enemy of all mankind. Beginning with an excess of generosity, he has ended ironically in an equally overgenerous squandering of invective. And in contrast with this "all or none" type, there is a factional hero, another enemy of Athens, but one who, having led rebellious troops victoriously against his native city, readily promises in a concluding couplet that he will "Make war breed peace, make peace stint war, make each / Prescribe to other, as each other's leech." Whereupon there is the quick martial ending, sans rhyme, "Let our drums strike."

But besides the stories of Timon and Alcibiades, there might be still one more element that needs mention, before we shall have covered the major aspects of this play's design. Some critics have doubted the Shakespearean authorship of many passages in which Apemantus figures. But he is so important to the symmetry of the play, if he wasn't an invention of Shakespeare's surely he was introduced by a playwright who had caught the very essence of Shakespearean dramaturgy. I have in mind particularly the episode in Act IV, scene iii, where Apemantus and Timon work themselves into a fury in their attempts to outcurse each other. Here is a dramatist's perfect way of embodying, by a wholly realistic altercation between two contestants, such a principle of reflexivity as would prevail if Timon were to have fallen into a fantastic quarrel with his mirror-image, under conditions that allowed it to answer back. Also, Apemantus serves to keep the play from falling simply into contrasted halves. For the presence of the scurrilous Apemantus from the start, even at the height of Timon's popularity, establishes thus early the style which will be stressed by Timon himself after his drastic change of heart which makes him into as sturdy a votary of vituperation as Apemantus. The nauseous presence of Apemantus in Act I, even while Timon was at the peak of his philanthropic expansiveness, is a dramatic way of saying that intrinsic to the very nature of such generosity as Timon's, there are always, in the offing, such nasty possibilities as Apemantus exemplifies.

In brief, the total motivational recipe, viewed "flatly," without regard to plot, would comprise these three major ingredients: (1) excessive universal generosity, exemplified by Timon; (2) a correspondingly excessive universal misanthropy, represented prophetically by Apemantus before Timon's crisis, and culminatively by Timon after the crisis; (3) a factional warlike opportunistic element (represented by Alcibiades) that holds to neither of such absolute attitudes, but has definite, limited ends, and will readily make peace if they are attained.

So much, I think, would be primary aspects of the pattern. The rest could be "derived," as the most obvious resources for filling out the pattern. For instance, if the pretext for Timon's misanthropy is to be a situation in which he is abandoned by his fair-weather friends, there must be an exhibit of fair-weather friends in action, to present this aspect of the unfolding. (Hence, such roles as Lucullus, Lucius, Sempronius, Ventidius.) If he is to be pressed for debt, there must be creditors to do the importuning. (Hence such characters as Varro and Isidore, and the Senator in scene i of Act II.) There should be other lords like Timon, to provide a typical pageantry for Timon's bounty. And Senators, as notables, serve also to make a bridge between the themes of Timon and Alcibiades.

Also, in trying to deduce the cast of characters by asking ourselves what sort of figures would be natural to such a plot, we might well observe that such a situation could obviously use a corps of servants as supernumeraries. But note that in this play they are given a more dynamic function as well. Usually, in the course of building up an audience's attitude toward a dramatic hero, playwrights find ways of having other characters help shape our sympathies. Often this effect is got "by contagion." That is, if some other character is obviously admirable and lovable, and if this character loves the problematical hero in an admirable way, then such suffrage "rubs off" on the problematical hero himself, thus indirectly persuading the audience to feel favorably disposed toward him, even at times when things might otherwise sorely try their loyalties.

In *Timon of Athens*, the protagonist's penchant for universal calumny is so far-reaching that such establishment of sympathy by contagion is hard to manage, particularly since Timon is so pigheadedly surly even to the winsomely unprincipled Alcibiades, and to Apemantus who, though himself surly on principle, reluctantly admits a fondness for Timon, only to be whipped into fury immediately afterward when his grudging hint of friendliness is viciously rejected. But the play finds ways whereby sheerly supernumerary characters, such as servants and strangers, can be manipulated in Timon's favor. The genuine, doglike loyalty of Flavius is a case in point. The image of the dog figures quite dyslogistically throughout the play, as Caroline Spurgeon has pointed out. It is almost as though Shakespeare were sytematically developing variations on the etymology of the word "cynic," as the term which the ancient Greeks would have applied to the "beastly" attitudinizings of both Timon and Apemantus, and which they would apply to the currish nature of mankind generally. But besides the fawning dog of flattery, and the mad dog of backbiting, there is the doglike loyalty of service. And Flavius's loyalty to Timon speaks well for Timon, as does the judgment of other servants, who despise the ingratitude of their masters with regard to Timon, even though, like the Stranger in Act III, scene ii, they themselves give us grounds to believe that they wouldn't have done much better had they been in their masters' place.

We should mention another kind of supernumerary. Since the play is almost wholly concerned with relations among men (as though all the world were a kind of secular monastery devoted perversely to a universal god of gold), women figure only in a supernumerary capacity. Thus the banquet scene of Act I offers a pretext to introduce a chorus. There is a dance, a group of girls is brought in, and the invitation for them to stay on after the dance is so worded that, immediately after this revuelike number, the playwright promptly gets them off the stage for good. (Also, the role of Cupid in connection with the masque suggests to me the thought that, whereas the absence of children is accidental in some plays, it is essential to this one.)

There was one other opportunity to introduce the theme of the girls; and it was used cunningly, when easygoing Alcibiades, who was equal to anything, passes by with two courtesans in his train. But though supernumeraries, they are made to function well indeed since they are woven so meaningfully into the play's constant references to gold (gold as filth and lucre). They are quite willing to accept with equanimity Timon's dirty comments on their trade, so long as his gestures of detestation include the act of showering them with treasure. "More counsel with more money, bounteous Timon," they call cheerfully, in the midst of his insults. They go well with Alcibiades.

Fittingly, there are no mothers, sisters, or wives in this play. Timon is an almost brutally end-of-the-line character, his life coming to a close in rabid talk of total human rot. And if there was to be any notion of a favorable Next Phase so far as the audience was concerned, this role was appropriately entrusted to that winsome rotter, Alcibiades, who did not resent Timon's beastly principles because he was not concerned with principles at all.

It is left for Flavius, in an episode questioned by some critics, to provide the one moment of pity (near the end of Act IV). This touch seems to me quite Shakespearean, at least in the sense that a Shakespearean tragedy regularly has a scene that softens the audience with tears of pity just before the final outbreak of victimage. (Desdemona's "willow" song, for instance.) Timon himself is on principle so pitiless, that here such a resource is almost necessarily ruled out. Yet in the play as we have it, this turn is circumspectly there:

FLAVIUS
The gods are witness,
Ne'er did poor steward wear a truer grief
For his undone lord, than mine eyes for you.
TIMON
What! dost thou weep? Come nearer. Then I love thee,
Because thou art a woman, and disclaim'st
Flinty mankind; whose eyes do never give
But thorough lust and laughter. Pity's sleeping.
Strange times, that weep with laughing, not with weeping!

Timon, weakening, then formulates "I do proclaim / One honest man. Mistake me not—but one." I submit that this moment, with Timon tugging at the outer limits of what we as the audience have learned to take as his new-formed nature, should most certainly be there.

If there are dubious passages, others seem better candidates for the charge. For instance, the scenes in which we see Timon's friends letting him down seem overly schematic. The movement was necessary, but it is executed a bit too bluntly. Though one might conceivably believe that Timon's former beneficiaries would abandon him somewhat, the ingratitude as here enacted seems too prompt, pat, and total. Yet, judged as a kind of dance, or as a reversion to such schematizations as went with the morality play out of which Shakespeare's drama had developed, these three episodes are seen to be quite ingeniously varied in their developments, and particularly trim as regards the neat device whereby the third case incidentally involves a fourth, thus suggesting that we have seen a wholly representative sample.

II

We are now in a position to consider a question we mentioned earlier, concerning the nature of Timon as a dramaturgic invention. This question has to do with Timon first of all as vilifier in the absolute, regardless of what he may happen to be vilifying. *Invective*, I submit, is a primary "freedom of speech," rooted extralinguistically in the helpless rage of an infant that states its attitude by utterances wholly unbridled. In this sense, no mode of expression could be more "radical," unless it be the closely allied motive of sheer *lamentation*, undirected wailing. And perhaps the sounds of contentment which an infant makes, when nursing or when being bedded or fondled, mark the pre-articulate origins of a third basic "freedom," *praise*.

Among these three, if rage is the infantile prototype of invective, it is a kind of "freedom" that must soon be subjected to control, once articulacy develops. For though even praise can get one into trouble (for instance, when one happens to praise A's enemy in the presence of A, who happens also to be both powerful and rancorous); and though lamentation can on occasion be equally embarrassing (if one is heard to lament a situation among persons who favor it), invective most directly invites pugnacity, since it is itself a species of pugnacity.

Obviously, the Shakespearean theater lends itself perfectly to the effects of invective. Coriolanus is an excellent case in point. Even a reader who might loathe his politics cannot but be engrossed by this man's mouthings. Lear also has a strong measure of such appeal, with his impotent senile maledictions that come quite close to the state of man's equally powerless infantile beginnings. (Such similarities, notably Lear's harping on the theme of human beastliness, have led critics to select 1607 as the approximate date of this play's completion, insofar as it is completed.) And that delightfully run-down aristocrat, Falstaff, delights us by making a game of such exercises.

But with Timon the function becomes almost total. For Timon can round things out by translating any particular situation into its corresponding absolute. If he digs for roots to eat ("Earth, yield me roots!"), they become universal roots. If in the course of thus digging in the "common mother" he finds gold, it is an ironically Midas-like gold, fecal gold, gold as defined by the touch that turns everything into the idea of corruption everywhere. When he talks of whores, he sees them as particular examples of a whole world a-whoring. If he encounters thieves, he almost demoralizes their very demoralization, causing them to question their trade, or "mystery," by assuring them:

> The earth's a thief,
> That feeds and breeds by a composture stol'n
> From general excrement; each thing's a thief. . . .
> All that you meet are thieves.

It is a foul form of gold that this play features, a quality of imagery in keeping with the fact that invective itself is a way of fighting by means of verbal filth, and Timon's absolute brand of it would besmear all mankind. In asking about the cathartic process in drama, I begin with the assumption that, wherever some unresolved tension plagues the human race, the dramatist can "perversely" appeal by transforming practical discomfitures into a source of aesthetic pleasure. For this reason, I have already discussed why I think that such a cantankerous character as Timon might have a certain categorical or universal appeal, since his aptitude for diatribe gave full expression to a desire that is intrinsic to the nature of language, but that becomes variously suppressed by the fears and proprieties that make up our "second nature."

Apemantus, since he is the character whom Timon subsequently imitates, can experimentally be taken as the one who enunciates the problem. At the other extreme from "the glass-faced flatterer," and a person who "few things loves better / Than to abhor himself" (Act I, scene i, lines 59-60), he ends Act I by a speech that in general terms give his formula for Timon's situation: Men are, he says, "To counsel deaf, but not to flattery." In brief he states explicitly the charge that several others have hinted at, the possibility that Timon is surrounded not by friends but by flatterers whose only real attachment to Timon is in their hope of favors.

Stated in its most general terms, the extradramatic tension which is here drawn upon for dramatic effect might be called the "predicament of substance (power, property, mine-own-ness)." Insofar as one aims to promote a sense of one's communion with others, one may seek to be of benefit to them; yet this means of establishing a bond with them is by its very nature suspect, for the attempt to please or reward friends can become but a way of attracting parasites. In this play, the suspicion is imagined as being drastically corroborated.

Thus, in Act II, scene ii, in lines generally credited to Shakespeare, when Flavius has told Timon of the impending financial disaster, Timon answers:

> Canst thou the conscience lack,
> To think I shall lack friends? Secure thy heart;
> If I would broach the vessels of my love,
> And try the argument of hearts, by borrowing,
> Men, and men's fortunes, could I frankly use
> As I can bid thee speak.
> FLAVIUS
> Assurance bless your thoughts.
> TIMON
> And in some sort these wants of mine are crowned,
> That I account them blessings; for by these
> Shall I try friends. You shall perceive how you
> Mistake my fortunes; I am wealthy in my friends.

The dialogue is obviously inserted as an ironic foreshadowing of precisely the blow which Timon will receive in full severity. And appropriately, he is depicted as not being the sort of person who could have been content with flattery alone (a kind of tribute he could have got for himself, on finding gold after his friends had abandoned him).

Perhaps, so far as the social ingredients in our "second nature" are concerned, this play is as radical in its concerns as is the anarchistic formula: "property is theft." There is what Marx would call the motive of "primitive accumulation," a motive of self-aggrandizement tinged also by the insecurity of such accumulation, the ways in which, in effect, private property severs one's bond with others, while also putting a person in constant jeopardy of loss. The contrary impulse, to share with others, was institutionalized in many cultures, one way being precisely the "lordly" habit of sharing one's bounty with a host of retainers (a variant of such promiscuous giving as many primitive tribes exemplify by the practice known as *potlach*, a way of distributing goods by giving, quite as in our society we distribute goods mainly by getting).

There is a sense in which any such generosity would be a squandering, and in the last analysis unrequited. And though, where there was no bounty to distribute, retainers would "naturally" fall away, in form this would add up to a kind of abandonment such as the play embodies thoroughly in the account of Timon's friends' ingratitude. True, not many in an audience would have a problem so grand as this to worry about. But *in principle* it would apply to Everyman in his relation to others.

To be sure, the play lacks the typical Shakespearean range. In its obsession with scurrility, it becomes as obstinate as Timon himself. In its devotion to an *idée fixe* it threatens to become as monotonic as a Poesque short story. And though, according to our modern depth psychologists, the infant's original relation to the fecal is on the slope of "love" rather than "hate," we early come to associate invective with the excrementitiously tabooed, hence the intensely pejorative nature of gold in this play. Of the three traits that Freud specifically associates with the "anal" character (orderliness, stinginess, obstinacy), the third figures most obviously. Timon's gift of persevering in his role as the perfect misanthrope is extreme. We have just been considering the ways in which the motives of parsimony are involved. As for the sense of orderliness: It is kept in constant agitation, both by the quality of Timon's language and by the extreme slovenliness of his ways either as a host or as a dedicated voluntary exile from the human race. Indeed, if we recall Ulysses' famous speech on order ("degree") in *Troilus and Cressida*, we see a repugnantly topsy-turvy equivalent (Act IV, scene iii) in Timon's words to his alter ego, Apemantus, ending:

> "What a beast couldst thou be, that were not subject to a beast; and what a beast art thou already, that seest not thy loss in transformation!"

Though the authorship of these lines is in dispute, we should not forget such a grandiloquently, sonorously, and maturely Shakespearean passage as the hymn of hate with which Timon begins Act IV, for here is the gist of Ulysses' speech, stated directly by antithesis, in lines such as these:

> Piety, and fear,
> Religion to the gods, peace, justice, truth,
> Domestic awe, night-rest, and neighbourhood,
> Instruction, manners, mysteries, and trades,
> Degrees, observances, customs, and laws,
> Decline to your confounding contraries,
> And let confusion live.

As for the cannibalistic food imagery in this play, one might at first question whether it fits the fecal theme. But as here used, it assuredly does. Man eat man, like dog eat dog. ("Destruction fang mankind!") Here eating is in the same category with fighting. We are invited to think of eating, not as the pleasant gratifying of a peaceloving appetite (as in the early church rites of the love feast, borrowed from the pagans and transformed into the Communion service) but as rending, tearing, biting, destroying. Eating here is the rabid use of claws and jaws, a species of hate (as in Act IV, scene iii, line 398: "Eat, Timon, and abhor them."). As so conceived, eating is but an incipient stage of excretion, in the same motivational bin with offal and invective.

All told, then, what we have, put together with an almost oppressive consistency, despite the forced marriage of the Timon and Alcibiades themes are: (1) Choice of a character with a vile tongue, as likely material for a drama. (2) Absolute misanthropy, as a motive about which to organize his cantankerousness. (3) Disappointment to justify his misanthropy. (4) Prior, overgenerous, prosperous hospitality, to set the conditions for his disappointment. (5) Two closely related characters, each like-minded in a notably different way, and both shunned by him. One is a misanthrope like him, but differs in that he was from the start what the protagonist became, and was never wealthy; the other, like him, is an enemy of Athens, but not on general principles as a corollary of misanthropy in general, and only so long as Athens effectively resists him. (6) Friends, guests, creditors, servants, and various other supernumeraries added, to meet incidental requirements of the plot; and they provide a spectrum of motivation that, though sparse for Shakespeare, far surpasses most dramas. (7) Since invective is motivationally fecal, gold provides a term that straddles both the theme of money and the theme of misanthropy. Also, its "radical" nature fits well with Timon's absolutist "digging." (8) Beastly imagery in general and dog imagery in particular serve as a variant source of misanthropic metaphors. (9)

The closely related imagery of eating (in a pejorative sense) fits well, as connoting corresponding kinds of appetition, either obsequious or rapacious.

Granted, the "radicalism" of this play is not pretty. Granted, for some reason or other the play needs more revision. But chalk one point emphatically in its favor: It is extremely thorough.

Chapter Three

Form and Persecution in the *Oresteia*[1]

I

This essay is a rewritten version of a longer section in a book that has since undergone much revision. The matters considered in these pages were immediately preceded by: (a) a section designed to show that the meaning of "imitation" in drama has become "scientistically" obscured, by failure to approach Aristotle's concept of *mimesis* through his concept of the *entelechy*, with its peculiar stress upon "fulfillment"; (b) a section on "allusion" in Greek tragedy, the gaining of dramatic forcefulness and stylistic dignity by allusion to contemporary situations and to religious rites; (c) a section on "civic tensions," for the *ad interim* resolving of which by poetic means Greek tragedy was "cathartically" designed.

Aristotle's famous formula refers to "pity, fear, and like emotions." For obvious reasons, we chose "pride" as the third major motive involved in tragic catharsis. But instead of treating pity, fear, and pride as simple motives, we tried to show how, as regards their bearing upon "civic" matters, each of them has notable complications. For instance, we cited Kierkegaard, on pity as a form of contempt. (Such complicated pity, whatever it was on its face, might be a kind of elevation bordering even on superiority, in offering the lowly man a chance to feel sorrow for the simulated sufferings of the great.) We cited Aristotle's *Ethics* to the effect that there is a *nobility* of fear, as a citizen can prove himself worthy by fearing the right things. And as for the "tragic flaw" (which Aristotle generally calls the *hamartia*, while

---

[1] The original, much longer version of this essay was an almost line-by-line analysis of the three plays' developments. Though such a treatment would be too unwieldy for present purposes, in closing I would at least restore a reference to the fatal formula that Clytemnaestra utters just before leaving to murder her husband: "Zeus, Zeus, that fulfillest, fulfill these my prayers. / To thee be the care of that thou wouldst fulfill." Here the notable word *telos* appears three times in two lines (as vocative case of the adjective, present indicative, and infinitive: *teleie, telei, telein*). The passage in many other respects has a jingle-like quality (for instance, *meloi de toi soi*); it is "vatic." And I submit that the combination of correlative and particle (*tonper an*) secretly, in a deflected pun, contains the makings of the adverb *peran* (which means "on the other side, the opposite shore," and the "transcendental" significance of which I discuss near the end of my essay on Emerson, in this same volume).

the playwrights usually prefer the more specific term, *hubris*, though they also often use *hamartia*): particularly by examining the uses of the term *hubris* in Aristotle's *Rhetoric*, we sought to emphasize its strongly civic and even legalistic nature, as a word for *social insult* (in contrast with the more purely theological or "universal" tinge now generally given to the notion of "pride" as a motive in tragedy).

All told: We were here generally concerned with stylistic resources whereby the important social relations involving superiority and inferiority could be translated into a set of "mythic" equivalents. Disorders within the *polis* could automatically attain tragic scope and dignity by translation into a corresponding "supernatural" terminology of motives. Hence, any civic issue could be reflected in a mythic idiom that transcended the political or social order, even if it did have reference to the political or social order (and to the corresponding disorders).

At this point in our inquiry, a kind of calamity occurred. Since "catharsis" also has analogues with bodily processes, we asked how "pity," "fear," and "pride" might figure, when translated into bodily terms. That is: Considered in the personal order, the terms may be taken at face value (as anyone who has felt pity or asked for pity is equipped to "understand" the term). Socially, there may be complications involving invidious relationships, matters of social or moral inferiority and superiority. And as regards "the thinking of the body," the purging of the emotions might reveal analogies with three privy functions of the "Demonic Trinity." Primarily, pity might involve the erotic, since pity is in essence a form of love. A study of the imagery in Wagner's *Ring* helped here, because of the maternal, nursing connotations by which he identifies the incipiently erotic. Fear would be diuretic, as with Coleridge's line, "Urine, the soft flowing Daughter of Fright." And "pride" would be anal, as with the proverb, "The higher the ape climbs, the more he shows his tail." But, inasmuch as the three functions are morally confused (in accordance with what Freud calls the "cloacal" ambiguities), there would be many interchangeabilities among the three.

In any case, to our great dismay, at this point a section of the book began writing itself, a systematic concern with "the thinking of the body." But since editors are still, on the whole, uneasy as regards matters to do with the Beauty Clinic, no one inquired after this Monster of a chapter, dealing with stylistic subterfuges whereby poetry mimics the body's purgative ways of giving off, when unburdening itself of impurities.

Suffice it to say that we had proceeded thus: Our study of Poetics had been concerned with the problem of carving out a poetics. We were thus trying to arrive at a poetics by a process of purification in our own essay, while at the same time we were working on the subject of purification in tragedy. And these two orders of motives so converged that we now found ourselves purgatively using body imagery in our own critical essay by talking about the use of it in poetry. Then, after so radical a purge, we had purified our subject to the degree where we could consider tragedy in its most dignified aspect; namely: in terms of tragic form.

Years ago, in *Counter-Statement*, we had analyzed form as the arousing and fulfilling of expectations. We now found ourselves again covering some of this same ground, but with a notable difference. Originally, we had meant by "form" all those devices whereby an audience is led to acquiesce in the destiny, good or bad, of the various characters in a tragedy. Now, we saw that such a network of expectancies and fulfillments can be summed up *dramatically* in such terms as Law, Right, Fate, Justice, Necessity. Accordingly, if tragic favorites like *Dike, Themis, Moira, Nemesis, Ananke* were dramatic equivalents for the principle of expectancy we had called "form," then there would be a "persecutional" element in formal propriety or "inevitability." So we were to be concerned with the Great Persecutional Words, and to watch the developments accordingly, in the *Oresteia*.

Whatever the social origins of such motives may be, once they are converted into the fullness of tragedy they have become *cosmologized*. Whereupon an almost terrifying *thoroughness* of human honesty is demanded of us, as audience. For we now are in our very essence *persecuted*, and there can be no comfort until we have disclosed and appropriately transfigured every important motive still unresolved within us. That is, once the irresolutions of the body, of personal relations, and of social relations have been heroically transmogrified by identification with the Great Persecutional Words, which are in turn identified with the vastness of Nature and the mystery of Super-Nature, no pleasantly pluralistic dissipation of outlook is any longer tolerable. Whatever the diversity of the world (a diversity which one would be a fool to deny or not to appreciate) one must become pious in doing homage to some underlying principle of oneness. One cannot deny the persecution; one must admit it: for by the nature of the cosmologizing, the persecution is integral, and everywhere.

We recall the man who had been working steadily on the Orestes trilogy, throughout the morning, afternoon, and evening of one day. He told how, awaking in the night, he lay in the dark, with somewhat the sense of looking down upon the world as though it were a kind of relief map, stretched out beneath him. He could "see," or "feel" its curving, from the coast off to the Great Lakes, then down towards the Gulf, and on across the Plains and the Rockies to the Pacific. The reasons for this fantasy were obvious. The half-awakened, half-dreaming sleeper was responding to what Henry Sams has called "the illusion of great physical space and magnitude" in Aeschylus and Job.

But there was another step here. To the man lying there in the dark, this notion of the great curved world stretching out through the night was somehow frightful, even monstrous. He felt as though he had awakened from a nightmare, and had not yet shaken himself free of it. And this further step seems to have resulted thus:

In using the ultimate vastness of scene to dignify the tragedy, which was likewise infused with the spirit of the Great Persecutional Words, Aeschylus had contrived to infuse nature itself with the terrors of tragedy (hence also with the civic virtues that gain much in authority if backed by such terrors). All the magic of dominion was operating here, in all its dimensions. By thus making fear universal, Aeschylus had made the universe fearsome. Hence, there was fear in the mere thought of all those places lying just where they were (though the sleeper, or semisleeper, had no sense of any specific danger threatening him). And when fear is thus made radical, an equally radical pity can be the only antidote.

But now we have (at least "in principle") a sufficient range of terms to consider the Poetic tactics of the *Oresteia* generally, and thus at least to get a glimpse into the kind of *thoroughness* to which the tragic playwright is necessarily vowed, once he sets out to cosmologize his fable in the spirit of the Great Persecutional Words.

II

First, to recall briefly the curve of the plot, in the trilogy as a whole, an aspect of form which Aristotle may have been led in part to slight because it is so "dialectical" (in its progress from one landing place to another), and Aristotle was reacting against Plato's dialectic emphasis:

The Orestes Trilogy

In the introductory play, the *Agamemnon*, Clytemnaestra, plotting with her paramour, kills her husband Agamemnon and Cassandra, the prophetess whom he had brought home as booty from the sack of Troy. Clytemnaestra justifies the murder on the grounds that, to obtain the victory for his armies, Agamemnon had slain their daughter, Iphigenia, on the sacrificial altar. The play ends with the Chorus praying for the son, Orestes, to appear and avenge his father's murder.

The second play, the *Libation Bearers* (*Choephoroe*), begins with Orestes' arrival. He kills both the paramour (Aegisthus) and the mother. But though he has murdered his mother in righteous retaliation, as the play ends he is beginning to be tortured by remorse. (Dramatically, this torture was objictified by his seeing of the Furies, ancient goddesses that punish bloodguilt.) And he is told that, to be cured, he must journey to the oracle at Delphi, called the "navel" of the world.

The third play, the *Eumenides*, deals with his final absolution. It begins at Delphi, where the Furies are still pursuing him, but have fallen asleep.

It ends at Athens, where Orestes is finally absolved. And in the course of this absolution, the Furies themselves change their nature, becoming much milder (or, as we expressed it in a brief account of the *Oresteia* reprinted in *The Philosophy of Literary Form*, they change their emphasis from the punishment of evil to the rewarding of good). Athena says that we are here witnessing the "first" trial for murder as contrasted with the earlier feudal practice whereby the victim was avenged by kinsmen. And the development also allusively solemnizes a treaty of alliance recently made between Athens and Argos (the land of Orestes, who has been freed by an Athenian court).

In these plays, the equivalent of "original sin" (dynastically or tribally motivated guilt "feudally" inherited, as distinguished from personal transgressions) is located in the crime of Atreus, who slew the children of his brother, Thyestes, and served them to Thyestes at a banquet which was supposedly to celebrate the brothers' reconciliation. Within the conditions of the tragedy as treated by Aeschylus, this is the mythic origin of the blood-guilt that curses the House of Atreus. And the guilt calls forth violence that in turn calls forth violence, until the playwright contrives in his third play to change the rules of vindication by changing the very nature of Justice and Conscience.

Since the "original" offense is in the category of eating, a corresponding strand of imagery is maintained throughout: biting (with its variants, devouring, bloodsucking, disgorging, and the like). The Furies themselves represent the image in the extreme. For their basic role (they call themselves "Curses") is to objectify the vicious bite of conscience ("remorse").

Secondarily, the dog image fits here. Hence, not only are the Furies "dogs," in their desire to hound the guilty. But also, there are treacherous dogs, loyal dogs, subservient dogs, alert dogs (at the very opening of the play, the Watchman is expectant "like a dog"). The dog-image is excellent for such purposes because, besides its close relation to the terms for biting, the dog serves so well "Aesop-wise" to sum up characteristic human relationships. For, above all, note how neatly this image represents a basic ambiguity of social relations: the wavering line between loyalty and subservience (an essential concern, if drama is to be *civically* motivated in the fullest sense).

We experience a special flurry when Clytemnaestra likens herself to a dog watching over the house. She is a woman, she is to kill, she is to be killed; and women (the Furies, the bloodthirsty hounds of conscience) are to preside over her avenging (as indeed, finally, a woman, Athena, presides over a deal whereby the matricide is pardoned and the Furies are given a new abode underground, in what we might call "the Unconscious of the State").

Whatever the ultimate guilt may be, there must also be guilt towards women as a *class*. Women, socially submerged, assigned to the innermost compartment of the house (the penetralia, or *muchos*), in an order where romantic love was best expressed homosexually, may thus come to stand for nearly all submerged motives. Their generic role as underprivileged would serve Euripides well, in fitting them to be dramatic personalizations for any aspect of the socially problematical. And in this trilogy, problems of social conscience, as reflected in the individual conscience, are finally resolved by an astounding intellectual (or even intellectualistic) feat whereby women's *biological* function of childbearing is in effect denied, through being interpreted in purely social terms.

We refer to the dramatized legalism of the third play, with its ingenious hagglings designed to prove (in proof attended by much pageantry) that men are not really descended from women. The woman is but a nurse for the fetus which descends through the male line only, as with patrilineal descent of property. Hence, Orestes' guilt of matricide is absolved because, strictly speaking, he had no mother. Similarly, when presiding over the trial that frees Orestes, Athena points out that she was born without a mother, from the head of Zeus. The "Justice" of the Parliamentary Zeus is thus essentially discriminatory with regard to women.

Hence, as a rule of thumb we assume: (a) That in the Athenian *polis* there was an unresolved civic guilt with regard to women; (b) and that they could accordingly serve well as dramatic vehicles (however roundabout) for the expression of social or political tensions in general. (For instance, recalling *Prometheus Bound*, consider what it may mean that, after the rebel deity has been so terrifyingly confined and tortured before our very eyes, the Chorus of Women enters, announcing that the reverberations had penetrated to the innermost recesses of their cave. For here again is the word *muchos*, that names the penetralia, the women's compartments, of a house. It also is the equivalent of the Latin word for an inner bay, *sinus*. And in our chapter on "the thinking of the body" we have offered reasons for believing that the motives of internality are here carried to the point where, in the course of the plot, as imaginally defined in the text, the terror is not merely felt by the audience as witnesses; rather, it is ingrained in the very behavior of the drama, which at this point, after its fashion, *micturates*. That is, the drama does not merely make us afraid; rather, it itself *is* afraid. And inchoately it calls forth appropriate movements from the innermost recesses of the frightened mind, as reflected in a correspondingly frightened body.)[2]

So much for the general view of the plays, and the place of our analysis in our concern with Poetics as a whole. Let us now list some of the major considerations that arose in the course of our making an index designed to follow the course of the plays step by step.

---

[2] In our chapter "The Thinking of the Body" (pp. 308–343) these speculations are developed more fully.

III

1) Two kinds of accountancy. Evil in first play (slaying of Agamemnon) leads to evil in second (Orestes' slaying of the slayers, the usual feudal pattern). But evil in second play leads to good in third, after the "conscientious" legalistic manipulations whereby tribal justice is replaced by parliamentary justice (which equals male supremacy). There are the great words for law and order (the *Dike* set). There are the corresponding words for threat, retaliation, vengeance, vindication, ruin (the *Ate* set). And there are the bridging terms, like those for pollution (*miasma*), pride, folly, venom, piety (*sebas*), with their correctives in rites of purification (rites that, since they involve blood sacrifices, are forever circling back into the feudal genealogy whereby conflict begets conflict).

2) We could make use of the distinction between a mathematics of continuity ("wave theories") and a mathematics of the discrete ("corpuscular theories"). See Eric Bell: *Mathematics; Handmaiden of the Sciences*. To "tick off" these plays step by step is to be astounded at the way in which the overall curve of the development proceeds through a succession of discrete points. The plot is like the ticks of a clock progressing through time.

Presumably the dance movements that underlie the logic of the choric utterances contributed much to this order. The lyrics of the chorus proceed by set stages (strophe, antistrophe, etc.). A sensitivity to this kind of form encourages a plot to proceed like a row of falling dominoes, each knocking down the next.

The allusion to religious forms helped to this end. For instance, if the stichomythia was felt not merely as *dialogue*, but as rather an adaptation of the catechistic, then it would figure not merely as a brisk kind of conversation, but also as the *announcing of a disclosure* in the development of the plot. Thus the progress of the story could with maximum pointedness sharpen our perception of the relationship between the characters, as viewed successively in various pairings, with a corresponding disclosure (or "doctrinal" moment) to sum up each such relationship. Thus the road goes from station to station. And you might say that each step can be *given a formalistic title*, as though the dramatist (within the resources of his medium) were saying, "This is an introduction," "This is a foreshadowing," "This is a transition," "This is a summing-up," etc.

The method points *beyond* purely aesthetic form, as usually conceived, to the view of the plot as being, in essence, not just this story or that, but a viaticum that carries us through the process of ritual initiation or cleansing proper to *any* such specific plot. . . .

Incidentally, we also suspect that, since stichomythia stood traditionally for disclosure, and since nurses traditionally recognized the child re-

132 PARTICULAR WORKS AND AUTHORS

turning incognito as adult, Aeschylus could solemnly spoof in the stichomythia in which Orestes' nurse fails to discover his identity. (We have
another reason to believe that there was spoofing here. For note how the
nurse uses the great terminology of tragic cleansing, but in terms to do with
her particular vocation, which involved the laundering of soiled diapers.)

3) Besides the influence of the Choric patterns in sharpening the perception of stages, there would be the tradition of the "oracular" in general.
Insofar as the culture took "Sibylline" ambiguities as the norm, it would
be on the lookout for "prophetic" utterances. And such a quality of attention greatly assists the kind of formalistic pointing we have in mind. Thus,
the play will not just somehow begin. In the choice of this particular beginning there will be an *announcement*. And so as regards all three plays. Similarly, the endings will be notable as such.

Or one must ask pointedly: Why the Chorus of *old men* in the first
play, why of *slave women* in the second, why of the *Furies* in the third—
why precisely these, at precisely these points? What formal "secret" underlies that progression? (Cryptology is all.) And, similarly, we will watch for
the slogan-like lines that, in summing things up, use tricks of sound observable even across the gulf of our insensitiveness to the Greek, once we know
what to look for. Or they may purposely use tricks of grammar that make
them vague as to head and tail, like the design of a snake with its own tail
in its mouth.

The problem of appreciation here is complicated by the accidents of
survival. For instance, prophesying after the event, we find it beautifully
appropriate that the second play should begin with an invocation to Hermes.
Yet, had it not happened that Aristophanes, when looking for asylum from
the risks of political criticism, chose Euripides as his victim, and in victimiz-
ing contrast quoted Aeschylus, the beginning of the second play would be
unknown. And as regards endings, there are problems which, competent
scholars tell us, still are not settled.

Meanwhile, "in principle" at least, we offer our suggestions. And even
if our answers are not wholly satisfactory since they are not complete, they
may at least let us see in flashes down long corridors . . . and piously, since
fearsomely . . . and fearsomely, since the logic of symbol-using becomes a
logic of persecution, with entanglement in the labyrinthine nets of Agamemnon's killing, until or unless there is emergence into the stage of Peace,
exulting as with the end of the *Oresteia* itself in the public celebration of a
Great Pact. "Without the shedding of blood, there is no remission of sins,"
wrote Paul. Forget it never, when meditating on the tragicomedy of vindication.

4) To consider a few of the strategic moments briefly: The first play
begins: "Gods" (in the accusative case, thus grammatically pushing us for-

ward); the second: "Hermes." The third: "First." So, for a beginning, a Watchman. What is he doing? He is watching and waiting. What will his first word be, to be appropriate? "Gods." Gods what? "Gods, I beseech." (This is a play by the civic-minded author of *The Suppliants*. And he well knew all the variants, complexities, refusals, and unwieldinesses, of supplication.) From the expectancy there will emerge, *gradatim et paulatim*, the annunciation looking towards Agamemnon's return—and the plot is on.

As for the second, *"Herme chthonie"* (Hermes, of the netherworld): This being the transitional play, and Orestes' murder of his mother being the transitional act, it is fittingly introduced by Orestes praying to Hermes, who is the tutelary deity of those on journeys (in transition), and is the power communicant between the living and the dead. (Maybe, in view of the parliamentary enlightenment which the third play is to celebrate, we should also note that Hermes was the patron of the Athenian businessmen; and later, during factional disputes, one conspiratorial night a gang of hoodlums in sympathy with the old aristocracy were to symbolize their political sympathies by mutilating all the statues of Hermes. But Aeschylus was writing at an earlier date, when the future of Athens, for all its factionalism, looked brighter.)

As for the final oracular beginning, "First" (*proton*): Surely, coming where it does, it is the most fitting of all. At the end of the second play, Orestes has been told that he must travel to the temple of Apollo at Delphi. In accordance with ancient Greek tradition, and the best modern psychology, the text refers to the center-stone of this temple as the "navel" (*omphalos*) of the world. So, after the murder of his mother, to be cured Orestes must be thorough. He must go back to beginnings. (For reasons of space, we shall omit our accountacy of the steps whereby the opening passage moves from maternal firsts to the male Apollo. But, look at the text, and you'll find it there, clearly enough.) All told, after the *Agamemnon* and the *Libation Bearers* have put us through the preparatory discipline of the father-murder and the son's avenging of it by a mother-murder, we are ready in the *Eumenides* to consider "beginnings" (whereat we move by degrees from the opening "First" to the final New Conscience as defined in the pageantry of the "First" legalistic trial, the turn from tribal "vengeance" to forensic "justice").

5) As for the endings: Textual difficulties plague us here. But the general logic would seem to be this: Last play ends in the spirit of a final "allusive" shout[3] (in contrast with a prior moment of ritual silence, while a kind of Recessional is being completed). The second play ends on a question:

---

[3] That is, the word was traditionally used to name a ritual shout made by women celebrating the Bacchic rites of the god's rebirth.

When will this fury cease (more specifically, when will it be *lulled to rest*)? We'd like to think that the incompleteness in the closing lines of the first play were not due merely to a defect in the codex but were intentional. For variants of the word for completion, fulfillment, run through this trilogy like an *idée fixe*. It is the word that Aristotle makes equally important in his philosophic stress upon the *teleological*, the word that, in the Greek New Testament translates Christ's dying formula, "It is finished." And to trail it through its many variations in these three plays, watching the imaginal associates with which it becomes successively identified as it proceeds, is almost like glimpsing the very essence of a culture. So we'd like to think that, when the stress upon the oracular is combined with such sensitiveness to fulfillment, the boastful lines at the end of the first play were deliberately left broken, as a device of stylistic prophecy, while the operatic nature of the medium might allow "naturally" for such an effect, since the words might at this point become submerged beneath a sudden swell of the music.

6) As for the propriety of the Choruses: For the first play, the Chorus of Elders provides a good variant of the fulfillment theme (as Orestes' brusque action and intense suffering will depict fulfillments of a different order, in the category of full manly vigor). Dialectically, we began to note how, in the three biological stages that had their corresponding social status (childhood, manhood, and age), childhood and age were "alike" as contrasted with manhood. But we did not need to argue for the point, since Aeschylus explicitly has his Chorus of Elders liken themselves to children, with the oracular addition that age is like a dream dreamed by day. So they are well suited to such speculations on motives as are best possible when the full range of life from infancy to late death sets the perspective. (Was not the dramatist near ninety when he wrote these plays, in which old age is called the evil of evils?)

Why the Chorus of Slave Women, for figuring the motives of the second play? It suits well the themes of sufferance, lamentation, supplication, that go with any Aeschylean tragedy. (See the *Suppliants* for the several lines wherein the mimetics of beseechment are explicitly discussed, as a kind of pious diplomacy when dealing with Powers of any sort.) And this second play concerns, above all, a kind of Babylonian captivity, a waiting for the moment of liberation, to be got ambiguously through sacrifices.

The propriety of the Furies as Chorus for the third play is obvious. In these female hounds of conscience, the dog image comes to fruition. (George Thompson, among others, has made clear their role as the personification of matriarchal-tribal motives, in contrast with the Olympian-patrilineal kind of motives that will be affirmed in the pageantry depicting the "first" trial in accordance with political justice.) And if there is still a problem of conscience to be settled, what better way to settle it dramatically than by putting the very principle of conscience itself, as symbolized by the Furies in a position where its transformation could be celebrated as pageantry?

Whereas the lyric function threatens the dramatic function in lesser dramatists, Aeschylus here finds a way of making it as dramatic as possible, since the Furies change their nature—and the great civic accomplishment in this enterprise comes from the skill by which the transformation of conscience is interwoven with political motives. The result is that the duplication of the State in the gods is dramatically presented as a derivation of the State from the gods.

And the transformations of conscience are, with astounding accuracy, related to emergent political institutions. As we have seen the primal curse previously translated into terms of personal relationship (specifically, relations between parents and offspring), it is now to be treated explicitly in terms of civic relationship. We could state this in another way by saying that, after the many stages of unfolding or uncovering, Aeschylus' search for the motivational origins of the plays has progressed to a point where the underlying civic motives can be explicitly (even systematically) disclosed. And the dramatic situation is such that, having passed beyond the stage of violence, the plot can treat of civic discord in a mixture of legalism and mythology that, by its conciliatory temper, gives us the happy sense of civic faction being transcended by civic unity.

7) Since the trilogy leads up to and away from the matricide, we are particularly careful to ask what themes gravitate about this act. And so, above all, we focus upon that word "amphisbaena," uttered by Cassandra (who, as prophetess is sure to state the motivational essence) when she is trying to decide what the murderous Clytemnaestra should be called. For if Orestes is to slay not just a mother, but an "amphisbaena" (naturally, for the best of reasons) we must meditate upon that term, since by the rules of the myth Cassandra *cannot* be wrong.

Amphisbaena: from *amphis*, both ways; and *bainein*, to go. It is a serpent, in ancient mythology, beginning or ending at both head and tail alike. Meditating upon it, we may also recall that Clytemnaestra is called a serpent, as is Orestes (in her dream). Confining ourselves here to the statement of a position that must slight the arguments for it, offered elsewhere, we sum up thus:

We take this "prelogical" monster to be the mythic representation of the ultimate dreaming worm, the sheerly vegetating digestive tract, that underlies all human rationality, and out of which somehow emerge the labyrinths of human reason. The purely social kind of "justice" which is finally celebrated in the third play's pageantry, having to do with the mythic founding of the Acropolis, is in the last analysis a dialectical "transcending" of the basic biological worm (even in its "secondary" form, the design of the fetus placentally feeding, as figured "tertiarily" in the design of the child at the maternal breast).

To arrive eventually (and by a dramatically "radical" course) at such a scheme of motives as sprang like Athena fully grown from the head of

Zeus, the playwright must somewhere depict the *ultimate* slaying (if the rules are such that the sacrificial rite requires an ultimate slaying, to be complete). Here even the slain *mother* must *stand for* something beyond herself. And Cassandra tells us what; namely: the amphisbaena, which we take to be the mythic representation of the ultimate, vegetatively, nonverbally dreaming worm, circling back upon itself in enwrapt self-engrossment (somewhat as with the self-love of Aristotle's God, and likewise of many later theologians' Gods).

When in the second play we have heard the cry of Aegisthus, slain by Orestes off stage, and when Clytemnaestra has rushed in, asking what has happened, the traditional messenger (here a servant) answers enigmatically: "The dead are killing the living, I say." But Clytemnaestra immediately calls the remark a riddle. She is pointing up its "oracular" nature. For the expression so utilizes the resources of Greek grammar that it can also be interpreted in reverse: "The living kills the dead." The formula is deliberately designed by the dramatist to have this, shall we say, "amphisbaenal" nature. She goes on to interpret her statement in accordance with the *lex talionis*: "We are killed by treachery, even as we killed."

The feudal nature of vindication (by victimage) gives us many variants of this design: "Meet hate with hate . . . repay murder with murder . . . as he does, be it done to him," etc. Even in the seven extant plays of Aeschylus, we could probably trace literally hundreds of variations on the formula.

Here is the labyrinthine puzzle at the ultimate verbally attainable depths of the trilogy. For there is a notable respect in which the logic of symbols would transcend the very material body by which symbols are made usable (and in the tragic idiom, this moment of transcendence is figured in terms of victimage, of an ultimate slaying).

Do we, then, imply, that these tragedies are, in their motivation, reducible to terms so biologically absolute that, in the last analysis, they are concerned but with the unresolved conflicts between the verbal and the nonverbal out of which it arises and in which it is necessarily grounded?

Decidedly, not at all. The confusions of anal and oral, the kissing of carrion, the uniting of efficient and final cause in one locus, the joining of potency and actuality (matter and spirit), the combining of "father" and "mother" in a term such as "parent," (or, technically, the fact that a "thesis" and an "antithesis" cannot join battle except insofar as they have a "synthesizing" ground in common)—such bepuzzlements are all about us. Yet, the perception of their ubiquity and universality should not be allowed to obscure from us an ambiguity of this sort, which has exercised the author in many ways (as his *Rhetoric of Motives* attests) but which gained especial clarity for him when, recently, he was reading of *ziggurats* (towerlike temples, "zoned" into a series of steps that, pyramidally receding, would seem hieratically to figure the principle of the social pyramid). The "top" of each stage, he dialectically mused, is the "bottom" of the stage immediately above it. *Telescope* that design, as you necessarily do when you reduce it to a matter of *principle*, and an "amphisbaenal" relationship seems to result. "Mouth" and "tail" are brought together.

So, beginning over again, hence again recalling that the great Greek tragedies were devices for treating of civic tensions (read: class conflicts), and for contributing to social amity by ritual devices for resolving such tensions: We would note how the "amphisbaena" belonged, here too, as the figuring of a pattern.

Unfortunately, our remarks here look "Swiftian." So, to mitigate such suspicions, let us ask exactly what the difference may be. And, to that end, let us apply our perspective to the analysis of a passage in Swift's own works. We have in mind Chapter VI of the *Voyage to Brobdingnag*, where tiny Gulliver makes a seat-bottom out of combings from her gigantic Majesty's hair. He goes on to say: "The Queen would have had me sit upon one of these chairs, but I absolutely refused to obey her, protesting I would rather die a thousand deaths than place a dishonorable part of my body on those precious hairs that once adorned her Majesty's head." He continues: "Of these hairs (as I had always been a mechanical genius) . . ." and at this point, as regards our kind of lurking, we would forthwith adjourn to consider that astounding, Swiftly tortured adumbration of psychoanalysis, his tract *On the Mechanical Operation of the Spirit*. For satire is best understood, as a variant of tragedy, quite as tragedy is best understood, not just "universally," but by remembering always that it is designed to resolve *temporal* tensions.

Incidentally, we have elsewhere in our text observed how well the use of the traditional "myth" in tragedy contributed to simplicity of design. For whatever the complexities of a unique situation may be, the myth reduces these to a few basic relationships. In this sense, the tragic playwright's use of myth enabled him to get, in his medium, the kind of functional simplification that we have learned to associate with Greek sculpture at its best.

And, for the general picture, perhaps we should add one further consideration, to take account of the fact that traditionally a tragic trilogy was in turn *completed* by a satyr play. For it would seem that all this astoundingly thorough concern with *completion* itself in turn was felt to require a completion. In our references to satire we have already hit upon a variant of such concerns but not wholly.

The satyr play that rounded out this particular trilogy is missing. From our point of view, the loss to those who would systematically lurk, and would piously spy on great texts, is perhaps the greatest in all human history. For though we do know that the satyr plays were *burlesques* of the very characters who were treated solemnly in the tragedies, we would like to think that, in the great days, the *same* characters were *finally* burlesqued who had been treated heroically in the tragic trilogy. Such an arrangement would be so very civilized. It would complete the completing.

Chapter Four

Goethe's *Faust*, Part I

In an earlier section of this essay, to be found in the Chicago Review for Fall, 1954, I proposed that four "offices" (derived in part
from Cicero's "three offices of the orator") be considered as essential
to the analysis of poetic symbolism. The first office is that of teaching
or informing; the second, that of pleasing; the third, that of moving
or persuading; and the fourth, that of expressing the "personality"
of the agent. It is with the fourth of these, and specifically with the
work's "personality" as expressed symbolically and socially determined, that I am concerned here; and I am to show how the symbolizing of perfect victimage relates to the "entelechial" principle natural
to the genius of language.

I
The Outline of the Work, as Pointed for Our Purposes

An elderly man, sick of sheer intellectual knowledge, regretful that worldly
delights and honors have passed him by, makes a pact with the devil. The
devil, restoring his youth, shall empower him to seduce a guileless girl. After
agreeing to a pact, but before encountering the girl, with the aid of diabolic
magic he takes part in a tipsy revel of adolescents and also visits a Witches'
Kitchen. Then follows the carefully paced seduction, which results in the
seducer's killing of the girl's brother and in her half-mad disgrace and death,
after she has in madness drowned her illegitimate child. The mounting turmoil of the plot culminates in an episode of Pandemonium, a perverse "preternatural" orgy that stylistically completes the episodes of the tippling
students, of Hell's Kitchen, and of the man's furious debate with himself in
a forest cavern. Also, its riot impressionistically duplicates a quasi-revolu-
tionary outbreak, here "channelized" in sexual terms. Of this sexual story
we could say that it recounts how a wealthy man seduced a trusting girl of
modest means by whom he was deemed "noble"; how his wealth had seemed
to her capable of making her look like a "lady of nobility"; and how her
guileless ways of failing to protect her sexual treasure had made her seem to
him like an "angel."

II

Negatives (or, rather, a Few of the More Notable Ones)

In the "Prologue in Heaven," the Lord classes Mephistopheles among the spirits that deny (*verneinen*). And when Mephistopheles discloses himself to Faust for the first time, he calls himself the spirit that always denies (*Ich bin der Geist, der stets verneint*). In the riot of Walpurgis Night, Faust calls Mephistopheles the "spirit of contradiction" (*Geist des Widerspruchs*). And the nature of the motives in the Witches' Kitchen is epitomized in the crazy mathematical design of a computation that nonsensically adds up to nothing.

But we should also note that Gretchen's first words are negatively couched, as she somewhat curtly says to Faust that she is neither a lady nor beautiful and can go home unaccompanied: *Bin weder Fraulein weder schön / Kann ungeleitet nach Hause gehn*. But subsequently we hear her admitting to herself how much she has been impressed by the talk of the great man, who makes her feel ashamed by comparison, while all she can do is say yes to everything he tells her: *Beschämt nur steh' ich vor ihm da, / Und sag zu allen Sachen ja*. Unlike the devil, she could not steadily deny. We might also note that the devil, in perhaps the most patly character-drawing device of all drama, pays handsome tribute to her in an aside, pityingly apostrophizing her as "thou good and innocent child" (*du guts unschuldigs Kind*), his negative here being couched almost in the accents of a doting parent.

In the first stanza of his opening speech, Faust had lamented that we can know nothing (*dass wir nichts wissen können*). Later he contemplates suicide, as a possible dissolution into nothingness (*ins Nichts*). And in the garden with Gretchen, when discussing the advisability of total yielding (*sich hinzugeben ganz*), he had avowed that the delight must be forever, since its end would be disaster: "No, no end! No end!" (*Nein, kein Ende! Kein Ende!*). Later, when reproaching himself for his impetuosity, he calls himself homeless and a monster (literally, "unhoused" and an "un-man": *der Unbehauste . . . der Unmensch*).

Gretchen's initial negative is understandable enough, as likewise the poetic justice of the disaster that went with her turn from nay to yea. Faust's negatives apparently involved philosophic speculations, plus his rhetorical adapting of these to the ends of certain worldly gains (here epitomized in the seducing of Gretchen). But the central consideration, for our purposes, is the negativity of Mephistopheles.

In the "Prologue in Heaven," the Lord explains why he does not hate the likes of Mephistopheles. Man inclines too easily toward sloth, he says

(*Des Menschen Tätigkeit kann allzuleicht erschlaffen*); and the devil serves as a companion, to keep men prodded into action. Previously the Lord had given Mephistopheles permission to tempt Faust, since man can be expected to err as long as he keeps striving (*es irrt der Mensch solang' er strebt*).

III
Striving (Streben)

With this reference to striving we have not only a *theme* but more specifically a *term* that we can trace in zigzags throughout the entire work. We have explicit authority in the text for connecting it with both "the Lord" and the "spirit of negation, or contradiction." And, if only because the play is for the most part in rhymes, we find the word itself quickly becoming interwoven with two others that rhyme with it: "soaring" (*Schweben*) and "life" or "living" (*Leben*). "Weaving" (*Weben*) figures secondarily. So far as sheer letters go, this "fatal" word is but *Schweben* without the initial *sch*.

To dispose of the more general motivational problem before tying ourselves down to purely "concordantial" connections, we should note, first of all, that the "Prologue in Heaven" makes no pretences whatever to an esoteric religious vision. Goethe is portraying a "heavenly" court, to be sure; but in the spirit of a conceiver of a *fiction*, of a masque or conceit, not in that of a pious prophet who might say that he is reporting on an actual dialogue in Heaven. In particular, we would lay great store by Mephistopheles' soliloquy, on which the Prologue ends. He likes to see the Old Man (*den Alten*) now and then, he says, and is careful never to break with him. And "it's quite decent of so great a lord to be so human when talking with the devil" (*Es ist gar hübsch von einem grossen Herrn, So menschlich mit dem Teufel selbst zu sprechen*). Clearly, this is the way an underling talks of his superior, as when the clerk feels proud that the boss has acted toward him "like a good fellow."

The "heavenly prologue" is thus seen to be the mythically transmogrified replica of a quite worldly situation: The three angels ("messengers") praising the Lord are analogous to three loyal ambassadors in audience with the monarch. And Mephistopheles is the inevitable nay that matches the three devoted angels' unswerving yea. We thus begin with a dramatized paradigm of an administrative center, a masquelike depiction of its "essence": the authority, the loyal underlings, the resistant underling (with the authority recognizing that there is a sense in which the resistant underling plays a necessary role in the authoritative structure). We should add: To the purely internal ends of greater vividness, the "heavenly scene" is cosmologized by the three angels' references to the astronomical heavens, which are as splendid (literally, "lordly," *herrlich*) as on the first day of the Creation.

There is an alternative prologue, the "Prologue in the Theatre." There, the theatrical manager would correspond to the Lord, the dramatic poet would be analogous to the angels, and the jester, or *lustige Person*, would match Mephistopheles. But the change of persons here naturally leads also to a slight dislocation of the three functions, so that the correspondences between the two matrices are not exact.

As for the "*Streben*-nexus," (the "courtly" motive localized in a few key words), the most famous *strebt* passage appears early in the drama, when Faust is talking to his bluntly devoted disciple, Wagner. Faust tells him man is born with a desire that presses forward and up (*hinauf und vorwärts*). There follows a transitional reference to skylarks; then comes the noted set piece, of the spread eagle that soars (*schwebt*) and the crane that over waters homeward strives (*strebt*). Next comes Faust's avowal that two motives ("souls") dwell within his breast—and out of that speech in turn evolves the appearance of the poodle, the first manifestation of Mephistopheles. (Though Wagner sees it only as a dog, while Faust from the start senses in it something vaguely portentous, the two views agree to this extent: Wagner lays great emphasis upon the *subservience* of the animal; and immediately after the "fog" has been dispelled, Mephistopheles presents himself in the guise of a person eager to *serve* Faust as his *master*: *Was steht dem Herrn zu Diensten?*) Later, when sizing up Faust's susceptibilities, Mephistopheles muses, "Fate has given him a spirit that ever presses forward irrepressibly" (*ungebändigt*). There is talk of overhasty striving that overleaps man's earthly pleasures. And "soaring" follows, in connection with the idea of unappeasable appetite.

In the "Prologue in Heaven," *schwebt* had appeared in a notable connection. The Lord, when addressing the loyal angels, likened eternal living to the condition of becoming (*das Werdende*); and he told them they must strengthen with enduring thoughts whatever wavers (the word *schwebt* itself vacillates among such meanings as soar, hover, and waver). But the most important further reference occurs in the episode of Walpurgis Night. Here, the riotous ride is said to take place among a whirlpool of fantastically inhuman creatures, a swirl (*Strudel*) that strives upward (*strebt nach oben*). Everything is so topsy-turvy in this incident, you think you're pushing and you're being shoved (*Du glaubst zu schieben, und du wirst geschoben*). Whereat we are reminded that, in the "Prologue in the Theatre," the dramatic poet refers to a *Strudel* into which the surging multitude draws us against our wills. And in the Dream that forms an intermezzo to the Walpurgis Night section, there is a quatrain recited by the crane (recall him in the earlier "striving" passage): He says that, because he loves to fish in both clear and muddy waters, that's why you see this pious gentleman mixing with the devil (a variant of the "two souls" theme).

IV
In Sum, On the Play as "Characteristic"

The foregoing observations should serve at least to indicate the sort of symbolism that figures in the work as a "natural sign" of the author (the work as approached in terms of the "fourth office"). However, in studying it as the portrait of a personality we aim to begin with the broadest possible frame of reference. The fact that Goethe was a romantic poet who became a minister of state would be relevant, certainly. But even if we knew nothing about him as a private citizen we should still want to contend that the "Prologue in Heaven" is a dramatized paradigm of the "courtly situation," the administrative motive reduced to a "basic design." Intrinsic to this, we would say, are problems of negativity variously classifiable in purely critical terms and here figured in terms of dramatic imitations (characters variously acting).

Even if we did not know that Goethe had translated Diderot's *Neveu de Rameau* or did not know that, in his capacity as an elderly statesman, he greatly feared and condemned such disorders as came to a head in the French Revolution, we should look for evidences of the "hierarchal psychosis" (of the "social pyramid") which we believe figures essentially in every work. (Indeed, we choose a full-bodied work such as this because, in its great intellectual clarity, it can clearly reveal motivational principles more readily overlooked in works that stress sheer imagery or "sensibility.")

The courting of Gretchen, we take it, translates the "courtly" motive into sexual equivalents. Paradoxically, there is thus a sense in which this seduction is more of an "allegory" than are the "supernatural" or "preternatural" episodes. For the reader does not take those as "real," but as "symbolical"; whereas the courtship of Gretchen is quite realistically rendered, even Mephistopheles' producing of the fatal jewels not being presented as a particularly "magical" happening. Yet what is this constant attempt to see behind or beyond the sheer seduction as such, if not a dramatist's way of reversing the motives, by looking for what we might call the "underlying forms" of this courtship? And in the light of these, the courting of Gretchen becomes like a kind of "case history."

One might look for "characteristics" in the narrowest sense. For instance, in the midst of a fantastic episode, there is even a quatrain about a "northern artist" contemplating a journey to Italy. Knowing the importance of Goethe's Italian journey as a stage in his development, and that it interrupted his relations with Charlotte, we might dig for the most particularized kind of biographical connections. But whereas there are not grounds for ruling out such minute portraiture (and especially in the case of a writer so autobiographical as Goethe), we are contending that inquiries into the "fourth office" should begin much farther afield.

Thus, as regards the notion that "man errs so long as he strives," the usual way of interpreting such a statement might be to think of "erring" as a mere undesirable risk, the generalized description of an "occupational hazard" to which those who strive are exposed. But another way of approaching the Faustian duality would be to think of the two words as but different terms for the same act, observed from different angles. If a person were wholly adequate he would not err; nor, if he were wholly adequate, would he have to strive. And we are thus suggesting that the inadequacy connoted by either of the terms is *categorical*, or "original." That is, it is intrinsic to the social order as such; and in this sense it is "inherited" by all mankind, being "prior" to any individual lapse into "actual sin." These remarks are offered not as a dialectical exercise in the Hegelian "reconciling of opposites," but to explain why we think that motives of "guilt" are inherent in social hierarchy as such. For if this were true, then we should be proved correct in our search for the *social* motives inherent in *poetic* "catharsis." Signs of such "original sin" might then be looked for in every work, both as a statement about poetic symbolism in general and as a way of suggesting something important to look for in any particular poet's strategy of expression.

"Categorical guilt," in this *political* or *sociological* sense (the need to "strive and/or err" in that scramble or *Strudel* wherein pushing is indistinguishable from being pushed), would not necessarily be taken as an alternative to "original sin" in the strictly *theological* sense. But the secular nature of secular poetry should justify us in expecting that, *at the very least*, secular poetry should mirror (or be the sign of) categorical guilt *in the merely political or sociological sense*. A secular poet might not have grace enough to understand original sin in the theological sense; but he might nonetheless exemplify the sociological variant without the slightest conscious effort. In any case, Goethe is at least talking about a *worldly* mode of striving—for that is what Faust explicitly chooses.

Such concerns naturally come to a head in problems of the negative, since the negative itself comes to a head in the perfection of the Decalogical (the thou-shalt-not's proper to a given order of property). Such motives are variously perverted and disguised, though great works such as this afford us the "missing links" connecting clear and direct manifestations with unclear and perverted ones.

An easily observable departure, in the present work, is in Faust's resounding set of itemized curses, which ends significantly on his cursing of patience above all else (*Und Fluch vor allen der Geduld!*) "Patience" sums up the attitude of social control, not as imposed *from without* or *from above*, but as a kind of self-legislation, the free imposing of law by the lawgiver upon the lawgiver. (We are talking here along Kantian lines.) In a similar vein, Faust said he didn't care whether there were Over and Under in the other world. Here is in principle the rejection of order, a rejection got by rejecting the principle of "mortification," or "renunciation" (*Entbehren*), that goes with any given order. Here is par excellence a *ministerial* value, though dramatized perversely, in Faust's curse (that prepared the way for Mephistopheles' appearance).

Later, musing in a romantic forest cavern, and turbulently nay-ridden as regards his designs on Gretchen, Faust likens himself to a cataract plunging down the mountain side, while Gretchen is as in a little Alpine hut standing quietly near by. His *im*patience is here expressed in terms imagistically positive, a thought that makes clear the ways whereby natural scenery can be endowed with motives of the social order, in this case even figuring a "fall." The correspondence may be even closer yet, as Faust further wishes that he could be like the stream in another respect, since the stream leaves the hut unharmed and expends its powers rather in tearing at its own rocks. (This kind of reflexive action would, as it were, get a semblance of self-control through a semblance of self-abuse, a motive that seems to flicker about the edges of the student scene in Auerbach's cellar, which ends when the bewitched youths awaken to find that the devil has set them all to pulling one another's *noses!*)

But regardless of how broadly or narrowly one conceives of the ways in which a work is the signature of personal (sociopolitical) motives, as soon as we begin looking for key terms, and for interrelations among them, we are turned in the direction of the "second order," as expanded in the omitted, earlier part of this discussion (and described there as the internal spinning of terms, from the standpoint of their intrinsic resources and obligations).

Thus the striving-soaring-living-weaving nexus is found, within this structure, to tie in with the philosophy of "Becoming." (In a song of Christ's resurrection it is called "delight in becoming": *Werdelust*.) But "becoming" itself, in being analyzable as moments between the limits of before and after, lends itself well to dramatization in terms of the youth-age relationship (the turbulent waterfall would obviously be on the youthful side of such a slope). And while watching lest the youth-age alignment itself be conceived in too naturalistic or biological a sense (while being on guard, that is, lest we overlook the social motivations implicit both in these terms and in the closely related sexual ones), we do have here central moments to do with the work as viewed in its internality.

V

The Heroine as Perfect Sacrificial Victim

When discussing a character from the standpoint of its formal perfection, we are obviously concerned with its "persuasiveness" as a symbol for arousing our sympathies or antipathies. Such a concern with the effectiveness of a character-recipe bears upon the "fourth office" insofar as we ask what social judgments are exploited in the endowing of the character with specific traits. The first seventeen chapters of Aristotle's *Rhetoric*, Book II, set down the main principles to be followed in such character drawing, though there are many remote or perverse ways whereby these principles can be complicated to the point where it seems that, in notable respects, almost the opposite policies are being followed, in writers given to "post-Christian" paradoxes.

But the mention of rhetoric in this connection suggests also that such considerations involve us in the poetic equivalent of the "third office," a work's capacity to "move" the audience. We say "poetic equivalent" because the use of these principles for poetic purposes is quite different from their rhetorical application, which is directed toward practical results outside the work, whereas the rewards of poetic application are intrinsic to their functioning within the work itself. To say as much is to indicate how such a concern with a character recipe involves us in the "second office," either in the narrowly Ciceronian sense of the entertaining or the wider sense of the self-consistent (self-developing). The "first office" (to inform) figures here, insofar as the poet uses "signs" for the traits he would have the reader attribute to the given character. (Under certain conditions, for instance, the doing of a kindly act would be a sign that the character is kindly; under other conditions, it would be a sign that the character is a hypocrite; and so forth.)

First of all, plotwise, there is Gretchen's guileless devotion to Faust. She must be the ideal victim, both in the sense that she is deemed admirable when "sinning," and in the sense that her victimage seems "logical" (at least in terms of "poetic justice"). She is very young; the sign of her youthfulness is dramatically "rendered" when we see her playing hide-and-seek with the great man. At that stage of the development (the "becoming"), he was still seeking what she still kept in hiding. The childish game was interrupted by Mephistopheles, in the dramatic interest of more protracted titillation for the audience. (He had previously pronounced the formula, observing that pleasure is increased by delay and slow preparation; there he had stated as a matter of psychology what the dramatist in this interruption embodies as a principle of form.)

Here are some traits that Faust identifies with her (indirectly, by associating them with her room): holiness through which sweet twilight weaves; quietude; order; peacefulness; a plenteousness in poverty; a blessedness in "this prison." He then imagines her piously kissing a grandfather's hand, says that the spirit of plenty and order has taught her like a mother, that she is a natural-born angel, that her divine image was made by pure and holy weaving (the two references to weaving might remind us that later she will sit at the spinning wheel, singing of her fatal love). Though he was drawn here by thoughts of pleasure, he now feels himself dissolving into a *Liebestraum.*

In another connection, roundabout, he attributes to her a simplicity and innocence that do not know their own holy worth, and a meekness and lowliness that are the highest gifts of lovingly bountiful Nature. He is talking to her about herself, but she is so much a case in point that she misses the point.

Such terms, as it were, provide the "sloganizing" for her character. Another kind of indirect portraiture results from her placement in a whole list of female *personae*, whose various ways of contrasting with her are in effect comments upon her, or illuminations of her, helping to differentiate her from other species of a genus. They are, in brief review: Gretchen's friend, Martha, so sexually designing that Mephistopheles, who must appear to be courting her (as a device for diverting her attention while Faust courts Gretchen), complains that she could hold even the devil himself to his word. (Gretchen is no such schemer.) Lieschen, who gossips with Gretchen by the well and talks unfeelingly about another girl involved in sexual scandal. Lieschen does not know that she is forcing Gretchen to realize how her own conduct will be interpreted by the villagers. (Gretchen is not thus unfeeling, though she admits ruefully to herself that once she would have been.) Bärbelchen, not a character in the play, but the subject of Lieschen's gossip. According to Lieschen, she had got into trouble acting the grand lady (by her *Vornehmtun*) and deserved all she got when her lover abandoned her to disgrace. (We shall return to her when on the subject of the jewels, involving Gretchen's kind of *Vornehmtun*.) Various other incidental figures, whose different ways of contrasting with Gretchen are obvious: the old prostitute, on the defensive but proud of her skill as a professional; a vague throng of marriageable young ladies, sexually unappeased and inquisitive, but primarily interested in making standard marriages; old crones of the Witches' Kitchen.

As for Gretchen herself: First of all, we must believe that she possesses all the virtues of malleability generously attributed to her by the man who would mold her. If his yearning for sexual domination is a cameo, it is dramatically matched by the intaglio of Gretchen's generous disposition. His designs adding up to guile, she is reciprocally a delightful vessel of guilelessness. Only Mephistopheles affronts her sympathetic tendencies. His presence, she says with naïve suggestiveness, makes her "close up inside" (*Und seine Gegenwart schnürt mir das Innre zu*); and he even troubles her so much that for emphasis she uses a double negative, avowing that he has "no sympathy with nothing" (*Man sieht, dass er an nichts keinen Anteil nimmt*).

But, above all, we would stress Gretchen's reception of the fatal jewels. Modestly undressing, unawares, before Faust and Mephistopheles, having sung to herself of the King of Thule who was loyal to a goblet (that seems to have stood ambiguously for motives both maternal and erotic), when she finds the jewels she says that such things as these could be worn on a high feast day by a lady of the nobility (an *Edelfrau*).

She also asks herself: "To whom might this splendor belong?" (*Wem mag die Herrlichkeit gehören.*) As we have said before, we would stress the literal meaning of this word as "lordliness." Beginning as an epithet applied to the Lord's Creation, in the "Prologue," the term has turned up at many strategic moments in the text. At one end, there is Faust addressing God as "great lordly Spirit," at a time when, in profound remorse, he is pleading for Gretchen to be saved. At the other end there is Mephistopheles applying the word to Walpurgis Night. Here Gretchen applies it to the fatal jewels, which had suggested to her the attraction of nobility, though none would say that she was putting on airs as Bärbelchen had done.

Musing about Faust, Gretchen is sure that he is of noble birth (*aus einem edlen Haus*). That would explain, she thinks, why he had been so self-assured (*keck*) when first accosting her on the street. Later she confides to Faust that she had been worried lest something immodest or improper in her manner (*Was freches, Unanständiges*) had led him on. Such guilelessness prompts Faust to call her an "angel," a "heavenly vision." And she does indeed look up to him with exactly such simple loyalty as the three angels of the Prologue manifest toward their Lord. Bärbelchen, who had put on airs, paid for her *Vornehmtun* with scandal. Gretchen is involved in a similar scandal—and there is the analogy of *Vornehmtun* in her relation to the jewels. But to say as much is to be reminded that her *perfection* as a victim for Faust's act was her undoing.

Perhaps we should mention two other traits. She had been like a mother to her younger, ailing sister, now dead. (A full analysis would certainly trace the "breast" theme through this work.) And she gives Faust a good description of her lower middle-class respectability, as with her references to the modest property left by her father and situated near the edge of town.

In sum, our point is this: While trying to characterize Gretchen as a *person*, we do so not in the interests of character portraiture as such but with reference to problems in the diplomacy of poetic symbolization. For instance, as a figure designed to arouse our sympathies, this child who later drowns her own illegitimate child is seen to have been a virgin-mother to her sister. This girl who dies in disgrace is seen to be intrinsically endowed with such spiritual inheritance as goes ideally with middle-class respectability, and extrinsically endowed with the ideal property requirements of such a status. When asking how "scandal" figures in such motivation, we confront subtler considerations of property and propriety, which move us into broader considerations of negativity—involving respects, for instance, in which the purely physiological facts of deflowering and extramarital impregnation can be poetically identified in relation to signs for social control (somewhat as when Mephistopheles, observing Gretchen's naïve attempts to reclaim Faust for religion, grumbles that girls catechize men because they feel that, if a man complies on this point, he'll yield to them in other matters).

But the reference to flowers brings up another mainly "internal" consideration: Goethe's use of the "flower" image, with its more immediate radiations.

VI
The "Flower" Image, and Ramifications

As regards the internalities of the story, we note the dramatic irony that Gretchen herself plucked the petals of a flower when in search of a sign that Faust loved her. The test "came out right," so far as its signifying of an intense attachment was concerned. But with regard to the specifically Goethean terminology (*Röslein, Röslein, Röslein rot*), she was off to a bad start. Similarly, later Lies*chen* tells Gret*chen* that Bärbel*chen* has lost her little flower, her Blüm*chen*. And before Gretchen, in unconscious shamelessness, had despoiled a flower by way of poetic prognosis, the devil himself had twitted Faust for talking pruriently of her as though her honor and her favors were flowers to be plucked.

When Faust enters the prison, intending to rescue her, and she mistakes him for her executioner, she tells him that her "friend," who once was near, is now far off. Then, impressionistically, she sums up: "The wreath lies torn, the flowers are scattered." (Nor should we overlook the *functioning perversity* of this scene, the principle of negativity concealed in the dramatic irony whereby Gretchen's mistaking of Faust for her executioner is "substantially" true, even while being *literally* a sign of her madness.)

Here is an instance of further radiations in the flower theme: In the "Prologue in the Theatre" the poet, after talk of the surging and crushing that draws us against our wills into the *Strudel*, offers an alternative ideal: "No," he says; "Lead me rather to some quiet corner in Heaven, where for the poet there blooms but pure delight, where love and friendship . . . ," etc. Recalling that Gretchen was Faust's "angel," we might also note that she repeatedly addresses him as "friend." It is questionable how far such correlations should be traced, particularly when the terms are so ordinary; but in any case it is a literal fact that the word for "love" here is abbreviated (*Lieb'*)—and it was similarly abbreviated in the punning formula of the students' song (about illegitimate pregnancy, *Lieb' im Leibe*), which poetically foretold the course of the Faustian seduction.

A bit later, after the director has said that, since it's hard to satisfy an audience, one should instead aim to mystify them, the poet remarks that a poet scatters the blooms of spring in the path of his beloved, whereat the jester (the *lustige Person* who, by our interpretation, is analogous to the Mephistopheles of the "Prologue in Heaven") tells him to engage in the business of poetry as one carries on a love affair.

He also tells the poet that "the most beautiful bloom of youth" will gather at his play. This elicits from the poet a gorgeous set piece, a nostalgic cry for the return of the early days, when he was still in the stage of un-folding, of becoming (*im Werden*), the Goethean fatality of defloration thus being interwoven with a key term in the German philosophy of Develop-ment (while the next line talks of *Liebe*, with *schwebt* to rhyme with *lebt*). The poet refers to a bud that, in the youthful days, promised wonders, and to the picking (literally "breaking") of endless flowers that richly filled the valleys. Then he had both the drive for truth and the delight in falsity (*den Drang nach Wahrheit und die Lust am Trug*). And he yearns for the return of the days when he experienced his impulses uncontrollably (*ungebändigt*).

The flower theme (*read*: the "deflowering" theme) obviously fits well with the theme of Faust's magically regained youth. But by approaching the youth-age alignment as we have, we hope to have provided the means of making clear how "politically" or "sociologically" tinged this biological imagery is. We are trying to suggest that, once a social order (with its "pyramidal" logic) has attained its scrupulous analogues in modes of "self-control" or "mortification," then imagery of youth can stand for general principles of *resistance*, however roundabout, symbolizing political or social motives not intrinsic to the biological condition as such.

In this sense, we believe, Gretchen's seduction becomes an imaginal substitute for the principle of riot (and of precisely such riot as a court minister, *né* romantic poet, would basically distrust if it were expressed politically rather than in terms of a sexual analogue). Poor Gretchen was, indeed, the sacrificial vessel of the negativistic principle, itself not essentially "sexual" or "biological" at all, but shaped by the thou-shalt-not's of gov-ernmental order. Age being the time when, physiologically, one must "rein in," the dream of youth regained can stand correspondingly for outbreak.

Incidentally, while such tendencies toward "riot" (in the sociopolitical sense) can be transferred to *sexual* terms, Faust's killing of Gretchen's brother points toward a subterfuge more often deemed "respectable" today: the imagining of violence in terms of physical brutality and murder. Here in the background of Goethe's play is an element that later came to the foreground, perhaps in keeping with the cult of the kill that overhangs the modern scene in general. But be that as it may, when the transference of sexual terms has been completed in the "flower" image, then seductive de-floration (with its peculiar kind of "violation") can fit well with the conditions of *becoming* that are also, *in principle*, identifiable with upheaval in general.

In sum, once social tensions (themselves compounded of both permanent and changing elements) have been translated into terms of a given "myth," the myth then brings up resources of its own. These resources are then capable of purely internal development within their own terms, though the use of such resources will reflect the personal bias of the user. That is, the dialectic is "in principle" absolute, being limited only by the scope of language as such; but in practice it is conditioned by the limitations of the particular practitioner.

We might here mention a pamphlet, *Love and Death* (by G. Legman). It is an attack upon the kind of murder mystery which has become a characteristic of our culture to a disturbing degree. With a certain slapdash brilliancy, and with some of the excessiveness "natural" to the pamphlet as a literary genre, the author undertakes to show how the imagery of physical violence serves as a legally and socially approved substitute for "indecent" thoughts of sexual violation. But we would want to go a step farther off, contending that the sexual fantasies themselves are a displacement of political motives.

Political, social ("hierarchal" or "pyramidal") motives would thus be present not just in imaginings of sexual "glamour" but in one's views of "nature" generally. Since a child begins his experience with natural images and personal relations, the social motives implicit in these "immediate" experiences are at first glimpsed but as vague forms beyond a fog, like premonitions of some "higher" reality. (Recall, for instance, how Wordsworth experienced the overtowering mountain when he had stolen the boat, a moralistic fear being translated into terms of a natural image sublimely threatening, hanging over him like a judgment, and even rising higher as he retreated.) In so far as one's perceptions of a "natural hierarchy" or "order" are an imaginative response to the morality of a given social order, there is a respect in which poetic "nature" is but the *incipient* manifestation of *society*. And in this sense, whatever might be the differences or even contrasts between "rural" and "urban" motives, there would be a sense in which Goethe, the "youthful" romantic poet, had already contained such potencies as attained fulfillment in Goethe the elderly court minister.

Such relations as the step from possibility to actuality, from hope to fulfillment, from *Werden* to *Gewordensein*, from sprout to seed, from emotion to intellect, from poetry to criticism, from "community" to "society," from plan to organization, from "culture" to "civilization," from "spring" to "fall," from internality to externality, can be dramatized quite fittingly in terms of the development from youth to age. Add to this the fantasy of an illicit sexual defloration, and you have plenty of incentives to get things reversed, thinking of the phantasmagoria in *Faust* as unreal and of the love

story as real; whereas the phantasmagoria comes nearest to disclosing the
social motives that shape the love story, causing *it* to be the *allegory* in this
work, while the "supernatural" and "preternatural" scenes bring us (within
the sources of this medium) nearer to the "literal truth."

VII
Walpurgis Night

Faust has said, "No" to the thou-shalt-not's. He has *essentially* violated the
sanctities of private property (beginning with the time when he furtively
entered Gretchen's bedroom and piously spied upon her privacy). He has
been "sexually radical." And the result is a pandemonium: all hell breaks
loose. The wild night could, with justice, be interpreted at least in all these
various ways:

It could symbolize the aftermath of the sexual violation, the general
spirit of perversity (*Widerspruch*) that was unleashed by the completing of
this plan, as though the seduction had been a preparation for something to
come next. Or it could be the symbolic or "mythic description" of the sexual
violation itself. (That is, whereas the literal act of copulation could not be
represented, it could be acceptably translated into "imaginal equivalents.")
Or it could be the kind of political subterfuge we have already mentioned,
an imagery whereby the *principle* of revolutionary overthrow could be expressed, but in a safer form, a form that turned the imagination away from
explicitly political considerations.

(There is the possibility that once political motives have become publicly transformed into their sexual analogues the psyche can spontaneously
dream its politics in sexual terms. If anti-authoritarian motives which could
not be confessed directly without embarrassment or risk were translated
into terms of sexual "sins of the flesh to which we all are prone," then the
psyche might cleanse itself by the confessing of untowardnesses not politically suspect. And this writer's admiration for the resourcefulness of the
psyche is great enough to make him feel sure that such kinds of consciousness
and/or conscience can be developed on a grand scale, particularly when
mankind has had centuries upon centuries during which to perfect itself in
such subterfuges. This shift in the psyche began to take place, we would
imagine, about the time when the pagan custom of "sacred prostitution"
began to be condemned as fornication, a praying to false gods.)

There is also a figuring of the topsy-turvy here, in the most literal
sense. Things are upside down, as if the riotous flight were really a *descent*.
Thus recall the passage in the *Strudel* of Walpurgis Night (the Dream intermezzo) where the Versatile (*die Gewandten*) announce that, in their merry
state, if they can't go on their feet, they'll go on their heads (*Auf den Füssen
geht's nicht mehr, / Drum gehn wir auf den Köpfen*). It is also worth noting

that they call themselves an army *von lustigen Geschöpfen*—and one of the three speakers of the "Prologue in the Theatre" is the jester, or *lustige Person*, whose analogies with Mephistopheles we have already mentioned.

A further indication of the same sort is that the Walpurgis Night episode has several "dirty" passages. Formally (as regards internal consistency, an aspect of the "second office") this fact helps accentuate the close linkage between the Walpurgis Night section and the earlier drunken student riot of Auerbach's cellar, which also is "dirty." Musically, the riot theme of Walpurgis Night is *incipiently* present, or announced, in the episode of Auerbach's cellar. This episode of the students precedes Faust's seduction of Gretchen (thus containing it "in germ," as sloganized in the refrain *Lieb' im Leibe*, concerning the girl extramaritally pregnant); and the witches' revels follow the seduction (thus "summing it up" in the various ways we are now considering).

We should also recall that the perversity is sloganized in sheer mathematical design in another episode that is quite like these in style: the scene in the Witches' Kitchen, also prior to the seduction. Here is where the witches' version of the multiplication table is given, in muddled counting from one to ten with vague additions and subtractions, all of which adds up to nothing (*Und Neun ist Eins, / Und Zehn ist keins. / Das ist das Hexen-Einmal-Eins*). In this scene Mephistopheles makes the first glancing reference to Walpurgis Night.

As regards the "sociality" of this episode in particular, and of the work in general: It is notable that, unless we overlooked the lines, nobody discusses the possibility of Faust's marrying Gretchen in the first place, though she would certainly have jumped at the offer. We take this to mean that the great man wanted not Gretchen, but what her sacrifice stood for: namely, riot, as revealed in the episode of Walpurgis Night. Here the incipiently perverse scruples of the poet (who ranged from romantic pre-minister to ministerial post-romantic) lead him to imagine the *perfect revelry*. And it, in turn, is announced in the student drinking scene, with its call: "Long live freedom! Long live wine!" (*Es lebe die Freiheit! Es lebe der Wein!*) And when thinking of that scene we should not fail to recall also, from the standpoint of the *Strudel*, Mephistopheles' rousing song of the flea who was made a minister, to the great embarrassment of the other courtiers, since they didn't dare scratch themselves (whereat the students exultantly join in the final refrain proclaiming their right to kill fleas).

There is a section in the work itself where such "hierarchal" motives as we are here considering are explicitly considered, though to an excessive degree made possible by the conditions of the drama. We have in mind an early, preparatory scene ("Before the Gate") where we are afforded a quick survey of classes and their motives. Here are such representative figures as a student praising beer, tobacco, and a well dressed girl; solid citizens praising

the comforts of peace; girl-conscious soldiers; respectable girls angling for
marriage; lower-class girls, who are thought more susceptible to sexual advances; the old whore, whom we have already mentioned with respect.

Faust says that all the citizenry are celebrating the Rerisen Christ,
since they themselves on this day have risen from all sorts of wretched
places: hovels, shops, mills, factories, and the like. This drastic analogy is
drawn by a man who is about to mortgage his immortal soul. So far as this
text is concerned, when trying to discern the social coordinates of poetic
"beauty," with its corresponding kinds of "catharsis," we would start from
the observation that the opening "Prologue in Heaven" is *not* concerned
with such esoteric lore of Heaven as, say, a Swedenborg might have dealt
with.

A moderate instance appears in Faust's opening monologue, and specifically in connection with the term *Strudel* (here the whirlpool of time,
Zeitenstrudel). The steps are these: First there was imagination expanding
in bold flight to infinity; but now we are content with trifles, as one joy after
another is shattered in time's whirlpool. Now Care nests deep within the
heart, causing hidden pains, restlessly disturbing rest and pleasure . . . and
so forth. The next step is particularly pointed to our purposes. This temporal
Care, we are told, lies concealed behind ever changing masks, such as house
and court, woman and child, water, fire, knife, poison, so that one trembles
before all things that never strike and must weep constantly for things one
never lost. To our way of thinking, this is a figurative way of saying that
the particulars of life itself have become infused with the spirit of the
Strudel, the pyramidal guilt or anguish. (We might remember it when looking for possible social motives in the *Angst* which Heidegger attributes to
wholly metaphysical causes.)

Long as this has been, we have omitted very many of the correlations
we noted when making our superficial index of the terminology in this work.
But perhaps we should mention one other primary problem of "signatures":
the historical or developmental problem, the "vatic" dimension of a work,
in metaphorically foretelling things that we can only know literally after the
event. Unquestionably such unfoldings occur, since conditions wholly here
now were emergently present in the past. The problem is in an embarrassment of riches: the resources of generalization and specification are such that,
in critical *vaticinium post eventum*, a critic is impoverished indeed if he can't
show how any given author anticipated the future, particularly if the critic
can make up his casuistry as he goes along, and if he never has to worry
about fitting all his casuistries together by schematizing their underlying
principles. (The critic usually solves the problem rhetorically by clamorously
despising schematizers, and thus frightening his reader into not daring to
do otherwise.)

Broadly: Once you discern in Goethe the idealistic philosophy of the becoming (tied to his key word, *Geist*) you are on the way to finding that he anticipated Hegel and thereby anticipated both communism and nazism. That's easy. But what of the *particulars*, then? When Gretchen, accosted by her seducer on the street, first refuses to be *led by him* (she will go home *ungeleitet*), we are helped to be modest in hindsight prognosis here by the fact that the word for street in this text is *Strasse*. Otherwise, when the becoming has been reduced to sex and flower, and the internal conditions call for a meeting on the street, we might be tempted to say that Gretchen's first intuition had been correct when she rejected what was, in sexual disguise, the political seductiveness of a *Gauleiter!*

VIII
Concluding Comments

Intrinsic to symbol-using as such there is the "principle of perfection," the delight in carrying out terministic possibilities "to their logical conclusion," in so far as such possibilities are perceived. This "entelechial" motive is the poetic equivalent of what, in the moral realm, is called "justice." It is equatable with both necessity and freedom in the sense that the consistent rounding out of a terminology is the very opposite of frustration. Necessary movement toward perfect symmetry is thus free.[1]

Extrinsically, the practical limitations of a given social order and of the given poet variously burden or complicate the search for perfect form in this purely technical sense. Diversities in their modes of life make people mysteries to one another. Discordant material interests produce "tensions" that complicate the ability to decide even in sheer theory what perfect justice would be, or what perfect poetic justice would be. Various kinds of partial advantage are rightly or wrongly deemed available, and personal "strategies" are developed in response to these partial purposes.

---

[1] However, a "principle of perfection," or "entelechial" motive, should by no means be thought of simply as a virtue to be saluted with delight. As exemplified in specialized disciplines, it can make for very ill-omened conditions. Apparently it can set the boldest scientific imaginations to dreams of artificial satellites, the "conquest of outer space," and similar "Faustian" grandiosities, while the humbler promises of applied science as a benefit to mankind are still ludicrously far from being redeemed. In its "aestheticism," its sheerly formalistic aim to carry the resources of a given medium to their ultimate conclusion, it can make for a variant of the perversely Gidean *acte gratuit*, but in a guise that fits only too well with the current "global" goads to victimage. Such unappeasability would seem to result when this purely speculative or technical adventurousness is combined with ambitions set by the pyramidal motives of the *Strudel* inevitable to even rudimentary kinds of political order, and drastically more so in the case of our present complex administrative problems. There is, of course, another kind of perfection conceivable: the perfection that a humanistic ideal of education might aim at. Yet at best, we sometimes fear, such an ideal would be but faintly compensatory.

Insofar as such "strategies" are "imitated" for their own sake, the extrinsic motivations are brought back within the orbit of the intrinsic, where resources natural to poetic mediums often allow for degrees of frankness not otherwise possible. Simplest example: the playwright can dramatically attribute to a "fool" or a "villain" some attitude which he might not otherwise be able to voice. And thereby at least he could *get it said* (thus satisfying a primary requisite of symbolic resourcefulness). The dialogue form offers the same diplomatic possibility in purely ideational matters. The lyric and the monologue-like essay are usually more confined in this regard. Satire is, of course, a risky form (a rhetorical danger to which, perhaps, we are partially indebted for the splendid fantasy of *Gulliver's Travels*, since its high percentage of universal satire helped in principle to protect the author's references to local personalities and issues).[2]

"Dramatistically," we would develop a view of language that permits us to watch always for the "social pageantry" of a given work, while always watching closely its purely internal developments. In this connection we look not only for "key words" and their bearings upon one another, but even for *puns* on those words. For though puns are grandest when they "make sense," the simple joy with which audiences often greet even sheerly nonsensical puns would seem to indicate that, within the limitations of the situation, such a response is mainly to a sheer internality of language as such. (We admit, however, that a sly pornographic suggestion in the offing helps intensify the explosiveness of the "yak.")

Puns, as so conceived, cover a wider area than is usually attributed to them. The punning of a good poet is complicated enough to make one dizzy, if one tries to see *clearly* all the possibilities that flutter vaguely about the blurred edges of his vision. And, methodologically, it is hard to make sure just how far this punning goes (since a given poet's puns are not necessarily identical with the puns that an appreciative reader may himself hear as the "overtones"). But we believe that a technique of indexing key words can

---

[2] In the London *Times Literary Supplement* of August 29, 1952, there is a relevant article, "The Soviet Dilemma," discussing the difficulties that beset recent Russian drama when certain theorists in authority decided that drama depicting contemporary situations within Russia should not depict conflict, "negative" characters, and the like, since the "new type of humanity" arising in the Soviet system had outgrown such conditions. Interestingly enough, this doctrine was later deposed by higher authorities. And there was always available, of course, the drama of conflict and negativism as regards the treatment of relations to foreign capitalism. Not having been able to follow the controversy at first hand, we do not know what all was touched upon. But motives can emerge in paradoxical ways, where art is concerned. In the theater of Corneille and Racine, for instance, the motives of the French Revolution emerged mainly in sexual terms. The principle of "control" being royal and masculine, the principle of "riot" was expressed in terms of feminine sensibility and passion. And Euripides seems often to have used feminine characters (such as Medea, and as Agave in the *Bacchae*) to stand for "submerged" principles of revolt in the political order.

help make more specific exactly how a terminology works in the idiom or dialect of a given author.

For instance, let us cite one purely terministic development we noted in *Faust* solely as a result of our indexing. (An ideally perfect memory, endowed with ideal accuracy of perception, plus ideal ability to recall the "annunciation" of a theme which had emerged at a stage in the development before its "future" was wholly graspable, might have been able to note this correspondence without the aid of indexing.) When Faust is making his bargain with Mephistopheles, he puts the matter thus: Let the devil enchain him, if ever he says to some moment of experience, "Tarry! Thou art so lovely." The words in German are, *Verweile doch! du bist so schön.* Surely, thereafter, each time the word for "lovely" or "beautiful" (*schön*) was uttered by Faust with regard to Gretchen, the Ideally Remembering Reader would have renewed the vibrancy of that passage.

But such an ideal reader would go further. In that line, the word for "tarry" is *verweile*. And, much later, it comes to fruition thus: When the seduction is near its tragic end, and Faust has furtively come into the prison where Gretchen is being held, he urges her to hurry and escape with him. In her pathetic confusion she answers, "Oh, wait! / I am so glad to wait, where you are waiting." In the light of our earlier entry, *this is a pun*. In German it reads: *O weile! / Weil' ich doch so gern, wo du weilest. Verweile* has become *weil'* and *weilest*. Yet we are not through. Faust answers, "Hurry! If you do not hurry, we shall pay dearly." But the words for "hurry" here are *eile* and *eilest*. Thus have we gone impetuously from *verweile* to *weile* to *eile*, a Faustian progression indeed. The impetuous Faust, we might say, cuts Gretchen short. And we might note further that the abbreviated verb form *weil'* sounds like the word for "because," *weil*. And we have a theory that a deflectively causal word, at such a revealing moment in the text, is well worth dwelling upon. For we dare have hopes that, once the necessary intermediate steps have been supplied, such a perturbation might be interpretable as the "natural sign" of some characteristic motivational kink in the Goethean tangle of motives.

Just what kind of ownership does figure in Faust's *Liebestraum* (the "exalted" aspect of his designs on Gretchen)? Clearly, Faust wants to possess her not just as a body, but as a person endowed with a whole catalogue of modest virtues. But he wants to possess her bodily too, even though (or because?) the conditions of his bodily possession will act as a mockery of these very virtues which he appraises resignationally in his initial stage of exaltation.

He would personally possess the personal virtues of a Gretchen, but at one remove, for he shows no desire to be himself endowed with these virtues. They are presumably feminine. He wants to possess them, we might say, *aesthetically*, by sheer *sympathetic appreciation* of them, in an appreciation that would not be confined to nonacquisitive forms of admiration. He wants to own the virtues by owning their owner (a treasure outside himself, yet brought within his dominion—not by compulsion, but by persuasion).

His ownership "necessarily" involves a despoiling, the transformation of Gretchen into a victim. (Indeed, as we have said, the virtues themselves add up to precisely such guilelessness as make her susceptible to victimage.) In saying that the despoiling is *necessary*, we have in mind the fact that this is the story of an act that was, in its essential origins, a *seduction*, a *conspiracy*, involving the *Lust am Trug* that we previously saw associated with the motives of youth in flower.

Also, there may be the motive of the explorer, the inventor, the promoter, the empire-builder, the discoverer of virgin soil, the man who fells virgin forests, the man who sails into new Keatsian seas. (By our interpretation, in Coleridge's "Ancient Mariner" the stage of drought or total depression begins immediately after the motives of sexual defloration have been indicated, the steps being: (1) "like God's own head, the glorious Sun uprist . . ."; (2) "We were the first that ever burst / Into that silent sea . . ."; (3) "Down dropt the breeze, the sails dropt down . . ."; (4) "the bloody Sun, no bigger than the Moon"—this second manifestation being the sun that fixed the boat at noon, a time that is at many places in Coleridge's verse, as in balladry generally, linked with the moment of marriage.)

Frankly, we don't know what all this adds up to. (Perhaps only to *keins*, like the *Hexen-Einmal-Eins*?) But we do believe that when in quest of basic human symbolism one should risk even many blind and pointless tentatives, in the attempt to understand what ideal types of human victimage there may be, and how they are related to whatever system of property and propriety, public and private, goes with any given social order. For human relations are dogged at every turn by victimage, and the freedom with which poetry can concern itself with these matters prompts us to inspect poetic symbolizations above all for their ability to express all variants of victimage.

At the very least, surely, Gretchen is a variant of beauty in distress, whatever range of motives that role may cover. More specifically, she is a variant of the wronged and forsaken maiden, another figure dear to balladry (and there are many ballad-like accents in the verse most immediately connected with her and her plight).

What *is* the "curative" function in such victimage? When considering Burns's lovely lyric, "Oh, wert thou in the cauld blast . . . I'd shelter thee, I'd shelter thee," one glimpses the possibilities of a man who, sensitive, unpretentious, and put-upon, turns not to self-pity but to kindly thoughts of someone still worse off, a beauty whom he imagines in dire misfortune, in order that he, himself so unfortunate, might nonetheless imagine himself coming to her aid. Then lo! we find: After he has thus imagined himself aiding her he next imagines that, in their happy amative union, they would be no less than royal, for she wad be his queen, wad be his queen.

Faust is frightfully torn by pity for Gretchen after he sees the drastic extent to which poetic justice has victimized her. But Goethe's vastly brainier project apparently involves him in a higher degree of self-consciousness than is found in Burns's lyric. We might put it thus: Where Burns begins by imagining the beauty already in a condition of distress, Goethe has gone a step farther back and imagined a character who, in his lust for a kind of power, himself brings upon his lady precisely the condition for which he will pity her. Indeed, prophesying after the event, we would say that in his original furtive penetration into her bedchamber Faust was so deeply moved by the "personality" of the room because this personality already contained the fate that he would impose upon it because, for "hierarchal" reasons, he needed to.

The desire for "power," as so translated into the terms of a sexual-personal "myth," is not absolute, we feel sure. It must be relative, involving subtleties of superiority and inferiority, with reflections going back and forth between these states, somewhat as when we see, on the sunless portion of a crescent moon, the solar light which reached it roundabout, by first lighting up the Earth, then being relayed to a portion of the moon hidden from the sun, and then coming back again to us, reflected from the moon. Which is probably to say, in effect, that we should consider the power motives as "luna-tic," even while recognizing how conditions compel them into intricate being.

Probably we should note also that seductionism, as dramatically defined in this work, has a homosexual aspect, too (along with the sadistic aspect, seen lurking behind its pity). For it reveals a resistance to the "norms" of heterosexual union, at least as defined by the orthodoxies of that particular society. Internal analysis seems to indicate that the scene of student revelry is *incipiently* the episode of Walpurgis Night. So among the "Faustian" strands might be that of homosexuality; though we should remember first that it is *radically modified* by the many other strands that go to make up the total weave and, second, that, from the standpoint of the "hierarchal psychosis," no "sexual" motive is deemed "primary," in so far as the sheer "biology" of sexual courtship is modified by *social* norms (that is, by *administrative* or *political* courtship).

However, poetic "catharsis" is not by any means confined to *victimage*. Croce, in his *Aesthetics*, identifies catharsis with expression in general—and there is certainly a sense in which, for a typically symbol-using animal, there would be a kind of "cleansing" got by the sheer fact of "getting something said." More subtly, there are modes of catharsis internal to the work, respects in which it "purifies" itself, and not merely through the "pity, terror, and similar emotions" which Aristotle associates specifically with catharsis in tragedy. Returning to our earlier point about "perfection," we might end this discussion by indicating how the "entelechial" principle operates in a certain kind of poetry which does not deal with "victimage" in the clear ways of tragedy, though attenuations of the sacrificial principle can be glimpsed here. This closing example is intended to indicate both how *external* reference would be involved in the hypothetical work and how a purely *internal* purification would take place, though here in the more Platonist form of a "revelation." Thus:

1) The "principle of perfection" could not be said to operate in any immediate purpose, as when a person reaches for something that he intends to eat.

2) But a kind of "ultimate projecting" is possible. For instance, when reaching for food, one may be said to do so, not just as a hungering organism, but as a *zoon politikon*.

3) Thus, one might not just "reach." One might "steal" the food, or "take what is rightfully one's own," or "be graspingly overeager," or "manifest good breeding," or "in one's zest, laughingly throw all proprieties to the wind and make a dive for it," etc.

4) Here would be a motive, in terms of "action," that would "transcend" the motive of sheer motion (the purely physiological processes involved in an organism's use of its hand as an instrument for helping to satisfy a purely physiological need).

5) Now consider an example of this sort: A storywriter of the "sensitive" school builds a story about some "mysterious moment" of childhood, some realistically described incident that is somehow felt to symbolize a "deeper meaning."

6) This would be the Joycean use of "epiphany," the discovering or unveiling of a moment that stands for much more than its sheer materiality.

7) Imagine such a story as so constructed that the sheer motion of reaching for food had, flickering about its edges, some such motive as is "dogmatically" symbolized in Eve's taking of the apple. (Here is an example we recently noted of such a "food-sex channel of affinity"; In the mathematical center of D'Annunzio's *Triomphe de la Mort*, just before the chapter headed "New Life," consider the "suggestive" connotations with which the girl's biting into the bread is surrounded. Beads of moisture about the mark of the bite are observed as pointedly as though one were witnessing a lewd kind of annunciation.)

8) Next, think of our hypothetical story as expressing a motive which was felt by its author to be the "ultimate" addition to such reaching (not in its nature as sheerly physical, but as personal).

9) Next, think of such a reaching as being similarly motivated even in

moments not thus touched with "revelation" (though the "transcendent" motive would here figure remotely and faintly).

10) The "ordinary" material act could thus always be felt as vaguely "striving" toward the "perfection" signalized at the moment of the "revelation." And this would be the "entelechial" motive, the fulfillment or realization of its particular nature, its sociality.

11) This sociality, or ideality, transcending the sheer physicality or materiality of the act could then be interpreted as the "principle of perfection" in the act (a "perfection" that could be interpreted supernaturally or sociologically or both, according to the preferences of the interpreter).

12) A design much like that of the Kantian *als ob* would be implicit here, if one looked upon each everyday motion of reaching *as though* it contained some measure of an ultimate reaching—whereat the everyday reaching would be viewed piously, as an act infused with spirit, rather than as "nothing but" the materially motivated behavior.

In sum, a catharsis purely internal to a poetic medium as such takes place when the cycle of a work's inner consistency is revealed or finished. Such emergence and completion being got in terms suited to the specific natures of the various literary genres, they will differ in accordance with the genres. As regards the "tragic pleasure," the completion is largely contrived in terms of "pity, fear, and the like emotions" that go with the imitation of a "perfect" sacrifice. But the story that, like many of Joyce's early pieces in *Dubliners*, is built about an "epiphany" makes for a different kind of purification: it involves a kind of Platonist transcendence whereby a "symbolic" motive is discerned in purely material things or situations.

While both such kinds of "perfection" are discussible in terms of a work's inner consistency, they also involve tensions extrinsic to the work and set by the "personality" of the social order. An "entelechial principle" in the social order (what we have called the "hierarchal psychosis") thus coincides with the purely linguistic kind, the need of symbolic systems as such to move "freely" toward the "necessity" of ideal consistency.

We believe that, as contrasted with the purely physiological motives of organisms that are not typically symbol-using, the motives of human beings are fatally pervaded by such dualism in the drive toward wholeness. Or, at least, such is the case with art under the conditions of empire, with what we might call the "poetry of statecraft" (most clearly exemplified in works like Aeschylus' *Oresteia*, Virgil's *Aeneid*, Shakespeare's *Coriolanus* or *Julius Caesar*, Corneille's *Cinna,* Goethe's *Faust*, but discernible in even tiny, "playful," "nonpolitical" forms, once we have the rules for "anticipating" the transformations proper to the various artistic species).

The revelation or fulfillment in "moments" suggests the possibility of a reverse situation whereby even trival acts can be remotely the exemplars of "perfect" acts, as though duration were but a departure, or temporary exile, from the culminative moment. (For instance, all details of the study preparatory to some particular professional career are, in a sense, variously "infused" with the spirit of the overall aim.)

We believe that the analysis of poetic forms, when approached from this attitude, points to the essential motives both of poetry in particular and of human relations in general. Such an approach would by no means deny the role of material factors in the shaping of human relations; but it would seek to analyze the modes of "magic" by which material elements become inspirited, when the quests for truth, goodness, and power (the useful or expedient) are translated into the corresponding quest for beauty.

Chapter Five

Faust II—The Ideas Behind the Imagery[1]

I

Our specific subject: the second part of *Faust*. But we must remember: not only was there a first part, quite different from the second; there was also a Faust Fragment and, finally, an Urfaust, which was found in the late nineteenth century, but had obviously preceded the Faust Fragment (originally published in 1790, when Goethe was about forty). Part I was published in 1808 (Schiller had died in 1805.) Most of the work on Part II was done 1824-31 (when Goethe was in his late seventies and early eighties). Yet his plans for the episodes between Faust and Helen had preceded the famous drama of Faust and Gretchen that became the major theme of Part I. In fact, it was a standard ingredient of the old Faust legend which Goethe had built on in the first place, but which he transformed from the drama of a villain who went to hell (as in the puppet plays well known to Goethe in his youth) into the drama of a hero who, despite a pact with the Devil, attained salvation. We could also be concerned with Goethe's borrowings, additions, omissions, and transformations as regards his use of the old legend of the puppet plays and chapbooks. There is a further store of details that Goethe apparently meant to add (Santayana cites from the *Nachlass* an excellent fragment of this sort: "*Des Menschen Leben ist ein ähnliches Gedicht; / Es hat wohl einen Anfang, hat ein Ende, / Allein ein Ganzes ist es nicht*"). There are many comments made by Goethe, to Eckermann and others. There are lights thrown on this work by other works of Goethe's—and so on, and so on, including the fact that, besides the enormous body of later critical and historical analysis, there was Goethe's peculiar way of working. Nearly everything he read, or every picture he saw, might suggest a possible insertion at one point or another, particularly since he had so many episodes that could serve as catchalls. For instance, episodes like Auerbach's Cellar, The Witches' Kitchen, the Walpurgis Night of Part I, the Masquerade and Classical Walpurgis Night of Part II, obviously allowed for as much detail as the poet's learning, invention, and industry might

---

[1] The substance of this essay was presented in a colloquium on "Theology and Literature" at Drew University, April, 1962.

provide. Such catchall episodes make for great fertility and variety of detail, but often they have less the form of a drama than of an encyclopedia, or perhaps more accurately, an anthology.

As we confront this almost bewildering mass of material, obviously some ground rules for my discussion must be laid down at the start. I shall try to proceed by what I would call a "logological" method of analysis. That is, I shall try to pick some key terms—or terministic functions, in Goethe's thinking—and shall try to show how, as I see it, the main lines of Part II should follow, if we track down the implications of these key terministic functions. In general, I shall proceed along the lines of an essay on "The First Three Chapters of Genesis," in my book *The Rhetoric of Religion*. I refer in particular to a chart entitled "Cycle of Terms Implicit in the Idea of 'Order.'" For a theology, a philosophy, a political system, or a drama are all alike in one notable respect: each involves a cycle or configuration of organically interrelated terms—and by featuring these and considering their implications we can hope to get the logic of the structure in general, and the parts in relation to the whole or to one another.

II

In his masterful essay on *Faust*, Santayana writes:

> The great merit of the romantic attitude in poetry, and of the transcendental method in philosophy, is that they put us back at the beginning of our experience. They disintegrate convention, which is often cumbrous and confused, and restore us to ourselves, to immediate perception and primordial will. That, as it would seem, is the true and inevitable starting-point.

Such a philosophy, as Kant said, "is a cathartic: it is purgative and liberating; it is intended to make us start afresh and start right."

Let us begin with this stress upon beginnings. But in keeping with our terministic emphasis, let us note that in German such considerations can be centered not just in one word, but even in a part of a word, that ingenious German prefix *Ur-*. While literally it means pre- or fore-, it subtly merges or confuses ideas of temporal and logical priority. Thus, if *Geschichte* is "history," *Urgeschichte* would be "pre-history." Added to *Mensch*, it transports us in a flash from "man" to "primordial man." We may speak of the "ground" or *Grund* of existence, or we can vaguely get the feel of a metaphysical ultimate if we speak about the *Urgrund* of existence (a term sometimes used synonymously with *Ungrund*—if one would add more clearly *meonic* connotations to such ideas of a transcendent ultimate or absolute ground of all possibility). The most ordinary word of this sort is the German word for "cause," *Ursache* (fore-thing, or perhaps better, "fore-sake").

Goethe's scientific studies were conducted quite explicitly under the aegis of this metaphysically resonant device. In studying botany, he sought for what he called the *Ur*-plant. In reducing optics to polarity of light and dark, he speaks of *Urpolarität*, while the contrast between light and dark is not just "initial" (*anfänglich*) but "*ur*-initial" (*uranfänglich*). He will be concerned with primal stone (*Urgestein*), with prototype (*Urbild*), not just with form, but with *Urform*.

All told, we are to be concerned with a search for *Ur*-motives, *Ur*-situations, not just the old, but the *uralt* or even the *urälteste*. Thus, in Act IV, Mephisto speaks of stuff from the *Ur*-mountain's *ur*-human power, *aus Urgebirgs Urmenschenkraft* (in Bayard Taylor's translation, "primal mountain's primal human might").

There are also synonyms that carry the same connotations (as with the use of either *Ursprung* or *Quelle* for "source"). In Faust's dreamlike love affair with Helen, the idea of the "source" also includes reference to her "motherly" breasts from which flows warm milk. Faust will tell her that she belongs to the "first" world. And since all such concerns involve thoughts of prime matter, there lurks beneath the whole search the fatal *materia-mater* pun.

And, of course, the search for beginnings in this sense of the word becomes indistinguishable from the search for endings, as we shall see. Efficient cause and final cause are hard to distinguish, in this realm of the *Urbeginn*.

In the meantime, when we consider *Faust I* from this point of view, we find a whole series of beginnings, thus: Title; Dedication; Prelude on the State; Prologue in Heaven; Faust in his study, meditating; he summons the Earth-Spirit; the development towards the important moment is next delayed by Wagner's entrance; then there are songs celebrating the beginning of Easter; then comes another intermediate scene before the city gate, dialogue among the vulgar; then Faust sees the black poodle (itself an incipient manifestation of a figure whose identity is yet to be disclosed); then, in his study, with the poodle now restlessly sniffing and growling, Faust opens to the gospel of John and reads, "In the beginning was the Word." He modifies this beginning three times: first, prompted by his Spirit, or *Geist*, he changes it to "Thought": *Im Anfang war der Sinn*; he modifies this in turn to "Power" (*Kraft*); then, aided by his *Geist*, he decides upon: "In the beginning was the act," the deed (*die Tat*)—whereupon are released the developments whereby the poodle becomes transformed into Mephistopheles, first dressed as a wandering scholar—and the drama is under way.

For the purposes of our present discussion, however, the main point is this: the entire first part of *Faust* is but the introduction to Part II. That is, Part II will involve the successive explicit disclosures, or revelations, of motives that were but implicit in Part I. Thus there is a sense in which the truly

Ur-motives lurking behind Part I should be sought in Part II, if they are to be found anywhere.

But before we turn to our next key term (should we say *Ur*-term?), we should add one final qualification about the nature of the revelations to be expected.

Affinities between Kant and Goethe are not hard to trace, since both the great metaphysician and the dramatist represent aspects of German idealistic romantic philosophy. But there is one basic terministic difference, and it shows up in the typical Goethean word, *Urphänomen*. You recall that the Kantian scheme came to a focus in the distinction between phenomenon and noumenon. The phenomenon is the sensible, the noumenon is but the intelligible. That is, it can only be *thought*, not perceived with the senses. But Goethe, the dramatist, or more specifically Goethe the lyric poet using some trappings of drama, could not work with noumena. The noumenon is, par excellence, a term for transcendental metaphysics. And Goethe's primary investment is in his role as *Dichter*, poet in the broadest sense, and thus often a philosophic poet (a role that the ideals of the current imagistic tradition in our poetic line would too thoroughly restrict).

As a dramatic-lyric poet, he must bring his ideas before our very eyes. And he revealed his leanings towards such expression by never seeking in his scientific studies to go beyond what he called the *Urphänomen*. There was nothing anti-Kantian in this. On the contrary. In Kant the realm of science is the realm of experience, whereas a noumenon cannot be experienced; it can but be dialectically inferred, or "thought." But note how the poetic search for an *Ur*-phenomenon operates, so far as the development of a vocabulary is concerned.

In brief, the term gives a clue to the subtitle of this essay: "The ideas behind the imagery." My notion is that, where a sheerly *poetic* search for *Ur*-motives is concerned, they must remain in a stage translatable into terms of imagery. For the time being, let us mention but the most obvious case: the episode of Faust's journey to the realm of "The Mothers."

Insofar as there is an *Ur-prinzip*, it must be reducible to terms of place, however vague that place. And if it is to be thoroughly dramatized, it must be personalized. Faust's journey to the realm of "The Mothers" is thus the poetic equivalent of Goethe's search for the *Ur-phänomen* in his scientific studies.

So much, for the time being, for our first key term, reducible to the terministic function of the prefix, *Ur-*.

III

The second key term marks the very essence of German idealism: the word for spirit, *Geist*. If you but took this one word, with its synonyms, out of the German language, I doubt whether a single German work of any stature could survive. Even Marxism would collapse, since so much of its materialism is concerned with plans to deflate the term.

Often it is so peculiarly German that there is no adequate translation at all for it in English. Generally, it has such meanings as ghost, spirit, breath, mind, intellect, disposition, genius, wit, essence, specter, phantom, demon. *Der heilige Geist* is the Holy Ghost, or Holy Spirit. *Ein Geistlicher* is a churchman, clergyman, church dignitary. (In the *Roman Elegies* we find the poet enticed with the conceit of masking as a *Geistlicher*, while enjoying a quite earthy love affair.) *Geistlos* is spiritless, lifeless, dead, torpid, dull. *Geistige Getränke* are alcoholic liquors. *Das geistige Auge* is the mind's eye. *Geistig* can mean incorporeal, immaterial, intellectual, mental. *Begeistern* is to inspire, fill with enthusiasm, electrify, enrapture. *Begeistigen* is, I believe, a special Goethean word, meaning to infuse with *Geist*. Animals, for instance, might encounter mere nature; but man, *Der Mensch*, is truly himself only insofar as nature is for him *begeistigt*, inspirited, given soul, or experienced in terms of idea.

(I might offer an aside here, as regards the problems that the word sometimes presents in English. Once, when I was translating a German biography, I found the word particularly bothersome. We were told that the character's *Geist* did this, the character's *Geist* did that, the character's *Geist* did the other, and so on. Did his spirit do it? Did his mind do it? Did his wit do it, or his essence, or disposition, or demon? I tried all sorts of synonyms, and none seemed quite natural in English. Then of a sudden, a breakthrough; whereupon, lo! I translated simply: "*He* did it.")

The *function* of the prefix *Ur-* is everywhere making itself felt in the successive unfoldings of the Faust-drama, even when the particle itself may be absent. But so far as *Geist* is concerned, the actual word occurs continually, like an *idée fixe*. And this is particularly so because, in its plural form, *Geister*, it lends itself spontaneously to that poetic device whereby all the things and processes of nature can be referred to in terms of their corresponding "spirits." Obviously, such a resource is made to order for the typical Goethean pageantry, which requires that every possible glimpse into some fragment of nature be presented in terms of a dramatic role. *Geister* are everywhere. Mephistopheles himself is apparently a portion of the Earth-Spirit, the *Erdgeist*, which so startled Faust when he summoned it in Part I. Goethe's considerable reliance on the ancient lore of alchemy also figured here.

Geist of itself could do the job. But there is a synonym, *Gespenst*, which has only dyslogistic meanings, such as: specter, phantom, ghost, goblin, hobgoblin. (While tough on the over-easy spiritualizings of *Geist*, Marx was gladly to announce, at the start of the Communist *Manifesto*, that the *Gespenst* of socialism was haunting Europe.)

Besides this direction (from *Geist* or spirit in general, to a realm of manifold spirits in particular, to a realm of specters wholly forbidding), there is another notable dialectical possibility: it would involve an ambiguously secularized variation on the theme of the spirit-matter, mind-body pair traditional to Western theology. That is, the term *Geist* will be manipulated with particular dialectical bearing upon a counterterm, *Natur*. The two will help define each other. *Geist* without *Natur* will necessarily be impoverished (somewhat like essence without existence). And *Natur* without *Geist* will be crude. Goethe worked *history* into this spirit-matter pair by conceiving of the ancient Greeks as having accomplished the perfect marriage of *Geist* and *Natur*: Greek genius, Greek *Geist*, was thought by him to have known the secret of perfectly *natural* artistic creativeness. Hence the opportunities for what would otherwise be a simple terministic paradox, the notion that one could come nearest to nature by the roundabout route of mere book learning, the very route which Faust renounced at the beginning of the drama, but in which his assistant (Famulus), Wagner, believed without the slightest hint of a doubt.

IV

Ur- is essentially "scenic" in its implications; it connotes the idea of some ultimate location in time or place, or in pre-time or in some realm of sheer *logical* priority. *Geist* is essentially a word for "agent," the spirit or character that performs some role. But recall those lines on origin that Faust uttered just before things began happening in earnest: I refer to the steps, "In the beginning was the Word . . . the Thought . . . the Power . . . the Act (or Deed)." To match *Ur-* for "scene" and *Geist* for "agent," do we not need a germinal word for "act"?

There is one—and it is, unquestionably, the word *streben*, "striving," a word that also by fatal accident happens to rhyme in German with the word for "live," *leben*, and the word for "float," "hover," "soar," *schweben*. The strive-live-soar complex (*Streben-Leben-Schweben*) is at the center of the *act* which is essential to the Goethean idea of Faust's redemption. It is so essential that one could almost derive from it alone the impulse to transform Faust from a villain destined for hell to a hero destined for salvation. It ties in with the change of values surrounding the idea of "ambition," with the emergence of Renaissance man out of the Middle Ages. Gradually, "ambition" was to drop its popular fearsome connotations (connotations much like those that theology—and Greek tragedy before it—had built around the idea of "pride"), and was to become a "good" word. The highly individualistic Goethe reflected this change in the radical transformation to which he (and some undistinguished contemporaries) subjected the traditional role of Faust as treated in the legend (which he himself, as a youth, had seen enacted in the puppet plays).

Streben also shades off into *sich sträuben* (to bristle at, to oppose). And it is but a slight acrostic modification of the verb, "to die" (*sterben*), an affinity not lost on Goethe. Recall, for instance, an early dialogue ("Artist's Apotheosis") that begins by linking nature with the "spirit of spirits," and later introduces the acrostic thus: *Es strebt unsterblich, wie es sterblich strebte.*

Insofar as such constant striving (*Streben*) can continue, it obviously involves the possibilities of development, transformation, becoming. And the most generalized equivalents are such terms as Becoming (*Werden*), and formation or transformation (*Gestaltung, Umgestaltung*). Also, obviously, the idea of *striving* implies the question of *purpose*, of *terminus ad quem*. Striving for what, towards what? Self-development, certainly, the Goethean equivalent of the Leibnizian entelechy. And, ultimately, it must be a striving towards the revelation of the *Ur*-motive. As a first rough approximate, at this stage in our analysis, we might note that, as often in terministic operations of this sort, Goethe solves the problem by treating the problem as its own solution. This is what Santayana calls "the official moral" and "general philosophy" of *Faust*; and he rates it lower than the incidental "vistas" that Goethe's scheme for "experience" opens up. The "official moral" also fits in well with the historical era of "Storm and Stress" (*Sturm und Drang*, the latter word doing great work in Schopenhauer's metaphysics and its contemporary psychological siblings), out of which Goethe's *Faust-Dichtung* emerged. But I intend to take up later, and from another point of view, this particular aspect of the drama's terministic economy. I think it can be shown how, in the course of solving one problem, Goethe's "official" solution involves the failure to solve another problem, with regard to the cult of endless *Streben*.

V

Meanwhile, let us try to "foretell" the second part of *Faust* by asking how it "ought to be," on the basis of the *Ur-Geist-Streben* nexus. And since we shall be prophesying after the event, we have an excellent opportunity to make sure that our hypothetical "foretelling" doesn't embarass us by getting too far out of line with the actual structure of the work. (Such a hypothetical "foretelling" is an expository device, a way of making clear what the structure is, and why it is as it is.)

We're now ready to begin the search for the *Ur*-motive, the *Ur-prinzip*. As an *Ur*-ground, it can't be quite the same as an *Ungrund*. That is, it can't be a "meonic" ground or ultimate. You may or may not agree with Bergson when he says that we can't have an idea of nothing. But one thing is certain—any *image* you have of "nothing" will necessarily be an image of *something*, otherwise it can't be an image. And Goethe must work primarily in that field. True, he will have his negative. But it is represented by that very ingenious and often quite personable *person*, Mephistopheles, who introduces himself as the principle of negativity (fittingly, the *Geist* who steadily denies). Also, he names himself in terms of origins: he is "a part of the part that initially was all" (*Ich bin ein Teil des Teils, der anfangs alles war*). So far as I can see, this sheer principle of negativity is enough to account for his serviceability to the cause of universal *Streben*. The negative sets the conditions for a moral code (since it makes possible a set of thou-shalt-not's, with their corresponding kinds of storm and stress). This terministic situation allows for some ingenious dramatic transformations, thus: the negative, which is the principle of evil, is also the principle of virtue (since it prevails in pronouncing the proscriptions which virtue willingly obeys); but it also sets the conditions for *Striving*, in the effort either to obey or to "soar" above any limitations imposed upon us. Thus, given the proper modes of conversion, the notion that "virtue is its own reward" can be transformed into the "official moral" that Striving is in itself a virtue—and a virtue that "ultimately" gets rewarded. Goethe's application of his *Ur-Geist-Streben* nexus will proceed along those lines.

Here is the general picture I have in mind. I think that the relation between the first and second parts of Faust is somewhat analogous to the relation between the first nine books of Augustine's *Confessions* and the last four. I have analyzed this relationship in my book, *The Rhetoric of Religion*. For present purposes, the point might be reduced to this: the first nine books detail a sequence of *memories*. But the tenth book shifts the angle of approach by asking: *what is memory?*

Similarly, as I see it, the first part of Goethe's drama tells us the story of Faust courting Gretchen. The second part asks in effect: what all was implied in that courtship?

But at the very start we must give full weight to this technical situation: the second part is not sheerly philosophic, or conceptual, but poetic in its own right; hence it must still deal with ideas in terms of imagery. Thus, it can't just talk about Beauty or the "Hellenic"—it must talk about *Helen*. It can't talk just about *change*—it must do so in terms of *Proteus*, the mythological figure that kept constantly changing. It can't talk about *origins*, about the *Ur*-principle as such—it must talk about *The Mothers*. And so on. (Good work has been done in showing how thoroughly Goethe, who at one stage in his life had actually set up an alchemic laboratory, adapted the nomenclature of alchemy to his purposes here, as well as his more obvious borrowings from classical mythology.)

This is what we had in mind when referring to the fact that, in his search for the ultimate ground of things, Goethe talked not of the noumenon, but of the *Ur*-phenomenon. His ultimates could not, as with Kant, be treated in terms of sheer "intelligibles" beyond the realm of appearances. Rather, they had to be conveyed in terms of what he took to be their most essential appearances. That's what I mean by saying that in both his poetry and his scientific speculations he thought not in terms of a noumenon (a merely "intelligible" entity) but in terms of an *Urphänomen* (a primal phenomenon). Insofar as the second part of Faust really is a breakthrough into a realm of motives underlying the first part, the question must still be discussed in terms of images, persons, and roles that correspond to the concepts and ideas they represent (and in terms of situations that permit of such images, persons, and roles).

VI

The first act opens lyrically, on the theme of Faust's refreshment. Interwoven with it, inevitably, there is talk of the depths and the abyss (here is the *Ur*-theme), and of *Geist* and *Streben*. We know it's the Faust of Part I, for there is talk of the waterfall (*Wassersturz*), and we remember a beautiful meditation in Part I, built around this pregnant proportion: Faust was to Gretchen as such a cascading, tumbling stream was to an Alpine cottage by its banks. There is talk of being blinded (a late development of the play being thus ambiguously introduced at the start). And there is talk of rule, and of such splendor (*Pracht*) as goes with the ostentation of governance—even though the theme enters but incipiently, in terms of moonlight's reigning splendor.

And with the next scene, which is more dramatical than lyrical, disclosures begin. The action is to take place in an Imperial Palace. We are to deal with a *court*. And translating imagery into ideas, I propose to prophesy thus: Part I had centered in the theme of a particular *sexual* courtship. Part II will say in effect: "Implicit in the idea of sexual courtship is the idea of courtship in general."

But this terministic situation immediately involves another development. Goethe can't proceed thus to *individuate* the principle or idea of courtship in general without depicting the life at some particular court. Poetry individuates. *Universale intelligitur, singulare sentitur.* In order that something may be brought before our senses it must be made singular, made precisely this entity or situation, and none other. This is but a different way of saying, as regards the poet's search for motivational sources (and in *Faust II* he has Helen refer to an *Urbeginn* in ancient night), it can only be represented on the stage as a *phenomenon*, an appearance, an *aisthesis*, not as merely that "intelligible" quantity x, a noumenon.

However, as soon as the poet has thus narrowed things down, he must choose details which, to him, seem most representative of court life as so conceived. He hits upon two major opportunities. First, since court life is usually distinguished by pageantry, masques, social display, there is the theme of the masquerade, the *Mummenschanz*. And that in turn can be expanded to the extent of the poet's inventiveness, with figures and sentiments that variously bear upon his own particular experience in court life and that can stand for such motives in general.

This episode (itself a jumble of episodes) is a kind of medieval morality play, an allegorical representation of the ills that come to beset the world with the gradual rise of complex modern conditions: problems of class, threats of socialism, cultural losses likely to follow the emancipation of woman (the author presumably had much greater admiration for Gretchen's ideally tragic seducibility), and the corruptive effects of great wealth (in contrast with the kind of wealth embodied in the profuseness of poetry). It was the kind of pageantry that readily allowed for the translation of court gossip into patterns as formal as a dance, and that could be expanded *ad lib*.

For our present purposes, the main thing to note is that such an incident serves the needs of localization (individuation). It is, in an idealized way, typical of such court life as Goethe was familiar with. And though but episodic, its display had topical relevance as a means of building up the life of the court. In brief, the steps from Faust's particular sexual courtship of Gretchen, to courtship in general, to court life in particular, to a *Mummenschanz* as a theatrical way of bringing court life before our very eyes, follow a quite reasonable chain of ideas. And the variety of the figures in the masque also suggests the many conflicting interests that come to a focus in the court.

However, another important motive has been presented, and I believe that it is much more problematical, though at first glance it looks obvious enough. I refer to the theme of the paper money, to which I shall return later. Meanwhile, we can agree that in a court such as Goethe is depicting, problems of finance urgently figure. Matters of finance sum up the material and administrative operations of a state; thus they are as representative in one way as the Masquerade was in another. (We might even say that, behind the masques there lurks always the question of funds.)

But what of the *particular* way in which this theme is developed? I refer to Mephisto's magic, in solving the Court's financial problems by the use of paper money; in brief, by inflation. The theme of inflation fits, on possibly three scores, but at present we have the equipment to deal with only two of them. Most notably, it gives Mephisto a role, since it is certainly one devil of a solution for the country's ills, so poor a one that, although by the rules of diabolic magic it is allowed to work, the King himself is scandalized and simply closes his mind to its risky possibilities. Also, its devilishness fits particularly well with basic Goethean motives, for it is essentially a burlesque, an ironic perversion, of spirit, *Geist*. The sheer inflating of a currency is *Geist* gone wrong. Thus, it's a perfect job for

Mephistopheles, as the master ironist in this drama. (Mephisto explicitly uses the term, "paper-specter," *Papiergespenst*.)

You might well ask: but why is *this* member of a terministic cycle implicit in the idea of courtship treated *dyslogistically*? One reason, as I already suggested, is that it is the work of the Devil. And that would be reason enough, since we are concerned with the story of a man who has made a pact with the Devil. But later, when we have seen other parts of the drama, I shall tentatively offer a further symbolic explanation for this theme.

Not being able to offer that explanation at this time, I must connect simply by "and" the episode of the Paper Money Scheme with the next, the episode of The Mothers. For the present, I can merely treat the episode of The Mothers as the introduction of a new motive. No, not wholly new. For Faust's terrified journey to this ominous realm (where Mephisto's powers fail, beyond his mere ability to give Faust the necessary "key," a small key that had grown in Faust's hand!) is obviously a search for the *Ur-* motive. In being primal mothers, they are obviously "beginnings" of some sort.

One's first impulse, under the aegis of psychoanalytic thought, would be to think of them as terrifying because they stand for the principle of ultimate *regression*. They suggest such threats of mental deterioration as character- ize neurotic yearnings for a return to the womb. The mere combination of their name and Faust's inexplicable fear would suggest this possibility, along with possible hints of incest awe. And these motives may figure, particularly inasmuch as Faust is given a "key," and the phallic connotations of keys are standard psychoanalysis. Also, recalling the origin of this episode, Goethe himself connects them with the idea of Faust as a person who, when feeling repugnance at contact with his fellow citizens, flees into solitude, and then, so as not to be wholly alone, makes a pact with the Devil. That development would indicate possible autoerotic impulses as one strand in the Mephisto- phelian motive (viewed as symbolizing a latent aspect of Goethe's own in- tense "individualism").

However, whatever may or may not be discoverable on the page, we at least have Goethe's word for it that, so far as his conscious intentions were concerned, The Mothers stood for a more precise role than that (though not necessarily a role that excludes such psychoanalytic implications). "When something has ceased to breathe," Goethe told Eckermann, "it returns to them [The Mothers] as spiritual nature" (*als geistige Natur*—there's our word *Geist* again)—"until it finds another opportunity to enter a new life. All souls and forms of that which once was, and in the future will be, range back and forth cloudily into the endless space of their abode."

In the text itself, Mephisto refers to them in terms of "Formation, Transformation" (*Gestaltung, Umgestaltung*). In their role as an ultimate source, they are also the principle of *rebeginning* (somewhat along the lines of the button-moulder in Ibsen's *Peer Gynt*). A synonym for their ways of transforming is *wandeln*, a verb that is here used transitively (in connection with a magic device, involving key and tripod) for transforming a mist of incense into gods. But in its intransitive form the word is synonymous with the word *wandern*.

This may sound a bit over-observant. But I incline to feel that, in scenes of this sort, such terministic subtleties are of major importance, hermeneutically. For (as one can verify in Paul Fischer's *Goethe-Wortschatz*) *Wanderer* is the word that Goethe repeatedly applies to himself throughout his writings. (Recall, for instance, that *Wilhelm Meister's Journeymanship* is, in German, *Wilhelm Meisters Wanderjahre*—literally, wander-years.) And the word will turn up later, at a most strategic moment, in this text. Indeed, we could say that, implicit in the storm and stress of *Streben* and its associations with Becoming (*Werden*) or Transformation (*Umgestaltung*), there is also the idea of the Wanderer (encompassing such connotations as the traveling scholar, the journeyman on his way to becoming a master, and the man astray on a pilgrimage through life in general).

We should also note that, when Mephisto describes the depths of this lonely, forbidding region, Faust says that his words "have the scent of a Witches' Kitchen, of a time long past," a statement that might justify us in viewing this scene in Part II as revealing connotations implicit in the Witches' Kitchen of Part I.

This is also the scene where the reification of Mephisto's negativity attains its ultimate formula: here, after talk of being sent on a journey into the Void (*ins Leere*), Faust says that he hopes to find the All in Mephistopheles' Naught (*"In deinem Nichts hoff' ich das All zu finden"*). Fittingly, also, we are told that, as he gets ready to take the magic key which gives him entry to the risky realm, he is *begeistert. Schweben* is there, in the notion that The Mothers are *umschwebt* (soaringly surrounded) by the images or prototypes of all creatures. And surely much that is still to unfold in later scenes is ambiguously announced in the "decidedly commanding posture" (*entschieden gebietende Attitüde*) which Faust assumes when grasping the key before his descent. No *Ur-* is there explicitly, though the theme of The Mothers obviously stands for precisely that. And the notion of a temporal ultimate gets its corresponding spatial analogue in Mephisto's statement that Faust will be in the deepest possible depths, *im tiefsten, allertiefsten Grund*.

At least one more observation should be made about this motivationally central scene (a scene which perhaps only in recent years, with the help of modern psychology, can begin to reveal the full range of its implications). We should note that Faust goes on this dangerous trip not simply of his own accord, but because the Emperor had expressed a wish to see Helen and Paris. It was an *Emperor* who wanted to behold the perfect model (*das Musterbild*) of woman and man.

This detail is made to order for my thesis, as regards the notion that, implicit in the courtship of Gretchen there was the principle of courtship in general. We had seen court life, we had considered the subject of finance with respect to such matters of governance. And now, we are to conceive of love itself in the perspective of empire.

If we had the time, here would be the place to consider Goethe's *Roman Elegies*, written after the "Wanderer," suddenly breaking away from Weimar and his attachment to Charlotte von Stein, went to Italy, and on his return to Germany, took up with a woman, Christiana Vulpius, whom he married some years later. These elegies seem to be a poetic merger of amative adventures he had while in Italy and his first delights with Christiana (though things weren't so pleasant later). But the point is this: the whole theme of these "Roman Elegies" is secret love with no claims whatever to the kind of gesture that attains fulfillment in Shakespeare's *Antony and Cleopatra*. Yet at the same time, the whole series is—if we may speak astrologically— "under the sign of" the statues, pictures, architecture, and literature surviving in Rome from the days when the classical culture was at its height. I suppose we should go on asking just what Goethe may have meant when he concerned himself with ways of uniting the romantic and the classical. But so far as the essence of his motivation was concerned, I think a reading of the "Roman Elegies" will make it quite apparent what the union of Faust and Helen meant to him personally. These poems bear witness that, while a Wanderer among the vestiges of the classical era, he had some romantic experiences. And he merged these poetically with a romance that he had when he got back to Weimar, a romance that later wasn't without considerable shoddiness, and that finally led to a marriage not without shoddiness. The "Roman Elegies" would seem to indicate that, by the union of Gothic North and Classic Greece, he meant primarily the sort of improvising he describes so charmingly in those poems. He gives the impression of having had an exceptionally good time—and in later years, he seems to be seeking for the predominantly *geistig* counterpart of such *Geist*-infused "Nature." We understand the "classical" nature of his "spirit" as he recounts how, by the body of his mistress, he got the feel of marble statuary. And he says that while he embraced her, though she did not know it he was composing lines of verse, and tapping out the hexameter rhythm on her back. Here was indeed the merging of *Geist* and *Natur*.

The next episode in Act I seems to be what other commentators have called a "bridge" scene. It is designed to establish the fact that Faust is away on his voyage. And, to this end, it has one line that may have been put there purely for business reasons, but does have a resonance that makes one want to look for deeper meanings. I have in mind where Mephisto apostrophizes: "O Mothers! Mothers! let but Faust go free!" (*"O Mütter, Mütter! lasst nur Fausten los!"*)

As for the rest of Act I: when Helen and Paris appear, there's obviously a good opportunity for some social comedy (basically along these lines: the gentlemen think that Paris leaves much to be desired, but they think well of Helen—and it's the other way around as regards the ladies). There is talk of the *grenzenlos* (the unbounded—for as long as possible, *Streben* must know no bounds; it must tug at the leash; otherwise it cannot be *Streben*).

We learn that, in being concerned with ideas of passion, we are concerned with the very fountainhead (*Quelle*) of beauty, whereupon, as you might expect, there is talk of a *stream*. Then Faust becomes agitated, himself calls upon The Mothers to aid him—and (surprise!) touches not Helen but Paris with his "key." There is an "explosion," Faust immediately thereafter lies upon the earth (*am Boden*), and Act I is over.

VII

Act II begins by transporting us back to another kind of *Ur*-situation: the Chamber in Part I where Faust had *originally* made his deal with the Devil. Mephisto says that the Devil is old—and that, to understand him, you should be old, too. Interpret this as you will; I incline to take it as a reflection of the poet's own difficulties. The Devil, like Faust and Goethe, is now to be viewed in terms of old age. Also, we are told that Mephisto is from the North and is at home only in the northern dusk. (There is a sense in which, on this score, too, Mephisto is a counterpart of Faust.)

This is the act in which Homunculus is born: a man-made man, invented in the laboratory; sheer intellect (another burlesque of *Geist*), lacking the existential immediacy of experience that goes with natural animality. Let's admit it: just as modern depth psychology can give new poignancy to the scene of The Mothers, so the recent development of computers gives this fantasy of Homunculus an explicit relevance that could have been but implicit in Goethe's time (though the motives were already there, as the possibility of a man made in a test tube had been among the dreams of the alchemists). And when Mephistopheles sums up the scene of Homunculus' birth by confiding to the audience, "Upon the creatures we have made / We are, ourselves, at last, dependent" (*Am Ende hängen wir doch ab / Von Kreaturen, die wir machten*), has he not perfectly summed up the paradoxical development, now plaguing us ever more insistently, whereby man becomes subject to his own inventions?

Drama being what it is, the dramatized version of even a purely mechanical man attains a certain kind of humanness. Indeed, it is an ironic fact that this intelligent half-man, lacking the warmth of animality, and perfectly capable of diagnosing his insufficiencies, is much more of a character (in the human sense) than many of the other dramatis personae, who are hardly more than motivational labels. But clearly he represents what Faust would avoid: a merely intellectualistic understanding of classic Greece, rather than a profoundly emotional reliving of its immediacies through the kind of personal responsiveness that must be grounded in man's animal nature, plus *Geist*.

The figure of Homunculus brings up another possibility; but this can be made clearest when we consider Act III, the *Helena*.

The remainder of Act II, the classical Walpurgis Night, is analogous to the romantic *Walpurgisnacht* of Part I. It also provides the kind of pretext Goethe likes, for the Pandora's Box aspect of his genius, a way to let motives run riot for a while. It ends on universal tributes to the four elements (possibly an adumbration of the development at the end of the next act?). Incidentally, in this section, Goethe also allegorically re-enacts a scientific battle he had waged at that time, a battle of so-called Neptunism vs. Vulcanism. Goethe is represented by Thales, who would derive all from water, and thus hails Ocean as the source.

VIII

As for Act III, the *Helena*:

Some critics contend that it was originally intended as an independent piece, and was later inserted bodily. Also, it is said to have been the part Goethe finished first (since it had been begun already). In any case, the theme is part of the Faust legend (in contrast with the story of the bourgeois girl whom he made the center of Part I). There are many complaints about it. But one thing is certain: you'll not often find an act that starts with so good an illustration of what I mean by a cycle of terms implicit in one another. Admiration (the first word is *bewundert*), family, power, order, slavery, beauty, jewels, fulfillment, theft, war—and talk of an *Urbeginn* in the lap, or womb (*Schoss*), of ancient night, with its horrors (here represented by the character who turns out to be Mephistopheles in disguise). That is, we here see, closely bunched, a cluster of strong motivational terms that are shown to involve one another, with the steps for successively disclosing their interrelationships.

There is one particularly notable development, poetically; up to the point where Faust and Helen meet and converse, Goethe had been using unrhymed, classical rhythms. At this point, of a sudden, rhyme is introduced, as Helen's lines begin rhyming with Faust's. Not long after that, we find the lovers worrying about Euphorion, their problematical love child, an idealized portrait of Lord Byron, whose reputation as the perfect poetic temperament was then at its height throughout Europe. Euphorion, alias Byron, comes to stand for the Faustian cult of the unbounded (*grenzenlos*) precisely at a time when Goethe, as citizen and poet, was coming to think quite otherwise. So, all told, we now get the first sacrifice of victims who die that Faust might live. The doting parents, who represent the union of classic Greece and romantic Germany, admonish their willful love child, a naïve representation of earlier motives that the aging Faust would radically modify. Whereupon, lo! like Icarus, he flies too high—and that's the end of Byron-Euphorion.

Whereas we had seen Faust go to the realm of The Mothers, after young Euphorion's death the queen mother Helen goes to join the son. And for the end of ends of that act, the deathy feminine figure of Phorkyas turns out to be none other than Mephistopheles.

Where are we now? I submit: we should make much of the fact that this whole Faust-and-Helen episode is concerned with *phantoms*. Should not that point be dwelt upon and pondered on? When we thus look more closely, we might even see reasons why Goethe originally abandoned the old Faustian legend of the fantastic union with Queen Helen, and substituted a story of bourgeois seduction. Goethe's *original* draft of the Faust story did not even consider at all the idea of an older man regaining his youth. It was written at a time when the poet was still young. And at such a stage, his Faust was not likely even to think of problems to do with the restoring of youthful motives. Goethe's chosen characters are too close to Goethe's own development for that.

But might we now be ready to deal with another line of motives (the discussion of which I have been delaying)? Do we not by now see a set of steps, beginning with the emptiness of a sheer paper money solution to social problems, becoming clearer in thoughts on Homunculus as a disembodied *Geist*, and still clearer when Goethe (now very late in life) is willing to turn from the immediacy of Gretchen to a concern with *Gespenst-Gespinste* Helen, a sheer phantom, albeit she stood for the true union of *Geist* and *Natur*? We should remember that we're talking about a work written by a man in his seventies and eighties, not the man who, when he *first* worked on the Faust drama, did not so much as mention the theme of rejuvenation, since he was still too young for it to be a matter of sufficient importance to him. This theme became important at the time of his first trip to Italy, with its corresponding sense of rebirth, after his state of great dejection when leaving Weimar. This is what we take him to mean personally by his hopes of putting classicism and romanticism together.

Act III ends on a theme that ambiguously represents the movement towards subsidence already indicated in the themes of paper money, Homunculus, and love reduced to sheerly spectral form. (We must remember that, for all Faust's engrossment with Helen, this ideal Queen of Love has been conjured forth simply as a dream, and not as the real girl whose sacrifice to

Faust's cult of *Streben* was the feature of Part I.) This movement towards death is presented pleasantly in terms of the decision, by the *Geister* of the classical *Walpurgisnacht*, that they will not return to Hades, but will instead merge with ever-living Nature (that ambiguous kind of life and/or death we first encountered in connection with The Mothers, and their powers of transformation, *Umgestaltung*). And as we noted, at the end of the Act the character of Phorkyas, supposedly a Greek goddess of death, is revealed as Mephistopheles in disguise.

Act IV represents another kind of dying. Faust here turns completely from sexual appetite to greed for sheer wealth and power. This act was apparently the one that Goethe wrote last. It has many weaknesses, but also many excellent moments. And above all, it does indeed make clear the grim ways in which the coldness of ambition can replace the warmth of love. (However, in the light of contemporary developments, we might pause to note that, greedy as Faust now is, he scorns Mephistopheles' attempt to offer him the moon.) The Act deals with war and acquisition. In its very structure it is as ironical as Mephistopheles himself ever was. For it ends on the theme of the Archbishop joining in the grab, to get part of the spoils of war for his Church.

IX

We are now ready for the final Act. Early in this Act there is a passage which clearly sanctions my interest in cycles of terms that imply one another. However, my gratification in having so authoritative a writer as Goethe to back me is considerably tempered by the fact that the principle is stated by Mephistopheles. I refer to his words: "War, Trade, and Piracy are three-in-one, and not to be divided." (*Krieg, Handel, und Paraterie, / Dreieinig sind sie, nicht zu trennen.*) He is referring to the fact that Faust's economic empire has been built on war, and that, in the process of trading under Mephisto's guidance, much subsequent profit had come from sheer piracy. Mephisto here states the formal principle I have in mind, when asking what may be implicit in the ideas of courtship that lie behind or beyond Faust's courting of Gretchen in Part I.[2]

---

[2] So far as the sheer sentiment is concerned, the war-trade-piracy equations must be discounted, since the formula is proclaimed by Mephistopheles. It is a "devilish" way of stating a situation (perhaps along the lines of the anarchist idea that property is theft). Yet, as regards its sheer form, note how the three might be "broken down" into the progressive form of a narrative. For Goethe proceeds precisely thus. First there are the episodes of war; out of these, Faust builds up a commercial enterprise; and in the course of his voyages, Mephistopheles returns with wealth-laden ships, some of the wealth got by piracy. To carry out the pattern completely, Goethe could have introduced an actual piratic episode. Also, note incidentally, the characteristic nature of Mephistopheles' trinity; not power, wisdom, love; but power, power, power, two of them clearly hellish.

The basic problem of Act V, it seems to me, is something like this: how so balance the accounts that a problem is transformed into its solution, that a man who is obviously in great debt gets rewarded? The transformations are in some ways so surprising, when looked at closely, I don't dare to be overly assertive about my analysis. But here's how it seems to me:

At first, there is the blanket solution: no matter what one is striving for, if one strives earnestly and long, the sheer activity as such makes the striver, the stormer and stresser, deserve salvation. This is what Santayana called the "official moral."

Goethe needed an ending as final as possible. As regards the traditional Faust story, the only complete ending was Faust's damnation. But with the changing attitude towards ambition (its transformation from a "temptation" to an "ideal") there was a corresponding need to transform the tragedy into a comedy (in keeping with the proverb, "All's well that ends well"). Lessing, among others, had considered doing a middle-class revision of the old legend. But he had planned to use wholly up-to-date imagery, omitting all the paraphernalia of black magic.

However, in so radical a redoing of a theme to make it a perfect fit with the middle-class cult of "climbing," even subtler bookkeeping was involved than is required of certified accountants who help a big corporation either show that its earnings are losses or that its liabilities are assets (depending upon whether the financial statement is designed for dodging income taxes or to help promoters unload the company's securities at the highest figure possible).

André Gide greatly admired Goethe, and in *The Counterfeiters* he also used the theme of bad money. (But whereas counterfeiting in Gide's novel explicitly reflects homosexual involvement, in Goethe's drama we take the paper money scheme to implicitly reflect sexual impotence.) As regards the "official moral" (that endless striving is a kind of divine discontent, and thus should end in heaven), it is somewhat as though, in Gide's novel, after Bernard had killed himself following his glorious night with Edward, alias Uncle Gide, the incident had led to great rejoicing in heaven, on the grounds that Bernard had shown his appreciation for perfection, and thus deserved to live in its presence forever.

But there are also subtler ways of contributing to such a transformation. One device operates along these lines: Faust is now one hundred years old. He has fought to keep back the sea, to turn from the Faustian world of mountaintops to the reclaiming of the flatlands, as with the dikes of Holland. The sea now, apparently, means *death*, and Faust is holding it back. I base my interpretation on a passage in Act IV, where Faust talks of the sea's barrenness—Unfruitfulness, *Unfruchtbarkeit*—and describes his plans to place borders, *Grenzen* around this unruly power, to push back this desert waste. This is an ingenious turn of events in itself, since Faust, vowed to the cult of the *grenzenlos*, the boundless, must here begin to hem it in, however externally directed his beginnings along these lines. But when Death threatens, a notable twist of motives is introduced; through no fear on his part, simply through a concern with one step more, he suddenly expresses the wish to drop all use of magic.

A most astounding thing has happened here, as regards the kind of accountancy I am now considering. When deciding that he would abandon *magic*, he apostrophizes *"Nature."* But in abandoning *magic*, he has abandoned *Mephistopheles*. He has foresworn the Devil. And thus, surprise! in abandoning magic for Nature in all its directness, he has implicitly set the conditions for a *super*natural resolution. I take this to be a subtler and more roundabout manipulation of the machinery which we saw operating in the case of the work's "official moral."

But more than that goes on here. The more thorough a poet is, the more likely he is not simply to cancel or transform guilt, but to *shift* it. If one vessel is to be disburdened, we are advised to ask whether some other vessel is to take on this burden. For the scapegoat principle dies hard—and the profounder the work, the greater the likelihood that, where a man with much guilt is saved, someone or something else must take on the load he is relieved of.

The device used to this end involves the decay of Mephistopheles himself. He loses his claims, since he doesn't even have his own character to back him. This turn is contrived by having him take a perverted liking for some boy angels. Even perverse love is love, and thus Mephisto is undone. For in his role as a genuine devil, he would never be on the slope of love, no matter how corrupt. And this leads to a further surprising development whereby the angels pelt him with roses, which burn him like fire, though they are *not* fire. (Also this ultimate disclosure of a homosexual strand in Mephisto's makeup reinforces our earlier suggestion that Goethe's original conception of the Faustian temptations, which Mephisto represents, involved at least incipiently an autoerotic strand.)

A still subtler kind of accountancy takes place as regards the pious old married couple, Philemon and Baucis, whose marital loyalty was essentially different from Faust's relation to either Gretchen or Helen, and whose modest hut spoiled Faust's view "into the endless," but who had refused to move, and whose chapel bell also irritated him. In getting rid of them forcibly, Faust becomes unintentionally responsible for their being burned to death, along with a "Wanderer" who honors them. We are told that this was a wildly burning hell; so I take it that here was the part of Faust which thus indirectly suffered the pangs of hellfire, leaving the purified part of him for a happier fate. Just before this episode, Faust himself was seen *wandelnd* in his palatial garden. I take it that the aged couple are to the Wanderer as parents to child. That is, there is a similar disparity of age; and the "Wanderer" actually addresses Baucis as *Mother.*

In the classic myth, Jupiter and Mercury had been the "wanderers." They had been received as strangers by the hospitable couple. As a reward they were saved, and the others who had turned the wanderers away were submerged beneath water. The couple had been led to a high place, where they lived, having asked to tend a temple to the gods. In Goethe's version this temple has been transformed into a chapel. And the couple's hospitality can serve as surrogate for parental harboring of a youth who is by nature a "wanderer" (stands for the *strebend* aspect of Goethe's poetic self). Note also that in substituting the "wanderer" for the wandering gods, Goethe's version of the old myth had implicitly given this figure "heavenly" attributes.

Faust died at the moment when he ceased to strive ambitiously (when, thinking of the good he may have done for others, he thought in delight of *their* freedom, and he called upon time to keep this moment in suspense). Shortly thereafter, Mephistopheles says of Faust the final words that the Bible gives to Christ: "It is finished" (*es ist vollbracht*). From then on, Faust but *receives* the celestial ministrations by which he cheats the Devil of his due. Also, in applying to Faust the last words that the Gospel attributes to Christ, Mephisto had made his contribution to the transforming of the Faust story from a tragedy to a kind of "divine comedy."

X

But is there not one problem still unresolved? If things do not come to a focus in a unitary principle of some sort, there is to that extent the problem of unresolved division. But insofar as things do culminate in a unitive focus, some universal oneness (as with the basic dialectic of the alchemists, or the general tendency of language towards an overall term of terms), this unitive principle must be either personalized or left unpersonalized. If it is *not* personalized, to that extent it has a degree of mere conceptuality, of inanition, certainly as judged by the tests of drama, which involves personalization. If it *is* personalized, secondarily there is the need to choose sexual imagery. But as soon as this step is taken, one confronts the ultimate need of hermaphroditic, narcissistic, or incestuous imagery (as the old alchemists had repeatedly kept discovering). A "sacred marriage" of two sexual principles is but a step along the way; for in the last analysis, the grand totality must be an intrinsic merger of the *two* sexual principles into *one.*

Faust, in his transcendent form, is called *Doctor Marianus.* Jung derives this choice from the name of an earlier alchemist. In the light of the terministic exigencies we have just been considering, we might also note that Marianus would be the masculine counterpart of the name for the Mater

Gloriosa. Doctor Marianus (the "Marian Doctor"?) hails her as "Virgin, Mother, Queen, and Goddess." The pagan connotations of this last epithet were made clear in an earlier reference to her as "of equal birth with the Gods" (*Göttern ebenbürtig*). Faust also refers to her as "pure in the most beautiful sense" (a designation that should be taken, I submit, as a *transcendent* device for merging the Virgin Mother with the principle of beauty that was otherwise connected with Helen, the "key" to whom Faust had obtained among The Mothers).

Mephistopheles accurately set the problem himself, in Act III, when he said that Beauty is indivisible (*unteilbar*). And as early as the third scene of Part I he had announced himself as "part of the part which in the beginning was all," a part of the maternal darkness from which the light had been born, depriving the maternal realm of its former rank. (*Ich bin ein Teil des Teils der anfangs alles war, / Ein Teil der Finsternis, die sich das Licht gebar, / Das stolze Licht, das nun der Mutter Nacht / Den alten Rang, den Raum ihr streitig macht.*)

I recall also a remark of Goethe's with regard to what was perhaps his greatest attachment, Charlotte von Stein. He said the quality of their relationship inclined him to believe in the transmigration of souls. For he felt as thought, in some earlier period, she had been his sister or his wife. Also, when thinking of the *Helena*, we should recall Goethe's concern with the era of Greece as the "foretime" (*Vorzeit*). Such idealized notions of priority can easily represent the merger of different stages or persons in an individual's experience. For instance, by his reference to Charlotte von Stein in terms of a previous incarnation, Goethe set up the conditions for implying that, along with her role as his mistress, she represented for him the role of symbolic mother. And ideas of Greece as a "foretime" can readily accommodate connotations derived from his own youth (ambiguities to keep in mind when thinking of Faust's relations to Helen). The design fits perfectly with Faust's idealization and seduction of Gretchen in Part I. When hiding in her room before possessing her, he becomes quite *schwärmerisch* about her motherly nature. And in *Psychology and Alchemy*, Jung observes: "The mother is the first bearer of the animal image, which gives her a fascinating quality in the eyes of the son. It is then transferred, via the sister and similar figures, to the beloved."

Obviously here, a merger into the "feminine" in general would raise unresolved problems. And things become still more complicated when we recall that none other than Mephistopheles himself assumes the role of Phorkyas, death as an old hag. Also, though nobody that I have read seems to find the point worth noting, there is that astounding development at the beginning of Act IV, where Faust has a vision of a gigantic, godlike feminine form, "like Juno, Leda, Helen." It recalls for him the dawn of love. The ecstatic passage is usually taken as referring grandly to thoughts of

Gretchen, since the passage ends on a reference to a gracious form that, like Spiritual Beauty, rises and carries with it the best of his inner being. Whereupon, abruptly there is the stage direction: "A seven-league boot trips forward: another immediately follows. Mephistopheles steps out of them. The Boots stride onward in haste."

I grant that the passage probably does refer to a vision of Gretchen. But I would also note the ironic ambiguity by which it is interwoven with the appearance of Mephisto, an abruptness obviously intentional. And in being likened to Juno, Leda, and Helen, the figure clearly merges several kinds of woman, the first distinctly in the category of the maternal.

All told, my notion is: the problem of dissociating the various feminine principles is not resolved. And the closing lines, "The Eternal Feminine / Draws us on," or better "up" (*Das Ewig-Weibliche / Zieht uns hinan*) implicitly proclaims this irresolution. Thus, from the purely logological point of view, I'd translate the *"ewig"* (eternal) as meaning: Given the kind of merger that goes perfectly with the *Ur-Geist-Streben* nexus, the problem of ultimate motivation, as personalized in sexual terms, necessarily remains unresolved. It has the "eternal" quality of the essentially unending.

And we can feel sure that, if Goethe were still living, he'd still be adding bit by bit to the second part of *Faust*, in his attempt to disclose there all the motives that were implied in the first part (the story of a man whose cult of striving had come to a focus in a courtship designed to despoil an ideal virginal-maternal heroine).

We have here been concerned with the more general aspects of *Faust II*. A much longer essay would be needed for even a remotely adequate treatment of the incidental beauties in Goethe's verse. Both tonally and epigrammatically there is a wealth of marvelous detail. Even his doggerel is as tuneful as Mozartian music. Furthermore, since he was an omnivorous reader, and since everything he read spontaneously suggested rejoinders of his own, the many "pin cushion" episodes lent themselves readily to his sententiously lyrical kind of amplification. Often the second part of *Faust* is weak in "progressive" form. But the grand theme of *Ur-Geist-Streben* was so comprehensive that, as regards the tests of internal consistency (or "repetitive" form) nearly everything Goethe thought of could be fitted in somewhere. He thought of many many things, both Mephistopheles-sly and Faust-moody. And he put very many of them, not just into sound, but into sound effects. His lines can be readily set to music—but at a risk, since they are already music, along with profuse imagery and much conceptual braininess. Ever in search of sources, he was indeed a source.[3]

---

[3] *Streben* for its own sake is analogous to the theological notion that God is an Uncaused Cause to whom no motive for creating the world could be imputed (since the imputing of any motive would imply a limitation of His being). Yet *streben* is an act, and implicit in the idea of an act is the idea of purpose. Hence there is always the

purely grammatical incentive to give the *streben* a teleological dimension (such as the good, or the Loved). But striving may also be conceived to have its bodily analogue—and in this sense the term would be a synonym for the organism's sheer will to live. Thus Faust's death (the turn from *streben* to *sterben*) in occurring just after he has repeated the fatal line of Part One (*Verweile doch! du bist so schön!*) might be interpreted (in the light of the *Geist-Natur* pair) as the equivalent of a sudden radical physiological willingness to give up the ghost.

I, Eye, Ay—Concerning Emerson's Early Essay on "Nature," and the Machinery of Transcendence

I

An enemy might want to rate this early essay of Emerson's as hardly other than a Happiness Pill. But I admit: I find it so charming and buoyant, I'd be willing to defend it even on that level.

Also, we need not confine our speculations to the one essay. I shall try to make clear what I take to be its salient traits, as considered in itself. But I also hope that what I say about it can be considered from the standpoint of symbolic action in general. Since Emersonian "transcendentalism" was quite accurately named, I shall discuss the work from the standpoint of "transcendence."

Though dialectical transcendence and dramatic catharsis have many areas in which the jurisdictions covered by the two terms overlap, there are also terministic situations in which they widely differ. And the simplicity of the procedures embodied in Emerson's essay is exceptionally useful in this regard, as a way to bring out the contrast between transcendence and catharsis.

Catharsis involves fundamentally purgation by the imitation of victimage. If imaginative devices are found whereby members of rival factions can weep together, and if weeping is a surrogate of orgastic release, then a play that produced in the audience a unitary tragic response regardless of personal discord otherwise would be in effect a transformed variant of an original collective orgy (such as the Dionysian rites from which Greek tragedy developed). Here would be our paradigm for catharsis.

But transcendence is a rival kind of medicine. Despite the area of overlap, the distinction between the two is clear enough at the extremes. And Emerson's brand of Transcendentalism is a thorough example of the difference.

There are traces of victimage even here. Similarly, in the Platonic dialogue, there are traces of victimage, insofar as some speakers are sacrificed for the good of the dialogue as a whole (sacrificed in the sense of being proved wrong—yet their errors were a necessary part of the ultimate truths in which the dialogue, ideally, culminates). A similar "cathartic" element is indicated in references to what has been called Hegel's "logonomical purgatory."

Though transcendence as we shall deal with it is a sheerly symbolic operation (quite as with catharsis by victimage), the process has an *institutional* base as well—and I can indicate my meaning quickly thus (or fairly quickly):

In the appendix to the revised edition of my *Attitudes Toward History*, there is an article, "The Seven Offices." It aims to decide how many and how few categories are needed, to designate the functions that people perform for one another. The first six are:

govern (rule)
serve—(provide for materially)
defend
teach
entertain
cure

But one further function still had to be dealt with. For a while, I thought of "console." After a person who has been governed, provided for materially, defended, taught, and entertained, but has gone beyond the point where he can be cured, there is nothing left to do for him but attempt to console him, as do the churches. But the priestly function could not be confined to consolation. A priesthood also assists in the processes of rule, insofar as promises of reward in the afterlife are matched by threats of punishment, though Gilbert Murray has pointed out that threats of punishment also have a consoling effect, insofar as we can tell ourselves that our unjust enemy must eventually suffer for his misdeeds—and revenge is sweet. But in any case, I suddenly realized that, regardless of whether a priesthood is promising rewards in the afterlife or threatening punishment, or even if the priesthood is discussing some other realm without reference to ultimate reward or punishment, a realm HERE is being talked about *in terms of* a realm ELSEWHERE—and there is a terminology designed to *bridge* these disparate realms. So, for my seventh office, I chose the term:

pontificate; that is, to "make a bridge."

Viewed as a sheerly terministic, or symbolic function, that's what transcendence is: the building of a *terministic bridge* whereby one realm is *transcended* by being viewed *in terms of* a realm "beyond" it. Once you consider this process purely from the standpoint of *symbolic functions*, you will see that it is by no means confined to such "tender-minded" modes of expression as we find in the explicit Transcendentalism of an Emerson.

Transcendence, as we shall see, is best got by processes of dialectic (quite as catharsis is best got through drama). And in borrowing so much from Hegel's dialectic, even so "tough-minded" a nomenclature as that of Karl Marx inevitably retained transcendental traces (as when conditions *here and now* are seen *in terms of* a broad historic sweep that quite *transcends* them, and thus imparts to them a kind of "ulterior" meaning).

II

The discussion of catharsis centers in speculations on the way in which an audience is purged by somewhat identifying itself with the excesses of the tragic hero. There are two main meanings of *hubris*: "pride" and "excess." (Both translations fit Coriolanus superbly. He is arrogant—and in his arrogance he embodies with great intensity a moral tension of society as we know it, the distinction between the privileged and the underprivileged.)

We must also consider a non-Aristotelian kind of catharsis, as with the Crocean stress upon the cathartic nature of sheer expression, the relief of getting things said (of turning brute impressions into articulate expression). Perhaps the most effective instance of such gratification in *Coriolanus* is the way in which the play reduces to a clear narrative line the bundle of overlapping complexities among the motives of individual, family, class, and nation.

In many ways, drama and dialectic are alike. Both exemplify competitive cooperation. Out of conflict within the work, there arises a unitary view transcending the partial views of the participants. At least, this is the dialectic of the ideal Platonic dialogue. Both drama and dialectic treat of persons and their characteristic thoughts. But whereas drama stresses the *persons* who have the thoughts, and the dialectic of a Platonic dialogue stresses the *thoughts* held by the persons, in both forms the element of personality figures.

However, dialectic can dispense with the formal division into cooperatively competing voices. The thoughts or ideas can still be vibrant with personality, as they so obviously are in the essays of Emerson. Yet we think of them as various aspects of the same but somewhat inconsistent personality, rather than as distinct *characters* in various degrees of agreement and disagreement, like in a Platonic dialogue.

Though the Hegelian dialectic lays much greater stress than Emerson's upon the cooperative *competition* (as with Hegel's pattern whereby antitheses become resolved in a synthesis that is the thesis out of which will arise a new antithesis, etc.) Emerson had his variant in his doctrine of "Compensation." (The scheme amounted to this: Show how evils will have good results, but play down the reciprocal possibility whereby good might have evil results. "There is no penalty to virtue, no penalty to wisdom; they are proper additions to being." In brief, work up a dialectic that would rule out an ironic concept such as Veblen's "trained incapacity," or the French proverbial formula, "the defects of its qualities.")

All told, however, at their extremes there is a notable difference between tragic catharsis and dialectical transcendence—and the Emerson essay serves as a delightful illustration of this difference. To be sure, the essay is a bit innocuous; but it is delightfully so. It has a kind of exaltation, thanks in large part to Emerson's profuse mixing of his ideas with ingratiating imagery. And we can readily understand why he was so enthusiastic about Whitman, before a more quizzical look at Whitman's poetic evangelism led him to see that it was beckoning "Come hither" to much more than a highly respectable vendor of uplift such as Emerson had bargained for. Both approached the conflicts of the century in terms that allowed for a joyous transcendental translation. To apply in a twisted way (and thereby twisting a twist) Rimbaud's demand for a poetry based on the "reasoned derangement of the senses," we might say that Emerson was as idealistically able as Whitman to look upon traveling salesmen and see a band of angels. There can be transcendence upwards (as when Coleridge studies the constitution of Church and State "according to the idea of each"). There can be transcendence downwards (as when, thinking of a Church, one speaks of it in terms of the sewer upon which a Church is necessarily built). And there can be a fluctuating between the two. (Cf. in E. M. Forster's novel, *A Passage to India*, the wavering as to whether India is a "muddle" or a "mystery.")

III

Emerson's essay is definitely an idealistic exercise in transcendence up. (There is also a down implicit in such a pattern—but as we proceed, we'll see how it differs from the angry or Beatnik downs.)

Since both tragic catharsis and dialectical transcendence involve *formal development*, by the same token both modes give us kinds of *transformation*.

In tragic catharsis (or, more generally, dramatic catharsis—for there are corresponding processes in comedy), the principle of transformation comes to a focus in *victimage*. The tragic pleasure requires a *symbolic sacrifice*—or, if you will, a *goat*. And the same is obviously true of the comic pleasure.

In dialectical transcendence, the principle of transformation operates in terms of a "beyond." It is like our seventh office, the "priestly" function, in that it pontificates, or "builds a bridge" between disparate realms. And insofar as things here and now are treated in terms of a "beyond," they thereby become infused or inspirited by the addition of a *new or further dimension.*

The Emerson essay is a delightful example of such a terministic process. But before we deal with it in particular, further preparatory considerations are in order, since they bear directly upon the distinction with which we are here concerned. They concern Friedrich Nietzsche's *Birth of Tragedy.* Though the histories of philosophy usually stress Plato's quarrels with the Sophists, Nietzsche was exercised rather with the difference between the Socratic medicine (as interpreted by Plato) and the medicine of the tragic playwrights. Celebrating the cult of tragedy (the cult of the kill, resolution in terms of extreme victimage), Nietzsche attacked Socrates for being a *reformer* whose policies implied the *death* of tragedy.

You might recommend a cause by tragic dignification (by depicting people of worth who are willing to die for it). Or (along the lines of Aristotle's *Rhetoric*) you might recommend it by showing the advantages to be gained if the cause (or policy) prevails (that is, you might argue in terms of expediency). Or there are the resources of dialectical transcendence (by seeing things in terms of some "higher" dimension, with the spirit of which all becomes infused). In Nietzsche's case the situation was further complicated by the fact that, even while attacking Plato, Nietzsche attributed to Plato a large measure of tragic dignification, owing to the stress that Nietzsche placed upon the figure of the "dying Socrates" who willingly sacrificed himself as a way of bearing witness to the virtues of the Socratic (Platonic, dialectical) method.

Essentially, the dialectical operations in the Emerson essay are to be built around the traditional One-Many (unity-diversity) pair. Emerson states it succinctly: "ascent from particular to general"; for if we say "furniture" instead of "tables, chairs, and carpets," we spontaneously speak of the more general term as in some way "higher." The process is completed when one has arrived at "highly" generalized terms like "entities" or "beings"— whereupon all that is left is a further step to something like "Pure Being," or the One, or First, or Ultimate, or some such. When we arrive at this stage, the overall term-of-terms or title-of-titles is so comprehensive it is simultaneously nowhere and everywhere. Hence, mystics can select just about anything, no matter how lowly and tangible, to stand for it (for instance, the enigmatic role of the wasp, as seen by Mrs. Moore and imagined by Professor Godbole, in *A Passage to India*). Dialectical transcendence depends upon these quite pedestrian resources of terminology.

In the case of Emerson's essay, the underlying structure is as simple as this: The everyday world, all about us here and now, is to be interpreted as a *diversity* of *means* for carrying out a *unitary purpose* (or, if you will, the

principle of purpose) that is situated in an ultimate realm *beyond* the here
and now. The world's variety of things is thus to be interpreted *in terms of* a
transcendent unifier (that infuses them all with its single spirit). And by this
mode of interpretation all the world becomes viewed as a set of *instrumen-
talities*. (Emerson more resonantly calls them, "commodities.") For we
should bear it in mind that Emerson's brand of transcendentalism was but
a short step ahead of out-and-out pragmatism, which would retain an un-
mistakable theological tinge in William James, and furtive traces even in
Dewey. I have in mind the ambiguity whereby, when Dewey pleads that
people use their "capacities" to the fullest, he secretly means their *"good*
capacities." He thus schemes to make a quasi-technical term serve a moralistic purpose.[1]

Where, then, are we? I am trying to do at least three things at once.
I am trying to build up a contrast between transformation by victimage
(dramatic catharsis) and transformation by dialectical "transcendence"
(modes of "crossing" whereby something here and now is interpreted in
terms of something beyond). I am trying to discuss precisely how these
operations are performed in one particular essay, by Emerson, on Nature.
(In brief, he so sets up "Nature" that it is to be interpreted in terms of
Supernature.) And I further hope to indicate that the design here being discussed is employed in all sorts of terministic schemes. For the same principle
is involved (there are tiny "transcendences") every time an author, no
matter how empirical his claims, mounts to a "higher" level of generalization and in effect asks that "lower" levels of generalization be interpreted
in its terms.

The third thesis should especially concern anyone who, while spontaneously shifting back and forth between different levels of generalization,
might incline not to see that all such procedures are operating within the
same rules, though in a fragmentary way.

---

[1] Money being a kind of universal purpose (since it can serve for an almost endless
variety of purchases), whereas one might ask, "Give our lives *meaning*," or "Give our
lives *purpose*," you are more likely to hear the pragmatic reduction, *"Give us jobs."*
It is well to keep such developments in mind when we read the Emerson essay. While
affirming much the kind of moralistic utilitarianism that one finds in the Discourses of
Epictetus, and with hankerings after the kind of moralistic "Progress" that one finds
in Bunyan's idea of pilgrimage, the essay must now be seen as inevitably, inexorably
placed along the way toward the confusions that beset the current combinings of
technological and monetary rationalization. "Under the name of commodity," Emerson writes, "I rank all those advantages which our senses owe to nature." Thus, under
the head of "Commodity," he can refer to "Nature, in its ministry to man." While
reading that section, perhaps we should not merely be sure to interpret "commodity"
in a moralistic sense that has since dropped away. When reading it we should also
have in mind the poignancy of the fact that, as we can now readily discern, since history is by nature a Damoclean sword, Emerson's use of the term already held in suspension the narrower contemporary meaning.

So, if one feels that Emerson's essay is not tough-minded enough (and I'd be the last to assert that it is, for all my love of it), I'd contend that such a judgment is not enough to dismiss it.

If only like loving a pleasant dream, love him for his idealistic upsurge. For *it reads well*. It is medicine. Even in those days, I feel sure, both he and Whitman suspected that they might be whistling in the dark. But they loved the gesture (if whistling is a gesture)—and it is an appealing gesture, albeit a gesture much more plausible then than now. Emerson's scheme for transcendence (like Whitman's variant) was propounded before his fellow townsmen had lost their sense of a happy, predestined future. There was not yet any crying need to turn, rather, and begin hoarding relics of the ancestral past, like an unregenerate Southerner's attic, with its trunkload of Confederate money.

IV

Here is what I take to be the underlying form of the essay:

It treats of Society in terms of Nature—and it treats of Nature in terms of the Supernatural. Thereby even the discussion of Society in its most realistic aspects becomes transcendentally tinged (somewhat as though you had made a quite literal line drawing with pen and ink, and had covered it with a diaphanous wash of cerulean blue).

In keeping with such an approach to the everyday materials of living, note how even the realm of the sensory can be interpreted as a kind of *revelation*. For whatever the world is, in its sheer brute nature as physical vibrations or motions it *reveals itself* to us *in terms of* sights, sounds, tastes, scents, touch, summed up as pleasure or pain. Thus you already have the terministic conditions whereby even the most material of sensations can be called "apocalyptic" (since the word but means "revealing")—and Emerson does apply precisely that word. In this respect, even the crudest of sensory perceptions can be treated as the revealing of nature's mysteries, though the revelations are confined to the restrictions imposed upon us by the physical senses that reveal them. Also, the resources of dialectic readily permit us to make a further step, insofar as particulars can be treated in terms that transcend their particularity. Within the Emersonian style, this convenience indigenous to terminology would be more resonantly stated: "when the fact is seen in the light of an idea."

If Nature is to be treated in terms of Supernature, another possibility presents itself. There could be stylistic procedures designed to serve as *bridges* (or intermediaries) between the two sets of terms. The simplest instance of such a bridging device is to be seen in the dialectic of Christian theology. If you make a distinction between "God" and "Man," you set up

the terministic conditions for an intermediate term (for bridging the gap between the two orders); namely: "God-Man." Similarly, in the dialectic of
psychoanalysis, one might be advised to inquire whether the term "preconscious" can serve (at least on some occasions) as a bridge between the
terms "conscious" and "unconscious." Fittingly, the major bridge of this sort
in Emerson's essay comes in the chapter halfway through, containing the
homily on "Discipline."

We'll discuss later how the chapter on Discipline operates as a bridge,
a "pontificator." Meanwhile we should note another kind of bridge: the
imagistic. There is such a profusion of images in the essay, at first I was
puzzled as to how I might discuss the imagery in the summarizing way needed
for a presentation of this sort. For to deal with the images in their particularity, one would need the kind of line-by-line analysis that is possible only
to a succession of sessions in the classroom.

So I propose a makeshift. Near the start of the essay, Emerson writes:
"If a man would be alone, let him look at the stars." Then he continues:

> The rays that come from those heavenly worlds will separate between
> him and what he touches. One might think the atmosphere was made
> transparent with this design, to give man, in the heavenly bodies, the
> perpetual presence of the sublime. Seen in the streets of cities, how
> great they are! [I fear that that line has become a victim of techno-
> logical progress.] If the stars should appear one night in a thousand
> years, how would men believe and adore; and preserve for many
> generations the remembrance of the city of God which had been
> shown! [This passage presumably refers to a spot in the Introduc-
> tion: "The foregoing generations beheld God and nature face to
> face; we, through their eyes." And at that point, of course, one might
> turn aside to mention the favored role of eye-imagery in Emerson's
> transcendental vision.] But every night come out these envoys of
> beauty, and light the universe with their admonishing smile.

Perhaps we should add the opening sentence of the next paragraph:
"The stars awaken a certain reverence, because though always present, they
are inaccessible; but all natural objects make a kindred impression, when
the mind is open to their influence."

On the basis of these sentences I would propose, for purposes of
essayistic efficiency, to suggest that Emerson's imagery in general is "starry-
eyed." Recall that all three canticles of the Divine Comedy end on references
to the stars; and put that thought together with the fact that Emerson's essay thus begins. Note also that, in keeping with the quality of Emersonian
individualism, he equates the stars with a desire to be alone. And when he
refers to the atmosphere as being "made transparent with this design," we
are advised to note the several other incidences of the term, thus:

I become a transparent eyeball.

. . . the universe becomes transparent, and the light of higher laws than its own shines through it.

If the Reason be stimulated to more earnest vision, outlines and surfaces become transparent, and are no longer seen; causes and spirits are seen through them.

The ruin or the blank that we see when we look at nature, is in our own eye. The axis of things is not coincident with the axis of things, and so they appear not transparent, but opaque.

And in his essay, "The Poet," with reference to reading a poem which he confides in "as an inspiration," he says: "And now my chains are to be broken; I shall mount above these clouds and opaque airs in which we live— opaque though they seem transparent—and from the heaven of truth I shall see and comprehend my relations."

Here is what I am aiming at: First, the essay involves a definite *crossing*, via the middle section on "Discipline," so far as the development of the *ideas* is concerned. But in the starry-eyed visionary imagery (as epitomized in the notion of the "transparent") the transcendence is *implicitly* or ambiguously there from the start, and permeates the style throughout the entire essay. To pick some instances almost at random:

. . . like an eagle or a swallow . . . the pomp of emperors . . . the live repose of the valley behind the mill . . . spires of flame in the sunset . . . the graces of winter scenery . . . this pomp of purpose and gold . . . the dewey morning, the rainbow, mountains, orchards in blossom, stars, moonlight, shadows in still water . . . the spells of persuasion, the keys of power . . . like travellers using the cinders of a volcano to roast their eggs . . . the azure sky, over whose unspotted deeps the winds forevermore drive flocks of stormy clouds . . . a leaf, a drop, a crystal, a moment of time . . . not built like a ship to be tossed, but like a house to stand . . . this transfiguration which all material objects undergo through the passion of the poet . . . the recesses of consciousness . . . faint copies of an invisible archetype . . . [Nor should we omit mention of this resonant set in his Introduction: "language, sleep, madness, dreams, beasts, sex." And characteristically, at one point he gives us the equation: "The eye—the mind."]

And here would be the place to cite from the transitional chapter on "Discipline," and at almost the mathematical center of the essay, his central bit of Uplift. In these tough times, I'd not even have the courage to repeat the passage, if I could not immediately hasten to propose a non-Emersonian translation:

Sensible objects conform to the premonitions of Reason and reflect the conscience. All things are moral; and in their boundless changes have an unceasing reference to spiritual nature. Therefore is nature glorious with form, color, and motion; that every globe in the remotest heaven, every chemical change from the rudest crystal up to the laws of life, every change of vegetation from the principle of growth in the eye of a leaf, to the tropical forest and antediluvian coal-mine, every animal function from the sponge up to Hercules, shall hint or thunder to man the laws of right and wrong, and echo the Ten Commandments. Therefore is Nature ever the Ally of Religion.

Going beyond the specifically theological level here, one might note the sheerly "logological" fact that a strategic feature of the Decalogue is its urgent sprinkling of Negatives. Elsewhere I have dealt with the all-importance of the Negative in the development of language, in connection with the complex property structures that depend upon the codifications of secular law (and its species of "thou-shalt-not's"), and with the modes of thinking that arise from the resources of Negativity (Alienation, or "Negativism," for instance).

But for present purposes I might offer a shortcut of this sort: You know of the great stress upon Negativity in much contemporary Existentialist philosophy. And you know of the ingenious talk about "Nothingness" (the Heideggerian concern with *nichten* and the Sartrian concern with *le Néant*). Well, in the last analysis, when Emerson grows edified at the thought that all things, for man, are permeated with the spirit of the "thou shalt not," is he not talking about the same situation, except that his particular dialectic allows him to discuss it in the accents of elation, thereby (if we may apply one of his own words) endowing his statements with the quality of the "medicinal"?

Indeed, once the pattern gets established, you will find Emerson's transcendentalism doing much the same as Whitman did with his infectious cult of the glad hand. Accordingly, since Nature is viewed as disciplinary, and since (as we have already noted) the Social Structure is viewed in terms of Nature, it follows that even the discords of "Property and its filial systems of debt and credit," can be welcomed transcendentally as a primary mode of moral discipline, thus:

Debt, grinding debt, whose iron face the widow, the orphan, and the sons of genius fear and hate—debt, which consumes so much time, which so cripples and disheartens a great spirit with cares that seem so base, is a preceptor whose lessons cannot be foregone, and is needed most by those who suffer from it most.

V

But I have not yet made wholly clear how the chapter on "Discipline" serves as a bridge between the *Hic et Nunc* and the "Beyond." To appreciate the dialectical maneuvers here, we should lay great stress upon the strategic sentence in the Introduction: "Let us inquire, to what end is nature?" This question sets the conditions for the pattern of development. Of all the issues that keep recurring in the maneuvers of dialectic, surely none is more frequent than the theme of the One and the Many. As I have said, to me it is grounded in the logological fact that terms for particulars can be classified under some one titular head. And thus, when we say "the Universe," we feel that we really are talking about the Universe, about "everything," though the term certainly includes an awful lot that we don't know anything about. (And I leave it for you to decide whether you can talk about something when you don't know what it is that you may be talking about.)

Be that as it may, given the typical resources of terminology, the question, "To what end is nature?" allows for a one-many alignment of this sort: The world of our Empirical existence can be viewed not just as a great variety of *things*, but as a great variety of *means*, all related to some ultimate *end*. In this regard we can see how Emerson's dialectic pattern (of *manifold means* in the world of everyday experience emblematically or hieroglyphically announcing some *unitary end* in a realm beyond everyday experience) set up the conditions for transcendentalizing maneuvers that would be progressively transformed into William James's pragmatism and John Dewey's instrumentalism. Though work, in its *utilitarian* aspects, amasses *material* powers, in its *ethical* aspects work can be felt to *transcend* utility. Hence "Discipline" serves as the means of crossing from sheer expediency to edification.

Before the bridge, Emerson's stress is upon *uses* (a subject dear to his countrymen, who were to build, by their technology, the highest Babylonian Tower of useful things the world has ever known, though many of the uses were to prove worse than useless). In his case, of course, the many resources of utility are moralized in terms of a transcendental purpose, itself in the realm *beyond* the bridge. On this side of the bridge, there are "Commodities," "Beauty," and "Language." "Beauty" endangers the design, inasmuch as it is an end in itself. But Emerson preserves the design by his concluding decision that "Beauty in nature is not ultimate." It is "the herald of inward and eternal beauty."

Nothing could more quickly reveal the terministic resources of the Emersonian dialectic (or, if you will, the Emersonian unction) than by contrasting his views on language with Jeremy Bentham's "theory of fictions." Bentham laid major stress upon the fact that all our terms for spiritual or psychological states are initially terms for sheerly physical things and processes. And by "fictions" he had in mind the thought that all moral or psychological nomenclatures are essentially metaphors carried over from the physical realm and applied analogically. But Emerson's transcendental dialectic allows him to apply a tender-minded mode of interpretation, thus:

> Words are signs of natural facts. The use of natural history is to give us aid in supernatural history; the use of the outer creation, to give us language for the beings and changes of the inward creation. Every word which is used to express a moral or intellectual fact, if traced to its root, is found to be borrowed from some material appearance. *Right* means *straight*; *wrong* means *twisted*; *Spirit* primarily means *wind*; *transgression*, the crossing of a *line*; *supercilious*, the *raising of the eyebrow*. We say the *heart* to express emotion, the *head* to denote thought; and *thought* and *emotion* are words borrowed from sensible things, and now appropriated to spiritual nature.

And so on. In any case, once you thus turn things around, you see why, if the things of nature are to serve us by providing us with terms which we can apply analogically for the development of a moral terminology, then the whole subject would come to a focus in a chapter on nature itself as a source of moral "discipline." Fittingly, the chapter begins by reference to the "*use* of the world" as a discipline. And at the beginning of the next chapter "Idealism" we read: "To this one *end* of Discipline, all parts of nature conspire." (Italics in both cases ours.) Thus, when the chapter on "Discipline" is over, we have gone from the realm of *means* to the realm of *ends*, or more specifically, one unitary end (or, if you will, the sheer *principle* of purpose).

Fittingly, now that we have crossed the bridge, into the realm of "Reason" and "Spirit," Nature suffers what Emerson himself calls a "degrading." For whereas Nature rated high when thought of as leading towards the Supernatural, in comparison with the Supernatural it comes into question, even as regards its material existence. (Incidentally, this change of rating in Emerson's dialectic corresponds, in the Marxian dialectic, to a step such as the transformation of the bourgeoisie from the class that is the bearer of the future to the class that is to be buried by the future. In a ladder of developments, rung five is "progressive" with regard to rung three, but "reactionary" with regard to rung seven.) However, in this later "degrading" of nature, he pauses to admonish: "I do not wish to fling stones at my beautiful mother, nor soil my gentle nest." He wishes, in effect, but to complete the tracking down of the positions implicit in his dialectic.

One final development should be mentioned, since it throws a quite relevant light upon the essay's methods. In his final chapter, "Prospects," while zestfully reciting the many steps that man has taken through the course of history towards the affirming of what Emerson takes to be the ultimate supernatural Oneness, the essay has so built up the promissory that we scarcely note how airily the problem of evil is dismissed:

Build yourself your own world. As fast as you conform your life to
the pure idea in your mind, that will unfold its great proportions. A
correspondent revolution in things will attend the influx of the spirit.
So fast will disagreeable appearances, swine, spiders, snakes, pests,
mad-houses, prisons, enemies, vanish; they are temporary and shall
be no more seen. [This comes close to the line in "Lycidas": "Shall
now no more be seen."] The sordor and filths of nature, the sun shall
dry up and the wind exhale. As when the summer comes from the
south the snow-banks melt and the face of the earth becomes green
before it, so shall the advancing spirit create its ornaments along its
path, and carry with it the beauty it visits and the song which en-
chants it. . . .

He envisions in sum: "the kingdom of man over nature."

One can't do anything with that, other than to note that it disposes
of many troublesome things in a great hurry. But the Marxist dialectic is
not without an analogous solution, in looking upon the socialist future as
"inevitable."

Two asides: As regards "the thinking of the body," there are strong
hints of a fecal motive near the end of the section on Language:

"Material objects," said a French philosopher, "are necessarily
kinds of *scoriae* of the substantial thoughts of the Creator, which
must always preserve an exact relation to their first origin; in other
words, visible nature must have a spiritual and moral side."

I have found that readers seldom look up the word *scoriae*. It comes
from the same root as "scatological." Here it conceives the realm of matter
as nothing other than God's *offal*. Such images are likely to turn up somewhere in the dialectics of transformation, especially where there is talk of
"discipline." And, thanks to an ambiguous use of the verb "betrays," I'd
incline to see traces of it in Emerson's statement that the principle of Unity
"lies under the undermost garment of Nature, and betrays its source in
Universal Spirit." In his later and shorter essay on "Nature," where we
are told that the universe "has but one stuff," the same tricky usage appears
thus: "Compound it how she will, star, sand, fire, water, tree, man, it is
still one stuff, and betrays the same properties." Surely "stuff" here is
synonymous with matter in the reference to Nature as God's *scoriae*. And
thinking along the same lines, we find it noteworthy that, though Unity is
the best of words when applied to the realm of the Supernatural, in the
chapter "Prospects" it is called "tyrannizing" when applied to the earthly
animal kingdom.[2]

---

[2] The grounds for my speculations here are made clearer in my essay on "Thinking of
the Body," particularly the section on the symbolism of "matter" in Flaubert's *Tenta-
tion de Saint-Antoine*. Similar connotations flit about the edges of an expression such
as "purge the eyes."

VI

At the end of the chapter on "Discipline," just before we cross to the realm of the Beyond, we find traces of victimage, in his solemnizing references to separation from a friend:

> When much intercourse with a friend has supplied us with a standard of excellence, and has increased our respect for the resources of God who thus sends a real person to outgo our ideal; when he has, moreover, become an object of thought, and, whilst his character retains all its unconscious effect, is converted in the mind into solid and sweet wisdom—it is a sign to us that his office is closing, and he is commonly withdrawn from our sight in a short time.

Is not this passage a euphemism for the death, or near-death, of a close friend? And thus, does not the bridge (that carries us across to the Beyond) end on strong traces of tragic dignification by victimage?

Similarly, I have tried elsewhere to show that James Joyce's story, "The Dead," should be analyzed primarily in terms of transcendence. (See the section from "Three Definitions" reprinted in my *Perspectives by Incongruity*, edited by Stanley Edgar Hyman.) But the very title indicates that the purgative force of victimage also figures here.

Without considering the story in detail, we might note this much about it: The "transcending," or "beyonding," concerns the final transformation whereby the situation of the living is viewed in terms of the dead. For if the world of conditions is the world of the living, then the transcending of conditions will, by the logic of such terms, equal the world of the dead. (And the Kantian transcendental dialectic could get in the idea of God by this route: If God transcends nature, and nature is the world of conditions, then God is the realm of the unconditioned. Or, otherwise put: given a term so highly generalized as the "conditioned," there's no possible context left but the "unconditioned.")

The final twist, what Joyce would call an "epiphany," is contrived by the transforming of "snow" from a *sensory* image to a *mythic* image. That is, in the first part of the story, the references to snow are wholly realistic ("lexical" snow, snow as defined in a dictionary). But at the end, snow has become a *mythic* image, manifesting itself in the world of conditions, but standing for transcendence above the conditioned. It is a snow that bridges two realms—but, as befits the behavior of snow, this Upward Way is figured in terms of a Downward Way, as the last paragraph features the present participle, "falling."

There is an interesting variant in Chaucer's *Troilus and Criseyde*. The poem tells a pagan story in a pagan setting. But in the telling, Chaucer infuses the story with the medieval terminology of Courtly Love. Now, it so happens that this terminology is a *secular* analogue of the language applied to *religious* devotion. Accordingly the story as so told sets up the conditions for the use of this language in ways that transcend its application to a pagan love affair. Accordingly, the book closes on the picture of slain Troilus looking down upon "this litel spot of erthe" in the traditional Christian attitude of the *contemptus mundi*, in contrast with "the playn felicite / That is in hevene above"—thence finally to an outright Christian prayer involving Mary and the Trinity.

In the early part of his trip to the Underworld, Virgil encountered those of the dead who could not cross Cocytus and the Stygian swamps. Charon would not ferry them to their final abode because they had not been buried. Then comes the famous line:

Tendebantque manus ripae ulterioris amore

(And they stretched forth their hands, through love of the farther shore)

That is the pattern. Whether there is or is not an ultimate shore towards which we, the unburied, would cross, transcendence involves dialectical processes whereby something HERE is interpreted *in terms of* something THERE, something *beyond* itself.

These examples involve modes of "beyonding" that overlap upon connotations of victimage where symbolic fulfillment is attained in the ambiguities of death and immortality (with technical twists whereby, if "death" means "not-life," "immortality" compounds the negative, giving us "not not-life"). Obviously, Emerson's dialectic of a transcendent End involves similar operations. But I would here stress the fact that the principle of transcendence which is central to his essay is not confined to its use in such thoroughgoing examples.

The machinery of language is so made that, either rightly or wrongly, either grandly or in fragments, we stretch forth our hands through love of the farther shore. Which is to say: The machinery of language is so made that things are necessarily placed in terms of a range broader than the terms for those things themselves. And thereby, in even the toughest or tiniest of terminologies, terminologies that, on their face, are far from the starry-eyed Transcendentalism of Emerson's essay, we stretch forth our hands through love of a farther shore; that is to say, we consider things in terms of a broader scope than the terms for those particular things themselves. And I submit that, wherever there are traces of that process, there are the makings of Transcendence.

Chapter Seven

"Kubla Khan," Proto-Surrealist Poem

Let's begin at the heart of the matter, and take up the "problems" after-wards. Count me among those who would view this poem both as a marvel, and as "in principle" *finished* (and here is a "problem," inasmuch as Coleridge himself refers to "Kubla Khan" as a "fragment").

Conceivably, details could be added, to amplify one or another of the three movements. And some readers (I am not among them) might especially feel the need of transitional lines to bridge the ellipsis between the middle and final stanzas. But as regards the relationship among the three stages of the poem's development, its unfolding seems to me no less trimly demarcated than the strophes of a Greek chorus, or (more relevantly) the Hegelian pattern of thesis, antithesis, and synthesis. Whatever may have got lost, the three stanzas in their overall progression tick off a perfect form, with beginning, middle, and end respectively. Thus:

Stanza One (Thesis) amplifies the theme of the beatific vision. Stanza Two (Antithesis) introduces and develops the sinister, turbulent counter-theme (plus, at the close, a notably modified recall of the contrasting first theme). And the Third Stanza fuses the two motives in terms of a beatific vision (the "damsel with a dulcimer") seen by a poetic "I," the mention of whom, despite the euphoria, leads to the cry, "Beware! Beware!" and to talk of a "dread" that, however "holy," in a sinister fashion is felt to befit the idealistic building of this particular air-castle.

In *The Road to Xanadu*, John Livingston Lowes brought an infectious combination of research and spirited delight to the tracking down of pos-sible literary sources behind Coleridge's great poems of Fascination (an enterprise further justified by the fact that Coleridge was so notoriously omnivorous a reader, and one of his memorandum books listed texts con-taining many references to caverns, chasms, mazes, sunken rivers, fountains, and the like). By consulting Lowes the reader will discover that nearly every notable term or reference in the poem appeared (often with quite relevant applications and combinations) in other passages that Coleridge is quite likely to have seen. But though greatly enjoying the charm of Lowes's presentation, and having on many occasions consulted his book when working on Coleridge, I should begin by pointing out that our present job involves a quite different trend of investigation (an investigation in which Lowes's book can be of great help, though his interest is directed otherwise).

There is a sense in which poets can be said to have special nomenclatures, just as scientists or philosophers do. But this situation is concealed from us by the fact that, rather than inventing a special word for some particular conceptual purpose, or pausing to define some particular application he is giving to a word in common usage, a poet leaves the process implicit, even though he uses the common idiom in his peculiar way. (For instance, the term "fish" in Theodore Roethke's poems would have little in common with the article of food we might buy in a market or order in a restaurant.) And by collating all the contexts that help define a word as it figures in a given poet's work, we can discern respects in which it is part of a nomenclature essentially as specialized as "entelechy" in the philosophy of Aristotle, or "relativity" with particular reference to the theories of Einstein. So, thinking along those lines, insofar as I'd risk looking up from the immediate text, I'd tend to ask about uses of a given term in other works *by Coleridge* rather than asking (like Lowes) about possible sources in *other* writers. For instance, people have doubtless talked about fountains since they could talk at all. And Coleridge's reference to the sacred river, Alph, does unquestionably suggest the ancient myth of the river Alpheus that sank into the ground and emerged as the fountain Arethusa (a belief which Lowes shows to have merged with notions about the sources of the Nile). I'd tend to start matters from a concern with the themes of submergence and emergence, with the Alpheus-Arethusa *pattern* as a symbolizing of *rebirth*, regardless of who else happened to speak of it. Or take this comment in Lowes:

> In April, 1798, Coleridge who had been suffering from an infected tooth, wrote as follows, in a letter to his brother George:
>
>> Laudanum gave me repose, not sleep; but you, I believe, know how divine that repose is, *what a spot of enchantment, a green spot of fountain and flowers and trees in the very heart of a waste of sands!*
>
> Now when Coleridge wrote that, he was recalling and echoing, consciously or unconsciously, something else. For in the Note Book (which, as we know, belongs to this same period) appears this memorandum:
>
>> —*some wilderness-plot, green and fountainous* and unviolated by Man.

Lowes then asks, "Is it possible to discover what lies behind this note?" He proceeds to discover, in Bartram's *Travels*, the expressions "blessed unviolated spot of earth!" and "the enchanting spot." And he notes that two pages earlier Bartram had written: "the dew-drops twinkle and play . . . on the tips of the lucid, green savanna, sparkling" beside a "serpentine rivulet, meandering over the meadows." As approached from Lowes's point of view, the serpentine, meandering rivulet would seem to touch upon the "sacred river, / Five miles meandering with a mazy motion"; the "dew-drops" might impinge upon "honey-dew"; and so on. But of primary importance for *our present investigations* is not the question of where Coleridge may have read words almost identical with "spot of enchantment," but the fact that he used the expression in this particular context (in association with laudanum). And the reference to "honey-dew" would lead us, not to such a reference as *Bartram's* "dew-drops," but rather to a pair of quite contrasting references in "The Ancient Mariner," the first a dew like the sweat of anguish ("From the sails the dew did drip"), the second the dew of refreshment after release from the dreadful drought ("I dreamt that they were filled with dew; / And when I awoke, it rained"). Or we might recall the voice "As soft as honey-dew" that, though gentle, pronounced a fatal sentence: "The man hath penance done, / And penance more will do." And above all, I should rejoice to encounter in another poem ("Youth and Age") an explicit recognition of this term's convertibility: "Dew-drops are the gems of morning, / But the tears of mournful eve." In a juvenile poem, there is a related expression, "inebriate with dew." And I should never feel wholly content until I could also fit in one of the jottings from *Anima Poeta* that widens the circle of associations by reference to "a voice that suits a dream, a voice in a dream, a voice soundless and yet for the *ear* and not for the *eye* of the soul" (for often eye and ear can represent quite different orders of motivation).

In brief, the student of any one poet's nomenclature has more to learn from a concordance of his work (a purely *internal* inspection of a term's "sources" in its own range of contexts) than from an inspection of possible borrowings (except in the broadest sense, as when a scholar cites usages by an older writer's contemporaries to help establish the likelihood that a given term was being used in a sense local to that period but now obsolete).

In fact, the many interesting documents which Lowes assembles as inductive proof of expressions which Coleridge derived or adapted from his reading, might with much justice be interpreted quite differently, as indication that Coleridge was but responding "naturally" to the implications of such imagery. For instance, one might conceivably not require a prior text to help him discover that the image of a maze can adequately stand for a certain kind of emotional entanglement or "amazement," and that the greenery of an oasis in a desert provides an adequate image for an idea of refuge. And presumably travel books select such things to talk about for the very reason that their sheer "factuality" follows along the

204   PARTICULAR WORKS AND AUTHORS

grooves of man's spontaneous imagination. Be that as it may, Lowes's
study of possible derivation with regard to possible private literary sources
contains much material that can be applied to the study of "associations"
in two senses that Lowes was not concerned with: (1) their relation to
"mythic" or "archetypal" forms of thought that do not rely on historical
sources for their derivation; and (2) their relation to a nomenclature that,
at notable points, may be uniquely Coleridgean (in that they possess
personal connotations not to be found in any dictionary, and not precisely
appreciated by us who read them, as it were, without quite the proper
accent).

In any case, for the most part, we shall interpret the poem by looking
for what now would often be called "archetypal" sources rather than for
Lowes's possible derivations from other sources (while occasionally considering the areas at which the two kinds of inquiry seem to overlap).

Even if, as regards its actual origin, we choose to accept without
question Coleridge's statement that the poem is the spontaneous product
of a dream (and thus arose without artistic purpose), when viewing it as
a work of art we must ask what kind of effect it "aims" to produce. I'd
propose to answer that question roundabout, thus:

In the *Poetics*, among the resources that Aristotle says contribute to
the effectiveness of tragedy as a literary species he lists a sense of the "marvelous" (*to thaumaston*). The overall purpose involved in tragedy is
"catharsis," while various other resources serve in one way or another to
make the sense of purgation most effective. The Cornelian "theater of
admiration" played down the principle of catharsis as exemplified in the
Attic plays. And it so altered the proportions of the tragic ingredients that
one particular kind of the "marvelous" (the cortège-like neoclassic pomp
of such plays' courtly style) rose in the scale from a means to an end. The
appeal to our sense of the marvelous takes many other forms, and among
the variations I would include Coleridge's great "Mystery" poems (or poems
of "Fascination"): "Kubla Khan," "The Ancient Mariner," and "Christabel." Indeed, they come closer to a sense of the marvelous that Aristotle
had in mind, since he was discussing ways whereby the playwright might
endow a plot with the aura of supernatural fatality; and in his *Biographia
Literaria* Coleridge says of his part in the volume of "Lyrical Ballads" containing work by him and Wordsworth:

> . . . it was agreed, that my endeavours should be directed to persons
> and characters supernatural, or at least romantic; yet so as to transfer
> from our inward nature a human interest and a semblance of truth
> sufficient to procure for these shadows of imagination that willing
> suspension of disbelief for the moment, which constitutes poetic faith.

And previously in the same text:

... the incidents and agents were to be, in part at least, supernatural; and the excellence aimed at was to consist in the interesting of the affections by the dramatic truth of such emotions, as would naturally accompany such situations, supposing them real. And real in *this* sense they have been to every human being who, from whatever source of delusion, has at any time believed himself under supernatural agency.

Though Coleridge does not mention "Kubla Khan" in this connection (it was not published at that time), when judged as a poem it obviously appeals by producing much the same kind of effect. That is, its *mystery* endows it with a feeling of *fatality*. Presumably "The Ancient Mariner" also had its "archetypal" origins in a dream, told to Coleridge by a friend of his, though greatly modified, as Wordsworth testifies, by Coleridge's own additions. And few works have a more strangely dreamlike quality than "Christabel." The sinister element that lies about the edges of these poems attains its blunt documentary completion in the nightmares of guilt, remorse, or woe he describes in "The Pains of Sleep," with such clinical testimony as the lines:

> The third night, when my own loud scream
> Had waked me from the fiendish dream,
> O'ercome with sufferings strange and wild,
> I wept as I had been a child;
> And having thus by tears subdued
> My anguish to a milder mood,
> My punishments, I said, were due
> To natures deepliest stained with sin,—
> For aye entempesting anew
> The unfathomable hell within,
> The horror of their deeds to view,
> To know and loathe, yet wish and do!
> Such griefs with such men well agree,
> But wherefore, wherefore fall on me?

Before considering "Kubla Khan" in detail, I cite this piece (which Coleridge himself specifically mentions as a "contrast") because of my conviction that it brings out the full implication of the sinister potentialities one finds faint traces of in the predominantly euphoric state symbolized by pleasure-dome, Edenic garden, and "a damsel with a dulcimer" (surely one of the most euphonious lines in the language). And now, to the poem in detail:

The first stanza, obviously, is the beatific vision of an Edenic garden, enclosed ("girdled round") in a circle of protection. In the third stanza the idea of encirclement will take on quite different connotations ("Weave a circle round him thrice"). To the generally recognized connotations of "Alph" as both "Alpheus" and "Alpha," I would offer but one addition;

yet I submit that it is essential to an understanding of many notable details in the poem. As I have tried to show in my *Grammar of Motives* (pp. 430-440 on "the temporizing of essence") and in my *Rhetoric of Religion* (particularly the section on "The First Three Chapters of *Genesis*"), the proper narrative, poetic, or "mythic" way to deal with fundamental motives is in terms of *temporal* priority. In this mode of expression, things deemed most basic are said to be *first in time*. So a river whose name suggests the first letter of the alphabet in an ancient language (one can as well hear the Hebrew form, "Aleph") is indeed well named. And fittingly, therefore, the forests are called "ancient as the hills." For this stanza is designed to convey in narrative, or "mythic" (or "archetypal") terms the very *essence* of felicity (the creative "joy" that, in his poignant ode, "Dejection," written about two years later, Coleridge will bemoan the permanent loss of, since his "genial spirits fail," and he "may not hope from outward forms to win / The passion and the life, whose fountains are within").

True, in the first stanza, there is no specific reference to a fountain. But when we recall the passage already quoted from a letter to his brother (concerning a "divine repose" that is like "a spot of enchantment, a green spot of fountain and flowers and trees in the very heart of a waste of sands"), we can see how, so far as the associations within Coleridge's private nomenclature were concerned, the reference to "sunny spots of greenery" (plus the connotations of Alph) had already set the terministic conditions for the explicit emergence of a fountain. And the thought might also induce us to ask whether, beyond such a "spot of enchantment" there might also be lurking some equivalent to the "waste of sands" for which it is medicinal.

In any case, given what we now know about the imagery of man's ideal beginnings, would we not take it for granted that the "caverns" traversed by the river are leading us "back" to such a "sunless sea" as the womb-heaven of the amniotic fluid by which the fetus was once "girdled round" in Edenic comfort? (In one of his fragments, Coleridge characteristically depicts a "sot" luxuriating on a couch and exclaiming: "Would that this were work—*utinam hoc esset laborare!*") In Lowes you can find literary "sources" for the fact that the caverns are "measureless." It is also a fact that they *should* be measureless for the simple reason that they connote an ideal time wholly alien to the knowledge of numbers. On the other hand, the garden spot is measured ("twice five miles") since such finiteness helps suggest connotations of protective enclosure, as with the medieval ideal of the *hortus conclusus* which Leo Spitzer has discussed in his monograph on "Milieu and Ambiance."

How far should we carry such speculations? We need not insist on it, but inasmuch as forests are of *wood* (thereby bringing us into the fate-laden Greek-Roman line of thought that commingles ideas of wood, matter, and mother: *hyle, dynamis, mater, materia, potentia*) the reference to them reinforces the feminine connotations of such a guarded and guardian garden.

So far as Coleridgean terminology in general is concerned, we might also note that green is not an unambiguous color. Christabel is to Geraldine as a dove is to a green snake coiled about her ("Swelling its neck as she swelled hers"). And when reading that Alph is a "sacred river," we might bear in mind the well-known but sometimes neglected etymological fact that in Latin usage either a priest or a criminal was *sacer*, as with the fluctuancies between French *sacre* and *sacré* (the same ambiguities applying to Greek *hagios* and to the Hebrew concept of the "set apart," *qodesh, qadesh*).

As for "stately": We might recall that Geraldine's bare neck was "stately" (l. 62). And cutting in from another angle, I might cite a prose passage that I consider so basic to Coleridge's thinking, I keep finding all sorts of uses for it. (See, for instance, *Permanence and Change*, Hermes edition, pp. 279-280.) It is from *The Friend*, where the exposition is divided into what he calls "landing-places." He is here discussing the sheer *form* of his presentation (the emphasis is mine):

> Among my *earliest* impressions I still distinctly remember that of my *first* entrance into the *mansion* of a neighboring baronet, *awfully* known to me by the name of the great house, its exterior having been long *connected in my childish imagination* with the *feelings and fancies* stirred up in me by the perusal of the Arabian Nights' Entertainments. Beyond all other objects, I was most struck with the magnificent staircase, relieved at well-proportioned intervals by spacious landing-places, this adorned with grand or showy plants, the next looking out on an extensive prospect through the *stately* window . . . while from the last and highest the eye commanded the *whole spiral ascent* with the marble pavement of the great hall; from which it seemed to spring up as if it merely used the ground on which it rested. My readers will find no difficulty in *translating these forms of the outward senses into their intellectual analogies.*

In sum, I'd say that references to the "decreeing" of this "stately pleasure-dome" combine connotations of infantile ("first" or "essential") felicity with concepts of hierarchal wonder. Though on its face the term fits well with the euphoria that so strikingly pervades the whole first stanza, and we shall later see the term applied to a hero, there is also the fact, as regards Coleridge's nomenclature in general, that it also applies to the sinister serpent-woman, Geraldine. Viewed in this light, it might be said to possess latent possibilities of trouble, an ambiguous announcement of a "problematical" theme that would become explicit later.

Similarly, despite my interpretation of "sunless" as uterine, I must concede its deathy connotations, particularly in view of the fact that the "sunless sea" will later be redefined as the "lifeless ocean." At best, we are on the edges of that midway, Life-in-Death stage which played so important a part in the sufferings of the Ancient Mariner. Or, otherwise put, any connotations of *rebirth* also imply connotations of *dying*.

In any case, the overall benignant tenor of the first stanza is so pronounced, the poetic conditions are set for a contrast, if the imaginative logic of the poem makes such a turn desirable. Thus, the second stanza is an amplification of the sinister meanings subsumed in the opening outcry: "But oh! that deep romantic chasm which slanted / Down the green hill athwart a cedarn cover!" On their face, chasms are cataclysmic, ghastly, and chaotic. "Athwart" on its face is troublous, to the extent that it has "thwart" in it. And as regards Coleridge's particular nomenclature, we might well adduce as evidence, from "Fears in Solitude," the lines, "the owlet Atheism, / Sailing on obscene wings athwart the noon," though part of the damage here may be associated also with the time of day, since it was "The bloody Sun, at noon" that visited such torture on the Ancient Mariner. (More on these lines later.)

Though you may have felt that I was straining things as regards the ambiguities of "sacred" in the first stanza, surely you will grant that in this middle stanza such disturbances come to the fore, as regards the synonym "holy" with reference to "A savage place! . . . enchanted" (recall the "spot of enchantment") and "haunted / By woman wailing for her demon-lover!" I take it that the theme of the demon lover will return in a slightly transformed state near the end of the poem. As for the phase of the moon, Lowes notes: It was under the aegis of the "waning moon" that the Mariner's cure began. (It would be more accurate to say his *partial* cure; for we should always remember that that "grey-beard loon" was subject to periodic *relapses*, and then his anguish again drove him to confess his sense of guilt.)

Coleridge has so beautifully interwoven description of *natural motions* with words for *human actions*, one is hardly aware of the shifts between the two kinds of verbs (beginning as early as the pleasure-dome, which is described as being *decreed*). Thus one hardly notes the "as if" in his reference to the "fast quick pants" with which the fountain is "breathing." All the descriptions are so saturated with *narrative*, one inevitably senses in them a principle of *personality*. (Ruskin's "pathetic fallacy" is carried to the point where everything is as active as in a picture by Breughel.) Though the observation applies to the poem throughout, we might illustrate the point by listing only the more obvious instances in the middle stanza: slanted, athwart, enchanted, waning, haunted, wailing, seething, breathing, forced, half-intermitted, vaulted, rebounding, flung up, meandering, ran, sank, heard, prophesying.

I would view this general hubbub as something more than a way of making descriptions vivid (though it certainly is at least that). I would take it also to indicate that this indeterminate mixture of motion and action is in effect a poetized *psychology*, detailing not what the reader is to *see* but what *mental states* he is thus empathically and sympathetically *imitating* as he reads.

I stress the notion because of my belief that it provides the answer to the problem of the "sunless sea" synonymized in the second stanza as a "lifeless ocean." Though the reciprocal relation between the destination of the river and the emergence of the fountain justifies one in looking upon them as standing for aspects of a life-force that bursts into creativity and sinks into death, I would contend that the central significance of this stream is somewhat more specific. The poem is figuring stages in a *psychology*—and in this sense the river is, first of all, the "stream of consciousness" (which is in turn inextricably interwoven with the river of *time*). That is, the design is not just depicting in general the course of *life and death*, plus connotations of rebirth. Rather, the poem is tracing in terms of imagery the very *form* of thinking (which is necessarily integral with a time process, inasmuch as the form of thinking must unfold through time.) It is as though, like Kantian transcendentalism, Coleridge were speculating epistemologically on the nature of consciousness, *except* that he is in effect talking of intuition in terms that are themselves the embodiment of what he is talking *about*. That's why Coleridge could say in his introduction to the poem:

> The Author ... could not have composed less than from two to three
> hundred lines; if that indeed can be called composition in which all
> the images rose up before him as *things*.

In this respect, I repeat, the poem could be viewed as a highly personal, *poetic* analogue of Kantian transcendentalism, which sought *conceptually* to think about itself until it ended in a schematization of the forms necessarily implicit in its very act of thinking.

I have several reasons for wanting to insist that the image of the sacred river, in its journey to and from an ultimate reservoir of the "sunless" or "lifeless," is to be viewed thus, as more specifically tied to the *psychology of idealism* than just a figuring of life and death in general. For one thing (as per my paper, "Thanatopsis for Critics: a Brief Thesaurus of Deaths and Dyings," *Essays in Criticism*, October 1952) since poets at their best write only what they profoundly know (and beyond all doubt, "Kubla Khan" is one kind of poetry at its best) and inasmuch as no living poet has experienced death, I take it for granted that, when a poet speaks of death, he is necessarily talking about something else, something witnessed *from without*, like a funeral, whereas this poem is wholly *from within*. Similarly, as regards fictions about the "supernatural," we need but consider the conduct of the "dead" sailors in "The Ancient Mariner" to realize that in the realm of the "supernatural" there *is* no death. Even in the "double death" of the orthodox Christian's Hell, the miserable wretches somehow carry on eternally. Or Whitman's paeans to Death indicate how Death becomes rather like the ultimate, maternal repository from which the forms of conscious life emerge (a pattern that also infuses thoughts on the ultimate end and source of things, in the second part of Goethe's *Faust*). Or think of the similar return to the "buttonmoulder," in *Peer Gynt*. And to cap things, recall Coleridge's "Epitaph," asking the reader to pray "That he who many a year with toil of breath / Found death in life, may here find life in death!"

Further, the realm of "essence" can never "die." For instance, what destruction of all existing life in the universe could alter the essential "fact" that, if *a* is greater than *b* and *b* is greater than *c*, then *a* is greater than *c*? And what obliteration can be so total as to alter the fact that Napoleon's character, or "essence," must go on having been exactly what it was?

If, on the other hand, we think of the river as more specifically interweaving the stream of time and the stream of consciousness (what Coleridge called the "streamy nature of association"), all comes clear. For there *is* a sense in which both time and thought continually hurry to their "death," yet are continually "reborn," since the death of one moment is incorporated in the moment that arises out of it, and the early stages of a thought process are embedded in its fulfillment. Nor should we forget Coleridge's original declared intention with regard to the "supernatural, or at least romantic" as a device to transfer from our "inward nature" various "shadows of imagination."

For these reasons, if you choose to see the river and the fountain as figuring ultimately the course of life and death, I'd ask you at least to think of these more specific "transcendental" qualifications as relevant adjectives to your nouns. And certainly a note like this, in the Gutch Memorandum Notebook, is on our side: "There is not a new or strange opinion—Truth returns from banishment—a river run underground—fire beneath embers—." Also, in his Notebooks, when saying that in the best part of one's nature man must be solitary, he adds: "Man exists herein to himself & to God alone—Yea, in how much only to God—how much lies *below* his own Consciousness."

In any case, there is no questioning the fact that the Coleridgean nomenclature elsewhere does clearly give us personal (moral, psychological) equivalents for fountains and streams with mazy motion. The most relevant for our purposes is in "Dejection," a poem specifically concerned with the loss of such impulsive poetic ability as distinguishes "Kubla Khan":

> My genial spirits fail;
> And what can these avail
> To lift the smothering weight from off my breast?
> It were a vain endeavour,
> Though I should gaze for ever
> On that green light that lingers in the west:
> I may not hope from outward forms to win
> The passion and the life, whose fountains are within.

In an expression some years later, he gives the word a decidedly moral twist, in referring to "my conscience, the sole fountain of certainty." In one letter, he refers to "the pure fountain of all my moral religious feelings and comforts,—I mean the absolute Impersonality of the Deity." And in a formal letter of condolence, written before the production of "Kubla Khan," he had given us a related moral significance for "chaff": "The pestilence of our lusts must be scattered, the strong-layed Foundations of our Pride blown up, and the stubble and chaff of our Vanities burnt, ere we can give ear to the inspeaking Voice of Mercy, 'Why *will* ye die?' " True, Lowes finds references to fountains that hurled forth various kinds of fragments, but he also cites a reference to an "inchanting and amazing chrystal fountain"; hence so far as "sources" in his sense are concerned, Coleridge could just as well have given us a fountain *without* "chaff." Thus, from the standpoint of "mythic" or "archetypal" sources, I'd say that Coleridge's creative fountain was a bit "problematical," as with the countertheme of this stanza generally; in effect this spirited (or breathy) upheaval had not yet separated the wheat from the tares, though it was intensely involved in the process of doing so.[1]

"Mazy" is a word that turns up often in Coleridge. It's as characteristically his as "dim." (Though there is no "dim" in the poem itself, the introduction quotes lines that refer to "the fragments dim of lovely forms.") And if you want the range of troublous moral connotations that are packed into that word "mazy," consult a passage in "Religious Musings" (an earlier, somewhat bombastic poem that Charles Lamb greatly admired). Here Enmity, Mistrust, "listening Treachery" and War are said to falsely defend the "Lamb of God" and "Prince of Peace," whom

> . . . (in their songs
> So bards of elder times had haply feigned)
> Some Fury fondled in her hate of man,
> Bidding her serpent hair in mazy surge
> Lick his young face, and at his mouth imbreathe
> Horrible sympathy!

"Religious Musings" is quite a storehouse for expressions that reveal the moral implications in many of the most characteristic images found in the Mystery, or "Fascination," Poems.

Though Lowes cites a text that refers to the prophecy of war (and in connection with *Abyssinia* even, an associative preparation, if you will, of

---

[1] In *Anima Poetae* there is an apostrophe "to a former friend" who, Coleridge says, was once a part of him, "even as the chaff to corn." The note ends bitterly: "But since that time, through whose fault I will be mute, I have been thrashed out by the flail of experience. Because you have been, therefore, never more can you be a part of the grain." May we thus take the spurt of the fountain to symbolize a personal condition prior to such dissociative "flailing"? (One might also mention some discarded lines from "The Ancient Mariner," regarding the tempest: "For days and weeks it play'd us freaks— / Like Chaff we drove along.")

the corresponding adjective in the final stanza), I'd view the line, "Ancestral voices propsheying war," as a narrative way of saying in effect: This tumultuous scene is *essentially* interwoven with such motives as we connote by the term "war." Or, otherwise put: The war that is to break out *subsequently* is *already implicit* in the nature of things *now*. That is, I would interpret it as a typical stylistic device for the "temporizing of essence." Such is always the significance of "portents," that detect the *presence* of the future.

The stanza does not conclude by a simple return to the pleasure-dome of the opening; for three notable details are added: We now learn of the dome's "shadow"; it is said to have "floated midway" on the waves; and the caves are said to be "of ice." Let us consider these additions.

In "The Ancient Mariner" we read that "where the ship's huge shadow lay, / The charmèd water burnt alway / A still and awful red." In a letter to Southey, written about three years after the probable production of "Kubla Khan," Coleridge says regarding troubles with his wife that his sleep "became the valley of the shadows of Death." (The same letter refers to "her inveterate habits of puny thwarting," a phrase which please bear in mind for later reference, "and unintermitting dyspathy," where the reader must decide for himself whether the participle throws connotative light upon the poem's reference to the fountain's "half-intermitted burst.") In the explicitly moralistic use of imagery in "Religious Musings," we are told that "Life is a vision shadowy of Truth; / And vice, and anguish, and the wormy grave, / Shapes of a dream!"

At this point it's almost imperative that we introduce an aside. For the pejorative reference to "shapes" all but *demands* our attention. "Shape" is characteristically a troublous word in Coleridgese. Thus, in "Religious Musings," see "pale Fear / Haunted by ghastlier shapings than surround / Moon-blasted Madness when he yells at midnight." Likewise, the ominous supernatural specter-bark of "The Ancient Mariner" was "A speck, a mist, a shape." In "The Pains of Sleep" he refers to "the fiendish crowd / Of shapes and thoughts" that "tortured" him. Many other usages could be adduced here. And though, in "Dejection," Coleridge explicitly regrets that he has lost his "shaping Spirit of Imagination," in one of his letters written during the same *annus mirabilis* when the first version of "The Ancient Mariner" and the first part of "Christabel" came into being, he speaks of his body as "diseased and fevered" by his imagination. Nor should we forget the essentially ironic situation underlying "The Eolian Harp," a poem that begins as an address to his wife, but develops into a vision of beatific universal oneness; whereupon he forgets all about his "pensive Sara," until he sees her "mild reproof"—and four lines after the appearance of his characteristic word "dim," he apologizes for "These shapings of the unregenerate mind."

So much for "shadow," and its membership in a cluster of terms that include pejorative or problematical connotations of "shape." "Float" is much less strongly weighted on the "bad" side than "shadow" and "shape." Things can float either malignly or benignly, as with the Mariner's boat at different stages in its journey. In Coleridge's play "Remorse" there is a passage that suggests Shelley's typical kind of idealistically easygoing boat:

> It were a lot divine in some small skiff
> Along some ocean's boundless solitude
> To float forever with a careless course
> And think myself the only being alive!

Thus in "Religious Musings," we read of Edenic delights that "float to earth." But in the same text there are "floating mists of dark idolatry" that "Broke and misshaped the omnipresent Sire." The poem itself has an interesting ambiguous usage, where talk of "Moulding Confusion" with "plastic might" (the Greek derivative "plastic" being his consistently "good" word for "shaping") leads into talk of "bright visions" that "float." And somewhere in between, there is a letter: "My thoughts are floating about in an almost chaotic state." So, when in the next stanza you come to the "floating hair," you are presumably on a ridge that slopes both ways. And the only fairly sure grounds for deciding which way it slopes is given to us on the surface: the accompanying cry, "Beware! Beware!"

We shall consider later the strategic term "midway." But before leaving it for the present, I'd like to suggest that, as regards Coleridge's poem "Love" (which transforms his troubled courtship of Sara Hutchinson into an allegory of knighthood), I doubt whether, under the modern dispensation, he'd have included the line, "When midway on the mount I lay."

We now have only the ice to deal with, and we shall have finished our consideration of the ways in which the closing lines of Stanza Two are not just a return to the theme of Stanza One, but a return *with a difference*. And that difference resides *precisely* in the addition of details more in keeping with the countertheme, though ambigouously so (yet not quite so ambiguously, if we read the poem not just as English, but as one particular poetic dialect of English, one vatic nomenclature subtly or implicitly different from all others).

Lowes (as might be expected!) turns up some caverns of ice in another text that Coleridge presumably read (even a quite rare kind of ice that waxes and wanes with the phases of the moon). But we still contend that a "source" in that sense is not relevant to our present problem. For we need but assume that the source chose to talk about ice for the same reason that Coleridge incorporated what had been said in the source; namely: because "ice" has a set of "mythic" or "archetypal" connotations which recommend it to a poet's attention. And we are concerned with "derivation" in that "nonhistoric" but poetically "principled" sense.

It is obvious enough what kind of attitude is linked with the iciness of ice in "The Ancient Mariner." There, ice is purely and simply a horror. And ice is unambiguously unpleasant, insofar as it stands for coldness in the sense that Coleridge had in mind when, in the letter to Southey about his wife's "puny thwarting," he characterized her as "cold in sympathy." And we are still to discuss Coleridge's play, *Remorse*, where "fingers of ice" are located in a "chasm" within a "cavern." (Here the sound of water dropping in the darkness is likened to "puny thwartings.") But regardless of what ominous implications may lurk in the ice, on its face the reference is euphoric.

We are now ready for the windup. In terms of the Hegelian pattern, we should expect the final stanza (a kind of poem-within-a-poem) to "synthesize" the two movements that have gone before. It does so. For the vision of the "Abyssinian maid" is clearly *beatific*, yet the beholder of the vision (as presented in terms of the poem) is also to be identified with *sinister* connotations (as with those that explicitly emerge just after a recurrent reference to the "caves of ice"). I refer to the cry, "Beware! Beware!"—and to the development that transforms malignly the principle of encirclement (introduced benignly in Stanza One).[2]

As for the fact that the maid in the vision is said to be "Abyssinian": Derive her as you will along the lines of sources in other books, there's still a tonal likelihood that the lady is "Abyssinian" because, among other things, as so designated she contains within this name for her essence the syllables that spell "abyss." And there, roundabout, would be the "chasm," euphorically transmuted for the last phase.

As for "Mount Abora": Regardless of its possible derivation from other texts (as Lowes suggests), in accordance with theories of "musicality in verse" that I have discussed elsewhere (in connection with Coleridge, an essay reprinted in my book, *The Philosophy of Literary Form*), I would lay great stress upon the fact that *m* and *b* are close tonal cognates, hence these vocables come very close to "Singing of Mount Amora," which is understandable enough.

As for the lines, "Could I revive within me / Her symphony and song": I see in them the euphorically tinged adumbration of the outcry that was to turn up, in "Dejection," only a few years later.

---

[2] This "synthesis" might also be viewed as a belated or misplaced "prothesis," Coleridge's own word for the kind of unity that *precedes* a division into thesis and antithesis. For, once the stages of a sequence are telescoped into terms of the principle that *underlies* the lot, who is to say whether this is a "first" (the *terminus a quo*) from which the narrative, or quasi-temporal sequence follows or the "last" (the *terminus ad quem*) in which it culminates? There is an eschatology of radical form (the secular equivalent of the theological notion according to which "God" is both "efficient" Cause and "final" Cause, the beginning and the end).

For some reason that it's hard to be clear about, though in a letter Coleridge admonished his son Hartley "not to speak so loud," again and again he applies this epithet to music (even to the bassoon, in "The Ancient Mariner," though that instrument cannot be loud, so far as sheer decibels go). All I can offer, along these lines, is the possibility of a submerged pun, as indicated by an early poem in which Coleridge speaks of "loud, lewd Mirth." Might "loud" *deflectively* connote "lewd," in the depths of the Coleridgean nomenclature? I won't assert so, but there does seem to be the possibility (though it would be a tough one to prove, even if it were absolutely true). In the meantime, we must simply await further advices.

The cavern scenes in Act IV of *Remorse* might well be mentioned in greater detail, since they help so greatly to reveal the sinister possibilities lurking beneath the surface of the terms in "Kubla Khan." Seen in a dream, the cave is "haunted," the villain appearing to his victim in "a thousand fearful shapes." There is a morbid dalliance with "shadows." The threat implicit in the very idea of a chasm is brought out explicitly by the nature of the plot, as the villain hurls his victim "down the chasm." (Chasms, that is, are implicitly a kind of gerundive, a to-be-bewared-of, a to-be-hurled-into). And whereas we are told that the "romantic chasm" of the euphoric poem "slanted / Down," these apparently innocuous words are seen to have contained, about their edges, malign connotations; for in the victim's premonitory dream of his destruction in *Remorse*, we learn that his foot hung "aslant adown" the edge. At the end of the act, the woman who is to be the *avenger* announces, "The moon hath moved in Heaven, and I am here," (a remarkable transformation of the prime motivating line in "The Ancient Mariner": "The moving Moon went up the sky").[3] At the start of the last act, the circle appears at its worst: "Circled with evil." (A previous reference to a threatening circle of people surrounding the villain had appeared in the stage directions.) A reference to the "fascination" in the eye of the hero (whom the loving heroine calls "stately") marks the spot from which I would derive the term, "Fascination Poems" as an alternative to "Mystery Poems."

In the light of our analysis, it should be easy to understand why, in the closing poem-within-a-poem, the references to the poet (who is ambiguously one with both the dream and the dreamer) should be so surrounded with connotations of admonition. Yet the poem is essentially euphoric. Hence, even though we are told to *beware*, and to view with *holy dread* (or rather, to deflect-our-eyes-from) the poet who both is this marvel and has conceived it, we end on *Paradise*.

Returning now to a point we postponed when considering "midway on the waves," should we not take into consideration the fact that in the

---

[3] Is the work of "moved" and "moving" done by "momently" in "Kubla Khan"?

middle stanza the notion appears not once but four times: The other explicit
places are: "Amid whose swift half-intermitted burst"; "And 'mid these
dancing rocks"; "And 'mid this tumult"—while a strong trace of the pattern
is also observable in "half-intermitted" and "the mingled measure / From
the fountain and the caves." (I take it that "measure," in contrast with
"measureless," includes connotations of poetic measure.)

At the risk of being charged with oversubtlety, I'd propose to view
that design (a kind of *spatial fixity* in these many motions and actions and
action-like motion) as a matter of basic significance. As regards the underlying principle of the poem (its essence or character as a *unity*) these conflicting elements (the beatific and the sinister) are but what we might
Spinozistically call two attributes of a common substance. Thus, in the last
analysis, the stages of its unfolding melt into a simultaneity, a nodus of
motivation that stands "midway" between the extremes. (A stanza of "Religious Musings" where Saints "sweep athwart" the poet's "gaze," develops
into agitation thus: "For who of woman born may paint the hour, / When
seized in his mid course, the Sun shall wane / Making noon ghastly!" I'd
hardly dare press the point; but we might at least recall that the midday sun
transfixed the Mariner's boat, and Christabel's troubles took place at midnight. And anyone who is concerned with the strange magic of reversal, as
in formulas like "Ave Eva," might also pause to note however uneasily that,
quite as Cummings in "God" saw "dog spelled backwards," so "mid" is but
a chiastic form of Coleridge's ubiquitous "dim.")

However, even if there is a sense in which the generating principle
represented by this poem's action is itself as much an unmoved mover as
Aristotle's God (with even an analogue of "negative theology" in "sunless,"
"lifeless," "measureless," and "ceaseless"), there is also the fact that, as
"broken down" into a quasi-temporal sequence, the translation of this essential unity into a series of successive revelations (or tiny "apocalypses")
can *begin* with a reference to an Edenic garden, and *end* on the word "Paradise." In this sense, despite the intrinsic immobility of the poem's organizing
principle (a "midway" situation that found more explicit dissociative expression in "The Ancient Mariner," both in the figure of the motionless
boat, and in the specter, "The Night-mare Life-in-Death"); despite the fact
that while the narrative relation between rising fountain and sinking river
goes on "turning," the *principle* behind the unfolding is "forever still"; despite these ups and downs en route, the poem as a whole can be called
"euphoric."

We are now ready to take up the problem that arises from our insistence upon calling the poem *finished* whereas the author himself called
it a "fragment." Here I can best make my point by quoting a passage from
my *Philosophy of Literary Form* (Vintage edition, pp. 26-27):

Imagine an author who had laid out a five-act drama of the rational, intricate, intrigue sort—a situation that was wound up at the start, and was to be unwound, step by step, through the five successive acts. Imagine that this plot was scheduled, in Act V, to culminate in a scene of battle. Dramatic consistency would require the playwright to "foreshadow" this battle. Hence, in Act III, he might give us the battle incipiently, or implicitly, in a vigorous battle of words between the antagonists. But since there was much business still to be trans-acted, in unwinding the plot to its conclusion he would treat Act III as a mere foreshadowing of Act V, and would proceed with his composition until the promises emergent in Act III had been ful-filled in Act V.

On the other hand, imagine a "lyric" plot that had reduced the in-trigue business to a minimum. When the poet had completed Act III, his job would be ended, and despite his intention to write a work in five acts, he might very well feel a loss of inclination to continue into Acts IV and V. For the act of foreshadowing, in Act III, would already *implicitly contain* the culmination of the promises. The battle of words would itself be the *symbolic equivalent* of the mortal com-bat scheduled for Act V. Hence, it would *serve as surrogate* for the *quality* with which he had intended to end Act V, whereat the poet would have no good reason to continue further. He would "lose interest"—and precisely because the quality of Act V had been "telescoped" into the quality of Act III that foreshadowed it (and in foreshadowing it, was of the same substance or essence). Act III would be a kind of ejaculation too soon, with the purpose of the composition forthwith dwindling.

Does not this possibility solve our problem? I believe that, in prin-ciple at least, Coleridge actually did dream all those lines, and transcribed them somewhat as an amanuensis might have done. For nearly every writer has jotted down a few bits that he woke up with, and there's no reason why someone couldn't wake up with more. And Mozart apparently could con-ceive of a work all finished before he wrote it down, so that in effect the act of composition was but the translating of a timeless unity (like a painting or piece of sculpture) into a temporal progression (quite as the observer "reads histories" into a static form when he lets his eye wander from place to place across it, thereby "improvising" developments within its parts). And even a long and complex structure which one works out painfully step by step may involve but the progressive "discovery" of implications already present in the "germ" that set him off in the first place. Why had it even struck him as worth working on, if it had not been for him like a knotted bundle of possibilities which he would untie one by one, as the loosening of each knot set the conditions for the loosening of the next (like a psychoanalyst's patient discovering by free association things that he somehow already knew but didn't know he knew)?

But "Kubla Khan" was the kind of poem that Coleridge's own aesthetic theories were not abreast of. His very attempts to distinguish between "Imagination" and "Fancy" at the expense of the latter serve to indicate my point. "Fancy" wouldn't come into its own until the time of Rimbaud, when it would take on dimensions that Coleridge never explicitly attributed to it. For his concept of Fancy got mixed up with purely mechanical doctrines of associationism which he strongly rejected (a kind of resistance that was probably also tied up with his moralistic attempts to resist the compulsive aspects of his addiction to opium, when it became integrated with the fountain of his creativity). In any case, at the very start of his collaboration with Wordsworth in plans for the "Lyrical Ballads," the kind of job he set himself really involved an ideal of "Fancy" (but not in the partly pejorative sense that the term took on, in the dialectic of his *Biographia Literaria*). And as an integral aspect of such possibilities there would be the kind of imagistic short-circuiting to which I have referred in my quotation from *Philosophy of Literary Form*.

Thus, when one contemporary critic finds that the expression, "ancestral voices prophesying war" is "too pointless," since "no further use is made of it," the objection would be like contending that, in Eliot's "Gerontion," a line such as "By Hakagawa, bowing among the Titians" is "pointless" because we learn nothing more about Hakagawa. On the contrary, as I have tried to show, the line does to perfection exactly what it is there for, as a narrative way of stating a motivational essence. Yvor Winters' label, "Reference to a non-existent plot," to characterize such usages as Eliot's, helps us see that Coleridge's poem was already moving towards a later elliptical manner, at a time when Southey could have turned "Kubla Khan" into a work as long as *The Ring and the Book*. In this sense, the poem was a "fragment." But it is complete insofar as no further movements are needed (or even possible, without the poem's becoming something else, as when one dream fades into another). The most one can imagine is the addition of a few details that amplify what is already sufficiently there.[4]

All told, the more closely we study the poem in the light of Coleridge's particular nomenclature, the more fully we realize how many of the terms have sinister connotations, as regards their notable use in other contexts. Imagery lends itself well to such shiftiness, and readily transcends the law of excluded middle. In fact, such susceptibility doubtless accounts for much of its appeal, since it can so spontaneously bridge the gulfs of dispute, and

---

[4] By the same token there is the embarrassing fact that, the more efficient the poet's brevity, the greater is the need for the critic to expatiate, in trying to show how condensed the work really is.

can simultaneously confess and be reticent. In line with contemporary interests, one might note that Coleridge explicitly equates the image of the fountain with the principle of what would now be called "creativity." On this point, in addition to references already cited, we might recall in his preface to "Christabel," his objections to "a set of critics . . . who have no notion that there are such things as fountains in the world, small as well as great." At another place he distinguishes between "Springs" and "tanks" ("two Kinds of Heads in the world of literature"). Elsewhere, when on the subject of "knowing" and "being," he sums up by thoughts on "the common fountain-head of both, the mysterious source whose being is knowledge, whose knowledge is being—the adorable I AM IN THAT I AM." In *Anima Poetae* he writes: "Nota bene to make a detailed comparison, in the manner of Jeremy Taylor, between the searching for the first cause of a thing and the seeking the fountains of the Nile—so many streams, each with its particular fountains—and, at last, it all comes to a name." Another note beautifully illustrates how the image takes on other connotations of delight: "Some wilderness-plot—green & fountainous & unviolated by Man." But "creativity" also has its *risks*. And whether or not you would agree that the "problematic" element was heightened in Coleridge's case by the interweaving of the Mystery Poems with the early stages of opium addiction, it still remains a fact that in "Kubla Khan" as enacted in detail, the principle of inspiration is simultaneously welcomed and feared (a secular attitude properly analogous to the theologians' doubts whether a vision of the divine is truly from God or from the Devil in disguise).[5]

---

[5] In later years, in his theological work, *Aids to Reflection*, when on the subject of Mysticism (a term which he explicitly says he is using in "a bad sense."), it is interesting to see how Coleridge allegorizes his theories by reapplying the imagery of his Mystery Poems (thus in effect saying that Mystery is to poetry as Mysticism is to religion). However, the Mystics to whom he is objecting are men for whom he had great affection (such as Boehme and Fenelon). He explicitly refers to "The Ancient Mariner," "Christabel," and "The Wanderings of Cain" in connection with his allegory, using the "creations" of his youthful fancy to illustrate the "errors" of Mysticism. (Note "Fancy," not "Imagination," though he had already published his *Biographia Literaria* in which Fancy was downgraded.) There is "an oasis or Islet of Verdure on the Sea of Sand"; a pilgrim here "wanders at leisure in its maze of beauty and sweetness." Moonshine is "the imaginative poesy of nature" that spreads "its soft shadowy form over all." Thus, if you "Interpret the moonlight and the shadows as the peculiar genius and sensibility of the individual's own spirit," you get but "a dream of truth," while in another connection there is "truth mingled with the dream." There is a wanderer who has "eaten of the fruits and drunk of the fountain," has been "scared by the roar and howl from the desert [sic]," and is confused because "shadows and imperfect beholdings and vivid fragments of things distinctly seen blend with the past and present shapings of his brain." There is a narrator whose "craving for sympathy . . . impels him to unbosom himself to abstract auditors." There is talk of an "enchanted land" and "refreshing caves." Throughout, the reservations on Mysticism are thus spoken of mildly and sympathetically. But the mood grows harsh when the subject shifts from Mysticism to Materialism, whereupon Coleridge says of Materialism and Subjective

ADDENDUM: I have here given the paper as written prior to a discussion of the poem in a seminar at the University of California, Santa Barbara, in the fall of 1964. I presented the substance of these pages in a lecture there, on the same day when members of the class submitted their own analyses, worked out independently of my observations. Some of their papers, and the discussion that followed, have led me to sharpen up the overall outline of the poem thus:

The fountain is so obviously scandalous when its behavior is considered from the psychoanalytic point of view, it prompts students to offer many ingenious speculations along those lines, ranging between extremes of heterosexual and homosexual motivations. The tendency is to lay great stress upon the orgastic aspects of the fountain's ejaculatory ways. I would but ask that any such interpretations do not confine themselves to the *erotic*, but also deal with the *familial* aspects of the imagination. Viewed in such wider terms, the steps in the poem could be summed up thus:

Kubla Khan's decree is the romantic counterpart of God's authoritative (parental, creative) fiat. The pleasure-dome and encircled garden are the analogue of happily enclosed Edenic *innocence*.

The fountain and the chasm figure the *fall*, as personalized in the wailing woman (the erotic woman) and the demon-lover.

When the lines that revert to the first theme add the shadow and the ice, the stage of "innocence" has been radically modified. It now confronts a conscience-laden way of life overshadowed by connotations of frigidity, or castration. Innocence being lost, there can at best be the straining after virtue.

The final synthesis (the song-within-a-song) reveals the personal figure that was missing in the garden (perhaps because the garden did itself stand for that figure in being inchoately maternal). If Kubla Khan is the father, and the poet is the child who had left the garden and erred, then the "damsel" is the counterpart of Mary, the heavenly mother, *gratia plena*, the erotic woman replaced by the maternal woman (*eros* replaced by *agape*), plus romantic ambiguities. The poet now grown up, is "set apart" by his profession, a role at once sacred and criminal. And appropriately the *hoi polloi* of everyday society are apostrophized and admonished with regard to him. The poem, in brief, is a "break down" of the romantic passion, involving analogues of the concern with "beginnings" in the book of Genesis.

Idealism: "the one obtruding on us a World of Spectres and Apparitions; the other a mazy Dream!"

In *Confessions of an Inquiring Spirit*, there is a passage that faintly suggests the kind of imagery with which "Kubla Khan" was concerned. But here the strong stress upon the fountainheads of creativity has definitely given way to image-tinged thoughts on life in general: "The unsubstantial, insulated Self passes away as a stream; but these are the shadows and reflections of the Rock of Ages, and of the Tree of Life that starts forth from its side."

The principles of what, in current cant, is called "creativity" are here stated narratively. Though they all imply one another (as a cycle of interrelated terms) they are here reduced to a sequence. There is a "problematical" element implicit in such romantically spontaneous waywardness; and biographical data permit us to speculate on the further possibility (lying outside the realm of poetics proper) that the fountain of productivity had also become interwoven with the instabilities of drug addiction (though in this particular poem, while the admonitory element is present the stress is predominantly euphoric).

In general, the papers that favored psychoanalytic modes of interpretation omitted what I have called the important *familial* aspect of the poem's development, and thus slighted the problem of accounting for the *successive stages* of the poem. Also, one member of the class contended that the poem could not be fully developed because a fuller development would have involved too much "self-revelation." To this notion I would only add the fact that there is a sheerly *formal* reason why any such implications could not be made explicit. For they would necessarily introduce doctrinal terms alien to the work's nature as a poetic species (somewhat as a "scientific" theory of "guilt" is alien to the experience of guilt in its intuitive immediacy). True, one might go back a bit farther, and note that all poems relying strongly upon imagery permit of much reticence, even in the midst of *implied* "confession." But by the same token, any *explicit* step outside this charmed circle is the fault of the reader or critic, not of the poet, intrinsic to whose "reticently" ambiguous medium is the rejoinder, *honi soit qui mal y pense.*

In closing I should also refer to a delightful article on "Kubla Khan" by Miss Kathleen Raine in the Autumn, 1964 issue of the *Sewanee Review.* I am happy to note that she allows for the "abyss" in "Abyssinia," hence I can retreat behind her authority. Also, she rightly points to Abyssinia's association with the symbolic motives implicit in Coleridge's Thoughts on the Sources of the Nile.

And her remarks on the dulcimer are a major contribution. I refer to her reminding us that it is "a one-stringed instrument, the monochord," upon which the Pythagoreans worked out their theory of the diatonic scale, and their application of it to the structure of the universe. Accordingly, when Coleridge's damsel plays a dulcimer, "she plays upon the chords of harmony which underlie all creation." It is most exciting to realize that Coleridge's line, so lovely as sheer music, has this added "doctrinal" backing.

But when Miss Raine comments on the Platonic doctrine of "anamnesis," I dare avow that, until critics get my point about the "temporizing of essence" (as discussed particularly in my *Grammar of Motives* and *Rhetoric of Religion*) they will not grasp the sheerly *linguistic* principle underlying the relationship between "mythic" and "philosophic" terms for "beginnings." Such analysis is needed to explain the position of the quasi-narrative "archetypes" that Plato's nomenclature situates midway between terms for logical priority and terms for temporal priority. It involves what I would call the step from a "mythological" to a "logological" study of such poetic structures as "Kubla Khan," with its obvious *bearing upon the very rudiments of poetic genesis.*

Chapter Eight

Social and Cosmic Mystery:
A Passage to India

I

Preparatory Definition

How begin? Three methods suggest themselves. In accordance with my "thesis," which is vaguely indicated in the title, I might say that I propose to treat E. M. Forster's novel rather as social comedy than in terms of cosmic mystery, though my analysis will qualify that formula somewhat. Or I might start with a generalized outline of the plot (particularly relevant in this case, since two quite different kinds of outline are feasible). Or I might propose a tentative definition of the book as a literary species, and work into it concretely by considering the various clauses of the definition. In choosing this third way-in, I do not pause to ask whether the definition would cover many books, or amounts to a treatment of this one as *sui generis*:

1) "A long realistic prose narrative, tinged with mystery, and employing dialogue and description." (I am not wholly happy with the word "tinged"; perhaps "enriched" or "embellished" would be better. But at least we may recall that in Aristotle's definition a metaphor is applied to "diction," which is said to be "seasoned" (or more literally "sweetened") by rhythm and melodiousness.

2) "The descriptions treat of the overall situation, of the particular scenes in which the many episodes take place, of the mental attitudes involved in the agents' acts and relationships, and of crises wherein private relations merge into the behavior of groups." This clause refers to the inclusive ways in which geological, historical, psychological, and sociological observations are used for poetic purposes.

3) "Though the descriptions contribute functionally to the total context, at times they have a design that sets them off like arias in music." I include this clause primarily because of my urgent conviction that the five paragraphs of Chapter XII (the description of the Marabar Caves) form an especially remarkable progression.

The first paragraph deals with the region in the most general sense, going back even to times of the "immemorial" and "prehistoric." It ends on a reference to "the incredible antiquity of these hills."

The second paragraph, with a sprinkling of negatives such as "un-touched," "unspeakable," "insanely," "uncanny," "unfrequented," envisions a time when this "primal" India that was "older than all spirit" and had never been covered by water, might sink beneath the sea, since it is already being silted over by the deposits of the Ganges.

The third paragraph describes the caves in general, their "extraordinary" nature, their total lack of differentiation. A visitor "finds it difficult to discuss the caves, or to keep them apart in his mind, for the pattern never varies, and no carving, not even a bee's-nest or a bat distinguishes one from another."

This stress upon their endless repetitiveness is an especially effective aspect of the description, and serves well as a transition into the theme of the fourth paragraph, where everything centers on a description of how a light behaves, when a burning match is mirrored in the "marvellously polished" walls. While the sense of the unbridgeable division between the flame and its reflection is, on its face, a merely picturesque description that incidentally treats the two as lovers close yet permanently and inexorably divided from each other, the figure also bears implicitly upon a major aspect of the plot.

The final stanza completes this principle of separation by culminating in as near an absolute as one could convey in terms of images. For all comes to a focus here in the thought of a cave that has no entrance tunnel, "a bubble-shaped cave that has neither ceiling nor floor, and mirrors its own darkness in every direction infinitely." The theme of a reflection has here come to completion in an image of total reflexivity, an ultimate withinness-of-withinness. And, fittingly, it is rife with negatives. At this point I should make clear: I would not view such a profusion of negatives as a mere in-stance of what some psychologists would call "negativism." Rather, I see it as a partly secular variant of what we encounter in "negative theology," that describes God as *in*comprehensible, *un*bounded, *un*ending, etc.

There are many other passages that have the quality of set pieces; and above all, we should mention the delightful episode at the end of Chapter VII, where the unctuous Brahmin, Professor Godbole, explains the song which he has been singing, and which had captured the attention of the native servants:

> "It was a religious song. I placed myself in the position of a milk-maiden. I say to Shri Krishna, 'Come! come to me only.' The god refuses to come. I grow humble and say: 'Do not come to me only. Multiply yourself into a hundred Krishnas, and let one go to each of my hundred companions, but one, O Lord of the Universe, come to me.' He refuses to come. This is repeated several times. The song is composed in a raga appropriate to the present hour, which is the evening."

"But he comes in some other song, I hope?" said Mrs. Moore gently.

"Oh no, he refuses to come," repeated Godbole, perhaps not understanding her question. "I say to Him, Come, come, come, come, come, come. He neglects to come."

Ronny's steps had died away, and there was a moment of absolute silence. No ripple disturbed the water, no leaf stirred.

But there is still one clause of the definition to be considered:

4) "The story is told from a novelistic point of view that transcends the perspective of any one character, and that is designed to evoke in the reader a mood of ironically sympathetic contemplation." It is essentially a comic mood, and essentially humane (in that the vices depicted in the book are viewed not as villainy, but as folly).

II
Situation

Let us now reverse things, by beginning with this last statement. Obviously, I am proposing that (for the definition of this modern Liberal novel, considered as a literary species) my formula, "designed to evoke in the reader a mood of ironically sympathetic contemplation" replaces the words "through pity and fear effecting the catharsis of such emotions" in Aristotle's recipe for Athenian tragedy. The project now lines up thus:

Note, first, how well the plot and the situation serve to provide us with the *materials* for a comedy of ironically sympathetic contemplation. The muddle of castes and classes in India itself, capped by the essential conflict between the natives and the British officials (whom one of their own compatriots refers to ironically as the "Army of Occupation"), allows for a maximum of interesting embarrassments in personal relations. Everybody is subtly at odds with everybody else; every situation treated by Forster acutely involves the "mysteries" that result from marked social differentiation—and these are further accentuated by the fact that, since India is in a state of acute transition, along with the *traditional formalities* due to such a clutter of social ratings there is much *improvising of protocol*. The embarrassments of the "Bridge Party" in which the British and the natives are expected to "bridge" their "gulf" are a good instance of improvised protocol. And precisely such embarrassed improvisings set up the conditions for the incident about which the whole plot hinges. I refer to the turn that takes place when the honest but sexually muddled English girl, Adela, who has accused the Mohammedan, Aziz, of making advances to her in one of the Marabar Caves, suddenly retracts her charge, to the utter confusion of her British champions and the orgiastic delight of the natives (for surely one of the most gratifying developments in the story is the scene of impromptu revelry that follows the abrupt termination of the trial).

Another notable form which the improvising takes is to be seen in the tentative relationship between this same Mohammedan, Aziz, and the prospective mother-in-law of the English girl, whose fiancé is one of the British officials (and a perfect exemplar of what in the novel is called "officialism"). There is a correspondingly tentative relationship between the girl and the administrator—for in this book the embarrasments of *empire* invariably have counterparts in *sexual* embarrassments, be they between members of the same or opposite sexes.[1]

If one stops, at this point, to say in outline form what this story is about, over the years students have taught me that the plot can be epitomized in two quite different ways. The first concerns a girl who is visiting a colony, where she hopes to make up her mind about marrying an official (like her, a citizen of the colonial power). The situation is so set up that she accuses a native of making advances to her in a cave, then she retracts the accusation. The colonialists, all except one, spontaneously line up against the native. The one, Fielding, sides with the native. For the two had become friends, despite the embarrassments of empire. But after the native is exonerated, the book closes on the theme of parting, since the native refuses to continue their friendship so long as his country is subject to imperial rule. The cause of ironic contemplation here is particularly favored by an ingenious development of the plot whereby the incidents of *personal separation* on which the story closes take place during a Hindu ritual proclaiming the principle of *universal unity*.

But a totally different kind of summary is possible. It is built around the figure of the elderly English woman, Mrs. Moore, who is accompanying her prospective daughter-in-law on this trip to India. I have seen this other strand so featured, that it might seem to concern a different story. The Mohammedan meets this elderly woman in a mosque. He becomes attached to her as a kind of All-Mother. In her absence (for she leaves India and dies on the way home) her presence (her *parousia*?) presides fatally over the course of the trial. And though she dies in a mystic state of drought, the mystery of her spirit pervades the entire course of the plot.

Such a strand is definitely there. And you may prefer to feature it, rather than the more pedestrian kind of outline we considered first. If you do, I would assume that my formula, "ironically sympathetic contemplation," would not serve best as the way in. And in any case this mystical element

---

[1] All sociopolitical relationships are expressible in terms of intimate, personal relationships—and these in turn are reducible to analogous sexual relationships. For instance, a general condition of conflict between classes can be stated in terms of private conflicts between individuals. And these in turn might be "dramatized" by expression in some such sexual terms as seduction, rape, or sadism.

must be considered as a subplot—and of a sort that is not merely incidental, but radically infuses the comedy with a dimension not generally deemed comical.

Once you view the novel in terms of the embarrassments due to differences of social status (be they among different castes or classes of native, or between natives and colonialists, or between the sexes, or between members of the same sex as affected by all these disparities) you confront a realm of compensatory possibilities. Such differences set the conditions that allow for new kinds of *gallantry* (modes of imagination neither necessary nor possible to ways of life that are not encumbered by such intensifications of difference). There is a *mystique* of such gallantry. And it's the point at which (in terms of this particular novel) "mystery" and "muddle" overlap. For there is always the opportunity for some kind of gallantry, when persons confront one another with respect (or polite tentativeness) while they experience at the same time a compelling sense of disparateness.

In such gallantry there is mystery, no matter how comic may be its origins or implications. Here the social mystery is reinforced by connotations of cosmic mystery, centering in the Marabar Caves, and their association with the muddled relationship between the English girl and the Mohammedan. Aziz's arrest as the result of Adela's accusation (a charge which she later impulsively or compulsively retracts after deciding that her suspicions were hallucinatory) takes place in almost the exact mathematical center of the book. The design of the social mystery is also repeated analogously in the hierarchal nature of the scene itself. Here is a typical instance (it follows comments to do with the failure of the "Bridge Party" that was designed to bridge the gulf between natives and British officials; considerations of social disparity shift to a series of layers in the natural scene itself, with glancing hints of further supernatural levels):

> Some kites hovered overhead, impartial, over the kites passed the mass of a vulture, and with an impartiality exceeding all, the sky, not deeply coloured, but translucent, poured light from its whole circumference. It seemed unlikely that the series stopped here. Beyond the sky must not there be something that overarches all the skies, more impartial even than they? Beyond which again . . .

The result is that, at strategic moments along the way, despite the novel's comic stress upon the dislocations of society as such, there are traces of a transcendental dialectic. For the presentation as a whole involves a stylistic device whereby *social* motives are viewed in terms of *nature*, and *nature* in turn is infused with glancing references to realms *beyond*. We shall return to this point later. Meantime, we should stress the primary functional fact that the realm of social discord provides the author with a constant underlying source of poetic entertainment: throughout the novel, we are entertained by the author's thesaurus of social embarrassments, and corresponding reports of things that go wrong.

Among the neatest maneuvers in this regard is the convergence of incidents whereby Aziz and Adela happen to be alone in the cave. Particularly apt here is the explanation that Fielding missed the train because he had arranged to accompany Godbole, and Godbole was late because he had miscalculated the length of a prayer. The skill in disposing of Mrs. Moore is of a different order, and is especially effective because of what it contributes to the quality of the plot. By having her refuse to enter a second cave because of her revulsion in the first, the novelist uses her absence both to reinforce the sinister aspect of the place in which Adela's hallucination will take place and to tie the caves in with Mrs. Moore's emergent sense of mystic drought.

III
Cast of Characters

All told, where are we? The most obvious human problem which is turned into a source of poetic pleasure is the "muddle" (or "mystery") of Indian social relations, culminating in the state of alienation that characterizes the relationship between the natives and British "officialism." This culminating tension sets the conditions for the gallant relationship between Aziz and Mrs. Moore, for her "mythic" translation in the minds of the natives during the trial, and for the central plot (involving Adela's hallucination with regard to Aziz, and the Englishman Fielding's own kind of gallantry, when siding with Aziz against his fellow countrymen during the ordeal before Adela had retracted her accusation). Among the most delightful stretches of high comedy is the account of the righteous indignation that edified the members of the British "Club" between the time of Adela's accusation and the retraction of her charges.

If, next, prophesying after the event, we seek to "derive" the dramatis personae, note how beautifully they fall into place. First, there is the tentativeness between Adela and her prospective fiancé, the British official, Ronny, the son of Mrs. Moore. One might treat this matter psychoanalytically in line with the fact that there are no wholly satisfactory heterosexual relationships in this book. Or one might consider the same situation from a purely social point of view, by observing that the principle of divisiveness, so "natural" to imperialism and its corresponding kinds of social pyramid, is here carried to completion, as regards even the possibilities of normal sexual intimacy. By far the strongest heterosexual attachment in the book is Aziz's attitude towards Mrs. Moore—and that is obviously not at all "erotic," but "agapetic" (if we may adapt Anders Nygren's *eros-agape* pair, and propose the adjective "agapetic" to designate the young Mohammedan's analogue of sheerly filial love with regard to Mrs. Moore). And one thing is certain: To Aziz, the young English girl whose hallucination leads her to accuse him is of no more interest erotically than is the elderly English-woman who serves him as a kind of adoptive mother ("mother symbol"), and whose corresponding erotic remoteness prepares her to become trans-formed (as regards the mystic or mythic dimension of the plot) into a kind tutelary deity overseeing the destiny of the natives. As regards our test of "ironically sympathetic contemplation," all this works out quite neatly. For even as her very name becomes converted into a magic formula, "Esmiss Esmoor," chanted by the natives during the trial, she has gone to a sullen death. Yet there is a sense in which the natives were right. For her sullen expression of disbelief in the very basis of all the excitement (" 'Of course he is innocent,' she answered indifferently") had been the exact thing needed to help awaken Adela from her trance, and thus indirectly to bring about the abrupt termination of the trial, with the corresponding orgiastic procession.

The state of misfit between Adela and her fiancé is developed with re-markable precision, as regards the aims of the plot. She is angular, stiff, breastless, with no genuine attachment to the natives, yet liberal on prin-ciple. While deploring the attitude of the officials, and wanting to transcend it, she causes the pivotal flare-up between the British and the natives. We are led to feel that she is in essence an outsider to any spontaneous love. Yet, just as she can but be friendly on principle, by the same token she can be honest on principle. And once she has decided (with the help of the imagery which we shall consider later) that she had falsely accused Aziz, Miss Adela Quested never questions her next step. She promptly and forthrightly retracts —and the trial is suddenly over, with a corresponding leap in the plot. In her pale way, she embodies a species of imperialist virtue.

Here I would stress the fact: In this work there is no villain. There is only a comic scale of errors. Thus, though it has no driving sexual love (no *amor*, or *eros*) it is essentially *charitable* (it has a contemplative brand of *charitas*, which is the Latin equivalent of *agape*). Thus, for these mean days, it is good medicine.[2]

Though Adela's fiancé, Ronny, is blunt and unimaginative, in his way he too is a person of principle. Accepting without question the assumptions of the colonial administrators, he abides by these rules. One finds it easy to believe that he does each day's work scrupulously, as tested by his scheme of

---

[2] However, we should note that, in the relation between Fielding and Aziz, the book does well by a third kind of affection: Friendship (*philia, amicitia*). It obviously suffers from the divisiveness of the colonial situation. Yet this same divisiveness is what gives it its great measure of gallantry, and makes it irreducible to terms of homosexuality, except where psychoanalytic snooping is exceptionally zealous. But one must admit: In saying "I travel light," Fielding uses a formula to which André Gide gives quite dif-ferent connotations. (Fittingly, one of Forster's ubiquitous negatives figures in Field-ing's mild oxymoron to explain why he has not yet married: "I'm a holy man minus the holiness.")

values. But just as Shakespeare, in *Antony and Cleopatra*, used the motives and motifs of empire to aggrandize a love affair, so that it takes place not between two individuals but between no less than Rome and Egypt, similarly now, when the empire was running down, the "politicalizing" of sexuality replaces grandeur with diffidence. Thus, fittingly, after a lovers' quarrel between Ronny and Adela, we are significantly informed that the reconciliation makes for but a "spurious unity"—and immediately following that moment there occurs the mysterious and portentous accident, just when the car in which they are being driven has crossed a bridge. It is the kind of incident one should especially watch, as a likely spot for key terms. We shall return to this point later (for the moment noting only that the typical "muddle-mystery" pair also figures ambiguously: "they felt adventurous as they muddled about in the dust").

The Mohammedan physician, Aziz (a poet on the side) is wholly functional with regard to the theme of social embarrassment. His primary reason for arranging the fatal expedition to the Caves is that he is sensitive about inviting the women to his home. Thus an aspect of his character is drawn upon to make this development seem "natural," just as we have seen how Fielding's frustrated compunctiousness, Godbole's ritualism, and Mrs. Moore's incipient acedia also assist in setting up the situation. And even in his attachment to his English friend, Fielding, he is never socially at ease. (This sensitiveness is ascribed by Ronny to the native Indian generally: "There's always something behind every remark he makes, and if nothing else he's trying to increase his izzat—in plain Anglo-Saxon, to score.")

Fielding (the educator who breaks with his countrymen and sides with Aziz during the trial), is not so different from Adela as one might at first assume. Like her, he acts on principle (in contrast with the spontaneous emotionality of Aziz). And though a hardened Freudian would doubtless insist that there are traces of homosexuality in his relationship to Aziz, they obviously never develop beyond the stage of tendencies, tendencies that come nearest to expression at the very end of the story, when these two friends are parting because Aziz avows that they cannot still be friends while India remains a British colony. At this very moment, their personal separation is charmingly infused with the gallantry of personal intimacy that transcends differentiations socially or politically imposed.

Mrs. Moore and the Hindu Professor Godbole serve in different but complementary ways to reinforce the mystery side of the muddle-mystery pair. The passing references to her momentary glimpses of cosmic unity set up the conditions for the state of drought that besets her after her revulsion when inspecting the caves. (This is the burden of Chapter XIV.)

As regards my interpretation of the novel's purpose (its overall poetic function in providing us with situation, plot, and dramatis personae that serve the ends of ironically sympathetic contemplation), when considered from this point of view Professor Godbole's contribution to the mystery-muddle pair is seen as the highest form of comedy. I have already referred to his song and his meticulous ritualism that caused him to miss the train. Another particularly delightful passage occurs near the end of Chapter XIX, where by many blandishments he transcends the factual and factional manner in which the issue of Aziz's guilt must be treated during the trial. His discussion is a stretch of beautiful, exasperating unction, and Fielding receives it "in gloomy silence." And there is no development in the book more felicitous than the use (as background for the story's outcome) of a "holy festival" over which Godbole is officiating. Fittingly, the rites being celebrated by this select Brahmin have their center in a radical denial, or perhaps we should say transubstantiation, of the entire social order:

> The Sweepers' Band was arriving. Playing on sieves and other emblems of their profession, they marched straight at the gate of the palace with the air of a victorious army. All other music was silent, for this was ritually the moment of the Despised and Rejected; the God could not issue from his temple until the unclean Sweepers played their tune, they were the spot of filth without which the spirit cannot cohere. For an instant the scene was magnificent. The doors were thrown open, and the whole court was seen inside, barefoot and dressed in white robes. . . . etc.

I submit: One must always look upon Professor Godbole's *social aloofness* in terms of such contrasting *ritual* or *formal oneness* not only with all mankind, but with the lowliest of things, even such a wasp as Mrs. Moore had once looked upon as vaguely one with the Universe.

To be thorough, we should go on, to "derive" the other characters. But you get the idea. They function. Thus, though Hamidullah, a friend of Aziz, is not sharply differentiated as a person, he is given traits enough to help us agree that he might misrepresent Fielding, thereby encouraging Aziz to surmise that Fielding had married Adela in England, and that intentions of this sort were involved in Fielding's persuading Aziz not to sue her for heavy damages. And the point is driven home when Fielding turns up with a wife (none other than a daughter of Mrs. Moore by a different marriage from the one that produced Ronny Hyslop). And above all, there is a most pleasurable thesaurus of minor characters, both men and women, connected with the English officers' club. They provide rich material for a comedy of manners, in giving us a scale of edified responses to the scandal of Adela's mistaken accusation. To be thorough, all these minor members of the cast could also be derived from the situation which is set up for our wanly liberal ponderings on the absurdities of man. But you get the idea. And if any sheerly sociology-minded student felt moved to treat that comic set of characters merely as "science," a most astute set of categories could result.

Surely, one other figure should be mentioned. I refer to the novel's gallant yet aloof treatment of the punkah wallah, the untouchable whose function it was to keep a breeze stirring in the stifling courtroom, a kind of "beautiful naked god" who had been nourished on garbage, but who "scarcely knew that he existed." After the abrupt termination of the trial, when all the others had left, "Unaware that anything unusual had occurred, he continued to pull the cord of his punkah, to gaze at the empty dais and the overturned special chairs, and rhythmically to agitate the clouds of descending dust." Here mystery and muddle meet. Here, tentatively, is a silently drastic step beyond Fielding's rationalism. Here one of the most supernumerary characters in the book is enigmatically invested with an unresolved tangle of motives such as one experiences at bewildering moments when "values" are not so much "transvalued" as thrown into a state of total suspension. The entire logic of both empire and resistance to empire becomes mute, merging into a realm of untouchability that is both vexing and enticing to a mind burdened with the norms of progress, tradition, and order. An incidental character is gallantly viewed as a kind of decerebrated god, an agent that threatens to sum up the farthest possible reaches of the book's ultimate scene. Here is another point where the zealously psychoanalytic might want to overstress the erotic connotations that are conceivably a fragment of the motivation as a whole. But even as we mention the possibility, we realize what a leap from *dramatis persona* to symbol this figure embodies —for, even as "he continued to pull the cord of his punkah, to gaze at the empty dais and the overturned special chairs, and rhythmically to agitate the clouds of descending dust," the rationale of the plot was developing into its next phase, the orgy of the impromptu celebration (a true revelrout) that followed upon the abrupt termination of the trial.

IV
Attendant Terms

(This will be a troublesome section for readers who would hurry on. It is necessary, though hard to follow in detail if one reads it without now and then referring to a previous statement. The discussion is necessary, since it throws important light on ways whereby recurrent terms help establish the internal consistency of the novel, an internal consistency that prevails at a level not likely to be noticed at a first, unanalytic reading. But such developments "in depth" frequently lack the progressive form of narrative, hence may seem to be more of a hindrance than a help, so far as observations on the orderly unfolding of the plot are concerned. As a visual aid to the exposition, the key terms are italicized.)

At the start, we'd certainly note (as others have noted) that the adjective "extraordinary" (applied to the Marabar Caves) appears in both the first and last sentences of the opening chapter. Here would be a minor instance of "eschatology" (concerned with the realm of "first and last things"). But we should also note (as others do not seem to have done) when the same word turns up *elsewhere* in the text. Among its incidences is an application to Ralph, who is a son of Mrs. Moore by a marriage other than the one that produced Ronny, and hence Fielding's brother-in-law. (Closer tie-ups follow, though I confess that I don't quite know what to make of them. For instance, the "extraordinary" Ralph is stung by bees, and his mother's sense of cosmic unity had centered in the sight of a *wasp*.) The term figures in many other important contexts. Thus, at the end of Part II we are told that, when leaving the Mediterranean on their way south, travelers "approach the monstrous and *extraordinary*." And in the first paragraph of Chapter XXVI, we realize that the word had come into its own, so far as the plot was concerned, since Adela (later called a "queer honest girl") here refers to her bewilderment in trying to account for her "*extraordinary* behaviour."

We have already mentioned the strong preference for *negatives* in the style of this book. Where others might incline to say, "It is x-like," Forster might rather say, "It is not non-x-like." His style often says in effect: If you *must* asseverate, do so by litotes.

Obviously, many other terms, if studied in all their contexts, would yield insights. I had not watched "*star*," for instance. Yet, having been alerted, I noticed: A few lines after the opening of Chapter XXVII, when Fielding and Aziz are lying near each other in the night, at a time in the course of the plot when their friendship was closest, we are told:

> Exactly above their heads hung the *constellation* of the Lion, the disc of Regulus so large and bright that it resembled a *tunnel*, and when this fancy was accepted all the other *stars* seemed *tunnels* too.

The interesting thing here is that the *passageways* in the Caves are regularly called "*tunnels*." In Chapter XVI, with regard to the *field glasses* that Miss Quested had dropped in her flight: "They were lying at the verge of a cave, *half-way* down an entrance *tunnel*." And from this passage one might radiate in another direction to the thought that the woman whom Fielding marries is named "*Stella*."

As for "*half-way*": It is remarkable how often the word "*half*" or some kindred term turns up in the text (the most notable variant being a reference to "the *twilight* of the *double vision*" with regard to Mrs. Moore). As for the sheerly tonal relationship between "*field glasses*" and "*Fielding*," I would but note that the long paragraph from which the mention of the *glasses* has been lifted (and in connection with the distress of Aziz over Adela's sudden, unexplained disappearance) is followed by this brief one concerning Aziz's delight on learning that the figure approaching in "an Englishman's topi" is not Ronny but *Fielding*:

"*Fielding*! Oh, I have so wanted you!" he cried, dropping the "Mr." for the first time.

The previous chapter ends as Adela enters the *tunnel* where, in her hallucinatory confusion, she will drop the *field glasses* "*half-way down*." "In her honest, decent, inquisitive way," she had asked Aziz whether he had "one wife or more than one." The novelist comments: "If she had said, 'Do you worship one god or several?' he would not have objected. But to ask an educated Indian Moslem how many wives he has—appalling, hideous!" And though he has been guiding her, in irritation he lets go of her hand. The chapter ends:

> She followed at her leisure, quite unconscious that she had said the wrong thing, and not seeing him, she also went into a cave, thinking *with half her mind* "sight-seeing bores me," and wondering *with the other half* about marriage.

A page or so previously we had read:

> But as she toiled over a rock that resembled an *inverted* saucer, she thought, "what about love?" The rock was nicked by a double row of footholds, and somehow the question was suggested by them.

Then she remembers where she had seen this design before. It had been "the pattern traced in the dust" by the wheels of the car in the accident following the moment of "spurious unity" in the relation between her and her fiancé. And she now decides that "they did not love each other."

As for the statement that the rock over which she "toiled" was "like an *inverted* saucer": In the penultimate chapter, immediately after the ceremony's "*half-way* moment" is said to have been passed, in the culminating celebration of cosmic unity "Mixed and confused in their *passage*, the rumours of salvation entered the Guest House." (One naturally watches "*passage*" because of its titular role in this book. "*Pass*" would also merit special attention; but as one might expect, the incidence of this term provides an embarrassment of riches.) Then the choir begins "repeating and *inverting* the names of deities." We might here incidentally recall the place where the pious formula, "God *is* Love," gets inverted by mistake into "God *si* Love" (though in one edition of the book either a helpful printer or an enterprising proofreader "remedied" this detail of the text by transforming "*si*" into "*is*").

If, following the novelist's own reference to an association of ideas, we go back (in Chapter VIII) to consult the account of the ambiguously portentous accident "just after the exit from a *bridge*," we find the reference to the design, "ribbons neatly nicked with lozenges." Other terministic details are notable. I previously mentioned the verb "*muddled*" in this episode.

When we are told that "they traced back the *writhing* of the tyres to the source of their disturbance," we have grounds for referring to a later context, where the echoes in the caves are like "a *snake composed of small snakes*, which *writhe* independently." (The lines are immediately followed by an account of the revulsion which decided Mrs. Moore "not to visit" a second cave.)

How many of the radiations should we consider here? Immediately before the reference to the *"spurious unity"* which preceded the accident, there is a reference to Professor Godbole's song, described in the previous chapter. Conveying states of mind in terms of the surrounding scene, the novel explains:

> In vain did each item call out, *"Come, come."* There was not enough god to go round. The two young people conversed feebly and felt unimportant.

And the way in which the mood of *"spurious unity"* is suddenly and significantly broken is recounted thus:

> They gripped . . . *bump, jump*, a *swerve*, two wheels lifted in the air, brakes on, *bump* with tree at edge of embankment, standstill.

How closely dare we tie in things here? *"Swerved"* will appear critically in the closing paragraph of the book, a step to be considered later. It appears in an incident on the visitors' way to the caves: "The elephant walked straight at the Kawa Dol as if she would knock for admission with her forehead, then *swerved*, and followed a path round its base." It appears in a quite exceptional usage, with regard to Mrs. Moore's son Ralph: "And with a *swerve of voice and body* that Aziz did not follow he added, 'In her letters, in her letters. She loved you.' " Ralph is referring to his mother. A few pages previously, there was the reference to Ralph as an *"extraordinary* youth."

I'd like to risk one more correlation with regard to the account of the accident. Twice, you will note, the strongly onomatopoeic word *"bump"* appeared in this context. Astonishingly enough, with regard to the train on which Adela is traveling toward the Caves, we are told: " '*Pomper, pomper, pomper*,' was the sound that the wheels made as they *trundled* over the bridge." ("trundled"—"tunnel"?) The railway here, we are told, "runs parallel" with the road on which the accident had occurred. And Adela begins thinking of Ronny. So I dare hear *"pomper"* as an enigmatic variant of *"bump*," the train thus in its vague way signifying the destiny implicit in its journey. In Chapter IX, there is a reference to "One, two, three, four *bumps*, as people sat down upon" Aziz's bed. Shortly after the reference to the *swerving* of the elephant, the beginnings of Mrs. Moore's revulsion are indicated in terms of a cognate sound: "Three hills encircled the tray. Two of them *pumped* out heat busily, but the third was in shadow, and here they camped. Mrs. Moore murmured to herself, 'A horrid, stuffy place really.' " And exactly in the middle of the book, when the train is on the way back from the Caves (about eight lines after we read "The train halted once under a *pump*, to drench the stock of coal in its tender. Then it caught sight of the main line in the distance, took courage, and *bumped* forward,") the Inspector of Police enters the car and announces: "Dr. Aziz, it is my highly painful duty to arrest you."

But I would risk one further correlation along these lines. In Chapter XIV, we are told of Mrs. Moore's revulsion in the cave: "For an instant she went mad. . . . For not only did the crush and stench alarm her; here was also a terrifying *echo*." And a few sentences later: " '*Boum*' is the sound as far as the human alphabet can express it or '*bou-oum*,' or '*ou-boum*,'—utterly dull." May we not hear in this sound a farther variant of "*bump*," "*pump*," "*pomper*"—along with the thought that, approached from another direction, it can be treated as a malign distortion of the sacred syllable "*oom*," symbolizing ultimate contact? I grant, there is no argument for the likelihood beyond the mere act of bringing up these possibilities for consideration, along with the thought that, in any case, the interrelationship among the *incidents themselves* is clear enough. And the onomatopoeic nature of all these words would justify us somewhat in asking whether they might be treated musically like variations on a single theme.

In any case, so far as sheer *terms* go, the novel's insistent use of the "*echo*" in connection with Adela's torment after accusing Aziz would certainly justify us in watching that term, and noting among other things how in Mrs. Moore's case the fact that "*echoes generate echoes*" is likened to the cave's being "stuffed with a *snake composed of small snakes*." Looking back, we find that the set piece (Chapter XXX) introducing the "Caves" section of the book had not mentioned sound. There things came to a focus in the notion that the flame of a match, mirrored in the polished walls, makes a design like lovers permanently divided; they "touch one another, kiss, expire." But here, stench and *sound* are featured—and the equating of the *echoes* with *snakes* undergoes a notable transformation when the riotous procession that is celebrating the sudden end of the trial is said to advance "Like a *snake* in a drain." Perhaps the figure was present incipiently when the visitors to the cave were said to be "*sucked in like water down a drain*" (followed, a few lines later, by the opposite movement: "And then the *hole* belched and humanity returned").

Many other internal relationships among terms are worth tracing. But one in particular should be dwelt on, since it bears directly upon the culmination of the plot. We have already mentioned the frequency of the "*half*-this . . . *half*-that" pattern. Towards the end of the book the pattern assumes almost aggressiveness. Chapter XXXV begins in the theme of the *severed* head, and the corresponding *two* shrines, The Shrine of the Body and The Shrine of the Head. We have already discussed the connotations surrounding the "*half-way*" moment" in the religious rites. There are several trivial instances, interesting only because of their bearing upon the pattern: "ran his little hospital at *half* steam"; "I wrote you *half* a dozen times"; "for one short *half*-hour"; "I feel *half* dead and *half* blind"; "the whole *semi*-mystic, *semi*-sensuous overture." A remoter variant: "They cantered past a temple to Hanuman—God so loved the world that *he took monkey's flesh upon him*—and past a Saivite temple, which invited to *lust*, but under the semblance of *eternity*." Previously: "They did not distinguish between the *God* and the *Rajah* in their minds, both were too far above them." Of a water tank: "Reflecting the evening clouds, it filled the netherworld with an equal splendour, so that earth and sky *leant toward one another, about to clash* in ecstasy." This symbolic clash of the elements was followed later by the *collision* between the two boats of worshippers. And all this, including a statement that "the *divisions* of daily life were returning," serve as thematic analogue for the relationship between Fielding and Aziz, who "must inevitably *part*." "They trusted each other, although they were *going to part*, perhaps because they were *going to part*." Then, after his challenge, "India shall be a nation! No foreigners of any sort! Hindu and Moslem and Sikh and all shall be *one*!" Aziz shouts to Fielding (they are both on horseback). . . . But let us quote the closing lines verbatim:

> "We shall drive every blasted Englishman into the sea, and then"—he rode against him furiously—"and then," he concluded, *half* kissing him, "you and I shall be friends."
>
> "Why can't we be friends now?" said the other, holding him affectionately. "It's what I want. It's what you want."
>
> But the horses didn't want it—they *swerved* apart: [there's our word "swerve" again] the earth didn't want it, sending up rocks through which riders must pass single file; the temples, the tank, the jail, the palace, the birds, the carrion, the Guest House, that came into view as they issued from the gap and saw Mau beneath: they didn't want it, they said in their hundred voices, *"No, not* yet," and the sky said, *"No, not* there."

Here, at the very end, and most effectively, we see the personal transformed into terms of the social or political, and that realm in turn transformed into terms of the natural background. But what of the supernatural?

V
Mystery

Let's end on that. The book had opened on the theme of the "extraordinary" Marabar Caves. The opening of the second section treats them in a series of steps that terminates in the symbolizing of total self-involvement, total withinness-of-withinness, with a great profusion of negatives that come to a head in the repetition of "nothing, nothing." Similarly on the subject of

Mrs. Moore's revulsion, we are told that the echo in a Marabar Cave "is entirely devoid of distinction." And a bit later:

> The crush and the smells she could forget, but the echo began in some indescribable way to undermine her hold on life. Coming at a moment when she chanced to be fatigued, it had managed to murmur, "Pathos, piety, courage—they exist, but are identical, and so is filth. Everything exists, nothing has value." If one had spoken vileness in that place, or quoted lofty poetry, the comment would have been the same—"ou-boum." If one had spoken with the tongues of angels and pleaded for all the unhappiness and misunderstanding in the world, past, present, and to come, for all the misery men must undergo whatever their opinion and position, and however much they dodge or bluff—it would amount to the same, the serpent would descend and return to the ceiling.

A few lines later, the essence of her sloth is summed up: "But suddenly, at the edge of her mind, Religion appeared, poor little talkative Christianity, and she knew that all its divine words from 'Let there be Light' to 'It is finished' only amounted to 'boum.' "

At the end of Chapter XX, there is an ingenious paragraph which describes how a "lovely, exquisite moment" had "passed" Fielding by, "passing the Englishman with averted face and on swift wings," leaving him untouched by any mood more accurate than a puzzled sadness. He was, on principle, a man who loathed the vast network of social distinctions under which India suffered. But he was spared the drought, through being denied the ecstasy. And as regards Mrs. Moore, one must admit that, at best, her sense of the ecstatic is to her state of drought as one is to a hundred.

All told, then, what do we have, for the joys of ironically sympathetic contemplation? Much indeed, as regards the comedy of manners, man's picturesque stupidities rooted in hierarchal motives that come to completion in the ills of empire. But how about a world "devoid" of all such "distinctions"? Could we be worthy of it? Could we be equal to its wholly different kinds of responsibility? A doubt of this sort seems to be at least implicit in the structure of *A Passage to India*. It is a dreadful doubt—but within the conditions of the fiction, it is there for our enjoyment.[3]

---

[3] As an addendum I'd like to end on a sort of puzzle not directly referable to the realm of Poetics, but tantalizingly relevant to the realm of linguistic action in general.

It concerns what I'd call a "perturbation," a term for various stylistic or formal "sports" that seem to involve motives abruptly alien to an explanation exclusively placeable in terms of poetics. For instance:

In Chapter VIII it is said of Mrs. Moore that "She was past marrying herself." When so competent a writer as E. M. Forster falls into an awkward and ambiguous usage of that sort, it might be worth storing tentatively, on the chance that something might tie in with it elsewhere. Whereupon, lo! a related usage does turn up, in one of Forster's early short pieces, "The Story of the Siren." It concerns a native who in primitive nakedness dived for a book that the author of the story had inadvertently let fall "downward through the waters of the Mediterranean." But there are plots-within-plots. For this simple man is said to have told of a myth concerning these same waters. And in the recounting of a local legend about two tragic lovers, we suddenly confront the line: "Who would have believed he would marry himself!" (exclamation point in the original). In both cases, the stylistic accident is the same. For obviously, it is meant neither that "she married herself" nor that "he would marry himself," but "she herself married" and "he himself would marry." I would especially note such a "perturbation" because of my conviction that the ambiguities of the reflexive and of identification necessarily continue to plague us.

Further internalities of a reflexive sort might be noted. Mrs. Moore's "double vision" has an analogue in the fact that her son Ronny is typical of British "officialism" while Ralph (her son by her second marriage) is "extraordinary." The close though divisive relationship between Fielding and Aziz splits into relationships whereby Mrs. Moore is a mother symbol to Aziz, and Fielding marries her daughter Stella. (At this point, we might again recall the beginning of Chapter XXVII, where Fielding and Aziz are lying together in the night, and we are told that all the stars seemed like "tunnels.")

The story "The Eternal Moment" is about a woman who is a writer, with an appealing "enthusiasm for the lower classes." Years before, a young native guide "had talked of love to her" upon a mountain. She had been alienated; but now, elderly, returning to the same region (which a book of hers had made into a tourist attraction), she realizes that she had been unconsciously in love with the man whose attentions she had resented. Embarrassments arise because, when she again meets him, though he is not at all the romantic figure of the past (he is now a portly concierge) she wants to talk over the whole episode with him. The story ends when a companion of hers, a Colonel Leyland, makes a secret sign to indicate that the authoress is mentally unbalanced:

> Much as Colonel Leyland disliked touching people he took Feo by the arm, and then quickly raised his finger to his forehead.
> "Exactly, sir," whispered the concierge. "Of course we understand—Oh, thank you, sir, thank you very much: thank you very much indeed!"

How closely we should inspect the verb "touch" here, I am not prepared to say. Certainly, at least, besides the fact that the Colonel "disliked touching people," there are the connotations of a pun in his gesture, which indicates that the authoress is mentally "touched." The punkah wallah was an "untouchable." And in Chapter XXII, when on the subject of the "cactus spines that had to be picked out of her flesh" after her hasty flight from the cave, Adela is sensitive to being touched, and repeats to herself somewhat vatically while the thorns are being extracted, "In space things touch, in time things part." The formula also ambiguously foretells the end of the novel.

This story was written before *A Passage to India*, quite as were the letters (most of them addressed to the author's mother) published in *The Hill of Devi*, which so often gives details similar to the picturesque embarrassments recounted in the novel. Though all fictional characters are transformed to varying degrees for purely formal purposes, I should work on the assumption that the author's mother is the prototype of Mrs. Moore, and that Fielding comes closest to being his personal representative in the novel. Adela is not so far from being a feminine Fielding as one might first assume. And Aziz's sensibility is but a special case of the sensibility that infuses the novel as a whole.

Chapter Nine

Version, Con-, Per-, and In-
Thoughts on Djuna Barnes's Novel *Nightwood*

To give an idea where I am going: I have been working on some problems to do with the relation between Rhetoric and Poetics. These matters figure strikingly, for instance, with regard to Cleanth Brooks's recent book on Faulkner.

Some years back, you will recall, Mr. Brooks set himself up quite definitely as an advocate of Formalistic criticism. But it seems generally agreed that, in his recent book on Faulkner, he has veered far from strictly Formalistic canons.

I do not object to such departures. Indeed, though at one stage in my analysis of a text I would try to meet strictly Formalistic requirements, I would hold that literary criticism should not confine itself within such limits. But one should certainly point out occasions where Mr. Brooks's own criticism seems to violate the strictly Formalistic canons by which he has tested other critics.

In the case of Mr. Brooks's book on Faulkner, as regards the relation between Rhetoric and Poetics the issue is quite clear. To make a book as entertaining as possible, an author might conceivably depict various kinds of violence. He might do so for the purely Formalistic reason that by the use of such themes he could develop a story with greatest forcefulness. But if this same fiction is presented as a quasi-*realistic* picture of one particular *region*, conditions are set up whereby the work can be interpreted sheerly as a "document." And this view can be personally embarrassing to the author, if he is especially partial to the region which he would represent in his fiction.

Obviously, two different systems of bookkeeping are here available. If an "outsider" to the region would interpret the violence as representative of the region, he can be rebuked for overlooking the sheerly Formalistic, or technical fact that violence is a device of storytelling, a resource of saliency. But many elements of the text that do not raise such embarrassments can be treated as instances of the author's true insight into his region.

There is a corresponding issue with regard to *Nightwood*. I shall consider the book essentially from the standpoint of Poetics. Yet we shall see how its stylistic tactics raise a Rhetorical problem, due to the nature of its theme.

I

James Joyce's *Portrait of the Artist as a Young Man* could be called the Bible of Aestheticism. Speaking in praise of its cause, it proclaims the *doctrine*, invents appropriate *symbols* (the bird-girl and the bird-man, the latter combining connotations of both flight and maze), and traces the kind of history (the story of Stephen's religious fall and romantically aesthetic rise) implicit in the doctrine and its symbols. There is the further twist that the doctrine itself is an attack upon indoctrination, in the sense that it propounds a theory of "esthetic stasis," in contrast with a "kinetic" that would be "improper" because it excited "desire or loathing." In brief, it would be an art essentially different from the kinds of effect represented by the sermon which had so terrified Stephen in Chapter III. It "arrests" the reader, rather than moving him as either the "pornographic or didactic" might do. In brief, though the aesthetic doctrine itself would come closer to a Poetic than to a Rhetoric, it has all the accoutrements of a gospel, with Stephen as the Logos, plus corresponding history and passion.

The novel *Nightwood*, by Djuna Barnes, also in its way takes the step from book to Bible, but in a different though related kind of Cause. In this case, however, the approach must be more roundabout. First, I would refer to the three "freedoms of speech" I discussed in the Laurel edition of Shakespeare's *Timon of Athens*: "freedom of praise," "freedom of invective," and "freedom of lamentation." Though such expressions, as developed in mature literary forms, are far beyond the limits of the infantile, I have suggested that their appeal can be grounded in our earliest preverbal responses. That is, praise, invective, and lamentation have their respective analogues in the infant's cooing with delight, shrieking with rage, or sobbing the unformed self to sleep. I would build a discussion of *Nightwood* around the notion that the book comes to stylistic fulfillment in the accents of lamentation. And I would approach the work as a set of devices ultimately designed to make lamentation a source of pleasure for the reader.

For there is one notable difference between a Biblical jeremiad and a purely literary variant of the species. However great the artistry of any document that gained admission to the Biblical canon (even so obviously literary an enterprise as the Book of Job), one should not approach a single sentence of the Bible purely in terms of literary entertainment. But in Joyce's *Portrait*, we are fittingly reminded that when Stephen began to doubt Biblical texts as true, he still loved them for their stylistic beauty. And a *literary* jeremiad must somehow be fun.

Another consideration presents itself, when you ask about this relationship between literary book and doctrinal Bible. If sheerly literary lamentation, then lamentation *in terms of what?*

Obviously, there are all kinds of things about which one might lament.
(At the moment, for instance, I personally wish I could write, not for
aesthetic purposes, but devoutly to the ends of persuasion, a resonant lament
with regard to what I take to be the lamentable errors of my country's
foreign policy.) The book we are considering must lament in terms of one
theme rather than another, with corresponding situation, plot, cast of
characters, and imagery. So, we necessarily take as "the given" the particular subject matter in terms of which the literary delights of lamentation
are to attain fulfillment.

In this book the literary appeal of lamentation will have for its pretext a subject that in one sense is quite orthodox: the sorrows of unrequited
love. More specifically, it exploits sex; more specifically still, homosex,
particularly Lesbianism (for even the primary "male" voice of Dr. O'Connor
suggests not so much a womanish man as a woman's perverse idea of a
womanish man, somewhat as with the major role in Susan Sontag's novel,
The Benefactor).

The book will be one more of the many works designed to celebrate
the grave responsibilities that Love places upon its votaries. And its plot
will gravitate about a conversion to perversion, or inversion.

In my book on *The Rhetoric of Religion* I deal with what I call the
"*vert*-family" of terms in Augustine's *Confessions*. I sometimes wonder
whether the good Bishop of Hippo could ever have written that work were
it not for the many Latin words that grow from this root, meaning "turn."
(Even the word "universe" belongs here.) There is a relevant text in
Lamentations, V, 21: "Turn thou us unto thee, O Lord, and we shall be
turned" (in the Vulgate, *Converte nos Domine ad te, et convertemur*). It
figures as the burden of Eliot's "Ash Wednesday": "Because I do not hope
to turn again" . . . "Although I do not hope to turn again" . . . and recall
the "turning" of the stairs. In *Nightwood* it appears in what I would call a
nova (the sudden flaring forth of a term) just at the point where Nora
first meets Robin. The italics are mine:

[*Since permission to quote was not obtainable from Miss Barnes, the
passage referred to has been deleted, with Mr. Burke's concurrence.
It may be found in* Nightwood *(New York, 1937), p. 69.—The
Publisher.*]

The word appears five times in that passage—and along with it there occurs another of the book's key expressions: "went down," the significance of which we shall consider later. (Incidentally, in *A Passage to India*, the last paragraph of Chapter XXIX, one form or another of "turn" appears eleven times within sixteen lines. For the most part the connotations in that text are theological, though muddled by irony.)

As regards Augustine's *Confessions*, the most notable use of the *vert*-family is in the contrast between Book II, concerned with what he calls his adolescent *per*versity in stealing pears (a Gidean *acte gratuit*), and Book VIII, that describes his *con*version. Nora's *turning* to Robin in this moment of their first meeting at the circus is indeed a romantic passion analogous to the religious passion. Some years ago, Dell Hymes, a former student of mine (now an expert in anthropological linguistics) offered an excellent suggestion when, in his paper on *Nightwood*, he characterized Robin as a kind of "unmoved mover" (the term that Aristotle applies to God). It is a kind of God notably different from the God of either the Old Testament or the New. It is the *eromenon*, the *loved*, a God that moves us not by paternal or paternalistic participation in our affairs, but purely as an impassive destination for us to aim at, like a target or a beacon.

The analogy is not perfect; for Robin can be moved by her emotions (somewhat as the Judaic-Christian God is said to become angry, like a parent, whereas such an attitude could not be applied even figuratively to Aristotle's God). But the idea of Robin as the "unmoved mover" in connection with Nora's conversion to perversion or inversion does help bring out the sense in which Nora's romantic passion is a secular variant of the religious passion, and thus involves the kind of motivational subtleties that Augustine worked out so ingeniously, in his doctrines of predestination, with the destination between those born to be saved and those born to be damned (the elect and the reprobates). And it all has to do with *turning*, turning towards or turning away (conversion, perversion, aversion).

True, the transforming of the religious passion into the romantic passion makes for quite paradoxical kinds of devotion and martyrdom. But I believe that, once you get the pattern in its simplicity, you can understand how it can lead to alembications. For the moment, the important thing is to note that, quite as Augustine, following the Old Testament, built his theology of motives around the subtleties of *turning*, so when Nora meets Robin, this term fittingly flares up. And, of course, one will do well to watch the term at all other places in the text. Here are a few, chosen almost but not wholly at random:

[Five brief extracts have been omitted here for the reason given above.—The Publisher.]

In a general way, I'd suggest that Robin's development is a symbolic *return* to the infantile. Fittingly, there is no dialogue in the last section of the book, a brief coda detailing Robin's transcendence (this book's alembicated equivalent of the way in which *Oedipus at Colonus* ends, as we see the hero at death becoming translated to the realm of a tutelary Beyond).

As regards the fact that Nora and Robin first meet at a circus, we might also do well to recall: Forty or more pages before this incident is described, in connection with another character (Felix) we were told with regard to "the pageantry of the circus and the theatre" that "In some way they linked his emotions to the higher and unattainable pageantry of kings and queens." And so, furthermore, we are to be involved here in an "aristocratic" realm of motives, though the elegance is going to be of a quite problematic sort. And at this point, I should give credit to a recent haphazard discussion by Kay Boyle, H. Nemerov, and K. Burke, which finally congealed into the pattern (none of us could take all the credit for this apocalyptic moment): "When Nightwood was in flower."

One more point by way of introduction. It involves from another angle the resources of "transcendence," which one sees exemplified with frank simplicity in Emerson's scheme for interpreting the "commodities" and disciplines of this world in terms of a Beyond, and which is treated with ironic fluctuancy in E. M. Forster's novel, "mystery" there being the tentative Beyond the "muddle." *Nightwood* aims at another mode of transcendence, a kind of "transcendence downward," if I may give further application to a term I worked with in my *Attitudes Toward History*. The terministic basis of the development is indicated in the titles of the first and seventh chapters: "Bow Down" and "Go Down, Matthew." The process is completed by stylistic devices and an enigmatic conclusion designed to make the plot seem absolute, and to present the Lamentations much as though this were the "primal" story of all mankind.

Thus, whereas a purely technical-minded critic might see in the work interesting modes of showmanship whereby a fairly narrow love triangle is made to seem like the deplorable tragedy of Everyman, in his laudatory introduction T. S. Eliot could say the same thing thus: "The miseries that people suffer through their particular abnormalities of temperament are visible on the surface: the deeper design is that of the human misery and bondage which is universal."

II

What's the plot? A "tall girl with the body of a boy" leaves her husband after she has borne him a son. She becomes involved in a love relationship with two women—and it serves as point of departure for lamentations by one of the women, seconded by a perverted doctor (who calls himself "an old worn out lioness," and who amplifies the theme by contributing many thoughts on human decay in general). Finally, after much promiscuity, and special interest in a child, the girl falls into a state of enigmatic communion with a dog.

Perhaps the quickest way to get inside the book is to restate, with minor modifications, some remarks I made on the subject in the *American Scholar* some years ago (Spring, 1951) in connection with a symposium on the so-called "New Criticism." Mr. Robert Gorham Davis had picked some terms to worry about (specifically "authority," hierarchy," "Catholicism," "aristocracy." "tradition," "absolutes," "dogma," and "truths"). And since, in my *Rhetoric of Motives*, I had made a particularly heavy investment in "hierarchy," I aimed to interfere with what I took to be the oversimplifications in his attitude towards such terms.

I noted that, when analyzing literary tactics, one is advised to be on the lookout for an author's modes of "dignification." And, of course, they may often be paradoxical, in employing twists whereby the apparent corruption of a character represents some higher values. In brief, we may find secular, and even blasphemous, variants of the transformations or miniature plots in the Sermon on the Mount. There is the "diamond in the rough," or "nature's gentleman"—or, recently, Sartre's showmanship in hailing "Saint Genet." And, similarly, what of the ending in *Nightwood*, where Robin sinks down on all fours, and becomes as it were the essence of dog?

Rather than starting from scratch (for the book contains no definite statement that the dog had fleas), I found in the author's own stories two

basic kinds of dog. I refer not to their breeds, but to their motivational
implications, both figurative: "put on dog," and "go to the dogs." And I
submit that the ending involves an ambiguity of that sort. Similarly, the
plaintive Dr. O'Connor sets the pattern when he aphorizes (not without
double entendre, I assume), "We don't rise to heights—we are eaten away
to them."

The ending settles on the image of an absolute, in line with a cult
of "pure" sensation, contrived by a perverse "ascent" in terms of decay
whereby corruption and distinction become interchangeable terms. The
same passage from which this problematical "beatitude" is formulated begins, "In the acceptance of depravity the sense of the past is most fully
captured." This observation can move us along one step further, by leading,
as it does on the same page, to the subject of "racial memory." But before
we deal with that, perhaps we should briefly review the cast of characters.

Since much of the story is unfolded by a succession of character
portraits, we might as well follow the same order. The first chapter is built
around Felix, Robin's husband, of Jewish, German, and Italian descent.
The novel particularly stresses the Jewish aspect of his lineage—and the
stress upon "blood" in this "folkish" sense serves as ambiguous introduction
to other connotations of this term, since the book's references to "blood"
place as much claim upon our attention as "night" and "wood."[1] Here the
problematic quality of the motivation begins farther off, in such expressions
as "the degradation by which his people had survived," "heavy with impermissible blood," "an alibi for the blood," "out of a diversity of bloods,"
and an obsequious respect for persons of superior social status (the "Bow
Down" theme that will later become the "Go Down" theme).

It will be Felix's function to make Robin a Baroness, though question-
ably. We learn in the chapter that the last name of Nora, Robin's lover, is
"Flood," whereupon I noticed that the consonants of his name, f-l-x, are
the same as in the word "flux." In this chapter we also get a first view of
O'Connor, the last syllable of whose name is also to be found in "Nora."

We note other affinities among the names (without of course equating
book characters with the author). "Baroness" has much the same structure
as "Barnes." "Robin" is an acrostic form of the b-r-o-n in "Baroness," an
affinity made still more apparent by the fact that she is often referred to as
the "Baronin." "Jenny," though she bears the brunt of the author's resentment, has obvious tonal affinity with "Djuna," as does an incidental character, "Nadja." Robin's name before marriage was "Vote," a bit puzzling

[1] In calling the author's use of blood "folkish," I have in mind the Hitlerite terminology;
but I most decidedly do *not* mean to imply that this novel has any political relations to
Nazism. Here is simply a point where two quite different cultural trends happen to
overlap.

until one observes that (*f* and *v* being cognates, *d* and *t* being cognates, and *oo* being modification of *o*) the word is tonally interpretable as "flood" without the *l*. A still more remarkable syllabic correlation is discernible in the fact that "Vote" in itself, without reference to the *l*, is a tonal variant of "food," with connotations symbolically relatable to O'Connor's previously quoted formula, "We don't rise to heights—we are eaten away to them." On page 51 we read, "Nora robbed herself for everyone." And on page 143 she says, if a woman is taken from you, "you cry that you have been robbed of yourself." But I will not object if you protest against my hearing "Robin" about the edges of those quotations.

In the second chapter, "La Somnambule," is built around the portrait of Robin. Her clothes were "of a period" that Felix, when he first came to know her, "could not quite place." (Yet, strangely enough, it is not here, but in another tale of jealousy, *Othello*, that we encounter the concluding exclamation, "O bloody period!" Here, near the close of O'Connor's summarizing chapter as spokesman, we find instead, "what a bloody time!" The theme of somnambulism (during her pregnancy she thought "unpeopled thoughts") contains in germ (entelechially) the trends that will be fulfilled in the absoluteness of her final crawling and barking "on all fours."

The theme of blood concerns the events of childbirth, which she looks upon "as if she had done something irreparable." One can readily understand her rejection of the child, and her "wandering," a theme that had been introduced deflectively in terms of Felix as a "wandering Jew." It is not wholly clear how she ever consented to have the child, though perhaps a sufficient reason is suggested by references to the trancelike quality of her experience, her "stubborn cataleptic calm," and "some hidden capacity, some lost subterranean humour." In any case, I would, though with much diffidence, mention the wholly unconfirmable possibility that in the expressions, "monstrously unfulfilled," and "monstrously alone, monstrously vain," the adverb accidentally contains a pun. Naturally, one can't say for sure. But one can say for sure that Dr. O'Connor, the male who is a kind of bearded lady, says: "To think is to be sick." And since the novel is of a single piece, I'd propose to remember here, ambiguity-wise, the passage in Nora's lament: "She sat up in bed and ate some eggs and called me, 'Angel! Angel!' and ate my eggs too, and turned over and went to sleep."

The third chapter, "Night Watch," is built around the character and psychology of Nora, "an early Christian," early American, with an almost orthodox conscience. After their meeting at the circus, Nora falls tumultuously in love with Robin. However, though this attachment marked her "turn" (her version, con-, per-, or in-), the novel is careful to introduce the principle of predestination, too: "there could be seen coming, early in her life, the design that was to be the weather-beaten grain of her face, that wood in the work; the tree coming forward in her, an undocumented record of time." Or, "She was one of those deviations by which man thinks to reconstruct himself."

By now we begin to see many motivational strands of the book coming together. The references to wood and tree point back, in line with the traditional associating of wood with the feminine principle of matter and mother (*materia, mater*) an association that shades into ideas of power antithetical to the masculine intellect, (*hyle* vs *nous*) hence ultimately equatable with some "primordial" motive, so far as the resources natural to dialectics are concerned. The motives of Christian vigil become transformed into the "night watch" of women like Nora in love or like Robin prowling.[2] Robin is now in Nora's heart, so that about her "ran Nora's blood," while "Robin was now beyond timely changes, except in the blood that animated her." The "bow down" theme noticeably takes on further dimensions: "down" into dreams, "down" into earth; and in a later chapter, "Watchman, What of the Night?" Nora diagnostically speaks for others:

> [*An extract has been omitted here for the reason given above. It may be found in the cited edition of* Nightwood, *p. 120.—The Publisher.*]

I have said that the primary appeal of this book as literature resides in its providing pretexts for the lament. Indeed, it employs such enterprise in working up to the jeremiads that precede Robin's enigmatic transcendence downward, it goes out of its way to present its world in terms of corruption. Whereupon we should note at least that things look more interesting that way.

However, the next chapter, built around the portrait of Nora's rival, Jenny Petherbridge, "The Squatter," is most accurately characterizable as *invective*. (There are also the many anonymous rivals due to the promiscuity of Robin's "wandering," but they exist mainly as vague and incidental

---

[2] In *Waiting for Godot* the same theme of Christian vigil is not thus romanticized, but deliberately burlesqued. Beckett also makes the theme serve another purpose. Form involves the arousing of expectations; here the audience is quite uncertain what to expect; but in effect the *formal principle* of expectation is transformed into a *problematical theme*. My early story "The Book of Yul" (republished in the collection, *Terms for Order*, edited by Stanley Edgar Hyman), begins on the theme of expectation *as expectation*. "While waiting, two men carried on a conversation that flapped and fluttered like an old newspaper. And a third was silent." Later: " 'Do you think she will come?' one of the other two asked." Later: "This waiting outside the gates of Heaven is cold business." Etc. The woman for whom they are vaguely waiting never appears. Instead, the story undergoes symbolic transformations; certain sounds that the men had heard while waiting ("scraping" and "thump") enigmatically reveal their unanticipatable implications by turning up again later, in a quite different context. In another early story, "First Pastoral," the theme of Christian vigil is romanticized, by the standard route. A monk, kept awake by fleshly hunger for a woman, struggles unsuccessfully to keep his beseechments directed toward a wholly spiritual advent.

aspects of Nora's complaints.) In contrast with Robin's trick species of "innocence" (about which more anon) and Nora's passionate sincerity, Jenny is "a dealer in second-hand." She had been married four times. "Each husband had wasted away and died." And in accordance with the norms natural to the cult of "nightwood," here is a telling blow that the novelist levels against her: "she gave off an odour to the mind (for there are purely mental smells that have no reality) of a woman about to be *accouchée*." Later O'Connor will say perhaps the worst thing against her, in describing her as but "lightly damned." Nor should we be overly timid about reading "squatter" two ways, in terms of both "squatter-sovereignty" and posture. The second usage, in a book by a woman, would be like a Jew calling another Jew a "kike," or an Italian calling another Italian a "wop," and so on. If we apply Bentham's triplicate vocabulary, Jenny Pxssxrbridge becomes the *dyslogistic* term for a necessary physiological attitude that could otherwise be characterized, if not *eulogistically*, then at least *neutrally*.

In the chapter we are now considering there also appears the child Sylvia who, while Robin is stroking her hand, is "smiling up into the trees." Sylvia, trees—and the reflexivity of the pattern is completed by the fact that the company, in carriages, is making the *tour du Bois*. Trees, trees, trees, and "turn." Later, there's to be a *corrupt* priest who complains that this is a *corrupt* age. (Again, the reflexive x-of-x pattern.)

To sum up, as regards the cast of characters: The child and the dog are *in the direction* of Robin. Felix had been ambiguously in the same direction, since his obsequiousness had introduced the "down" theme, while he had also represented a species of "wandering," and he had made her a problematical sort of Baroness (a not irrelevant item as judged by these twisted tests of election). In Nora, there is vigil, to match Robin's sleep. In Jenny there is the ordinary, to match Robin's oddity. And finally, in O'Connor there is an appointed garrulity to match Robin's silence.

Though this "gynaecologist" is nominally a man, all sorts of details are presented to help cancel out that curse. In the chapter, "Watchman, What of the Night?" where Nora comes to consult him, we find him surrounded by all sorts of female paraphernalia, lying "in a woman's flannel night-gown." Much earlier, we had been told that his voice can be "as irritable and possessive as a maddened woman's." He speaks of a possible earlier age when he was a girl with a sailor in Marseilles. Later we find him calling himself "the last woman left in this world, . . . the bearded lady." And in ultimate thoroughness he refers to God as feminine "because of the way she made me." And the novelist tells us that "the doctor had a mother's reverence for childhood." But whereas Nora has only her troubles with Robin to lament about, he has ailments besides. "Do you think there is no lament in this world but your own? . . . I have falling arches, flying dandruff, a floating kidney, shattered nerves *and* a broken heart!" So he is better qualified by his physical disabilities to have a more generalized approach than Nora to exercises in lamentation, that come to fulfillment just before the brief epilogue detailing Robin's ambiguous translation into pure beastliness: "The end—mark my words—now *nothing, but wrath and weeping!*" (Incidentally, I have found that many readers miss the point about the problematical display when O'Connor is in church with "Tiny O'Toole," who is not someone else, but none other than a part of O'Connor.)

One puzzle in the book, as viewed from the standpoint of sheer terministic accountancy, is the fact that O'Connor is called "the Squatting Beast." That comes dangerously close to the epithet for Jenny, "The Squatter," who is the book's only personalized victim of invective. The best we can do for this is to note that it is said by a mere someone who is obviously *outside* the range of sympathy and understanding with regard to the doctor, who a moment later boasts, "I'm damned, and carefully public!"

III

And now, for epitomizing purposes, let us put together various passages that most directly indicate the book's terministic tactics. First of all, we might contrast the "blood" theme here with its incidence in a work such as the *Oresteia* of Aeschylus. There it centers in the cult of the kill, the bloody sacrificing of the tragic victim. In *Nightwood* there is no such cult. Instead, it merges integrally with night and wood, as a badge of woman wholly alien to connotations of masculine courage or military violence.

No, I should qualify this. On the first page of the book we are told that Felix's mother, who died shortly after childbirth, was a "Viennese woman of great strength and military beauty." Yet I still would hold that, in the large, "blood" here, as a "red badge of courage," is a sign naturally and necessarily alien to male soldiers and their damned heroic bloodletting by war (whatever kind of Amazon all this might add up to).

As early as page 5, with regard to Felix's mother, we read of her having "played the waltzes of her time with the masterly stroke of a man, in the tempo of her blood." And her study "harboured two rambling desks in rich and bloody wood." O'Connor says that, when you "turn" to the Catholic church, you respond to "something that's already in your blood." Such usages can spread to talk of an "eternal river," a "river of sorrow," with "corruption," which is "the Age of Time . . . the body and the blood of ecstasy, religion and love." In being an "enigma" to Felix, Robin always "seemed to be listening to the echo of some foray in the blood that had no known setting." It gets mixed up with Nora's dreams of her grandmother wearing a "billycock," and " 'drawn upon' as a prehistoric ruin is drawn upon," while talk of the "prehistoric" leads elsewhere via "the cooling of the earth" and "the receding of the sea" to Nora's lament of her having chosen "a girl who resembles a boy." And, of course, O'Connor who proclaims himself the "last" of his "line," and whom Nora admires as having been "dead in the beginning," is "a man with a prehistoric memory," quite as, having equated "love with death," he says that every child is "born prehistorically." Similarly, there has been talk of "racial memory." An extension in another direction gives us a variant of the Demonic Trinity: "excrement, blood and flowers" as "three essential oils" of the human plight. (By "demonic trinity" I refer to a concept I first developed in my *Grammar of Motives*. It concerns the terministic fact that the three persons of the Trinity have their burlesqued analogues in terms of the fecal, diuretic, and genital respectively. [Here most Freudians cut corners.])

What I am aiming at is to show how the "essence" of motivation ties in with terms of one sort or another for the *temporally* prior, even the temporally primal. I mean: Instead of saying that something "essentially *is* such-and-such," the narrative style says that "it has been this way from away back," or "it was so from the very beginning." The amalgam widens in another direction via the novel's various formulas for the responsibilities of love, which is "the first lie; wisdom the last." "It rots me away," Nora complained to O'Connor, and Robin said of Nora's jealous possessiveness, "You make me feel dirty!" O'Connor calls Nora "blood-thirsty with love." She avows, "There's something evil in me that loves evil and degradation—purity's black backside!" She asks, "Have you ever loved someone and it became yourself?" Robin is also her child, hence she "is incest, too." She is "a mirage of an eternal wedding cast on the racial memory." She is "eaten death *returning*, for only then do we put our face close to the blood on the lips of our forefathers." (italics ours) To Nora "a woman is yourself . . . on her mouth you kiss your own." "Love of woman for woman" is an "insane passion for unmitigated anguish and motherhood." She is "the eternal momentary . . . the second person singular." Such love equals "the inbreeding of pain." And Robin is called "innocent" because "she can't do anything in relation to anyone but herself." It is a "fearful sort of primitive innocence" that others may consider depraved. She is infantile, playing with toys —yet she had given them both a doll, "their child." Love for "the invert, boy or girl" all ties in with the stories of prince and princess upon which we were "impaled" in childhood. (Here is a twist whereby one woman's giving of a doll to another woman stands somehow for impregnation, gestation, parturition and parenthood linking the two.) Nora was " 'a good woman,' and so a bitch on a high plane"—and Robin "a wild thing caught in a woman's skin, monstrously alone, monstrously vain." Sleep, death, love, "the evil of the night"; "Love, that terrible thing!"—all tied in with the ambiguous range of meanings for "Go down."

Might we make one more try? As I view the general background of terms for motivation in this book, they merge into an amalgam not unlike the merging of terms in the dialectic of Hitler's *Mein Kampf*. But in that book there are clearly *two antithetical* sets, all built around a spurious contrast between "Aryan" and "Jew." Again, I should warn that I am decidedly *not* calling this book "Hitlerite." The Nazis adapted "race" and "blood" to their purposes; but here, we might say, such a view of seeing and placing things is almost as "innocent" of political organization as is childhood itself.

Also, here the focus is rather upon one vast coalescence of terms, all born of one source and built in keeping with a dialectic that involves a considerably recondite secular variant of the relation between the Old Testament and the New. For here the analogue of Old Testament motives is Felix, under a social cloud in run-down Christianity; and the analogue of New Testament motives is Robin, whose "wanderings" represent a problematic sexual motive. Here the differentiation is so set up that one realm of motives is treated as *leading into* the other rather than as being *antithetical* to it.

I mean: Hitlerism set up "Jew" *against* "Aryan." But here, the relation between the "impermissible blood" of the Jew (Felix) and "blood-thirsty" Nora is analogous to the relationship (in traditional Christian theology) between the Old Testament and the New. "In the Old Testament the New is concealed, In the New Testament the Old is revealed." (*Novum Testamentum in Vetere latet, Vetus in Novo patet.*) But here, the analogue of the Old Testament was a Jew among the ambiguously anti-Semitic possibilities of Christianity at its worst; and the analogue of the New Dispensation was the troublous gospel of Nora's *con*version to *per*version.[3]

Thence, by the dialectical resources of *amalgamation*, the entire coalescence of terms is born of the *Night* (their universal identity deriving from this all-Mother whose claims to origin were recognized even by Olympian, patrilineal Greeks, and whom Nora's dreams individuate in terms of a grandmother dressed like a man).

IV

And so to our windup.

O'Connor tells Felix, "Calamity is what we are all seeking." Maybe yes, maybe no, so far as life is concerned—*but certainly yes, as regards the stylistics of lamentation*. I remember my fright on first clearly realizing

---

[3] At this point we might pause to note a different kind of maneuvering in James Baldwin's novel, *Giovanni's Room*. Here the analogous problem of the Negro is in effect "transcended." Instead of the social stigma that Baldwin has fought so valiantly and competently in the United States, the novel deals with the more tenuous dubiousness of homosexuals in Paris. Here the analogue of an Old Testament stage is discernible, if at all, in nothing but the *imagery*, as with that marvelous expression where the skin of an old degenerate white roué is said to look like "sour milk."

that there are two totally different ways of recommending a cause: (1) in terms of expediency, by showing the advantages to be gained if the proper policies are adopted; (2) in terms of "tragic dignification," by showing people who are willing to undergo sacrifices in behalf of the cause. Here was a flat contradiction at the very center of human advocacy, enough in itself to make unlikely the building of a world order in which all important issues could be decided purely on the basis of calm, rational deliberation.

I submitted an article propounding this concept to one editor who rejected it with dispatch: "Snap, back it comes like a rubber check." Then I was more frightened than ever. But eventually it got published, in a magazine, the *Symposium*, edited by Philip Wheelwright and James Burnham. And it is reprinted in my *Philosophy of Literary Form* under the title, "War, Response, and Contradiction." It doesn't look very startling to me now. Yet I still believe that it may happen to deal with a permanently unsolvable problem at the roots of human relations. And I submit that a variant of this situation figures in the structure of this book, as looked at from the stylistic or formalistic point of view.

That is, in this analysis we are considering the theme of sexual inversion without any regard to specifically moral judgments. We would note simply that, in the course of using this theme as a pretext for the accents of Lamentation, the novel naturally and necessarily seeks for ways to make the theme lamentable. Hence the reliance upon ethical or religious values, even though they are exemplifid in *re*verse (in terms of "decay" treated as a recondite species of distinction). Accordingly, the "cause" is recommended in terms that are a variant of "tragic dignification" rather than in terms of rational expediency, or sophisticated relaxation (as were the subject treated *ridendo*, in the manner of a Henry Miller). In brief, the pleasurable effects of the novel will be weakened except insofar as it can build up, for aesthetic purposes the sense of a Puritan morale even while running counter to the Puritanical.

Some such rhetorical situation, it seems to me, underlies the poetics of this book. In celebrating the modes of invert love (in the course of taking on Biblical accents to the ends of artistic entertainment), it must find ways to make the plot "serious" (*spoudaios*). Devices for harping on love's sorrows and its attendant degradations serve this purpose. The impression of "completion" (the *teleios*) is sought through the absoluteness of Robin's translation into identity with sheer beast. And for the sense of "magnitude" (*megethos*), there are the expressions we have considered for, in effect, treating the story in terms of a Beyond, by viewing certain personal relationships as impingements upon the realm of the "racial memory" and such.

Chapter Ten

The Vegetal Radicalism of Theodore Roethke

Perhaps the best way-in is through the thirteen flower poems that comprise the first section of *The Lost Son*. The two opening lyrics, "Cuttings" and "Cuttings (Later)," present the vital strivings of coronated stem, severed from parental stock. Clearly the imagistic figuring of a human situation, they view minutely the action of vegetal "sticks-in-a-drowse" as

> One nub of growth
> Nudges a sand-crumb loose,
> Pokes through a musty sheath
> Its pale tendrilous horn.

The second of the two (that sum up the design of this particular poetic vocation) should be cited entire, for its nature as epitome:

> This urge, wrestle, resurrection of dry sticks,
> Cut stems struggling to put down feet,
> What saint strained so much,
> Rose on such lopped limbs to a new life?
>
> I can hear, underground, that sucking and sobbing,
> In my veins, in my bones I feel it,—
> The small waters seeping upward,
> The tight grains parting at last.
> What sprouts break out,
> Slippery as fish,
> I quail, lean to beginnings, sheath-wet.

Severedness, dying that is at the same time a fanatic tenacity; submergence (fish, and the sheer mindless nerves of sensitive plants); envagination as a homecoming.

To characterize the others briefly: "Root Cellar" (of bulbs that "broke out of boxes hunting for chinks in the dark," of shoots "lolling obscenely," of roots "ripe as old bait"—a "congress of stinks"); "Forcing House" (a frantic urgency of growth, "shooting up lime and dung and ground bones" ... "as the live heat billows from pipes and pots"); "Weed Puller" (the poet

"Under the concrete benches, / Hacking at black hairy roots,— / Those lewd monkey-tails hanging from drainholes"); "Orchids" ("adder-mouthed" in the day, at night "Loose ghostly mouths / Breathing"); "Moss-Gathering" (the guilt of moss-gathering); "Old Florist" (genre portrait, lines in praise of a man vowed to the ethics of this vegetal radicalism); "Transplanting" (a companion piece to the previous poem, detailing *operations* in ways that appeal to our *sensations*); "Child on Top of a Greenhouse" (the great stir below, while the young hero climbs, smashing through glass, the wind billowing out the seat of his britches); "Flower-Dump" (the picturesqueness greatly increased by a strong contrast, as the catalogue of the heap and clutter ends on a vision of "one tulip on top / One swaggering head / Over the dying, the newly dead"); "Carnations" (where the theme shifts to talk of "a crisp hyacinthine coolness, / Like that clear autumnal weather of eternity," —a kind of expression, as we shall later try to indicate, not wholly characteristic of this poet).

From this group we omitted one item, "Big Wind," because we want to consider it at greater length. It reveals most clearly how Roethke can endow his brief lyrics with intensity of *action*. Nor is the effect got, as so often in short forms, merely by a new spurt in the last line. No matter how brief the poems are, they progress from stage to stage. Reading them, you have strongly the sense of entering at one place, winding through a series of internal developments, and coming out somewhere else. Thus "Big Wind" first defines the situation (water shortage in greenhouse during storm) with a five-line rhetorical question. Next come fifteen lines describing the action appropriate to the scene, the strained efforts of those who contrive to keep the pipes supplied with hot steam. Then the substance of this account is restated in a figure that likens the hothouse to a ship riding a gale. And after eleven lines amplifying the one turbulent metaphor, there are two final lines wherein the agitation subsides into calm, with a splendid gesture of assertion. We cite the summarizing image, and its closing couplet:

> But she rode it out,
> That old rose-house,
> She hove into the teeth of it,
> The core and pith of that ugly storm,
> Ploughing with her stiff prow,
> Bucking into the wind-waves
> That broke over the whole of her,
> Flailing her sides with spray,
> Flinging long strings of wet across the roof-top,
> Finally veering, wearing themselves out, merely
> Whistling thinly under the wind-vents;
> She sailed into the calm morning,
> Carrying her full cargo of roses.

The unwinding of the trope is particularly fortunate in suggesting tran-scendence because the reference to the "full cargo of roses," even as we are thinking of a ship, suddenly brings before us a vision of the greenhouse solidly grounded on *terra firma*; and this shift apparently helps to give the close its great finality. Thus, though you'd never look to Roethke for the rationalistic, the expository steps are here ticked off as strictly as in the successive steps of a well-formed argument. And thanks to the develop-mental structure of such poems, one never thinks of them sheerly as descrip-tive: they have the vigor, and the poetic morality, of action, of form un-folding.

To round out this general sampling, we might consider a poem written since the publication of *The Lost Son*. It is "The Visitant," and in contrast with "The Big Wind," which is robust, it possesses an undulance, a hushed-ness, a contemplative, or even devotional attitude, that makes of love an almost mystic presence. Roethke here begins with such a natural scene as would require a local deity, a *genius loci*, to make it complete. Hence as the poem opens, the place described is infused with a *numen* or *pneuma*, a con-centration of spirit just on the verge of apparition.

The work is divided into three movements: the first anticipatory, the third reminiscent, the second leading through a partly secular, yet gently pious, theophany. The mood is beautifully sustained.

The introductory stanza evokes a secretive spot by a stream, at a time of vigil ("I waited, alert as a dog") while, with a shift in the slight wind (figuring also a breath of passion?), "a tree swayed over water." Nine lines establishing expectancy, a state of suspension as though holding one's breath. ("The leech clinging to a stone waited.")

The second stanza is of the "coming." We quote it entire:

> Slow, slow as a fish she came,
> Slow as a fish coming forward,
> Swaying in a long wave;
> Her skirts not touching a leaf,
> Her white arms reaching toward me.
>
> She came without sound,
> Without brushing the wet stones;
> In the soft dark of early evening,
> She came,
> The wind in her hair,
> The moon beginning.

The wind is thus there too, so the ambiguities of the advent may now pre-sumably stand also for erotic movements sometimes celebrated by poets as a "dying." The swaying tree of the first stanza has its counterpart in the swaying "fish" of the second.

The third stanza is of the same scene, now retrospectively: The spirit is there still, but only through having been there, as in the first stanza it was there prophetically. Thus, at the end:

> A wind stirred in a web of appleworms;
> The tree, the close willow, swayed.

The peculiar mixture of tension and calm in this poem is of great felicity. The talk of "swaying," the key word repeated in each stanza, has its replica in the cradle-like rhythm. And the whole effect is gratifyingly idyllic, even worshipful.

As a comment on method, we might contrast "The Visitant" with another poem where Roethke was apparently attempting, in a somewhat "essayistic" manner, to trace the birth of Psyche. It begins

> The soul stirs in its damp folds,
> Stirs as a blossom stirs,
> Still wet from its bud-sheath,
> Slowly unfolding.

Cyclamen, turtle, minnow, child, seed, snail—each in turn is exploited to define how the spirit moves, "still and inward." The lines are the poet's *De Anima*: and the emergent soul is seen ultimately in terms of an inner Snail-Phallus. As there is a mind's eye, a spirit breath, an inner ear, so he would seem to conceive a kind of transcendent sex-within-sex, the essence of pure snailhood ("outward and inward" . . . "hugging a rock, stone and horn" . . . "taking and embracing its surroundings"). But though the poem is almost a review of Roethke's favorite images, it is far less successful in combining Psyche and Eros than "The Visitant." For it is weaker in action, development, being rather a series of repetitive attempts to arrive at the same end from different images as starting point. Roethke could have got to this poem by translating the theories of mystical theology directly into his own impressionistic equivalent. In "The Visitant" he has moved beyond such mere correspondences by introducing a dramatic situation and building around it. A comparison of the two poems shows how the essayistic (that moves toward excellence in Pope) could be but an obstruction to Roethke.[1]

We have said that the mention of "coolness" and "eternity" was not characteristic of Roethke's language. We meant this statement in the strictest sense. We meant that you will rarely find in his verse a noun ending in

---

[1] Since this comment was written, the poem has been greatly revised, mainly by omission of about half its original contents. In its final form, there is a progression of but three images (blossom, minnow, snail) culminating in a catachresis ("music in a hood"). One epithet ("a light breather") is lifted from the body of the poem to be used as title. And the last six lines diminish gradually from ten syllables to two. The poem has thus finally been assimilated, has been made developmental.

"-ness" or "-ity." He goes as far as is humanly possible in quest of a speech wholly devoid of abstractions.

To make our point by antithesis: glancing through Eliot's "Burnt Norton," we find these words:

> abstraction, possibility, speculation, purpose, deception, circulation, arrest, movement, fixity, freedom, compulsion, *Erhebung* without motion, concentration without elimination, completion, ecstasy, resolution, enchantment, weakness, mankind, damnation, consciousness, disaffection, stillness, beauty, rotation, permanence, deprivation, affection, plentitude, vacancy, distraction, apathy, concentration, eructation, solitude, darkness, deprivation, destitution, property, dessication, evacuation, inoperancy, abstention, appetency, silence, stillness, co-existence, tension, imprecision, temptation, limitation.

If Roethke adheres to his present aesthetic, there are more of such expressions in this one Quartet of Eliot's than Roethke's Vegetal Radicalism would require for a whole lifetime of poetizing.

In one poem, to be sure, they do cluster. In "Dolor," lines detailing the "tedium" of "institutions" (notably the schoolroom), we find, besides these two words: sadness, misery, desolation, reception, pathos, ritual, duplication. But their relative profusion here explains their absence elsewhere, in verse written under an aesthetic diametrically opposed to such motives. (In one place he uses "sweetness" as a term of endearment, yet the effect is more like an epithet than like an abstract noun.)

Accordingly, in the attempt to characterize Roethke's verse, you could profitably start from considerations of vocabulary. The motive that we have in mind is by no means peculiar to this one poet. It runs through modern art generally. And though few of the artists working in this mode are interested in formal philosophy, the ultimate statement of the problem would take us back to some basic distinctions in Immanuel Kant's *Critique of Pure Reason*: notably his way of aligning "intuitions," "concepts," and "ideas."

If you perceive various sensations (of color, texture, size, shape, etc.), you are experiencing what Kant would call "intuitions of sensibility." If you can next "unify" this "manifold" (as were you to decide that the entire lot should be called a "tree"), in this word or name you have employed a "concept of the understanding." "Intuitions" and "concepts," taken together, would thus sum up the world of visible, tangible, audible things, the objects and operations of our sensory experience. And because of their positive, empirical nature, they would also present the sensible material that forms the basis of a poetic image (however "spiritual" may be the implications of the poet's language in its outer reaches).

"Intuitions" and "concepts" belong to Kant's "Aesthetic" and "Analytic" respectively. But there is also a purely "Dialectical" realm, comprising "ideas of reason." This is the world of such invisible, intangible, inaudible things as "principles." The various "isms" would be classed as "ideas of reason." In carrying out an idea, men will at every turn deal with the concrete objects that are represented in terms of "intuitions" and "concepts"; yet the idea itself is not thus "empirical," but purely "dialectical," not available to our senses alone, or to measurement by scientific instruments.

Do not these distinctions of Kant's indicate the direction which poetry might take, in looking for a notable purification of language? If one could avoid the terms for "ideas," and could use "concepts" only insofar as they are needed to unify the manifold of "intuitions," the resultant vocabulary would move toward childlike simplicity. And it would be cleansed of such unwieldly expressions (now wielded by politicos and journalists) as: capitalism, fascism, socialism, communism, democracy (words unthinkable in Roethke's verse, which features rather: cry, moon, stones, drip, toad, bones, snail, fish, flower, house, water, spider, pit, dance, kiss, bud, sheath, budsheath, ooze, slip-ooze, behind which last term, despite ourselves, we irresponsibly keep hearing a child's pronunciation of "slippers").

Kant's alignment was designed primarily to meet the positivistic requirements of modern technological science. And since he himself, in the *Critique of Judgment*, talked of "aesthetic ideas," the issue is not drawn by him with finality. The modern lyric poet of imagistic cast might even with some justice think of himself as paralleling the scientific ideal, when he stresses the vocabulary of concrete things and sensible operations; yet the typical scientist language, with its artificially constructed Greek-Roman compounds, seems usable only in a few sophisticated gestures (as with the ironic nostalgia of a Laforgue). This much is certain, however: Whatever the complications, we can use the Kantian distinctions to specify a possible criterion for a purified poetic idiom. The ideal formula might be stated thus: *A minimum of "ideas," a maximum of "intuitions."* In this form, it can sum up the Roethkean aesthetic. (The concept would be admitted as a kind of regrettable necessity.)

For further placements (as regards the problems of linguistic purity set by urbanization), we might think of Dante's *De Vulgari Eloquentia*, Wordsworth's Preface to the *Lyrical Ballads*, and D. H. Lawrence's cult of the "physical" as contrasted with the "abstract."

Dante introduced the criterion of the *infantile* in the search for a purified poetic idiom. Choosing between learned Latin and the vernacular, he noted that the "vulgar locution" which infants imitate from their nurses is "natural" and "more noble," hence the most fit for poetry. But though he set up the infantile as a criterion for preferring Italian to a learned and "artificial" language, his criteria for the selection of a poetic vocabulary within Italian itself encompassed a quite mature medium. Thus, the ideal speech should be "illustrious, cardinal, courtly, and curial"; and in such a language, one would necessarily introduce, without irony or sullenness, many "ideas of reason." Indeed, what we have called the "infantile" criterion of selection we might rather call a search for the ideal mother tongue (had it not been for the Fall, Dante reminds us, all men would still speak Hebrew, the language of the Garden of Eden). That is, we could stress its *perfection*, its maturity and scope (its "mother wit"), rather than its *intellectual limitations* (though in the first great division of labor, separating those who specialize in being males and those who specialize in being females, the class of womanhood would seem to be the "more noble," so far as concerned its associations with the *medium* of poetry). The ideal language, we might say, was under the sign not of the child but of the Virgin Mother; though even, had the infant Jesus been the ultimate term for the motivation here, his essential kingliness would have been enough to derive the illustrious, cardinal, courtly, and curial from the infantile alone, as so modified.

In any case, as early as Dante's time, though prior to the upsurge of the industrial revolution, the division of labor was sufficiently advanced for him to assert that each kind of craftsman had come to speak a different language in the confusion of tongues caused during work on the Tower. The diversity of languages was thus derived from specialization, quite as with particular technical idioms today—and the higher the specialized activity, Dante says, the more "barbarous" its speech. His principle of selection could thus acquire a new poignancy later, when the learned language he had rejected had become an essential part of the vernacular itself, and when the relation between mother and child is not formally summed up in the infancy of a universal ruler (though, roundabout, in furtive ways, there are the modern mothers who are by implication ennobled, in giving birth to offspring they encourage to be child-tyrants).

By the time of Wordsworth's preface, after several centuries of progressively accelerated industrialization, the search for a principle of selection, for a "purified" speech, involves another kind of regression, a romantic reversion, not just to childhood simplicity, but also to "low and rustic life." For in this condition, "the essential passions of the heart . . . can attain their maturity, are less under restraint, and speak a plainer and more emphatic language." Though Wordsworth is talking of the rustic life itself, approaching the problem in terms of language (as Wordsworth's own explicit concern with selection entitles us to do), we should stress rather the *imagery* drawn from "the necessary character of rural occupations." Such imagery, he says, would be "more easily comprehended" and "more durable"; and by it "our elementary feelings" would be "more forcibly communicated," since "the passions of men are incorporated with the beautiful and permanent forms of nature."

Wordsworth is also explicitly considering another threat to poetry, the journalistic idiom which by now has almost become the norm with us, so that poets are repeatedly rebuked for not writing in a style designed to be used once and thrown away. Thus, on the subject of the causes that now act "with a combined force to blunt the discriminating powers of the mind," bringing about "a state of almost savage stupor," Wordsworth writes:

> The most effective of these causes are the great national events which are daily taking place, and the increasing accumulation of men in cities, where the uniformity of their occupations produces a craving for extraordinary incident, which the rapid communication of intelligence hourly gratifies.

"The rapid communication of intelligence hourly"; this is Wordsworth's resonant equivalent for "journalism." In such an expression he does well by it, even while recognizing its threat to poetic purity as he conceives of such purity.

He goes on to state his belief that, despite his preference for the ways of pretechnological nature as the basis for a poet's imagery, "If the time should ever come when what is now called Science . . . shall be ready to put on . . . a form of flesh and blood, the Poet will lend his divine spirit to aid the transfiguration." Maybe yes, maybe no. Though concerned with the purification of vocabulary for poetic purposes, Wordsworth does not show (or even ask) how the technological idioms themselves can be likened to the language learned at the breast.

We should note, however, one major respect in which the terms of the new technology are in spirit a language close to childhood. For they have the quality of death rays and rocket ships, and other magical powers the thought of which can make the child wonder and in his imagination feel mighty. Indeed, the pageantry of the technological (the new lore of the giant-killers) can appeal to the infantile, long before there is any concern with such romances of love as, variously, concern Dante, Wordsworth, and Roethke, all three. What you put around a Christmas tree reflects no longer the mystery of the Birth, but the wonders of modern technological production. So, surprisingly, we glimpse how a poet's nursery language may be more mature than at first it may seem. It may be no younger than the adolescent in spirit, though this adolescense is on the side that leans toward the universal sensibility of childhood (and of the maternal) rather than toward the forensic, abstract, and journalistically "global."

A bridge-builder, no matter how special his language, has successfully "communicated" with his fellows when he has built them a good bridge. In this respect, the languages of the technological specialties confront a different communicative problem than marks the language of the specialist in verse. And even if, with Wordsworth, you believed in the ability of poetry to poetize any conditions that modern technology might bring into being, you could question whether this result could be got through the Wordsworth aesthetic. Hence a century later, D. H. Lawrence, whose flower poems could have been models for Roethke, warns against a kind of *abstraction from the physical* that accompanies the progress of scientific materialism.

The doctrine infuses all of Lawrence's writings. But one can find it especially announced in his essay, "Men Must Work and Women as Well," reprinted in the Viking Portable. We think of statements like these: "Mr. Ford, being in his own way a genius, has realized that what the modern workman wants, just like the modern gentleman, is abstraction. The modern workman doesn't *want* to be interested in his job. He wants to be as little interested, as nearly perfectly mechanical, as possible." . . . The trend of our civilization is "towards a greater and greater abstraction from the physical, towards a further and further physical separateness between men and women, and between individual and individual." . . . Such displays even as "sitting in bathing suits all day on a beach" are "peculiarly non-physical, a flaunting of the body in its non-physical, merely optical aspect." . . . "He only *sees* his meal, he never *really* eats it. He drinks his beer by idea, he no longer tastes it." . . . "Under it all, as ever, as everywhere, vibrates the one great impulse of our civilization, physical recoil from every other being and from every form of physical existence." . . . "We can look on Soviet Russia as nothing but a logical state of society established in anti-physical insanity. —Physical and material are, of course, not the same; in fact, they are subtly opposite. The machine is absolutely material, and absolutely anti-physical— as even our fingers know. And the Soviet is established on the image of the machine, 'pure' materialism. The Soviet hates the real physical body far more deeply than it hates Capital." . . . "The only thing to do is to get your bodies back, men and women. A great part of society is irreparably lost: abstracted into non-physical, mechanical entities."

One may object to the particulars here; the *tendency* Lawrence discusses is clear enough. And though machinery (as viewed in psychoanalytic terms) may stand for the pudenda, and though the abstractions of technology and finance may even make for a compensatory overemphasizing of the sexual (Love Among the Machines), Lawrence was noting how the proliferation of mechanical means makes for a relative withdrawal, for a turn from intuitive immediacy to pragmatist meditation; hence his crusade against the intellect (and its "ideas").

As a novelist, Lawrence confronted this problem in all its contradictoriness. His crusade against the intellect was itself intellectual, even intellectualistic. Along with his cult of simplicity (which, going beyond Dante's infantile-maternal criterion and Wordsworth's rustic one, became a super-Rousseauistic vision of ideal savagery) there was his endless discussion of the issue. But though few modern novels contain a higher percentage of talk that might fall roughly under the heading of "ideas," (talk under the slogan, Down With Talk), in his verse he sought for images that *exemplified* the state of intuitive immediacy rather than expatiating on the problem of its loss. For whereas the novels dealt with people, the verse could treat of animals and inanimate beings that imagistically figured some generalized or idealized human motive (as with the heroic copulation of whales and elephants, or the social implications in the motions of a snapdragon). All told, he loquaciously celebrated the wisdom of silent things— for the yearning to see beyond the intellect terminates mystically in the yearning to regain a true state of "infancy," such immediacy of communication as would be possible only if man had never spoken at all (an aim often sought in sexual union, though both sexual barriers and the breaking of those barriers are preponderantly conditioned by the many "ideas of reason" that are the necessary result of language and of the social order made possible by language).

All told, then, we can see in Roethke's cult of "intuitive" language: a more strictly "infantile" variant of the Dantesque search for a "noble" vernacular; a somewhat suburban, horticulturist variant of Wordsworth's stress upon the universal nature of rusticity; and a close replica of Lawrence's distinction between the "physical" and the "abstract."

With "prowess in arms" (*Virtus*) he is not concerned. The long poems, still to be considered, are engrossed with problems of welfare (*Salus*), though of a kind attainable rather by persistent dreamlike yielding than by moralistic "guidance of the will." As for *Venus*, in Roethke's verse it would seem addressed most directly to a phase of adolescence. The infantile motif serves here, perhaps, like the persuasive gestures of sorrow or helplessness, as appeal to childless girls vaguely disposed toward nursing. The lost son's bid for a return to the womb may thus become transformed into a doting on the erotic imagery of the "sheath-wet" and its "slip-ooze." And in keeping, there is the vocabulary of flowers and fishes (used with connotations of love), and of primeval slime.

We have considered representative instances of Roethke's poetic manner. We have viewed his choice of terms from the standpoint of three motivational orders as described by Kant. And we noted three strategic moments in the theory of poetic selectivity (Dante on the infantile, Wordsworth on the rustic, Lawrence on the physical). Now let us ask what kind of selectivity is implicit in Roethke's flower images (with their variants of the infantile, rustic, and physical).

In particular, what is a greenhouse? What might we expect it to stand for? It is not sheer nature, like a jungle; nor even regulated nature, like a formal garden. It is not the starkly unnatural, like a factory. Nor is it in those intermediate realms of institutional lore, systematic thanatopses, or convenient views of death, we find among the relics of a natural history museum. Nor would it be like a metropolitan art gallery. It is like all these only in the sense that it is a museum experience, and so an aspect of our late civilization. But there is a peculiar balance of the natural and the artificial in a greenhouse. All about one, the lovely, straining beings, visibly drawing sustenance from ultimate, invisible powers—in a silent blare of vitality—yet as morbid as the caged animals of a zoo.

Even so, with Roethke the experience is not like going from exhibit to exhibit among botanic oddities and rarities. It is like merging there into the life-laden but sickly soil.

To get the quality of Roethke's affections, we should try thinking of "lubricity" as a "good" word, connoting the curative element in the primeval slime. Thus, with him, the image of the mire is usually felicitous, associated with protection and welcome, as in warm sheathlike forms. Only in moments of extremity does he swing to the opposite order of meanings, and think rather of the mire that can hold one a prisoner, sucking toward stagnation and death. Then, for a period of wretchedness, the poet is surprised into finding in this otherwise Edenic image, his own equivalent for Bunyan's slough of despond.

Flowers suggest analogous human motives quite as the figures of animals do in Aesop's fables (except that here they stand for relationships rather than for typical characters). The poet need but be as accurate as he can, in describing the flowers objectively; and while aiming at this, he comes upon corresponding human situations, as it were by redundancy. Here was a good vein of imagery to exploit, even as a conceit: that is, any poet shrewdly choosing a theme might hit upon hothouse imagery as generating principle for a group of poems. Yet in this poet's case there was a further incentive. His father had actually been a florist, in charge of a greenhouse. Hence, when utilizing the resources of this key image for new developments, Roethke could at the same time be drawing upon the most occult of early experiences. Deviously, elusively, under such conditions the amplifying of the theme could also be "regressive," and in-turning.

The duality, in the apparent simplicity, of his method probably leads back, as with the somewhat mystic *ars poetica* of so many contemporary poets, to the kind of order statuesquely expressed in Baudelaire's sonnet, "*Correspondances*," on mankind's passage through nature as through "forests of symbols," while scents, sounds, and colors "make mutual rejoinder" like distant echoes that fuse "in deep and dusky unity."

In "Night Crow," Roethke states his equivalent of the pattern thus:

> When I saw that clumsy crow
> Flap from a wasted tree,
> A shape in the mind rose up:
> Over the gulfs of dream

> Flew a tremendous bird
> Further and further away
> Into a moonless black,
> Deep in the brain, far back.

One could take it as a particularized embodiment of a general principle, an anecdote of *one* image standing for the way of all such images, which are somehow felt twice, once positivistically, and once symbolically.

In this connection, even one misprint becomes meaningful. In "Weed Puller," he writes of flowers "tugging all day at perverse life." At least, that is the wording presumably intended. The line actually reads: "tugging at preverse life." In Roethke's case, this was indeed a "pre-verse" way of life. In the flowers, their hazards and quixotisms, he was trained to a symbolic vocabulary of subtle human relations and odd strivings, before he could have encountered the equivalent patterns of experience in exclusively human terms. As with those systems of pure mathematics which mathematicians sometimes develop without concern for utility, long before men in the practical realm begin asking themselves the kind of questions for which the inventor of the pure forms has already offered the answers; so, in the flower stories, the poet would be reverting to a time when he had noted these forms before he felt the need for them, except vaguely and "vatically."

The opposite way is depicted in a drawing (we falsely remembered it as a caricature) printed in *L'Illustration* and reproduced in Matthew Josephson's book on Emile Zola. It is entitled "Zola Studying Railroad Life on a Locomotive; Drawing Made on the Scene, During a Voyage Between Paris and Le Havre, When He Was Seeking the 'Living Documents' for his Novel, *La Bête Humaine*." Zola, standing, stiffly erect, between the cabin and the coal car, dressed in a semiformal attire that would suit a doctor or a lawyer of that time, is all set to make the trip that would supply him with certain required documentary observations for a "scientific" novel.

What, roughly, then, is the range of meaning in Roethke's flowers? In part, they are a kind of psychology, an emphatic vocabulary for expressing rudimentary motives felt, rightly or wrongly, to transcend particular periods of time. Often, in their characters as "the lovely diminutives," they are children in general, or girls specifically. When we are told in "The Waking" that "flowers jumped / Like small goats," there is a gracing of the bestial motive referred to as "the goat's mouth" in the "dance" of "The Long Alley," section three. The preconscious, the infantile, the regressive, the sexual—but is there not in them a further mystery, do they not also appeal as a pageantry, as "positions of pantomime," their natural beauty deriving added secular "sanctification" from the principle of hierarchy? For the thought of flowers, in their various conditions, with their many ways of root, sprout, and blossom, is like the contemplation of nobles, churchmen, commoners, peasants (a world of masks). In hothouse flowers, you confront, enigmatically, the representation of status. By their nature flowers contribute grace to social magic—hence, they are insignia, infused with a spirit of social ordination. In this respect they could be like Aesop's animals, though only incipiently so. For if their relation to the social mysteries were schematically recognized, we should emerge from the realm of intuitions (with their appropriate "aesthetic ideas") into such "ideas of reason" as a Pope might cultivate ("whatever is, is right" . . . "self-love, to urge, and reason, to restrain" . . . "force first made conquest, and that conquest, law" . . . "order is heaven's first law" . . . "that true self-love and social are the same"). A Roethke might well subscribe to some such doctrine, notably Pope's tribute's to "honest Instinct"—but in terms whereby the assumptions would, within these rules of utterance, be themselves unutterable.

Other of the shorter poems should be mentioned, such as "My Papa's Waltz," which is dashing, in its account of a boy whirled in a dance with his tipsy father; "Judge Not," a more formalistic statement than is characteristic. Some of the short pieces come close to standard magazine verse. "The Waking" risks a simple post-Wordsworthian account of pure joy. And "Pickle Belt," recounting "the itches / Of sixteen-year-old lust," while not of moment in itself, in its puns could be listed with the crow poem, if one were attempting to specify systematically just how many kinds of correspondence Roethke's images draw upon. But mostly, here, we want to consider the four longer pieces: "The Lost Son," "The Long Alley," "A Field of Light," and "The Shape of the Fire."

Roethke himself has described them as "four experiences, each in a sense stages in a kind of struggle out of the slime; part of a slow spiritual progress, if you will; part of an effort to be born." At the risk of brashness, we would want to modify this description somewhat. The transformations seem like a struggle less to be born than to avoid being undone. Or put it thus: The dangers inherent in the regressive imagery seem to have received an impetus from without, that drove the poet still more forcefully in the same direction, dipping him in the river who loved water. His own lore thus threatened to turn against him. The enduring of such discomforts is a "birth" in the sense that, if the poet survives the ordeal, he is essentially stronger, and has to this extent *forged himself* an identity.

The four poems are, in general, an alternating of two motives: regression, and a nearly lost, but never quite relinquished, expectancy that leads to varying degrees of fulfillment. In "Flight," the first section of "The Lost Son," the problem is stated impressionistically, beginning with the mention of death ("concretized," of course, not in the name of "death," which would be at the farthest an abstraction, at the nearest an abstraction personified, but circumstantially: "At Woodlawn I heard the dead cry"). When considering the possible thesaurus of flowers, we were struck by the fact that, in the greenhouse poems, there was no overt reference to the use of flowers for the sickroom and as funeral wreaths. Deathy connotations are implicitly there, at the very start, in the account of the Cuttings, which are dying even as they strain heroically to live. And there is the refuse of "Flower Dump." But of flowers as standing for the final term of human life, we recall no mention. Roethke has said that he conceives of the greenhouse as symbol for "a womb, a heaven-on-earth." And the thought of its vital internality, in this sense, seems to have obliterated any conscious concern with the uses to which the products of the florist's trade are put. In any case his present poem, dealing with a lyric "I" in serious danger, fittingly begins in the sign of death.

The opening stanza, however, contains not merely the theme of death-like stagnation. There is also, vaguely, talk of moving on:

> Snail, snail, glister me forward,
> Bird, soft-sigh me home.

In the society of *this* poet's lowly organisms, there is a curative element, incipiently. And throughout the opening section, with its images of rot and stoppage, there is likewise a watching and waiting. Even a rhetorical *question* is, after all, subtly, in form a *quest*. Hence the call for a sign ("Out of what door do I go, / Where and to whom?"), though it leads but to veiled oracular answers ("Dark hollows said, lee to the wind, / The moon said, back of an eel," etc.), transforms this opening section ("The Flight") into a hunt, however perplexed. Thus the stanza that begins "Running lightly over spongy ground," is followed by one that begins, "Hunting along the river." The section ends on a riddle, in terms contradictory and symbolic, as befits such utterance. The connotations are Sphinxlike, oracular; the descriptions seem to touch upon an ultimate wordless secret. What is the answer? Put all the disjunct details together, and, for our purposes, we need but note that the object of the quest is lubricitous (in the mode of furtive felicity). End of Section One.

Section Two: The Pit—nine lines, in very subdued tonality, about roots—in general an amplification of the statement that the poet's search is radical. We cite the passage entire, since it is a splendid text for revealing the ingenuity of Roethke as Rhetorician:

> Where do the roots go?
>   Look down under the leaves.
> Who put the moss there?
>   These stones have been here too long.
> Who stunned the dirt into noise?
>   Ask the mole, he knows.
> I feel the slime of a wet nest.
>   Beware Mother Mildew.
> Nibble again, fish nerves.

Considered as topics ("places" in the traditional rhetorical sense), the stanza could be reduced to a set of images that variously repeat the idea of the deep-down, the submerged, the underground. Roots . . . "under the leaves" . . . stones long buried beneath moss . . . the sound of moles burrowing . . . these are details that variously repeat the same theme in the first six lines. The last three, while similar in quality (the dank, hidden, submerged, within), add a further development: the hint of incipience, ambiguously present in lines seven and eight ("I feel" and "Beware"), comes clear in line nine: "Nibble again, fish nerves."

For the moment confining ourselves to the first six: note how this series of lyric images is dramatized. Surprisingly, much is done by a purely Grammatical resource. Thus, the underlying assertion of the first couplet (this mood is like roots, like under-the-leaves) is transformed into a kind of "cosmic" dialogue, split into an interchange between two voices. The next restatement (it is like moss-covered stones) is broken into the same Q-A pattern, but this time the answer is slightly evasive, though still in the indicative ("These stones have been here too long," a "vatic" way of suggesting that the mood is like stones sunken, and covered heavily). The third couplet (it is like the sound of moles burrowing) is introduced by a slightly longer and more complex form of question. (The first was where-roots-go, the second who-put-moss-there, and the third is who-stunned-dirt-into-noise, a subtly growing series). Also the answer is varied by a shift into the imperative ("ask the mole").

All this questioning and answering has been as if from voices in the air, or in the nature of things. But the turn in the last three lines is announced by a shift to the lyric "I" as subject. The image of mildew is made not only personal, but "essential," by being named as "Mother Mildew." The indicative in line seven ("I feel") shifts to imperatives in lines eight and nine ("Beware" and "Nibble"); but whereas in the first of these imperatives the topic (mildew) appears as object of the command, in the second the topic ("fish nerves") is given as subject.

Thus, though the stanza is but a series of restatements, it has considerable variety despite the brevity of the lines and despite the fact that each sentence ends exactly at the end of a line. And the Grammatical shifts, by dramatizing the sequence of topics, keep one from noting that the stanza is in essence but a series of similarly disposed images (symbolizing what Roethke, in a critical reference, has called "obsessions").

As for the closing line, the more one knows of the fish image in Roethke's verse, the more clearly one will feel the quality of incipience in the nibbling of "fish nerves."

The third section, "The Gibber," might (within the conditions of a lyric) be said to culminate in the *act* that corresponds to the attitude implicit in the opening scene. It is sexual, but reflexively so: the poet is disastrously

alone. Listening, "by the cave's door," the poet hears an old call ("Dogs of
the groin / Barked and howled," and sinister things, in the mood of a Walpurgisnacht, call for his yielding in a kind of death). Against a freezing fear,
there is a desperate cry for infantile warmth. "I'm cold. I'm cold all over.
Rub me in father and mother." The reflexive motif is most direct, perhaps,
in the lines: "As my own tongue kissed / My lips awake." The next lines
(Roethke has called them a kind of Elizabethan "rant") culminate in a
shrilly plaintive inventory of the hero's plight:

> All the windows are burning! What's left of my life?
> I want the old rage, the lash of primordial milk!
> Goodbye, goodbye, old stones, the time-order is going,
> I have married my hands to perpetual agitation,
> I run, I run to the whistle of money,

the lamentation being summed up, by a break in a different rhythm:

> Money money money
> Water water water

Roethke's Vegetal Radicalism is not the place one would ordinarily
look for comments on the economic motive. Yet you can take it as a law
that, in our culture, at a moment of extreme mental anguish, if the sufferer
is accurate there will be an accounting of money, too. It will be at least implicit, in the offing—hence with professional utterers it should be explicit.
So, the agitation comes to a head in the juxtaposing of two liquidities, two
potencies, one out of society, the other universal, out of nature. (And in the
typical dichotomy of aestheticism, where the aesthetic and the practical are
treated as in diametrical opposition to each other, does not this alignment
encourage us to treat art and the rational as antitheses? For if money is
equated with the practical and the rational, then by the dialectics of the case
art is on the side of an "irrational," nonmonetary Nature.)

After a brief rush of scenic details (cool grass, a bird that may have
gone away, a swaying stalk, the shadow of a worm, undirected clouds—all
developed by the Grammatico-Rhetorical method we noted in "The Pit")
the section ends on a world of white flashes, which the poet finally characterizes as of the essence of cinder "falling through a dark swirl."

Into the funnel: down the drain. The dream-death. Though the second
section was *entitled* "The Pit," here actually is the poem's abysmal moment,
after which there must be a turning.

Hence, Section Four, "The Return." Recovery in terms of the "father
principle." Memory of a greenhouse experience: out of night, the coming of
dawn, and the father. After the description of the dark, with the roses likened
to bloody clinkers in a furnace (an excellently right transition from the ashes
theme at the close of the previous section to the topic of steam knocking in

the steam pipes as a heralding of the advent), the movement proceeds thus (note that the theme of white is also kept and appropriately transformed):

> Once I stayed all night.
> The light in the morning came up slowly over the
>   white
> Snow.
> There were many kinds of cool
> Air.
> Then came steam.
>
> Pipe-knock.
> Scurry of warm over small plants.
> Ordnung! ordnung!
> Papa is coming!

We happen to have seen a comment which Roethke wrote on this passage, and we cite it for its great use in revealing his methods:

> Buried in the text are many little ambiguities that are not always absolutely necessary to know. For instance, the "pipe-knock." With the coming of steam, the pipes begin knocking violently, in a greenhouse. But "Papa," or the florist, often would knock his own pipe (a pipe for smoking) on the sides of the benches, or the pipes. ... Then, with the coming of steam (and "papa"—the papa on earth and heaven being blended, of course) there is the sense of motion in the greenhouse—my symbol for the whole of life, a womb, a heaven-on-earth.

Recalling De Quincey's comments on the knocking at the gate after the murder scene in Macbeth, and recalling that we have just been through a "suicide" scene, might we not also include, among the connotations of this sound, the knock of conscience? Particularly in that the return to the paternally (or "superegoistically") rational is announced in terms of an admonition (*Ordnung! ordnung!*)—and we should note, on the side, as a possible motivating factor in Roethke's avoidance of ideational abstraction, that this German word for order is one of his few such expressions, though here it has practically the force of an imperative verb, as "sweetness," in another context, was not in function an abstract noun but rather a *name*, an epithet of personal endearment. (Roethke has said that he had in mind the father's Prussian love of discipline, as sublimated into the care of flowers; and he wanted to suggest that the child, as a kind of sleepy sentry, "jumped to attention at the approach.")

The final section (sans title) amplifies the subject of illumination (that we have followed from darkness, through "white flashes," to dawn). But its opening suggests its unfinishedness (as with a corresponding midstage in Eliot's *Four Quartets*):

> It was beginning winter,
> An in-between time . . .

And after talk of light (and reflexively, "light within light") the poem ends on his variant of religious patience and vigil, as applied to the problem of superegoistic rationality:

> A lively understandable spirit
> Once entertained you.
> It will come again.
> Be still.
> Wait.

Again the funnel, in the narrowing-down of the lines. But not, this time, the funnel of darkness that had marked the end of Section Three. There has been a coming of light after darkness, a coming of warmth after cold, a coming of steam after powerlessness, a coming of the father and of his super-egoistic knock—and now at the last a fuller coming is promised. And within the rules of this idiom, "understandable" is a perfect discovery. It is perhaps the only "intellectualistic" word (the only word for "rational") that would not have jarred in this context.

All four of the long poems follow this same general pattern. Thus, "The Long Alley" begins with a sluggish near-stagnant current (from sources outside the poem we have learned that this brooding, regressive stream is "by the edge of the city"). Direction is slight but it is there:

> A river glides out of the grass. A river or serpent.
> A fish floats belly upward,
> Sliding through the white current,
> Slowing turning,
> Slowly.

But the way out is roundabout, a way in. Next there are apostrophes to an absent "kitten-limp sister," a "milk-nose," a "sweetness I cannot touch," as our hero complains that he needs "a loan of the quick." And the stanza ends narcissistically. In the third section, after a plea again reflexively addressed ("Have mercy, gristle") there is an agitated "dance," a simulated *argutatio lecti* (Catullus 6, 11) conveyed somewhat impressionistically, symbolically, enigmatically. After this "close knock," again struggling toward warmth ("Sweet Jesus, make me sweat," a musically felicitous cry, in that the last word is an umlaut modification of the first: sw——t sw——t), there is a somewhat idealistic vision, a gentle name-calling, in which girls ("tenderest") are "littlest flowers" with "fish-ways," while the talk of light ("drowsing in soft light" . . . "Light airs! A piece of angels!") prepares for the closing stanza with its talk of warmth. The progress of the sections might be indicated by these summarizing lines: (1) "My gates are all caves"; (2) "Return the gaze of a pond" (an ingenious inversion of the Narcissus image); (3) "I'm happy with my paws"; (4) "The tendrils have me"; (5) "I'll take the fire."

The shortest of the four long poems, "A Field of Light," begins similarly with "dead water" and evolves into a celebrating of "the lovely diminutives," while the poet walked "through the light air" and "moved with the morning." The mood is most succinctly conveyed, perhaps, in the line: "Some morning thing came, beating its wings." The poem is in three stages: (1) The "dead water," but almost pleasantly, a "watery drowse"; (2) the question-like and questionable act ("Alone, I kissed the skin of a stone; marrow-soft, danced in the sand"); (3) Exhilarated sense of promise.

However, despite the alleviation here, in the final poem, "The Shape of the Fire," the entire course is traveled again. Indeed, if we can accept the ingenious suggestion of one commentator (Mr. Bill Brown, a student in a poetry class of Roethke's), the line "An old scow bumps over black rocks" is about as regressive as human memory could be. It suggests to him "the heart-beat of the mother," as the fetus might hear it dully while asleep in the amniotic fluid, the ultimately regressive baptismal water. (Such reminiscence from prenatal experience would be a purely naturalistic equivalent for the "clouds of glory" that Wordsworth Platonically saw the infant memory "trailing" from its "immortal" past.) In any case, at the very least, the line suggests the state of near-stagnation, a stream so low that a boat of even the shallowest draught scrapes bottom. And after a reflexive section ("My meat eats me," while before this there was but half a being, "only one shoe" and "a two-legged dog"), and a section on vigil ("The wasp waits"), and one to announce awakening promise ("Love, love sang toward," a pleasantly impressionistic idyll of early happiness at the age when childhood was merging into puberty), now the boat can again figure, but transfigured, to assert direction:

> To stare into the after-light, the glitter left on the lake's surface,
> When the sun has fallen behind a wooded island;
> To follow the drops sliding from a lifted oar,
> Held up, while the rower breathes, and the small boat drifts quietly
>   shoreward;
> To know that light falls and fills, often without our knowing,
> As an opaque vase fills to the brim from a quick pouring,
> Fills and trembles at the edge yet does not flow over,
> Still holding and feeding the stem of the contained flower.

Thus, at the end, the cut flower with which the book began. And though the image of the gliding boat (as contrasted with the bottom-scraping one) has moved us from stagnation to felicity (here is a resting on one's oars, whereas Shelley's enrapt boats proceed even without a rower), note that the position of the poet in the advancing craft is backward-looking. Still, there is testimony to a delight in seeing, in contrast with Baudelaire's poem on Don Juan crossing the Styx, similarly looking back: Charon steered the craft among the shades in torment,

> Mais le calme héros, courbé sur sa rapière,
> Regardait le sillage et ne daignait rien voir.

As for all the possible connotations in light, as used in the final illumination of the Roethke poem, spying, we may recall that the last line of the second section was: "Renew the light, lewd whisper."

All told, to analyze the longer poems[2] one should get the general "idea" (or better, mood or *attitude*) of each stanza, then note the succession of images that actualize and amplify it. Insofar as these images are of visible, tangible things, each will be given its verb, so that it have sufficient incidental vividness. But though, in a general way, these verbs will be, either directly or remotely, of the sort that usually goes with the thing (as were dogs to bark, or pigs to grunt), often there may be no verb that, within the conditions of the poem, the noun objectively requires.

For instance, at the beginning of "The Shape of the Fire," there is a line "A cracked pod calls." As an image, the cracked pod belongs here. It is dead, yet there is possibility of a new life in it. Hence, topically, the line might have read simply "A cracked pod." Similarly, there is the line, "Water recedes to the crying of spiders." If spiders stand in general for the loathsome, the line might be translated formalistically: "The principle of fertility is overcome by the principle of fear." However, though pods may rattle, and spiders may weave or bite or trap flies, pods don't call and spiders don't cry.[3]

In considering this problem most pedestrianly, we believe we discovered another Rhetorical device which Roethke has used quite effectively.

---

[2] Incidentally, there are records of "The Long Alley" and "The Shape of the Fire," as read by the author (Poetry Room, Harvard College Library: *The Harvard Vocarium Records*). Some of the tonalities are strikingly like those in the record of Joyce's readings from *Anna Livia Plurabelle*.

[3] Though our "formalistic" version here would be acceptable as a "first rough approximate" of the meaning, there are further possibilities in the offing. Psychoanalytically, insects are said to figure often in dreams as surrogates for children. And in an earlier version of the lyric, "Judge Not," a reference to "the unborn, starving in wombs, curling" had used the same image: the fetuses were described as curling "like dried spiders." The line, "Water recedes to the crying of spiders" might thus, if trailed far enough, bring us into the region of the "birth trauma," as figuring an infant cry at separation from the placental bath. And since the line is immediately followed by "An old scow bumps over black rocks," the child as crying spider could fit well with the already cited interpretation of this second line. (The matter of the order would not be all-important. In the elliptical style, the stages of a development may readily become reordered.)

That is, whenever there is no specific verb required, Roethke resorts to some word in the general category of *communication*. Thus, though "shale loosens" and "a low mouth laps water," a cracked pod calls, spiders and snakes cry, weeds whine, dark hollows, the moon and salt say, inanimate things answer and question and listen or are listened to. To suggest that one thing is of the same essence as another, the poet can speak of their kissing, that is, being in intimate communion (a device that has unintended lewd overtones at one point where the poet, to suggest that he is of the essence of refuse, says, "Kiss me, ashes," a hard line to read aloud without disaster, unless one pauses long on the comma). The topic is clouds? Not clouds that billow or blow, but that would just *be*? The line becomes: "What do the clouds *say*?"

There are possible objections to be raised against this sort of standard poetic personifying, which amounts to putting a communicative verb where the copula is normally required, or perhaps one could have no verb at all. But it does help to suggest a world of natural objects in vigorous communication with one another. The very least these poetic entities do is resort to "mystic participation." The poet's scene constitutes a society of animals and things. To walk through his idealized Nature is to be surrounded by figures variously greeting, beckoning, calling, answering one another, or with little groups here and there in confidential huddles, or strangers by the wayside waiting to pose Sphinxlike questions or to propound obscure but truth-laden riddles. One thus lives as though ever on the edge of an Ultimate Revelation. And as a clear instance of the method as a device for dramatization, consider a passage in "The Lost Son," which, topically considered, amounts to saying, "This is like dying in a weedy meadow, among snakes, cows, and briars," but is transformed by communicative verbs thus:

> The weeds whined,
> The snakes cried,
> The cows and briars
> Said to me: Die.

Somewhat incongruously, we have expressed the underlying statement in terms of simile. Yet similes are very rare in Roethke. The word "like" appears, unless we counted wrong, but three times in the four long poems; "as," used as a synonym for "like," occurs not much oftener. Indeed, one way to glimpse the basic method used here is to think, first, of simile, next of metaphor, and then (extrapolating) imagine advancing to a further step. Thus, one might say, in simile, "The toothache is like a raging storm," or metaphorically, "The raging tooth." Or "beyond" that, one might go elliptically, without logical connectives, from talk of toothache to talk of ships storm-tossed at sea. And there one would confront the kind of *ars poetica* in which Roethke is working.

The method may be further extended by the use of a word in accordance with pure pun-logic. Thus, if in "reach" you hear "rich," you may say either "reach me" or "rich me" for the reach that enriches. ("Rich me cherries a fondling's kiss.")

Much of this verse is highly auditory, leaving implicit the kind of tonal transformations that Hopkins makes explicit. And often the ellipses, by weakening strictly logical attention, induce the hearer to flutter on the edge of associations not surely present, but evanescently there, and acutely evocative (to those who receive poetry through ear rather than eye).

Surely in a poem still to be considered, "God, give me a near" is a barely audible extending of the sense in "God, give me an ear" (here the tonal effect is surest if approached through visual reading); and in the same poem, "tree" and "time" have been "irresponsibly" transposed, with suggestive effects, thus: "Once upon a tree / I came across a time." "The ear's not here / Beneath the hair" (in the opening stanza of Section Two, "The Shape of the Fire") is tonal improvising, which leads one vaguely to think of the ear as surrogate for a different order of receptacle. And in the lines immediately following ("When I took off my clothes / To find a nose, / There was only one / For the waltz of To, / The pinch of Where"), besides "to" in the sense of "toward," there are suggestions of "two" (here present in its denial, but the meaning most prominent to an auditor who does not have the page before him), while there are also connotations of "toe" as in toe dance (which in turn stirs up a belfry of bat-thoughts when we consider the narcissistic nature of this particular "toe dance," recall similarly the "last waltz with an old itch" in "The Long Alley," and then flutter vaguely in the direction of the infantile "polymorphous perverse" as we think of the briskly and brilliantly conveyed corybantics in the brief lyric, "My Papa's Waltz," the account of a child snatched up and whirled riotously in a dance by his tipsy father). And since "t" is but an unvoiced "d," we believe that, on the purely tonal level, "God" may be heard in "gate." In any case, in "The Long Alley" there are but three lines elliptically separating "this smoke's from the glory of God" and "My gates are all caves."

Though Roethke's lines often suggest spontaneous simplicity, and though the author has doubtless so cultivated this effect that many lines do originally present themselves in such a form, on occasion the simplicity may be got only after considerable revision. Thus, in an early version of "The Shape of the Fire," there had been a passage:

> The wind sharpened itself on a rock. It began raining.
> Finally, having exhausted the possibilities of common sense,
> I composed the following: . . .

"It began raining" was later changed to "Rain began falling." An earlier version had been, "It rains offal," but this, though more accurate, had to be abandoned presumably because of its closeness to "It rains awful." Eventually the reference to rain was dropped completely—for if the essence of this rain (its quality as motive) could not be specified, the reference was perhaps better omitted. The second and third lines were changed to: "Finally, to interrupt that particular monotony, / I intoned the following." Both versions thus sounded self-conscious and formalistic, whereas the final version is naïvely vatic:

> The wind sharpened itself on a rock;
> A voice sang: . . .

The "I" of the versifier at work has been replaced by a cosmically communicating "voice."

Stanley Kunitz, reviewing *The Lost Son and Other Poems* in POETRY, justly observes:

> The sub-human is given tongue; and what the tongue proclaims is the agony of coming alive, the painful miracle of growth. Here is a poetry immersed in the destructive element. It would seem that Roethke has reached the limits of exploration in this direction, that the next step beyond must be either silence or gibberish. Yet the daemon is with him, and there is no telling what surprises await us.

Reverting, in this connection, to our talk of intuitions, concepts, and ideas, and recalling the contrast between the vocabulary of these poems and that of Eliot's *Quartets*, we might put the matter thus, in seeking to characterize Roethke's "way":

There is a realm of motives local to the body, and there is a possible ultimate realm, of motives derived from the Ground of All Existence, whatever that may be. In between, there are the motives of man-made institutions, motives located generally in the terminologies of technology, business, politics, social institutions, and the like. Here are many titular words, abstractions, "ideas of reason," to name the realm midway between the pains, pleasures, appetites of the individual body and the Universal Ground.

Since the body emerges out of nature, its language seems closer to the ultimate realm of motives than do the abstractions of politics. However, the pleasures, pains, fears, and appetites of the body are all, in subtle ways, molded by the forms of the political realm; hence what we take as "nature" is largely a social pageant in disguise. But the vocabulary of traffic regulation is alien to the "noble" speech of childhood emerging from infancy. (Parker Tyler, so often excellent in his insights, convincingly points to the "aristocratic" element in Charlie Chaplin's child motif. And Nietzsche, in his *Genealogy of Morals*, might better be talking of a child when he cites, as his example of the aristocrat, the person whose resentment

"fulfils and exhausts itself in an immediate reaction, and consequently in-
stills no *venom*," while this resentment "never manifests itself at all in
countless instances," since "strong natures" cannot "take seriously for any
length of time their enemies, their disasters, their *misdeeds*," and forgive
insult simply because they forget it.)

In any case, as tested by the simplicity of the "natural" vocabulary,
the forensic sub-Ciceronian speech is "barbaric." And though we may, by
roundabout devices, disclose how politics, through the medium of family
relations, affects the child's experiences at the very start of life, the *ideas*
are certainly not there—hence the "purest" vocabulary is that of the
emotionally tinged perceptions (the "intuitions of sensibility").

But how much of human motivation is the poet to encompass in his
work? Or, next, how much is he to encompass *directly*, *explicitly*, and how
much by *implication*, by resonances derived from sympathetic vibrations in
the offing? There comes a time, in life itself, when one flatly confronts the
realm of social hierarchy (in the scramble to get or to retain or to reward-
ingly use money, position, prestige). Will one, then, if a poet, seek to discuss
these motives just as flatly in his poetic medium? Or will he conceive of
poetry by antithesis (as so many of our poets, now teaching poetry, place
it in direct antithesis to their means of livelihood, hence contending that
the "aesthetic" is precisely what the "didactic" is not)?

It is not for critics, in their task of characterization, to legislate for
the poet here. It is enough to note that there are several methods of confronting the problem, and that Roethke's work has thoroughly and imaginatively exemplified one of them. He meets, in his way, the problem which
Eliot met in another by expanding his poetry to encompass theological
doctrine, and thereby including a terminology which, within the Roethke
rules, would be ungainly (unless used ironically—and children don't take
to irony). Eliot added winds of doctrine. Roethke "regressed" as thoroughly
as he could, even at considerable risk, toward a language of sheer "intuition."

However, our use of the Kantian pattern will deceive us, if we conclude that such intuitions really do remain on the level of "sensation." For
not only do they require the "concept" (as a name that clamps intellectual
unity upon a given manifold of sensations); they also involve motives beyond
both sense and understanding: we go from intuitions of a sensory sort to
intuitions of a *symbolic* sort (as with the motives of the "unconscious"
which make variously for fusion, confusion, diffusion). In scholastic usage,
by "intuition" was meant the recognition that something is as it is. The
term was not restricted merely to sense perception. Not only would color,
sound, or odor be an intuition; but there would be intuition in the recognition that two and two make four, or that a complex problem is solvable
in a certain way, or that a science rests on such and such principles. Applied
to modern poetizing, the word might also be used to name a situation when

the poet chooses an expression because it "feels right," though he might not be able to account for the choice rationalistically. The judgment would rely on such motives as are, under favorable circumstances, disclosable psychoanalytically, or may be idealistic counterparts of hierarchic motives (a "beauty" involving *social* distinction between the noble and the vulgar, mastery and enslavement, loveliness and crassness); and there may also be included here responses to the incentives of pun-logic.

Thus, if in one context the image of a flower can stand for girlhood in general, and if in other contexts a fish can have similar connotations, in still other contexts flower and fish can be elliptically merged (for reasons beyond the fact that the one can be plucked and the other caught), producing what we might call a "symbolic intuition" atop the purely sensory kind. Or we might consider such idealistic mergers a symbolist variant of the "aesthetic idea" (as distinguished from "ideas of reason" in the more strictly rationalist sense). They are "fusions" if you like them, "confusions" if you don't, and "diffusions" when their disjunction outweighs their conjunction. And they are a resource of all our "objectivist" poets who use "positive" terms to elicit effects beyond the positive. Particularly we are in a purely idealistic (rather than positivistic) order of intuitions when we extend the motifs, going from fish to water and from flower to warmth or light, and hence from water to motions that are like pouring, or from flowers to motions that are like swaying (so that a sudden influx of birds might be a symbol descending through the fish-water-girl line, or a swaying tree might descend through the flower-warmth-girl side of the family, the two branches being reunited if the tree is swaying over water, after talk of a swaying fish).

This is the liquescent realm in which Roethke operates. But by eschewing the "rationality" of doctrine (a "parental principle" which one may situate in identification with father governments or mother churches, or with lesser brotherhoods themselves authoritatively endowed), the poet is forced into a "regressive" search for the "superego," as with talk of being "rubbed" . . . "in father and mother." Eliot could thus "rub" himself in dogma, borrowed from the intellectual matrix of the church. But Roethke, while avidly in search of an essential parenthood, would glumly reject incorporation in any cause or movement or institution as the new parent (at least so far as his poetic idiom is concerned). Hence his search for essential motives has driven him back into the quandaries of adolescence, childhood, even infancy. Also, as we have noted elsewhere, the search for essence being a search for "first principles," there is a purely technical inducement to look for definition in terms of one's absolute past; for a *narrative* vocabulary, such as is natural to poetry, invites one to state essence (priority) in *temporal* terms, as with Platonist "reminiscence"—an enterprise that leads readily to "mystic" intuitions of womb heaven and primeval slime.

The battle is a fundamental one. Hence the poems give the feeling of being "eschatological," concerned with first and last things. Where their positivism dissolves into mysticism, they suggest a kind of phallic pantheism. And the constant reverberations about the edges of the images give the excitement of being on the edge of Revelation (or suggest a state of vigil, the hope of getting the girl, of getting a medal, of seeing God). There is the pious awaiting of the good message—and there is response to "the spoor that spurs."

Later poems repeat the regressive imagery without the abysmal anguish. Thus, in "Praise to the End!" our hero, expanding in a mood of self-play ("What a bone-ache I have" . . . "Prickle-me" . . . "I'm a duke of eels" . . . "I'll feed the ghost alone. / Father, forgive my hands" . . . "The river's alone with its water. / All risings / Fall") follows with snatches of wonder-struck childhood reminiscence mixed with amative promise:

> Mips and ma the mooly moo,
> The like of him is biting who,
> A cow's a care and who's a coo?—
> What footie does is final.

He ends by asking to be laved in "ultimate waters," surrounded by "birds and small fish." And a line in the opening ("stagnation") section of "The Long Alley" ("My gates are all caves") is now echoed in an altered form happy enough to serve in the upsurge of the final stanza: "My ghosts are all gay." Along with the nursery jingles, some lines are allowed to remain wholly "unsimplified":

> It's necessary, among the flies and bananas, to keep a constant vigil,
> For the attacks of false humility take sudden turns for the worse.

"Where Knock Is Open Wide" is a placid depiction of childhood sensibility and reverie, in a post-Blake, post-Crazy Jane medium close to the quality of Mother Goose, with many "oracular" lines, in Sibylline ways near to the sound of nonsense. The poem progresses thus: thoughts about a kitten (it can "bite with its feet"); lullaby ("sing me a sleep-song, please"); dreams; the parents; an uncle that died ("he's gone for always" . . . "they'll jump on his belly"); singing in infancy; an owl in the distance; "happy hands"; a walk by the river; a fish dying in the bottom of a boat ("he's trying to talk"); the watering of roses ("the stems said, Thank you"). But "That was before. I fell! I fell!" Thereafter, talk of "nowhere," "cold," and "wind," the death of birds, followed by a paradigm of courtship: "I'll be a bite. You be a wink. / Sing the snake to sleep." And finally: "God's somewhere else. / . . . Maybe God has a house. / But not here."

The title, though borrowed, is extremely apt in suggesting the kind of motivation which Roethke would reconstruct for us. Recall, for instance, Coleridge's distinction between "motive" and "impulse" (a distinction later revised somewhat in his theological writings, but clearly maintained while his reasoning was in accordance with the aesthetic of "The Eolian Harp"). By "motives" Coleridge meant such springs of action as derive from "interests." Bentham's utilitarian grounds of conduct, for instance, would be "motives." But "impulse" is spontaneous, a response free of all *arrière-pensée*, all ulterior purpose. Here, the answer would be as prompt as the call, would be one with the call. In the world of the adult Scramble, such a state of affairs would indeed be a happy hunting ground for hunters— and whoever is in fear of loss must, at the startling knock on the door, hasten to hide the treasure before opening. However, in the theme of childhood reverie, as ideally reconstructed, the poet can contemplate an Edenic realm of pure impulsiveness.

Yet perhaps it is not wholly without *arrière-pensée*. For is the motivation here as sheerly "regressive" as it may at first seem? Is not this recondite "baby-talk" also, considered as rhetoric, one mode of lover-appeal? And considering mention of the wink and the bite in connection with talk of the fall, might we not also discern an outcropping of double meanings, whether intended or not, in reference to a "mooly man" who "had a rubber hat" and "kept it in a can"? The cloaking of the utterance in such apparent simplicity may not prevent conception of an adult sort here, particularly as the lines are followed immediately by talk of "papa-seed."

What next? The placid evocation of childhood might well be carried further (the period of anguished evocations has presumably been safely weathered). Further readings in mystic literature could lead to more developments in the materializing of "spirit" (as in "The Visitant"). But a turn toward the doctrinaire and didactic (the socially "global" as against the sensitively "ultimate") would seem possible only if all this poet's past methods and skills were abandoned.

There is another already indicated possibility, however, which we might define by making a distinction between "personification" and "personalization." And we might get at the matter thus:

Though Roethke has dealt always with very concrete things, there is a sense in which these very concretions are abstractions. Notably, the theme of sex in his poems has been highly generalized, however intensely felt. His outcries concern erotic and autoerotic motives generically, the Feminine as attribute of a class. Or, though he may have had an individual in mind at the moment, there is no personal particularization in his epithets, so far as the reader is concerned. He courts Woman, as a Commoner might court The Nobility (though of course he has his own "pastoral" variants of the courtly, or coy, relation).

But because his imagism merges into symbolism, his flowers and fishes become Woman in the Absolute. That is what we would mean by "personification."

By "personalization," on the other hand, we would mean the greater *individualizing* of human relations. (Not total individualizing, however, for Aristotle reminds us that poetry is closer than history to philosophy, and philosophy seeks high generalization, whereas historical eras, in their exact combination of events, are unique.) In any case, we have seen one recent poem in which Roethke has attempted "personalization" as we have here defined it: "Elegy for Jane (My student, thrown by a horse)." Though not so finished a poem as "The Visitant," it conveys a tribute of heartfelt poignancy, in a pious gallantry of the quick confronting the dead, and ending:

> If only I could nudge you from this sleep,
> My maimed darling, my skittery pigeon.
> Over this damp grave I speak the words of my love:
> I, with no rights in this matter,
> Neither father nor lover.

Perhaps more such portraits, on less solemn occasions, will be the Next Phase? Meanwhile, our salute to the very relevant work that Roethke has already accomplished, both for what it is in itself, and for its typicality, its interest as representative of one poetic way which many others are also taking, with varying thoroughness.[4]

---

[4] I had long planned to revise this article (which was published sixteen years ago). I had hoped to bring it up to date by discussing Theodore Roethke's later work, and to make some of my original observations more precise. But I have finally decided to leave the piece just as it was, along with its several fumblings. For I cannot better contrive to suggest the rare, enticing danger of Roethke's verse, as I felt it then, and still do. Looking back now, in the light of his body's sudden yielding into death, can we not see the end vatically foretold when the connotations of vibrancy in his image of the fish become transformed into connotations of putrescence? And, if the heart stops at a moment of total mystic drought, do we not find that moment ambiguously and even jauntily introduced, through the delightful lines on "The Sloth"? With both this essay and the one following, my memory of voice and manner is imperious in ways that I have not at all been able to indicate.

Chapter Eleven

William Carlos Williams, 1883-1963

William Carlos Williams, poet and physician. Trained to crises of sickness and parturition that often came at odd hours. An ebullient man, sorely vexed in his last years, and now at rest. But he had this exceptional good luck: that his appeal as a person survives in his work. To read his books is to find him warmly there, everywhere you turn.

In some respects, the physician and the poet might be viewed as opposites, as they certainly were at least in the sense that time spent on his patients was necessarily time denied to the writing of poetry. But that's a superficial view. In essence, this man was an imaginative physician and a nosological poet. His great humaneness was equally present in both roles, which contributed essentially to the development of each other.

"There is no thing that with a twist of the imagination cannot be something else," he said in an early work, whereby he could both use flowers as an image of lovely womanhood and speak of pathology as a "flower garden." The principle made for great mobility, for constant transformations that might affect a writer in late years somewhat like trying to run a hundred yards in ten seconds flat. At the same time, such shiftiness in the new country of the poet's mind allowed for imaginal deflections that could be at once secretive and expressive. Also (except that the simile fails to bring out the strongly personal aspect of the work) his "objectivism" was like inquiring into baseball not in terms of the rule book, but rather by noting the motions and designs which the players in some one particular game might make with reference to the trajectories of a sphere that, sometimes thrown, sometimes struck, took various courses across a demarcated field. Such constant attempts to see things afresh, as "facts," gave him plenty to do. For he proceeded circumstantially, without intellectualistic shortcuts —and with the combined conscientiousness of both disciplines, as man of medicine and medicine man.

An anecdote might help indicate what I have in mind about Williams. (For present purposes, I think, we should refer to him thus, though the usage does greatly misrepresent my personal attitude.) Some years after Williams had retired from his practice as a physician, and ailments had begun to cripple him, we were walking slowly on a beach in Florida. A neighbor's dog decided to accompany us, but was limping. I leaned down, aimlessly hoping to help the dog (which became suddenly frightened, and nearly bit me). Then Williams took the paw in his left hand (the right was now less agile) and started probing for the source of the trouble. It was a gesture at once expert and imaginative, something in which to have perfect confidence, as both the cur and I saw in a flash. Feeling between the toes lightly, quickly, and above all *surely*, he spotted a burr, removed it without the slightest cringe on the dog's part—and the three of us were again on our way along the beach.

I thought to myself (though not then clearly enough to say so): "And here I've learned one more thing about Williams' doctrine of 'contact.' " It concerned the "*tactus eruditus*," and I quote words that he had tossed, as a line all by itself, into a somewhat rough-and-tumble outburst, "This is My Platform," he had written in the twenties.

Some forty years earlier, when I had first haggled with him about this slogan (which is as basic to an understanding of him as the statement of poetic policy he makes several times in his writings, "No ideas but in things"), the talk of "contact" had seemed most of all to imply that an interest in local writing and language should replace my absorption in Thomas Mann's German and André Gide's French. Next, it suggested a cult of "Amurricanism" just at the time when many young writers, copying Pound and Eliot, were on the way to self-exile in Europe while more were soon to follow. (I mistakenly thought that I was to be one of them.) Further, it seemed to imply the problematical proposition that one should live in a small town like Rutherford rather than in the very heart of Babylon (or in some area that, if not central to the grass roots of the nation, was at least close to the ragweed).

But over the years, as Williams persisted unstoppably in his ways, the nature of his writings gradually made it clear that the implications of "contact" and its particular kind of "anti-poetry" were quite different, and went much deeper. I feel sure that, whatever may be our uncertainties about the accidents of his doctrine, its essence resides in the kind of physicality imposed upon his poetry by the nature of his work as a physician. Thus, as with the incident of the dog, my understanding of his slogan took a notable step forward when, some time after giving up his practice, he said explosively that he missed the opportunity to get his hands on things (and he made gestures to do with the delivering of a child). However, my thesis is not made any easier by the fact that, while including Aaron Burr among his band because Burr felt the need "to touch, to hear, to see, to smell, to taste" (thus being "intact" in the ways of contact), at the same time Williams disapproved of Franklin, "the face on the penny stamp," and complained with regard to Franklin's perpetual tinkering: "To want to touch, not to wish any-thing to remain clean, aloof—comes always of a kind of timidity, from fear."

The point is this: For Williams any natural or poetic concern with the body as a sexual object was reinforced and notably modified by a pro-fessional concern with the body as a suffering or diseased object. (Think how many of his stories testify to his sympathetic yet picturesquely enter-taining encounters with wide areas of both physical and social morbidity.) The same relation to the human animal in terms of bodily disabilities led him to a kind of democracy quite unlike Whitman's, despite the obvious in-fluence of Whitman upon him. "After some years of varied experience with the bodies of the rich and the poor a man finds little to distinguish between them, bulks them as one and bases his working judgments on other matters." (In any case, the political editorializing in Whitman's come-one-come-all attitude had lost its meaning, other than as a pleasant sentiment, in propor-tion as Congress erected legal barriers to the flow of immigrants by a quota system.)

The same stress upon the all-importance of the bodily element ac-counts also for the many cruel references to subsidence that are scattered through *The Collected Later Poems*. (We shall later get to the earlier, more athletic stages.) Consider "The Night Rider," for instance, that begins, "scoured like a conch / or the moon's shell / I ride from my love / through the damp night," and ends: "the pulse a remembered pulse / of full-tide gone." The theme naturally lends itself to other kinds of imagery: "The old horse dies slow": the portrait of an old goat, "listless in its assured sanc-tity"; a time of drought ("The Words Lying Idle"); the tree, stretched on the garage roof, after a hurricane; homage to the woodpecker, "stabbing there with a barbed tongue which *succeeds*"; apostrophizing the self, "why do you try / so hard to be a man? You are / a lover! Why adopt / the reprehensible absurdities of / an inferior attitude?"; with the mind like a tidal river, "the tide will / change / and rise again, maybe"; there is the theme of "The Thoughtful Lover" who finds that "today / the particulars of poetry" require his "whole attention"; and of a "Bare Tree" he writes, "chop it down / and use the wood / against this biting cold." In this group, certainly, would be-long "The Injury," an account of the poet lying in a hospital bed; he hears "an engine / breathing—somewhere / in the night:—soft coal, soft coal, / soft coal"; in terms of the laboring engine's sounds as he interprets them, he makes plans for the next phase, "the slow way . . . if you can find any way." This expression of dispiritedness wells up so simply, so spontaneously, it is itself a poignantly beautiful instance of spirit. And for a happy and charm-ing variation on such themes, there is "Spring is Here Again, Sir," ending:

We lay, Floss and I, on
the grass together, in

>   *the warm air a bird flew*
>   *into a bush, dipped our*
>   *hands in the cold running water—*
>   *cold, too cold; but found*
>   *it, to our satisfaction,*
>   *as in the past, still wet.*

The sudden reference (already quoted) to using the "bare tree" as firewood reminds us that whereas in an early poem fires came "out of the bodies / Of all men that walk with lust at heart," in later poems the theme of fire could be modified by merging with connotations of the purgative. Thus, there is the ecstatic section to do with fire in *Paterson*. And his rightly well-known piece, "Burning the Christmas Greens," interweaves this elation of the purgative with the color that is always the best of omens in Williams' work. I have at times got courage from the thought that a poem of his, entitled "At Kenneth Burke's Place," has for its ending a reference to a greening apple, "smudged with / a sooty life that clings, also, / with the skin," and despite a bit of rot "still good / even unusual compared with the usual."

But this moves us to a further step in his benignly nosological approach to the subject matter of poetry. I refer to his interest in the sheer survival of things, so that he would record the quality of an ungainly apple from a gnarled old unpruned, unsprayed tree, "as if a taste long lost and regretted / had in the end, finally, been brought to life again." Thus it seems almost inevitable that he should get around to writing a long poem, "The Desert Music." Along these lines, I have thought that an ideal subject for a poem by him would be a gallant description of weeds, wildflowers, bushes and low trees gradually carving out a livelihood for themselves in the slag piles around Scranton. This would be done without sentimentality. (Poems of his like that can't be sentimental, for they say what's actually there in front of him, as with his lines on the rat, surviving even infections deliberately imposed by the hellish ingenuity of man-made plagues, an animal "well / suited to a world / conditioned to such human 'tropism / for order' at all cost.") Here would belong his many poems that, by the very accuracy of their description, testify to his delight in scattered, improvised bits of beauty, as with things one can see during that most dismal of transitions, "Approach to a City" (tracks in dirty snow, "snow / pencilled with the stubble of old / weeds," dried flowers in a barroom window, while "The flags in the heavy / air move against a leaden / ground." In such observations, he says, he can "refresh" himself. Cannot one easily see how his doctoring figured here, teaching him never to overlook "a mud / livid with decay and life," and where the doctor had found sheer life, challenging the poet to go a step further and spontaneously find it beautiful, as a theologian might have striven to find it good?

See, on this point, "The Hard Core of Beauty," describing things on "the / dead-end highway, abandoned / when the new bridge went in finally." Just stop for a while, go back over that line, ponder on each moment—and I'm sure you'll agree that, whatever its cruel, spare sharpness, there's something softly nostalgic like a voice heard through a mist. Within it there's the thought that never left him, the beauty and cleanness of the river around the falls at Paterson, before its rape by the drastic combination of raw politics, raw technics, and raw business. (In earlier years, he referred to the area as "the origin today of the vilest swillhole in christendom, the Passaic river.") All the time the poet-doctor is pointing out, again and again, what survives, there is also the poignancy of what is lost. And in *Paterson*, along with the love, there is the tough, unanswerable, *legalistic documentation* of man's brutal errors, and their costliness to man. As he put it in another book, "Poised against the *Mayflower* is the slave ship." This too was *contact*. And he has done for that damned botched area just west of the Hudson (that hateful traffic-belching squandering of industrial power atop the tidal swamps) something quite incredible: he has made it poignantly songful. He went on singing, singing, singing, while the rivers and the soil and the air and the fires became progressively more polluted in the name of Progress, while more and more of the natural beauties were ripped apart, singing while each year there spread inexorably farther west a cancerous growth of haphazard real-estating that came to enclose his own fine old house in some measure of the general urban sprawl. When the sun rises behind "the moody / water-loving giants of Manhattan," eight miles to the east, they must cast their shadows for a time on the houses west of the Meadows. And in any case the troublous monsters at a distance, magical in the morning or evening mist, did unquestionably cast their shadows on his work.

I have said that Williams was never "sentimental." But I must say more on this point, in view of Wallace Stevens' remark in his preface to Williams' *Collected Poems 1921-1931*: " 'The Cod Head' is a bit of pure sentimentalization; so is 'The Bull.' " But, as you must expect of Stevens, the word is used in a quite alembicated sense, to name "what vitalizes Williams," and to serve as a proper accompaniment to his "anti-poetic" side. To see most quickly how the two motives work together, one needs but think of a gruffly beautiful line like "the moon is in / the oak tree's crotch." Or "Little frogs / with puffed-out throats, / singing in the slime."

I meant that Williams' typical use of imagery does not involve *false* or *forced* sentiment. If I correctly interpret Wallace Stevens' "Nuances of a Theme by Williams" (in *Harmonium*), Stevens meant by sentiment any personal identification with an object, as distinct from an appreciation of it in its pure singularity, without reference to its possible imaginary role as a mirror of mankind.

In this sense, Williams is "sentimental." For all his "objectivist" accu-

racy, Williams' details are not in essence descriptions of things but portraits of personalities. Typically in his poems the eye (like a laying on of
hands), by disguised rituals that are improvised constantly anew, inordinates
us into the human nature of things.

As regards the two poems that Stevens specifically mentions, the ending
of "The Cod Head" ("a severed codhead between two / green stones—lift-
ing / falling") involves associations that might ultimately fit better with a
title somehow combining "severed godhead" and "codpiece"—and something similar is obviously afoot at the end of the poem "The Bull": "Milk-
less / he nods the hair between his horns / and eyes matted / with hyacinthine curls." As with Marianne Moore, Williams' observations about animals
or things are statements about notable traits in people. Along with their
ostensible nature, the sympathetic reader gets this deeper dimension as a
bonus, an earned increment. Let's be specific. I shall quote a brief item that,
if it doesn't seem almost like nonsense, must seem like what it is, a marvel:

> *As the cat*
> *climbed over*
> *the top of*
>
> *the jamcloset*
> *first the right*
> *forefoot*
>
> *carefully*
> *then the hind*
> *stepped down*
>
> *into the pit of*
> *the empty*
> *flowerpot*

Here is the account of a consummate moment in the motions of an unas-
suming cat, an alleycat (I like to think) that just happened to have a home
—plus the inanity of the consummation, as hinted by the empty flowerpot.
How differently a dog would have managed, barging in and doubtless bump-
ing the flowerpot over! What trimness the poet brings to his representation
of trimness! And in its perfectly comic study of perfection, it is so final, I
could easily imagine it being used as the epilogue to something long and
arduous. Inevitably, he called the lines just "Poem."

Stevens' point led us away from our main point. But in his own way he
leads us back again, when he ends by observing that an alternative preface
might have been written presenting Williams as "a kind of Diogenes of contemporary poetry." Diogenes wrote when Greek culture was decidedly in a
valetudinarian condition; and though neither poet nor medico, in his proverbial downrightness he could properly be taken to stand for Williams'
particular combination of the two.

There are many cases where Williams' diagnostic eye, modified by an urge toward encouragement, becomes the sheerly appreciative eye. (Cf. Stevens: "He writes of flowers exquisitely.") But it's also a fact, for instance, that whenever Williams bears down on the description of a flower, connotations of love and lovely woman are there implicitly, and quite often explicitly. Thus, in *Stevens'* sense, the poems are inherently "sentimentalized." Whatever the gestures of *haecceitas* (the sense of an object in its sheer thisness), with Williams lyric utterance is essentially a flash of drama, a fragment of narrative, a bit of personal history mirrored as well in talk of a thing as in talk of a person.

And for this reason, given his initial medical slant, the tendency always is towards a matter of welfare. Dante said that the proper subjects for poetry are *venus*, *virtus* and *salus*. The "anti-poetic" strain in Williams' poetry gives us a medical variant of *salus*, nowhere more startlingly contrived than in this neat abruptness:

> *To*
> *a child (a boy) bouncing*
> *a ball (a blue ball)—*
>
> *He bounces it (a toy racket*
> *in his hand) and runs*
>
> *and catches it (with his*
> *left hand) six floors*
> *straight down—*
> *which is the old back yard*

When the child, successfully clutching the ball, hits "the old back yard," by God he is home.

Stevens' use of imagery is more airy than Williams', quite as the world of a part-time insurance man differs from the world of a part-time medical doctor, though each of these poets in his way is strongly aware of the appetites. That great "heavy" of Williams, "The Clouds," is interesting in this regard. The deathy horses, in a "charge from south to north" while a writhing black flag "fights / to be free," are racing in a gigantic turmoil (something like a visual analogue of Wagner's Valkyrs). It's a vision of such death as goes with fire, famine, plague and slaughter. That's how it starts. The second section is a kind of inventory, a quick sampling of the great dead, and done somewhat haphazardly, like glances at the scurrying clouds themselves. It brings the poet forcefully close to a vision of pure spirit despite himself: "The intellect leads, leads still! Beyond the clouds." Part three is a "scherzo," a kind of joke, grisly in this context, about a "holy man" who, while "riding / the clouds of his belief" (that is, officiating at a service) had "turned and grinned" at him. And the final stanza gets torn into unfinished uncertainty, quite like "the disordered heavens, ragged, ripped by winds." It is a gorgeous poem, at times almost ferocious, and stopped abruptly, in the middle of a sentence, as with the boy who had conscientiously caught the ball.

Elsewhere Williams aims at less drastic kinds of spirit, the most puzzling or puzzled contrivance being perhaps at the end of the long late poem, "Asphodel, that Greeny Flower." To be sure, the flower is green, and that's all to the good. But a few lines before the close we are informed, "Asphodel / has no odor, save to the imagination." Yet in an earlier poem we had been assured: "Time without / odor is Time without me." And one of Williams' most amusing early poems was an itemized rebuke to his nose for the "ardors" of its smelling.

At this point, another personal anecdote occurs to me, for its bearing upon Williams' character. On one occasion, when visiting us, he told me ruefully of misbehavior on his part (an incident that also falls under the head of "contact"). A little delegation of solemn admirers had come to pay him homage. Naturally, he was grateful to them. But as his poems overwhelmingly testify, he was also mercurial. And in the very midst of their solemnity at parting, since one of the little band happened to be a pretty young woman he gave her a frank, good-natured smack on the fanny. It was all part of the game, done on the spur of the moment, and it had seemed quite reasonable. It was the *tactus eruditus* in capricious relaxation. But his visitors were horrified, and he realized that he had spoiled the whole show. He confessed to me his gloom at such unruly ways. But is it not a simple scientific fact that the poet they had come to honor owed much of his charm to precisely such whimsicality as this? One might class it with another occasion when, in a talk at a girls' school, he earnestly exhorted them, "You must learn to be a man." Maybe some of them did—but all were furious. How were they to be reminded precisely then that he was also the man who has written: "Anyone who has seen 2,000 infants born as I have and pulled them one way or another into the world must know that man, as such, is doomed to disappear in not too many thousand years. He just can't go on. No woman will stand for it. Why should she?"

I wish that, to commemorate Williams, some publisher would now reissue his *Al Que Quiere*, just as it was in the original 1917 edition. It shows with such winsomeness this quirky aspect of his genius. Consider the crazy "Danse Russe," for instance, a poem delightfully alien to the pomposities that Eliot did so much to encourage; yet in their way the verse and prose of this "Diogenes" have been written into the very constitution of our country:

> *If I when my wife is sleeping*
> *and the baby and Kathleen*
> *are sleeping*
> *and the sun is a flame-white disc*
> *in silken mists*
> *above shining trees,—*

if I in my north room
danse naked, grotesquely
before my mirror
waving my shirt round my head
and singing softly to myself:
"I am lonely, lonely.
I was born to be lonely.
I am best so!"
If I admire my arms, my face
my shoulders, flanks, buttocks
against the yellow drawn shades,—
who shall say I am not
the happy genius of my household?

Here also was first published the well-known "Tract," his instructions to his "townspeople," on "how to perform a funeral," lines that were read by the minister, as a final goodbye, at the side of Williams' own grave. That was exactly right. And at the end of the book there is a long poem ("The Wanderer, a Rococo Study") which, though it was written before the poet had fully got his stride, and is a kind of romantic allegorizing that he would later outlaw, yet is in its way notable, particularly as a stage in Williams' development. For after several preparatory steps which it would require too much space to detail here, it leads up to a ritualistic transformation involving an imaginary baptism in the waters of "The Passaic, that filthy river." These lines should be enough to indicate how the merger of poet and physician initially involved a somewhat magical process, thus:

Then the river began to enter my heart,
Eddying back cool and limpid
Into the crystal beginning of its days.
But with the rebound it leaped forward:
Muddy, then black and shrunken
Till I felt the utter depth of its rottenness
The vile breath of its degradation
And dropped down knowing this was me.

Here, surely, was the essential ritualistic step by which he began his "contact" with "anti-poetry"—and though often, in later years, he turned to the sheerly beautiful, even sheerly decorative, here we see the tubes and coils and sluices of the powerhouse. Or am I but tricked by the occasion into going back forty-plus years, and seeing him too much as I saw him then? Yet recall (in *Journey to Love*) that late poem, "The Sparrow," dedicated to his father, "a poetic truth / more than a natural one," and thus a delightful contribution to the *comédie humaine*. As you follow the great variety of *aperçus* that use as their point of departure this busy mutt-bird, his ways of congregation, his amours and family life, you heartily agree it's "a pity / there are not more oats eaten now-a-days." Here is no less than Aesop singing.

In the course of doing this piece, I found among my notes a letter dated May 10, 1940. Presumably I had sent Williams some pages which he had read with his usual mixture of friendliness and resistance. He writes (enclosing a poem):

> If I hadn't been reading your essay and thinking my own thoughts against it—I shouldn't have stepped on the word "prebirth" and so the poem (completely independent of the whole matter otherwise) might not have been written.
>
> THEREFORE the poem belongs to you. I like it as well as anything I have written—

Then, after some other matters, he returns to the subject abruptly: "All I wanted to do was to send you the poem."

At the time I assumed that he meant the gift figuratively. But after inquiring of John Thirlwall, who has spent so much effort tracking down Williams' scattered work, I think it possible that friendly Wm. C. Wms., strong man two-gun Bill, may have meant the gift literally, and I may possess the only copy of the poem. In any case, I append it here, since it is a lovely thing to end on. It has a kind of reversal which crops up somewhat mystically, every now and then, among his poems, and which is probably implicit in many other passages. In the light of such forms, when he writes "It is merely pure luck that gets the mind turned inside out in a work of art," we may take it that he had such reversals in mind:

> CHERRY BLOSSOMS AT EVENING
> In the prebirth of the evening
> the blue cherry blossoms
> on the blue tree
> from this yellow, ended room—
> press to the windows
> inside shall be out
> the clustered faces of the flowers
> straining to look in
>   (Signed) William Carlos Williams.

PART III

FURTHER ESSAYS ON SYMBOLISM IN GENERAL

Note

In this section the articles "The Thinking of the Body" and "*Somnia ad Urinandum*" relate most directly to Chapter 4 of Part One. "Myth, Poetry, and Philosophy" and "Rhetoric and Poetic" relate most directly to Chapters 2 and 5. "What Are the Signs of What?" and "A Dramatistic View of the Origins of Language" relate most directly to Chapters 1 and 3. The essay on Marshall McLuhan is placed among the general articles because of its relation to the Dramatistic perspective as a whole.

The discussion of myth from the standpoint of rhetoric and poetic is designed to correct a typical error of naturalism which, in being conceived antithetically to supernaturalism, tends to overstress the notion of magic as bad physical science. That emphasis obscures the role of magic as an effective structure of persuasion. Rituals designed to "cause" the regular sequence of the seasons derive from natural regularities a kind of "pragmatic sanction" that would convey authority to the practitioners of the corresponding rites. "Success" as so defined would help such institutions to survive and proliferate. And the concept of the "scapegoat" would also be of use, since it would explain why a rite failed. If, for instance, a ritual designed to "cause" rain in the rainy season happened to encounter an unseasonal drought, some "unclean" power could be suspected. Thus, without deliberate scheming on the part of a priesthood, myths and rituals that conform to the regularities of nature would best meet the requirements of natural selection—and their contribution to the structure of authority would provide a strong *social* incentive for their perfecting and institutional backing.

The discussion of signatures aims to correct an error usual with overly realistic commonsensical notions regarding the relation between language and the nonlinguistic. The issue boils down to this: Instead of viewing words as *names* for *things*, we should view them as abbreviated *titles* for *situations*.

The final piece, originally presented at the University of Texas Symposium on Formalistic Criticism (in February, 1965) has a summarizing function that might have recommended it for inclusion in the first section of this volume.

Chapter One

Rhetoric and Poetics

Recently I heard a discussion on the Poetics of motion pictures. One speaker attempted to build his theory about the respects in which the medium is unique. The other pointed out that some aspects of motion pictures were present in other arts. For instance, in some respects the motion picture is analogous to drama, or narrative.

Is not Aristotle's *Poetics* the proper example to keep in mind here? When turning from Tragedy to Epic, Aristotle considers both the elements they have in common and the respects in which they differ. Similarly, as regards Rhetoric and Poetics, is it not true that, whatever their differences, they also have an area of overlap, since either Poetry or the exercisings of Rhetoric can be enjoyed for their own sake?

And now I am already in a bit of trouble. In general, I approach the problem thus:

Language is taken as "the given." Man is viewed as the kind of animal that is distinguished by his prowess in symbolic action. The poetic motive is viewed as symbolic action undertaken in and for itself. Just as, in being an animal that lives by locomotion, man moves not merely for purposes of acquisition or avoidance but also through the sheer delight in being free to move, so in being the typically symbol-using animal he takes a natural delight in the exercising of his powers with symbols. In extreme cases, we can distinguish between the Poetic and the Rhetorical here when we think of "Art for Art's Sake" in contrast with deliberative and forensic oratory as discussed in Aristotle, or with the third office of the orator, as discussed in Cicero.

But does not epideictic readily become transformed into a display art, pure and simple? Indeed, as Charles Sears Baldwin's histories of Rhetoric and Poetic make clear, there seem to have been times when, the less men had to say, the greater was their delight in the saying. The anthropologist Malinowski proposed the term "pathic communion" to designate the social satisfaction of sheer chatter. And we should have a hard time trying to make sure whether the renewed interest in glossolalia should be treated in terms of poetics or rhetoric (though some, I assume, would class it purely under the head of manifestations to be studied by psychiatry).

Our problem is further complicated by the fact that, terms like poetic and rhetoric having been used in many different situations, one cannot expect them to stay put. Since it is a sheer fact of history that their meanings have shifted, we must admit as much, then try to show the logic of their transformations. And if Longinus can quote equally from poet and orator (Homer and Demosthenes), the equal availability of examples from the two fields is doubtless due in part to the fact that, though Demosthenes was definitely a rhetorician at the time he wrote, his persuasiveness becomes more like sheer literary appeal, once the occasions on which he spoke cease to be felt as immediately burning issues.

In *Shakespeare's Use of the Arts of Language* Sister Miriam Joseph illustrates from the plays of Shakespeare (surely the realm of Poetics par excellence) many figures listed in such authors as Quintilian (Books VII-IX). And in her *Elizabethan and Metaphysical Imagery; Renaissance Poetic and Twentieth-Century Critics*, Rosemond Tuve cites many instances of works in which the persuasive and dissuasive resources of rhetoric were imitated for purely poetic purposes.

(In my *Rhetoric of Motives*, I have suggested the possibility that the appeal in the sheer *forms* of expression—be they called poetic or rhetorical —is *universal*. Hence, an audience can readily yield to this aspect of an exhortation. And in thus responding to the *doctrinally neutral* aspects of the address, the audience is in more of a mood to accept by contagion the rest of the author's plea.)

As for the probable source of the divergence between rhetorical and poetical expression (where they do diverge!): I would assume that rhetoric was developed by the use of language for purposes of cooperation and competition. It served to form appropriate attitudes that were designed to induce corresponding acts (the *flectere* or *movere* of Cicero's third office). But Poetics could still be concerned with symbolic action for its own sake, without reference to purposes in the practical, nonartistic realm. It could exploit, to the ends of entertainment, the *conflicts* that arise among the tribal attitudes. Consider, for instance, how many plays (such as Sophocles' *Antigone*) have given poetic pleasure by exploiting variations on the theme of the conflict between love and duty. Or one might prefer simply to view the play as a device for exploiting a conflict between two kinds of duty.

In sum, where a rhetorician might conceivably argue the cause of Love rather than Duty, or the other way round, in Poetics a profound dramatizing of the conflict itself would be enough; for in this field the imitation of great practical or moral problems is itself a source of gratification.

As regards the relation between the two fields in the *Rhetoric* and *Poetics* of Aristotle: When, in the *Poetics*, on the subject of Thought (*dianoia*) the reader is referred to the *Rhetoric*, I take it first of all that we are expected to find in the *Rhetoric* the kind of things a person should say, to fit the kind of character the dramatist would have him be, and to arouse the kind of attitude the dramatist would arouse in the audience with regard to that character.

But could there not also be a wider application? Many of the topics in the *Rhetoric* are in effect epitomized situations—and insofar as actions speak louder than words, the topics might also be said to have a corresponding Poetic application. For if a man can mollify us or enrage us by saying gentle or arrogant things respectively, then it is all the more likely that gentle or arrogant conduct can have the same effects. Thus, the poet can produce characters by conceiving of plots in which his puppets (by imitation) *do* as well as *say* the sort of things listed in the topics.

Where the topics are reflected in actual *statements* on the part of the characters, I would incline to feel that, as far as possible, all such dialogue should be treated as *poetic functions* rather than as *philosophic* or *religious* "*truths*." That is to say: As far as possible, one should treat a play not as "about" religion or fate, and such (in the sense of being contributions to theology, science, history, and the like), but as *using* religion or fate or revolt and such for the production of poetic effects.

But one might ask: If the poetic motive involves symbolic action for its own sake, what do we do as regards the last clause in Aristotle's definition of tragedy, "through pity and fear effecting the catharsis of such emotions"? This has to be discussed, though I am aware that, no matter what one might say on this subject, one is bound to encounter some resistance.

From the standpoint of our present specific concerns we must ask: Is this clause wholly in the realm of Poetics? Or does it bulge over into the realm of Rhetoric? Here is my suggestion for finding our way around in this problem:

Since it is stated in the *Politics* that the subject of catharsis is to get further treatment in the *Poetics*, I assume that there was such a section, and that the two are closely related. In the *Politics* the treatment seems to be rhetorical in the sense that music is there viewed as having utilitarian (medicinal) effects upon an audience. And since the subject is discussed in connection with disruptive tendencies in the State, I assume that there must be some analogous (though not necessarily identical) effect with regard to Greek tragedy. Also, on this point, we might recall that a performance of Greek tragedy was probably much nearer to opera than to straight drama as we know it.

We have already considered the natural grounds for human delight in symbolic action. Similarly, the greater the range and intenseness of the opportunities for the exercising of our symbolic prowess, the greater might be our delight in such modes of action. Symbolic action for its own sake, in so great range and intensity, is of course supplied by the kinds of work that are the primary concern of Poetics. They are works that excite our sense of wonder and terror, artistic imitations that move us to laughter or tears.

At first glance, one might think that the notion of symbolic action for its own sake would not be consistent with doctrines like the Aristotelian view of tragedy as purgative. Yet, just as people who are expert at solving puzzles will prefer hard ones, so the delights of symbolic action will be increased by the imitation of grave and serious conflicts.

If, then, in the case of tragedy, a dramatist contrives to imitate some of the most poignant situations conceivable, in bringing them to a state of formal resolution he will have contributed just about as much as possible to the delights of symbolic exercising. Also, inasmuch as the ending really is a "resolution," all the turmoil will somehow have been "cleaned up." Through the pleasurable exciting of our capacities for pity and fear as related to one particular set of individuations, when we come to the formal resolution we shall in effect have *gone beyond* this very tangle.

At this point, an aside is in order. It involves a step of mine in arrantly amateurish etymology. It has to do with the fact that a resolution "goes beyond" the motivational tangle exploited for the purposes of poetic enjoyment. (And maybe, at this point, along with reference to Aristotle on the tragic "pleasure," I should bolster my position by also citing from Coleridge, *Biographia Literaria*: "A poem is that species of composition, which is opposed to works of science, by proposing for its immediate object *pleasure*, not truth.")

As for "going beyond": In the final clause of Aristotle's definition (usually translated in some such way as: "through pity and fear effecting the catharsis of such emotions"), I find it of significance that the word that is translated "effecting," or "producing" (*perainousa*) is etymologically from the same root as *peran*, which means "opposite shore." And I'd relate it to the line in the sixth book of the *Aeneid* where the shades are said to have "stretched forth their hands through love of the opposite shore" (*tendebantque manus ripae ulterioris amore*).

So, experimentally, I would propose to make up an English verb, "to beyond," and thus to translate the Aristotelian formula: "through pity and fear *beyonding* the catharsis of such emotions." This tentative invention fits perfectly for the one surviving tragic trilogy, Aeschylus' *Oresteia*, a kind of form which is not even mentioned in the extant portions of the *Poetics*. In the *Agamemnon*, the *Libation Bearers*, and the beginning of the *Eumenides*, we confront the fearful and the pitiable. But towards the end, we *go beyond* pity and fear, feudal justice gives way to the justice of the law courts, and the Furies themselves become transformed, their emphasis henceforth to be not so much upon the punishing of evil as upon the rewarding of good.

Similarly, in the *Divine Comedy*: Fear is central to the Inferno, pity to the Purgatorio (recall the singing of lines from the Miserere)—and we are *beyond* these states in the Paradiso. In the single kinds of tragedy that Aristotle deals with, the "beyonding" is, as it were, like a fan folded, so that all three stages can transpire at once. The clearest instance is Sophocles' *Oedipus at Colonus*. We feel pity and fear at his death precisely when he is transcending the miseries of this world—that is, *going beyond* them, and becoming a *tutelary deity*.

We must go a bit round about, to make clear just how this issue bears upon the relation between Rhetoric and Poetics. The Poetics of tragedy explicitly deals with transformation by victimage. The audience is edified by sympathetically witnessing the imitation of a "good" (*chrestos*) character being sacrificed.

At the extremes (as made clear by Nietzsche's rage against the *dialectic of reform* in contrast with the *cult of tragic sacrifice*) there is the different medicine got along Platonic lines by transcendence.

We have already considered (in *Oedipus at Colonus*) a kind of work in which the two overlap. But there are cases where they are clearly different, the most direct case I can think of being the dialectic of Emersonian transcendentalism, in his early essay on *Nature*. Here the stress upon the kill is at an absolute minimum, though there is a sacrificial motive (notably in the chapter on "Discipline"). But we can discern a strong *rhetorical* ingredient implicit in the *dialectic*, which is designed to interpret *social* motives in terms of *nature*, while nature in turn is interpreted in terms of the *supernatural*; hence *social* motives become infused with the spirit of the *supernatural*. The rhetorical implications of such a dialectic become obvious as soon as we stop to realize, for instance, how such a terministic setup would make a Marxist dialectic impossible, and thus would automatically rule out the corresponding rhetorical ingredients implicit in the Marxist dialectic.

The dialectic of transcendence amounts to a mode of interpretation by treating of empirical things-here-and-now *in terms of a Beyond* (be this, in its simplest form, but a way to view terms of lower generalization as inspirited by terms of higher generalization). Obviously, such a dialectic has notable rhetorical implications since the view of things *hic et nunc* in terms of a Beyond implies a corresponding attitude towards them, with corresponding implications of policy, or action.

However, such modes of transcendence can also be confined to purely poetic functions. E. M. Forster's novel, *A Passage to India*, is well worth considering in this regard. I postulate as its effect "ironically sympathetic contemplation." (That is, I would offer this formula as the equivalent, in this kind of modern novel, for the clause that Aristotle discussed in terms of catharsis, as regards Greek tragedy.) The book centers in ways whereby the modes of mystery or embarrassment associated with social divisiveness (the social ladder) are infused with imagery of cosmic mystery. All this gets sloganized in the question whether India is a muddle or a mystery. The novel leaves the issue fluctuant, in contrast with Emerson's simple and happy transcendental solution.

As regards these shiftings back and forth between the realms of Rhetoric and Poetics, many aspects of the matter must be left undiscussed. But I might at least reiterate a couple of paragraphs I wrote in connection with a recent Symposium on Formalist Criticism, at the University of Texas. They concern a problem having to do with the novels of William Faulkner (as treated in a book by Cleanth Brooks).

In Faulkner's case we confront a situation which almost inevitably involves (these days at least) an invasion of Poetics by a problem in Rhetoric. For instance, whatever relevance Shakespeare's *Coriolanus* may have had to conditions in London at that time, the play on its face was about factionalism in ancient Rome. Similarly, indications are that in *The Trojan Women* Euripides was alluding to a contemporary incident, the outrageous sack of Melos that the war party of Athens had engineered about six months before the production of the play; but the work itself got a kind of "distance" by treating of such issues in terms of "primal" Greek tradition, the sack of Troy.

Regionalist literature proceeds in a quite different manner. Its kind of "verisimilitude" is strongly influenced by modern, scientific concepts of realism, which has dispensed with much of the ritual in older forms. . . . Fiction is often made to look not just like an artistic "imitation," but rather to have the quality of a documentary "record." In contrast with Shakespeare's play about "Rome," or Euripides' play about "Troy," Regionalist literature is written as by someone who "was there," hence it has a suggestion of expert "field work."

Accordingly, if the author would entertain his public by trying to make his work seem representative of some Region, and if at the same time—if only for formal reasons—he weaves into his background some tales of violence, corruption, "outrage," he will necessarily confront a dilemma. For if his readers take his books at face value, and are outsiders ("outlanders"), they may irritate him by interpreting his books simply as an indictment. Yet, though he would like the "outlanders" to read his work and be persuaded by it, he must feel that they are like intruders in the dust of his homeland. For the true Regionalist does not write like an exile who has fled from his country and is appealing to the world against a regime that has it in bondage. Rather, the Regionalist is one who, at least in principle and in Faulkner's case actually, remains at home. Though he tries to make his plots look "real," he naturally resents it if critics of Marxist cast, or the sociologically-minded in general, look upon them simply as the "evidence" which (in a purely *poetic* sense) he strives to make them resemble. For many of his readers approach the work from the outside, whereas he had written it from the inside, with corresponding differences of attitude. Thus the books are like what Mr. Brooks aptly calls Charles Mallison's "lover's quarrel" with his neighbors; yet the nature of publication has in effect invited all the world to listen in.

But I'd like to end on a question that has to do primarily with Rhetoric (though, as always, it provides material for corresponding but different application to the realm of Poetics).

It concerns the feasibility of doing what I did in my *Rhetoric of Motives*, when I introduced the concepts of *Identification* and *Administrative Rhetoric*.

Administrative Rhetoric is most clearly illustrated by Machiavelli's *The Prince*. (Ovid's *Ars Amatoria* turns much the same sort of topics into a Poetic, by fancifully treating them as a species of *Rhetorica docens*.) The concept of Administrative Rhetoric involves a theory of persuasive devices which have a directly rhetorical aspect, yet include operations not confined to sheerly verbal persuasion. One example will suffice. It is a variant of what I would call the "bland" strategy. It goes back to the days when the German Emperor was showing signs of militancy—and Theodore Roosevelt sent our fleet on a "goodwill mission." Ostensibly paying the Emperor the compliment of a friendly visit, the President was exemplifying his political precept: "Speak softly, and carry a big stick." His "goodwill" visit was clearly rhetorical insofar as it was designed blandly to use a display of force as a mode of persuasion.

Even Aristotle touches upon such a Rhetoric, in his brief discussion of "inartificial proofs": laws, witnesses, contracts, tortures, and oaths. Here was a kind of *inventio* that might be treated as an extention of "bearing witness."

The concept of Identification begins in a problem of this sort: Aristotle's Rhetoric centers in the speaker's explicit designs with regard to the confronting of an audience. But there are also ways in which we *spontaneously, intuitively*, even *unconsciously* persuade ourselves.

In forming ideas of our personal identity, we spontaneously identify ourselves with family, nation, political or cultural cause, church, and so on. In this regard, when Marx applies the term "class consciousness" to the *Weltanschauung* of the bourgeoisie, he is concerned with a kind of identification that could as properly be called "class unconsciousness."

The concept is also relevant because it admonishes us to look for modes of Identification implicit or concealed in doctrines of "Autonomy" that figure prominently in our theories of technological specialization. Simplest instance: If the shepherd is guarding the sheep so that they may be raised for market, though his role (considered in itself, as guardian of the sheep) concerns only their good, he is implicitly identified with their slaughter. A total stress upon the autonomy of his pastoral specialization here functions *rhetorically* as a mode of expression whereby we are encouraged to overlook the full implications of his office. Identifications can also be *deliberately* established, as with the baby-kissing politician's ways of kissing women on their babies.

There is another possible extension of Rhetoric, concealed from us by the terminologies of the sciences: By "topics" Aristotle obviously has in mind something quite close to what contemporary sociologists would call "values." Much that in the old days would be called "persuasion" might now, following the lore of anthropology, be treated as "word magic." "Style" becomes "ritual." And in modern psychology the word "myth" has taken on meanings that considerably alter and extend the scope of the term as used in the *Poetics*. Even a popular expression such as "bedside manner" obviously has its *rhetorical* implications—and much stress upon *love* and *transference* in psychoanalytic remedies for sick souls might serve to deflect attention from the analyst's schemes for building himself up as an *authority*.

Before closing, I'd like to bring out one notable feature implicit in the *combining* of Identification and Administrative Rhetoric. I refer to the great increase in the tendency of faculty members to identify themselves in a partly administrative way by signing petitions of protest against governmental policies that they find questionable. Such performances are saying in effect: "Whatever the autonomy of our field, in the mere act of remaining silent we are *in effect* identified with certain policies. So, *in effect*, we abandon the customary resources of the secret ballot; and by affixing our signatures (along with the names of our schools and departments) to certain public statements, we identify ourselves with the alternative policies proclaimed in this statement."

This is no place to discuss the rights or wrongs of such procedures. But it does decidedly fit this talk for me to point out that implicit in signatures of this sort there are strong elements of Identification and Administrative Rhetoric.

To sum up: I would propose to view the relation between Rhetoric and Poetics thus:

The two fields readily become confused, because there is a large area which they share in common. Also, although some works lend themselves more readily to treatment in terms of Rhetoric than in terms of Poetics, or vice versa, even a work of pure science can be shown to have some Rhetorical or Poetic ingredients. With your permission, I shall end this talk by shifting my approach and giving an *illustration* rather than an argument.

Some time ago I happened to be working on a kind of satiric poem for which I wanted some especially resonant tonalities of invective. But, although I regularly find much to grumble about, I couldn't become furious enough long enough about things, to turn out the particular kind of turbulence I needed. Then a possible subterfuge occurred to me. Why not go through the Pauline Epistles, and assemble "efficiently" in one place the various bits of vituperation that are scattered through the books as a whole?

I tried the experiment, and I'd like to end up by exhibiting the result. It should illustrate the main point of this talk because, though the selected passages in their original application would obviously fit well under the Aristotelian heading of epideictic, or demonstrative oratory (or under the heading of Cicero's third office), they are not being applied here for hortatory ends at all (so far as Paul's kind of persuasion was concerned) but because their particular saliency served to provide the kind of verbal music I wanted at this stage in the poem.

The lines can serve as illustration, if the Poetic Motive is treated as an engagement in symbolic action for its own sake, for love of the art. A corresponding change of attitude would be involved, since such expressions were not used originally for their sheer picturesqueness (a "poetic" aim which could itself be called "rhetorical," though not in the sense that the term would signify as applied to their function in the Epistles proper).

> Hark, while I plunder harshness from the Thirteenth Apostle.
> Bah! There are those greedy of filthy lucre, blind of heart, alienated from truth, heady, highminded, lascivious, slothful in business, of cunning craftiness, given up to uncleanness, the double-tongued, those of darkened understanding, covenant breakers, without natural affection, implacable, unmerciful, deceitful workers, ministers of sin, transgressors, false apostles, adulterers, those given to idolatry, witchcraft, hatred, variance, emulations, wrath, strife, seditions, heresies, those who do not cast down imaginations, those who do not give cheerfully, those filled with all unrighteousness, fornication, wickedness, covetousness, maliciousness, full of envy, murder, debate, deceit, malignity, whisperers, backsliders, backbiters, the despiteful, the proud, boasters, inventors of evil things, adulterers, blasphemers, menstealers, liars, perjured persons, slanderers, brawlers, purloiners, thieves, traitors, those with the mouth full of cursing and bitterness, railers, drunkards, those of feet swift to shed blood (destruction and misery are in their ways), trucebreakers, false accusers, incontinent, fierce, despisers of those that are good, apostates, subverters, heretics (such as are condemned of themselves), lovers of their own selves, disobedient to parents, unthankful, unholy, extortioners, persecutors, partakers of other men's sins, those who wrong and defraud their brethren, those marked by filthiness, foolish talk, and jesting (rather than giving thanks).
> In this realm of strife and vainglory, of much filthy communication among rulers of the darkness of this world, with its spiritual wicked-

ness in high places, where novices are lifted up with pride, and men of corrupt minds, reprobates (teachers of the law, who do not understand what they say), exhort servants to be disobedient to their own masters and to answer back, many are puffed up, and have swerved aside into vain jangling, not avoiding foolish questions, and contentions, and vain, unprofitable strivings about the law, giving heed rather to fables and endless genealogies, proud, knowing nothing but doting about questions and strifes of words (perverse disputings of men of corrupt minds from which come envy, strife, railings, and evil surmisings), ever learning, and never able to come to the knowledge of the truth.

There are the effeminate, abusers of themselves with mankind, men leaving the natural use of women, and burning in their lust toward other men. And there are others which creep into houses, and lead away captive silly women laden with sins, led away with divers lusts.

And of women, there are wives who are not grave, not faithful in all things; they are idlers, tatlers, busybodies, wandering about from house to house speaking things which they ought not; and there are young widows that wax wanton, and women who do not learn in silence with all subjection, or who would teach, or usurp authority over a man, and are not silent.

In sum, there are the foolish, disobedient, deceived, serving diverse lusts and pleasures, living in malice and envy, hateful and hating one another for their envyings, murders, drunkenness, revellings, chambering, and such like, after hardness and impenitent heart, treasuring up unto the self wrath against the day of wrath, and thus, condemning themselves in judging others.[1]

This piece was presented in a Symposium on the History and Significance of Rhetoric, 1965, at the University of California, Los Angeles. An address on the same subject was delivered by Dr. Wilbur S. Howell. The major difference, as regards questions of method, is indicated by the subtitle of Dr. Howell's paper "A Plea for the Recognition of the Two Literatures." In brief he argued for the strict distinction (between the realms of Rhetoric and Poetic) that I confessed myself unable to maintain. But though Dr. Howell's address was given on the day following mine, it had been planned before my talk, hence did not directly refer to these particular pages. However, at the start it did deal with some statements of mine already printed. And I might properly add a postscript repeating some of the comments I made during the discussion period.

I cannot do well by his thesis as a whole. Much of it I missed entirely. For during the latter portions that did not directly concern me, I necessarily used the time trying to assemble my badly scattered forces. (I

---

[1] From "Introduction To What," *Location*, Spring 1963.

refer to the scattering within my own mind.) First, I wish to thank him for the several generous things he said in my favor; but I shall here review only the matters I mentioned in reply to his reservations:

As regards the large area of overlap which the realms of Rhetoric and Poetics have in common, I repeated my point about Longinus' quoting equally well from Demosthenes and Homer, or Sister Miriam Joseph's illustrating by quotations from Shakespearean *drama* the kinds of figures enumerated in Quintilian's work on *rhetoric*. In the nomenclature of *Counter-Statement*, these would be called "minor forms." And quite as they are to be found in both Rhetorical and Poetic texts, I still submit that the three fundamental principles in the dynamics of form (progressive form, repetitive form, and conventional form) are to be found in both Rhetorical and Poetic structures.

I regret that Dr. Howell did not discuss these principles *seriatim*. And though, when inquiring into the dynamics of a literary work, I still lay great stress upon the three principles of form as described in *Counter-Statement*, I naturally regret that Dr. Howell did not discuss my further extensions of Rhetoric, in my *Rhetoric of Motives* and *Rhetoric of Religion*.

Basically, the situation is this: I began in the aesthete tradition, with the stress upon self-expression. Things started moving for me in earnest when, as attested in *Counter-Statement*, I made the shift from "self-expression" to "communication." The theory of form (and "forms") centers in that distinction. For quite a while, as with many critics, I found it enough to work with these two terms, treating them as principles that variously correct and reinforce each other. But I am always happiest when I can transform any such dyad into a triad—and I subsequently did so by adding what I call "consummation." One can "track down the implications of a terminology" over and above the needs of either self-expression or communication (for instance, Beethoven's last quartets in his time, or James Joyce's later works)—and I'd want to treat such formal thoroughness as not strictly reducible to the arousing and fulfilling of expectations in an audience. Also, there are certain phenomena to do with the shift between terms for *logical* priority and terms for *temporal* priority which figure in the vocabularies of religion, viewed as modes of "persuasion" capable of both Rhetorical and Poetic analogues.

In leading up to his plea for a hard-and-fast distinction between the realms of Rhetoric and Poetics, Dr. Howell gave quite a list of distinctions made by various authors. For instance, De Quincey's distinction between literature of "knowledge" and literature of "power." Or Fenelon's statement that "good oratory is almost poetry," while "poetry paints with ecstasy." Or Baldwin's equating of Rhetoric with idea and Poetry with image (a distinction I have always found troublesome, since by this alignment such effective rhetorical images as Churchill's "iron curtain" or "power vacuum" would belong in the realm of Poetics). Whereas Dr. Howell presumably cited such distinctions as an argument on his side (there were several more that escaped me), they really are an argument against him. For every one of them cuts at a different angle—and that's precisely why I think the best we can do is to show the logic behind the *various* cuts that can be made in the Rhetoric-Poetics pair. (Incidentally, though I did not say so at the time, when going over my article I realized that Dr. Howell could well have turned his dyad into a triad by adding dialectic as the third term, particularly in view of the fact that Aristotle somewhat metaphorically calls rhetoric the *antistrophos* of dialectic.)

In his discussion of my little parable about the author who, out of self-pity, writes a story about a King and a Peasant, Dr. Howell neglected to make clear the main point of the parable. It was designed to show why, even though our hypothetical author might begin his work out of nothing better than sheer self-pity, in the course of developing a persuasive story he would have to master many artistic problems not at all derivable from self-pity.

As I have said elsewhere with regard to the "extending" of Rhetoric (along the lines of such a "New Dispensation" as the modifying of persuasion by identification, or the study of rhetorically administrative acts after the fashion of Machiavelli, or by taking literally the usage whereby religions are called "persuasions"): The issue has its methodological grounding in the rise of *aesthetics*, with the corresponding exile of literary and academic traditions that had placed the stress upon Rhetoric, Poetics, and Dialectic. The exiled subjects found asylum in the "new sciences," so that many of the older concepts now have new names—and often the new names open up implications not discernible in the old names. The job here is not to be simply "purists," but rather to ask just how much of the new material should be added to the study of Rhetoric, Poetics, and Dialectic—and how much should be definitively abandoned to the jurisdiction of the "new sciences" themselves.

But insofar as such abandonment is advocated, let us at least bear it in mind that the principles of Rhetoric, Poetics, and Dialectic (and the corresponding dynamics of form, or order) are to be found, *mutatis mutandis*, within the modes of symbolic action generally. And though questions to do with the arousing and fulfilling of expectations are, in the last analysis, but ways of asking pointed questions about a work's *unity* and though they probably cannot be recommended on "purist" grounds, they do serve well as goads, or arrows, prodding us to take a close look at the dynamics or *musculature* of either Poetical or Rhetorical performances.

Thinking back about Dr. Howell's reservations, I wonder whether they might boil down to a charge we have heard leveled against others in other quarters and in other connections; namely: "revisionism." For though I find myself quite in sympathy with the traditions which Dr. Howell would extoll,

I must concede: My "Dramatistic" theory of "symbolic action" does not permit me to use categories that draw the lines at precisely the same places where he would prefer to have them drawn. Also, frankly, I am much more interested in bringing the full resources of Poetics and *Rhetorica docens* to bear upon the study of a text than in trying to draw a *strict* line of demarcation between Rhetoric and Poetics, particularly in view of the fact that the full history of the subject has necessarily kept such a distinction forever on the move.

Chapter Two

The Thinking of the Body
Comments on the Imagery of Catharsis in Literature

The following pages are concerned with ways in which the functions of bodily excretion attain expression (sometimes direct, more often indirect) in works of the imagination. They were written in connection with a book I am writing on the subject of Poetics which, since the days of Aristotle's famous treatise, has variously concerned itself with processes of "catharsis" in art.—K.B.

Catharsis is usually considered in the grand style (in terms of such sacrifices and victimage as attain their fulfillment in the ritualistic use of the "scapegoat" for poetic purposes). But there are humbler modes of "mortification" available to imaginative writing. And I have here illustrated the point by close inspection of certain famous texts: *Alice in Wonderland*, Wagner's *Ring*, Flaubert's *The Temptation of St. Anthony*, the *Prometheus Bound* of Aeschylus, the poetry of Mallarmé—also some poems and stories of my own. Persons who insist on keeping the subject of the poetic imagination *salonfähig* (or, as the dictionary might put it, "suitable for discussion in the drawing room") will resent such analysis. So let us offer these pages simply as a contribution to what I elsewhere call the "Beauty Clinic."

Since the idea of purgation readily includes connotations of physical excretion, and since good writers are thorough in the range of their imaginings, it is almost inevitable that (through the subterfuges of poetic invention) good literature would readily and naturally encompass this area of expression, though often by ingenious subterfuge, as particularly in the case of our first example.

Alice in Wonderland

In this ingenious fantasy, we submit, the chapter "Pig and Pepper" is to be viewed as a circuitous description of "child-training." Here, by the subterfuges (the "miraculism"?) of nonsense and fantasy, the disciplinary punishment for *crepitus ventris* can be humorously transformed into the advice given in the Duchess's song: "Speak roughly to your little boy, / And beat him when he sneezes." In brief, when we read this perverse reference to "sneezing," I am suggesting that here is a time to remember the euphemisms in Gilbert Murray's translation of *The Frogs* (where the translator systematically substitutes "sneeze" for Aristophanes' references to a farcical nether noise). As for the grunting which began when the child "had left off sneezing," and which led Alice to say, "that's not at all a proper way of expressing yourself": The double meaning (the "self-expressive" grunt as "purgative") is simultaneously concealed and revealed by the developments of the plot: the grunting child becomes a grunting pig. Or, more literally, what at first was taken for a grunting child turns out to be a pig. This is a roundabout way of saying that such a grunt is piggish, an animal noise. And as we shall see in a few moments, there are good reasons for locating this "grunt" with relation to the reverse end of the animal.

What about the conceit of the Cheshire Cat, which "beginning with the end of its tail" disappeared all but its grin, until that too was gone? By what labyrinthine route did the author hit upon this ingenious invention? If our interpretation about the sneeze and the grunt is correct, then it might well follow that the vaporous grin is the deceptive translation of odor into terms of sight. To introduce a Grammatical element here: The grin would be the *essence* of the "cat." And what kind of essence? The associational bridge might be contrived through "Cheshire," which would belong in the olfactory bin by reason of its connection with the almost proverbial Cheshire Cheese.

The whole kitchen scene would be a reversal of motives, a "dizzy" transcendence by concealment through nonsense, so that food could perversely stand for its opposite, offal. (See Freud's *Basic Writings*, Modern Library Edition, p. 366: "The ugliest as well as the most intimate details of sexual life may be thought of or dreamed of in apparently innocent allusions to culinary operations.") Hence the ambiguities of the kitchen "pot" which "seemed to be full of soup," and into which the cook put too much sternutatory "pepper."

"The only two creatures in the kitchen that did *not* sneeze" were the "cook" and the cat. Presumably it did not disturb the "cook" because she stood for mother or nurse. And it did not disturb the cat because the cat was the very "soul" of the creation (its transcendent actuality). Other pertinent details: the fishlike and froglike footmen, with their impaired *dignity*; the Fish-footman's remark, "I shall sit here . . . on and off, for days and days"; his irrelevant *whistling* that leads to nothing;[1] the Duchess on a "stool" (she is the unpresentable counterpart of Alice's primness). The theme was introduced by the episode of the insolent caterpillar, "smoking," and seen by Alice

---

[1] Recall in this connection the Aristophanic detail in Samuel Beckett's story "Yellow" (*New World Writing, No. 10*), explicitly concerned with a reference to bowel movements in a hospital: "He whistled a snatch outside the duty-room."

"beyond" the mushroom (that is, beyond the phallic?). Alice here was worried about a "poem" that *wouldn't come out right* ("It all came different," she complained). It was a poem about a busy bee (a creature proverbial for its attention to "duty," which we here interpret in the French sense of *devoirs*).

The anal-oral reversibility is continued in the scene of the Mad Tea Party, with its rudeness so embarrassing to Alice, the prim, well-trained potty-girl. The reversal centers about the theme of the eating from dirty plates. It is paralleled intellectually in the inventions that get things inside-out, upside down, and backwards—and is repeated in the principle of reversal that is clearly indicated in the title of the sequel, *Through the Looking Glass*. The set of the footmen's heads in the previous chapter, (being held so far back that they are turned upwards rather than forwards) is thus seen to represent not just the comic exaggeration of a servant's pride in his master's dignity, but also the principle of a burlesqued human face such as is suggested by a *cul nu*. The three at the dirty table (Mad Hatter, March Hare, and Dormouse) presumably include connotations of the Demonic Trinity (the one asleep, to reflect the dormant sexuality of the child?). And a glance at Tenniel's drawing of Mad Hatter and March Hare, attempting to stuff the Dormouse into the teapot, now makes the cloacal "ambiguities" here startlingly clear.

This principle of reversibility is incipiently present as early as the initial "fall" down the rabbit hole. The internality of this fall is represented in Alice's speculations during her descent, "I must be getting somewhere near the centre of the earth." The principle of *reversibility* with regard to food is ambiguously introduced when she sleepily decides that there is no difference between the two questions, "Do cats eat bats?" and "Do bats eat cats?" The jingle of the final episode (with its interpretation, " 'If she should push the matter on'—that must be the Queen") leads into the "stuff and nonsense" of the Queen's intellectualistic putting of the hind end foremost: "Sentence first—verdict afterwards."

The circling about the table, and the reference (in the epilogue) to this "never-ending meal," suggest that we might eventually trail the fantasy back to the digestive tract as primal worm, Ouroboros, ever circling back upon itself, the "mystic" dreaming stage of vegetal metabolism in which the taking-in and the giving-off merge into one another (a kind of possibility which, at this stage, we shall mention without further argument).

But, for one final set of observations designed to indicate the puns underlying this "nonsense," we might note that the author himself ambiguously attests to such enigmas, in saying that the story follows the pattern of a chess game (a "Cheshire" game? a "cheese" game?) where Alice is to "win in eleven moves." Here our point about the "Duchess" is born out by Alice's "coronation," in line with popular witticisms about the "throne." And the outline of the game tells us exactly when Alice "leaves egg on shelf," a double meaning in keeping with popular witticisms involving the outlaw meanings of "egg."

Wagner's Ring

Wagner's opera, *Das Rheingold* centers about a problem of purification that seems never quite resolved. In the higher terms of "Justice," the Nibelungen tetralogy concerns a battle between love and lovelessness. In the first scene of the cycle, Alberich gets possession of the problematical gold (which stands specifically for property and in general for the principle of evil) by renouncing love—whereupon a long succession of misfortunes follows, culminating in the death of the manly young hero, Siegfried, and in the twilight of the gods.

The heroics of the entire cycle are discussed by Wagner in a letter to August Röckel, January 25, 1854, quoted in *The Letters of Richard Wagner*, selected and edited by Wilhelm Altmann, translated by M. M. Bozman (Dutton, 1927). Wagner there treats the subject in its grandest aspects: freedom, integrity, development in accord with the laws of one's being, love of absolute truth, self-immolation, love (of which the highest form is the love between Man and Woman), salvation by the ability to will one's own death (since lovelessness arises from our inability to will the inevitable end, as Wotan and Fricka are constrained to lovelessness through their attempt to maintain their outworn marriage "in opposition to the law of eternal transmutation and renewal"). Wotan attains the tragic dignity of willing his own destruction; and the "creative power of this highest, self-annihilating Will" attains its culmination in Siegfried, a hero who loves fearlessly.

The letter is particularly interesting because the humble Herr Röckel happened to stumble upon some embarrassing questions about the logic of the plot; and in the course of both rebuking him and attempting to answer him, the Master refers to the "great revolution" in his rational concepts, "ultimately effected through Schopenhauer." Thus in another letter to the same correspondent (August 23, 1856) Wagner refers to a conflict between concepts and intuitions, saying that conceptually he had built his plot in accordance with an "Hellenic-optimistic model," but intuitively (as revealed particularly through the music) he had come upon a realization of the world's "nothingness." And this conflicting revelation was to be derived from an "exposure of a first wrong, from which springs a whole world of evil." *It is the imagery of this "first wrong" that concerns us here.*

Inasmuch as this change of plans, whereby "a conceptual universe upon the Hellenistic-optimistic model" became transformed by "intuitions" into a stress upon the world's "nothingness," was attributed to the philosophy of Schopenhauer, we might well look to the philosophy for motivational hints. Schopenhauer's major work, *The World as Will and Idea*, should serve best, since it pointedly *ends* on the word "nothing."

Near the beginning of Book IV, on "The Affirming and Negating of the Will" (§54), "life" is explicitly equated with sexual and nutritive appetites; and "death" is explicitly equated with *bodily excretions*. Nourishment and growth are distinguished from procreation (*Zeugung*) only in degree. And the constant process of excretion (*die beständige Exkretion*) is distinguished from death only in degree. Death is merely excretion *in erhöhter Potenz*. And excretion itself is defined as "the constant exhaling and expelling of matter (*das stete Aushauchen und Abwerfen von Materie*)," a formula to bear in mind when we come to Flaubert's *Temptation of St. Anthony*. We might also mention a handwritten commentary which Schopenhauer has left, with reference to Buddhist Nirvana, just a few lines before the book's culmination in "Nothing." Here he discusses the relation that positive and negative have to pantheistic philosophies which view the world as an emanation from God, with an eventual return after a "purgative cure" (*Reinigungskur*).

As for the overall design of the Cycle, we learn from the letters that it developed somewhat regressively. It seems to have begun with the theme of Siegfried's death (which we might call a dignification of love by the imagery of tragic sacrifice). This in turn was found to need a preparatory grounding in Siegfried's youth. But what might be prior to that, in turn? The incestuous love affair between the sister and brother who became his mother and father. But have we even yet gone back far enough? No, there is still "original sin." So we progress, in reverse order, from Siegfried's Death (finally called *The Twilight of the Gods*), to Young Siegfried (later simply *Siegfried*), to the origins and adventures of his parents (*The Valkyrie*), to *The Rhinegold* (where the golden ring, stolen from the Rhine-maidens, stands for "a first wrong, from which springs a whole world of evil").

First of all somewhat punningly, we go from "Rhinegold" (*Rheingold*) to "pure gold" (*reines Gold*), in the lament of the Rhine-maidens at the close of the first opera. Their lament is "from the depths" (*aus der Tiefe*). As regards the imagery of the body, what are these depths?

For all the apparent scope of the dramas, they fit neatly into the pattern of *one* life. The fourth deals with complications after marriage (the troubles of Wotan and Fricka). The third deals with the manly wooing of a bride (Siegfried and Brynhilda). This union has traces of the incestuous; for Brynhilda is Wotan's daughter, and Siegfried was the grandson of Wälse (who had been a human incarnation of Wotan). The second play deals with the somewhat narcissistic motives of childhood (as symbolized in the incestuous relation between Siegfried's parents, Siegmund and Siegliende). In contrast with Siegfried's "high spirits and impetuous self-confidence," his father celebrates love as the mild light of spring. Siegliende calls him mild spring (*Lenz*). All this I would interpret as the stage of early adolescent love (the incestuous element standing for the strongly narcissistic motive still prominent at that stage of human development). From the standpoint of our familial metaphor, the lovers and Valkyrs are like a throng of spirited children, watching the disturbed marital relations between Wotan and Fricka. They are half-rebellious, half-respectful, playing the elder gods off against each other, and capable of working themselves into a frenzy (as with their famous ride).

We say all this about the three plays to make more apparent the infantile nature of the first, *The Rhinegold*. In this prelude, which we might call the "ultimate source" of the tragic developments, the pun on the name of the Nibelungen (as the "mist-people") is systematically developed. In the very first scene, at the depths of the Rhine, the atmosphere is pervaded with mist (*Nebel*). And repeatedly throughout the work, there are these scenic references to the emergence from mist, the glimpses through the mist, the return behind the mist. (Psychologically, we take such mist to symbolize the transitional state when infancy is merging into language. The beginnings of verbalization would seem "misty" in contrast with the clarity towards which language is striving. Recall a related incidence of mist at the beginning of creation in Genesis.) The plot is a typical early childhood tale of weird ogres; and the orchestra gives forth heavy oathlike body sounds, in spirit suggesting what the giant's voice might be like who thunderously chanted "fe fi fo fum" when smelling a live child's blood.

But if "original sin" is to be imagined in terms proper to infancy, what then would be the essence of this problematical "gold," viewed not as metal but as symbol? As evil, it should be "dirty," "nasty," "unclean." Yet Freud admonishes us that, although the child is eventually taught to have such an attitude towards the feces, its first response is of a totally different sort. Insofar as the Rhine-maidens stand for the principle of the gold which is in their possession, this "gold" can in effect be wooed by Alberich indirectly through his wooing of them, as its personalized equivalent. And he (whom they call a "toad," to perfection a dirt-creature) can stand for the infantile desire that by training is made equatable with the forbidden.

In any case, once the fecal motive has been "broken down" and personalized in the roles of pursuer and pursued, conditions are set for the opening scene, in which the infantile act of playing with the feces is staged as a pursuit in terms of dirtiness sliding and slipping through hands and feet, of a dampness that fills the nostrils and causes sneezing, of "play" that must suffer a penalty, of making love with eels, of the bratlike goblin as loathesome, of tauntings ("shame on you"), of the gold as an "awakener" that laughs into the depths (sign of awakening to greater consciousness and conscience?), of delicious bathing in the bed (ostensibly riverbed), then an admonition (half guilt, half transformed into a moralistic sanction): "Our father told us to regard the bright treasure wisely (*klug*)." There had also been an initial reference to bed: "You are guarding poorly the sleep of the gold; watch better the slumberer's bed." The scene ends on the act of dissociation within the cloacal ambiguity, as Alberich gains control over the gold by renouncing love (that is, he chooses the fecal, in rejecting the sexual).[2]

Flaubert's Temptation of St. Anthony

Insofar as asceticism would renounce the world of the flesh for the realm of the spirit, it is almost "logically inevitable" that in Flaubert's fertile phantasmagoria Anthony's temptations would take the form of "body thinking" that lured him in the other direction, from "Spirit" to "Matter." So we might well begin by selecting as our text (from among the succession of monsters by which the Saint's imagination is depicted as being incessantly assailed) some lines by "Crepitus," recalling the days of his ancient honor and dignity:

> J'eus mes jours d'orgueil. Le bon Aristophane me promena sur la scène, et l'empereur Claudius Drusus me fit asseoir á sa table. Dans les laticlaves des patriciens j'ai circulé majestueusement! Les vases d'or, comme des tympanons, résonnaient sous moi;—et quand plein de murènes, de truffes et de pâtés, l'intestin du maître se dégageait avec fracas, l'univers attentif apprenait que César avait diné!

Fittingly for our purposes, Crepitus says that those were his "days of pride" when, by the resonances of his release, "the whole attentive world learned that Caesar had dined well." And he ends dejectedly, "But now, I am confined to the common people, and there are protests at the mere mention of my name." So greatly had his powers diminished, in the new religion. Whereupon the author adds a stage direction: "And Crepitus departs, emitting a sigh." Surely this is perfect style. Crepitus is reduced from the ostentation of his former trumpet-like grandiloquence to an utterance barely audible. Here is the burlesque of a tragic plot in miniature, a fall from the majesty of high estate to piteous abasement. Not even a "whistle"; just a "sigh."

But the obscenity of the Saint's temptations becomes clear by association, for the next apparition is none other than Jehovah, as war god, the Lord

---

[2] In German, the relevant lines are: *"Des Goldes Schlaf / hütet ihr schlecht; / besser bewacht / des Schlummernden Bett, / sonst büss't ihr beide das Spiel!"* ... *"Garstig glatter / glitschriger Glimmer! / Wie gleit ich aus! / Mit Händen und Füssen / nicht fasse noch halt ich / das schlecke Geschlüpfer! / Feuchtes Nass / füllt mir die Nase"* ... *"verfluchtes Niessen!"* ... *"so buhle mit Aalen, / ist dir eklig mein Balg!"* ... *"Deine Krötengestalt"* ... *"Schäme dich, Albe!"* ... *"Lugt, Schwestern! / Die Weckerin lacht in den Grund."* ... *"Umfliessen wir tauchend, / tanzend und singend, / im seligen Bade dein Bett. / Rheingold!"* ... *"Was ist's, ihr Glatten"* ... *"der Vater sagt'es, / und uns befahl er / klug zu hüten / den klaren Hort."*

of Hosts, definitely suffering from what might now be called a "Jehovah complex." He is a jealous hater of rivals, a lover of power who once struck down the proud, but now in turn laments his fallen glory. And the obscenity of this vision derives from the fact that the discussion of power so clearly grows out of the earlier explicit linkage between power and anality (whereby reference to the earlier incident functions as an interpretative comment upon this one).

Next, Anthony's disciple Hilarion appears. He here represents the boastful powers of Science—and the downward turn comes this time by the disclosure that he is, in disguise, the Devil—and on this disclosure the chapter ends.

In another place there is a related development in the recital by a Gymnosophist, who begins by deriving "existence from corruption, corruption from desire, desire from sensation, and sensation from contact"; hence he had "avoided all action, all contact"; and "meditating upon the ether in my spirit, the world in my members, the moon in my heart," terms uniting human body and world's body, "I dreamed about the essence of the great Soul from which there continually escape, like sparks of fire, the principles of life." From this you can go back to the opening statement, that all existence "comes from corruption." Or you can go forward to the thought of the Great Universal Mind in everything—whereat God, the heavens, and the human body are all of the same essence, namely: corruption. For the body is the central moment here, and the body is corruption. Hilarion had earlier taunted St. Anthony with a related proposition: *"Ta chastete n'est qu'une corruption plus subtile."*

These quotations have been concerned with the "anality" of power. But by our interpretation, the next references are in the category of fear and thus inchoately urethral.[3] Following the terrifying discovery that the Devil has appeared, and that he represents Science, the next chapter is in its very essence an "effortless" flight (a point to remember when we consider Aeschylus' *Prometheus Bound*). Now, with the Devil as guide, Anthony flies "like a swimmer . . . without weight," soaring lightly above sands, rivers, oceans, and on through the immense expanses of infinite space.

It is wholly an absence of stricture; and Anthony cries "I am afraid," fearing that he will "fall into the abyss." (The relation between flying and fear is etymologically indicated in the fact that "flight" refers to both "flying" and "fleeing.") There is also talk of the "perpetual flux." And Anthony mentions *cette dilatation du néant*, translatable perhaps as "this dilating (or enlargement) of the void" (literally "the nothing"). Perhaps we are here

---

[3] This refers to pages where I treat pity, fear, and pride as "spiritual" analogues of the genital, urethral, and anal images respectively, though the correspondences are not exact. (Pride is anal since pride is disdainful.) For the urethral I quote Coleridge's line, "Urine, the softly flowing daughter of Fright." This point is discussed in my article, "On Catharsis, or Resolution," in the Summer 1959 issue of the *Kenyon Review*.

making too much of an accident; but it's a fact that the word has a common medical usage (indicated in our Webster's by the definition for a dilator: "An instrument for expanding a part; as, a urethral dilator").

A girl who appeared at the beginning of the work is called "Ammonaria." Ammonia is said to be so named because it was obtained by the burning of camel's dung, near the temple of Jupiter Ammon. And the article on horticulture in the *Encyclopaedia Britannica*, when discussing liquid manures, notes the production of ammonia from stale urine. Such associations may explain why, at the first mention of her, we are told that her tunic, open at the hips, floated in the breeze (*sa tunique ouverte sur les hanches flottait au vent*). In this apparently trivial detail suggesting looseness, there was enigmatically foretold her relation to the micturition of fear. For she reappears at the beginning of the next chapter, after this terrifying flight through the Nothingness of Knowledge has been completed (that is, by our reckoning, under the sign of such diuretic release as goes with fright).

And she appears in a context having to do with Anthony's memories of his childhood. As the chapter starts, he finds himself lying on his back, ambiguously near dawn or in moonlight. He is cold, his teeth chatter. He laughs bitterly at the memories of the flight, and at his former hopes of union with God. Now, "the sand smoked" (or reeked: *fumait*) "like the spray" (dust: *poussière*) "of a censer." He remembers a trip he took with Ammon, "when looking for some lonely place" where they might establish monasteries. A page later, he is recalling his childhood, when he liked to play at building a hermitage with pebbles. He thinks of his mother, and of her corpse, with a hyena sniffing through a crack. Thence to the thought of Ammonaria, taking her garments one by one from a tub, while her body gave off the fumes (*vapeur*) of cinnamon. Note these olfactory images, which I interpret as "euphemistic"; for his thoughts immediately become transformed into self-disgust as he exclaims: "I can't endure myself."

Then, after his response to a condition that is, thus roundabout, like the distress of a child awakening after having been unclean, and that has interwoven with it the "conscientious" monastic motive, there is a further set of transformations that are almost breathtaking in their implications. (Indeed, just before the final disclosure, Anthony will hold his breath.) Suffice it here to say that the story now depicts a frenzied series of regressions, and regressions beyond regressions, and others beyond those in turn. They are unresolved ambiguities to do with the relation between mother and sweetheart.

These become transformed into a mythic statement of the relation between motionless secret and unending labyrinthine strivings, Sphinx and Chimera, with Chimère finally inviting Sphinx to mount her. A bit later, the Chimera barks, the Sphinx growls—then from his breath arises the mist: *"brouillard"* . . . *"brume"*—and beyond that Anthony perceives rolling clouds and vague curves.

Here, by our calculations, is the step from childhood back into infancy. It is marked by a jumble of fabulous forms, fragmentary creatures, that represent dissociation, disintegration: Astomi, like air bubbles; Nisnas, each like a person sliced down the middle; Blemmyes, headless ("we think digestion, we refine secretions . . . making our way through slime, on the edge of each abyss"); Sciapodes, upside down, for true happiness; and so on . . . each kind figuring some drastic malproportion. This is a fantastic assortment of bodyheresies, to match the earlier pageantry of theological heresies paraded in Chapter IV, on the other side of the mist.

Above all we should mention the Catoblepas, with its piglike head, so large that the body cannot sustain it; it lies flat, its head on the mud, eating venomous grasses soaked with its own breath, and once it ate its own paws without noticing. Heretofore, Anthony has but suffered the vision of these horrors. But he admits that this reflexive, uterine monster attracts him. In a sense, it is the perfect fetus. The gigantic head, given to the consuming of portions of its own being, is it not a sheerly physical burlesqued replica of Aristotle's God, the Thought of Thought, engrossed in the contemplation of itself? Hence, Anthony's greater temptation here.

The race continues, *"Au galop! Au galop!"* the Licorne cries. What then could all this be moving toward? Toward the maternal source as the sea. Hence, punwise, we come to "the Beasts of the Sea" (*Les Bêtes de la Mer*; punwise, because we hear in the offing, *Les Bêtes de la Mère*).

Much earlier, when the advent of the Savior had been awaited, there had appeared the form of a python. Its tail, going through a hole in the wall, lost itself in the remote regions of the sea. The figure had thus represented, in spatial design, the trend that this tail-end kind of plot was to unfold, in temporal design.

One possible penultimate stage: the point at which "plants are confused with stones" (Thus the grounding of the animal in the vegetal, and of the vegetal in the mineral). Hence there is talk of stalactites like breasts. And of pebbles like brains. Then he holds his breath . . . for the ultimate revelation is due. We are near to pure potentiality. Insects are eating without stomachs. Dried ferns are flowering again. Missing members grow back. Then he perceives tiny hairs, and pulsings. He ejaculates: "O happiness, happiness! I have seen the birth of life, I have seen the beginnings of motion."

What is there left?

The disintegration into an infinity of possibilities: "I would fly, swim, bark, bellow, howl. I would have wings, shell, rind. I would breathe smoke, have a tail, squirm, divide everywhere, be in everything, emanate in smells, unfold like plants, trickle like water, vibrate like sound, gleam like light, pervade every form, penetrate each atom."

Then, out of this drastically infinite diversity, of a sudden there emerges, for the finale, the equally drastic unity: "I would go down to the depths of matter—I would *be* matter!"

He would be one with the very essence of excrement, as so conceived within the conditions of this fiction. *Antoine se fait le signe de la croix et se remet en prières.* We might recall this great epic of rejection, when recalling how, while Rodolphe romantically wooed Emma Bovary, from outside came the word of the auctioneer: "Dung-heap" (*fumier*).

Aeschylus' Prometheus Bound

Because of the relation between fire and water, Freud views *enuresis nocturna* as the symbolizing of a "burning" ambition. Also, he treats urethral excitations as a deflection of genital impulses. Thus, in his essay on "The Acquisition of Power over Fire" (*Collected Papers*, Vol. V), Freud analyzes the Promethean myth in terms of *sexual* "fire" and its "extinguishing." Though his observations thus differ considerably from the interpretation we are about to offer, he clearly sanctions our stress upon the theme of micturition as a motivational strand in the myth of Prometheus (whose very name fits in with our scheme relating the urethral with fear, since it means "Forethinker," is a word for *caution*, "Promethean rule" meaning "provident rule"). Beneath the awe and grandeur of the fable, this play seems to offer an almost schematically clear instance of fear expressed in terms of micturition. Our reasons are as follows:

As the play opens, Power delivers a pounding, eleven-line speech in which he establishes the situation for the audience. Hephaestus has been commanded to bind Prometheus on the crag, and Power is present to see that the order is carried out. Prometheus has stolen the fire for mankind. And whatever its relation to a sexual motive, its *civic* nature is made explicit; it is called "pantechnic" fire. Prometheus must now satisfy the needs of Justice. He must be taught not to resist the sovereignty of Zeus. He must cease his "philanthropic ways."

Thus Prometheus has been introduced, but in startling accents. "Audience identification" with the hero is established in three ways. First, since he stole the fire for mankind, he is a kind of revolutionary Redeemer, who represents their best interests. Second, though a god, he is a gruff and blustering fellow, even pigheaded; hence in this respect he is reduced to average human proportions by a flaw. (In *Aeschylus and Athens*, George Thomson offers convincing reasons for believing that in the later part of the trilogy, the plays that are lost, both Zeus and Prometheus mellowed.) Third, we can suffer with him, since suffering is reduced to its most immediate physical aspect. The reader cannot help but wince at the mere mention of the wedge that Hephaestus drives through Prometheus' chest. The sense of physical torture is established with a brutality that is relieved only by the Aeschylean grandeur of this beginning, which is in quality like muscles held painfully tense.

We might also note how, despite the torture of the binding, Prometheus has been silent. But the suffering gets verbal expression through Hephaestus, who is acting against his will, and who mingles remarks on the progress of his task with expressions of profound pity for the victim. After the binding is complete, and Power with his silent partner, Force, has left, then Prometheus raises his voice in a mighty lamentation, calling to the Earth Mother in his wretchedness (calling thus to the very Essence of Motherhood). Yet, as indicated by his name, "Forethought," he had known that this destiny was in store for him even when he made the fatal decision. He reaffirms this fact—then tells himself that he must somehow be resigned to the miseries now imposed upon him by Necessity. (Dramatically, his ability to foretell compensates for his inability to move.)

The term for Necessity, *ananke*, originally meant "force" in the purely physical sense, the opposite of "persuasion." But in time it took on cosmic connotations, whereby the principle of social compulsion could be thus mythologically dignified. In Liddell and Scott we find that *tyche anankaia* meant the *lot of slavery*, and *hemar anankaion* the *life of slavery*, literally *day of constraint*. So Prometheus, who stands for such invention as leads to the division of labor, here undergoes the mythological equivalent of enslavement.

Next the drama introduces a countertheme. Just as Prometheus' condition suggests *muscular tension* and *painful confinement*, so now the Daughters of Oceanus enter, amid connotations of buoyancy and freedom. They are in a winged car. A light rush of whirring pinions is mentioned. These Maidens, the Chorus, have flitted here with speed. Everything is fluent, and as unresistant as feathers. The contrast in this amplification of the theme of easy motion is about as great as could be. But I submit that, in looking for the "appropriateness" of this imagery, we should seek motivations deeper than mere contrast.

At this point, we might better proceed by a detour. Let us consider two remarkably radiant Aeschylean words: *muchos* and *muchothen. Muchos* means literally the inmost part, nook, corner. It also means the inmost part of the house, specifically, the women's apartments, the *penetralia*. A third meaning: bay or creek running far inland. Latin equivalents: *sinus, recessus*. (We are here following Liddell and Scott.) *Muchothen* then, in general, would mean: *from* such innerness (as *theothen* means: from God). And the range of physical, personal, and social connotations in the term *muchos* thus suggests the possibility that, whichever meaning was explicitly uppermost, we might think of the others as implied. And accordingly, as regards analogies between houses and bodies, a reference to the female *penetralia* (*muchos*) should connote internality in general. Hence the possibility that such a theme could be symbolized by such women as the daughters of a water-god, who are moved to pour forth their expressions of pity for Prometheus. (In the article on Aeschylus in the eleventh edition of the *Encyclopaedia Britannica*, they are said to enter "dripping with pity.") Thus, we would place the same interpretation upon their role as we placed upon the river of lightning in Coleridge's poem.[4]

Thus appropriately, when they enter, they announce that the sound of the riveting had pierced to the inmost recesses of their cave. Here, fittingly, our word *muchos*! The *penetralia*, the inwards, are responding behavioristically to this torture of the mankindbefriending god. (In Flaubert's *Temptation*, Maximilla had spoken of "*l'épouvante dans les entrailles*.")

Thereupon there is talk of *shame*, or *modesty*. The sound of these terrors, we are told, had shocked their *modesty* (in this sense, the corresponding word in Latin is *pudor*, from which we get *pudenda*.) Whereat they set out hastily, on a winged car, barefoot.

What was there for them to be embarrassed about: That is: why did this report, penetrating even to the *muchos*, shock their *modesty*? The verb here is translated as: drive out of one's senses by a shock; scare; frighten out of one's wits. The word for shame or modesty (*aido*), also has such equivalents, in the Greek-English dictionary, as: dignity, majesty, regard, reverence, mercy, pardon. In the *Suppliants* there is a reference to "tears of sorrow and pity," the word here translated "pity" being the genitive form of *aido*.

Near the end of this episode the Chorus tells Prometheus "to seek some *release* (*eklusis*) from this ordeal." There is talk of pity for his plight. Prometheus makes a rousing speech that centers in the cry, "Willingly, willingly, I offended" (here using the verb form of *hamartia*, as the Chorus had twice done a few lines previously, when referring to his rebellion in behalf of human kind). Then, after a passage that again introduces obliquely the theme of lightness, speeding, and birds, Oceanus enters. Whatever the Daughters were, here in their father is their single summing-up. Appropriately, therefore, he also is riding on a bird. And he has made his way here, he tells us, *without the use of a bit*.

---

[4] This refers to a discussion of lines in Coleridge's poem, "The Ancient Mariner," where (in a magically fearsome situation) lightning is described as pouring:

> Like waters shot from some high crag,
> The lightning fell with never a jag,
> A river steep and wide.

Entry 1000A in Coleridge's *Notebooks* refers to a witch who transformed her urine into a raincloud that she could discharge by her command.

How appropriate is that detail?

One translation we consulted has him say that he arrived "guiding" the bird "by mine own will." This would put us wholly to rout. A few lines previously, Prometheus, for all his wretchedness, vaunted that he had acted of his own deliberate choice (*hekon, hekon*). If now Oceanus similarly advertises the motive of his flight, our whole theory of the inchoate diuretic movement here is greatly weakened. Another translation says: "Directing the flight by my thought." And that is better; for by our interpretation, this flowing flight should be moved by sheer *attitude*, not by an act of *control*.

The original is *gnōmē*. And insofar as it ovelaps upon "will," it does so not in the sense of deliberate choice (as with the *proairesis* that Aristotle says is the touchstone of Character), but rather in the sense of awareness. (It is related to the Indo-European root, *gna-* or *gno-*, from which comes our word "know.") This would be exactly right. We would then have: A plot that progresses from suffering, to pity, to such fluent "flight" as directs itself without reins and bit.

Its essence is mythically symbolized by a deity associated with the *primeval waters*. His abode is called a "stream" (*rheuma*); and a neat bit of condensation occurs when Prometheus explosively prophesies to him that "rivers of fire" shall burst forth from Mount Aetna. We might further note that the word for "bit," being a diminutive of *stoma*, has the following range of connotations: aperture, opening, curb, mouth, outlet, such as mouth of a river.

New motives enter, with the entrance of Io, who is also in her way persecuted. But at this point we should tend rather to note how she rounds out a triad of major motives. For the play began with variants of Power and Wisdom: and Io obviously represents the motive of Love. We might also note that the play ends on the subject of a torrential storm, a terrifying downpour in which sea and sky become confounded.

There are traces of the same theme in Aeschylus' *Libation Bearers* (*Choephoroe*) in which the Chorus is composed of mourners sent to pour libations (*choaí*) to the shade of Agamemnon. The corresponding verb (*chéo*) means: to pour; to pour liquids, as to make rain; it can also apply to the shedding of tears. Other meanings: to flow, stream, gush forth, become liquid, melt, dissolve (so of ground in spring, like Latin, *resolvi, laxari*). In the perfect passive, it can refer to one wholly engaged in something, as *effusus in Venerem*. It can also mean: to be shed, scattered; or to embrace. The lexicographers observe that "these usages, though we call them metaphors, are hardly so in the old poets; the voice is to them a *stream*, beauty an *effluence*, death a *mist*."

The corruption of a dead body (as with the euphemistic use of the word "ashes") would naturally suggest acts associated with the body imagery of fear. So I append, for its possible relevance, this observation I made about the magic rites of children when confronting death: "The woodchuck was finally slain, after a fight that must have seemed spectacular to the two young boys. Now, as it lay stretched out dead, they solemnly wet thereon—not in derision, but with the gravity of Indian chieftains paying last honors to a noble warrior who had been vanquished in combat." (And in the light of the fact that so many sensitivities of this sort can be expressed in exactly opposite ways, as with the use of many comic obscenities in early religious rites, we should not consider such speculations invalidated by such old formulas as: "*sacer est locus, extra meiite,*" and "*hospes ad hunc tumulum ne meias.*" Indeed, do not these very injunctions against urinating in sacred places indirectly suggest their relation to the fearsomeness of solemnity?)

The "Pure" Poetry of Mallarmé

In the choice of examples, it suddenly occurred to me: Since Mallarmé's standards of stylistic elegance were the most exacting of all, we might well find that he had carried these matters to their ultimate state of paradox. His desire to write the perfect poem led him, in reflexive self-involvement, to write poem after poem about the process of writing a poem. Thus he confronted such absolute tests as come nearest to fulfillment when they contrive, however maturely, to reaffirm the motivational design of the infantile. (Imagery related to the realm of the infantile necessarily provides a radical terminology for the poetic expression of first principles, because the search for essence can so readily be conceived in terms of the mind's beginnings, when emerging from what Mallarmé's Hérodiade calls her *monotone patrie,* and the "somber sleep" of the *terre première.*)

Also in the Freudian dialectic, a poem so conceived as the "essential" (thus "first" and "purest") creation would almost necessarily belong in the category which is assigned to such offspring. Further, we saw how we might in effect enlist the aid of an expert collaborator. For in his splendid exegetic work on Mallarmé (surely among the few best pieces of critical analysis in contemporary criticism) Wallace Fowlie happens to give us as much help from the sheerly literary side as Freud does from the medical side. The difficulty is that Mr. Fowlie does not *explicitly* discuss this possible motivational strand in Mallarmé's aesthetic.

However, remarkably many of his expressions *imply* such a view; and to see them in our light, we need but systematically read them as *double-entendres,* though it is possible that they have such double meaning simply because the critic has so spontaneously and sensitively put himself into the spirit of the lines he is analyzing. One such usage, Mr. Fowlie's frequent translation of *Néant* as "void," even brings out connotations that are hardly there in the French (except in the remote sense that among the definitions for "nothing" in our Larousse is "*situation infime*"). Our "collaboration" will consist in reading as a *double-entendre* Mr. Fowlie's remark on page 116 concerning Mallarmé's *Igitur*: "An identification is established between the Absolute and the Void." And we shall similarly read as *double-entendre* other remarks of his in this vein.

Mr. Fowlie sums up his analysis of Mallarmé's poetic motives in these three words: angelism, hermeticism, narcissism. If, as Mr. Fowlie explains, "angelism" creates its own world, then here would be the burlesque of Paternal Power. If "hermeticism" guards the secret, here would be the burlesque of Wisdom. And "narcissism," being entranced with its own image in the glass, is clearly the burlesque of the Holy Spirit's Love.

Behind these we should look for signs of the Demonic Trinity, since such an absolute pattern of "creativity" can have its beginnings only in ideas of bodily power and creativity ("gift" or "treasure") so primary that they necessarily merge into an analerotic grounding. Thus the poem, as imagined in terms of such "primeval" essences, must be of lowly ancestry. And, ironically, the more scrupulous and thorough the poet would be in his meditations, the more drastically he will confront the paradox: That his absolutely "pure" poem must be of the same symbolic substance as, when it is tested by other criteria, is absolutely "impure." Surveying Mallarmé's terminology in the large, here is the kind of constellation we see emerge:

Gold and jewels and metals and sand-colored hair, *purs ongles*, and pride, mummies, *pourriture*, the severed head of John the Baptist, fascination with the void, problematical perfumes (as though *odeurs* secretly meant *ordures*), poems like things expelled, or like such wreckage as can be called a "throw of dice," aesthetic parsimony and the withholding of the secret, the mirror of self-love conceived as a "black hole," a scene of poetic vigil that begins with the words, "*surgi de la croupe*,"—such details suggest an *ars poetica* wholly in keeping with Mr. Fowlie's formula (p. 126): "He became so much a part of the poem that he was always fearful of being unable to project it outside of himself."

When Mr. Fowlie notes that Hérodiade rejects perfumes because she wants her hair to resemble "gold and the sterile coldness of metals," he adds much to our armory. And on pages 131-132 he adds a statement that clinches the argument, if his words are read as *double-entendre* along the lines of our remarks on the Rhinegold (that is if, along Freudian lines, we see in words for treasure euphemisms for fecal motives):

> Hérodiade is flowering for herself, not in the usual kind of garden, but in a garden of amethysts and precious stones. Her beauty is like the hidden beauty of jewels deep in the earth which contain the ancient secrets of the world. The first part of the aria describes the beauty of Hérodiade's eyes and hair as essentially a sterile beauty. Her eyes are like pure jewels and her hair is fatal and massive be-

cause it reflects the colour of metal. Jewels and metal, originally buried in the earth, are as sterile and useless as the eyes and hair of Hérodiade, concealed in her tower away from the world of men.

A page later he refers to "the perpetual night inside the earth where the jewels and the metals sleep; the night of the mirror which is like a black hole into which Hérodiade looks in order to see all the remembered and forgotten memories of her life." A bit above this, he had said that Hérodiade's narcissism "is narcissism pushed one degree farther than the limit which Narcissus reached." A variant of Wagner's theories is suggested when he says that this farther degree "might be called the myth of self-destruction which lies at the core of every human being," a motive that could also be called "the principle of transformation or metamorphosis." And when he further explains that the hair and eyes of Hérodiade "are not only compared to jewels and metals but seem to be converted into the inert material world," we might well recall the kind of transformation into matter we observed as the ultimate of Anthony's temptations. For when we read that the Mallarméan poet who is "the guardian of creative secrets" is "engaged in the alchemy of his own language," we might well ask what base metals this hermetic alchemy would transform into aesthetic gold (a thought the reader is asked to keep in mind when later we turn to the subjects of "miraculism" and alchemy).[5]

The "sterility" of such treasure is related by Mr. Fowlie to problems of poetic "impotence," with which Mallarmé was apparently much concerned. But the tenor of our *double-entendre* would indicate rather that a more accurate diagnosis would be poetic constipation. However, we do not say so in the spirit of levity. For instance, when analyzing the sonnet, *Victorieusement fui le suicide beau*, Mr. Fowlie notes how the last word of the poem "is the deliberate reduction of the long expansive second line, the symbol of a symbol." Here is the perfect instance of ways in which the anal principle of parsimony, whatever its infantile associations may happen to be, can lead to the most exacting kind of poetic purity. Mallarmé hoarded words like a miser with a piggy-bank—and his economizing is a permanent source of expert interest in his work.

More problematical, perhaps, is the fact that the paradox of such "purity" can lead to a kind of logical blocking in poetic composition, a methodic pudency with regard to the function of the term, "Therefore." This shows in the Hamletic battles of an autobiographic figure to whom Mal-

---

[5] These pages are not included in the present exhibits. They deal primarily with the fecal and diuretic imagery in alchemy, owing to the alchemists' concern with "our water" and the transforming of "base metals." Since John Crowe Ransom has written an article on what he calls the "miraculism" of the transformations in poetry, I use the imagery of the alchemists as a device for revealing the same processes in poems about what Mr. Ransom has suggestively called "the world's body."

larmé gave the name of "Igitur," which is the Latin word for "thence" or "accordingly," and is translated "thus" in the first verse of the second chapter of Genesis, the statement about creation from which Mallarmé is said to have got the name: "Thus the heavens and the earth were finished" (*igitur perfecti sunt caeli et terra*).

If one's notions of poetic purity happen to be so absolute that they almost necessarily go back to primal infantile associations, and if one would nonetheless erect a "priestly" edifice atop such a *cloaca*, there is likely to be a constant prodding towards illogicality in the development of a work written under such auspices. Many shifts and subterfuges should result—and though these may in themselves produce results that engage our interest, the artist who embodies them may be made uneasy by them to the extent that his meditations are thorough. Conceivably he could even carry such a scrupulous tangle to the point where he would fear for his own reason, as Mallarmé often apparently did.

Civically, we may seek the loci of irrationality to the extent that the perpetuation of social injustice is implied in a writer's code of values (for instance, where traditions that function as the protectors of special privilege are advocated as "good in themselves" or as "inevitable"). But the incongruous relations between the thinking of the body and the reduction of poetic propriety to the canons of mere social propriety can also provide a locus of irrationality. For the aesthetic may automatically vow its practitioner to remain vague as to the basic relation between poetic pathos and bodily bathos. On the contrary, "logic" is made comically, Aristophanically supreme in the vulgar lines about "the fabulous bird that eats sand and ————s bricks, and *hence* the pyramids." It is one of the most "efficient" démarches in the lore of expressiveness—and we had it in mind, as authoritative corroboration of our motion that the Egyptian pyramids are "mighty stylized replicas of the dung-pile" (see p. 832 of *A Grammar of Motives and A Rhetoric of Motives*, combined in Meridian paperback edition).

Mr. Fowlie has some exceptionally able pages on the "Symbol of Hair" in Mallarmé's verse. When his remarks regarding its association with jewels, metals, *arôme aux farouches délices*, warm rivers, and the like are viewed in connection with the thought that Hérodiade's jealously treasured hair can be conceived as "detached from her body," and when we add, the observation that it can be "the symbol of her immortality," we see how schematically the motives converge (particularly if you both recall Freud on hair, and agree that, in body-thinking, talk of "immortality" implies the *pourriture* of death).

Mr. Fowlie gives a skillful summary of "Les Fenêtres," a block of ten quatrains built around a contrast between a sick man in a hospital and the poetic possibilities of the sky beyond the glass of the window. It is presumably an early poem, written before Mallarmé had perfected the method that in effect merged the themes here kept logically distinct, though the possibilities of such merger are indicated in the opening reference to hospital odors as "fetid incense / Which rises in the banal whiteness of the curtains / Towards the large bored crucifix of the empty wall." And at the end, he interrupts the description of his contrasting poetic elation, to avow in Baudelairean fashion that the *vomissement impur* of Stupidity makes him hold his nose *devant l'azur*. The transitional element is glass, which he equates with art and the esoteric: *Que la vitre soit l'art, soit la mysticité*. And the poem ends on the thought of his having wings "without feathers," whereupon we might recall that although Dante applies the word "bird" (*uccello*) to both devils and angels, the wings of his Satan were without feathers.

From the standpoint of our present concerns, this poem seems the best point from which to consider the perfect Mallarméan muddle, once his principles of condensation have attained their proper method (as they had not yet done in this poem). Suppose we *telescoped* all three motivational stages into a single moment. That is, instead of conceiving the "incense" as separated from the *azur* by the artful glass, suppose that we put them all together as aspects of one substance, for which there is no name, except perhaps the kind of thinking made possible by the "Chimera" of poetry ("Chimera" being Mallarme's synonym for the poetic imagination). With a merger of this sort, all three stages would become but phases of one identity; as with the ultimate merger in Flaubert's *Temptations* they would be related as three terms all implying one another, rather than as steps *from* the first term *through* the second *to* the third.

The lines in which such condensation, or telescoping of motives, becomes startlingly complete are his *Don du Poème*. Here the idea of a poet flying without feathers (*sans plumes*) has been jammed into the idea of a poem as a bird born featherless (*déplumée*). The description of it as a "relic" reminds us that, though it has the connotations of a fetus, these suggestions of parturition merge with the more "primal" associations of evacuation. The "black hole" of the glass here figures in the notion that the bird, which is black, has been brought "through the glass burned with aromatics and gold," an expression that, taken in itself, seems hard to explain, but that is seen to belong here, once we think of it in terms of its "humbler" associations.

Mr. Fowlie has a comment that, if read by our rules, helps bring out the fundamental nature of this "gift," even though it also has connotations of parturition. He has just been referring to Mallarmé's poem on the beheading of John the Baptist. And now, with reference to *Don du Poème*, he says that it "contains especially the image of the poem separated from the poet (as the head is separated from the saint)." This comment, if read by our heuristic rules, also explains how the poem on the head of John the Baptist, though its treatment is quite different from the Hérodiade, continues the theme of that poem. Indeed, we might say that both the *Cantique de Saint Jean* and the *Don du Poème* complete the act of bodily severance which *Hérodiade* begrudged: the featherless "bird" is in effect expelled from within, and separated, like a fecal "egg."

We have by now built up such an investment in Mallarmé's terminology, we could readily move to other pieces and note how the same telescoping of terms takes place, often without any clear explanation as to just what the "glass" might be, or just why something is said to *surgir* (the word that is applied to the severing of the saint's head, and that appears in many contexts, most notably the poem beginning *Surgi de la croupe et du bond*).

Before ending, we should note some others of Mr. Fowlie's penetrating observations, particularly when viewed from the standpoint of our speculation about the "telescoping" of terms. When discussing the poem, *Une dentelle s'abolit* (which he translates "a lace is effaced," though he himself notes that *abolir* is a word of some special though unclear significance for Mallarmé), Mr. Fowlie refers to "the 'window' with which the 'mandoline' tries to communicate." This sense of objects in an active relation to one another is most important; for it helps make clear how *things* can be the *scenic* equivalent of *acts*. And this is an important consideration, in connection with our theory that Mallarmé's great stress upon the *state* of vacuity (a theme that is almost an *idée fixe* with him) could stand for a corresponding evacuative *act*. The *emptiness* concerns an *emptying*.

If you will experimentally read, in the spirit of *double-entendre*, and in keeping with Freud's suggestion that the body can be conceived architecturally, Mr. Fowlie's pages on the poem beginning with "his pure fingernails" (*Ses purs ongles*), you will find that this "picture of the poet's room, emptied" is perhaps as far as one can go towards regaining the essence of "creating" as imagined in terms of infantile "firsts." The theme is interwoven with ideas of Phoenix, ashes, and cinerary urn. And in his notes Mr. Fowlie quotes an early version which brings out the theme with startling clarity. Here we are told that "approving night" makes the nails gleam, in connection with a kind of "torchbearer" that is a "pure Crime." "Pure Crime" is perfect for our purposes. In the final version, "A torchbearer at night holds up his hands with no torch in them, and what he supports is a void created by the dreams that have been burned so completely that no ashes remain." The reference to the "torchbearer" (who is descending to the Styx) might also be recalled in connection with the poem, *Tout Orgueil*, where Pride is equated with a torch that smokes after having been put out. As regards the theme of the Styx, by the way, it is also worthy of note that the search for the essence of creativity is a *descent*. "Igitur is the adventurer of what is most primal in oneself. The stairs lead down to that region." Here he would "plunge into some cosmic underground fluid." (p. 114)

The esoteric connotations of "aromatic" (after the analogy of *l'encens fétide*) show clearest in one of the *Chansons Bas*, "The Woman Who Sells

Aromatic Herbs." Following a reference to a hypocrite who would use them to paper the wall *"De lieux absolus lieux / Pour le ventre qui se raille / Renâitre aux sentiments bleus,"* the associative chain turns next to talk of putting them in the "penetrating" hair (*envahissante / Chevelure*), so that the healthy shoots might smell of it instead; and the poem ends on the rhyming of spouse with the plural of louse. Clearly, *chevelure* is *ordure* problematically redeemed. And (in view of the fact that "privy" is among the meanings for *lieux*, though no such meaning was deliberately intended here) the reference to *lieux* as "absolute" is another notable point in favor of our thesis, as regards the infantile implications in the search for the poetic absolute, where *on reviens toujours à ses premiers amours*.) "The hair," Mr. Fowlie says, "is closely associated for Mallarmé with a moment of stillness coming after a strong experience of power and colour." Caressed in darkness, it is as that of a "child empress."

As regards Mallarmé's great preference for the word *abolir*, if you will allow that words can contain words, there is the possibility that he especially liked it because it enigmatically contained the word *bol*, which is defined in our Larousse either English "bowl" or *grosse pilule*, and *nom donné aux argiles ocreuses* (ochre-colored clay fitting well indeed with his cult of sand-colored hair). The Larousse derives this second meaning from a Greek word meaning clod or clump of earth. The same possibility would apply to the word *Hyperbole*, the gonglike exclamation with which the *Prose pour des Esseintes* begins, and a term that Mr. Fowlie describes as "a formula resembling some algebraic condensation." We are suggesting how far such condensation might be carried, and in what direction.

A similar line of speculation might account for several unclear uses of the word *ignoré*. There is gold embedded in its middle syllable, as there is also in Mallarmé's word, *mandore*, for the mandoline that would communicate with the window. In *Hérodiade* there is a doubled form, *ors ignorés*. In *Une dentelle s'abolit* the *mandore* is rhymed with *dore*, in *Sainte* with *dédore*.

In referring to "the image of sunset committing on itself the sin of self-destruction," Mr. Fowlie would seem to be saying in effect that the principle of vacuity, as tinctured by narcissism, can also take on the attributes of self-abuse transmogrified to cosmological proportions. But on the whole, we believe that the Mallarméan regression in the search for aesthetic origins is more "radical" than that. Even in his most erotic poem, *The Afternoon of a Faun* (the plot of which, by the way, has some of the backward-turning we noted in Flaubert's *Temptation*), towards the end there is a notable change. Just as things are about to reach fulfillment, a figure involving grapes is abandoned for a figure involving volcanic lava. After mention of the hour when the woods are the color of gold and ashes, and when Venus sets foot on the lava of Aetna, only then the Faun cries, "I hold the queen!"

However, in ending this section we might be admonished: Although,

judged as imagery, the work of Mallarmé would seem to gravitate continually about euphemisms for the modes of bodily catharsis, when it is judged
as sheer principle or idea all this can properly be interpreted as meditations
on the Negative (somewhat as though a poet were to spend a lifetime translating into terms proper to poetry the mysteries inherent in the square root
of minus-1). Yet we could not possibly do justice to the poetry if we attempted to treat of it solely in such sheerly "grammatical" terms. To realize
the inadequacy all over again, we need but turn to the opening lines of *Le
Tombeau de Charles Baudelaire*, the reference to the buried temple with
mud and rubies dripping from its sepulchral sewer-mouth.

(Addendum: Despite the thoroughness of his book, Mr. Fowlie does
not mention even the existence of the poem beginning, *Une négresse par le
démon secouée*, surely one of the most startling curiosities in all literature.)

Conscious and Unconscious
(Ab Intra and Ab Extra)

Let us take as our text this sonnet on the mythical island of Atlantis. The
first stanza was intended to describe Atlantis in its happy days, before suffering calamity. The second describes its cataclysmic sinking. The sestet
imagines its buildings, now submerged, but still standing somewhere, at the
bottom of the sea:

> *There was an island of Antiquity,*
> *Well-favored with an equatorial sky,*
> *Where Babylonic galleys used to lie,*
> *And inland music sounded cumbrously.*
>
> *Though long accustomed to such clemency,*
> *It felt obscure disturbances, whereby*
> *Emitting a huge geologic sigh*
> *It lurched, and gently sank beneath the sea.*
>
> *Its marbles now, in pale aquatic hues,*
> *Stand aimless, posturing on heavy floors*
> *Where parchments waver, limp and yellowish,*
> *And houses front on darkened avenues*
> *Bearded with sea-growth, promenades for fish*
> *With mournful faces peering through the doors.*[6]

The author wrote this without any *arrière-pensée*. Yet when he submitted it for publication, he was surprised to find himself composing an
almost slavishly apologetic letter. The sensitive editor to whom the sonnet

---

[6] The lines are reprinted in the author's *Book of Moments: Poems 1915–1954* (Hermes
Publications, Los Altos, California, 1955).

was submitted returned it after a long delay, and with such a sense of embarrassment that the author was puzzled. For nearly a year, at odd moments, he wondered about this incident. True, the sonnet has obvious weaknesses. It is too adjectival, for instance. The rhymes are commonplace. And the first stanza in particular pauses too patly at the end of each line. Yet its workmanship is not as unspeakably bad as would seem to be indicated by his excessively apologetic letter and by the otherwise friendly editor's strange evasiveness.

One day the secret was revealed to him in a flash—and he saw the design he had systematically though unconsciously followed. The glare of our present inquiries makes quite clear now what the author had not realized, yet what he must have been "preconscious" of from the start, as indicated by the excessively apologetic nature of his letter, a tone which he interpreted at the time as purely professional embarrassment. After the "breakthrough," the "equatorial sky" of the world's body was seen as referring to the region of the human body's belt; the "inland music" was obviously a euphemism for visceral rumblings—and as for the "huge geologic sigh," it is hard to believe that the significance of the bodily analogy could escape notice for so long. It is equally difficult now to understand how the connotations of the "parchments" could have been missed. And subsequently it was discovered from puns and misprints, that "faces" is a screen word for "faeces."

A remarkable thing about the incident is the fact that, whereas the analogies were wholly unconscious, the writer followed them so strictly, while the embarrassed letter indicated that he simultaneously knew and did not know what he was doing.

For better or worse, the sonnet was a kind of "universal," half-somnambulistic thing, written at a time of divisiveness in the author's life (a divisiveness that may have had something to do with the "schizoid" combination of awareness and unawareness). And as contrast, we might quote some "civic" verses explicitly designed to exploit a related form of imagery for satirically partisan purposes. Whereas the sonnet was a grotesque (and thus involved the use of essentially "comic" imagery without the intention of being "funny"), these lines are "rationally vituperative":

NEWSPAPER EDITOR'S PRAYER

I pray thee, God,
Send us for tomorrow's copy
Some great flood or earthquake or disastrously erupting volcano
Or picturesquely havoc-bearing storm
Or other natural calamity such as we
In piety
Call "acts of God."

Or may there transpire some big new step towards greater global
*   malice*

Or may the peaceful work of the U.N.
Be disrupted by a new flare-up, with corresponding walk-out.

Or may some admiral or general
Blowhorn about the ever-mounting power
To spread misery.
Or if there is to be no true disaster for this day
Then I pray thee
Send us at least conditions for some rumor
That we may flaunt it before the nation
In foot-high front-page headlines
(Being to truth dedicated
We can deny it later,
In a small item well hidden).

Give us, I pray thee,
Some such monstrosity
As a way of drawing gapers to market
That our merchants may the better peddle their wares.

And then happily
Many thousands more acres of stately trees
(Such as young Keats called "solemn Senators")
Trees that make a Cathedral of the forest
Will have been successfully processed,
Transformed into the printed yellow matter of journalism
By the rules of hygiene
To use once and throw away . . .

Here, for obvious satiric purposes, the author's closing lines about a "transformation" deliberately aimed at the "miraculism" of "alchemy in reverse." Though when writing the grotesque sonnet he had both known and not known what he was up to, here he proceeded as consciously as with much of the fecal imagery in Swift.

On the subject of the conscious, unconscious, and "preconscious" relation to problems of negativity and body-thinking, in some respects an author can have no better evidence than observations about his own former writings. For often there is a sense in which they are now wholly alien to him, things which he could not now write any more than he could write the works of some other author. Yet he may still retain the memory of experiences to do with the writing, and thus come as near as one possibly can come, to seeing the object simultaneously *ab intra* and *ab extra*.

For instance, in my *Book of Moments*, page 20, there is a piece of nonsense verse called "Stout Affirmation." As you might expect, this "affirmation" (the final impulsive "Yes!!!") grows out of negatives: "And by never, / And lessermost from beneath not." Hence, by the logic of this chapter, we should be justified in looking beneath the nonsense for traces of such body imagery as we have here been considering. And, of course, the very fact that the poem deliberately aims at "nonsense" indicates the likelihood that its No-no's might be "radical" enough to draw upon the infantile.

Thus, I now think of two lines: "I shall be concerning sank ships / Throughout the entire Endure-Myself." I had consciously in mind something vaguely of this sort: "I shall persist in my sympathy with unpopular causes, though the pressure of adverse criticism greatly depresses me; and insofar as people won't go along with what I advocate, even while persisting in my ways I'll tend to feel self-disgust."

But while revising this very manuscript, I was struck by some relevant lines I wrote about Flaubert's Temptation of St. Anthony. I had been discussing the vapeur that came from the body of Ammonaria. And I concluded: "Note these olfactory images, which I interpret as 'euphemistic,' " since the Saint's thoughts "immediately become transformed into self-disgust, as he exclaims: 'I can't endure myself.' " There's the "Endure-myself" of my lines. But there is more. The previous stanza of the nonsense poem runs:

A great amt. of beauties emplenish the world,
Wherein I would o'erglance upon.
There are those which you go out and exclaim:
"Why! How brim-brim!"

Now, it so happens that I particularly enjoy the somewhat rare figure of anacoluthon, which is defined in Webster's as: "Abandonment in the midst of a sentence of one type of construction in favor of one grammatically inconsonant." And I intentionally used such a figure in the last two lines of the above quatrain. But it so happens that the figure of anacoluthon is immediately and invariably associated in my mind with these lines from an early story in which an anacoluthon was intentionally "embedded":

There are, for those who love such things, rains which come ripping along the valleys, attacking whole forests, bending around gaps between the mountains, driving things before them. Further, there are patchy rains; they piddle for a while, then pour, then even cease entirely, so that the rain gets at the landscape here and there in shafts. [Then comes the anacoluthon.] And there are still other rains which you go out on the porch and exclaim, "Why, it is raining!" they have sneaked into being so imperceptibly. While after any sort of rain the woods are even smellier than usual.

Since the figure involves a disruption of logic, by our theory it should especially fit in contexts involving a shift between body imagery ("they piddle for a while, then pour") and imagery of the world's body (the "beauty" of natural rainfall).

The next paragraph in the story, also involving an anacoluthon, begins with a still more "problematical" body image:

> Oh, vomit of loveliness! Let us rise in the night and give thanks for the pure horizons that remain to us. Exult, for the heavy hills are patient to be climbed upon / willingly they suffer us to paw at their necks and sit across the peaks of their ears. And looking down from them, we see the valley, as it dips and waves, and how the shadows of the clouds . . . the shadows of the clouds, there being any number of clouds that day, though there was also the night when I went to the door / and found the whole world snuggled away under snow / that spread off and over the hills / blue in the full moon / sifting softly against the fences of the meadows / and drooping from the fir trees.

The quotations are from a story entitled "The Death of Tragedy,"[7] built around the antithesis between moody but aloof recollections of childhood and a "mature," vulgar, journalistic kind of competence. ("Let us erect a dirty little monument to these intellectuals. There is even the possibility that we shall be driven into the Church by the scurviness of our free-thinkers.") At that time I was reading much in modern French Catholic polemic literature, which struck me as more concerned with worldly vituperation and holier-than-thou posturing than with the love and fear of God— but I enjoyed it because I have always enjoyed the stylistics of vituperation. And I early realized that the religious terminologies of the Christians and Jews provide a mighty grounding for moralistic resonance. But obviously, such a preference implicitly involved a vote against religion, too. And the story, as indicated by the descriptions I have quoted, turned to the temporary solution that has been quite common, the cult of virgin nature (*not* the alembicated nature of modern power-plagued physics). Yet having inside info on the subject, I personally happen to know that nature, as so conceived, was but the vast female landscapes of Baudelaire's grand sonnet, "The Giantess"; and I had in mind such lines as "*ramper sur le versant de ses genoux énormes*" ("to crawl across the slope of her enormous knees") when I wrote of the hills that they "suffer us to paw at their necks and sit across the peaks of their ears." Ultimately, as regards the relations between world's body and human body, it was a nature ambiguously erotic and "agapetic" (sexual and parental, its *caritas* essentially confused with *amor*).

I have explained in my essay on "The First Three Chapters of Genesis" (*The Rhetoric of Religion*) how the "mythic" attempt to state principles of motivation in narrative terms leads to great stress upon *beginnings*, moments *first in time*. Whatever personal disappointments and frustrations may lead

---

[7] *The White Oxen, and Other Stories.* Albert and Charles Boni, 1924, O.P.

a writer to "regress" towards memories and fantasies of childhood, there is this purely *technical* motive, also. Quite as the Bible, in trying to indicate the *essence* of human temptation, did so in terms of the *first* man's *first* transgression, so all storywriters, sheerly as storywriters, confront this invitation to think about *beginnings* thus in terms of childhood, whenever they are trying to be as radical as they can be in depicting the essence of the human condition as it seems to them. A similar incentive was involved, I think, in these early stories of mine, parts of which I am now discussing because, besides the fact that they permit me to discuss things both *ab intra* and *ab extra*, the stories often use infantile fantasies; and, of course, the body imagery we are discussing has its roots in early familial experience. (Our discussion of the way in which Wagner developed his *Ring* tetralogy was designed to show how such "regressive" tendencies can emerge, through the sheer attempts to be as thorough as possible.)

In another of these early stories, there is a development which is quite relevant to our present subject. The story, "In Quest of Olympus,"[8] begins with what was obviously the symbolism of birth (confused emergence from a cave, in which the mythic "I" had been wandering, lost). Next comes an episode of symbolic parricide (the tiny figure, "Treep," cuts down a big tree, and thereby becomes transformed into a giant). Next there are his experiences in a kind of Nordic warriors' heaven, where he conquers a rival god, Arjk, usurping both Arjk's domain and his name (after which he boasts "I, Treep become Arjk, can drink and carouse in Heaven and yet retain the most powerful arm among the gods"). Next comes his gallant attempt to prevent the Blizzard God's rape of the goddess Hyelva. The attempt is unsuccessful, as Arjk is outwitted by the magic of beauty—and the chapter ends:

> . . . Then the Blizzard God hurried again after Hyelva, falling among her garments like a hawk among the feathers of a dove. His appetites were so ravenous that he tore everything which covered her body . . . and the little bits, whirling about in the tempest, spilled finally out of Heaven, and falling, covered whole states and provinces of the earth, so that some houses were sunk up to their second stories in snow.

Descending with the snow, the story now shifts to an apartment in New York City, a scene arrived at thus:

> The air was almost black with snow; it was so thick that at times stray flakes, falling down the particular air-shaft, swerved and sifted through the partly open window of the particular kitchen. This kitchen was dark, with dirty dishes showing up here and there, while

---

[8] It has been reprinted in selections of my work *Perspectives by Incongruity*, edited by Stanley Edgar Hyman.

the other rooms of the suite were lighted. All were empty, however, except the one in the extreme front, where James Hobbes was lying on Esther MacIntyre.

From here on, the story builds around the contrast between a somewhat sordid metropolitan seduction and the grandeurs of such natural violence as had been described previously. After the seduction scene the story again looks upward, this time describing the stages of a development from a hot night in the country, through increasing heat the next day, to a great downpour, followed by "a new wind . . . from the northwest" that "shoves the entire storm out of my knowledge"—whereupon in crystal clear night the northern lights play, and finally the sun arises "as clean as a brand-new dollar . . . As rash as a blast of unexpected music." This leads to a brief three-line prayer beginning "Praise to the Three-God, Father, Son, and Spirit."

The prayer marks the end of the chapter, but also introduces a theme that will be developed in the final section: the second coming of Christ. The treatment is built around a paradox: Those who seek to honor Christ treat him indecently without knowing what they do. The story ends with Christ's sorrowful return to Heaven. And if you will bear with me, I shall quote the last few paragraphs:

> As Christ heard a faint noise now, He bent His ear to the ground, discovering that the noise came from one unusually minute cricket which was rubbing its wings across its back to produce a little whir of gratitude for the Divine Food it had received. A second later the entire swarm joined in, the graveyard trembling with their praise. Then, with a blare of Hosannahs, an Angelic Horde flew toward Him out of the sunset.
>
> Other battalions answered from the West, as they likewise advanced steadily upon Jesus. And still others, from all corners of the the compass. The sky was churned with song and Seraphic Manoeuvres. For these great fleets of God's Elect, multiplying egregiously, began winding in among one another, melting together, separating, deploying in the shape of V's like wild geese, or banked up like pyramids, or upside down, or advancing in columns . . . while miracles were scattered upon the earth like seed. The sun, the moon, the stars, the planets and all the wandering bodies shone together. Fountains burst forth; wild beasts lolled among the clouds.
>
> All motion and song stopped . . . some thunder was climbing across the sky. Then, as it disappeared in the distance, things began revolving, a Sublime Vortex sucked up into Heaven. In the very centre, unmistakably wide open, stood the Gate, with squadron after squadron of Angels already hurrying within. Christ, too, began rising, while God called out to Him, smiling, AHRLOM AHRLOMMA MINNOR. And Christ answered, MAHN PAUNDA OLAMMETH. Thus had one

spoken and the other answered. Then He entered Heaven, the rear
armies of the Angels following Him rapidly.

> *Olammeth! . . . the seed*
> *. . . This sudden certainty!*
> *Fulfillment, bursting through the mists*
> *Olammeth, His Breasts!*
> *Across night*
> *Projected . . . (latent) . . .*
>   *when lo! the* Sun!

Heaven's Gate swung shut.

When I was writing this final "Ascension" (it will soon become clear
why I put the word in quotation marks), I had no conscious meaning for
the two utterances by Father and Son except that to me they sounded like
a mixture of Sanskrit and Hebrew (fitting tongues for divinity to speak at
this "eschatological" moment when, just as the story began *ab ovo*, things
now attain a grand and total culmination). Also, when I was writing the
story, one detail took me quite by surprise. I refer to the description of God's
elect flying "in the shape of V's like wild geese, or banked up like pyramids,
or upside down, or advancing in columns." More specifically, it was the
notion of their flying "upside down" that suddenly occurred to me. It was
so unexpected, that I nearly omitted it. Then I decided to retain it, on the
grounds that, since this would be a time when lions and lambs lie down
together, any such topsy-turvy detail would "fit."

Yet, since I have always been interested in experiences of that sort
(as has been said of Paul Valéry, I am often more interested in the processes
of poetry than in the poetry itself), I kept puzzling about that "breakthrough." And many years later, I realized the secret when I asked myself:
When have you ever actually seen such a situation as you describe here, a
vortex in which everything whirls around a central point until suddenly
everything is "shut"? To which the answer was: Not when something is
going "up" into the sky, but when unclean waters are going *down* the drain.
Earlier in the story, when the Blizzard God was pursuing Hyelva in the
grand rape meteorologically transmogrified, he had called to her, "Hyelva!
Hyelva, open the great gate of thy body! The great gate of thy body, that I
may enter in!" And at the end, there is a Gate into which all finally enters
whereupon, in spondees (for I always try to pronounce the first word as
much like a single syllable as possible), "Heaven's Gate swung shut." It
thus becomes reasonable to infer that the design of the vortex was ambiguously introduced as early as the reference to the Elect flying "in the
shape of V's"—for lo! as regards the look of V on the pages the vortex *is*
pointed down. And my previous references to "pyramids" in this chapter
suggest why this term has similar connotations (though, of course, I did not
think of this at the time). As a matter of fact, the "Divine Food" mentioned

at the start of this ambiguous "Ascension" had been described as: "A boo from His nose." And now we can decipher the two enigmas:

For some reason or other, a favorite witticism of my father's, when speaking of me in my mother's presence, was to call me "our lamb." I don't know why he did so. But at least there's this to go on: Since I was an only child, we made a sort of "trinity," with him as father, "our lamb" as son, and the final cry, "His Breasts!" possibly adding the maternal principle (having it emerge through the masculine, somewhat as, in Christian thinking, the Holy Spirit, or Love, begins grammatically as a masculine, yet out of it there gradually emerges the role of Mary). In any case, it turns out fittingly that, at this ultimate moment, the figure of Christ is addressed as AHRLOM, which I have since deciphered as "our lamb." And, in the light of the fact that the "Ascension" is but a "euphemistic" descent down the drain, the magic formula, AHRLOM AHRLOMMA MINNOR, enigmatically proclaims: "Our lamb, our lamb a manure."

In the answering formula, "our lamb" becomes "Olamm-" (the "-eth" being intentionally added because it sounds Biblically archaic, while there's also the fact that it's the final syllable of the author's first name). As for the first two words of the second formula, they become clear when I explain that I called my mother and father "Maw" and "Paw." Thus, the entire second formula (MAHN PAUNDA OLAMMETH) means: "Maw 'n' Paw 'nd Our Lamb-eth." In this second form, "our lamb" becomes the theme of the closing verses, which go from "Olammeth! . . . the seed" through "Olammeth, His Breasts!" to the final enfolding in womb-heaven. And it's a further fact, which I never noticed until this moment, that the words "His Breasts!" happen to be exactly in the middle of this final formula, preceded and followed by twelve words.

All told, then, this "eschatological" transfiguration was, unintentionally, a *scatological* one, describing the essence of the poetic Ego in narrative terms *ab ovo* to a final flush down the drain. It was unintentionally "Satanistic" in that, whereas the thinking was essentially theological in *pattern*, it translated the Holy Trinity first into a purely human family and next into the sheerly fecal. Thus, once again, as regards "the thinking of the body," I recall that Luther (whose fundamental vision of man's relations to God and the Devil came upon him while he was in the act of evacuation) avowed that we cannot keep the commandments, that all human virtues must be mixed with some modicum of vice.[9]

To be sure, mine enemies can use these observations to my embarrassment, in effect thanking God that they themselves are pure and exemplary in their treatment of body imagery. But it is implicit in the nature of poetics that such lowly "miracles" must be found to lie about the edges of

---

[9] The closing lines also reflect orgastic fulfillment.

the motives involved in aesthetic production, and possibly in other kinds of production as well—for at the very least we have grounds to fear the "break-through's" in the analities of contemporary physical science, particularly in its close association with the powers of the military (powers that threaten to make any such speculations as these quite irrelevant, like Books of Etiquette for social climbers, or the poetry of Pope, in a devastated world where all life as we know it will have gone down the drain).

Meanwhile, let us close this section on "Conscious and Unconscious" with one last set of personal observations, this time to do with the author's early novel, *Towards a Better Life*, which ends: "Silence, that the torrent may be heard descending in all its fullness." This glum conclusion was the ironic fulfillment of an avowal made in Chapter One: "I would speak as a gargoyle would speak which, in times of storm, spouted forth words." Here, obviously, the flow of vituperative speech was conceived after the analogy of water being drained off tumultuously in a storm. This brand of "Oedipal complex" involves us in the labyrinthine task of trying to solve the Riddle of the Sphincter.[10] For I take it that the sentence also symbolizes, within the conditions of the fiction, an ideal regression towards the "infantile" state of speechlessness. Our hero is choosing to fold up within himself, as though he were encased in his own internality, while the storm raged as though without.

Though the world hurried on its way (particularly since the novel appeared at the height of the great financial depression following the market crash of '29), the course of the plot disturbed the author considerably. For he believes that writers do sometimes hit upon things which prophesy their future (not the accidents that may befall them, but the quality of mind with which they will meet these accidents, and thus which will give the accidents one particular kind of meaning, thereby effectively enclosing a man within the limits of his own personality). And he feared that this ending overhung him like a sentence, a most severe condemnation which he had pronounced upon himself.

Then came a "breakthrough," thus: Some years before, the painter Carl Spinchorn had found him the place in Maine which suggested most of the nature imagery used in the previously mentioned story, "In Quest of Olympus." The author now remembered that this painter had shown him some reproductions of primitive paintings done by a Chinese peasant who had been converted to Christianity. They were illustrations of Bible stories, appealingly ardent. One, for instance, depicted the parable of the lost sheep —and it was the lostest sheep you could imagine, in a fantastic clutter of jagged bushes and rough rocks. Another depicted the story of the Ark, show-

---

[10] I thought the pun was mine. But you'll find it in entry 1184 of Coleridge's *Note-books*. Whereupon, as regards the formula, "Heaven's gate swung shut," we might glimpse further possibilities by experimentally spelling the last word thus: "sh—t."

ing the Ark snugly enclosed, while rain fell all around it in furious cascades. Of a sudden I memembered: I had had this picture in mind when writing my sentence about the torrent. In brief, I had ended on a symbol of *rebirth*!

Maybe I could also refer to another such ambiguous "omen," even though, at the time of writing it, I had consciously meant it in a malign sense only, as with a man who is shown making hopeful plans for tomorrow when we know that he is to be slain today. I refer to the words: "*resurgam*! *resurgam*! I shall rise again! Hail, all hail! Here is a promise: *resurgam*!" Yet somewhat in the spirit of Dryden's formula, "The corruption of a poet is the generation of a critic," I would now read that passage, along with these two passages, as prefiguring a change:

> The sword of discovery goes before the couch of laughter. One sneers by the modifying of a snarl; one smiles by the modifying of a sneer. You should have lived twice, and smiled the second time. . . .

> all I have pondered in malice, some one, coming after me, will consider comfortably. What I have learned through being in grave extremities, he will handle with ease.

In brief, I interpreted the tale as foretelling a transformation from the novel's grotesquely tragic narrative to my later concern with criticism as a theory of "comedy." And, in the light of comic analysis, looking back on that early book's heroics, I saw how it had ended grandly on a meteorologizing of the micturition of fear. Also, I inclined to suspect that, of all English prepositions, "towards" is the most suspect, where puns on body-thinking are concerned, as one can discern readily enough by pronouncing it in one syllable, "tords." This suspicion has ever since pervaded the author's attitude towards titles under the sign of that highly moralistic word.

In one of the earlier stories, "Portrait of an Arrived Critic," the issue of *alternative motives* had been treated quite differently, in a choice-that-was-no-choice. There a shrewdly up-to-date, self-assured, and self-contained man about town was identified with criticism, while the alternative (poetic and narrative expression) was represented by an uncouth wretch whose spontaneity was alcoholic and infantile.

After Words

A colleague to whom I had shown some of these speculations replied: "I can't feel a particle of emotion about micturition and stools. Those members of the Body Trinity don't stir me, though I have often seen sense in libido. There's a heap of water, all shapes and sizes in this world; and such a little bit of it trickling and micturing." (One might answer by recalling the story of the man marrying the girl who was "just a little bit" pregnant.)

And on another occasion my colleague stated his "belief that defecation and micturition do *not* ordinarily survive as passionately engaging the attention after the small boy has become a man, or even a big boy. Nothing like it in my experience. You are so good in your understanding of pure libido that you don't need or deserve a triad of powers on the ejaculative level." To which I answered:

"As for the functions of the privy parts (fecal, urinary, and genital) and their 'spiritual' analogues: I am a confirmed trinitarian. Recall that even Freud, despite the strong monotheistic tradition of his upbringing, and despite the popular idea of him as concerned solely with the 'genital,' was led by his clinical experience to recognize the motivational pressure of what, in my *Grammar of Motives*, I call the 'Demonic Trinity' (that is, the bodily parody of the heavenly set). I like Emerson. Indeed, I class him with Mark Twain as one of my two favorite domestic authors. But I say emphatically: down with Unitarianism where the Thinking of the Body is concerned. True, as I said in an article of mine on catharsis published in the *Kenyon Review* (Summer 1959), the body is not limited to these three purgative outlets. But our culture's featuring of them as the *parties honteuses* gives them their special power as hidden sources of cathartic imagery." I could have added: as regards the norms of the aesthetic, the presence of fecal and diuretic imagery must often be disguised not because it is "wicked," but because it is unbeautiful or unheroic (or, if you will, infantile).

Freud has convincingly developed the idea of anality as a character syndrome. He has also pointed to the ambiguities of the diuretic, but not so thoroughly. For instance, he has noted the relation that fire imagery bears to water (a relation exemplified satirically on the "grand" scale when Gulliver unceremoniously puts out the fire in the castle of the Lilliputian king). And Freud treats *enuresis nocturna* as a symptom of "burning" ambition (an equation that might testify to special diuretic tendencies in his own character, which certainly manifested much "burning ambition," particularly in the study of mental associations revealed by what William James aptly named the "stream" of consciousness).

Another line of speculation fits here. Drugs are, in a sense, caricatures of personality types. Thus, hasheesh reinforces a penchant for the fantastic, the opiates naturally make for quietude, and alcohol fits well with ideals of assertiveness. In this respect, much of our literature could be said to embody the "aesthetic of alcohol," including trends towards a pleasant dizziness, towards such breaking-away from all constraint as is exemplified in the plot of Flaubert's *Legend of St. Julian the Hospitaler*, or the "*au galop*" section of *Temptation of St. Anthony*, trends also exemplified in the cult of speed and flight. Here also belongs the spontaneous flow of ideas, words, and yes, the flow of urine in which, so far as *bodily* "expression" is concerned, the drinking of alcohol *terminates* (whereupon, with regard to theories of "fulfillment" as "essence," we might well ask to what extent, in the secret correlations between body and mind, imagery of this same "fulfillment" might serve to "name" or "sum up" the "meaning" attached to the process of intoxication in the imaginative deviousness of "body-thinking").

Or, here is another line of speculations: Even if one disagrees with Freud's notion that there is a special "death instinct," we do know it for a fact that Freud's stress upon the "wishes" of the Unconscious developed a psychology in line with Schopenhauer's metaphysics of the "will." We also know it for a fact that, in Schopenhauer's scheme, death is equated with excretion. And the body could certainly be said to have an "excretion instinct," in the sense that excretion is a natural aspect of metabolism. That is, despite Schopenhauer's equating of excretion and death, natural excretion is in itself not at all "deathy"; on the contrary, only by excretion can the body remain *healthy*, and it is the *arresting* of excretion that is deathy.

The thought suggests the possibility that, in Freudian theory, talk of a "death instinct" could serve stylistically as tragic dignification of an "excretion instinct." Dramatic grandeur here sneaks into the Beauty Clinic, transforming bathos into pathos. (Similarly, in my *Rhetoric of Religion*, pp. 257-265, I indicated how Theodor Reik's remarks on Freud's idea of a "primal crime" with cannibalistic connotations could be interpreted as a tragically dignified version of an infant eating its feces.) Here, in the very midst of the Clinic, we find tricks of poetic "miraculism" intruding, by the unrecognized transforming of lowly physical functions into terms quite pretentious (what I have called the turning of bathos into pathos).

Motivationally, we might put the terministic problem thus: When several ideas integrally imply one another, we may take any one as ambiguously standing for the others. But unless this situation is made explicit, and the kinship between the supposedly quite different members of the set is made clear, the "problematical" members of the set are likely to be denied their rights, particularly if they are problematical in a way that interferes with some "ideal" involved in the use of this motivational set (as with tame ideas of the "aesthetic").

Except in works of frankly Rabelaisian, Aristophanic, or Swiftian cast, aesthetic ideals are such that any tendencies towards bathos will, if possible, be so transmuted that they bear the guise of pathos. However, as regards our exegesis, we are *not* reducing the whole set to the genius of the "problematical" member. Rather, we are trying simply to show that the problematical elements remain, however disguised by euphemism.

But before closing, let's ask specifically just how the imagery of death as such might figure. As I write these words I am living on a Florida key, where I love to walk among the whole and broken shells (skeletons and parts of skeletons) that the waves toss up on the beach. Never for a moment do I cease to think of these things as the detritus of *death*, aspects of life's *offal*. I live with the thought that digestion and fertilization involve the life-giving properties of *corruption*, that life grows out of *rot*.

Then, suddenly, an idea of this sort invaded me, when I was comparing and contrasting these natural forms with, say, the forms of sculpture. Sculpture carved from wood or stone, I thought, is of material that in one sense really does transcend the skeleton; for beneath its surface there are no analogues of the body's bones. But sculpture cast from clay forms built on frames retains the "principle" of the skeleton beneath the flesh. Here would be a halfway stage between skeleton and skeleton transcended. By the same token, sheerly structural forms would be all skeleton, insofar as they are, however remotely, imitations of bodily articulations. Insofar as they are not thus "bodily" at all, presumably they are attempts to transcend death. The aim at the transcendence of death is revealed in another way by the story of Pygmalion and Galatea, or by the thought of carving a human form out of the "living" rock.

All told, though the principle of the negative is often embodied in "No-no" kinds of imagery, it is itself neither "life-affirming" nor "life-denying." It is a marvel of language, perhaps *the* marvel of language—and though "Don't" can constrain us (thus, to an extent, "mortifying" our desires) it can also save us (when inducing us to guard against a real danger).

The negative could in itself be "deathy" only in the sense that, while man cannot properly use language at all unless he has a feel for the principle of the negative, all symbolism can be a mockery. That is, although symbolism may help us get food, as sheer bodies we live or die not by the words for food, but by the food. As a person, we want another person, not just a symbol for that person. In this sense, all such "transcending" of the thing by its name is towards death. And in this sense, even the most "vital" of language is intrinsically deathy. It is a realm of "essence" such that, without the warm blood of live bodies to feed it, it cannot truly "exist." The "spirit of all symbol systems" could be said to "transcend the body" in this sense, thus taking on a dimension that can also be named by our "good" word for death: "immortality."

But even if one concedes that symbolism is "intrinsically deathy" in this ultimate sense, the fact remains that the great utility of language in helping men cooperate and prosper and praise and give thanks endows it with plenty of "vital" associations. By the same token, however, the negative becomes integrally woven with the motives of shame or guilt ("conscience" in general) because of its role in shaping and transmitting ideas of propriety and impropriety. Next, particularly in cultures that lay great stress upon toilet training and a corresponding set of proprieties associated with the pudenda, the genius of the negative (now strongly moralistic) comes to pervade the realm of the aesthetic, though often in disguise (except in comedy, satire, invective, and the like). In aesthetic forms where it is categorically excluded by the rules of the game, it must enter by subterfuge if it is to enter at all. Insofar as it does not enter at all, the work can not be "thorough." Hence, insofar as the work is thorough in its use of body imagery for the theme of purgation, the expression must be transformed in accordance with the rules "proper" to the aesthetic species (modes of expression ranging from the solemnities of tragedy to the coy Victorian primness, or teasing, of Lewis Carroll's "infantile" fantasies).

Another kind of subterfuge seems likely. Imagery of the fecal and urethral may figure not solely in its own right, but as *substitution* for the genital (that is, as a kind of castration fantasy). There seems to be something of this sort going on in Beckett's story, "Yellow," with regard to the sickroom jokes about laxatives and the patient's operable toe, as he is being prepared for a more serious operation that results in his death.

Once one asks about a possible imaginal correlation between human body, world's body, and body politic, all such likelihoods present themselves. The problem is to discuss the subject intelligibly without discussing it too much. Yet the mere omission of it would be an "idealistic lie," in conformity with merely superficial tests of parlor "propriety," as though great poetry could ever be reduced to the modes of "delicacy" one finds in a book of etiquette designed for teaching the vulgar how to be "elegant." In sum, insofar as poets "give body" to their thoughts, look for Aristophanes, Rabelais, Swift, and Company in the offing, however roundabout.

And one may expect to find all sorts of related paradoxical variations in our way of life, with its special stress upon hygiene as the modern equivalent for the ritually clean. There is, for instance, the ideal of floor wax that does not "yellow," when the floors are compulsively kept polished to the point where they become a major menace to life and limb (a kind of dream-life that matches the military man's ideal of fighting his dirty wars with "clean" bombs). Or there are the millions of dollars spent on detergents that add disgracefully to the pollution of our waters, and all for some slight extra edge of white in our fabrics that is wholly worthless except as the obedient response to a commercially stimulated idea of purely ritual cleanliness. Precisely while loading up the world with murderous atomic wastes in the name of power and progress, or with dangerous chemicals that add some useless gloss or luster to the looks of a food, people have so "disciplined" their critical faculties, they do not want to realize just what all, so far as "body-thinking" is concerned, would be implied in the fact that we necessarily "anthropomorphize" nature.

These pages are offered, not in the belief that the issue has been settled, but in the hopes that its relation to much more important matters has been indicated.

Chapter Three

Somnia Ad Urinandum:
More Thoughts on Motion and Action

As regards the dynamics of a dream, I take it that the Freudian view could be summed up thus: Any indirect or "inaccurate" symbolizing of a motive is an instance of "repression," and of the dreamer's attempt to evade the "censorship" by subterfuges. But, given the proper analytic methods, these disguises can be unmasked, and the true underlying motives revealed. Or there is the Jungian stress upon the theory of "archetypes" that emerge naturally and without repressive distortion from an archaic "Collective Unconscious," and that, given the proper analytic methods, can be shown to retain their primitive perfection.

But even if, for the sake of the argument, we conceded the possibility that one or the other or both of these theories (whether distortions due to conscience-stricken repression, or representations that stem from archaic modes of thought still somehow preserved in our tissues) might account for many major aspects of dreams, is there not at least one other possibility that should be considered at least sometimes?

Suppose that you have been reading about some complicated situation, a current political muddle, for instance. And you want to tell someone just what it seems like to you. You might say, "When I read of that situation, and try to decide what should be done about it, I feel like a fly caught in the old-fashioned flypaper we used to have when I was young, though there hasn't been any of it around for years." Or you might say, "It's like a serious version of W. C. Fields trying to pick his way with dignity through a barbed wire fence, and getting hilariously entangled." Or, "It's like trying to sleep while being attacked by a swarm of mosquitoes." And so on.

Some similes might serve better than others to represent the situation. But none would be likely to represent it in its detailed accuracy, for that's not what similes are designed to do. They *sum up* rather than *analyze*—yet their way of summing up provides relevant material for analysis. (Here, approaching from another angle, we touch upon the theory of "entitlement" in our chapter "What Are the Signs of What?")

This hypothetical example suggests the following tentative proposition: *A wide range of analogies, more or less adequate as judged by conscious, critical tests of representation, can serve to symbolize a motive. But in sleep, when the critical faculties are less exacting than during times of maximum alertness, a dreamer might be temporarily "satisfied" with any mode of representation that remotely resembles the motive or complex of motives with which his dream happens to be preoccupied.*

In this connection, the "repressive" nature of sphincter-training, plus its relation to bodily processes that are unquestionably "archaic," offers especially convenient opportunities for observation. For though the interpretation of many dreams is open to question, surely such doubts are at a minimum when a dreamer, dreaming of a search for a place where he might urinate, awakens to find himself under pressure purely and simply to attain precisely this culmination. Dreams under such conditions may serve to show how, along with the symbolizing of "repressive" and "archaic" motives, the dream resorts to analogies that vary considerably in their accuracy.

If the reader inclines to feel that any given dream seems to include motives and motifs other than that of micturition, he should know that I do not dispute the point. Indeed, such a possibility would explain why one might assume that a dream representation is likely to be somewhat inadequate, as regards the symbolizing of any one motive. (For instance, there is always the likelihood that diuretic motives could involve at least secondarily, outright erotic connotations.) Insofar as a dream condenses several motives into one symbol, the sheer complexity of the problem that the dream synthesis is "solving" would be enough to account for inadequacies in the dream's symbolism, even without the workings of "repression." For, as I tried to show when asking about similes to suggest one's attitude toward a muddled political problem, analogies can be variously inadequate not just owing to "repression," but because of the brute technical fact that *no* analogy can meet the tests of step-by-step analysis for which it was not designed.

To be specific, let us consider the case of an elderly gentleman who, since he was a confirmed valetudinarian, will here be referred to as "Mr. V." Being a light sleeper, Mr. V. was easily awakened by the slightest discomfort. Accordingly, he was exceptionally responsive to any such disturbance as even mild pressure on the bladder. But almost invariably, just before awaking under these conditions, he had a dream in which some detail or other served as an alarm that terminated his sleep abruptly; and thereafter he could not hope to sleep again until he had relieved himself.

Being especially interested in the thinking of the body as it affects the imagery of poetry (and acting on the assumption that *all* bodily processes must have their effect upon human imagery if men are to avoid the charge of "angelism," that is, the claim to think, like angels, in ways purely intellectualistic, without the intervention of bodily imagination), Mr. V. began experimentally taking notes on the dreams which awoke him to the full consciousness of his physical need. For he thought that, by observing the symbolism of these dreams, he might discover just how wide a range of analogies could have served as signals of his immediate condition (over and above any other motivational quandaries that they might happen, directly or indirectly, to stand for).

Often the dreams were explicitly on the theme of urination (though usually under quite "problematic" circumstances, as when they involved a sequence of unsuccessful attempts, despite increasing urgency, to find a place sufficiently private for the fulfillment of his task in a manner deemed decent). Such imaginary interferences, he surmised on awaking, were probably themselves a reflection of "repression" designed to prevent *enuresis nocturna* and doubtless stemmed partly at least from childhood experiences in sphincter-training.

At other times Mr. V. would be awakened, though with equal suddenness or urgency, by a dream that was but remotely analogous to the dreamer's immediate physical condition. Often, for instance, the only obvious relevance that the content of the dream seemed to have was in the fact that some detail of the dream was the occasion of his suddenly awaking, as with the conviction that while asleep he had heard the telephone ring, or a knock at the door. Yet on further thought, "signals" of that sort seemed relevant enough, since they clearly symbolized a warning, or "call" to "duty."

On one occasion, in his dream a voice from nowhere was saying in the accents of an oracle, "Ask him: Just what does it mean? On these elements the chapter might end"—and on the word "end" the state of sleep abruptly ended. We shall revert to this dream when on the subject of "consummation."

Many were dreams of climbing, in situations so hazardous that Mr. V. awoke in a state of fright. (For instance, he might dream that he was losing his grip, and that either he or something he held was about to fall into the vague depths below.) Another variant involved dreams of going interminable distances to find the men's room. These clearly seemed to provide a bungling way of postponing the moment of risk, when the body might somehow contrive to dream of release even while actually still not losing its powers of containment (a moment of conflict on which Mr. V. frequently awoke). Or dreams of actually relieving himself sometimes introduced an admonitory, or repressive principle by imagining the act as being consummated in a highly embarrassing situation, such as a theater foyer or hotel lobby, with an endless stream of strangers passing by. Or he might even dream of soiling others, though against his will and though, despite his great chagrin at the whole performance, the persons whom he was treating thus outrageously seemed strangely unconcerned, as though they were in a wholly different plane of existence.

Among obvious analogies were dreams of heavy rain, with puddles everywhere, while Mr. V. sought to avoid stepping in them. Or in analogies farther afield, the body seemed getting ready to "go" by inducing images of vaguely destined "boat trips" (thereby secondarily introducing the theme of "water").

High among the remote analogies (and here is the point at which we would recall Mr. V.'s dream of awaking at the pronouncing of the fatal word, "end") was a dream that, in one form or another, recurred several times (and probably also reflected his occupational psychosis as a lecturer). In this dream there was usually an audience of great but indeterminate magnitude, distributed in various rooms, galleries, and corridors of some enormous hall or church. Mr. V. saw none of the people individually, they were present simply as a vague churning mass. He was there to make an address. But he could not think of one single word to say. Indeed, the experience was so essentially *aphasic*, he had not even the slightest idea of what he was expected to say. Though no one else seemed bothered by his plight, he stood there in the most wretched confusion, completely blank, until the discomfiture became intense and persistent enough to awaken him.

Mr. V. was particularly puzzled by this species of dream. At first it seemed so far afield, he inclined to doubt whether there was a single strand of diuretic motivation in it. But when reflecting on the *blocked flow of words*, and asking how it might be interpreted from the standpoint of analogy, he began to speculate along these lines:

The situation could be easily accounted for if the inhibited *flow of words* stood for the inhibiting of *diuresis*. Such a relationship might be all the more likely since sphincter-training ordinarily takes place at the time when the child is emerging from infancy (speechlessness) into the ways of verbal expression. If such a tie-up does lurk at the roots of speech, then one can see why the "conscientious" aim to prevent *enuresis nocturna* could attain representation though the analogy of total verbal blocking. If the inability to speak stands for a lack of completion or culmination (a "failure to bring a job to fulfillment"), one could now understand why the reference to the "end" had had an awakening effect in the case of the previously mentioned formula, "On these elements the chapter might end." And similarly, dreams of searching for things under generally inadequate conditions, or of trying to "answer" someone who was "calling" whereas all sorts of contretemps interfered with the attempt to complete the effort, would seem analyzable along the same lines (though, doubtless, the kind of "fulfillment" could also figure).

Such explanations might also account for a different kind of case. Mr.

V. awoke from a dream about a clock that showed the time as a quarter to three. However, when awaking on this occasion he felt no urgency, and dozed off to sleep again without rising. But in the interim, while he was free-associating, on the basis of "three o'clock" as his starting point, the first notion that occurred to him was "One-two-three-*go*." But he didn't have to "go." Hence, the time was registered *not* as three o'clock, but as only a *quarter to three*. Another possibility occurred to him. Mr. V. had often said (and he recalled the comment now) that, what with our later hours for re-tiring, 3 A.M. is the modern equivalent of midnight, old style. So, three o'clock would stand for the moment of "crisis"—and by the same token the dream analogically stated that the moment of "crisis" was not yet. So Mr. V. could confidently resume his struggles with slumber.

A lady of distinguished lineage with whom I happened to be dis-cussing Mr. V.'s observations proffered a reminiscence that throws further light on our present concerns. She told me of a dream in which she was using a *pot de chambre* such as was once considered the height of fashion, in earlier and simpler and more Edenic stages of our culture. Her act, if we may so designate it, was in connection with last-minute preparations for a trip with various members of her family, who kept calling her impatiently, since she was delaying their departure. But despite her hurried efforts, she never seemed to finish, nor did the receptacle get filled. And in the midst of this continuing dilemma, she awoke to find that the dream was relevant to the physical pressure which required her conscious attention.

Note how especially felicitous the analogy was which the dream in-vented in this instance. The imaginary process could not *end* since it had not actually *begun*; and by the same token, despite the interminable flow, the receptacle remained unfilled (or should we say "unfulfilled"?). In a paradoxical way, the dream thus worked out the "proper logical implica-tions" of the protective sphincter contraction whereby, despite the dream's imagining of fulfillment in one respect, in another respect this embarrassing eventuality was successfully inhibited. One does not usually think of "logic" as so deep-lying in connection with body imagery. But it does seem to have been so in this case.

As regards folktales, this anecdote made me wonder whether the story of the "Widow's Cruise" that miraculously never emptied but con-tinued to provide nourishment no matter how often it was poured from, could have arisen through a fantasy that embodied the same principle in reverse, in keeping with Freud's claim that—by a characteristic mode of reversal in dreams—culinary imagery can often represent not food but the excretory.

Also, I might cite an episode from a recently published novel, an in-genious psychological fantasy, *The Benefactor*, by Susan Sontag. Being at once playful and profound in its "free-associating" on the subject of guilt, it almost inevitably includes at some points imagery that shows signs of dating back to such infantile connotation as would go with "ideas of right and wrong" formed during the stage of sphincter-training. Fittingly, in accordance with the narrative "temporizing of essence," such quandaries would be radically represented, in imaginal analogy, if the "principle" of guilt were conceived *in terms* of one's *first* conscience-ridden experiences undergone at the time of emergence from infancy into speech, a time when "No-no" is learned in connection with the control of excretory functions. The "infantile" element also shows in the book's eulogistic references to silence and aphasia. And when considering the book's cult of dreams, we might also do well to keep in mind Coleridge's formula, "the streamy nature of association."

The particular episode I would consider here is in Chapter Seven, and concerns a "Dream of an Elderly Patron." Fittingly, the same chapter contains a treatise on "the doctrines of the Autogenists," who are surely a mock-intellectualistic counterpart of the early "autistic" stage in a person's biological and psychological development. For our purposes, it is not necessary to recount the dream in detail; the following excerpts should be enough to indicate its tenor:

> I was repelled by the cat's strong odor. I flung it on the ground but it remained by my side, so I picked it up again and put it in my pocket, thinking I would wait until I found a place to dispose of it. . . . The doctor . . . passed around sheets of paper for each of us to fill out. . . . I was dismayed at this request. . . . He told me to adjust the large bath towel which I realized was all I was wearing and led me to another part of the garden where I was given a shovel and told to dig. I began earnestly enough, though the towel which was knotted around my waist kept coming loose. The ground was hard and the digging strenuous. And when I had dug a fair-sized trench, water began seeping into it. Soon the trench was half filled with muddy water. There seemed no point in continuing, so I stopped digging and threw the cat in. . . . "Have you forgotten it's time for your operation?" he said. . . . Everything is too heavy," I said, to distract him. "Besides," I added ingratiatingly, "I'm asleep." . . . I could not understand how I was continuing to provoke him. "There's nothing unhealthy about that," I continued. "I get up very early." . . . I was aware that something was wrong with my body, and looking under the towel I saw to my horror that, from the middle of my ribs to my hip, my entire left side was open and wet. . . . The butcher's view of myself was revolting. I wrapped the towel around me even more tightly and, with both hands pressed against my side to prevent my entrails from falling out, I started to walk. At first I felt dignified and brave, and I determined to ask the help of no one. . . . I felt weak now from the loss of blood and could barely walk. . . . I dared not go inside and tell the old man how I had failed to carry out his advice. [At

the start of the dream this old man was seen spilling tea on his shirt, the infraction thus presumably being also such a risk as even the superego is not safe from.] . . . The unfamiliar streets were empty. I pressed my left side, holding back my tears of humiliation. I wanted to lie down, but I was reluctant to dirty my white towel on the pavement. The feeling of heaviness on my left side increased. I was draining away and struggled to lean toward the right. It was then that I died. . . . "This dream is too heavy," I said to myself when I awoke. . . . This dream told me all too plainly how burdened I was and how I despised myself. Who am I to aspire to being free? I thought. How dare I go about disposing of others, when I cannot even dispose of myself.

As I read of this dream, in the light of my previous remarks I began to feel sure that I knew more about this dream than the author did. And in particular, the fictitious narrator's statement that, on awakening from the dream, he found it "too heavy," was interpreted by me as an analogical way of saying that, despite the diuretic nature of the dream, its literal "fulfillment" had been "conscientiously" resisted. But in the story itself, "a scholar whose special field of study was ancient religious sects" is reported as having interpreted the dream thus:

> According to certain theological ideas with which I shall acquaint you . . . this may be interpreted as a dream of water. You dug a ditch and it filled with water. And in the end you were not heavy. You were—how shall I say?—liquefying.

It is interesting, by the way, that the statement, "in the end you were not heavy" follows the appearance of three terms, "heavy," "heaviness," and "burdened," with regard to the immediate content of the dream.

I take it for granted that many of the dreams here mentioned lend themselves to other explanations that, though they could not rule out the dream's possible relation to a fortuitous symptom of bodily unrest, would attribute the imagery to more serious planes of motivation. And in the case of the dream just cited, another strand of even sheerly physical motivation seems indicated, despite the fact that the authoress is attributing the dream to a man. (I refer to the sheerly feminine connotations of blood.) One can readily detect the possibility of erotic motives in dreams of falling, and thus at one remove in dreams of flying. Some of Mr. V.'s dreams would also seem to involve an exhibitionistic motive, others sadistic (his imaginary soiling of others, for instance). And we might reasonably find traces of a concern with death in any theme having to do with "ends" or "fulfillments."

In this connection, Mr. V. recounted one dream so obviously ambiguous that the very subject matter of the dream involved a fluctuancy of motives. In the dream, he was worried about some task, the exact nature of which he could not remember, but which could be accomplished in one of two quite different ways. One kind of solution would be gradual, the other decidedly abrupt. (He could recall the contrasting *quality* of the solutions, but not their *content*.) Conceivably, so far as the bearing upon sheer bodily behavior was concerned, this confusion could represent a situation that indeterminately involved both erotic and diuretic impulses. The "abrupt" solution would represent such an "explosion" or "orgastic" outcome as would be associated with spontaneous seminal emission. The "solution" by measured, gradual release would represent the decidedly less heroic course of micturition. And Mr. V. awoke just after having decided on the "moderate" policy, his sudden awaking at this moment obviously being quite "proper" with regard to his humbler needs of the moment. Possibly, if he had been a much younger man, Mr. V.'s dream would have hit upon the more ardent solution, and died rather with a bang than with a whimper.

Such ambiguities are attested to in many common ways of speaking; e.g., in classical Latin *meiere* could be used as slang for *semen emittere*. And Mr. V. himself told me of a game that he and some little girls had invented when he was very young (indeed, this was among his earliest memories). The game was called "playing cow." It involved his going into a nearby field and picking daisies—an act that stood for the cow's grazing. Then, at a signal, he was called in to be milked by the little milkmaids, who used an old tin can for this purpose. To this day, though he is now quite elderly, among wild flowers Mr. V. is particularly partial to the daisy, which among other things he associates with that humble pastoral pastime so near the innocence of his infancy.

In sum, if dreams are condensations of several motivational strands (and they almost inevitably are, since the material they adapt for their analogies obviously comes from many sources, some accidental and some integral to both superficial and profound problems of the personality), there is all the more cause for the analogies to be inadequate, as regards the representation of any *one* motive. And insofar as the dreaming mind rarely meets the tests of rationality that a wholly awakened critical mind would demand of an analogy, there is all the greater likelihood that any analogies (for which the uncritical dreamer finds *pro tem*. use) will be confused.

But this thought does bring up one further possibility, along this line:

Religion serves two functions that sometimes reinforce each other and sometimes are in conflict. The one function is purgative, redemptive. To the sick soul that feels lost, religion offers solace. The other function is designed for a quite different purpose; namely: the service of religion as an instrument of social control. And whereas the first requirement might be sufficiently met if a person most in authority directly relieved a man by assuring him that he was henceforth free of all guilt, such a simple legalizing of bankruptcy would not meet the requirements of religion as an instrument of social control. Thus, often, to meet both tests, the cleansing of guilt must be contrived in ways that reinforce the very assumptions on which the sense of guilt was based.

Orthodox psychoanalytic cures presumably aim to operate on a different basis. *They would introduce a radical questioning of the very assumptions on which the sufferer's sense of guilt was based.* However, certain principles of dramatization keep pressing for embodiment just as strongly in the psychoanalytic treatment of sick souls as in religion. Hence, if the psychoanalyst would become the *complete* secular counterpart of the father confessor, he must not merely sweep away the assumptions on which the confessant's sense of guilt was based. His catharsis must also, however roundabout, serve to reinforce either these assumptions or the conditions that, however roundabout, reinforce these assumptions.

It is quite possible that he may be content to save the individual at any cost, and let the social order take care of itself. But insofar as he is a secular counterpart of the religious priesthood, functions that resemble the use of religion as an instrument of social control will figure willy-nilly in his techniques.

At this stage in our discussion, the reader might suspect me of getting ready to trot out the sound but somewhat shopworn notion that psychologists who treat people for so much an hour will, in the last analysis, work out a kind of cure in which "guilt" (or "debt") of the money-paying sort is somehow still soundly upheld. But, taking that for granted, let's consider a more complicated step, thus:

When Freud tells us that our guilt is as though stemming from an original father-kill (a scheme that under other conditions might be extended to encompass vague notions of parricide in general), he has still left us with a quite heroic source for our anxieties. Whereupon I ask: Might this opportunity for heroizing serve paradoxically to reinforce all over again a kind of aim that is *in its very essence opposed to the sheerly clinical aspects of psychoanalytic cure*? (In other words, might it secretly build up the very thing it is supposedly tearing down? And thus might it, however roundabout, imitate in its own way the same religious pattern which, on the surface, it would seem to replace?)

Perhaps I can best make the point clear thus:

Suppose a dreamer dreamed of guilt. Suppose he dreamed of guilt because, among other things, he wanted humbly to piss without either getting up or wetting the bed. But when the dreamer brought his dream to market (the psychologist's couch) what if he was assured that his dream was an analogy for tremendously honorific motives (such as are associated with the Big Kill)? Might not the introduction of such analogies reinforce a dramatic picture of human dignity that is as regrettable in its way as the cult of a Hitler or a Napoleon? Might not quasi-clinical dramatizations of that sort act to encourage all over again the kind of meditations that we must abandon, if we are to become truly humble?

By all means, please don't read this as an "attack on Freud." For he has offered ingeniously many clinical observations that I could have cited in behalf of my thesis in these pages. I am merely suggesting that the old Adam was in him, as in all of us; and at times it showed up as a tendency to make an explanation as dramatically effective as possible. Obviously in such cases a more pretentious explanation is more dramatic than a less pretentious one, unless we are formally considering human motivation in terms of comedy, burlesque, or farce. Yet many customers would resent paying their good money for too unimpressive an interpretation of their dreams, when they could just as well get a "nobler" one. And, by a kind of purely "*formal* countertransference," the analyst might tend to satisfy such demands for dignification, even though (as compared with theological ideas of "sin") the psychoanalytic enterprise deliberately aims to dispel all sense of truly magnificent depravity. I am merely suggesting that, though psychoanalysis is programmatically designed to free us of such sickly "grandeurs," since drama lends itself so well to the producing of catharsis there is a "natural" tendency to re-establish the kinds of cure that go best with theatrical solemnities.

This is not the place to attempt deciding whether or not psychoanalysis should build up on one side the conditions that it would remove on the other (thus secularly paralleling the two different and often conflicting functions of religion with regard to the saving of sick souls). Our point for the present is simply this: Might the pressure for dramatic dignification often lead to a greater stress upon serious causes than is actually the case?

I mean: If a dream represented, let us say, both an immediate trivial bodily motive for dream imagery of guilt, and a profound personal motive, and if the analysis focused attention only on the serious motive, would there not be implicit in such a choice a kind of dramatizing that at least misrepresents the case, and thus builds up in the patient a too thoroughly "heroic" view of the imagery improvised by his dreaming body? In such a situation, should one not at least allow for a kind of "double plot," with the analogy operating simultaneously in two different motivational planes, one of them involving such a "high-born" or "Cornelian" motive as the Oedipus Complex, the other such a vulgar "meiotic" motive as the vague desire to urinate under conditions that reactivate in the dreamer a sense of guilt surviving from domestic fears to which he was conditioned as a child, with regard to the risks of bed-wetting? (Incidentally, the thought also suggests the possibility that, under some conditions, tendencies to insomnia may originate in early sphincter-training.)

However, let us end on a "dramatization" decidedly in the heroic mold. It concerns a dream in which Mr. V. was awakened to his "duty" by thinking that he had heard a brutal pounding on the door. When he awoke he was immediately reminded of an episode in *Macbeth,* much to our purposes: Act II, scene iii, just following the murder of the king. There has been a "knocking within." Macbeth has breathed his conscience-stricken avowal: "Awake Duncan with thy knocking! I would thou couldst!" And then comes the famous Porter scene, which we should quote through line 41:

> *Porter.* Here's a knocking, indeed! If a man were porter of hell-gate he should have old turning the key. (*Knocking within.*) Knock, knock, knock! Who's there, i' the name of Beelzebub? Here's a farmer that hanged himself on the expectation of plenty: come in time; have napkins enough about you; here you'll sweat for't. (*Knocking within.*) Knock, knock! Who's there i' the other devil's name! Faith, here's an equivocator, that could swear in both the scales against either scale; who committed treason enough for God's sake, yet could not equivocate to heaven: O! come in, equivocator. (*Knocking within.*) Knock, knock, knock! Who's there? Faith, here's an English tailor comes hither for stealing out of a French hose: come in, tailor; here you may roast your goose. (*Knocking within.*) Knock, knock; never at quiet! What are you? But this place is too cold for hell. I'll devil-porter it no further: I had thought to have let in some of all professions, that go the primrose way to the everlasting bonfire. (*Knocking within.*) Anon, anon! I pray you, remember the porter.
>
> (*Opens the gate.*)
> *Enter* MACDUFF *and* LENNOX
> *Macd.* Was it so late, friend, ere you went to bed, That you do lie so late?
> *Port.* Faith, sir, we were carousing till the second cock; and drink, sir, is a great provoker of three things.
> *Macd.* What three things does drink especially provoke?
> *Port.* Marry, sir, nose-painting, sleep, and urine. Lechery, sir, it provokes, and unprovokes; it provokes the desire, but it takes away the performance. Therefore much drink may be said to be an equivocator with lechery; it makes him, and it mars him; it sets him on, and it takes him off; it persuades him, and disheartens him; makes him stand to, and not stand to; in conclusion, equivocates him in a sleep, and, giving him the lie, leaves him.

Here, first of all, we find objectified the "knock of conscience." And properly so, since we are on the subject of guilt (here "rationalized" in terms of murder). On one point, as regards our thesis, there is no doubt: The subject of "urine" is *specifically* introduced by name. Beginning with a first rough approximate, the reference to "turning the key" (surely a preparation for a release of some sort) will lead, step by step, to the Porter's opening the gate. Looked at in the light of the analogies with which we are here concerned, the progressive unfoldings are quite remarkable. Talk of a farmer that "hanged himself on the expectation of plenty" would obviously be a way of including the notion that a "harvest" (a *yield* of some sort) is in the realm of the problematical; for otherwise, why should connotations of self-punishment turn up precisely in connection with an "expectation of plenty"? However, at this stage, there seems no indication that the "plenty" might be of the "liquefying" sort.

But we apologized too soon. For, before the sentence is over, we read: "have napkins enough about you; here you'll sweat for't." Yet, obviously, "napkins" and "sweat" are still in the far outlying areas of the locus towards which, as we already know, these "streamy" associations are surely leading. Later we shall consider the possibility that the reference to an "equivocator" is itself an equivocation. But at the moment it is developed through a pun on "hose," indeterminately an article of clothing, a flexible tube for watering plants, and a male member. Obviously, we are here coming closer to the "fulfillment."

Once we accept Freud's observations on the ways in which "fire" can stand for "water," we realize that, in the reference to "the primrose way to the everlasting bonfire," things are drawing still closer to the culminative formulation. After the opening of the gate (surely an important qualitative step in this direction) there is talk of "carousing till the second cock," with corresponding symptoms having to do with "drink." The word "cock" may or may not be an "equivocator"; in any case, "drink" is but the first stage in a process that terminates naturally in "urine," quite as does the Porter's diagnostic statement that drink provokes "nose-painting, sleep, and urine." (I introduce the word "diagnostic" here because of my feeling that, once the "gate is opened," a more explicitly "rational" kind of consciousness enters with the entrance of Macduff and Lennox.)

If, next, we allow that the reference to "nose-painting" is itself somewhat of an equivocation, while sleep and urine are to be taken quite in the spirit of our present aesthetico-clinical speculations, then the remainder of the Porter's speech, on drink as an "equivocator," seems all the more perfectly to derive from what has gone before—and obviously, it embodies the very equivocation which we have already discussed, with regard to erotic and urethral motives. Nay more, it deals with these ambiguities in quite diagnostic fashion, ending on the assurance to us that, in having "made a shift to cast him," the doughty Porter had not wet his bed. Nor, we assume, would the audience, responding first in urine-causing fright, as attested by the insistent knocking, but finally in terms of the Porter's comic diagnostics, terms that were designed to help the audience keep control, terms that, for all their seemingly haphazard sparkle, are themselves under the keenest clinical control, as attested by their shrewd talk of equivocation diuretic and erotic.

And so it goes . . .

Addendum:

Persons better acquainted with the range of psychoanalytic literature than I am have corroborated these speculations at least to the extent of assuring me that many other theorists have, in one way or another, already formulated and subscribed to the basic principle underlying these pages. That is, they have contended that certain aspects of dreams might best be explainable not in Freudian terms, as an ego's attempts to express its id despite the repression imposed by the superego (or in Jungian terms, as survivals of archetypal imagery), but as a dream's fumbling attempts to represent situations by which the dreamer is vaguely afflicted. In particular I should certainly mention a splendid article entitled "The Hinterland of Thought." It is by a British psychologist, D. W. Harding; it appears in a collection of essays, *Metaphor and Symbol*, edited by L. C. Knights and Basil Cottle (Butterworths, 1960). In a course on "Poetics and Linguistics" I gave at Bennington in the spring of 1961, I called my students' attention to both this article in particular and to the collection in general—and I have since been praising them elsewhere. And though I had already been working along these lines, the article by D. W. Harding in particular enabled me to sharpen my ideas of the difference between such notions and Freud's on repression or Jung's on archetypes. Consider, for instance, these paragraphs, pages 19, 20:

> We are still obliged to use similes and metaphors in describing these things, and I think the metaphor of distance as well as depth is needed. We stand at the harbour of our mind and watch flotillas of ideas far out at sea coming up over the horizon, already in formation of a sort; and though we can re-order them to a great extent on their closer approach, we cannot disregard the organization they had before they came in sight. They are all submarines, partly under water the whole time and capable of submerging entirely at any point and being lost to sight until analytic techniques undo the repression. But it constitutes a fundamental difference whether an idea is out of mind because it has been forced to dive or because it has not yet come up over the horizon. Sometimes repressed ideas may be close inshore, forming the co-conscious that interested Morton Prince. Others may be both under water and at a great distance; they find expression in some sorts of dreaming, especially the sorts that have most interested the Jungians. And in creative work great numbers of ideas, more or less organized, are simply out of sight beyond the

horizon and can be brought into view only through the redispositions we make amongst the in-shore mental shipping that we *can* see and control.

The main emphasis of Freud's work was on the unconscious that has been formed by repression and it was Jung who gave more attention to the emergence of ideas out of the remote distance of the non-mental. In his elucidation of dream-work Freud identified the over-determined symbol, one combining multiple meanings, which seems very likely to be a possible way by which at an early stage of thinking potential ideas are held in a common matrix without being organized through articulate relationships. But Freud attributed it to "condensation," implying that defined ideas (whether or not repressed) have been brought together; there is in the dream, he says, "an inclination to form fresh unities out of elements which in our waking thoughts we should certainly have kept separate" (*An Outline of Psycho-Analysis*, Ch. 5.) The alternative view that certain symbols are the undifferentiated totalities out of which clear ideas may emerge, each representing only an aspect of the whole, has been put forward with great insistence by Jung in his doctrine of archetypes. It seems to me a matter for regret that because of Jung's quality of mind symbols of this kind should have been given that name and made to seem more mysterious than most thinking.

I do not claim that my stress upon a dream's bungling attempts at analogy accounts for all cases. I am merely reminding that even the most conscious and critically astute terminology for the representing of a complex situation will necessarily bungle somewhat, either by oversimplifying the representation for some particular purpose or by seeking indeterminately for analogies that can encompass the situation in its full complexity (the process which Freud would presumably call "condensation"). I am saying, in effect, "It may be necessary to employ the concepts of either 'repression' or 'archetypes' or both in your schemes for the interpretation of dreams. But it still remains a methodological fact that certain aspects of dreams are adequately explained in terms of the dream's sheer *inadequacy*, as tested by the norms of a wholly conscious and mature representation (tests which the laxities of a dream are not designed to meet)." Freud would doubtless treat such motives as simply the "occasional cause" of the dream.

If a certain person wears a garment of a certain color, in a dream a garment of this color may *stand for* that person. It may stand for the person, not because the dreamer is trying to conceal from himself the fact that he is dreaming of this person, but simply because the dream, as per the normal resources of synecdoche, can use this image *as a sufficiently acceptable representation* of the person. Thus, in the case of Poe's "The Raven," we can imagine that a mere dream would have been satisfied with his original plan to have the vatic syllables uttered by a parrot (perhaps sitting on a black object); but the conditions of the poem were more exacting, and required revision by substituting a raven.

A further possibility here would be of this sort: If the dreamer has strong feelings about a person, and some sign stands for that person, then the dreamer may be tentatively organizing a new symbolic order by trying to fit the sign into his symbol system while taking vaguely into account the further fact that the sign also possesses motivational claims *outside* its particular role as a sign for the given person. The situation would be analogous, in a bungling way, to something of this sort:

Suppose that a certain location happened to have unpleasant associations for a certain person. For instance, suppose it were an amusement park at which he happened to have suffered some important loss. Next, imagine friends who did not know of this situation, and who arranged to have an outing in that park. The person would then have to clear up this conflict, which is not intrinsic to the place itself. He would have to consider it in two lights: as his friends saw it, and as he saw it from the past.

Next, imagine a duality of this sort being treated in the laxities of a dream. Would not the dream's bungling be explainable simply on the basis of the fact that the problem was too difficult for the relaxed dreamer, rather than as the unconscious' way of getting around repression?

In referring to a synecdochic process whereby a garment of a certain color might "stand for" a person who was, in the dreamer's mind, identified with that garment, I had in mind the expressionistic cinematic version of Poe's "Fall of the House of Usher" (Webber-Watson, 1928). At several points in this work, like the visual counterpart of a Wagnerian *leitmotif*, a certain character's hat appears in scenes that involve the character as a motivational ingredient but do not require his physical presence.

Chapter Four

What Are the Signs of What?
A Theory of "Entitlement"

There are two quite different senses in which we can say that a word has a context. There is the context of the other words among which it is used in a sentence (or, by extension, in an article or book or entire universe of discourse). And there is a nonverbal or extraverbal context (what the anthropologist Malinowski has called "context of situation"), the circumstances involving many elements that are not verbal, though many are named and all are at least in principle nameable.

The two kinds of context can be quite different. For instance, a word that has connotations of "friend" (as defined by its place in a strictly verbal context) might figure in a "context of situation" where the same word would connote "enemy" (as with reversals we encounter in the shifting alliances of international politics). Insofar as the word itself can be considered a kind of act, in effect it becomes a different act by reason of its placement in a different scene (a logic of transformation which, in my *Grammar of Motives*, I call a "scene-act ratio").

By the "symbolic" or "symptomatic" nature of terms (in the strictly psychoanalytic sense) we mean their significance, not as defined in a sheerly lexical context (as in a dictionary) but as secretly infused with some "repressed" or "forgotten" *context of situation* that was in some way "traumatic" (as per my remarks about the "primal" dog, in my previous chapter on "Mind, Body, and the Unconscious").

There is a strict sense in which, whenever you cry "Wolf," you repeat the same act (as regards the meaning of the word in a dictionary, the "lexical" wolf). But there is another sense in which your cry is quite different if there is no wolf, or if there is a wolf, or if you had been repeating the cry when there had been no wolf but this time there is one. Here, obviously, the nature of the term as an "act" is defined not just by its place in the context of a certain language, but by its extra-verbal "context of situation."

Furthermore, such a nonverbal scene or context of situation is capable of being defined in terms of varying scope, or "circumference." (For instance, I am writing these words "in Florida this January," or "during a lull in the bombing of North Vietnam," or "in a period following the invention of the atomic bomb but prior to a soft landing of electronic instruments on the surface of the moon," and so on.) Thus, the "same" act can be defined "differently," depending upon the "circumference" of the scene or overall situation *in terms of which* we choose to locate it.

Not only words, but also persons and things are defined by such scenes of varying scope. And in this sense, if I happen to have had some "traumatic" experience involving a hammer in some kind of situation which you have never experienced the likes of, it's possible that even the sheer *word* "hammer" will imply, for me personally, a cycle of terms quite different from your cycle. (In terms of the previous chapter already mentioned, I'd here tentatively put together a "primal" hammer and a "tautological" hammer.)

As I see our problem, we shall here be radically involved with variations on Spinoza's concept of substance (as overall situational context). Thinking along such lines, we ask: In the last analysis, how could even some one tiny pinpoint exist, or be "determined," except insofar as the entire context of the universe lets it be there, in exactly the conditions by which it is conditioned (or lets it be determined in exactly such terms as do define its existence)?

This article is the revised, but not essentially modified, version of a paper originally presented at the Human Relations Center, Boston University, in the spring of 1956. It was published in *Anthropological Linguistics* because a linguistically anthropological expert, Dell Hymes, happened to tell me about a field worker's discovery that, as I saw it, added up to this: If a tribe has one name for a raccoon in one nonverbal situation, and another name for a raccoon in a different nonverbal situation, and you show a member of that tribe the sheer picture of a raccoon, he may not be able to tell you what it is called. He is puzzled because he conceives of the word for raccoon *situationally*, whereas the sheer *picture* of a raccoon sans setting is in effect but *lexical*. I felt that the embarrassed tribesman would here be proving himself, unbeknownst to himself, an excellent Spinozist. And I dug out these pages, which might profit by being read in the light of such considerations.

This chapter proposes to inquire into the problem by asking what could be said in defense of a somewhat paradoxical proposition that experimentally reverses the commonsense view of the relation between words and things. The commonsense view favors the idea that "words are the signs of things." That is, various things in our way of living, are thought to be singled out by words which stand for them; and in this sense the words are said to be the "signs" of those corresponding things.

But, if only as a tour de force, we here ask what might be discovered if we tried inverting such a view, and upholding instead the proposition that "things are the signs of words." That is, might words be found to possess a "spirit" peculiar to their nature as words? And might the things of experience then become in effect the materialization of such spirit, the manifestation of this spirit in visible tangible bodies?

If such verbal spirits, or essences, were enigmatically symbolized in nonverbal things, then their derivation (so far as causes within the natural world are concerned) could come both from the forms of language and from the group motives that language possesses by reason of its nature as a social product.

This chapter examines both these possibilities. First, it proposes that language be viewed, not directly in terms of a word-thing relationship, but roundabout, by thinking of speech as the "entitling" of complex nonverbal situations (somewhat as the title of a novel does not really name one object, but sums up the vast complexity of elements that compose the novel, giving it its character, essence, or general drift).

Thus, with the sentence, "The man walks down the street": To realize that it is more like the "title" of a situation than like the description of an act, we need but realize that the sentence, as stated, could not be illustrated. For you'd have to picture a tall man, or a short man, a dark man or a light man, etc. He'd have to be pictured as walking upright or bent over, with or without a hat, or a cane, etc. And the street would have to be wide or narrow, with a certain kind of curbing, paving, and the like. It is in this sense that the sentence is to be viewed after the analogy of a title, which sums up an essence or trend or slant, rather than describing the conditions that would be required for the thing named really to happen or exist.

Next, the chapter considers modes of abbreviation whereby the whole sentence, considered as a title, can be summed up in one word, as were we to sum up the sentence "the man walks down the street" by saying that it had to do with either a "man-situation," or a "walk-situation," or a "street-situation." "Entitling" of this sort prepares for the linguistic shortcut whereby we can next get "universals" such as "man," "dog," "tree," with individual men, dogs, and trees serving as particularized instances or manifestations of the "perfect forms" that are present in the words themselves (which so transcend any particular man, dog, or tree that they can be applied universally to all men, dogs, or trees).

Next the chapter considers the social content in such words, their nature as receptacles of personal attitudes and social ratings due to the fact that language is a social product, and thus builds the tribe's attitudes into its "entitlings" and into their "abbreviations" as words for things. Thereby, the things of the world become material exemplars of the values which the tribal idiom has placed upon them.

Thus, in mediating between the social realm and the realm of nonverbal nature, words communicate to things the spirit that the society imposes upon the words which have come to be the "names" for them. The things are in effect the visible tangible material embodiments of the spirit that infuses them through the medium of words. And in this sense, things become the signs of the genius that resides in words. The things of nature, as so conceived, become a vast pageantry of social-verbal masques and costumes and guildlike mysteries, not just a world of sheer natural objects, but a parade of spirits, quite as the grass on a college campus has its meaning for us, not just as physical grass, but because of its nature as symbolic of the promises and social values associated with the order of formal education. In a subtler way, it is suggested, all nonverbal "nature" is in this sense not just itself for man, the word-using animal; rather, for man, nature is emblematic of the spirit imposed upon it by man's linguistic genius.

The author considers his approach a linguistic counterpart of Emerson's Transcendentalist views, in his early long essay on "Nature," the difference being that this essay treats as an empirical aspect of language many elements which Emerson would treat in terms of supernatural "spirit."

In this chapter, the plan is experimentally to reverse the usual realistic view of the relation between words and things. Generally, people assume that a child learns its first language somewhat like this: As an infant, it receives through its senses the impressions of nonverbal things. At the same time, it hears words used in connection with these things. And so, gradually emerging from infancy into linguistic articulacy, it comes to associate the words with the things, whereupon the words become in effect the conventional signs of the things.

Though Augustine eventually refers everything back to a supernatural source, in his *Confessions* he substantially gives this account of the relation between words and things whereby words are to be viewed as the signs of the things which they signify. And we quote it for its succinctness in stating the case:

> I afterwards observed how I first learned to speak, for my elders did not teach me words in any set method, as they did letters afterwards; but I myself, when I was unable to say all I wished and to whomsoever I desired, by means of the whimperings and broken utterances and various motions of my limbs, which I used to enforce my wishes, repeated the sounds in my memory by the mind, O my God, which Thou gavest me. When they called anything by name, and moved the body towards it while they spoke, I saw and gathered that the thing they wished to point out was called by the name they then uttered; and that they did mean this was made plain by the motion of the body, even by the natural language of all nations expressed by

the countenance, glance of the eye, movement of other members, and by the sound of the voice indicating the affections of the mind, as it seeks, possesses, rejects, or avoids. So it was that by frequently hearing words, in duly placed sentences, I gradually gathered what things they were the signs of; and having formed my mouth to the utterance of these signs, I thereby expressed my will. Thus I exchanged with those about me the signs by which we express our wishes, and advanced deeper into the stormy fellowship of human life, depending the while on the authority of parents, and the beck of elders.

One may complicate the design by a quaternary relationship, such as is usually involved in primers used for teaching children to read. The relation there is between two kinds of writing; namely: pictures and words, with the pictures as the signs of the corresponding nonverbal things, and the written words as the signs of the corresponding spoken words. But the overall design is substantially the same: a correspondence whereby the words are learned as conventional signs of the things (and of the predicates of those things).

There is so much that is substantially correct in this commonsense view (summed up in the proposition that "Words are the signs of things"), we tinker with it at our peril. But we would here ask, if only as a tour de force, if only as an experiment tentatively tried for heuristic purposes, what might be said for the reverse proposition, "Resolved: That things are the signs of words." And even if we didn't dare assert that it should flatly replace the traditional view, we still might hope that it could supply a needed modification of that view, like adding an adjective to a noun.

Unfortunately, there is a sense in which we can't place over-much faith in any statement as to how a human being emerges from infancy into word-consciousness. For if we have great trouble understanding verbal processes even at their clearest in mature adult speech, there are less hopes of learning something at this point, where the materials of the problem are vaguest. The exquisitely evanescent state of awareness that goes with the fluctuant emergence from infancy into speech is much vaguer by far even than the realm of dreams, since in dreams many of the signs are often quite clearly rememberable.

Accordingly, if we propose to reverse the realistic account of the word-thing relationship, we must correspondingly modify our view of the meaning that we should attach to any treatment of linguistic signs in terms of their possible origin.

That is: If we get around to discussing the logical sign-thing relationship in terms of its possible temporal evolution, we must not take such an account as evidence designed to prove the validity of our position. Any such statement about the emergence of language out of infancy can be but an "arbitrary anecdote," the pedantic counterpart of a picturesque story, which one might make up simply as an illustration of his theory. That is, a theory of origins would not serve as adequate grounds for any purely logical or linguistic speculations; but the logical position might serve as its grounds. Or, more simply: the theory of origins would be a translation from logical terms into corresponding narrative or temporal terms.

To illustrate what we mean here, when we speak of translating logical terms into their narrative or temporal counterparts, consider Jefferson's proposition that "all men are created equal." As phrased, it is a statement about origins, about a condition in which men were "created," and thus which they presumably in some way inherited (as a kind of "original virtue" to match "original sin"). Men are here said to have some kind of equality that derives from a prior natural condition, itself possibly deriving in turn from a supernatural source, if "created" is to be understood in the traditional sense of the word.

But suppose we wanted to state this same proposition sheerly as a matter of principle, without reference to any grounding in temporal origins. Translating it into terminese, we might get some such statement as this: "Resolved: That within this universe of discourse, all men are to be considered *in terms of* ideal equality, or of equality 'in principle' (quite as, at other times in history, men have been asked to consider their sociopolitical relations *in terms of* ideal *in*equality)."

Next, beginning now with this purely *logical* proposition (that "in principle" men are to be treated as equal) let us imagine trying on the basis of it to set up an ideal calculus for the placement of human relations. And suppose that we wanted to translate it into the narrative or quasi-historicist style of temporal precedence.

First, we might say that all men somehow began equal. Then, if we wanted to make the statement as thorough as possible, we might derive this initial essential equality from some still earlier and higher First and Foremost beginning, such as is contained in the idea of God as Creative Source of human equality (an idea that in the Declaration of Independence's formula is not enlisted outright, but is coyly courted when the principle of equality is phrased as men's being "created" equal). Thereby the terministic proposition has its corresponding translation into the style of narrative, the temporal, the story, or myth.[1]

---

[1] Malinowski's *Myth in Primitive Psychology* cites one creation myth that happens to illustrate this relationship with beautiful simplicity. According to this myth, the tribe is descended from a race of supernatural ancestors (or in this case, subterranean ancestors, since they had lived underground). These mythic ancestors had a social order identical with the social order which currently prevailed, having been inherited from the tribe's mythic progenitors. Since philosophic terminologies appear late in a

Similarly, whatever proposals we make must be considered on their merits. The theory of signs that arises from our terms must be based on the logic of the terms themselves. And the corresponding notion as to how language takes form at the point of a human being's emergence from infancy must be offered, not as a proof of our position, but as a speculative deduction from it, a deduction that can be justified only as an illustration, a narrative device for translating a theoretical position into a corresponding temporal or narrative design.

When working with a set of terms that mutually or circularly imply one another, we must necessarily pick one of them to begin with, though we might as well have begun with any of the others. But whichever one we do start with becomes in effect "foremost among the equals." And with it as a starting point, we could then proceed to a second, a third, and so on, treating each successive term as though it had been developed solely from the situation as defined by the particular order in which we had been considering the whole lot up to this point. That is, if terms A-B-C all imply one another in such a way that we might just as well take them up in C-B-A order, or B-A-C, or C-A-B, etc., whichever one we do start with becomes our "first" —and the one we take up next is in effect "derived from" our discussion of the first, etc. Yet we could just as well have had a different sequence of such derivation, by choosing from our circle of terms a different one to begin with. Any such procession from one term to another is a stage midway between logical implication and temporal narrative. For as we read an account of interrelationships among terms, we go from one term to the next in a succession of unfoldings or disclosures—and in this sense the exposition follows a narrative course. Yet insofar as the terms mutually imply one another, the whole family circle is already contained in any one of them, before we begin to proceed analytically from any one of the terms to any of the others. We here confront a situation somewhat analogous to Hegel's shifts between the logical simultaneity of the "Idea" with its implications, and the translation of such simultaneity, or "pure present," into terms of nature and

---

society, and terministic terminologies perhaps even later, a tribal account of the essence implicit in its social order here and now would naturally resort to narrative (temporal) terms for the placement of such relationships. Secondarily, of course, we should note how, owing to the sanctions of custom (morality of the mores), the current order of relationships is in effect sanctioned by the shifts that first ideally duplicate it in prehistory; and next derive the contemporary order from this storied past. In our *Grammar of Motives* (pp. 431-432) we discuss how Freud, borrowing Darwin's fiction of the "primal horde," similarly translated a familial situation now into a corresponding ideal of pre-history, and next explained the prevailing familial order as an attenuated derivation from this purely mythic source. We there suggest that the style typical of nineteenth-century historicism tricked Freud into thus adding two irrelevant steps, as needed by a "temporal, evolutionary" way of saying: "Intrinsic to a certain kind of family relationships, there are certain corresponding kinds of tension, or disrelation."

history narratively or temporally unfolding. A shift of the same sort is involved in the difference between the "logical" statement that "All men are 'in principle' equal" and its quasi-temporal translation, "All men are 'created' equal." And similarly, our statements here about the way in which children learn to name things should be viewed rather as the translating of a logical or terministic consideration into its most likely narrative parallel (its quasi-temporal parable) rather than as a proof of our theory.

There is still one more caution needed. We must try to indicate at least as much of our general position as seems necessary for placing the present inquiry. Briefly, then:

We view language as a kind of action, symbolic action. And for this terministic perspective we have proposed the trade name of 'Dramatism' precisely because we would feature the term "act." At one notable point within this alignment, there is a variant of the Cartesian split. For, from this point of view, the human or social sciences, dialectics, logic, language, poetry, rhetoric, grammar, and the like all call for treatment in terms of action. But by the same token, the realm of physics (with related sciences, such as chemistry, geology, mechanics, electronics) calls for inquiry in terms of sheer motion. The distinction at its extremes is clear enough. "Action" encompasses the realm of entities that respond to words as such (not just to the mere physical vibrations of the syllables, as with electrically discriminatory devices, which have taken a big step forward recently, in the direction of Cybernetics). And "motion" encompasses the realm of entities that do not respond to words as such. (A telegraphic instrument does not respond to words as words, but a person does who can respond to the message properly only when it is decoded.)

Unfortunately, there is an intermediate realm, as when sheerly physiological processes (properly to be charted in terms of motion) are affected by men's attitudes, passions, reasonings, and the like (properly to be charted in terms of action). Simplest example: The thought of a physiologically wholesome food may produce repugnance in a person whose mores have not established the normality of this food. This margin of overlap is further made possible by the fact that, so far as the empirical realm is concerned at least, though there can be motion without action (cf. the realm of physics, at least as that realm is studied and applied by humans), there can be no action without motion (since every idea, concept, attitude, or even every sheer word, if you will allow man no more consciousness than that, requires its corresponding set of purely physical processes; for though we still may not accurately know what a word is like as regards its sheerly physiological counterpart, we do assume that, within our logic of empirical knowledge at least, its happening even in thought requires certain living functions in a certain neural order, as the physically nonexistent rules of a ballgame cannot be enacted in a game except by eighteen bodies that move, with appropriate physical paraphernalia, by which we mean, at the very least, ball and bat and specified grounds).

Regrettably, such a view of language does not spontaneously favor a theory of signs. In keeping with the rules of this calculus, language must be approached primarily in terms of its poetic and rhetorical uses (its functions as expression and as persuasion, or inducement to action). For such is the "Dramatistic" emphasis (in contrast with a "scientist" or epistemological one, that properly lays primary stress upon considerations of knowledge). Accordingly, whereas the scientist emphasis spontaneously, almost automatically, begins with problems of the direct relation between the verbal sign and its corresponding nonverbal referent, a Dramatistic approach to the analysis of language starts with problems of terministic catharsis (which is another word for "rebirth," transcendence, transubstantiation, or simply for "transformation" in the sense of the technically developmental, as when a major term is found somehow to have moved on, and thus to have in effect changed its nature either by adding new meanings to its old nature, or by yielding place to some other term that henceforth takes over its functions wholly or in part).

Such an approach can become so engrossed in a work's *unfoldings as such*, that in extreme cases, it might even treat an avowedly scientific tract as a "poem," or as the unwitting "portrait of a personality."

"Knowledge," in the strictly scientific sense, enters such a view secondarily. Insofar as the material assembled is properly managed, a Dramatistic view of it should be a contribution to knowledge; and in this sense, it would be "scientist" roundabout. Also, somewhat like Galileo, when he referred to scientific experiment as an ordeal (thereby borrowing a Dramatistic term to designate a process in many notable ways different from the kinds of evidence adduced in the nonscientific or prescientific trials of his days) the tactics natural to a Dramatistic terminology would spontaneously call for a roundabout design of this sort: One acts; in the course of acting, one organizes the opposition to one's act (or, in the course of asserting, one causes a multitude of counter-assertions to come running from all directions, like outlaws in the antique woods converging upon the place where a horn had sounded); and insofar as one can encompass such opposition, seeing the situation anew in terms of it, one has dialectically arrived thus roundabout at knowledge. In this way, the setting up of laboratory situations for testing one's hunches or one's *ad hoc* conclusions would be viewed as a series of devices whereby one deliberately gave voice to the opposition, by a selection of means that addressed such questions to speechless nature as enabled nature to give unequivocal answers. In sum, thus roundabout, we'd say that

action leads to passion (or suffering of the opposition)—and passion leads
to revelation.

But, alas! no matter how roundabout may be a terminology's approach
to a theory of signs, there still must be that theory, if a terminology would be
complete in its statements about language. And the theory should ideally
be condensable into a single proposition. And so, in case we have already
got lost, let us start anew by recalling that we are here vowed, experimentally at least, to see what can be said for the mildly paradoxical reversal
whereby, instead of treating words (in ontological realism) as the signs of
things, we would maintain (in linguistic realism) that "Things Are the
Signs of Words."

Though I would hold that poetry *qua* poetry (or, if you will, art *qua*
art) lies outside the orbit of knowledge, I grant that poetry (and I here
mean the imaginative arts generally) can contribute to knowledge in at
least two notable respects.

First: Its particular discipline cuts across the departmentalization
proper to the academic principles of discipline.

Second: There is a sense in which poetry can contribute vitally to
knowledge by being naturally itself, despite all its efforts to be artificial. In
this sense, poetry's contribution to knowledge is limited only by the observer's nonpoetic or extrapoetic prowess at diagnosis, his ability to read the
signs like a competent medical doctor interpreting a syndrome of symptoms.

If we start by trying to analyze the terms in a work of art, such as a
poem, drama, or story, we automatically begin with problems of sheer internality among those terms. No one, for instance, would think of contending
that the validity of Shakespeare's Hamlet or Flaubert's Madame Bovary depends on the necessity of showing that there actually were precisely such
referents in history. And if one were to start analyzing such a structure of
terms, one's first job would obviously be to spot the internal terministic relationships as such, whatever one might finally take to be the allusive element. (We mean the terms' possible direct or indirect reference to a universe
of discourse beyond their internal relations to one another.)

If we are analyzing such a structure, we look first of all for key terms.
(Thus, "Hamlet" would certainly be a key term in *Hamlet*, and "Emma
Bovary" in *Madame Bovary*.) Then we look for their transformations (as
when we ask what sufferances and changes a character undergoes). But,
however we analyze such material, the main thing is that we are first of all
vowed to let the words have their say. At this first stage at least, we should
not heckle. Thus, if a novelist writes a story with Australia as his background, we could not reasonably heckle him at the very start, even if we
wanted to do so at the end, because he had placed his story in Australia
rather than in Norway or New Zealand. Even if we were preparing even-

tually to demur, our first step would require us to note (insofar as we are able) how the writer's words proceed. And in this sense, a Dramatistic approach to language vows us first of all to considerations of pure verbal internality, as we seek to chart the transformations within the work itself (for that's what we get, even in a superficial outline of a story's plot, and in a placing of the main characters with relation to one another, though newspaper reviewers may not care to recognize in their report of a book such a sheerly terministic enterprise). In this sense, the most haphazard of reviewers indexes a book, noting what he considers notable relationships and transformations among the work's key terms.

So, though we are all properly concerned with the relations between the verbal and the nonverbal, and though this chapter has contracted to deal with such a relation, after several pages it is still entrammeled within the verbal. And we must get out somehow. For bold, bald behaviorism reminds us that even the noises and stenches of industry can become pleasant, through signifying the means of livelihood, and thus secondarily being identified with the very essence of the vital, while one may by dialectical opposition come to place the sweet, silent fragrance of flowers on the side of disease and death.

When dealing with terms in poems and fictions (still not asking about their possible reference to things in the world), we note three stages. First, there is the perfect certainty that ranges from sheer word-counting to a comparison of all the contexts in which a given word appears (aiming ideally at the discovery of a development in the succession of such contexts). But, though this is probably the nearest men can ever come to perfect "factual certainty" (in saying that there is a certain incidence of a particular word in a particular text), we cannot usually go far enough by staying within these limits.

There are radiations of a term, for instance. That is, if a term notably appears and reappears in connection with some other term, we can begin to build up equations whereby the terms are treated as overlapping in their jurisdiction, and maybe even sometimes identical. The most perfect instance of this wider step is the decision to treat two different words as synonymous in a given verbal structure. Here, in effect, we expand from word to theme. This step is necessary to mature analysis, but risky. For instance, in noting wherein two different words are synonymous, we may fail to note an important motivational distinction between them (as the implications of one may be favorable, the other unfavorable).

But there is a further step in this same outward direction: and it is the one we most need for our present inquiry. Insofar as a poem is properly formed, suppose you were to ask yourself what subtitle might properly be given to each stanza. Or suppose you were to break up each chapter of a novel into a succession of steps or stages, giving titles to such parts of a chapter, then to chapters, then to groups of chapters, and so finally to the whole work. Your entitlings would not necessarily agree with any that the author himself may have given, since titles are often assigned for fortuitous reasons. And, of course, other readers might not agree with your proposed entitlings. But the point is this:

Insofar as the work is properly formed, and insofar as your titles are accurate, they mark off a succession of essences. Each title would sum up the overall trend or spirit informing or infusing the range of details that are included under this head. And as we progressed from parts of chapters, to chapters, to groups of chapters, and so finally to an ultimate title of titles, we would have in effect a set of terms ever-widening in scope, until we got to the all-inclusive title that was technically the "god-term" for the whole congeries of words in their one particular order. There would thus be a sense in which the overall title could be said to be the infolding of all the details, or the details could be treated as the exfoliation-in-time of the eternal now that was contained in the rational seminality of the title.

It is this final step that we would take as our starting point for the analysis of the relation between the verbal and the nonverbal situations in which words are used. In short, instead of thinking of the relation between words and things after the analogy of the relation between written word and spoken word, or between picture and thing, we propose to ask how the problem looks if we begin with what we have now arrived at; namely: titles.

Thus, instead of starting with the relation between words and the things of which the words are the signs, we start with verbal expressions (even whole sentences) that are to be treated as ways of entitling, or of summing up, nonverbal situations. (While such situations are themselves largely outside the realm of the verbal, they may also involve attitudes that are influenced by verbal elements.)

Thus, with our sentence, "The man walks down the street," to realize its nature as a title, or summary, rather than as description, we need but reflect that, as stated, it could not be illustrated. If the sentence properly described the situation, it would have to contain enough details to make the situation empirically possible—and many are obviously lacking, even as regards a merely ocular image of such a situation.[2]

---

[2] We are here adapting, for other purposes, a kind of speculation which Berkeley employs in his *Treatise Concerning the Principles of Human Knowledge*, and which had an important influence upon Hume's *Enquiry Concerning Human Understanding*. Berkeley points out that though we may draw a line that stands for sheer rectilinearity, and may then proceed to demonstrate the way of bisecting it, our illustration must use a long line or a short one, a thick one or a thin one, drawn in ink or pencil, etc., all such details disregarded as irrelevant to the demonstration. Berkeley uses such reasonings to deny the possibility of abstract general ideas. But whether or not one agrees with his metaphysics, one must concede that he throws much light on the part

Next, just as a sentence may be considered as a title that sums up the nonverbal context of the situation to which it is applied, one may look for terms that abbreviate the title. Hence our suggestion that "The man walks down the street" might be in turn summed up, or entitled, as a "man-situation," or a "walk-situation," or a "street-situation," depending upon the direction of selectivity of your interests.

If you said, "There are trees bordering the street," the most obvious abbreviations would be got by classing this sentence as title for a "tree-situation," a "bordering-situation," or a "street-situation."

Insofar as you called it the extended title for a "street-situation," it could be in the same general class with "The man walks down the street" (which is likewise the extended title for a sentence classifiable more summarily as a "street-situation").

Thus, these two sentences, or extended titles for situations, have allowed for at least five major classificatory abbreviations: as man-situation, walk-situation, street-situation, tree-situation, border-situation. But at one point these classificatory abbreviations (or shortened titles) overlap. Both sentences can be the titles for street-situations. Or, more briefly, both situations could have as their titles: "street."

The redoubtable Horne Tooke did great service, in his *Diversions of Purley*, by pointing out the nature of language as abbreviation, though he does not give the notion this particular twist. In any case, the important thing is to note that, once you carry the principle of entitlement to this final step (proceeding from the view of the sentence as the title for its nonverbal context of situation, to the view of some one element in the sentence as being capable of serving as title for the whole sentence), then you are ready for the linguistic shortcut whereby we can next get "universals" such as "man," "dog," "tree."

Such a process of abbreviation, whereby some one element of a context can come to be felt as summing up a whole, is no rarity. It is a normal resource of the representative function that the old rhetoricians called synecdoche, the resource whereby a part can come to stand for a whole. (Fetishistically, for instance, some portion of a person's garments can call forth

---

that language plays in such notions. Berkeley claims, for instance, that one cannot really think of extension or color or motion without thinking of some extended thing, or of some particular color, or of some object moving at a certain speed and in a certain direction. He contends that, merely because we can have a word such as "extension," we wrongly assume an ability to prescind the sheer idea from other ideas that necessarily accompany our actual perception of extension. According to him, it is as impossible to conceive of sheer extension as it would be to conceive of a four-sided triangle. Jeremy Bentham deals with the same problem, in calling such terms as "extension" linguistic fictions, and proposing rules (such as archetypation and phraseoplerosis) for disclosing and discounting the fictitious element in them. (However, an overstress upon imagery can close our minds to the role of other terministic factors, such as grammar, in shaping consciousness.)

responses connected not just with the garment in itself, but with the person it is felt to represent.)

In sum, then, the dialectical resources intrinsic to entitlement and abbreviation would be these: (1) There can be a verbal expression, of varying duration, that sums up, or entitles, a nonverbal situation; (2) this expression can be so abbreviated that a portion of it stands for the whole of it, the shorter portion thus in effect being the title-of-a-title; (3) similarly, an actual object can have this same abbreviative role, as when something identified with a person ceases to be merely what it is in itself, but becomes in effect an aspect of that person, or we may think of a particular tree as the "essence" of a situation involving house, yard, sky, season, mortgage, and so on; (4) when an expression is thus reduced to a portion of itself (a word) and a nonverbal situation is represented by some one fragment or portion that is felt to stand for the essence of the situation (which is in effect its context), conditions are now ripe for a shortcut whereby the *summarizing object* can be paired with the *summarizing word*. And if one starts merely at this point, one can with justice make a corresponding shortcut in his theory, by simply treating the correspondence between the summarizing word and the summarizing object as a state of affairs wherein the word is the sign of the thing.

Such shortcuts give us "universals," such as "man," "dog," and "tree" in general, without reference to *any particular* man, dog, or tree. The literary critic usually thinks of such words as very concrete, on the grounds that they bring things vividly before the imagination and thereby avoid abstraction. Spinoza, on the other hand, shows how such concrete images can be instances of the abstract, insofar as they conceal our perception of essence by centering attention upon some partial aspect abstracted from the whole. See his *Ethics*, Book II, Prop. XL, Scholium I, where in discussing the limitations due to imagination, he says: "Those who have more frequently looked with admiration upon the stature of men, by the name man will understand an animal of erect stature, while those who have been in the habit of fixing their thoughts on something else, will form another common image of men, describing men, for instance, as an animal capable of laughter, a featherless biped, a rational animal, and so on, each person forming universal images of things according to the temperament of his own body."

We here suggest that the notion of abbreviated entitlements makes a somewhat different linguistic cut across this subject, but in a way that bears directly upon the problem of abstraction with which Spinoza is centrally concerned (in his insistence that things must be understood in terms of their overall context). Similarly, see my reference to the "paradox of substance" in the essay on *Coriolanus*, p. 84.

We should also here recall Plato's theory in which the things of this world are said to be but imperfect exemplars of the perfect forms that have eternal being in the realm of the transcendent. However little faith one may happen to put in this scheme considered as metaphysics or as theology, its possible analogue in linguistic theory is much to our purposes.

For, when you have abbreviated the verbal expression by using some one word as its summarizing title, and when you have next abbreviated the nonverbal context of situation by featuring some one object that serves as the material equivalent of a title by standing for the essence of the situation, and when finally you have completed your method of shortcuts by leaping from the word that sums up the expression to the object that sums up the nonverbal situation, then you have a condition wherein the thing can be taken as the visible manifestation of the "universal form" that resides spiritually in the corresponding word. Thus, if you consider any individual man as abstracted from the kinds of contexts in which alone a living man is possible, he has become, from the linguistic point of view, a sign or manifestation or imperfect exemplar of the "universal" word for his type or class of entity (the universal in this sense being "prior" to any particular entity that is included under this general head).

"Things" are now the signs of words, quite as, if someone asked you the meaning of bicycle, you might define the word by showing him one. Here the thing would obviously be a visible, tangible sign of the essence or spirit contained in the word itself. For you can't see a meaning, though you may point to things that, as it were, make that spiritual condition manifest to the nonverbal senses.

But what is the context of a word or situation? Besides the local contexts of situation that call for correspondingly local entitlings, there is also the structure of a given language in general. Each language has its peculiar genius, which figures in its modes of entitling, and by suggesting that we entitle some situations rather than others. Also, there is some kind of overall context beyond all language, whether natural or supernatural, serving as a nonverbal, or less-than-verbal, or more-than-verbal ground that informs language. The problem of that is still to be considered.[3]

Let us think of four terministic pyramids, each of which contains words for a certain realm, or order. These four are: (1) words for the sheerly natural (in the sense of the less-than-verbal, the realm of visible tangible things and operations, the realm that is best charted and described in terms

---

[3] I have since come to think that the theory of language as entitlement could best be illustrated by thinking of a sentence as a theme song, for instance, as "East Side, West Side, all around the town" became the theme song for Al Smith's presidential campaign. It thus summed up the motives of the whole campaign, and a few bars of it could serve as an appropriate abbreviation.

of motion and position); (2) words for the verbal realm itself, the terms of grammar, rhetoric, poetics, logic, dialectic, philology, etymology, semantics, symbolism, etc.; (3) words for the sociopolitical realm, for personal and social relations, including terms like "justice," "right," and "obligation," etc.; (4) words for the "supernatural."

These four should cover the ground, though they are not mutually exclusive. For instance, a word such as "person" belongs in the sheerly *natural* insofar as a person must have a living body subject to the laws of motion; it is in the *verbal* order inasmuch as the rationality of a person is involved in kinds of mental maturity that require a high degree of aptitude at symbol-using; it is in the *sociopolitical* order because of the sociopolitical relationships and roles involved in personality; and it is in the *supernatural* order at the very least to the extent that it involves attitudes towards words for this order and towards the institutions representing this order, while furthermore the person is often said to be derived from some transcendent principle of pure personality that is designated by whatever term may be the Title of Titles for this fourth realm.

We draw a line between terms for the three empirical, worldly orders and terms for the supernatural order because, whatever the supernatural order may or may not be in reality, the terms that describe it are necessarily borrowed from our words for the three worldly orders; Thus, a metaphor for God's power, such as the "arm" of God, would be taken from the natural order; the notion of the divine creative Fiat, or of Christ as The Word, would be taken from the verbal order; and the reference to God as father or lord would be from the sociopolitical order. Words being in the realm of the worldly, it follows by the very nature of the case that any words designed to describe a realm by definition transcendent must be inadequate to their real or supposed subject matter.

But note, now, some of the complications that have entered, as regards the way in which the demands of extraverbal reality impose themselves upon this fourfold scheme. In the first place, there are words for all the four realms (as "table" and "chair" for the natural order, "subject" and "predicate" for the verbal order, "democracy" and "dictatorship" for the sociopolitical order, "thrones," "dominations," "princedoms," "virtues," and "powers" for the supernatural order). Though there are many differences among them with regard to their referents, all four are equally real so far as their nature as sheer words is concerned. And if we were making a concordance of their incidence in a given test, they would all have equal claims to be counted.

For our purposes, from the standpoint of sheer words, the second (or linquistic) pyramid is foremost among the equals. For though all four pyramids are orders of words, this one is an order of words about words. And of all situations having to do with language, the only time when something can be discussed wholly in terms of itself, is when we are using words about words. Insofar as nonverbal things are discussed in terms of words (or symbols generally), they are necessarily discussed in terms of what they are not.

As regards reference beyond words, words for the natural order generally enjoy the most unquestionable reality of reference. True, when we penetrate the remoter areas of the natural order, there is much questioning, and this questioning may return to complicate or sophisticate our speculations about the nature of even the most visible and tangible of objects for which languages have names. But, however we may choose to qualify our statement, the fact still remains: The world is run on the commonsense realistic assumption that there is a fairly accurate correspondence between the realm of everyday sensory objects and the vocabulary that names them. Words of this sort allow for the kind of definition *per genus et differentiam* that Bentham considered ideal, his "theory of fictions" being designed for the definition of words that by his tests did not lend themselves to such a mode of definition.

As regards terms for the sociopolitical order: We should note first of all: They depend upon the verbal order in a way that the natural order does not. If I say "table," and you don't understand me, there is at least the possibility of my using the physical object as the source of communication between us. Or, at one remove, I might show you a picture of a table. But if I say "democracy" or "dictatorship" or "rights" or "crimes" or "obligations," despite the vast institutional backing that such words may come to have, there is no clear "natural" counterpart to the word (and recall that we are here using "natural" in the sense of the nonverbal, to designate the sort of less-than-verbal world that would be left if all word-using creatures and their verbalizings were suddenly obliterated).

Sociopolitical institutions, with the personal and social relations involved in them, and the vast terminology of attitudes, acts, and motives that goes with them, do not enjoy exactly the kind of extraverbal reality we find in the commonsense vocabulary of the natural realm; yet they are not identical with the verbal order as such (the order of words-about-words). "Motherhood" for instance may be a word for a relationship between two biologic organisms which are not merely verbal at all, but are in the natural realm of physiological motion—and similarly, though "criminality" is a sheer word, the functioning of this term may imply such purely natural resources as prisons, or such natural sanctions as the infliction of physical suffering by way of punishment.[4]

But though political institutions and the terms that they variously implement are dependent upon language for their high or complex development, they cannot be simply equated with the verbal order—and this is all the more so, since the terms for the sociopolitical order are interwoven with words for the sheerly natural instruments that variously serve as rewards or punishments for sociopolitical conduct, or as promises of reward and threats of punishment.

Thus, of these four orders, the only two that can claim wholly non-verbal referents are the natural and the supernatural. This must be narrowed still further, to the natural alone, if you deny the existence of the supernatural, or if you stress the fact that, even if there is a supernatural realm, the "science" of this realm is sheerly verbal; namely, "theology," or "words about God." But at least so far as the technicalities of the case are concerned, the natural and supernatural orders could have wholly extra-verbal referents, whereas Bentham's analysis of such legal fictions as "property," "rights," and "obligations" (or of such personifications as "the Crown" for the king, or "the law" for lawyers, or "the Court" for judges) is enough in itself to show conclusively that the sociopolitical order is inextricably interwoven with man's terministic genius.

Here, then, is the crucial lesson that we would draw from this alignment:

No matter how firm may be one's conviction that his terminology for the supernatural refers somehow to a real order of existence, there is the obvious fact that he necessarily borrows his terms from the terms prevailing in the three worldly orders. At the very start, therefore, he must concede (and if he is thoroughgoing, he does willingly concede): His statements are but metaphorical, analogical, mere makeshifts for talking figuratively about a supposed superhuman realm that, no matter how real it may be, cannot be adequately discussed in human terms. Consider Augustine, for instance,

---

[4] The mention of sanctions here reminds us: These four pyramids coincide quite closely with the four legal sanctions that Jeremy Bentham uses in his *Principles of Legislation*, and that he apparently derived from the four moral obligations in John Gay's *Dissertation Concerning the Fundamental Principle of Virtue or Morality*. In our modification of this alignment, the moral sanction is replaced by the verbal order. This shift has to do with the fact that our terms are adjusted to linguistic rather than to ethical or legal analysis. Linguistically, the moral motive is in all four orders, as with the personal. But for reasons we have explained elsewhere, it is particularly identifiable with the 'Idea of No' (as per the thou-shalt-not's of the Decalogue), and we would contend that the negative is a peculiarly linguistic addition to the positive sensory world of nature. Technically, the negative "perfects" nature in a sense analogous to the theologian's "grace."

seeking to explain the relations among the three persons of the Trinity, and becoming involved in a theological variant of the shift between temporal and logical. For he admonishes that, whereas the Father is said to "generate" the Son, we are not to conceive of such a process in the temporal way that the terms Father, Son, and generation suggest; for the Father, the Son, and the Holy Spirit that arises from the relation between them (a relation expressed in familial terms that are not to be taken literally) are coeternal, no one of them narratively preceding another.[5]

Clearly, the naturalist has one notable advantage over the supernaturalist, for only by failing to be frank or thorough, can the supernaturalist avoid the charge of using a terminology that is by definition insufficient for his purposes. But precisely here, there is room for a paradoxical possibility. And we would approach it thus:

If our naturalist is of a debunking sort, he can lay devastating stress upon such considerations as the ways whereby God is named after the analogy of autocratic or feudal social systems now in many countries obsolete, with obsequious underlings doing obeisance to a mighty overlord who, for all his overwhelming might, jealously demands their loyalty. Our debunker points out that, insofar as the eternal supernatural pattern is but the ideal duplication of a more or less obsolete temporal social pattern, the here-and-now on earth can be made to seem like the dim analogue of its ideal otherworldly perfection.

See, for instance, Coleridge on "The Constitution of Church and State," with its revealing subtitle, "according to the idea of each." And recall how he used his idealizing principle of motivation, *a Jove principium* (we might now say "from the top down"). For in accordance with it, any imperfection in the worldly social order could be sanctioned by being viewed in terms of its corresponding perfection in the ideal order.

To be sure, the resources of dialectics being what they are, this terministic relationship would allow for a contrary policy too. For the thought of

---

[5] Linguistically, the analogue of the Trinity would be: "Father" equals the thing named (*esse*); "Son" equals the name (*nosse*, Christ as "the Word"); "Holy Spirit" equals the perfect concordance or communion between named and name (*velle*), a relations of conformity that is properly expressed, from the personal point of view, as love. ("Love" names an ideal, desired state of communion that, as technically attenuated, amounts to "communication.") As for the difference between the Father's "generating" of the Son, and the process whereby both are united in a Holy Spirit, the linguistic analogies might be of this sort: The thing-to-be-named could be treated as the ground of the name; but the step from the to-be-named to the name implies a relationship of correspondence in which both named and to-be-named must take part as participants that mutually imply each other. This would be the "logological" analogue of the difference between the Father's "generating" of the Son and their combined "spirating" of the Holy Spirit. Such logological analogies of the theological are discussed at length in my *Rhetoric of Religion*.

an ideal perfect order might make men all the more exacting when they considered the respects in which the actual worldly order fell short of this ideal. But insofar as Coleridge did not stress such possibilities, his ideal duplication of an imperfect social order could serve rhetorically as an apparent sanctioning of the prevailing society's imperfections (imperfections that would be necessary insofar as no actual order can be expected completely to embody its ideal counterpart, or transcendent archetype). We discuss (in Note I) a similar case that we found in Malinowski's references to origin myths. But that myth presented a purely narrative ideal duplication of the prevailing social order. It thus dealt with a much more primitive notion of priority. Coleridge's notion, on the other hand, is close to the kind of semitemporal, semilogical (or terministic) priority we find in Plato's notion of archetypes, though ideals can also have a semitemporal dimension in their role as final causes.

But we are mainly concerned with the ironic possibility that, even as the naturalist scores, he may do so by a device that deflects attention from similar ambiguities in his own position.

Our approach here might be summed up thus: Whereas Anselm propounded the "ontological necessity for the existence of God," we base our position on the analogous linguistic necessity for the existence of god-terms. We here have in mind the nature of language as a means of entitling, since a god-term would be an overall title, or title of titles. And insofar as man, the word-using animal, approached nonverbal nature in terms of his humanly verbalizing nature, is there not a sense in which *nature* must be as much of a linguistically inspirited thing for him as *super-nature*?

And next, since language derives its materials from the cooperative acts of men in sociopolitical orders, which are themselves held together by a vast network of verbally perfected meanings, might it not follow that man must perceive nature through the fog of symbol-ridden social structures that he has erected atop nature? Material things would thus be like outward manifestations of the forms which are imposed upon the intuiting of nature by language, and by the sociopolitical orders that are interwoven with language (sociopolitical orders that are in turn indicated by the linguistic thou-shalt-not's inhering in a given set of property relationships).

In sum, just as the Word is said by theologians to be a mediatory principle between this world and the supernatural, might words be a mediatory principle between ourselves and nature? And just as the theologian might say that we must think of the Word as the bond between man and the supernatural, might words (and the social motives implicit in them) be the bond between man and the natural? Or, otherwise put, might nature be necessarily approached by us through the gift of the spirit of words?

If this were possible, then nature, as perceived by the word-using animal, would be not just the less-than-verbal thing that we usually take it to be. Rather, as so conceived and perceived, it would be infused with the spirit of words, and of the social orders that are implicit in any given complex verbal structure. Nature, as the early Greek metaphysical physicist put it, would thus be full of gods, gods in essence linguistic and sociopolitical. The world that we mistook for a realm of sheerly nonverbal, nonmental, visible, tangible things would thus become a fantastic pageantry, a parade of masques and costumes and guildlike mysteries (such as Carlyle treats of, in his *Sartor Resartus*).

But if such does prove to be the case, there is this notable difference between the naturalist and the supernaturalist, so far as terminology is concerned: Whereas the supernaturalist has had to recognize explicitly that his words about the supernatural are but analogical, figurative, metaphorical, the naturalist would persuade us that his observed nonverbal realm is available to us in its immediate sensory aspects, completely free of verbal and sociopolitical elements. But if the things of nature are, for man, the visible signs of their verbal entitlements, then nature gleams secretly with a most fantastic shimmer of words and social relationships. And quite as men's views of the supernatural embody the forms of language and society in recognized ways, so their views of the natural would embody these same forms, however furtively.

In this sense things would be the signs of words.

Chapter Five

Myth, Poetry, and Philosophy

I. General nature of combat myth; general nature of difference between problem of origins as viewed folkloristically and as viewed in terms of Poetics.
II. Main themes of the combat myth—and preparatory account of how the various clauses should be "derived" in terms of Poetics.
III. How principle of negative is translated into terms of rival temporal purposes; and how "Eros" and "Thanatos" serve as mythic terms for purpose.
IV. Dialectic of Love and Death, with combat myth as "cause" (*aition*) that serves as sanction for the Order with which it is associated.
V. Contrast between folkloristic and "entelechial" ways of viewing variations on a theme.
VI. Different implications in statements that at first glance seem alike.
VII. Intrinsic tests of combat myth's "perfection" as a story are not identical with its "perfection" as *aition*; thus there are two different sets of questions to be answered.
VIII. Our very stress upon the "use" of the combat myth now enables us to go back and theoretically prescind this element. Since the combat myth contains the designs of both tragedy and comedy, the problem of these species is introduced.
IX. Summary: on combat myth, tragedy, and comedy viewed entelechially.
X. Dialectics of monotheism and polytheism, the "perfection" in which problems of generalization concerning the combat myth would culminate.

I

Though *mythos* originally meant but "word" (being the Homeric equivalent for *logos*), the important consideration for present purposes is that it came to mean a tale, story, fable, a *narrative* form. Such expansion (from a word that meant word to a word that meant a tale composed of many words) is like the step whereby the title of the play *Hamlet* becomes expanded into all the words and simulated actions, characters, and situations of which that play is composed. The title is in effect an "essence." And in the narrative expansion that comprises the drama, the "essence" that is named in the title acquires in effect a kind of "existential definition." It is the relation I had in mind when writing these lines, that are perhaps too "ideological" as judged by current imagistic canons but that at least serve to sum up my point:

> And may we have neither the mania of the One
> Nor the delirium of the Many—
> But both the Union and the Diversity—
> The Title and the manifold details that arise
> As that Title is restated
> In the narrative of History
> Not forgetting that the Title represents the story's Sequence,
> And that the Sequence represents the Power entitled.[1]

Here "History" is but a more "cosmic" word for "story," a usage in line with the analogy between books and the "Book of Nature." What we have called the "existential definition" would be the expansion of the title in terms of poetry; a discussion of the theoretic principles involved in its construction would be an expansion in terms of *poetics*.

In an essay entitled "The First Three Chapters of Genesis," I try to show how the "creation myth" of those opening chapters was a way of propounding "principles of governance," by translation into terms of narrative rather than as they might be formulated in philosophy, metaphysics, or theology. The problem, involving the relation between terms for "logical priority" and terms for "temporal priority," concerns ways of shuttling between the two kinds. In my *Grammar of Motives*, the translation of logical principles into terms of temporal "firsts" is called "the temporizing of essence"; for when the narrative style makes a statement about essence, it does so in quasi-historical terms (terms referring to the "primordial" or "prehistoric").

While revising my poetics I came upon a recent work of quite stupendous scholarship (*Python, A Study of Delphic Myth and Its Origins*, by by Joseph Fontenrose, University of California Press, 1959), concerned with the origins and transformations of what it calls the "combat myth." The investigation is so admirably thorough it even points beyond itself; essentially folkloristic in its approach, it impinges upon problems of Poetics. Consider, for instance, this closing paragraph of the book proper:

"So we may look upon the whole combat in all its forms as the conflict between Eros and Thanatos. It is that opposition between life instincts and death instincts that Freud was the first to formulate, albeit tentatively, as the central principle of all living organisms from the beginning; though

---

[1] Quoted from "Dialectician's Prayer," reprinted in my *Book of Moments* (Hermes Publications, Los Altos, California, 1955), p. 41.

it was seen dimly and expressed in dramatic or metaphysical terms by poets and philosophers before him. But in life the two kinds of instincts, though opposed, are always mingled. Thus do the fantasies of myth disguise the fundamental truths of the human spirit." (p. 474)

Unfortunately, we cannot stop here and merely appreciate the book's great skill in tracking down "versions" and "variants" of the "combat myth." Instead, we must use it somewhat tendentiously, and even in a supereroga-tory way. For though the author accomplished a plenty, yet in effect we are asking him to do still more, and to concern himself with a problem that is ours rather than his.

Accordingly, I must admonish that my points of difference with the book do not imply criticisms of it as such. Our reservations derive mainly from the fact that we would use its material for an "ulterior" purpose, mak-ing central what the author considers but peripherally, somewhat as a final afterthought: the relation between myth's "fantasies" and "fundamental truths" (a relation which we would further shift into a concern with the dif-ference between myth's narrative modes of statement and what Coleridge would have called the style of the "philosopheme").

Taking as its point of departure the myth of the combat between Apollo and Python, the book inquires into the origins of all such "combat myths" in Greek literature. It seeks for "origins" in the sense of the probable place or places from which the myth spread, the probable ways in which the spreading occurred, the various transformations involved, etc. In the course of its speculating, it outlines two main types of the myth. The later type concerns a struggle between an "older" god and a "new" god, with the new god triumphing and founding a cult; but this is said to be derived from an earlier type, concerning a struggle between dragon and sky-god, with the sky-god triumphing.

As we shall see, the two types are more complicated than this first statement of their nature would suggest. But for the moment the important thing to note is that, in the course of discussing these types, the author re-duces each of them to a paradigm. And as soon as he has done so, he has provided material for speculating on "origins" in a quite different sense. We can now ask about "origins" in the sense of the logic implicit in the forms of these paradigms. The study of the "combat myth's" emergence in history would be "folkloristic" or "anthropological." The study of the motives in-volved in such paradigms (the principles of the myths' structure as progres-sive forms having beginning, middle, and end) would belong to Poetics.

Also in the course of his study the author considers another problem of origins. He offers good reasons for doubting that the "combat myths" which are associated with particular cults ordinarily derive from the rituals associated with those same cults, though he grants that there can be con-siderable "interpenetration" between myth and ritual. By and large, however, he would incline to infer that the "combat myth" begins in legends of struggle that may themselves have developed originally out of men's literal experiences with hunt, war, and the like. And he assumes that the "combat myth" thus arose independently of cults, but was adopted by them because it lent itself particularly well to use as an *aition* for a cult, a mythic explanation for the cult's origins and services. Thus, in its final development, a myth is said to be a traditional story having beginning, middle, and end, and purporting "to tell of the occasion on which some religious institution, a cult or certain of its rites and festivals, had its beginning." (p. 3)

II

The main "themes of the combat myth" are given as follows on pages 9 to 11 (all told, including the subdivisions, forty-three are listed, though of course no particular version or variant is likely to embody the whole lot):

1) The Enemy was of divine origin.
2) The Enemy had a distinctive habitation.
3) The Enemy had extraordinary appearances and properties.
4) The Enemy was vicious and greedy.
5) The Enemy conspired against heaven.
6) A divine Champion appeared to face him.
7) The Champion fought the Enemy.
8) The Champion nearly lost the battle.
9) The Enemy was finally destroyed, after being outwitted, deceived, or bewitched.
10) The Champion disposed of the Enemy and celebrated his victory. (In connection with this last stage, after being "purified of blood pollution," the Champion "instituted cult, ritual, festival, and built a temple for himself.")

A glance at this list, from the standpoint of Poetics, suggests a problem of "derivation" quite different from an attempt to retrace the myth's probable development and diffusion through history. Consider, for instance, Theme 7, which along with 8 concerns the stages of the actual combat. Subdivision 7c is: "The other gods were panicstricken: they appeased the Enemy or fled." Much later in the book, on that subject the author writes: "The gods are afraid and take to flight. . . . in this way the champion god's bravery is emphasised." (p. 250) Here obviously, the author is concerned with a kind of "origin" that has nothing to do with the spread of a theme from Mesopotamia, Egypt, or wherever. Clause 7c concerns a function within the story as such, a dramatic device for building up the character of the champion. From the standpoint of Poetics, then, the question becomes: Regardless of where the "combat myth" came from, and/or how many transformations it may have undergone, to what extent can we derive its form from the logic of that form? In other words: To what extent does the paradigm give us, not some "first" story from which the many versions and variants were derived, but rather a "perfect" form towards which such a story would "naturally" gravitate? And could we so define its nature that such an "entelechy" would seem natural? In brief, Poetics would ask: In order to be a "perfect combat myth," what form "ought" the story have?

Scattered through the book there are numerous observations that can be used to this end. Here is one, for instance, with regard to the earlier of the two myth types: "The hero-gods of the displaced peoples tended to become cast in the role of dragon or brigand." (p. 424) One can readily see why such a development could take place without the need of a previous example to borrow from. For a variant of this response takes place after every successful revolution, which views the losers from the standpoint of the winners. We do not need a prototype to account for it, but can explain it dialectically by the fact that, when one orientation is replaced by another, the first is "naturally" viewed in terms of its successor.

However, when noting that such adjectives as "insolent" (*hybristês*), "violent" (*biaios*), "lawless" (*ánomos*) and "impious" (*asebês*) are applied to various forms of the enemy character, the author seems to consider this overlap as the sign of a common historical origin. Yet whether or not such epithets indicate a myth in common, should we not note that their application to an enemy of the cult's particular deity would be wholly "natural" and would need no historical strand in common, just as atrocity stories "naturally" arise in war time, without necessarily having some particular past atrocity story to start from (the atrocity of war itself being enough to make sure that the human mind will gravitate towards the imagining of the "perfect" atrocity story)?

Looking again at the author's ten major themes, and seeking to "prophesy them after the event" in terms of Poetics, we can see many good purely "internal" reasons for the paradigm. For instance, as regards the first clause, concerning the Enemy's divine origin: Unless the Champion fights someone his own size, it's not a "perfect" combat. Hence, the "natural" tendency here would be for the Enemy to be of divine origin, like the figure he is opposing. The subclauses deal with particular ways of amplifying this detail, by giving the Enemy parents or companions appropriate to such a role. (Another way of stating the case would be: The most "perfect" combat would be "heroic" in scale; and in a polytheistic age the most "heroic" scale would involve a conflict between gods.)

Clause 2, regarding the Enemy's "distinctive habitation" (usually in places where monsters and demons dwell), represents an appropriate scene-agent ratio, the principle of artistic consistency whereby characters are given their proper settings.[2]

Clause 3, regarding the Enemy's "extraordinary appearance and properties," builds him up as an enemy. Clause 1 built him up as a worthwhile enemy; Clause 3 builds him up as an enemy in the sense that our sympathies should be turned against him. The subclauses (which I do not here cite) list various ways in which he can be physically repugnant.

Clause 4 deals with the Enemy's repugnance morally. To this end he is shown as being the kind of vicious, lecherous, greedy character and doing the kind of atrocious things that would make you glad to be rid of him.

Clause 5, regarding the Enemy's conspiring "against heaven," in a desire to rule the world, is the "perfection" of the charges leveled against him. Here the enemy becomes as *complete* as he can be, in his role as a repugnant power. (In this sense his ambition is the "ultimate conclusion" of the traits considered in Clause 4.)

Clause 6 introduces the Champion (a young "weather god or sky god"). For the time being, I doubt whether we have the grounds for fully "prophesying" why the Champion "should be" this particular kind of god. We must be content with a purely "tautological" explanation. If the myth is used as *aition* for a cult devoted to a sky god, then by the same token the most perfect hero would be that sky god himself, including whatever attributes were associated with such a god in that particular culture, regardless of what a story of combat may have been in its origins. But this also brings up a problem which is best considered in connection with Clause 7.

First of all, obviously, Clause 7 is a response to the principle of *enargeia*. If there is to be a combat, it must be fought before our very eyes— otherwise the storyteller has not lived up to the obligations of his trade. Tautologically stated: If a combat myth, then certainly a combat. Hence also, under this head, we consider the various kinds of force and fraud available to combat as so conceived (including the resources of magic as defined by the modes of priestcraft then current).

Later, we shall consider other reasons why there should be a "combat myth" at all. For the moment, taking it as "the given," we observe that if there is to be a combat, there must be at least two combatants (Clause 7 thus pointing back to Clauses 6 and 1). But there might be a kind of combat with only one combatant who vanquished himself, though at present we don't have enough material for the adequate treatment of that possibility. Meanwhile, any athletic contest or war is sufficient evidence that, so far as drama and narrative are concerned, a combat to be "perfect" in form needs at least two combatants. Even in solitaire, one plays against "the Jack."

---

[2] On scene-agent ratio see my *Grammar of Motives*, Meridian edition, pp. 7 ff.

The book also refers to many ways in which the two sides can be amplified by the addition of allies.

Clause 8, in which the Champion nearly loses the battle, lends itself as beautifully to Poetics as though the primitive narrators of the "combat myth" had read Aristotle on the dramatic value of plots complicated by reversal ("peripety"). Obviously, a story about someone who simply goes out and wins is much less effective (hence less perfect) than a story about someone who nearly loses, then wins at the last moment as the result of a new development. Also, because of certain ambiguities regarding death and immortality among the gods, the period of near-defeat can even be carried to the "perfect" point where the Champion is slain and lamented, as per five subclauses which the author lists under 8.

Clause 9 marks the victory of our hero, by rival use of force and fraud (including, of course, magic). For in one sense the "combat myth" is misnamed. It is really a "victory myth." It isn't just the story of a fight; it is the story of a radical triumph (with qualifications still to be considered).

Clause 10 completes the form by detailing the final triumphant celebration of the Champion and those loyal to his cause. It attains its last touches of perfection in the author's subclauses 10c and 10d, regarding the Champion's purging of bloodguilt and his setting up of institutions devoted to his worship (the myth's *telos* thus coming to a head in its priestly use as sanction for the institutions associated with it). Thoughts on this last point suggest that we might even want to give the combat myth some such revised name as the "inaugural agon," having in mind its way of merging a mythic account of "origins" with a theory of *sanctions* for a given order of priestly governance.

III

So far, it must be admitted, our comments on the author's ten-clause paradigm, as viewed from the standpoint of Poetics, have been superficial, being intended merely to suggest the general slant. We shall now try to dig beneath the surface. For our point of departure, let's select this good formulation, from among the sixteen "important observations and discoveries" which the author lists by way of conclusion on pages 465 through 466: "The combat-myth is a myth of beginnings, a tale of conflict between order and disorder, chaos and cosmos."

We should begin by noting that, considered simply as terms, the members of these pairs imply each other. Though both types of the combat myth, in their simplicity, proceed *from* disorder *to* order, there is no such progression in the relation between the terms themselves, considered as logical opposites (or "polar" terms). We can say with equal justice either that "order" implies "disorder" or that "disorder" implies "order"—and the same will be found true of "chaos" and "cosmos," insofar as they stand opposed.

We would derive this state of affairs not from such *historical* "origins" or "firsts" as men's primitive battles with nature, wild beasts, and one another, but from the nature of that peculiarly linguistic marvel, the *negative*. The negative as such offers a basis for a tendency to think in terms of antitheses (yes-no, good-evil, true-false, right-wrong, order-disorder, cosmos-chaos, success-failure, presence-absence, pleasure-pain, clean-unclean, life-death, love-hate—or, recombining these last two sets, Eros-Thanatos).[3]

Hence, were one to ask, "Why the combat myth?" while having such considerations in mind our specifically "logological" answer would be: Insofar as negatives imply their opposites (as "disorder" implies "order"), the opposition between them is in effect "timeless." In themselves, as "polar" terms, they have no progression or priority, but merely imply each other. *When translated into terms of mythic narrative, however, such opposition can become a quasi-temporal "combat" between the two terms,* with the corresponding possibility that one of the terms can be pictured as "vanquishing" the other. Or they can be thought of as alternatively uppermost, in periodic or cyclic succession (an arrangement that comes closer to retaining the notion of their mutual involvement in each other, even while distinguishing between them and giving each a measure of predominance). Similarly, the pattern can be further modulated by the thought of an *interregnum*, with one of the terms not an out-and-out victor but a temporary *interrex*, eventually to be replaced by the other.

Note, also, that once you have translated the logical principle of antithesis into terms of narrative combat, by the same token you have set the conditions for a *purposive* development. Thus, for instance, the principle of disorder can be pictured as *aiming to win* over the principle of order, and

---

[3] However, one must guard against the temptation to interpret such groupings too symmetrically, with all the "good" on the "positive" side and all the "evil" viewed as "negative." Consider, for instance, the theological pair, "finite-infinite," where the Grammatically negative term is immeasurably the superior (whereby ingenious dialectical operations are employed to show that the finite is "really" the negative, and vice versa). Or consider the fact that freedom is the *destruction* of bondage, purification the *elimination* of guilt, redemption the *canceling* of debt, etc. One great fatality overhanging the Freudian nomenclature in this regard is that Freud approaches the negative from a *biological* emphasis rather than as an intrinsically *linguistic* phenomenon—hence the tendency towards an oversymmetrical equating of "positive" with "life" and "negative" with "death." Yet surely, it is not a "death instinct," but a "love of life," that makes us seek for ways of *negating* our distresses. There is nothing essentially deathy about zero or the minus sign in mathematics. Such negatives are purely a resource of symbol systems (though they can come to take on psychological associations extrinsic to their nature as sheerly technical signs and functions, and such associations may for some people be of a deathy sort). Killing ceases to be equatable with sheer negativity as soon as one thinks of "negating the negation," thereby piling on still more negativity, as with Donne's challenge, "Death, thou shalt die!"

vice versa, so that the purely directionless way in which polar terms imply each other can be replaced by schemes intensely teleological, as with "quest-myths" recounting the earnest effort to attain some greatly desired object or destination (a category wide enough to include all mythic narratives insofar as such narratives involve action and all action implies purpose).

Python does not deal with the "quest-myth" as such. But when the author finally arrives at his reduction to Eros and Thanatos, he is really doing in his way what the proponents of the "quest-myth" are doing in theirs: By such a trend towards "mono-myth," the motives for narrative development are in effect reduced to dramatic synonyms for "purpose." This is made obvious by the very term "quest-myth." And it should be clear enough in the case of Eros, the basic meaning of which is "desire for" (whereat we also readily realize the strong teleological ingredient in such Freudian concepts as "wish-fulfillment" and "purposive forgetting").

To show that Thanatos is similarly but a dramatic synonym for purpose, we must be a bit more roundabout, but not much. First, we recall the two meanings of "end," as cessation or aim. The two merge in the sense that the fulfillment of an aim and the completion of a development are characterizable as the "death" of that aim or development, once you permit yourself to describe the process in so dramatic a term. The attaining of any given end marks the "death" of such efforts as went with the attaining of it.

"Death" also figures in another sense. For besides the "killing" of a desire by its *attainment*, there is also the *frustrating* of a desire. Here again, permitting ourselves a dramatic vocabulary, we could introduce the Thanatos theme, since any frustrating of a desire can be treated as a species of "mortification."

Thus in two opposite ways a *purpose* can undergo *transformations* which, if stated in terms of Love and Death, could be called modes of "dying." And insofar as the sheer Grammar of such semimythic language is concerned, reduction to terms of Eros and Thanatos is in effect reduction to the three categories: purpose, fulfillment of purpose, frustration of purpose. In this sense, the terms are intrinsically as "mono-mythic" as reduction to the "quest." And insofar as they are reductions to the one category of "purpose," they are necessarily insufficient; for obviously there are other loci of motives.[4]

IV

However, though semimythic when applied to action generally, the terms can be literal when applied specifically to the biological realm of sexual desire and to the presence or absence of life in an organism. And this literal

---

[4] In my *Grammar of Motives* I reduce such loci to five: act, scene, agent, agency, and purpose.

reference adds plausibility to their universalistic usage. But obviously, their "universalistic" usage (as terms for aspects of purpose) quickly takes us beyond any possible restriction to natural conditions alone, as when we are told that Eros helped Zeus conquer "by putting into Typhon's soul a readiness to be charmed by Kadmos' music," or when we recall that in the combat myth the divine contestants both "die" and are "immortal."

Not only does polytheism provide a style of expression whereby the terms for gods can duplicate the vocabulary of human psychology (as a desire can be attributed to a god of desire, a fear to a god of fear, etc.); it also allows for a further complication whereby the gods themselves can be treated sometimes as having purely personal motives and sometimes as having motives which were induced in them by other gods (as a god might directly be said to experience a desire, or the desire might be said to have been aroused in him by the action of Eros). Hence note that, when Desire itself becomes a god, a frustrated desire can become in principle "immortal," to the extent that it *persists*, in however gnarled or imperfect or imprisoned a form. That is, insofar as a desire can be "killed" by its *fulfillment*, in failing to be fulfilled it can "live on."

In this sense, the ambiguous relation between death and immortality in the combat myth can be seen to be a perfect narrative translation for the underlying polarity of the antithetic principles (expressed in terms of warring principals). Insofar as one term excludes the other, if we had to state this logical relation in terms of a mythic combat, we could properly say that one term "slays" the other. Yet insofar as the term timelessly implies its opposite, we could say that the "slain" term remains "immortal," and though vanquished, is ever ready to make a comeback if the opportunity offers, like Typhon fuming beneath Aetna. For insofar as narrative involves *action* and action implies *purpose*, the relation between the terms would remain one of purposive combat.

The underlying dialectic of the Love-Death pair is further complicated by the fact that they are not directly antithetical in the way that order-disorder and cosmos-chaos are. Strictly, the antithesis of Love would be Hate, and the antithesis of Death would be Life. By crossing the pairs, we get the invitation to equate Hate with Death (Styx meant the "hateful") and Love with Life. But as viewed in terms of death, there are at least two major incentives to equate Love *with* Death rather than treating them as contestants. Physiologically, the sense of release through sexual orgasm can be likened to a pleasurable form of dying (an association frequently found in poetry). Sociologically, there is the fact that the lovers' immersion in a common identity implies the "death" of whatever separate identities they may have outside the circle of their mutual engrossment. It is a way of "transcending" ordinary "mortal" concerns, a kind of claim to "immortality" (though the principles of dialectic are so inexorable that such "im-mortality" can be but a species of "mortality," so far as the experience of mortals is concerned). As regards the vagaries of poetic catharsis, the love-death equation has the further advantage that, while symbolizing sexual union, it can also symbolize "punishment" for such union, thereby merging guilt, gratification, and redemption.

Thus, when following Professor Fontenrose's purely folkloristic efforts to derive the "Venusberg theme" from earlier stories of a trip to the underworld of the dead, we should keep in mind also such sheerly "entelechial" concerns as the above. As a principle of operatic "perfection," the Wagnerian theme of the *Liebestod* is to be derived not from an original version of the "combat myth," but from the implications of the Wagnerian canon. Poetics would study it not as a derivation, but as a kind of culmination, an entelechy that is implicit in *Tannhäuser*, but that attains its full narrative expression in *Tristan*, since it is the theme on which the opera closes. The plot of *Tristan* might be viewed as the "perfect paradigm" for a "myth" so equating Eros and Thanatos that any "combat" between them becomes transformed into a species of "concerted action." (We say "concerted," having in mind that the Latin verb *concerto* meant to strive, rival, dispute, and that such connotations are present in the idea of a musical *concerto*, which involves a kind of "contest" between the orchestra and the solo instrument.)

To sum up the steps already taken: First, we considered the combat myth purely as a narrative way of handling "polar" opposition, a response to the genius of the negative. Next, when the author ended on Freud's Eros-Thanatos pair, we noted that, besides their bearing upon love, hate, life, and death as ultimate terms of combat, they functioned as somewhat dramatized synonyms for aspects of *purpose*.

This point about purpose is particularly important because, as the author of *Python* repeatedly makes clear, the combat myth comes to a head in its use as *aition*. Here is its *purpose*, its function as a story to account for the cult or services associated with it. In this regard, the author calls it a myth of "origins," whereupon we would add the important reminder that such an account of "origins" is also a way of establishing *sanctions*. Its narrative stating how things *were* in the past thereby substantiates the principles of governance to which the faithful *should be* vowed in the present.

V

Such an "entelechial" perspective ("deriving" the many versions and variants not from some one story that may have originally been going the rounds, but rather from poetic and rhetorical principles that would attain their perfect embodiment in Fontenrose's paradigms) would locate the "principles" of a form not in temporally past moments that a form develops *from*, but in possibilities of perfection which reside in the form as such and *toward* which all sorts of stories might gravitate. Similarly, as considered from the entelechial point of view, the "principles" of Greek tragedy would be sought not in the incunabula of tragedy, but in *late* developments, such "perfect" tragedies as those of Aeschylus or Sophocles, in line with Aristotle's statement, in Chapter IV (Section 15) of the *Poetics*: "After going through many stages" in its gradual evolution, tragedy "stopped when it had found its natural form."[5]

But note that, even as regards the "entelechial" perspective itself, we have come upon two sources of motives. Besides the combat myth's way of translating contraries and contradictories into narrative terms of combat (involving a search for a corresponding perfection of dramatis personae and plot), there is the aetiological use of myth for a somewhat "propagandistic" purpose, to account for the "origins" of the cult with which the myth has become identified. The matter of such "origins" brings up further considerations, which we shall deal with next.

First, there is one problem that plagues us at every stage of this inquiry. The author of *Python* encounters it in his way when, having equated sea and death, he seeks to answer a critic's objection "that sea and death do not belong to the same level of concept." In reply he observes that by the use of personification mythic thinking does frequently place "concepts of different levels . . . on the same level." (p. 142) Also, he notes that folklorists generally interpret the sea as a "realm of death."

Insofar as myth is poetic, it naturally expresses its ideas in terms of imagery and personification. Thus, the *idea* of death will be replaced by the imagery of a realm in which the dead reside and which can be duplicated in terms of a supernatural power presiding over this realm. Hence, whatever details may be used in the amplifying of the idea, they are necessarily somewhat extrinsic to the idea as such. If for instance, the realm of death is equated with the sea, there is also the fact that the sea, *qua* sea, is not a realm of death. In fact, it may be gloriously fertile with life. Or if the idea of death is equated, say, with absence, we recognize that absence *qua* absence is not identical with death. For instance, a person may be absent from some gathering not because he is dead, but because he is having a good time elsewhere.

Now, reversing the matter, suppose that you come upon the theme of a god's absence. Are you to treat it categorically as a surrogate for the theme of his death? Or can it sometimes refer simply to absence *qua* absence, without any reference to death? For instance, if at some point in a story the exigencies of the plot require that a certain character be absent, any suf-

---

[5] The tendency to treat of motivational *principles* ("beginnings") in terms of the primordial past is central to the method of myth (which expresses essence temporally, in terms of narrative). To end by borrowing Freud's highly imaginative Eros-Thanatos pair comes close to explaining a myth by a myth.

ficient reason might serve. If he is said to have gone on a trip, must this necessarily be interpreted as a disguised variation on the theme of a trip to the dead? In *Python* there are references to such absence on pages 381 through 382. Here the god's absence is interpreted as the sign of his death, though it was certainly a highly qualified form of death, since it had to do with months during which Apollo spent the winter in "the northern paradise of the Hyperboreans" (p. 345), a form of "death" not unlike that of healthy tourists who, during the bleak northern winter, sunbathe and water-ski in the tropics.

The entelechial perspective suggests a third possibility. Here would be the steps: (1) In a narrative, the theme of "absence" may be a motive in its own right, a narrator's convenience in accounting for a development that could not have taken place so "naturally" had the absent character been present. (2) The theme of absence might be variously motivated (two obvious possibilities being either that the absent person had gone on a trip or that he was dead). (3) For a heroic combat myth, the most "perfect" explanation would be one which equated absence-on-a-trip with absence-through-death, hence arriving at absence-on-a-trip-to-the-world-of-the-dead.

Thus instead of treating the theme of absence as a variation on the theme of death, we should treat each as designed to solve a problem within the story, a problem that was solved by the theme of absence as such. However, once the narrator starts accounting for the absence, entelechial pressures attract him towards terms for death as the "most thorough" explanation. Such an entelechial view of the situation would not require us to assume that the theme of absence stood for the theme of a journey to the realm of the dead. Far from a situation whereby the theme of absence as such indicates the theme of death, it could indicate merely that the given version was not so "thorough" in accounting for the absence as it would have been had the explanation been in terms of death. Indeed, lack of "thoroughness" in this regard can often result from the fact that the narrative is being "thorough" in quite different ways, to quite different ends. Such considerations would figure particularly if, in the examination of myths from many lands, every reference to a stage in which a god is absent were interpreted as a disguised, fragmentary variation on the theme of his death.

Similarly, one man might write a story about gambling for money, and another about gambling for one's life. There is no reason to assume that the story about gambling for money is a mere variation on the theme of gambling for one's life (though both stories may be studied as variations on the theme of gambling, with its motivational range from symbolic self-abuse to the *beau geste* of "aristocratic" adventurousness). But we could say that, *caeteris paribus*, the theme of gambling for one's life is more "thorough" than the theme of gambling for money; and certainly the theme of losing one's life at gambling would be heroically more thorough than the theme of winning money. Yet to say as much is to suggest a further ironic possibility: The hero wins a fortune in gambling for money; but this very success leads ironically to events that culminate in his downfall and death, and that would not have "transpired" had he lost.

Or a woman, dreaming of being jilted by her lover, might punningly dream so in terms of an incident that involved his dropping a garment of hers. Or the dream might be of an incident in which she was about to fall over a cliff, her lover was rescuing her, then he too began to slip, and to save himself he let her go—whereat she awoke in terror, after the plunge to her certain death had begun. Both versions would be on the theme of her being "dropped." But the milder version would not be a surrogate for the more drastic one. Each of the two variations on the same theme could arise without necessary reference to the other. But one would be more "complete," so far as tests of tragic fulfillment are concerned.

In all such cases, *caeteris paribus*, we might expect an entelechial pressure in the direction of the more drastic version, as regards the motives of a "perfect paradigm."

VI

In an excellent introductory summary of the variations which a theme may undergo (pp. 7-8), the author makes two kinds of observations which might at first glance seem the same; yet when viewed from the standpoint of our "entelechial" concern they can be shown to have quite different implications.

Here is an example of a statement that can mislead: "A striking feature of one variant may be reduced in another to something less striking, or it may be disguised. Death may be changed to wound, sleep, defeat, exile, disappearance." (p. 8) In the light of our analysis, would we not be justified in saying that the author himself here spontaneously exemplifies, without proper safeguards, the entelechial principle of tragedy, in taking the most drastic member of his series as the essence of the lot? His statement, if uncriticized, becomes an invitation to see a disguised reference to death in every mention of a contestant's wound, sleep, defeat, exile, or disappearance. By such a rule, Thanatos is bound to turn up just about everywhere, universalistically joining with its partner, Eros, to encompass the whole field.

Here, on the other hand, is an example of a statement which seems to avoid such an invitation to error: "The mode of combat may change from one variant to another. One kind of punishment or deception may be replaced by another." (p. 7) The statement is so generalized that no one example is offered as basic, with others treated as departures from it. All examples would be equally valid, so far as their inclusion under this head is concerned, though we might next proceed to show why one particular example was more "perfect" for a particular context.

The statement that "There may be expansion or doubling of themes, persons, episodes" can be somewhat misleading. (p. 8) For though it is often more "perfect" to have a principle summed up in the role of an individual contestant, a work like *The Iliad*, or stories of "titanomachies," "theomachies," and "gigantomachies" indicate that in many narratives a principle of opposition as such can be properly represented by assigning several contestants to one side, a consideration that also applies specifically to the combat myth, since both Enemy and Champion can have allies (including defectors from the opposition).

The statement that "A deed may become merely the attempt to do it" would require the addition of the words "and *vice versa*"; otherwise the assumption is that deed is primary and attempt is derivative. In the next paragraph, this kind of corrective is actually introduced, when the author notes that "deeds or traits may be transferred from one character to another . . . even from champion to enemy and *vice versa*." (p. 8)

Insofar as the author's summary here is to be taken merely as a convenience for the reader, there is no particular reason why it should have been written any more exactly than it is. As regards the test of sheer preparatory serviceability, the outline is wholly adequate, and we are straining at gnats if we seem to be asking that it be legalistically holeproof. Our point is simply that, though there is no particular need for having those clauses any more accurate than they are, they happen to be of two sorts whereas at first they all seem to be of one sort. And insofar as we distinguish between them, we can make clear the distinction we are after, regarding the relation between themes and variations as viewed from the standpoint of Poetics.

You might put the matter thus: Christian theologians treat figures in the Old Testament as "types of Christ." Another approach might be to pick such a figure in the Old Testament, and to treat Christ and Christian martyrs, and all similar Old Testament figures as variations on this theme. A third way would be to treat both Christ and all such characters in the Old Testament or later as examples of a more generalized category, such as: The principle of sacrifice, exemplified in various roles that embody this principle with varying degrees of "perfection." Here would be the "entelechial" approach. Clauses ending "and *vice versa*" would allow for it, whereas it would not be accommodated by clauses that imply the temporal priority of one among the lot, with the others treated as variants (derivatives) of this ancestral term.

Professor Fontenrose's use of thematic paradigms is like the first view insofar as the paradigms are a kind of ideal summing-up. It would be like the second, insofar as certain early figures were taken to be the probable thematic originals and all others were treated as variants of these. It is strongly influenced by the *pressures* of the third; but the folkloristic stress upon temporal priority keeps the entelechial aspect of the paradigms from attaining its full rationale, and makes it look as though the "variants" were descended from ideal prototypes which came *first in time*, whereas actually the paradigms are prototypes only in the sense that they possess the "perfection" of overall generalizations or schematizations.

VII

If the combat myth were nothing but a story of combat, designed to appeal simply as a story in keeping with the aesthetic canons of Art for Art's Sake, the study of its paradigm from the entelechial point of view would require only such considerations of internal symmetry. But a cult is a system of *governance*. Thus its moral authority is a direct or indirect means of influencing the dispositions and habits of the believers. And insofar as the myth of "origins" serves as a precedent on which to base this authority, it must be designed not merely to account for "origins," but also to account for them in ways that provide *sanctions* for the given order. This aetiological factor complicates the entelechial perspective by so localizing the tests of a myth's "perfection" that a version which would best sanction one authority would need revision if applied to the sanctioning of a different authority.

Thus, whereas the mythic translation of opposition into terms of a contest allows ideas like order and disorder, cosmos and chaos to be represented by personified contestants that can triumph over each other or succeed each other, there still remains the fact that any system of order implies corresponding kinds of disorder. This persistence of the logical opposites despite the possibilities of mythic victory can be best handled in these two ways: (1) By a myth according to which, though one of the contestants has been vanquished (or, in the most thorough terms, "slain"), he still somehow survives (like Typhon buried by Zeus beneath Sicily and fuming through Aetna), with the constant threat that he may again rise in revolt. (2) By a myth according to which the vanquished principle does periodically take over, to reign for a season, and to be periodically replaced again by the opposing principle. (Obviously, the resources of dialectic being what they are, under certain conditions such *opposition* can be translated into terms more like *cooperation*, with both powers or principles being necessary to make a world, whereby the principle of "disorder" becomes in its way a species of order, too. Even the Kingdom of Darkness is not just rebellion against Light, but has its own modes of organization.)

The design of human combat itself would seem to provide the basic imagery for the first of these versions, according to which one side conquers but can never remain wholly sure of his victory. And obviously, the periodicity of the seasons provides the basic image for the second version, which translates the principle of opposition into terms of cyclical succession. The second primarily concerns us now, since the paradigm calls for the victory of a sky-god or weather-god, and seasonal change is most readily associated with such a power.

There is one notable difference between rituals designed to influence irregular phenomena (like magic for ending drought in a season normally rainy) and rituals designed for influencing regular phenomena (like magic for "causing" the return of spring at a time when spring is normally due): The second kind of rite can possess a measure of "infallibility" not possible to the first. And insofar as a priesthood can associate its rites with the orderly production of inevitable processes, it has optimum conditions for establishing its authority. For what system of priestly magic could possibly be more authoritative than one which had obvious pragmatic sanction, since its services proved "successful" year after year?

Too great a stress upon primitive magic as "bad science" (a faulty method of *coercing nature*) can deflect our attention from its efficacy as "good rhetoric" (an authoritative method of *persuading people*). No one could say with certainty whether magic began with the attempt to influence the irregularities of nature or in a "poetic" responsiveness to nature's regular cycle of transformations. But one can say with certainty that, insofar as a cult could associate its rites with the lore of the calendar, it had the best basis for establishing the authority of those rites, since it could then work out ritual ways of "bringing about the inevitable." Thus, whatever may have been the beginnings of magic, its rites attained a certain "perfection" when identified with the seasons. And in this sense, with the translation of polar opposition (order-disorder, cosmos-chaos, rule-misrule) into terms of powers whose jurisdiction fluctuated with the seasons, the combat myth was brought to a state of "aetiological perfection."

We now can see clearly the two kinds of "perfection" that the "entelechial" perspective must deal with, in the case of the "combat myth." There is its perfection simply as a story that translates polar opposition into terms of narrative. And there is its perfection as an instrument in the establishing of a cult's authority. For this second kind, we have suggested, there is the added factor of identification with seasonal regularities. But obviously, in taking responsibility for seasonal *regularities*, the magician also had to take responsibility for the correcting of seasonal *irregularities*. It has often been pointed out that there was an irrefutable explanation within the system itself whenever such rites failed, since any failure could be ascribed to counter-magic. But that would not be a "perfect" answer, since it would tend to impugn the power of the cult's own magic, by implying that there could be stronger rival powers.

The "perfect" answer involved merely a further extension of a principle already present in both contestants of the myth: the principle of *victimage*. The Champion's period of suffering was in the cause of order.

And *a fortiori* the Enemy had also participated as a victim in the contest, so that his suffering was a major contribution to the maintenance of order. This principle could be further extended, not simply to the use of human sacrifice as a way of appeasing offended powers, but also to the notion of the "hidden imposthume," the undetected offender *within* the tribe, the problematical source of moral or ritual uncleanness still to be located by the experts (as with Sophocles' Oedipus). The "perfect" answer, in this sense, may not always have been resorted to. But it was there. And it really did involve an "abscess" hidden *within* the tribe—for our ideas of the *threats* to order arise from our ideas of order itself, guilt thus being intrinsic to the system (the very means of purgation reinforcing the sense of uncleanness, as the flying of flags in Tibet to *drive away* evil spirits reinforces the sense of their *presence*).

For a complete discussion of "teleological perfection," we should have to know a great deal about the particular "interests" which a given cult favored, though sometimes such proclivities may be inferred from the nature of the version itself, as when the relation between Apollo and Dionysos was presented rather in terms of alternate rule than rivalry. (A similar development seems to have occurred in early Christianity, when a threatened doctrinal rivalry between followers of Christ and followers of John the Baptist became transformed into the account of the Baptist as the Savior's forerunner). This problem is further complicated by the fact that, though religious institutions contribute to governance, thereby using religion as a means of "social control," they are sounder when the identification between priesthood and secular administration is not too close, as then they can better survive shifts in secular authority.

In general, for a wholly accurate account of the "teleological perfection" which a given version of a myth might have, while making such latitudinarian allowances for its relations to secular authority we should have to know a great deal not only about the local conditions of a given cult through the various stages of its history, but also about its relation to different economic systems (hunting, agriculture, trade, etc.), and to such social distinctions as patrilineal-matrilineal and patrician-plebeian (with the apparent merging of popular and aristocratic trends in the forms of Greek tragedy). Though the subject is not discussed systematically, there is material for such speculation scattered through the book. For instance: "It is possible that political changes in the Delphic state brought with them corresponding changes in the slant of the Charila myth, so that the heroine was transformed from demoness to a humble girl of the people." (p. 460)

This issue adds complication atop complication because of the fact that, although we tend to view religions as systems of internally generated doctrines, they are often *polar* terms, being best defined at a given time in history by some other doctrine they are *against*, though if they last long enough, they may be shaped by a changing series of such opponents, even to the extent of incorporating many of the opponents' principles.

VIII

Insofar as the nature of the combat myth as *aition* involved a discussion of uses to which the myth was put in different historical situations, it could not be described purely in terms of Poetics. The discussion would require considerations which modern anthropology would analyze in terms of ritual and magic, but which in the categories of classical education would fall under rhetoric."[6]

However, by the very fact of having so greatly stressed the problem of the myth's specific "propagandistic" utility, we are in a position to go back and ask what kind of form the myth is seen to have, if this complication is dropped out of account (theoretically prescinded).

Considered as sheer design, the combat myth comprises two modes of plot that are related to each other as obverse and reverse, concave and convex. The contesting principles (or principals) of the combat are so related that the gains of one are the losses of the other. If we next add the "entelechial" notion that a combat, to be dramatically perfect, requires a peripety, the complementary designs are seen to be so formed that one contestant meets with increasing success until there is a reversal of fortune and he fails, while by the same token the opponent meets with increasing failure until the same reversal of fortune brings success.

There are two major ways of distinguishing between comedy and tragedy: (1) Tragic characters are said to be "better" than ordinary people, comic characters "worse"; (2) Comedy has a plot that builds towards a "happy" ending, tragedy towards an "unhappy" ending. Each in its way involves the entelechial principle. But for the moment we are concerned with the more obvious case, the test by endings (an "entelechial" consideration because endings, like entelechies, are culminative, formal fulfillments).

The mere combat pattern as such is most directly illustrated by an athletic contest in which there is no need to have the sides so distinguished that the one is "virtuous" and the other "villainous," one for "cosmos" and the other for "chaos," etc. (though partisan sympathies can make for such a response among the spectators). Judged as sheer form, the most "perfect" game would be one in which at the last minute the losing side breaks through and wins ("complex plot" with "peripety"). Since one side's gain would be the other side's loss, the pattern thus contains simultaneously the designs of both tragedy and comedy (as tested by the outcome).

---

[6] At various places in my *Rhetoric of Motives*, now available in a Meridian paperback edition, I have aimed to show how the "Hierarchal" motive figures in the sense of mystery.

However, in a well-formed work, the ending is not something that can merely be tacked on (as though the poet were to write his drama without reference to its ending, and at the last minute tossed up a coin to decide whether he'd have his hero end in anguish like Sophocles' *Oedipus Rex* or end up with a banquet and two girls like Dicaeopolis in Aristophanes' *Acharnians*). To be perfect, an ending must be perfectly prepared for. And such preparation when most thorough involves not merely the curve of the plot but the choice of appropriate characters. For if the action is to be tragic, the characters must be of a sort that is appropriate to tragic action.

The question of tragedy and comedy thus shifts from considerations of outcome to considerations of dramatis personae. Although, simply as regards the test of endings, the outcome of an athletic contest would be in principle "comic" for the victors and "tragic" for the losers, the test of dramatis personae suggests that in principle both sides are "tragic." For they are "better" than most people (in the sense that, in their role as athletes, they represent a skill which people ordinarily do not possess). Thus in this technical sense they would meet the requirements of Aristotle's formula. Insofar as he performs properly, each player has his peculiar way of being "serious" (*spoudaios*).

The analogue of a "comic" game would be one in which, instead of directing all their efforts earnestly, the players complicated things by clowning. In this technical sense they would be "worse" even than ordinary people who took the game seriously.

In Chapter XV of the *Poetics*, the word that Aristotle uses when giving his total recipe for a tragic character is *chrestos*. Though it is usually translated as "good," we might well remember that its primary meaning is goodness in the sense of usefulness, serviceability. Particularly in view of the fact that the Greek idea of service has the same range of pragmatic and ritualistic connotations as in English, we submit that the notion of a tragic character's "goodness" might best be approached through a hypothetical example of this sort:

Think of a funeral service. Think next of an usher officiating at that service. Insofar as he performed his function properly, he would contribute to the austerities of the occasion by being "better" than he ordinarily was. He would accept the responsibilities of his tragic role, and act accordingly. Only the most discreet kinds of bodily expression would be permitted, nothing more "purgative" than a barely audible clearing of the throat. Even if he smiled, it would be a wan smile, a sad smile, by all means not a carefree beaming smile. (On the contrary as regards bodily purgative imagery in Aristophanic comedy: just as a comic character was ornamented with a large stylized phallus, so in a state of comic fright he might befoul himself, such manners obviously being "worse" than those of ordinary people.) Similarly, despite the low rating placed on a slave in Greek culture, the character of a slave could be introduced into tragedy. But those aspects of the role must be stressed which "live up to" the solemnities of the occasion.

The striking difference between the low status of women in Athenian society (except for an occasional famous courtesan like Aspasia) and the tremendous roles assigned to them in tragedy is a perfect instance of the way in which tragic figures could be called "better" than the ordinary, even though many of Euripides' women were "better" in quite horrifying ways, thereby providing the plot for Aristophanes' comedy, the *Thesmophoria-zusae*, built around the theme of Athenian women who organize against Euripides in indignation at his slandering of their sex (a comic situation that is at its best when Mnesilochus, who undertakes the defense of the playwright, makes things still worse by reciting the many evil things that Euripides might with justice have said about women but left unsaid).

Again, by the test of "better" and "worse," what would you do with a character like Iago? Is he to be called "better" than ordinary people? Or must he be denied a "tragic" character, despite the fact that, had he been any less enterprising in villainy than he was, the whole tragedy would have collapsed? He is a tragic character, since he contributes so well to the tragic roles of Othello and Desdemona. But he is "less tragic" than they. For no wholly tragic character can be loathed, and Iago is loathed except insofar as a critic might feel sorry for an inventive soul who so thoroughly took upon himself the playwright's serious job of keeping the tragedy in motion, a sturdy role for which we must always give the Devil his due.

The tragic "flaw" or "error of judgment" (*hamartia*) is matched by what we might call the comic "blotch" (*hamartema*, a word incidentally that in the New Testament came to mean "sin"). Comic characters are "worse" than ordinary people in the sense that caricatures of public figures look "worse" than if simply "lifelike." Such picturesque disfigurement and distortion also applies to characters with whom we are meant to be in sympathy, though the kinds of overemphasis will differ. Thus the political cartoonist might exaggerate a large mouth by picturing it as disproportionately still larger, but he could still choose between giving this "comic blotch" a grin or a leer.

To the test by endings and the test by character we might add the related test by response. Tragedy naturally attains its culmination in tears, comedy in laughter. But there are complications such as the *comédie lar-moyante* (which may be seasoned with incidental tearful "endings," such as an episode depicting the pitiful death of some pathetic secondary character). And the Shakespearean theater allows for the "perfect" possibility of a double plot in which a sympathetically unhappy ending for heroic characters is interwoven with a vindictively unhappy ending for similarly "serious" villainous characters, along with an out-and-out happy ending for some comic characters, and a measure of minor vengeance for their comic enemies. The tearfulness would relate predominantly to the tragic set, the laughter

to the comic set. Yet there could be incidental crossing of the borders, too.
(I say that the canons of the Shakespearean theater would allow for this as
a "perfect possibility." But I do not think of any play that fully embodies
such a range.)

As regards the test by endings alone, the design of Christ's sacrifice
combines tragedy and comedy. For whereas the death of Christ on the Cross
is in itself a tragic ending, Christ's resurrection and return to Heaven sets
the pattern for a "divine comedy." As with the combat myth, the hero goes
through a stage in which he "dies" and is lamented, followed by a stage of
rebirth and celebration. The idea of Christ-Jesus as God-man allowed for
a greater dissociation between the idea of the Christian Champion's "death"
(as a man) and his "immortality" (as a divine Person).

As regards the test by character and response, though the Christian
agon was weak in comedy, this defect was remedied somewhat in the semi-
secular Miracle Plays that re-enacted Biblical stories. (Cf. the stock comic
character of Noah's wife as a scold, and the devices whereby actors who
were assigned the role of devils made their hard lot bearable by giving such
devils the character of comic imps and pranksters.)

By progressing from Hell through Purgatory to Paradise, Dante gives
his epic the design of a happy ending, particularly since the poet's pilgrimage
is presented as a kind of object lesson intended for his salvation. However,
behind this "temporal" unfolding there remains the fact that Hell is not
merely a stage along the way but as long-lasting as Paradise. Thus, though
the epic *ends* on the theme of Paradise, one-third of it is concerned with
characters whose sufferings are *unending*. In this sense it is one hell of an
idea of comedy, though technically the way out of the difficulty would probably be along these lines: (1) Tragedy involves pity; (2) according to
Aristotle we feel pity only for suffering that is undeserved; (3) the eternal
hellish suffering of the damned is said to be a "just" punishment; (4) hence,
in the last analysis, it should not awaken pity—and, according to St. Thomas,
does not arouse the pity of the saints in Heaven; (5) however, being a mere
mortal, in some circles of Hell Dante does feel pity; but mostly his attitude
is one of fascinated fear and repugnance; and sometimes he is moved by
vindictive satisfaction, an attitude that the saints would not share; (6)
Aristotle also says that we feel pity for people like ourselves—and Dante's
sudden feelings of pity concern sufferers with whose temptations he most
readily identifies himself.

IX

Fontenrose says (p. 22) that "Often in the following chapters the name
Python will be used merely as a convenient designation for Apollo's opponent without regard to sex or species," and (p. 70) "I shall henceforth

use the term *dragon* broadly to mean any kind of monster or animal or mixed shape." Here we confront in another way the kind of problem we encountered when asking whether the terms "Eros" and "Thanatos" might be interpreted as mythical equivalents for the concept of "purpose." (We noted that the word "quest," stressed by some literary folklorists, could be similarly analyzed. And we might also have noted that in philosophic writings the word "good" is similarly analyzable, as per the definition at the beginning of the *Nichomachean Ethics*: "The Good is that at which all things aim."[7])

We dealt with a similar problem when considering the author's use of "Enemy" and "Champion" in his paradigm for the final type of combat myth with which he is concerned. We contended that they might be shown to imply in turn a principle of sheerly logical opposition (as with "polar" terms), for which they provide a quasi-narrative equivalent.

But now we might also supply an intermediate step, along these lines:

If we wanted to stress purely narrative opposition (but in terms that would be as highly generalized as possible without losing the idea of sheerly logical opposition), we might designate the contestant principles simply as Negative and Positive. In doing so, however, we should immediately confront the fact that there would be no basis for deciding which of the opposing principles should be called Positive and which Negative. This situation is made apparent in a succinct footnote (*Python*, p. 240) where the author says that he applies the term "rebel gods" to the "older generation of gods" which the "victory-destined younger gods" displace. He also notes here that in the Hesiodic Titanomachy, "the younger gods are those who revolt." And we might add: In a sense it is always the younger gods who revolt, as with the Champion who goes forth to end the tyrannical reign of the Enemy; but the displaced gods are the rebels because, once the new order has become the norm, the old order stands for the corresponding principle of disorder which constantly threatens to regain control and can even be said to reign periodically (but not permanently, thanks to the efficacy of the cultic rites with which the myth is associated).

Considering the pattern as sheer design, all we can say is that either side negates the other. But despite the traditional associating of law and order, and despite the fact that law is essentially negative (a structure of thou-shalt-not's), there is also the traditional tendency to associate the Negative with "bad" and the Positive with "good." So we might arbitrarily use the Negative as the mark of the Enemy, though the negative would be in our attitude towards him.

Building from there, we should next ask how things should be if both sides were perfect examples of their kind. The answer to this question would

---

[7] Chapter I, Section I.

give us our first step from sheer pattern to mythic particularization: Both sides should be "gods." We have now translated our Negative and Positive into terms of *body*, though a kind of body which also shades off into ideas of the *disembodied*.

Next should follow the ways of "amplifying" the two principles, as when the Unfavored Principle is placed in terms of a habitat deemed unfavorable, a set of details which introduce many terms for body (as with descriptions connecting the Unfavored Principle with some forbidding place where monsters and demons are traditionaly thought to dwell). Association with a set of similarly unfavored physical traits (such as a monstrous form) would carry the process of amplification further in terms that myth traditionally associated with the physically repulsive. The principle would now have been given still more body. Yet however monstrous, and however identified with superhuman or nonhuman powers, this principle, to be narratively "perfect," must be a *person*. Hence, amplification in terms of moral traits (powers and habits) upon which men look most strongly with disfavor. And this unfavored character must cap the climax by association with a purpose that is the most thoroughly (or "perfectly") disfavored. This should be his ambition for total tyranny, absolute misrule.

If the narrative structure is to be as neat in its internal adjustments as possible, this culminating purpose on the part of the Unfavored Principle (or Principal) must serve as motive for the action of the rival Positive Favored Principle (endowed with correspondingly favored background, physical and moral powers and habits, all culminating in the intention to undo the Negative Principle's culminating intention).

The two principles must come to terms—and the most fitting way to do so narratively is in terms of a contest. In some respects, a sheerly physical combat is not "perfect" for all conditions, as we realize when we come to the agons of tragedy and comedy. But we are here concerned with principles, or "*firsts*,"—and terms for physical combat are prior in our imagination (as in our experience) to terms for moral combat. (Recall that, behind the account of rule and misrule in the opening chapters of Genesis, there lies the account of Lucifer's rebellion; and though the tragedies deal with moral scruples, they generally come to a focus in the imagery of physical violence.)

The combat, in turn, must be amplified by appropriate details, centering in accounts of force and fraud (the only resources of combat) which also attain their proper supernatural completion in terms of magic. This combat, to be perfect as a plot, must undergo a peripety whereby the Positive principle is first defeated, then successful. Given the nature of the contestants, the defeat can be expressed in the most thorough terms possible: The Positive principle can actually be said to "die" (a proper juncture for lamentations on the part of those who favor the vanquished principle). For "death" under such conditions is not incongruous with "immortality" (and the two taken together make a perfect narrative equivalent for the under-lying Paradox of the Negative whereby polar terms both exclude each other and necessarily require each other).

When, by the use of similar resources (force and fraud aided by such magic as was deemed "natural" to the gods) the Reversal in the narrative occurs and the Positive principle ultimately prevails, conditions are set for the appropriate aftermath: cleansing of guilt, celebration of victory, and (when the myth is "put to use" as an *aition*) inaugurating of rites (rites rationalized in accordance with the principle-of-principles whereby the Posi-tive still goes on implying its corresponding Negative).

We should now add that, when the myth is given body by translation into descriptive details, not all the details are explainable solely in terms of their identification with one or the other of the contestant principles. Many will be "neutral." Indeed, the contestants can "come to terms" only insofar as they have grounds of altercation in common. Thus, a battlefield or a banquet hall will merit some details in its own right. So, in our search for explanations in terms of perfection, we must also keep in mind the pressures that keep the contest from becoming too simply itself, and that call for an underlying neutrality of details designed to help the narrative look real. This ambiguity is true of all characters in fiction. Some things they do because of their specific roles; but they do other things simply because they are "people."

Up to this point, the design is not unambiguously describable as either tragedy or comedy. The ambiguity prevails all the more in that under the conditions of polytheism, as Professor Fontenrose reminds us (p. 425): "The enemy, although and precisely because he is fearful, always receives cult: there can be no doubt about the worship of most dragons and demons that have been mentioned in these pages." So, particularly when you get to comparing fragmentary versions of myths that have come down through many sources, the symmetry becomes impaired, even to the extent that favored and unfavored traits can change sides; and only in the theoretically perfect paradigm towards which the myths were gravitating would the sym-metry be as unerring as here suggested. For various reasons, mortal nar-ratives will "fall" from such a state of Paradisiac innocence.

For one thing, as becomes apparent when you turn from thoughts of the combat myth to speculations about tragedy and comedy (a field with which Professor Fontenrose is not concerned at all and which we have intro-duced into the discussion purely for reasons of our own), the principles of perfection shaping the combat myth are found to differ intrinsically from those shaping tragedy and comedy, though there are also overlaps, quite as Aristotle recognized overlaps between the principles of drama and epic de-spite the considerable differences between these poetic species. Though, as we have tried to show, the design of the combat myth has the makings of both tragic and comic plots, we need but think of a clown like Aristophanes' Dicaeopolis to realize that here much different entelechial principles are operating.

As regards test by endings, the themes of banqueting and celebration at the end of comedy are closer to the combat myth than tragedy is. As regards test by character, tragedy is the closer. But the main point is that, whereas the combat myth is not to be viewed simply as incipient tragedy or incipient comedy but as a form responding to potentialities of its own, so either the "drastic" preferences which tragedy cultivates or the comic poet's emphases should be taken as final only with regard to one particular poetic species. Along with both the heroics of tragedy and the extremes of the comic blotch, there must be rules for many kinds of understatement to which they are closed, and which work further refinements on the distribution, nature, and proportions of favorable, unfavorable, and neutral terms in the given work. While admiring the drastic aims of a Dostoevsky, we turn with relief to a Chekhov, whose modes of exasperation range from the hilarious to the moody, but who consistently aims to avoid the very effects that Dostoevsky aims to produce. Aristophanic burlesque was replaced by Menander's sentimental comedy of errors, an elaborate adding of tangle to tangle until all came out benevolently at the end. The picturesque assortment of rogues in Ben Jonson is a different world (representing different "perfections") from the prim, subdued comedy of Jane Austen. Tartuffe is a kind of "comedy" built around a kind of villain close to melodrama (not a butt of derision but almost an Iago in the scope of his viciousness). And so on.

Our point is: One might undertake to show how each such art is derivative (as a development out of some previous art) or prophetic (as a forerunner of something that developed out of it. But from the standpoint of *Poetics*, the rules of "derivation" are of an essentially different sort. Each species has aims intrinsic to itself. The *Poetics* remains remarkable because Aristotle makes this problem clear by so exemplarily solving it in the case he is discussing.

Should criticism, then, but try to do the same job on all other species? Beyond doubt, it would be a worthy cause. For in the effort critics would correct the current catch-as-catch-can procedures which might be pardoned as a concession to human weakness, but which are usually put forward as something to be *desired*. The attempt to codify principles, as Professor Fontenrose has codified his views on the combat myth, would be a notable step forward, but one for which I find slight reason to have hopes, literary criticism being the haphazard pursuit it now generally is and is expected to be.

However, in my zeal I should not be too thorough. For it is true that much tentativeness is now called for. The problem of man as the symbol-using animal is *not* a subject to be treated as *settled*. And the risk in the "entelechial" approach is that it may maneuver us into too great love for the "finishedness" of such a method.

But beyond all procedures and observations there looms the vexingly unsettled question, "Just what does it mean, to be the symbol-using animal?"

Close to the essence of this animal is the problem of the negative, of words for nothing, minus, thou-shalt-not, hence the yes-and-no of "polar" terms which, since man is an organism living in time whereas logical relations as such are timeless, can provide mythic-narrative equivalents for nontemporal aspects of symbolism (equivalents which, if pursued persistently enough, are found to track back upon themselves, thus ultimately denying the very progression whereby they seemed to progress).

But along with the problem of the "slain" principle's "immortal" survival (involving the guilt-laden paradox whereby each new law implies new crimes, each rule its corresponding misrule), there is the further logological fact that the "cosmos" of every clear definition fades into a "chaos" of implications, making a "chaos of clear ideas" that lead from one to another in an endless circle, and are best symbolized by the mythic design of the serpent Ouroboros with his own tail in his mouth (I started to say "like a dictionary"!). The thought of such "formlessness," such a Daedalian maze, lurking behind the paradigms leads to considerations on which we shall end this essay.

X

When discussing ways in which at Delphi Dionysos merged with Python, Fontenrose observes (p. 380): "It may be true that both alike are derived from an ancient Mediterranean deity who assumed a different name and complexion in every region, perhaps in every village, and that the cult and name of Dionysos spread out from its native land and absorbed many of the cults that had worshipped the ancient god under other names."

The conjecture but carries one step farther the author's decision (already quoted) to use the name Python "merely as a convenient designation for Apollo's opponent without regard to sex or species." And it involves fascinating possibilities with regard to the hazy relationship between polytheism and monotheism. For in effect it is suggesting a development whereby one god split into many.

As regards the sheer dialectics of the case, is monotheism as monotheistic as we usually take it to be, and polytheism as polytheistic? Are the Jewish Yahweh, Islam's Allah, the Johannine Logos, and the Roman Deus Dominus all the "same God" under different names? Or, within Christianity, is there no difference between the God of a devout Catholic and the God of Jehovah's Witnesses, no difference between the benign God of a Unitarian and a severe, Calvinistic God who condemns many wretched mortals to hellish suffering eternally? Or if the idea of "one" God spreads over many areas, and if that "one" God is necessarily conceived within the terms peculiar to each particular area, is this situation to be viewed as no different from, say, the choice of *Baum* or *arbre*, depending upon whether you would speak of trees to a German or a Frenchman?

The history of Mediterranean paganism is the history of gods whose attributes variously overlap upon one another, variously merging and dividing like language itself, with its many modes of "condensation" and "displacement" (modes of transformation not at all confined to the symbolism of myth, dream, and neurosis, but also present in symbol systems at their most mature stage of development). The polytheistic nomenclature provided resources whereby any motive, habit, habitat, natural power, institution, or means of livelihood could by linguistic abstraction become a "god." Often the process was hardly more than the effect we get by capitalizing a word, writing "Thunder" instead of "thunder," plus mythic personifying of such abstractions. Where we might go from "finance" to "Finance," polytheism could readily go a step further, to the personal god, Plutus. In brief, polytheism could easily designate as gods many motives which monotheism would tend rather to define "a-theistically," yet monotheistic theologians are wont to warn that men "make gods" of many such "godless" things, a proclivity which we might at least call "moral polytheism," as distinct from an out-and-out ontological variety.

On the other hand, the polytheistic personifying of motives made possible a kind of duplication that in turn pointed in the direction of monotheism. For if a desire could be either just that, or the action of a god of Desire, here was a situation whereby the gods were profundly implicated in one another, since every personal motive experienced by them could also be treated as the action of whatever god was most directly associated with that motive (a situation whereby in effect two gods would be one). Conversely, one god becomes two when the Homeric epithet for Ares, "Warlike" (*enyalios*) is treated by later authors as a separate person, a subaltern of Ares.

Also, obviously, where a combat myth figured, along with the fact that all gods had to be propitiated there were further incentives for traits to overlap. Before we ever get to the ultimate problem of polar terms, there is the comparatively superficial fact that ambiguities and shifts of allegiance could confuse the allocation of favored and unfavored attributes. Hence, when all the versions and variants of a myth are collated, from sources that did not all represent the same attitude towards a given combat, Champion and Enemy are found to overlap, with corresponding confusion as regards the "perfect" distinction between "favored" and "unfavored" contestant.

Hellenistic imperialism itself also provided a step towards the "monotheizing of polytheism" in that it tended to treat all gods simply as regional motives, each of which could be represented by its appropriate temple in the capital city. Such convergence of outlying deities provided a visual incentive for the sort of thinking that could culminate in the idea of a temple to "The Unknown God." And this idea in turn could culminate in Paul's assurance to the Greeks that he represented precisely that God, the *Deus absconditus* of nascent Christian *trinitarian* monotheism.

But above all, *note this sheerly linguistic fact*: Whatever else gods are or are not, they are *terms*. And as terms their nature is such that, when you put all the gods together, you get a group with one overall trait in common: Each of the many gods is divine, godly. Thus all the polytheistic nouns merge into one common monotheistic adjective.

So far as Greek was concerned, this adjective in turn could be transformed into a neuter noun, "the divine" (*to theîon*). The same word, astoundingly enough, also meant brimstone—and the related verb, *theióō*, meant: to smoke with brimstone, to fumigate, hence to purify, to hallow. This range of meanings seems spontaneously to bring dragon and champion together!

But note one further significant fact about a word for the "divine." However generalized the idea of any particular god may be (as a term for powers or motives), the idea of the "divine" is still more highly generalized, since all words for particular deities could be classed under this one head. But central to our theory of words is our concern with the mythic tendency to state logical priority in terms of the temporally prior, to define principles in terms of the primordial. Following this pattern, the "mythic" way to say that the one principle of the divine is logically prior to particular examples of it would be to say that monotheism "came first" and was broken down into polytheism, when the unitary principle of godhead got different names (and eventually different attributes) in different places.

Thus, as seen from the logological point of view, you can "begin with" either monotheism or polytheism, depending upon whether you would stress the element of "the divine" that all gods have in common, or the theological differences that characterize people and peoples who supposedly worship the same God.

We are not here discussing a question of theology as such. For present purposes, our concern is with the turn from *mythos* to *logos* (both of them originally words for "word")—and thus from mythology to logology. We are trying to show how, as the approach through *mythology* led to overall generalizations in mythic terms of Love and Death, so an approach through *logology* leads to overall generalizations in dialectical terms of composition and division, as shaped by the role of the negative and its translation into quasi-temporal terms of narrative combat. The problems of generalization underlying Fontenrose's paradigms, his reduction to Eros and Thanatos, his generalized use of the term "Python," and his thoughts on a unitary principle of godhead possibly underlying the names for many gods, thus are seen to reach their peculiar kind of "perfection" in speculations on the shifting relation between polytheism and monotheism.

The book we have been considering (and using as our point of departure!) is so thorough, it admirably helps us to confront these issues. Thus, in closing, we would again admonish that we have been attempting to *use* the book, not to argue with it. If peace is ever to be attained in this world, it will be attained through an educational system that can systematically study the principles underlying precisely the ways whereby man, the symbol-using animal, makes his peculiar contributions to the "combat myth," in all its variations.

Chapter Six

Medium as "Message"

Some thoughts on Marshall McLuhan's *Understanding Media: The Extensions of Man* (and, secondarily, on *The Gutenberg Galaxy*)[1]

There are many loci of motives. For instance, an act may be attributed to the nature of the agent; Marxists lay major stress upon the motivating force of the "objective situation" (the Dramatistic nomenclature would call it "scene"); McLuhan's book on "media" necessarily puts the main emphasis upon the role of *instruments* (means, agencies) in shaping human dispositions, or attitudes and habits. And though men's technical innovations are but a fraction of the "human condition" in general, the great clutter of such things that characterize modern life adds up to a formative background. Thus, we confront the pragmatistic trend I discussed in my *Grammar of Motives*, whereby the accumulation of agencies becomes viewed as the major aspect of man's motivating scenes (or, as I put it in my Definition, man is "separated from his natural condition by instruments of his own making").

But though McLuhan's title features Agency as a locus of motivation, his subtitle provides a different twist. The agencies, in turn, are derived from the *agent* (namely "Man"). Thus, as the title suggests a brand of *pragmatism*, the subtitle suggests a somewhat *idealistic* modifier. (As explained in my *Grammar*, the Dramatistic perspective classes as "idealistic" all terminologies that have for their *Ausgangspunkt* some intrinsic aspect of "man" or his "consciousness.") But even here, the initial pragmatist emphasis ultimately prevails to the extent that by "extensions" is meant such instruments as are to be found *primarily* in our technical devices, such as wheels, printing presses, radio, television. (I say "primarily" because the category has some vague edges. For instance, there is a chapter on Games as extensions of man; and language is called "a human technology." But it is typical of McLuhan that whereas, from the full Dramatistic point of view, one would necessarily include a chapter on "War" when discussing the problems

---

[1] Much of this material parallels part of a paper on "Dramatism" presented at the Second International Symposium on Communication Theory and Research, 1966, the proceedings to be published in a volume edited by Lee Thayer and issued by Spartan Books, Washington, D. C.

of human culture, he writes instead on "Weapons." This shift permits him to end on the sunshine thought that "weaponry is a self-liquidating fact," whereas alas! a fully developed Dramatistic way of meditating on such matters goads us to realize that *any* new power, or mode of control (such as control over the weather) is potentially an instrument of war.

Obviously, when man's "extensions" are viewed thus narrowly, insofar as most of the instruments considered are physical (things in the realm of sheer *motion*), they will be viewed as extensions of human *physiology*. But this pattern is impaired somewhat, and for the better, in the chapters on language and games, which impinge upon the Dramatistic in the full sense of the term. (Basically, I am contending that since Agency is one member of the Dramatistic pentad, McLuhan's bright book is at least inconsistent enough to keep straying beyond the realm of motion into the realm of action—and, of course, this step shows up most clearly when he turns from such mere technical mechanisms as the *wheel* to such media as newspapers printed on a rotary press.)

The word "dramatic" keeps turning up at many points in the text, and at least once there is a shallow reference to the "cathartic." But drama and its motives get head-on treatment in only about three pages of the chapter on games. This omission is particularly important because the stress upon the media in the narrower sense reduces to a minimum such considerations as we find in *The Gutenberg Galaxy* (with regard to the dialectical nature of the medieval manuscript). Fundamentally, the term "extensions" is used along these lines: Instruments prior to the "electric" age are said to have been extensions of *particular* bodily parts (such as eye, hand, or foot), but the inventions of the new "electric age" differ from those to the extent that electricity is viewed as an extension of the "central nervous system" in general. This distinction serves as a quasiphysical basis for McLuhan's claim that the electric media (by "extending" the nature of the nervous system *in general*) will eliminate tendencies toward specialization characteristic of the earlier "mechanical" inventions that were extensions of *particular* bodily parts.

We should introduce two admonitions here. First, we should note that man's symbolic prowess in general is not derived from particular bodily parts, but in its own way reflects the central nervous system as source. Hence, throughout the whole era of "mechanical" specialization, there has been a realm of motives grounded (by his scheme) in physiological beginnings that *naturally transcend* such specialization, even though it may include specialized terminologies. (I would contend, of course, that McLuhan's great skimping on *drama* as a "medium" necessarily leads to an overly simplified view of media in general and their role in our culture.) I would also call it to your attention that although many human inventions conceivably might *not* be "extensions" of the human body, the whole subject is sufficiently vague to allow for McLuhan's mediumistic genealogy. I mean: Maybe the sight of birds flying is what induced man to try and invent flying machines. Nevertheless, by McLuhan's derivation the airplane would be an "extension" of the human body. A club could be thought of as a kind of "extended" arm and fist; but when McLuhan puts major emphasis upon the notion that the wheel is an extension of the feet, I can't help recalling a newspaper dispatch that observed: "Your body contains virtually every engineering device except the wheel." And it gave this list: "The cylinder, ball joint, dome, tripod, hinge and reinforcing beam." But no matter. What is really involved here, as viewed from the standpoint of sheerly terministic resources, is: If, instead of saying that certain media are *analogous* to parts of the body, you say that they are "extensions" of such parts, and if you allow for great latitude in the use of analogy, anything will fit in somewhere. In fact, since the body is itself an aspect of nature, and thus embodies the same kinds of goings-on that we can observe in other parts of nature, even if an invention did happen to arise from observation of nature rather than by "extension" of the inventor's body, lax rules for the application of analogy here would allow you to find some analogical process in the body itself—whereupon, in keeping with the prime resources of the McLuhan nomenclature, you could call such an *analogy with* the body an "extension of" the body, that is to say a *derivation from* the body. The wheel could conceivably have been derived from looking at a disk like the sun or moon; or it might conceivably have been derived by slicing a log, or whatever. The main point is that even though the body has no wheel, this major invention in McLuhan's scheme is, by terministic fiat, derived from the "circular" motion of the feet (a derivation made easy by the fact that if you treat analogy with latitude enough, the *repetition* of a *reciprocating* motion can be called "circular," or even more broadly, the regular repetition of *anything* can be called "circular"). To haggle with McLuhan on this point is necessarily a waste of time. All we should do is recognize what's going on here. And what *is* going on? Simply this: Any analogy, however lax, between an invented medium and some part of the human body can be presented as an "extension" of that part, whether or not it actually is so. We here confront a mere matter of terministic policy. And since the body does, beyond question, affect our thinking by providing us with analogies, to that extent the policy can serve. We'd go along with him, just for the ride, were it not that he later uses this terministic device to the ends of faulty interpretation as regards our current quandaries. On that point, more anon.

But here we need a brief interpolation; namely: Suppose you ground the whole thing, as McLuhan does, in a distinction between the "mechanical" wheel and an "electric age" that wholly transcends the old-fashioned era of the wheel, an era that rejects both wheel and mechanism. Then suppose that, on looking up the definition of an *electric* dynamo, you learn that this *new-age medium* is defined (italics ours) as "a *machine* for converting *mechanical* into electric energy by *rotating* coils of copper wire in a magnetic field." In brief, all these electric dynamos are *machines* that *rotate*. Yet the new "electric age" is to be presented as *antithetical* to the "mechanical" and the "rotatory" (the wheel). No matter. All you need do is say that the wheel is "obsolescent," or "in principle" obsolete.

But to the key formula, "The medium is the message." And we should keep to it, not allowing the book to dodge it, even though I heard McLuhan over the air engagingly suggest that maybe one had better change "message" to "massage." If he wants to rewrite his book by revising all his chapters in keeping with this pun, and thus showing that all media, or "extensions of man," are best understood as variations on the art of massage, I'll gladly read it. Indeed, I can even glimpse some ribald fun here, based on lewd conceits about a man's extension. But in the meantime, let's cling to the formula as given in the book now before us. The first implication of the formula is obvious enough, and McLuhan recognizes it when he summarily dismisses any and all who would approach a message in terms of "content analysis." If the *medium* is the message, obviously the important thing is not what somebody *says* in a given medium, but what medium he uses, regardless of what he says. Since this oversimplification is the very soul of *his* message, we must never let it get out of sight when considering his book. Though we all may disagree as to just what the effects of men's accumulated media are, anyone of intelligence recognizes that media must have had great effects of some kind upon our thinking, so that they have become a kind of "second nature" with us. McLuhan here profits considerably by a recent increase in the ambiguity of the words "information" and "communication." If you give someone a hard blow on the head, this "happening" can now be classed as a kind of "information" that is physically "communicated" to the nervous centers of the victim's brain. Hence, whatever the difference between an electric light and a comic book, or between a chemical and the "iconic" image on a television screen, all can be classed as media in McLuhan's nomenclature. And he keeps incidentally talking about "forms" in ways that would cover the same range (a point to which I shall revert when discussing Lessing's *Laocoon*—for I believe that even a mere glance at that book quickly makes clear the fatal fallacy in McLuhan's formula). And, of course, stress upon media as such fits in well with current hankerings after various kinds of "nonobjective" or "nonrepresentational" art (trends that are justifiable responses to the many new textures and materials supplied by modern technology).

The medium is the message. Hence, down with content analysis. We should at least pause en route to note that the formula lends itself readily to caricature. Primus rushes up breathlessly to his friend Secundus, shouting, "I have a drastic message for you. It's about your worst enemy. He is armed and raging and is—" whereupon Secundus interrupts: "Please! Let's get down to business. Who cares about the contents of a message? My lad, hasn't McLuhan made it clear to you? The *medium* is the message. So quick, tell me the really crucial point. I don't care what the news is. What I want to know is: Did it come by telegraph, telephone, wireless, radio, TV, semaphore signals, or word of mouth?" The moral of my tale is simple. Though McLuhan's quixotic formula serves well as a slogan, any such over-simplification is likely to show up, sooner or later, as a flat contradiction. Hence, after outlawing "content analysis" as an approach to the effects of media, toward the end of his book he comes close to a terministic orgy in his enthusiasm for "information-gathering." But if the "information" that is fed into an electric computer isn't "content," what is it? The issue always keeps turning up in the most amusing fashion when McLuhan is being questioned. For, inevitably, he is questioned about the *contents* of his position, whether these contents are being considered in his book, or in class-room discussion, or on radio or television. And it's fun to watch how he somehow manages to dodge his questioners. For he uses question periods not as opportunities to make his position more precise, but rather as chal-lenges that he must deflect and confuse to the best of his ability (which along these lines is considerable).

Looked at most broadly, I think his terministic lineup can be seen to operate thus: Viewing technological development in terms of a *continuum*, one might note how invention has progressed pari passu with the increase of specialization. And one might conclude that the growth of specialization will continue, though modern trends (in automation and computers) might greatly modify its nature. Or one might use a terminology that introduces a principle of *discontinuity*. Thus instead of discussing the "overall situation" in terms of technology in general, one might propose a distinction between two kinds or eras of technology. McLuhan's terms opt for this latter policy. He builds everything around a radical distinction between an earlier "me-chanical" stage of technology and a presently emergent "electric age." And whereas the "mechanical" stage led to extreme division of labor, he promises that in the "electric age" this tendency toward "specialism" will be reversed. The earlier "explosion" becomes an "implosion," which is somehow some-thing quite different, despite the great *expansion* of markets for the new electric devices (and I leave it for the reader to decide whether we might compromise on simple "plosion"). By talk of the new electric age's pen-chant for "information-gathering" (of data to be fed into computers) he uses this overall titular term to suggest that all specialization dissolves in this single common task. True, information gathered from many diverse sources can be fed into a computer; and the results will transcend the limits of any specialized pursuit (except, of course, the highly specialized pursuits that have to do with the programming and perfecting of computers). But what of the information itself? Would not chemical data require specialized knowledge of chemistry; biological data, specialists in biology; etc.? Though the computer may "process" such material in ways hitherto impossible, the treatment of the data does not at all eliminate the need for specialists to gather it. Now that any and every animate and inanimate process in all the world can be classed as a kind of "information," we must not let McLuhan use the term to suggest that merely because it can be applied to all "information-gathering," all information-gatherers would be engaged in an identical enterprise. McLuhan rightly becomes zestful in his use of the term; for high among its "subliminal" effects (if we may adapt a favorite word of his for a different purpose) is its ability to deflect the reader's attention away from the question: *Insofar as technology, under any form, produces a great diversity of media, must there not be a corresponding diversity of occupations concerned with the production, distribution, and servicing of such varied devices (whether they are in the realm of communication specifically or are to be classed as economic commodities in general)?* In sum: The highly generalized nature of his sheer *term*, "information-gathering," conceals the fact that a whole army of specialists will be needed to supply the analytic material that the computers presumably will synthesize after their fashion (*and within their limits*).

Though, as with "dramatic," the book contains many passing references to language, here again it skimps, as regards the full range of the Dramatistic nomenclature. For instance, by linking perspective with "point of view" in the *literal* sense, McLuhan can persuasively advance the notion that certain new media present a kind of "mosaic" not characterized by "point of view." Hence he can treat "point of view" as obsolescent, along with the kinds of individualism and specialism that marked its rise (in connection with the developments of printing). But tactics of that sort "subliminally" conceal from us the strictly terministic fact that any particular nomenclature (such as the one used in McLuhan's book) *functions* as a "perspective," or "point of view"; and to idealize a problem in its particular terms is to consider the problem *from that special angle of approach.* McLuhan's own book is, of course, a case in point—just as, similarly, while writing a monologue, he asks for the kinds of tolerance that would belong to a dialogue.

Similarly, he will talk about "repeatability" as though it were simply a matter of mass production by machines. But a more methodically *terministic* approach to his thesis would remind him that there is also a prior kind of "repeatability" intrinsic to the very nature of terministic generalization. Give me the *word* "wheel," for instance, and I thereby have a principle of repeatability much more extensive than the mass productions of any printing press or assembly line. For the word applies to every wheel-like thing that ever has been, will be, or could be—and all the more so, if you will add to

the rules for McLuhan's nomenclature a "variance" whereby even reciprocating motion can be classed as "rotatory." Yet surely not a machine, but the
broad relevance of such generalized terms in his nomenclature is what induces McLuhan so often to repeat the word "repeatable" when he is promising that in his "electric age" this touchstone of the "mechanical" will cease
to prevail.

Since practically any artifact can be classed as a medium, and the
current widened use of the term "communication" allows McLuhan to
treat any such invention as a medium of *communication*, we might here
propose a working distinction, for present purposes. We might speak of
directly communicative media (such as telephones or television) and *indirectly* communicative media (in the broad sense that cars, refrigerators,
foods, clothing, and guns could be called communicative). "Forms" would
extend things further (as with the difference between television as a medium
of communication and soap opera as a medium of communication). Here's
where we get to Lessing's *Laocoon*. I submit that had McLuhan taken that
text to heart, he would have had a much better chance of arriving at a
properly matured revision of his slogan, "The medium is the message."
Under Lessing's guidance, with regard to *directly* communicative media
and their tie-in with particular forms, or artistic modes, McLuhan could
have systematically asked himself *just what kind of content* is favored by
the peculiar nature of a given medium. Actually, the sheer pressure of his
subject matter does impose such a procedure upon McLuhan at many points.
For instance, in *Understanding Media* we find him concerning himself with
the notion that one kind of character is a better fit for television, another
kind a better fit for radio. That's the way he should have proceeded throughout, rather than merely admitting such observations without explicitly recognizing that they imply the need for the revision of his slogan (whereas the
inaccuracy of that slogan served instead to keep him from recognizing exactly what all his concern with media did imply). In brief, as Lessing shows:
The point is not that a given medium (in the sense of a directly communicative form) does its full work upon us *without* the element of "content."
Rather, his study of the difference between painting (or sculpture) and
poetry indicates how expert practitioners of a given medium may resort to
the kind of contents that the given medium is best equipped to exploit. Obviously, as so approached, the issue is quite different from the blunt proposition that "the medium is the message." Yet McLuhan's muddled method
does have one advantage, rhetorically. For it seems to have caught the attention in ways that Lessing's kind of treatment can no longer match.

McLuhan is prominent among current idea-men whose thought-style
might be summed up as: "Down with the political, up with the apocalyptic."
And there's no denying: It's much more pleasant to speculate about the
possible subliminal magic of "participation in depth" when looking at the

iconic image (any image) on a television screen than to suffer the burden
of an explicit analysis concerned with the miseducation clearly implicit in
the contents of particular programs that line people up by exploiting one set
of "topics" rather than another in the concocting of their motivational
recipes. Incidentally, there's a news program that I regularly follow with
some confidence; yet I can't help worrying about the fact that it is sponsored
by the damnedest batch of poisons and quack drugs, so I keep fearing that
the show is somehow being built up for a sellout, come the strategic moment.
In any case, whether you like it or not, we are here concerned with the
contents of the programs and the ads, and not just the nature of the *medium*,
in the sense of the "mosaic" screen on which they are shown, whatever its
"subliminal" effects may be.

One could go on and on. But two more points should be enough for
now. First, there's the problem of the "visual," and its corresponding effects
in promoting a "lineal" point of view. I question whether most readers
have got that matter clear. Or maybe I'm the one that has it wrong. I see it
thus: One could hardly say with conviction that "lineal" thinking is essentially due to the lineal nature of phonetic writing. Other kinds of writing
follow in a sequence, too, since sentences (like melody) are sequential, in
contrast with a picture or piece of sculpture (which is "all there at once").
Codes of literary and musical notation allow us to approach the overall
form of a work step-by-step, but the relation among the parts "just *is*,"
nontemporally. On the other hand, works such as painting and sculpture
first confront us in their totality, then we impart a kind of temporal order
to them by letting the eye rove over them analytically, thus endowing them
with many tiny "histories" as we go from one part to another, feeling the
developments and the relationships among the parts. But although no work
can come to life as an artistic medium unless we, by our modes of interpretation, sympathetically and "empathetically" (or "imaginatively") endow its *positions* and *motions* with the quality of *action*, there is a notable
difference between paintings or sculpture on one side and notations for
words or music on the other. The colors and forms of the "static" media
(painting and sculpture) appeal to us directly, sensuously, as they are,
right there in front of us. But codes of literary or musical notation do not
thus directly appeal. Rather, they are but *instructions* for performing,
whereas painting and sculpture are themselves performances, as a drama
is, not when read, but when actually witnessed in a theater. In this sense,
such "instructions" need not have the "tactility" of painting and sculpture.
True, insofar as type is actually designed for its visual appeal, to this extent
it *is* "tactile." And, ironically enough, it is the sheer data fed into computers
(without either visual beauty or appeal as language and melody) that lack
"tactility," though McLuhan tries to make up the difference by hailing
electricity as a "biological form," and talking about the electronic "scanning

finger" of a digital computer in terms of "forms" that "caress the contours of every kind of being." (The basic trick about McLuhan's "extensions" of man resides in the fact that his rhetoric induces you to forget their wholly *nonhuman* nature, albeit that humans can make their human inventions be "as though" human. To grasp this issue clearly, consider the notable difference between an "extension" of man in the sense of the wheel, and an "extension" in the sense of human offspring, or less immediately, such complexly developed artistic *forms* as drama, dance, song.) Be that as it may, this entire set of responses should be distinguished from a different kind of visuality, as when, for instance, one transforms sounds into a sheerly visual pattern. Ironically enough, many typical *electric* devices such as the cardiograph or the oscilloscope have added notably to such possibilities; yet McLuhan is probably correct when he says that writing provided a big step forward in such modes of translation (though I personally can't see why a fairly imaginative savage couldn't have picked up "lineal" thinking through the sheer problem of tracking an animal's footprints in the sand, with corresponding recognition that this sheerly *spatial* series represented a *temporal sequence*, depending on the direction in which the animal's traces showed it to be moving). But in any case, I see no reason to object if phonetic script and phonetic printing are given special credit, or blame, for such "lineality" of placement with regard to nonlineal matters, while bearing it in mind that McLuhan himself gives us a lineal theory of the steps into the mechanical age and through it into the electric age. Maybe he'd probingly concede that on this score, his own book (in being printed) is necessarily a somewhat obsolescent way of heralding the anti-Gutenberg future; or maybe not. The main point is this: Unless you are willing to worry through all those considerations I have listed, I question whether you can accurately deal with what McLuhan's quite reasonable speculations on print actually boil down to.

And the final point: There is a sense in which I have been most unfair to our author and his in many ways admirable volumes. For though I would contend that his skimping as regards the Dramatistic perspective in its fullness greatly misrepresents the scope and center of our necessary major worries, and though I would particularly protest if such a truncated scheme is allowed to look as though it really could cover the ground, I must concede that his books (particularly as modified by the many borrowings in *The Gutenberg Galaxy* which he seems to forget in *Understanding Media*) are often incidentally incisive and delightful. Though I seriously question whether his basic slogan would ever allow you to put that puzzle together, McLuhan's admirers have already demonstrated that one can make pretty playthings of the bits.

Chapter Seven

A Dramatistic View of the Origins of Language and Postscripts on the Negative

SECTION ONE

Le néant n'est qu'un mot. Dictionnaire des Sciences Philoso-
phiques.
*Die Bejahung ist erst die Verneinung einer Verneinung. Fritz
Mauthner,* Wörterbuch der Philosophie.
Let your communication be Yea, yea; Nay, nay. Matthew v. 37

I
The Negative as a Marvel of Language

This chapter is a kind of *tour de force*, locating the specific nature of
language in the ability to use the Negative. We are obviously indebted
to Bergson's remarks in *Creative Evolution,* on "The Idea of 'Nothing.' "
But whereas Bergson is aiming primarily to buttress his notions about
"pseudo-problems" in philosophy, we are adapting his concerns to linguistic analysis.

Bergson points out that there are no "negative" conditions in nature.
Every situation is positively what it is. For instance, we may *say,* "The
ground is *not* damp." But the corresponding actual conditions in nature are
those whereby the ground *is* dry. We may say that something "is not" in
such and such a place. But so far as nature is concerned, whatever "is not"
here is positively somewhere else; or, if it does not exist, then other things
actually occupy all places where it "is not."

There are many notable aspects of language, such as classification,
specification, abstraction, which have their analogues in purely nonverbal
behavior. But the negative is a peculiarly linguistic resource. And because it
is so peculiarly linguistic, the study of man as the specifically word-using
animal requires special attention to this distinctive marvel, the negative.

Consider the *via negationis* in theology; or those related projects in
which "non-being" is taken as the ground of being (cf. Boehme's *Ungrund,*
or even Kant's dialectic whereby, having summed up the positive world as
the "conditioned," he grounds this in the idea of God as the "uncondi-

tioned"); or Spinoza's strategic definition in his *Ethics*, "all determination is negation"; or Hegel's principle of Negativity, proclaimed in his *Phenomenology of Mind* as the character of existence; or the adaptation of this in the Marxist dialectic.

There might even be a sense in which we could derive the linguistic faculty itself from the ability to use the Negative *qua* Negative. Or, insofar as this statement must be modified, once we have made the proper allowances we may find that we are still left with some basic insights into the nature of language, and of human relations as shaped by language. In line with these observations, which seem to us not only solid but fertile, we would like to spin some tentative theories built around the following proposition: *The essential distinction between the verbal and the nonverbal is in the fact that language adds the peculiar possibility of the Negative.* We hope to show how the Negative developed from earlier forms and to indicate the many areas in which it operates. We shall later attempt to analyze some typical passages in the light of the Negative.

II
Verbal Realism and the Negative

The problem of the negative is complicated by confusions in linguistic usage. For instance, if you say, "There are no negatives in nature," someone might ask in rebuttal, "Then how about negative electricity? Isn't that as 'natural' as positive electricity?"

Yes, there is the positive phenomenon called "negative electricity." But it might just as fittingly have been called "cathodic electricity," since it appears at the so-called "negative" pole, which is also called a "cathode." And sometimes it actually is called "resinous electricity." Or it might have been called "positive" electricity, whereat the positive kind could have been called "negative" or "anodic."

If you arbitrarily called an entrance "positive," then by the same token an exit might be called "negative"; but there is nothing intrinsically more positive about one than about the other. Either is defined by exactly the set of conditions that make up its positive existence or function. A ditch is as positive as a dyke, though each might be classed as a "negation" of the other.

Since language so often applies the negative to physical conditions, we tend to think that the conditions really are a kind of "negative" in their actual nature. But Bergson makes it quite clear how such *apparent* kinds of negativity can come to be. For instance, if you are *expecting* something to be damp and it is found to be dry, then its dryness is expressible not just as dryness, but as the *negation of your expectation* (as "not wet"). Or, if you wanted a thermometer to show 32, then any and every other reading could be classed as "not 32," though each such reading would be exactly what it positively was.

A great many terms like *opposition, antithesis, alternation, contrast, contradiction, reciprocation, balance,* and even *succession* can be summed up as pairs of elements or processes that "negate" each other. There is no difficulty here, if you employ the terms under properly controlled dialectical conditions, discounting them for their linguistic factor. For instance, if we make a distinction between personal "action" and mechanical "motion," we can discount for language when somebody referred to "the action of a motor." There is a brand of naïve verbal realism, always ready to permeate any terminology. For instance, whereas there is nothing in Marxist "dialectical materialism" as such to require that the concept of negativity be interpreted literally, as though some situations in nature actually *said "no"* to others, the linguistic usage itself can be confused with a state of nature.

All told, the metaphorical resources of language being what they are, we can comfortably say that a man walks down the street by motions whereby one foot "negates" the other; or we can speak of the reciprocal motions as acting to produce out of their antitheses a synthesis. Or, though all natural conditions are positively, materially, what they are, we might say that the bud "negates" the blossom, or that the day "negates" the night. And particularly, as Bergson helps us see, we may use such expressions where intention or expectation is involved.

III
The Perfect Dramatistic Starting Point

By a "Dramatistic" approach to the negative, as contrasted with the somewhat "Scientist" emphasis in Bergson, we mean: Whereas Bergson starts from problems of truth or falsity, we start from problems of action. Each approach obviously involves the other. And the situation is further complicated by the fact that Bergson's point about the importance of *expectation* in the functioning of the negative is, in our terms, quite "Dramatistic."

Bergson approaches the problem of the negative in terms of the negative *proposition*; but we would approach it in terms of the negative *command*. Where he would build his analysis of the negative about a sentence in the indicative mood, such as "The thing is not here," we would build ours about a sentence in the imperative, such as "Do not do that." We would say that the negative must have begun as a rhetorical or hortatory function, *as with the negatives of the Ten Commandments.*

And we would call ourselves "Dramatist" rather than "Scientist" because, whereas there are many places in Bergson's analysis that fit beautifully with such a thesis, it nowhere breaks through clearly to such an example. Bergson's account contains many references to the admonitory, or pedagogical, or social origins of the negative. And you see how the pragmatistic strand in his thinking helps him in this direction. He also includes a citation from Kant similarly pointed: "The peculiar function of negative propositions is simply to prevent error."

But the ultimate necessary step is missing, because Bergson does not make the final readjustment required by his own theories. For if he is going to stress the *admonitory* function of the negative, or its use "to prevent error," then by the rules of Dramatism he *should look for the most thorough kind of admonition*, the *completion or perfection of the admonitory*, the admonition of admonitions. And where would such *fulfillment* of the admonitory be but in the thou-shalt-not's of the Decalogue?

By our "Dramatist" approach, we leap to such a form as the "essence" of the negative. The steps are these: (1) A totally formalist approach might try to deal with "negative propositions" as such; (2) a "scientist" approach might incline to bring out their use in giving information or instruction; (3) an anthropologically pragmatist approach might widen the notion of informative usefulness by such social terms as *admonitory* and *pedagogical*; (4) a Dramatistic approach would look for the "essential" instance of an admonitory or pedagogical negative—and it would find this to perfection in the negatives of the Ten Commandments. Hence we would "start" in the thought of the negative command. Such reduction to the "Complete Hortatory Negative" has its special kind of simplicity, to be distinguished from atomistic reduction.

IV

The "Positive Pre-Negative"

Unfortunately, however, as soon as we decide on such Codification of Conscience for our model of the Perfect Negative, we find another shift necessary. Though we want to derive the very essence of language from the ability to use the negative as negative, and though we derive the very essence of the negative from the form of the negative commandments, we must ask whether the negative need originally have been such at all.

There are several grounds for thinking of this possibility. If the negative of command is a perfection, or flowering, then by the same token we might well expect that it itself *evolved* from a form relatively imperfect. Further, the imperative negative being closely interwoven with the "sense of right and wrong" that is taken as the mark of mature "reason," one might look for its origins in a "more unreasoning" form. Third (a very weak third, but not to be too promptly dismissed), the "One" family and the "No" family do seem surprisingly close for words so logically at odds. There is the fact that something of great price can be called "priceless," that double negatives sometimes cancel out and sometimes intensify the negative, that Latin and Greek verbs of fearing reverse the normal indicative use of negatives. Nor is it hard to see how the Latin words for *with* and *against* (*cum* and *contra*) can come from the same root, when we think of these two usages in English: "I fought with the enemy; I fought with my friends against the enemy"; and *contra* in the sense of "over against" or "in contact with" has given us the word *country*.

So, at least tentatively, we try to imagine the possibility of an original purely *positive* kind of negative, one closer to those conditions of nature in which there is no negative of the peculiarly linguistic sort.[1]

Dramatistically, in our ideal Genealogy of the Negative, the primal ancestor would be closer to a verb than to any other part of speech. At least, it would be verbal in the sense that it had strongly *imperative* or *hortatory* connotations, and grammarians usually grant such functions only to verbal modes. Such a "pre-negative" verb could have been a mere tonal gesture for calling-attention-to. It would have been less like a negative than like the gruntlike sounds an incipiently vocal infant makes when handing something to an adult, or when asking something of an adult, or when noticing something in which it takes an interest.

This sound would come to have a deterrent or pejorative meaning be-

---

[1] In his article on the negative, Mauthner writes: "In some era of prehistory, negation was perhaps a wholly physiological voicing of disgust and refusal, an abrupt expulsion of breath through the nostrils, probably intended to symbolize a spewing-forth of disagreeable food." From this usage, he says, it eventually assumed the grammatical form of a noun, whereupon philosophers sought ways "to make a thinkable nothing into a knowable something." Since dislikes are as sensorily real as likes, Mauthner suggests a different kind of positive as origin for the negative: the experience of purely physical revulsion (which is a negative in the *attitudinal* sense, as were we to call thumbs-up positive and thumbs-down negative). Unfortunately, his article does not consider the thou-shalt-not kind of negative. But the indications are that, if he had discussed it, he would have derived it from such sensory beginnings. For though he knows how to "dramatize" most entertainingly his treatment of philosophic terms, his point of view is predominantly "scientist," rather than "dramatistic." Dramatistically, we should not derive the linguistic negative from physical repugnance. But we should note how, once such a negative has taken form, it can on many occasions so affect the body that the violating of moralistic proscriptions may produce acute bodily distress and revulsion. Dramatistically, we watch always for ways in which bodily attitudes can affect the development of linguistic expression. (We like Paget's theory of "gesture speech" for this reason.) But we also watch for notable respects in which symbolization is an order of motives not reducible to purely nonlinguistic terms. In any case, however, we are not obliged to attempt disproving Mauthner's genealogy. It can be classed as another kind of "positive pre-negative." And it has the advantage of a more attitudinal beginning than our notion of the negative's start in an expression half-demonstrative, half-imperative. In fact, perhaps at this point we shift a bit to the "scientist" side, whereas Mauthner's feeling of disgust is more "dramatistic," through being incipiently "factional." See, Fritz Mauthner, *Wörterbuch der Philosophie* (Munich & Leipzig, 1910), II, 149-156.

cause the calling of attention to *danger* is of greater significance than the calling of attention just to *something*—somewhat as our verb *look out* usually has admonitory connotations, though it need not have. Such a "verbal demonstrative" could also be well adapted to serve as a word for *one*, insofar as forty elephants can be said to constitute "one" manifestation —or, if you will, one herd. Anything, even a conglomerate, would be a "one," if conceived as a single subject or object of attention. Or the same sound could convey the command "look," or "look out!" Distinctions among the usages could be suggested by changes in tone of voice.

Once this "verbal demonstrative" for "attitudinally calling-attention-to" had come to signify attention in the specifically sinister sense, it would be translatable by some such expressions as *Beware!* or *Caution!* Note that it would *not* be a negative in the *formal* sense at all. But it would have the *force* of a negative command, insofar as it implied: "Stop what you're doing," or "Change your ways of doing what you're doing."

We have postulated a prehistorical beginning of language in which a word such as *no* meant something positive like "Look at this," or "Look at that." Insofar as it called attention in the admonitory sense, while *implying* a negative it would still not be felt as an out-and-out negative command. It was as positive as any word like *run*, or *eat*, or *fight*, and the like, except that it had a hortatory nature which such words do not primarily possess. We can imagine it containing in germ a range of meanings as different as these: thou, look, don't, there, give, one, a, the, that.

However, once human speech had a positive word with admonitory connotations, it was well on the road towards the discovery of the peculiar genius implicit in the negative as such. We can thus readily imagine an intermediate stage during which the admonitory word came to function *like an auxiliary verb in the imperative*. In this stage, an expression like *man no run* would be literally translatable not as "the man does not run" or even as "the man should not run," but as "man beware run" or "man caution run." A little further along would be: "man stop run."

V

Later Steps in the Development of the Negative

Gradually the implied negative in connotations of deterrence would become the explicit negative of command. Yet between it and the propositional negative there would be intermediate stages. There would thus be an adaptation to ideas of fear. An expression like *No lions* would mean not "there are no lions," but "I fear lions" or "You should watch for lions." Here an observation on the evolution of Latin grammar stands us in good stead. Though we should ordinarily translate *timeo ne accidat* as "I fear lest it happen" or "I fear it may happen," we read this pregnant remark in Allen and Greenough:

With verbs of Fearing the subjunctive with *nē* is hortatory in origin: *timeō nē accidat* is literally *I fear, let it not happen.* The subjunctive with *ut* may have been either hortatory or deliberative . . .[2]

The next step would seem to involve words of *Doubt.* Here the perturbations are obvious enough even in modern English, despite its great sloughing-off of inflections. If you say in English, "I don't doubt that he won't come," one is not quite sure whether you expect him or don't expect him, though *legally* the statement says that you don't expect him.

Nevertheless terms for doubt would probably be the point at which the out-and-out propositional negative emerged. We mean that from this point on, the negative *qua* negative would be felt in a given linguistic system. It would have come of age, no longer being felt merely as a modification of admonitory verbs, but as the kind of particle used in the purely *indicative* distinction between "it is" and "it is not."

In brief, when you get to *doubt,* you're within the *scientist* area of *information.* So your next step is the outright *No* of "negative propositions" that affirm a "negative fact."

You would then be on the road to the kind of thinking that flowers in *formal definition.*

VI
"Behavioristic Pre-Language"

Implied in the use of the negative, there is both the ability to generalize and the ability to specify. That is, you cannot use the negative properly without by the same token exemplifying the two basic dialectical resources of merger and division. For you can use *no* properly only insofar as you can classify under one head many situations that are, in their positive details, quite distinct from one another. In effect, you group them under the head of "Situations all of which are classed in terms of the negative." And in the very act of so classifying, you distinguish them from another class of situations that are "*not* No-Situations."

However, classification and discrimination are not peculiarly linguistic processes. The senses classify, when they "translate" some vibrations into terms of sound, others into terms of color, or record still others as smell, etc. And insofar as each biological organism selects the kind of food proper to its species, it is in effect discriminating, making distinctions between wanted and unwanted classes of objects. The necessary limitations imposed upon a

---

[2] *Allen and Greenough's Latin Grammar*, Rev. and Enlarged by James Bradstreet Greenough, assisted by George L. Kittredge (Boston & London, 1892), n., p. 361. According to the same grammarians, the subjunctive is the adaptation of a form originally future.

biological organism in its "act of being itself" make for a kind of "behavioristic classifying."

In this rudimentary sense, a mere paucity of sense organs is enough to make a kind of "abstraction" and "classification" inevitable. Three lambs, each with a history of unique details, become reducible to sheer mutton, when we ignore their "personal histories" and abstract from the totality of their special natures the one generic quality they possess as meat. In this respect, "behavioristic classification" is like that of scales, which can abstract and record but the one quantity, weight, and hence indifferently report a man to weigh a certain amount, whether he be a genius or an imbecile.

Since any paucity in the means of recording a given situation implies *classification* and *abstraction*, there is thus a sense in which discrimination is by the same token lack of discrimination. For inasmuch as discrimination by abstraction and classification implies the ignoring of detailed differences among things bunched under the same head, discrimination is "insensitive." And "insensitiveness" of this sort is as observable in "behavioristic pre-language" as in language proper.

Every warm day is, in its particularity, distinct from every other warm day. But insofar as we sense it merely as "warm," we have classed it with many other days past and possible, distinguishing it grossly from a class of cool or cold days. The principle of classification here would seem to be the same as the principle embodied in behavioristic pre-language. Thus, if a dog barks on some occasions, whimpers on others, growls on others, grovels on others, and wags his tail on others, he has in effect "classified" these various *kinds* of situation. However, inasmuch as there are many unique details of motion on each occasion, there is the possibility that *we* are classifying more than *he*. Each time he salivates may be for him "unique," though our linguistic approach leads us rather to class all such occasions under some such general heading as "salivation-situations." It is thus possible that sensory experience in a nonverbalizing animal allows every moment of existence to be felt as *totally new*, even as successive pairs of lovers feel that they have invented love.

When we call attention to the rudiments of generalization, specification, classification, and abstraction in the conditioning and adaptations of nonlinguistic organisms, we do not mean to derive "rational" human language by a simple "graded series" from the "behavioristic pre-language" of sensation and gesture. On the contrary, we subscribe to the view that there is a "qualitative leap" between the motives of pre-language and those of language. But we are trying to narrow the gap here, in the interests of method asserting no greater differentiation than the evidence seems to justify.

We say as much while also reminding ourselves that, once a qualitative leap has been made, even those ingredients taken over from the previous structure have a new nature because of their place in a new motivational

cluster. Hence, to say that the principles of abstraction, classification, generalization, and specification (or division) are present in prelinguistic behavior is not the same as saying that their linguistic analogues are "nothing
but" more complicated variants of the prelinguistic. But we must be on
guard lest, in our zeal to make much of the negative, we give too much
credit to it in particular and to language in general because of the negative's
attribute as a peculiarity of language.

Though we would treat the motives of a specifically language-using
organism as qualitatively different from those of nonlinguistic animals,
hence not derivable by the *lex continui* from natural behavior and not reducible to such terms, we must even admit that there is a kind of purely
behavioristic negative. Either infant or animal in effect "says no" when
turning the head away from something that it does not want. Coleridge once
attributed to such a source the use of the headshake as a sign of negation.
The alternative nod, to indicate assent, might have arisen as a "negation of
this negation." For though either nod or headshake serve, to turn away the
mouth (hence though either could serve, on this basis, as a sign for negation), the other would seem to be left for the complementary sign of assent,
as the only completely "opposite" kind of gesture available.

All told, we find ourselves steering between opposite extremes of interpretation. We want to uphold an "entelechial" interpretation of language,
according to which even the simplest infantile sounds would have in them
the possibilities of linguistic *fulfillment*. Their simplest *beginnings* would
implicitly reveal their mature potentialities, if we were but discerning enough,
so that the first "nonlinguistic" cry of a language-using species could be
found to contain a motivational element not present in the first cry of a
nonlinguistic species. At the same time, we would retain an emphasis upon
the *evolutionary* processes whereby a language is built from generation to
generation by gradual accretions.

Evolution-wise, we would even incline to believe that most rudiments
of language were taught to adults by children, as the mother imitated the
child's sounds in the efforts to communicate with him. But "entelechy-wise,"
we would incline to believe that *no* was the peculiarly "mature" contribution
to language, the "moralistic" non-sensory "idea" that adults imposed upon
children. The child's brain has to be such that any moralistic "transcending"
of the sensory can gradually become understandable. In other words, there
must be the "entelechial" factor that made the "evolution of no" possible.
And once this feeling for the linguistic *no* is present, all sorts of words can
become permeated with its genius as they accumulate with the gradual
growth of language.

Though Socrates started his analysis of dialectic from the distinction
between words that put things together and words that take things apart,
and we note here an area where verbal dialectic and *Naturdialektik* overlap,

we find reason to look for a double genesis of language. For we cannot bring ourselves to say that *words* for abstracting and classifying are "nothing but" the analogous use of such principles implicit in the selectivities of purely biological behavior.

So we glimpse here two quite distinct sources for the development of language, each of them contributing in its way to linguistic enrichment. First, there would be the "scientist" source, knowledge received or perceived through the medium of the senses in their role as bearers of information. Second, there would be a "dramatistic" source, conceived in "tribal" terms that are still to be made clear. "Abstraction" would be through the "sensory," or informative line. And "generalization" would be through the *action* line. Leibnitz's equating of *substance* with *action*, and the Spinozistic equating of *substance* with *causality* would suggest the ways whereby "generalization" would involve the "tribal." For *substance* is a thoroughly "tribal" concept; and *causality* is as "tribal" as parenthood.

Sensory abstraction would yield the simple positives, a language of things and of doings and of the sensations that we typically experience in connection with them. Dramatistic generalization would yield the "idea of the negative," the "ability to distinguish between the yes and no of 'right' and 'wrong,' " in the sense not just of avoidances (such as any animal can be conditioned to) but of a thou-shalt-not which, though originally directed at someone else, is universalized to the point where it circles back upon the self—the "tribal" thus being made total.

But since the Dramatistic-tribal negative involves "reason," we should consider more fully how it compares and contrasts with the "behavioristic pre-language" that man, the verbalizing species, shares with nonverbalizing kinds of natural organisms.

VII
Image and Idea

There seems to be a kind of "behavioristic pre-language" in the sounds and posturing of animals—expressions which are to some extent "interpreted" by other animals, at least to the extent that they call forth relevant changes in behavior. But when we analyze "behavior" in the strictest sense, "expectation" does not exist. For expectation involves a future, whereas behavior can only be observed in the present. Behavioristically, a state of "expectation" is identical with a set of neuromuscular conditions *now*. Let us illustrate. Once we watched a cat that had caught a chipmunk. He was toying with it, even to the extent of letting it loose and looking away, only to reach out an expert paw at the last moment just as the victim, taking new heart, seemed about to escape. As this incident was repeated several times, the chipmunk gradually edged nearer to a tree. Finally, victim and tormentor were both so near the tree that, when the chipmunk was again released, he made a dash for it, and by climbing spiral-wise, escaped. Whereupon the cat lifted its head, looked straight at its master, and gave a most emphatic yowl. Here was decidedly a change from an "is" situation to an "is not" situation. *So far as the logical diagram of the case was concerned*, the chipmunk first *was*, and then *wasn't*. But behavioristically, what you had was simply each positive motion, in exactly that positive order, including, of course, unseen motions that must have occurred within the body when the "salivation-situation" was suddenly replaced by the new austerity-situation. We might say that the second situation "negated" the first. But as regards behavior there was no negative, for there could not be; every step of the way was an engrossing positive.

Such stories prove nothing in themselves. But they do help make clear that there is a qualitative distinction between the sensory (rooted in the images of "behavioristic pre-language") and the rational (rooted in the ideas of language proper).

The empiricist strategy would account for an idea such as "whiteness" along nominalist lines, as a summarizing word got by abstracting the single quality of "white" from the perception of many different white things. It would reduce the "idea" to an "image." The Dramatist strategy would (though coyly) incline to the realist side, where "whiteness" would be thought of as an "activity," a way of belonging to one kind or family of color, rather than belonging to some other family of color (with its particular tribal nature or "substance"). Here the "image" (of any particular white thing) would owe its meaning as a *word* to its participation in the "idea of whiteness in general."

Obviously, the distinction between sensory (imaginal) abstraction and rational (ideal) generalization must be lost almost as soon as it is made, quite as we often use the two words *abstraction* and *generalization* interchangeably. And if *both* idea and image contribute to the development of language, we can expect to find each influencing the other. A distinction between mother and father ultimately involves substantial relationships; but it must begin in purely sensory perceptions, distinctions in the sensory ways by which the two relatives manifest themselves.

Empiricist reduction of idea to image is particularly deceptive because of the ways in which it conceals the social animus contained in sensations. And "Dramatism" aims always to make us sensitive to the "ideas" lurking in "things," which might even as social motives seem reducible to their sheerly material nature, unless we can perfect techniques for disclosing their "enigmatic" or "emblematic" dimension.

Though idea and image have become merged in the development of language, the negative provides the instrument for splitting them apart. *For the negative is an idea*; there can be no image of it. *But in imagery there is no negative.*

Here, recalling Bergson's just and penetrating observations on "the idea of 'nothing,' " we might distinguish between "the idea of nothing" and "the idea of no." If you would form an idea of nothing, you require an image —and, as Bergson points out, an image must be of something. But you need no image to form an idea of no. All you need is to "get the drift," to understand in what sort of situations you would employ this particular linguistic function. For "ideas" don't have to be of "things." If, for instance, you learn how to use the expletive "there," in a sentence like "There are many men here," you "get the idea." You might try to picture the many men, but you would not try to picture the expletive.

The negative is not picturable, though it can be *indicated*—as by a headshake, or the mathematical mark for minus, or the word *no*. It is properly shown by a *sign*, not by an *image*. For a "negative image" would be a contradiction in terms. Even a photographic "negative" is "positive," so far as its effect upon the retina of the eye is concerned. Its negativity derives from our *ideas* of its place in a total purposive process, involving "expectation."

Spinoza stresses that if you would imaginally cancel the effects of one image, you can do so only by introducing a stronger image. In effect, he is saying that there is no negative in imagery. The negative is in the realm of *idea*. And its "rational" nature is implicit in Spinoza's stress upon the "adequate idea" as the means to freedom of action.

If we take the image as devoid of negatives, and the idea as the realm of the negative, we glimpse in Spinoza very remarkable transformations of the tribal thou-shalt-not. First, we recall that by him the *positive* world is characterized by "negation." For the world of our positive, natural sensations is determined; and in Spinoza's central formula all determination is negation. Such a determined world is, by the same token, inevitably, a realm of "necessity." In this respect, note that it is what we might call a realm of "natural *command*," with thou-shalt-not's supplied, not by authority, but by the nature of things. We thus glimpse the possibility that part of its "negativity" may derive from its nature as a cosmologizing of the Tribal No.

Yet this Tribal No resides basically in the realm not of sensory image, but of supersensory idea. If sensation is the realm of motion, idea is the realm of action. And action is possible only insofar as the rational agent transcends the realm of sheer motion—sensory image. He does so, however, by forming adequate ideas of the limitations defining this sensory realm. And insofar as his understanding of the world's necessities approaches perfection, he is correspondingly free: he can *act*, rather than merely being *moved*, or "affected." But just as one cannot keep the sensory and the rational kinds of classification distinct, so the essential nolessness of image becomes confused with the essential no of the rational-tribal idea. Hence, though the injunction, "Thou shalt not kill" is in essence an *idea*, in its role as *imagery* it can but strike the resonant gong: "Kill!"

VIII
Reason, Understanding, Imagination, Fancy

Approaching the traditional reason-imagination pair in terms of the negative, we find them distinguishable thus: Reason is the ability to use the negative *qua* negative, the moralistic equivalent being "the ability to distinguish between right and wrong"; and it either is or is not—there being a difference in kind between the presence or absence of reason. But imagination, having no negative, induces or deters by changes of intensity; its presence or absince are thus a matter of degree.

We must hasten to qualify this statement. It applies to the typical classical relation between the two terms. In classical usage, imagination is a "low" faculty which humans share with brutes. But in romantic usage, imagination is often a higher faculty than reason, for in this usage it transcends mere image, though the transcendence is through the cultivation of images. The "aesthetic" in Kant is sensory; the "idea" is rational; but a term such as *the aesthetic idea* applied to works of art sets up possibilities whereby imagination in general and artistic imagination in particular can be said to possess the highest synthesizing powers—the direction completed in Schelling.

Coleridge treats the situation thus: In the *Biographia Literaria*, when dealing with poetry, he uses a fancy-imagination pair; in *The Friend*, when dealing with philosophy, he uses an understanding-reason pair. Fancy is close to mere sensation in the poetic realm. And understanding is the correspondingly lower term in the philosophic realm. Fancy in poetry is to understanding in philosophy as imagination in poetry is to reason in philosophy or theology. Hence as regards our previous distinction: reason is something that one either has or does not have, as one either sees or does not see a joke; and understanding is the kind of accumulative factual knowledge one can have more or less of. The presence-or-absence element figures in poetic imagination mainly through Coleridge's equating of wholeness with imagination; and the matter of quantity or degree in fancy figures mainly as an equating of fancy with the mechanistically motivated.

Obviously, there are dialectical transformations whereby, within a given controlled system, a "low" word can become of the highest. And we are not here trying to argue for or against any such usage, except insofar as we hold that one's analysis of such terms should begin with the classical distinction between sensation and reason, a distinction which we would reduce to a feeling for the negative as such. Since we take it that the negative is not (in Kantian terms) either a "sensation" or a "concept," at least so far as its beginnings *in the imperative* are concerned, we class it as an "idea"; hence, again in Kantian terms, we situate its essential function in the "dialectic" of "reason."

Therefore, all we ask is that you consent to *enter* the field by this route. Look at any house, and the house you see is the "image" of that house. Call it a house, and you have given it its appropriate "concept." But the "idea" of a house is not empirically reproducible. As Kant puts it, ". . . we can have no knowledge of an object, which perfectly corresponds to an idea, although we may possess a problematical conception thereof."

Glimpse the admonitory motive lurking within that term, *problematical.* You are thereby discerning the pressure of the moralistic *Critique of Practical Reason*, ambiguously proclaiming its genius behind and beyond the quasi-intellectualistic *Critique of Pure Reason.* You are glimpsing from afar the Essential No at the roots of the Categorical Imperative.

IX
In Sum

In analyzing the negative we arrive at these various distinctions:

1) Primitive positives, as with the animal taking what it wants.

2) Primitive negatives, as with the animal turning away from what it doesn't want, or what it wants but fears to take—or is "conditioned" not to take.

Since 1) and 2) are aspects of "behavioristic pre-language," they are not *bona fide* positive and negative in the peculiarly linguistic sense. Indeed, the turning-away is as "positive" an operation as the "taking," so far as its sheer materiality is concerned.

3) There are rational or dramatist positives, in the sense that the intelligent carrying-out of an act for an intelligent purpose is positive.

From the standpoint of 3) both 1) and 2) are called negative, insofar as "enslavement" to the "necessities" of "the senses" is a "negation" of "freedom."

4) There is the linguistic positive of words like *stop, caution, look out,* which have negative *implications* insofar as they are admonitory or deterrent in meaning. For such meanings can be phrased outright as negative command, once such a grammatical form is available.

5) There are the out-and-out negatives, ranging from "thou shalt not" to "it is not."

And our main point is: Once the Perfect Negatives of 5) have taken form, their genius permeates the motivations of the other four. For instance, whereas one might otherwise want to treat "Yea" simply as a combination of 1) primitive positives and 3) rational positives, we would admonish always to look for respects in which it might more accurately be treated as a negating of No.

A perfect illustration of our point is Nietzsche's nihilistic cult of Yea-saying. Nietzsche was trying to say no to the customary ways in which we say yes to the tribal thou-shalt-not's. His stylistic tactics involved him in exhorting us to cultivate a realm of primitive-positive motives.

But the primitivism was false. His Zarathustra was in essence as admonitory as a Hebrew prophet. And what more perfectly symbolizes the negativism of his perception than Zarathustra's poem on the striking of the clock at midnight? Each of the first eleven strokes has its corresponding sentence. But, when we get to the stroke of twelve (the all-important moment of *fulfillment*) the expected completion is missing. Precisely where the form attains its culmination, its symmetry is broken.

> Eins! O Mensch, gib acht!
> Zwei! Was spricht die tiefe Mitternacht?
> Drei! "Ich schlief, ich schlief—
> Vier! "Aus tiefem Traum bin ich erwacht!
> Fünf! "Die Welt ist tief—
> Sechs! "Und tiefer, als der Tag gedacht.
> Sieben! "Tief ist ihr Weh,—
> Acht! "Lust—tiefer noch als Herzeleid!
> Neun! "Weh spricht: Vergeh!
> Zehn! "Doch alle Lust will Ewigkeit—,
> Elf! "—Will tiefe, tiefe Ewigkeit!"
> Zwölf!

The "revelation" in the twelfth line is in the very negating of the form which we had been led by the pattern of the previous eleven lines to expect. And through this *perfection* of the surprise ending, we may glimpse the genius of the negative lurking in all surprise, when used as a device of literary form.

Nietzsche's greatest insight concerned the ways in which positive-seeming acts can be concealments of the great Tribal negatives. For the astounding genius of the negative includes its ability to manifest itself in disciplinary disguise. Ironically, his discoveries can also be carried to the point where we never lose sight of the moralistic negatives underlying his nihilistic cult of the primitive-positive.

Once you have society, with the thou-shalt-not's indigenous to its order, there can be no primitive-positives. Those who kill themselves with eating doubtless do so in the belief that they are motivated by sheer physical appetite. And physical appetite is probably the nearest to a primitive-positive we can come, outside the inevitable positiveness of physical development from childhood to old age, with perhaps only the years between twenty-one and forty being thought of as wholly positive, in our culture. But insofar as physical appetite is *compensatory* (insofar as one overeats because one feels frustrated in some other area of expression or "has nothing else to do") here are the same negativistic motives crowding in on the supposedly most positive behavior of all.

With regard to the erotic motive, the simplest way to realize how far it is from the primitive-positive is to walk about Times Square, looking at the advertisements for the "nature in the raw" movies regularly being shown there. In an environment far from the "natural," the posters blatantly proclaim a cult of what is supposedly sheer natural sexuality, depictions of violent sexual heat in a welter of imported jungle imagery. Of course, you might say that the cult of "nature" here is attained through sheer reaction to the excessive unnaturalness of the city. But we question whether "nature" is so easily won. And we would ask instead whether people so unnaturally surrounded could accurately appreciate anything truly "natural." In either case, one will grant that the appeal of such quasi "primitive-positives" is largely in their expression of imaginary trespass upon the thou-shalt-not's of private sexual property.

In sum, however positive sexual potency *in itself* may be, we should always distinguish between it and a *cult* of sexual potency. The "I can" of the cult (as distinguished from the "I can" of the sheer material condition) involves thou-shalt-not's of private property that have only a remote and roundabout connection with sex as such, however enjoyable in its sheer material positiveness sexual coupling may be.

Yet the mention of private property brings up another point. We have already indicated, and shall later consider more fully, how moral negatives can become positives through universalization. For if everybody were in debt to everybody, to this extent nobody would owe anybody. At least, the indebtedness would cancel out, so far as sheer mathematics is concerned. But we must consider a twist whereby the genius of the moral negative, as thus made positive, can add a new kind of negativity, in the very midst of its positivizing. For if everybody has something that he would keep for himself, to the exclusion of everybody else, to this extent everybody is guilty with regard to everybody, so that the accumulation of such positive possessions adds up to universal indebtedness. In such straits, the individual debtor may seek no less than Nietzschean consolations for his discomfitures; and like Nietzsche, he may persuade himself that such negations-atop-negations-atop-negations are a rediscovery of primitive-positives, somewhat as though bathing beauties on the beach were there sunning themselves just like turtles, and not as candidates for preferment.

In the terms of our present inquiry, "Reason" differs from "Conscience" in that "Reason" translates Yea and Nay as True and False, "Conscience" translates them as Right and Wrong. But since the Yeas of Conscience are headed in a code of Negative Commandments, techniques for "mortification" of "the senses" can be developed by conscientious priesthoods who would transform the negatives of guilty trespass into a corresponding regimen of "positive" athleticism. For since all acts have the positiveness of being what they are in their sheer materiality, a schematically penitential mode of living has positiveness of this sort; yet, implicit in its motivation, there is the admonitory genius of self-punishment.

Beyond such modes of cancellation as prevail in penance, mortification, and pietistic or Puritanical austerity of living, we catch a glimpse of the debt-negative, that apparently contributed to the development of the minus sign in mathematics. In failing to abide by the tribal or institutional thou-shalt-not's, or in fearing that one might fail, one piles up a measure of guilt after the analogy of a debt that needs repayment by corresponding positive sums. One here sees how the religious sin-penance pair, the secular debit-credit pair, and the plus-and-minus of mathematics all share ultimately in the same motivational cluster.

Zero is the negating of any plus. What, then, of minus? Is it a kind of super-negation or sub-negation, in turn to be negated by a compensatory plus that brings us to zero? In any case, as regards the special realm of moral debt, there can be a moment when the sheer cancelation of such a heavy minus is a kind of zero that *positively levitates*. For just as a man carrying a burden on his back might fall forward if it were suddenly released, so freedom from guilt, like freedom from debt or responsibility, can be felt as buoyancy.

Accordingly, any authoritative constraint, willingly accepted, that negates guilt or temptation by a regimen of "positive Law" (if we may wrench a term egregiously from its usual usage) can be felt as "freedom." And freedom is the most "positive" of all experiences, despite the obvious negatives in the word itself, which should prompt us always to ask, "Freedom *from what?*"

Victimage is another variant of the negative lurking in a quasi-positive. For the victim is positively there, in the most thoroughly materialistic sense. Yet insofar as the victim is a scapegoat, being symbolically or ritually laden by the victimizer with the guilt of the victimizer, he is a positive-seeming vessel of the victimizer's conscience-ridden response to the Great Negations of his tribe. "Our sins, in all their negativity as regards our tendency to trespass upon the thou-shalt-not's, are positively out there, in the enemy. Let us organize against them!" What could be more sanctimonious a sanction?

SECTION TWO

X
Dramatistic Introduction to Kant

Of Kant's three great Critiques (of Pure Reason, Practical Reason, and Judgment) the second leans most toward the Dramatistic. You might expect as much, since it concerns ethics; and by the very nature of the case, ethics builds its terminology around the problem of action.

Let us summarize Kant's position in *out-and-out Dramatistic terms*:

What kind of *agent* must there be for an act to be possible? And what kind of *scene* must there be for such an *agent* to be possible? Or, if we cut directly across from act to scene, what kind of *scene* must there be for an *act* to be possible? In form, the three questions would be, respectively, an agent-act ratio, a scene-agent ratio, and a scene-act ratio. (See *A Grammar of Motives*, pp. 3-20.)

An act is by definition "free." If it were but the conditioned "response to a stimulus," it would be not an act but sheer motion. Terministically, the *possibility* of an act is grounded in the "will" of an agent. (That is: Regarded from the standpoint of terministic tactics, the *word*, "will," states the motivational place where an act might originate in an agent.) And this "will" in turn must be grounded in the "idea" of an ultimate scene that lies outside the compulsions of strict causality. (That is: If an act to be an act must be willed, and a will to be a will must be free, then the will's freedom must in turn be grounded in some scenic freedom.)

The scene of causality is the totality of conditions and conditionings we call "nature." It is the world of our sensory experience, the world about which we can accumulate information, or knowledge. Such knowledge attains its fulfillment when science formulates the "laws" of any given causal chain, and of causality in general. But a world of "law" in such a purely necessitarian sense would not allow for "action," insofar as action must be *free*.

If "nature" equals "causality," then "freedom" must derive its grounding from a realm *beyond* nature. But because our sensory experience is by definition confined to the realm of "nature," if we equate "knowledge" with such sensory experience we cannot *know* of any realm beyond it. However, insofar as ideas are not sensory, we might have an "idea" of some ultimate realm.

Or, by sheer dialectical operation: If the realm of natural experience is summed up as the realm of the "conditioned," we could have the "idea" of (or at least the *term* for) an ulterior realm of the "unconditioned." Or if the world of nature is a realm in which things are experienced by us as "appearances," then we could have the "idea" of (or at least the *term* for) an ulterior realm of "things in themselves," beyond their nature as appearances. Then, if the realm of appearances is the realm of causality, it follows dialectically that the realm of things-in-themselves would be under the sign of "freedom."

Man as a purely sensory animal, with natural desires and inclinations (*Begierde* and *Neigungen*), is in the realm of causality. As such, in Dramatistic terms, he could but move (or, more accurately, be moved). He could not "act." So, to find a theoretical ground for the possibility of action, Kant resorts to a double system of accountancy. Insofar as we "act," we do so by reason of our affinity with the realm beyond mere appearances, our ability to share intrinsically in the supernatural realm of "things-in-themselves," or the "unconditioned."

You will note that, so far as the world of positive natural experience is concerned, such a transcendent realm of "pure being" is indistinguishable from "nothing." For "things" as we know them are in the realm of "conditions," each thing being conditioned by its relation to other things, yet "things-in-themselves" are "unconditioned" and by definition beyond such conditioning relationships. So, in the mere "idea" of a transcendent realm, we have a positive-seeming word for what is really the *function* of the negative. As Bergson makes clear by an ingenious mixture of introspection and logic, we can't really *think* of nothing. The nearest we can come to it is to think of annihilating something, a feat which on closer inspection will be found to force upon us the thought of the annihilator or of a substituted image such as a black spot, etc.[3]

From the Dramatistic point of view, the negative is an "idea" in the

---

[3] As regards this notion of Bergson's that, in trying to think of "nothing," we often think of something being annihilated: Note that this is another way of defining what Hegel calls the *Aufheben* of dialectic.

Such *Aufheben* is reducible to this process: Starting from A, we get a view of B in terms of A; next we advance to a view of B that transcends A; and then, looking back, we can view A in terms of B.

Bergson's discovery that "nothing" is seen in terms of "annihilation" (a process involving *steps*) helps us glimpse the genius of the negative underlying dialectic generally. In Hegel's case, this motive reveals itself most clearly in his notions as to the ways in which the "thesis" is "negated" by "antithesis." But when such negations are negated in turn, we reach a state of affairs which gives us, according to Mauthner, "almost an equating of thinking with nothing (*beinahe eine Gleichsetzung von Denken und Nichts*)."

Indeed, since Hegel equates Thinking with Being and since Hegel himself reminds us that "pure" Being is indistinguishable from Nothing, and since thought according to Hegel is essentially dialectical, we here have the means for spinning Thought, Being, and Dialectic from the principle of negation, as Mauthner helps us see in his related articles on *Sein* and *Nichts*.

verbal sense, an *act*. One never expects to see a verb "exist" as such. One doesn't expect to see a "*running*" or an "*eating*." One expects to see some particular thing or other running, eating, etc. Or you might put the matter thus: You can picture many kinds of houses; but you can't picture "housiness," which is sheer "principle," the name for an ideal "way of being a house."

When you think of this possibility, you can understand why Platonic realism, with its strong linguistic bias, thought of objects as having existence by reason of their ability to share in an absolute "idea" that transcended sensory experience. For the sheer *idea* would be indistinguishable from "nothing," so far as sensory experience was concerned; and the attempt to "think" such a "nothing" would be plagued by men's inability to transcend completely their tie with images. But if you think of "running" as an ultimate reality, for instance, then each person or thing that runs partakes of this ultimate, itself a supersensory "idea," capable only of being imperfectly embodied in one or another kind of running thing. Any individual runner would in effect give body to the "pure idea" of running, and thus would bring it down to the lower world of immediate sensory experience.

Bergson brought out the nature of the negative as an act rather than a thing when he found that the attempt to form a perfect idea of *nothing* leads furtively into the imagining of *annihilation*. We would only want to add that the same embarrassments figure when you try to think of the pure idea beyond *any* image. The *idea* of whiteness is invisible, you can only see white things; the *idea* of sweetness is tasteless, etc. Indeed, the more closely you look, the closer becomes the kinship between our feeling for the *-ness* words and our ability to use the negative *qua* negative.

But though we have glimpsed the linguistics of the negative in Kant's treatment of the "idea" as he uses it to characterize the ultimate ground of a "free" act, we still have to show specifically how the negative figures in his treatment of the "Categorical Imperative." For by our notions, it should reveal precisely the same genius as is manifest in the form of the Decalogue.

XI
Language and the Ethical

Our problem is complicated by the fact that for the most part Kant's terms for ethical motivation are almost resonantly positive. The very key term, *freedom*, seems strongly affirmative, as in a way it is. But a glance at any dictionary reveals its essentially negative nature. We pick some definitions at random: "Exempt from subjection . . . not under restraint, control, or compulsion . . . not dependent . . . not under an arbitrary or despotic government . . . not confined or imprisoned . . . not subjected to the laws of physical necessity . . . guiltless . . . innocent . . . unconstrained . . . unreserved . . . not close or parsimonious . . . released . . . liberated . . . not encumbered or troubled with . . . acting without spurring or whipping . . . unrestricted . . . not obstructed . . . not gained by importunity or purchase . . . not arbitrary or despotic . . . not united or combined . . . unattached . . ." etc.

Sometimes, however, the synonyms for such definitions are themselves more positive-seeming. Here are such entries as: "able to follow one's own impulses . . . capable of voluntary activity . . . frank . . . familiar . . . communicative . . . lavish . . . open-handed . . . clear . . . charming . . . easy . . . spirited . . . accessible . . . gratuitous . . . spontaneous . . . admitted to special rights . . . certain or honorable . . ." etc.

Surely, here is an alignment worth pondering. The first list clearly reveals the "unnish" or "nonnic" nature of the concept, "freedom." Then by reading the second list with the first list in mind, we catch glimpses of ways whereby a whole universe of positive-seeming words might arise to conceal their affinity with the *principium negationis*. And the double list culled from the dictionary should prepare us to look for something similar in the Kantian Ethics of the Categorical Imperative.

Kant's views in their most "positive" aspect rise to an urgent and persuasive eloquence, when he would avow the "majesty of duty," *die Ehrwürdigkeit der Pflicht*. Man as a mere animal creature in nature is driven solely by "desires and inclinations." Here is sheer compulsion. But man is also capable of "ideas," or as we would say, capable of a language which adds the negative to nature. And the theory of the possibility of action is grounded in man's ability to have an *idea* of freedom, itself grounded in the *idea* of a world beyond natural compulsions. This higher, *moral* realm is available only to man, as distinct from other animal species, or from himself as mere animal.

What, then, is a moral act? It is an act in which man himself freely lays down the law. He does so, not for mere personal gain, but because there is a joy in righteous lawgiving as such. In fact, since the righteous lawgiving involves the constraining of purely natural "desires and inclinations," it may even be a vexation to the lawgiver, inasmuch as it imposes restrictions upon his own individual yieldings to sheer natural impulse. The mark of lawgiving, as so conceived, is voluntary self-legislation. One asks of others only what one, in principle, finds it just to ask of oneself.

Here is, obviously, a mode of moralizing that splendidly transcends any purely "utilitarian" theory of morals. If there is to be satisfaction, it is not in the satisfying of natural appetites (headed in "self-love"), but in the thought of a task scrupulously and honorably done.

"Respect" (*Achtung*) is a term that plays a resonant role here. Respect applies to persons, or indirectly to things insofar as they pertain to persons:

Fontenelle says, "I bow before a great man, but my mind does not bow." I would add, before an humble, plain man, in whom I perceive uprightness of character in a higher degree than I am conscious of in myself, *my mind bows* whether I choose it or not, and though I bear my head never so high that he may not forget my superior rank.
. . . *Respect* is a tribute which we cannot refuse to merit. . . .

Who could refuse to respect such pronouncements on "respect"? Yet our treatment of it involves us in a kind of analysis that may not, at first glance, seem to give the Kantian cult of moral dignity its due. That is: The sentences being, by the nature of the case, verbal, we approach them linguistically, thus:

Since language has its own peculiar motives, a language-using species could not be motivated solely by nonlinguistic motives. There are many "local" motivations possible to language, as when a given word is, by "conditioning," associated with a special thing or person or political cause, and the like. But by its very nature, language also drives toward the "ultimate" of itself. And the ultimate is "Justice," a kind of *completion* whereby laws are so universalized that they also apply to the lawgiver.

Completion by universalization, considered as a linguistic resource, is not simply such an extension from image to idea as makes idea reducible to image. An idea, insofar as it is a "principle," is intrinsically *beyond* image. From the standpoint of image, it is as "nothing."

Such universalization comes easy to language. Merely round out a terminology, and "justice" is found to involve "self-legislation." But though we say that universalization, or following-through-to-the-end-of-the-line, comes easy to language, we should add two qualifications: (1) The orderly perfection of such thoroughness, in art or thought, brings up strains intrinsic to the medium; (2) morally, a further strain arises when we attempt to embody in practice what we have conceived in principle. In both kinds of cases, note that the efforts are *linguistically* motivated, in contrast with motivations of "the senses." And to this extent our respect for technical and moral attainments is linguistically grounded.

We do not thereby obligate ourselves to say that the grounding is "nothing but" language. We say merely that it is *at least* language (as distinct from "the senses"). And if one so desired, one could say that though these two sources of "respect" are grounded in the nature of language as "lawgiver," language itself is grounded in some kind of ultimate "language-giver."[4]

---

[4] Here would be the simplest way of stating, in sheerly grammatical terms, Kant's principle of moral universalization: Suppose that I begin with a purely selfish, utilitarian command, "*Thou* shalt not kill *me*." Next, I universalize the pronouns, so that everyone is a *thou* and everyone is a *me*. When this cycle is formally completed, I end by "freely" commanding *myself* not to kill *others*.

XII
"Negative" and "Positive" in Kant's Ethics

According to Kant, "What is essential in the moral worth of actions is *that the moral law should directly determine the will*." When the will is moved, not by mere sensory impulses but by the motives of justice and duty, it is being moved by moral law, and awakens respect. Respect for the "moral law in its solemn majesty" is "the one indubitable moral motive." Respect for the law is the "consciousness of a *free* submission to the will of the law." And since such devotedness derives not from mere fear of punishment, and the like, but "through the legislation of our *own* reason," it elevates, edifies, entitling us to a dignified kind of self-respect totally different from mere self-love. Where the will of a perfect being is concerned, the moral law is no less than "a law of *holiness*"; and for every merely finite rational being it is a "law of dutiful constraint," inspirited "by respect for such law and by reverence for such duty." "We stand under a *discipline* of reason," of the "pure practical reason" which is "no other than the pure moral law itself," awaking us to the "sublimity (*Erhabenheit*) of our supersensible existence," majestically superior to the "pathology" of *Begierde und Neigungen*, mere "animal desires and inclinations."

In this presentation, the thou-shalt-not's of moral law retreat behind the positive accents of a noble righteousness. True, you glimpse *admonitions* in the offing, when you take a closer look at words like *submission* (*Unterwerfung*), *constraint* (*Zwang*), *duty* (*Pflicht*: recall our etymologically related word, *plight*), and *discipline*. But we need not merely "glimpse," since Kant himself has explicitly distinguished between "negative" and "positive" motivations, thus:

The "effect of the moral law as a motive is only negative" insofar as it involves merely "the checking of inclinations," including "selfishness." In its negative aspects, "the moral law, as a determining principle of the will, must by thwarting all our inclinations produce a feeling which may be called pain." But since the moral law is "a feeling which is produced by an intellectual cause," it "is something positive in itself." "The negative effect on feeling (unpleasantness) is *pathological*, like every influence on feeling, and like feeling generally." This "feeling of a rational being affected by inclinations is called humiliation [*Demüthigung*] . . . but with reference to the positive source of this humiliation, the law, it is respect for it." Such respect for the law "is not a motive to morality, but is morality itself subjectively considered. . . ." Insofar as the moral law "restricts all inclinations, including self-esteem," it has a merely "negative effect." But "practical esteem for the law itself on the intellectual side" is a "positive feeling." Hence, in sum, "Respect for the moral law . . . must be regarded as a positive, though indirect" influence upon "feeling."

We should here dramatistically interject some reminders as regards the overall pattern. That is, if the Kantian ethics were reduced purely to an exercise in linguistics, the scheme would proceed thus: (a) If there is to be an act, there must be free will in the agent (since things merely sliding on a slope, in accordance with its *Neigung*, or inclination, are not *acting*); (b) free will manifests itself in freedom to *lay down the law*; (c) law just to somebody else?; (d) nay more, *universal* law; (e) whereat *universal* legislation comes to fulfillment in legislation imposed by the self upon the self; (f) since each completion is, in its way, *admirable*, this "moralistic" completion of completions wholly justifies Respect (*Achtung*); (g) and insofar as we can, by good criticism, be sure that we have thus rounded the circle, out of the negatives has arisen, lo! a positive, as Kant said it could arise;— (h) whereupon, the ability to respect *is* a "positive." It is "positive" in the sense that it makes an ethical affirmation. It affirms the superiority of "duty" over every other motive. But it makes clear that such duty is a "command," founded on "obligation," not "inclination." Respect "*demands* obedience to the law." If we were virtuous spontaneously, we should not be "virtuous," but "holy," like duty itself. Duty requires sacrifice (*Aufopferung*), and self-compulsion (*Selbstzwang*); and one might again recall that Kantian "freedom" comes to fruition in legislation, while legislation comes to fruition in self-legislation, so that the free are *free* to practice *self-control* in accordance with moral principle as motive (*Triebfeder*), a kind of motive not within the competence of sheerly natural organisms.

In its mere "restricting" of "natural inclinations" (including the inclination to "self-love"), moral law is "negative." Insofar as "respect for the law" has this merely deterrent function, it is "*far from being* a feeling of pleasure." It is a "resistance to the motives of the sensibility." Such "negative effect upon feeling" is "*pathological* (like every effect upon feeling)." But such "humiliation on the sensible side" is an "elevation (*Erhebung*) on the intellectual side." And since its cause is intellectual (or as we linguistically would say, since its "cause" is the completing of the verbal to the point where it rounds the circle), in this regard Kant calls it "positive." Whereupon, "dignity" (*Würde*) arises from such a "*free* submission of the will to the law" as amounts inevitably to "constraint put upon the self."

Perhaps we should insert an aside here. Within the Dramatistic scheme, any reference to the "senses" must be examined for possible motivations not specifically "sensory" at all. For, once "the senses" begin operating in a given socio-semantic context, their sheer biological nature as "senses" is by the same token already transcended. Why? Because the "senses" as such are not a fit for any one social order.

The main motivational strands would be as follows: (a) There is some particular kind of social order; (b) it has its corresponding system of property relationships; (c) it has its corresponding system of controls, to inculcate and protect the system of property relationships and its corresponding "values"; (d) control (the code of thou-shalt-not's) is not "positive" until it contains its fulfillment in the citizens' will freely to practice self-control; (e) such self-control is synonymous with control over "the senses," insofar as "the senses" are credited (or more accurately, debited) with all tendencies to deviate from the *ideals* that go with the given social order; (f) insofar as techniques are found for "mortifying the senses," their "positive" nature as material operations reinforces their "positive" nature as an "assertion" that negates the motives of "the senses"; (g) the language factor thus shows in the ability to develop a complex human social order, in the corresponding ideas of status and property, in the thou-shalt-not's indigenous to such a structure, and in the various "positives" that arise out of such negations.

Returning specifically to Kant:

"The *consciousness* of having *voluntarily subjected oneself*" to the spirit of a code of *don'ts* can be *subjectively* called a "positive" motive. But, for our purposes, please note that Kant himself explicitly situates the *beginning* of the process in a *command* (the Categorical *Imperative*). And such command begins, as he himself explicitly says, in the mere "negating" of certain motives (or "inclinations"). This is the "negative" found in sheer *constraint*.

In his heavy way, Kant is working out a scheme that corresponds to the step from the "negative" attitude in the *lex talionis* to the "positive" attitude in the Golden Rule. However, he is worried by the thought that love cannot be "commanded." Commands are addressed to our sense of fear (a "negative" motive) or to our sense of Duty (which Kant makes "positive" by universalizing where the Dutiful freely commands himself). Here is Kant's own discussion of the point:

> *Love God above everything, and thy neighbour as thyself.* . . . as a command it requires respect for a law which *commands* love and does not leave it to our own arbitrary choice to make this our principle. Love to God, however, considered as an inclination (pathological love), is impossible, for He is not an object of the senses. . . . To love God means . . . to like to do His commandments; to love one's neighbour means to like to practise all duties towards him. But the command that makes this a rule cannot command us to *have* this disposition in actions conformed to duty, but only to *endeavor* after it. For a command to like to do a thing is in itself contradictory. Because if we already know of ourselves what we are bound to do, and if further we are conscious of liking to do it, a command would be quite needless; and if we do it not willingly, but only out of respect for the law, a command that makes this respect the motive of our maxim would directly counteract the disposition commanded. That law of all laws, therefore, exhibits the moral disposition in all

its perfection, in which, viewed as an Ideal of holiness, it is not attainable by any creature, but yet is the pattern [*Urbild*] which we should strive to approach . . . and become like. . . . In fact, if a rational creature could ever reach this point, that he thoroughly *likes* to do all moral laws, this would mean that there does not exist in him even the possibility of a desire that would tempt him to deviate from them . . . being a creature . . . he can never be quite free from desires and inclinations, and as these rest on physical causes, they can never of themselves coincide with the moral law, the sources of which are quite different. . . .[5]

The sources of moral law, then, make it necessary "to found the mental disposition of one's maxims on moral obligation, not on ready inclination . . . not on love, which apprehends no inward reluctance of the will towards the law." If we acted wholly from love of the law, "then morality, which would have passed subjectively into holiness, would cease to be *virtue*"; and holiness is the "constant though unattainable goal" of our virtuous endeavors. The law of duty which *commands* does not allow us to choose what may be agreeable to our inclinations.

Fortunately, for our purposes, by our way of cutting across the issue, we need not choose between the claims of Love and Duty as rival kinds of "positives." Our aim, rather, is to stress the fact that both terms, considered as "styles," owe their genius to the genius of that specifically linguistic marvel, the negative.

XIII
Arts of "the Senses"

As regards the transforming of the negative command into an attitudinal positive, William Ernest Henley's overly confident "Invictus" is an obvious illustration, beginning even with the title. "Out of the night," a negative ground, the poet thanks God for his "unconquerable soul." He has "not winced nor cried aloud." His head is "unbowed." He is, and will remain, "unafraid." If the road is narrow, "it matters not." Nor will he worry that he may be "charged with punishments." For, he concludes,

> "I am the master of my fate:
> I am the captain of my soul."

One need not be in the literary business long to detect a considerable amount

---

[5] We would say: The sources of the "moral law," as stated in books, are linguistic; but not in the simple sense of "conditioning," with people simply responding to whatever associations between one thing and another may have been established by one means or another; on the contrary, you must add the to-the-end-of-the-line motive, the completion-that-rounds-out-the-circle, and so, as regards "justice," brings the act of legislation back upon the self.

of whistling in the dark here. We don't know the facts of the case, but we shouldn't be surprised to learn that, about this time, the poet had been scaring himself intensely. In any case, the poem is obviously infused with the genius of the moralistic negative. Pressing upon it are implied Commandments of this sort:

> Thou shalt not be conquered;
> Thou shalt not wince nor cry aloud;
> Thou shalt not bow thy head, even be it bloody;
> Thou shalt not fear;
> Though thou art burdened with threats,
>   thou shalt not fail to say:
> It mattereth not.

Whereupon, we note how the exaltation in the words *master* and *captain* derives from their sylistic transcending of this hortatory negativity by two positive-seeming propositions. The zest is in the fact that, behind the word *master* there lurks, "Thou shalt not be enslaved," and behind the word *captain* there lurks "Thou shalt not fail in self-guidance."

Arthur Hugh Clough's poem, "Say not the struggle nought availeth" is in the same hierarchically burdened mode. The two negatives of this opening, titular line clearly set the motivational quality. Then, after filmy description of battle, with its hopes despite fears, there emerges the "positive" assertion of the third stanza:

> For while the tired waves, vainly breaking,
>   Seem here no painful inch to gain,
> Far back, through creeks and inlets making,
>   Came silent, flooding in, the main, . . .

Quite an interweaving of threads can be distinguished in the simple tactics of this ardent but ailing poem. But to make them clear, our approach must be roundabout, thus:

To begin with purely moral positivizing such as we have considered in Kant, let us state the point in terms of a relationship between the Old Testament and the New, as characterized in one of our other works (*Permanence and Change*).

> In the earlier confusion, the golden rule seems to have been brought forward as a lowest common denominator of appeal. It was a truly "catholic" basis of reference, or sanction for human values, which might unite all cultural integers despite their many differences. It formed a rock-bottom of communication, having about it sufficient self-evidence as a desirable end to gain it at least acceptance in principle among people of many sects and cultures with wholly distinct systems of piety or customs. There are even grounds for suspecting that the doctrine had a double qualification.

For besides its validity as a universal criterion, a basic formula for smearing a single cultural reorientation across a host of economically united but spiritually disunited cultural integers, it had its roots in the patterns of vindictiveness. Was it not the "tooth for a tooth and eye for an eye" formula rephrased? Had not the *lex talionis*, so basic to human notions of justice, been simply lifted by the golden rule out of the vindictive category and placed in the *caritas*-category?

If you consider the vindictive element in justice as "negative," then the golden rule is a translation into a "positive." But once you arrive at some such positive as universal love, you are in a position to go back and seek its grounding in purely "natural" motivations. That is, you can treat the positives of sheer animal appetite as an incipient manifestation of ideal love (thus reversing the procedure of simple materialism, which would treat ideal love as a mere projection of the animal's erotic appetite). Even the crudest or most brutal forms of desire can then be interpreted, not as wholly outside the ideal motive, but as the remotest manifestation of it.

If even the abstractions of the philosopher or theologer thus seek to restore the very kind of sensory positives which they began by denying, we have all the more reason to ask always how the poet will proceed to ground his statement of moral motives in the imagery of the senses.

In sensory imagery itself, there are the well-known devices of metonymy whereby states of mind can be expressed in terms of physical states. And there are the devices of the "pathetic fallacy" whereby behavioral symptoms of the individual body can be conveyed in terms of scenic parallels, as when a state of mental agitation is expressed, not just in terms of a person's corresponding physical agitation, but of some broader scene or incident, like storm or shipwreck.

We now have sufficient motivational elements lined up to help us call the plays in this simple poem:

1) The poem is designed, in its way, to build affirmatives out of negatives (being in this regard like Henley's).

2) It will do so first of all by countering fears (negatives) with reassurances (positives).

3) But such purely *moralistic* positivizing will be matched by another kind, the attempt to express the ethical *ideas* in terms of sensory *images*.

4) The poet will thus proceed from *images* suggesting fearsome struggle to *images* suggesting release. (And though we might distinguish between these two kinds of imagery morally, calling the fearsome sort negative and the consolatory sort positive, we could lump all imagery together as a realm of "poetic positives.")

5) The "idea" of release is here translated into the "positive image" of a *flooding*.

6) On the assumption that, in accord with the "thinking of the body,"

purely "scenic" details might also be relevant to purely bodily processes, we might tentatively ask what would be the bodily equivalent of release by "flooding."

7) Insofar as poetry deals with "cathartic" matters, we assume that such scenic imagery, when referred to the imagery of bodily behavior, would remotely figure diuretic release.

8) But since such release is purely *imaginal*, it would *transcend* "the senses," being in the realm of "idea" rather than in the realm of outright bodily behavior. Its motivation would thus differ qualitatively from such bodily surrender as would take place if an actual micturition in fear had occurred.

9) This incipient bodily correspondence is further transcended by being stated not directly in biological terms at all, but in terms of natural scene, whereby the "shameful" symptoms are made grand, and so universalized as to be observable *ab extra*.

10) And the final stanza of the poem takes us still another step from the symptoms of purely bodily release, as it turns from the watery flood to the flood of light:

> And not by eastern windows only,
>   When daylight comes, comes in the light,
> In front, the sun climbs slow, how slowly,
>   But westward, look, the land is bright.

Thus, quite as imaging of diuretic release has advanced a further step from its purely sensory relevance to the theme of the poem as enacted in "the thinking of the body," so the motive of fear itself has gone from fear, through assured relief, to a most positive variant of man's uneasiness, a reverent glorification of the day's brightness, a *Schwelgerei* of moralized delight in nature when nature is most reassuringly happiest. The negativity of "shame" is transcended, though implicit, in the ecstatic vision of a *clean* landscape, *bathed* in light.

We may be wrong in particular here. And admittedly, we have not adduced sufficient evidence to support our analysis conclusively even if we are right. For the moment, all we aim to do is indicate the sort of motivational pattern we think is likely, when the poet "Platonically" translates an "idea" into its corresponding "positive" realm of imagery. Given a social order, with its thou-shalt-not's that begin in training of the body's purgative functions, one can properly look for ways whereby, in the thoroughness of a poem, fear symptoms are thus simultaneously expressed and transcended.

Though these are not the best of poems, they appear in many reputable anthologies. Among major English poems clearly indicating the tactics of the negative, surely one of the greatest is Milton's lyric on his blindness, "When I consider how my light is spent." This sonnet (with its notable irregularity of form, in the run-over line that bridges octave and sestet) is built about the kind of negative Aristotle would call privation (*steresis*).

The moral problem here is not with "the senses," as placed in Kant's alignment. For the poet is writing not on rebellious or excessive sight, but on sight deficient. The conclusion ("They also serve who only stand and wait") is Kantian in its glorification of service as a positive, though such service is given a somewhat neutral aspect, to fit the conditions of the privation.

As the treatment well suits the nature of the lyric arrest, *Samson Agonistes* treats the same sensory privation in keeping with the nature of a dramatic form. There the service to God is made almost ferocious; and in Samson's physical strength the excess of another bodily resource in effect negates the visual privation.

Since arts such as painting, music, and the dance are so obviously mediums for reaching us through the senses, the reader might conclude that the Idea of No is not important here, or does not figure as a motive. On the contrary! Insofar as an artist rigorously develops a method, his selectivity is but the obverse of his exclusions, exclusions that implicitly (and often explicitly) follow his code of thou-shalt-not's. Or, think of the many times in the history of art when a new development was made possible by the deliberate rejection of some canon previously accepted.

True, in a painting, the forms and colors are positively what they are. In that sense, a painting is "nothing but" an imagery, and so by our test can have no negatives. The genius of the negative is present, however, in the fact that the work's principles of *organization* and *selectivity* follow what Kant would have called the "aesthetic idea"—and the force of the negative figures in this aspect of painting as a symbol system, a "terminology."

Sometimes we can even glimpse moments on the canvas itself when *signs* of the negative can be seen. What modern painter, for instance, shows a more positive delight in form and color as such than Cézanne? Yet consider his early painting, "The Black Clock," built about the theme of a clock that *has no hands*. He omitted the hands, we assume, for "a-horological" reasons, since his painting, unlike that of his impressionist contemporaries, not only did not aim to establish any precise time, but even deliberately flouted such purposes. Recall a later work, for instance, showing the shadows of chimneys cast in various directions, as though the sun were in several places at once. And the same *principle* (that is, "idea") was applied in the painting of a figure in two perspectives at once, the upper and lower halves of the body being viewed from two different angles in the one painting. At such moments, we can see the artist, in effect, saying no to certain established thou-shalt-not's, in the development of methods that would be guided by admonitions of its own.

Or, recall that many modern composers have delighted in consecutive fourths, which have a somewhat stark effect, providing an *Ersatz*-primitivism.

You may take them "positively," simply hearing the sounds as they are. But in the "dialectics of history," they were also loved as negations of the harmonic rules against consecutive fourths and fifths. And if popular harmonization gives up its overdoses of thirds and sixths, as it now often threatens to do, we then have only the *positive* nature of consecutive fourths and fifths. Whereat we might even forget their role as *negations* of other effects.

We also mentioned the dance. It would seem that, precisely at the time when the cult of the sensory-positive was at is greatest, the best teachers of the best modern dance taught the new art by noting always what rules of the old art their modern method was negating. Similarly, we recall an instructor in the modern dance explaining: "In the ideal modern dance, there must be no use of merely conventional signs. For instance, we give the student this job: How say good-bye in gestures, if you're not allowed simply to wave good-bye, if you can in fact do anything but that?" Here was the genius of the negative, reinvigorating the most positive of forms, so far as the sheer surface physicality of the medium is concerned.

You may say: Such negative motives are not the best that the modern mediums have to offer. And we would agree with you. Ideally, every artistic method should be statable in wholly positive terms, as Aristotle analyzes Athenian drama in the extant portions of his *Poetics*. But in noting these negatives, we have further purposes in mind. We want to make the presence of the No sufficiently apparent, so that the reader will not take a profession too seriously when it doth profess too much its positive nature. The more zealously a positive is proclaimed, the more we are admonished to inspect it for evidence of its guidance by a set of thou-shalt-not's.

XIV
Negative and Positive in a Bossuet Sermon

We would comment next on a notable piece of rhetoric, a few paragraphs from an Easter Sermon by Bossuet. Besides its excellence as sheer eloquence, it particularly serves our purposes because it embodies in a short space perhaps all the major motives relating moral idea and bodily imagery:

"Man's life is like a road leading to the fearsome edge of an abyss. At the very start we are warned of the end. But the law has been decreed; all must keep pressing forward. I would retrace my steps. *Marche! marche!* We are dragged by an unconquerable weight, an unconquerable force. We must advance towards the precipice, unceasingly. A thousand obstacles, a thousand cares, weary us and distress us, as we move on. If I could but escape that fearsome pit! No, we must walk, we must run—such is the swiftness of the years."

Next come some qualifications: a brief account of solaces along the way. The author does not do much in their behalf. He but grants that we are

momentarily diverted "by flowing waters and passing flowers"; then he has-
tens to remind us how such delights fade even as we enjoy them, how everything behind us falls into ruin, even as we are drawn towards our engulfment:

> Already things are beginning to blur. Flowers are less brilliant,
> colors less bright, meadows less cheery, waters less clear. All grows
> dull, all loses lustre. The shadow of death is present; we feel our
> nearness to the fatal fall. But we must advance to the brink—one
> step more. Already horror troubles our senses, we are confused, and
> wild-eyed. We must keep on. We would turn back; we cannot; all
> has fallen, all has vanished, all has slipped away.

Next comes the moralistic interpretation of the parable, presenting the
choice between an eternity of *sensory* positives (made negative by torture)
and the *moral* positives of eternal salvation:

> I need not tell you that the road is life, and the steep descent is
> death. But in ending past evils, does death end itself? No, no; in this
> pit there are voracious fires, the gnashing of teeth, an eternal weep-
> ing, a flame that burns for ever, a worm that never dies. Such is the
> road of him who abandons himself to the senses, shorter for some
> than for others. One does not foresee the end; sometimes one falls
> unexpectedly and of a sudden. But the man of faith stands firm.
> Jesus Christ is with him always, to sustain him. He scorns what he
> sees perishing and dwindling away. At the last, when he is near to the
> abyss, an invisible hand will take hold of him. Or rather, he will enter
> there like Jesus Christ; he will die like Jesus Christ, to triumph over
> death. Whoever has this faith is blessed.

In sum:

"Such is the joy of the resurrected Jesus, who holds passing joys in
contempt, but will give joy eternal."

Note that the orator, like the poets and artists we have considered,
grounds his idea in a sensory or animal fact, in this case the purely physical
inevitability of death. But his recital of the physical worldly journey with its
risks is interwoven with the idea of a worldly journey in the moral sense, a
journey in which one accepts responsibilities as defined by the social order.

The strands here are as follows:

1) There is the distinction between abandonment to "the senses" and
the saying of nay to such a realm of sheer bodily positives.

2) There is an implied likeness between the inevitability of physical
death and the inevitability of social burdens. It is the likeness stated more
realistically in the proverbial expression, "as sure as death and taxes," which
makes no distinction between a purely natural motive (in the realm of "the
senses") and a situation socio-linguistically motivated (in the realm of gov-
ernmental authority).

3) Since, by our theories, the proscriptions proper to the given social

order are summed up moralistically as "self-legislation" against "the senses," or as "mortification" (in the disciplines of theology), "the senses" reinforce commands physically and are themselves to be legislated against morally.

They reinforce commands insofar as they equate the *absolutely unavoidable* fact of physical death with the *relatively avoidable* fact of social burdens. Bossuet's reference to "the senses" here says in effect: The need to accept the moral tax of burdens all along the way of life is as undeniable as the need to accept the ultimate physical tax, the capital levy of death.

But "the senses" are to be questioned, in ways that lead to mortification, insofar as they stand in general for tendencies to trespass against the prevailing ideals of property. And such nay-saying to "the senses" is like a tax willingly laid upon the self. This self-taxing in principle usually implies an argument for acceptance of the ruler's taxes in particular; but we decidedly do not assume that "self-taxation" must thus always exact obedience; for one might, under certain conditions, so tax oneself morally that, like Thoreau, one refused to pay taxes literally. Here we are somewhere among the Higher Complications of No.

A further step in Bossuet's admonitions involves the fact that the proscriptions against moral trespass are grounded, not in the positive laws protecting the prevailing norms of property, but in an *extension* of the idea of inevitability. What can *not* be avoided is not just physical death, but an *undying* continuation after physical death. The sensory fact of *physical* inevitability has its analogue in the idea (threat or promise) of *moral* inevitability, the idea of life-after-death rhetorically reinforcing the idea of moral responsibility. And moral responsibility is thereby said to transcend the limits of physical existence quite as, with Kant, the "moral law" transcends the limits of "the senses."

It is not for us to decide or even ask whether this symmetry has more than a purely dialectical basis. But we do want to note how the Kantian step from a "negative" to a "positive" morality is complicated here. The cult of Christian love attains its ultimate positive in the promise of eternal salvation. This positive itself motivates the thou-shalt-not's directed against "the senses." And these negative commands are reinforced by a negative of another sort; the threats of eternal damnation. And the whole hortatory structure gains credibility by being grounded in the positives of sensory experience, positives however which culminate in a *negative* idea (the *threat* of death, which Lucretius presented as a *positive promise*, negating the claims of pagan priests who threatened mortals with divine pursuit after death).

This brings us to our final point about the ways in which positives are negatively infused in the realm of such "sublime" theological admonitions as are found in the Bossuet passage:

Recalling Cicero's three offices of the orator (to instruct, to delight, to move), note that the third is in the fullest sense the hortatory, in the spirit of the imperative. In his *De Doctrina Christiana*, applying this design to Christian models, and discussing the kind of style appropriate to each of the offices, Augustine naturally assigns to the "grand" style the office of moving. But note the kind of remarks he makes about texts written *granditer*:

The grand style is used "when something ought to be done, and we are speaking to those who ought to do it but do not want to." It is adapted to the bending of their minds (*ad flectendos animos*). By it a disinclination is impelled to change. We might use the language of embellishment when praising God: "but if He is not worshipped, or if idols (demons or other creatures) are worshipped with Him or even before Him," the grand style should be employed to show "how evil such things are," and "to turn men from such evil." Augustine cites a passage in Paul where "the Apostle urges that for the ministry of the gospel all evils of this world be borne patiently, with God's gifts as solace." He cites another passage where Paul "urges the Romans to vanquish persecution with love." Another where Paul, exhorting the Galatians, leads up to the judgment, "I am ashamed for you." He quotes another passage where Paul is inveighing against the women of the congregation who, despite their good conduct, become "adulterous" before God by the pollution of cosmetics. Applause may follow the acumen of the subdued style or the embellishments of the temperate style, Augustine says; but the grand style "by its weight usually imposes silence and calls forth tears." He then tells how at Caesarea in Mauritania, when he was exhorting the people against a ruinous custom of feuding at a certain period each year, to the best of his ability he employed the grand style. Yet he did not take their applause as a sign that he was making headway with them. It indicated that they understood and were pleased; but only when they wept did they show that they were moved, and that an old custom had been conquered. He ended, he tells us, on the giving of thanks to God; and he notes that, in the eight or more years since he spoke there, the people have not reverted to their inveterate custom. This and other experiences led him to conclude that grandeur in diction manifests its effects not in shouting, but in groans, tears, and a change in men's way of living (*vitae mutatione*). In sum, all three styles aim at persuasion. The subdued style would persuade that what the speaker says is the truth; the temperate style would persuade that he is speaking beautifully and elegantly; but the grand style is employed to make us choose good ways and shun evil ways.

We interpret the tenor of these remarks to indicate that the grand style (and its secular equivalent, the poetically "sublime"), operates in the regions of the *fearsome*, the "negative" realm from which the idea of deterrence, of the thou-shalt-not, is never absent. To make this moral negative effective, the speaker may conjure up a set of purely "imaginal positives," sensory details designed to bring the fearsome condition "before our very eyes." But such positives are "negatively" motivated insofar as they are used for reinforcement of the moralistic exhortations.

There is also the kind of "positives" one gets by transforming the threats into promises (as when Bossuet wound his vision of hell into a vision of heaven, or when Augustine turned from admonition to thanksgiving). The underlying negative genius here is not disclosed until we stop to realize that *any promise is in function a threat if it can be withheld*. If a promise can, under certain conditions, be withheld, then the more fully we build it up as a promise, the more fully we build up our sense of its possible loss.

The same negativistic genius lurks behind the promises of secular reward for secular efforts, as with the supposedly "positive emphasis" in economic doctrines of "free enterprise." One may think of another seculari-zation, as when we go from the grand style of the moralizing sermon to the grandeur of the *poetically* sublime. There is, unquestionably, a "positive" motive here, in the love of the medium and its resources as such (a motive that we can also detect even in works of grand moralistic urgency). But there is also the concealed negative. First, the sublime itself has a strongly moral-istic element. Second, it is in the realm of the fearsome. Third, even where it is not directly explainable as a quasi-secularized variant of its theological forebears, implicit in its norms of style there are the promises rightly or wrongly associated with such style in the given social order (promises that are threats in disguise inasmuch as they can be withheld).

Philosophers regularly justify their exhortations in terms of statements about the ultimate scene in which men act. These exhortations, to be such, must be somehow infused with the spirit of the thou-shalt-not. And they are justified in abstract terms that, by their transcending of the sensorily positive, lead us through ingenious paths into "the idea of nothing."

Let us sum up by saying that, however "positive" a style, or moral injunction, may contrive to be in its wording, behind it always lurks the Basic Negative, the Great, Tragic, Feudlike *Lex Talionis*, itself a universal principle of Justice, and one without which the art of an Aeschylus would be meaningless. And we hope to have so treated the distinction between "the senses" and "the law" that the reader both sees how it looks when reduced to the distinction between nonlinguistic and linguistic motives, and sees that such reduction by no means imposes impoverishment or distortion upon the analysis of human motives.

SECTION THREE

XV

Negative Theology

In the preceding essay we analyzed Kant's writings on Ethics, passages from Bossuet, Augustine, and others to indicate the pervasiveness of the Negative and thus to support our proposition: *The essential distinction between the verbal and the nonverbal is in the fact that language adds the peculiar possibility of the Negative.* Let us proceed with a more general survey of the Negative. We shall also suggest some positive aspects of language, ending on a theory of Definition.

"If you pile Pelion upon Ossa," Mauthner writes, "out comes a handsome hyperbole. But if you toss a Nothing into the Bottomless Pit (*ein Nichts in den Abgrund*), out comes nothing."

Nevertheless, in an almost diabolically ingenious essay (*Was Ist Metaphysik?*) Heidegger offers a new variant of that very old dialectical resource whereby the sum total of Being is said to be grounded in Nothing, or Non-Being, considered as an ultimate reality which is beyond sensory perception but of which we might on occasion have inklings. In his treatment of "Nothing" as the ultimate ground of all positive, worldly existence and knowledge, he gives his claims at least an appealing literary twist by introducing a verb. The Ultimate Nothing (*Nichts*) can *enact* its identity; for it can non-do (*nichten*). Or, heavily cavorting, we might translate the verb *nichten* into English thus: *Things* can *be*; and their Being is grounded in *Nothing's* ability to *noth*.

In a further step, Heidegger brings his exposition to a point that opens quite a vista. He asks: If Nothing has a kind of actuality, in its role as the ground of Being, might there by empirical signs of its nature? And he suggests that, insofar as we experience pure metaphysical fear, an anguish or uneasiness (*Angst*) not explainable in terms of immediate discomfitures or dangers, in this feeling there is manifest the communicative link with the realm *beyond* nature.

Even if we agree with Heidegger's views, we could still note strands of motivation here that should first be considered without reference to a supernatural realm. For instance, if you agree that, in terms of natural experience, the negative *Command* is prior to the purely *Propositional* negative, and may be glimpsed "beyond" it or about its edges, you see a possibility that the metaphysician could be rediscovering, through the labyrinthine virtuosity of his dialectic, the respect and awe of the original No, communicated to him as a child by parents who represented the principle of personal authority.

Here the adult thinker would be recalling an early *attitude*. But in accordance with the nature of the medium he was using, he would not recall it directly as a former personal experience now explicitly recollected. Rather, he would treat it indirectly, and somewhat "scientistically" (in terms of metaphysical "knowledge"). Similarly, the *temporal* priority of the childhood *attitude* would be expressed in terms of a *metaphysical* priority; for "Nothing," in its role as the "ground" of Being, could be called "prior" to Being.

Again, a terminology essentially metaphysical would also incline to interpret as purely metaphysical any kind of uneasiness stemming from the *social order.* In our *Rhetoric of Motives* we have called this motive the "hierarchal psychosis." And, as we saw in the case of the Bossuet sermon, theological dogma could intensify such *Angst* by adding the fear of hell.

Then there is the fact that Death itself, as the privation of Life, is the Great Negative. While it is not itself an experience available to direct sensory knowledge and report, the *idea* of Death can lend solemnity and authority to other motives, or can provide an ideal seriousness that dwarfs other motives by comparison. Because of Death's nature as a *culmination*, there is a sense in which the feeling for the genius of the negative in general can "naturally" head in the idea of Death. And as a proper name can survive its owner, like a spirit-self eternal in the realm of essence, so the intensely linguistic feeling for the negative, that in one direction leads to the idea of Death as its completion, leads in another direction to the feeling for the undying identity of that other linguistic marvel, the *name* (whereat, recalling the Latin's notable doctrinal pun on *nomen* and *numen*, we find one as much beyond the sheer realm of "the senses" as the other).

However, though we treat language as a positive natural faculty which requires us always to explain its operations and effects naturalistically, there is a notable difference between our position and that of, say, an outright behaviorist. The discussion of language in terms of "conditioning" is purely behavioristic. It culminates in experiments that reveal how certain words can become associated with certain things or situations. While not wanting in the least to deny such laws of association (the "conditioned reflex"), we stress the further fact that, once associations have been established between words and extraverbal situations, a new order of motivation arises through resources internal to words as such. And above all, we have suggested, there are the purely verbal (or "rational") incentives to "complete the circle" of language, following-through or rounding-out internal verbal relationships to the point where such sensorily nonexistent things as "ideas" and "principles" press for complete universalization (whereat thou-shalt-not becomes I-will-not).

Thus, when confronting the verbal tactics of negative theology, we would always stress the purely linguistic elements operating here. At the same time, there is nothing in our position requiring us to deny the possibility that language, with its basic No, is grounded in a transcendent ground. As we observed in our *Rhetoric of Motives*, though one may *scientifically* distinguish simply between words and things, *philosophically* there must be not only the verbal and the nonverbal, but also the more-than-verbal, since "Reality" as a whole comprises not only the verbal and the nonverbal, but also the more-than-verbal.

We can even at times see in negative theology hardly more than a mere psittacism of word-slinging, without thereby feeling obliged to conclude that the motives of such dialectical exercising are merely verbal, natural, social. Linguistically, *God* can be nothing but a term. Some such term is required as a title of titles, when we are spinning out the resources of language in a to-the-end-of-the-line way until an overall term is reached. And though such a term is, by its very nature as a generalization, almost devoid of content (as content is tested by terms for particular sensory experiences), we can understand how it may come also to sum up the realm of duties and admonitions (being essentially negative in the Decalogical way, a kind of Universalized Gerundive, the Ultimate Principle of the To-be-done, with the promise of rewards that, insofar as they can be withheld, are threats). We could note such purely linguistic resources to the end of time, and still not find in such inquiry a compelling reason to believe that they are "nothing but" purely linguistic resources. If language derives from the realm of a "more-than-language," and if the Realm of No is the special domain of language, then there would be a sense in which all having to do with No, and especially all Negative Theology, could be taken as a manifestation of this transcendent motive (which demands at least that it be named, since no man can think thoroughly without coming upon the need of some word for ultimate ground, and in its nature as a highly generalized idea it will necessarily involve us in "negative theology," regardless of how positive it may seem at first glance).

However, having granted as much to theology, we should go on to say that methodologically as students of language we proceed in the other direction. Often, the study of theology is particularly rewarding to the secular student of language, first because much of the best linguistic analysis in the past was approached in theological terms, and second because theology, as a design, almost inevitably drives one to that thoroughness of statement we take as the culminating attribute of the linguistic faculty. But where the theologian says "God," for secular ends we might rather say "overall term for ground" or "overall term for purpose." Where the theologian says "love," we might rather say "communication." Where the theologian speaks of "sin," we might ask how his terms serve as a rhetoric ideally preserving or modifying the social order. Etc.

In sum: Once you have a word-using animal, you can properly look for the linguistic motive as a possible strand of motivation in all its behavior, even in such *actions* as could be accounted for without this motive in the corresponding *motions* of a nonlinguistic species. In this sense, just as the theologian would say that "God is ever present," we should say that in a language-using species "language is ever present." And "No" is the basis of language somewhat as Boehme grounded his positive-seeming "God" in a still remoter source he called "deity" (his "-ness" word, which he appropriately described as God's "un-ground"). So it would seem that, quite as the only way to say "No" systematically is to say "the godly" (as a word for the ultimate ground), so the only way to speak of "the godly" systematically is to say "No" (as with negative theology, or the negatives essential to Kant's categorical imperative). And in this sense, we can always find theological scruples interchangeable with the subtleties of language. (In materialistic philosophies, terms like *inevitability* or *historical necessity* replace *God* as the overall name for ultimate motivational ground.)

The simplest route to negative theology is to make negatives of all terms that designate positive availability to sensory perception (as *invisible, unknowable, boundless*). Such a description of *God* is also, necessarily, a statement about resources of language. And so with the next step, when we find that, insofar as the "infinitely inclusive" is the "all-inclusive," the "infinity" of "everything" is as negative as zero. Whereat we are involved in the purely linguistic paradox whereby words of greatest generality have the least empirical content. This, again, is a statement about negative theology, inasmuch as "God," the "most perfect being" (*ens perfectissimum* or *ens realissimum*) would be the most-inclusive term; hence the approach to him would be as the mystic approach to total negation or as the linguistic approach to total generality. Thus, just as the "ontological argument" for the existence of God proves itself out of itself, by saying that if there is being there must be perfect being, so our equivalent in linguistics would be our contention that *language by its nature necessarily culminates in the Negative, hence negation is of the very essence of language.*

XVI
General Survey of Negatives

Since we are here dealing with words about words, sometimes we need a distinction between a word like *No* and a word like *negativity*, which are related to each other as are *sweet* and *sweetness*. One may never learn to use the *-ness* words (particularly in their more formal reaches, as with the ideas and principles that philosophers specialize in). In accordance with our "principle of completion" as regards language, we would incline to believe that an organism cannot learn to use language at all unless it possesses the genius of *-ness*. In No (as a command) there is implicit the invitation to discover Nothing (as a "reality"), Negativity (as a principle), negativism (as an attitude), and Nihilism (as a doctrine).

We have seen how the ability to go from No to Negativity (or rather, the fact that the ability to use No intelligently, and not merely like an automaton, is grounded in the implicit ability to intuit the *no-ness* of No) makes for easy transformations whereby "positive" and "negative" change places. First, you can call things "negative" by sheer convention; as when a statistician, having divided a group into persons younger or older than a certain age, calls one of these sets positive and the other negative. Or a positivist will speak of negative electricity (without thereby assuming that it is any less positive than positive electricity is, so far as its availability to empirical operations and recording devices is concerned). And many concepts of conflict, balance, sequence, and the like may be classed together if one term is treated as the negation of another.

Next, we noted positive terms that are implicitly negative, insofar as they had connotations of deterrence or admonition. We suggested that words for No might have arisen out of such expressions.

We thus soon encountered the "attitudinal negative." That is, though both "sweet" and "bitter" are positive sensations (in the sense that a positivist might call any physical sensation positive), if you think of "sweet" as pleasant and "bitter" as unpleasant, you might call the latter negative.

When you extend this principle into the realm of ideas, you get the various alignments that put malice, vengeance, hate, fear, doubt, etc. on the negative side, with faith, hope, charity, etc. on the positive side. And once you have thus moved from the sensory realm to the moral realm, you encounter the kind of transformations we watched in Kant, with the motives of "the senses" in general being called negative. By now we have reversed the usage that would call all sensations and physically observable operations positive, in contrast with the realm of ideals, principles, "isms," and the like, which have no visible or tangible ("physicalist") existence.

Ironically, though Kant's Ethics is so strongly on the side of Ideas, his own way of using the term *intuition* gave impetus to the positivist usage. For in his terminology, human "intuition" was narrowed to the realm of *sensation*, the "Aesthetic." Earlier, it meant any immediate recognition that something is as it is. In Kant's usage, when you look at a house the sensations experienced through the retina of the eye are intuitions. In earlier usage, the term would also cover your intellectual awareness of the fact that, if the house is here, somebody must have built it, or it is not somewhere else, or it must be an appearance, etc. The word was often used to translate Aristotle's term *nous*, the faculty by which we recognize the first principles of a science, principles that might guide our sensory observations but could not themselves be sensorily observed.

Behavioristic pre-negatives (such as an animal's positive ways of avoiding an unwanted thing) would lead into human attitudinal negatives (as with Mauthner's suggestion that the negative may have begun as a sign of physical repugnance). Where Mauthner stresses an original *expressiveness* in No, we stress its original *persuasiveness*. His emphasis is aesthetic, ours is rhetorical. The two are not mutually exclusive, since persuasion is expressive. And both agree in beginning with No as an *act*-word rather than as a *scene*-word for "stating propositions" about what is and is not.

The moral equating of positive with thumbs-up attitudes and of negative with the thumbs-down set should also gain reinforcement from the contrasting behavior of the body under ideas of promise and ideas of threat, though new complications enter when, fear having turned to rage, the body that had drooped and sagged may suddenly be made assertive and erect by an internal flood of such hormones as stimulate pugnacity (adrenalin, for instance?). The negative of vengefulness here becomes the dubious but irrefutable "positive" of "moral indignation."

We have said that questions imply a feeling for the negative, since the "perfect question" is so phrased as to permit of a yes-no answer. And with Socrates in mind, we may also recall that the negative element in questions can be exploited ironically or even "negativistically," if the questioner chooses to be the bland adult counterpart of a vexatiously inquisitive child. Would you say no to this, that, and the other? You need but be persistent in your questions, piling one atop another, and stopping just short of the point where the person questioned is about to explode with anger, if only as a protection against the Heideggerian metaphysical *Angst* one experiences when the thought of ultimate questions makes one feel the underpinnings of one's beliefs melt away. Do we not here glimpse, in the Socratic questioning, the particularly ardent feeling for the negative that animates all persons strongly moralistic, as Socrates was, and that makes them plague themselves at least as much as they plague others?

The journey from the command negative, through the attitudinal negative, to the out-and-out propositional negative (with, beyond it, the sheerly arbitrary negative used for convenience) is marked also by the zero-negative (including "infinity"), the privative negative (like blindness in an organism with eyes), and the minus-negative (which presumably owes its origin to ideas of financial debt and moral guilt).

The training of Laura Bridgman and Helen Keller well illustrates the negative of privation. Here we observe how the loss of senses that are normal to the human organism was matched by a corrective positive, the compensatory refinement of senses still functioning. Also, the published records of the educational methods employed corroborate our view of the negative's origins. The matter is not explicitly discussed, but in both cases the records show a strong use of the hortatory negative from the start, with propositional negatives emerging later.

Since positive quantities can negate negative quantities, or since "positive" *acts* can negate the guilt-negatives, we move thereby into the class of positive-seeming motives negatively infused. Here we considered the negative genius in penance, mortification, victimage, property ("mine" as a "keep off"), sexuality (in its role as a cult), neoprimitivism (at its best in the quasi-positives of Nietzschean nihilism). Here belong: all ascetic regimens, all rites (in their stress upon propriety), all affirmations (atop misgivings), all "freedom" through knowledge of "necessity," all truth through study of error, all rewards that imply threats (insofar as the rewards can be withheld for failure to deliver), all things that, no matter how material they seem, are endowed with the moral judgments of the social order through which men are related to things (or you could say, all images that, insofar as they are infused by ideas, are infused by the Realm of No).[6] Similarly, psychogenic illnesses would be infused with the "Decalogical negative" insofar as they derive from repressions, inhibitions, self-punishments, and other judgments pronounced against the body by the mind it houses. The clearly theological negative in struggles with "the senses" becomes secularized in men's struggles with "nature," "environment," calamity, etc. (an edification arising from fire, famine, pestilence, and slaughter, said to be sent by God's grace as a cosmic means of saying nay to tribes when they have grown morally so blunted that they cannot understand admonitions less radical). Thus, in a minor way, there was the negative in the love that goes with the kind of misery that loves company, as with the "earthquake love" said to have prevailed for some days after the great quake and tidal wave in San Francisco.

But that brings us to a further distinction, still harder to maintain: There are positives in which the negative is necessarily implied, even though

---

[6] In our notion of an image infused by idea, we encounter a form that might be used to embarrass us. For if we began by distinguishing between image and idea on the basis that there is no No in imagery, and if we said that the realm of idea is infused with No, have we not thereby said that the realm of imagery is infused with No insofar as it is infused with idea? In which case, what happens to our original distinction between idea and image?

We here but encounter, in another way, the distinction between "image" as a sheer sensory perception and "image" in its nature as an aspect of language. It is the distinction that led to the two ratings for the term *imagination*, which in one sense meant the mere physical receiving of images as such, and in another sense meant the ability even to transcend the world of image and sensation entirely. (In between, would be the mere recombinations of sensory images that Coleridge called fancy. And memory would figure, as a name for the distinction between the perceiving of an image when the perceived thing is actually present, and the wholly or partly reminiscent imagining of an image voluntarily or in a dream when the imaged thing is not actually present.)

In saying that one cannot say no in imagery, we certainly did not mean that one cannot *imply* no. If, when a would-be thief is eyeing some valuable property that is not his, you pointedly show him a picture of a jail, you have pictorially implied, "Don't steal, or else . . ." But it is not the mere *physical* aspects of the image that make such implication possible. It is the *idea* of a jail that implies the negative. Further, the negative can but be implied, in imagery, whereas it can be stated directly through the negative command, with its *clear verbal sign* for the idea of no.

Images, in their role as verbal counters, are on the side of idea, hence are infused with the order and the disorder of ideas (being above all capable of great transformation, and even obliteration, through the powers of negativity). In brief, this is their bond with the realm of *action*. In their reference to physical sensation as such, they are "primitive-positive"—and this aspect of their nature connects them with the no-less realm of sheer motion, where everything can be only what it is.

Insofar as reduction to sheer motion is not possible to a creature endowed with the motives of verbal action, imagery will most likely indicate some kind of *passion* (ranging anywhere from the intense passion of great poetic drama to the eager *passiveness* often characteristic of contemporary lyric sensibility, that receives sensations like a dry sponge being soaked with water until it becomes so heavy that it drips).

we would deny or overlook its presence. And there are positive or neutral aspects of language that imply a feeling for the negative, though the person who exemplifies this feeling may not think of the matter as having anything to do with either positives or negatives.

"Earthquake love" would be of the first sort. The calamity having broken the established structure of routines (with the many keep-off's indigenous to it) a new sociality could flare up. It was doubtless felt as completely positive; and it should have been, since it was a spontaneous communal "love." But, willy-nilly, it owed its spirit to two orders of negation: The negating of the calamity and the negating of the rigidities that had arisen in the established order.

The other kind of negative is more "positive" (if we may coin a word!) in this sense: Language, considered in itself, is a wholly "positive" phenomenon, even in the most strictly *positivistic* usage of the term. Words, as words, are *positively* what they are. If Mr. Xavier says, "I am Napoleon and none other," he is positively saying just that.

But since we also contend that the genius of language resides in the genius of the negative, here is the point at which we must bring together these two apparently conflicting strands of motivation. We do so thus:

A man may feel his "earthquake love" as purely positive; he may even *deny* our assertion that it is negatively infused; but to do so, he must have a feeling for positive and negative as such. He may not know that he is "negating" a situation itself partly nonlinguistic or nonsymbolical; but in order to use language at all, he must have a *spontaneous feeling* for the negative.

Why? And in this linguist's variant of the ontological argument to prove that the "perfection" of the negative is implicit in the very nature of language, we would answer, first of all: Because man must spontaneously recognize that his *word* for a thing is *not* that thing. And we would now proceed to sum up that third order of the negative, where the feeling for the negative is implied in the ability to use correctly certain resources that are *purely linguistic* though no negative as such figures in their expression. Thus, in general we might say: To use language properly, you must know how to *discount* language. (That is: You must know when something is *not* quite what language, taken literally, states it to be.)

Irony is the most obvious specific example of the implied feeling for the negative. If one says, "What a beautiful day!" when the day is obviously wretched, the remark makes sense because we know it to be ironic, in flatly negating the real state of affairs.

We have already noted that the appreciation of surprise, as a formal device, implies a feeling for the negative (since the reader is led to expect one outcome, and a *different* outcome is felt as its *negation*). The feeling for the negative, in this sense, is also implicit in the comic enjoyment of incongruity, as the comic art embodies the thou-shalt-not's of social proprieties by devices that disrupt them. We thus "glimpse the missing link" between man as the rational animal and man as the laughing animal (hyena excepted), since laughter is seen to be one with the "reason" of "conscience" and the sheer nay-saying or no-understanding of verbalization.

Something "prior" to a positive will be implicitly negative. Consider, for instance, that ingenious German prefix, *ur*. *Mensch* is "man"; *Urmensch* is "prehistoric man," the kind of man that now is not. *Grund* is "ground, source, cause." *Urgrund* is "the original, primal cause." And we saw Boehme calling it the *Ungrund*. (Accordingly, when we use an expression like "behavioristic pre-language," we are by the same token talking about something that is *not* language.)

We should conclude this chapter by noting how one quite positive aspect of language, its progressive enrichment by metaphor, relies greatly on the "feeling for no." For we could not properly use a metaphor unless, as with the closely related trope, irony, we spontaneously knew that things are *not* as we literally say they are. So, on the assumption that we have, "in principle," reviewed all the cases of implied negativity, we would move ahead and end this chapter by briefly surveying the ways of metaphor.

First, we should recall the respects in which metaphor could be described as "linguistic poverty." When using the same word for the *head* of a bed, the *head* of a nation, the *head* of a man, and the *head* of a pimple, we are, in a sense, being quite limited. When you add the atrociously mixed metaphors that necessarily arise from the use of verbs, you find, as often, that the quick enrichment of language through poverty leads even to barbarism. What does a head draw away from, for instance? Well, if it is the head of an embodiment it can draw away from the praises for its weighings-out. We mean: The head of a corporation can deduct allowances for his expenditures.

One uses metaphor without madness insofar as one spontaneously knows that the *literal* implication of the figure is *not* true. Hearing an expression like "the hammer of his diction," we never for a moment think that a literal hammer is involved. We language-users are too essentially "negative-minded" for that. We spontaneously know that *this* "hammer" is *not* a hammer.

True, there are complications here. Thus, if we find that, over a long stretch of time, a given person's metaphors all seem to be pointing in the same direction, we can legitimately suspect that there is a compulsion within the freedom. Hence, despite the *freedom* of the rational discount, there may be sheer *necessity* in the trend of the images as such. Insofar as terms, metaphors, "models," fictions generally, are positive, they may compel us despite our genius for the negative; that is, we may not "discount" them enough, not fully recognizing how imaginally positive they are.

We should also note, among the ways whereby metaphor (transference, "carry-over") can occur: there is its arising through sheer error. Particularly, we have in mind shifts between genus and species (the kind of metaphor sometimes differentiated as synecdoche). We see these operating when children are first learning to speak. Thus, recall the many anecdotes about the child who, taught to call *one particular person* "Papa," embarrasses the mother and amuses the fellow travelers in a railway car by delightedly shouting "Papa!" when a strange man goes by. Particularly, as regards words for relationship, there is a spontaneous shifting between specific and generic usage. Similarly, unique designations, such as *Caesar*, can come to have purely relational or functional meanings (as with *Kaiser* and *Czar*).

Thus, metaphor can creep up on us, too, sometimes to very good effect. We need merely remind ourselves that, in its essence, it implies such feeling for the "discount" as could not completely be, unless it were logically reducible to the yes-no distinction.

XVII
Positive Aspects of Language

In one sense, all language is positive, in the most positivistic sense of the term. For the structure of each sentence is positively what it is, even though the sentence itself might be nonsense or a lie.

Within such positiveness, there are ways of introducing positive-negative distinctions. For instance, we have pointed out that a generalized term like *act* is a *question*, when set against specific terms like *eat, run, fight*, which are like answers to that implied question: "Was the act this, or that, or the other?"

But even a specific verb becomes in effect a question, insofar as there is something problematical about the way of carrying out the act it designates. Q: "What did he do (that is: What was his act)?" A: "He won." Q: "But *how* did he win (that is: He won by *doing what*)?" And Q might add: "In what order?" That is, in effect: "Did he do this, that, or the other first? Answer yes or no on each count," etc.; "Did he do such-and-such second?" etc. But by asking questions *in general*, one can somewhat conceal the yes-no design implicit in them. Or, if you will: Once the yes-no design becomes subtilized by an intermediate realm of maybe, questions can be phrased in the spirit of this intermediate realm, with the result that we conceal the logic of their ultimate design: the yes-no, true-false, right-wrong kind of terms or propositions that are "contradictory" since they confront each other as negations of each other.

However devoid of positive content such words as *act* and *scene* may be (when contrasted with words that specify particular acts or give the details of particular scenes), one can work out an algebra concerned with positive relations between such terms. Thus, by a "scene-act ratio" we designate a substantial relationship between scene and act whereby some ingredient of the scene is analogically present in the act; hence, with regard to this ingredient, the act can be called a derivative or function of the scene. The thought suggests that, however negative-minded the problematical x of Arabian algebra may be as the sign of the unknown quantity, and whatever may be its hidden cultural bonds with the prohibitions that Mohammedanism placed upon imagery in art (prohibitions which led to subterfuges whereby imagery in disguise was smuggled into the algebra-like "arabesque" traceries), out of this negation-mindedness intrinsic to the symbol there arises a realm of positives intrinsic to the medium as such.

It is not our province in this chapter to discuss the positive aspects of language. But we might consider them at least "in principle," lest our stress upon the ubiquity of linguistic negativity leave the reader with the impression that we would reduce language to "nothing but" the negative. In the first place, even the relations among a batch of negatives would be positively what they were. Similarly, our intuiting of them would be positive. And by the same token, all tactics and developments of language are to be studied and enjoyed in their positive nature.

Once language is developed to any extent, all sorts of evolutions are possible that need not or can not be referred to the negative. Out of interrogative pronouns, for instance, can come relative pronouns (as with the step from "Who is here?" to "The man who is here . . ."). Or demonstratives can weaken into articles (as with the many forms that Latin *ille* took, in becoming *il, elle, la, lo, les, las,* etc. of the modern Romance languages). Verbs can readily become prepositions, as with a word like *during.* In popular speech, an interesting transformation of that sort is to be seen in an expression like, "He'll be twenty-one come next Thursday," where "come" has about the same grammatical force as though one had said, "He'll be twenty-one by next Thursday," though the sense is slightly different.

But let us round out our positives "in principle," by a theory of definition. Whereas we shall find the genius of the negative present as a necessary motive, our main concern will be with the positive element in definition.

XVIII
Dramatistic Theory of Definition

Here are three major ways in which a language helps us to make our meaning precise:

1) By order. (Even in a language that allows for much freedom of word order, the fact remains that, once a sentence is formed, it is necessarily a series of words released in a certain order.)

2) By differentiation of grammatical function.

3) By growth of vocabulary, either through new words or through the metaphorical extension of old words.

All three ways, even the *latitudinarian* way of metaphorical (or analogical) extension, are in the direction of definiteness. Whereat we would liken a sentence to a series of successive siftings-down. It narrows its meaning in much the same way as the address on an envelope locates one person among millions. For instance, consider a sentence such as: "This good man runs very swiftly."

In the first three words (partly defined by a conventional word order that abides by our established expectations), we have narrowed down the substantive *man* by a demonstrative and an adjective. Logically (as distinguished from the actual word order) we "began" with a noun that applies to everyman; we "next" narrowed it with an adjective that applies to some men; "then" we further narrowed it by the demonstrative for selecting one man.

Perhaps we should add a further distinction, in line with Hegel on "this-ness." Any actual sensory thing is a "this" *uniquely*. But the word *this* is a *universal*. Whereas *man* and *good* can properly be applied only to *some* things, *this* can be applied to anything and everything (except insofar as a distinction between *this* and *that* is involved). So there is a sense in which you could say that *this* is the most general term of the three, with the other two progressively narrowing its reference. *Good* and *man* here function like grammatical inflections of the demonstrative: *man* indicates that *this* is masculine in gender, and *good* indicates that it is honorific.

Insofar as the first three words of our illustrative sentence make a cluster of terms mutually modifying one another, in their totality they designate their subject by a process of sifting-down. The same reasoning applies to the predicate. *Runs* is progressively narrowed by *swiftly* and *very*. Then, taking the first three words as part of one system and the second three as part of another system, we note how these two systems mutually narrow each other. That is, we could say that the "man" system "belongs to" the "run" system (*man* being in effect a medium through which the "pure" act of running is made to exist in time). Or we could say that *runs* belongs to *man* much as though it were a participle, as in *running man*.

Such would be, in sum, the Dramatistic view of definition. It would be our version of the classic formula: *per genus et differentiam*.

In the ideal conditions for making a statement, we begin with enough resources to choose from. And then we narrow down our meaning by selections from among these resources. The selections are related to one another by an *order*; and each selection is to the others as if this one selection were the widest field and each of the others contributed to the narrowing of that field.

Insofar as the field of available terms was not wide enough to begin with, it must be extended by new terms or by the metaphorical extension of old terms. And insofar as the new terms designate not empirical objects and physical operations but principles, ideas, and the like, even new terms will be clarified with the help of metaphorical extensions from the previous terminology. Such metaphorical extension is, from one point of view, but the principle of latitude, needed before we can have sufficient range to choose from; or from another point of view, it has itself begun the work of specification done by any term, even a universal "this."

In one notable respect, the narrowing is "circular." For instance, when describing how "This good man runs very swiftly" filters down to its meaning, we might begin with *very*. *Very* is then the widest field covered by these terms. It might go with an endless number of adjectives or adverbs. As soon as we say "swiftly," we have cut its field greatly. But we might have to do with very swift riding, walking, flying, thinking, growing, raining, dying, etc. As soon as we add *runs*, we have eliminated that range of possibilities—but we next must select from among the many kinds of things that can run, etc. Start with *man*, and our series of progressive narrowings takes another course.

In actual practice, however, even with a language like Latin, with its wide range of word orders that will be intelligible and "seem natural," the form or order that the sentence actually takes will determine the sequence in which the successive narrowings-down will be presented by speaker or writer and thus experienced by auditor or reader.

All told, a sentence proceeds by establishing an order by which the domain of terministic coverage is successively narrowed. The order of such narrowings might have been different, so far as the sheer logic of the case is concerned. But in any case, even cases where the principle of circularity holds, some order must be chosen and followed, even if but arbitrarily. Once an order is chosen, *through* it, in its "temporizing," we can readily move beyond it, to the fixing of an *essence* (the *meaning* that the sentence *adds up to*, or rather, *narrows down to*).

However, we decidedly do not want to suggest that, as regards definition in the large, "order" is always thus a somewhat arbitrary matter. In logic, as well as in rhetoric and poetic, there are *proprieties of unfolding*, despite circularity among one's terms, or despite the ways whereby a work finally *adds up to* (or is *reducible to*!) certain overall or underlying equations. True, an experienced author writes his introduction last. So, in a sense, he begins where he ended. (And, had he thus begun, he would have ended somewhere else, unless he is a marvel either of steadfastness or of stodginess—we'll let the reader decide on the probabilities here.) But, once the die is cast, from then on a succession *of some sort* is *unavoidable*; and the farther one proceeds, the more inexorably a succession *of one sort* becomes *inevitable*, or *should* become so.

But to show how terms and order can so work together that even terms on their face *inaccurate* can function as wholly *definite* or *defining*, let us consider this hypothetical case:

You would have a picture placed appropriately on a wall. A friend is aiding you to this end. He holds the picture, while you stand back, giving directions. You say: "A little higher . . . no, that was too much . . . now a bit to the right . . . now down just a tiny bit more . . . now revolve the whole thing slightly . . . no, I meant: revolve it in the other direction . . ." etc.

Here is a hopelessly vague set of directions. Your friend might have asked, "What do you mean, 'a little higher'?" etc. He might have challenged you at each stage of the way to define your terms, as one might hold you up (in our hypothetical sentence about "this good man") by demanding definitions for *this*, *good*, and *man*. But he knows, as you know, that certain definings here can be got through sheer *order*. He knows that even if he does swing out of line a bit (as the first term in a sentence is way out of line), nevertheless the next step will help to narrow things down—and so on.

The important thing to note, for our purposes, is: However vague any given direction might have seemed when you examined it *in isolation* as a term, it may function quite specifically if it appears in *precisely that* ORDER *of terms*.

Thus, out of even *arbitrary* first choices, there may emerge *necessary* orders of expression. And once you add the concept of order to your notions of definition, you discover that even the "vaguest" of terms can serve quite adequately to *define*, if their "order of appearance" is proper to the situation.

Of course, there are two kinds of situation here. There are the *purely* linguistic situations, as regards for instance the kind of order needed for making an intellible remark in English, which must rely greatly upon word order because it has been able to shed the many inflections that give Latin its great latitude in this respect. And there are the pragmatic norms of order (grounded in what Malinowski calls "context of situation") whereby, however "vague" a word might seem when approached in the absolute, it is *perfectly* clear as used in a particular situation. (What could be vaguer, for instance, than an expression such as "Do this"? And the more you tried to define it in the absolute, the more difficult your task might be. Yet if you say it when doing exactly what someone is asking about, think how perfect an indicator the words are.)

However great a feeling for propriety (and thus for the admonitory negative) may be involved in the building of an order, order as such is wholly positive. That is, (as regards the directions for hanging the picture) the various directions, each vague in itself, acquired their collective precision by being given *in exactly that order and no other*. And order, in this sense, applies even more compellingly to "imaginative" literature, where the terms may not be strictly defined as individual counters, but where the particular kind of unfolding that results from this one particular arrangement allows us to experience a mood not otherwise definable.

Dramatistically, we might think of key terms as *Characters*, like the characters in a fiction. Characters do not mutually exclude one another, no matter how clear they may become for us, as we watch their words and acts and situations and relationships unfold in accordance with the order of the author's exposition.

Or, Characters are like empires, which have strong centers of jurisdiction that become vague at the outer edges. You know well enough when you are at the center of one jurisdictional system rather than another. But the outer areas may overlap upon the outer areas of other jurisdictional systems. Or, to change the analogy, words are like planets, each with its particular gravitational pull. The gravitational pull weakens, the farther away from the center a body is—and it may move so far away that it falls within the gravitational pull of some other planet.

Since Characters do not flatly exclude one another (as a proneness to "Over-Negation" may prompt the fiends of definition to require), a new Character can come to set up an area of jurisdiction within the realm once occupied solely by another ruler. Thus, there was Don Quixote. Then, later, there was Emma Bovary. Before the arrival of Emma Bovary, Don Quixote covered an area of personal motives that largely included Emma Bovary's. After Emma Bovary arrived, Don Quixote had to move over. Or many nineteenth-century Characters carved for themselves small areas of jurisdiction within the general empire covered by Hamlet. We believe that all terms for the "ideas" used by philosophers, historians, psychologists, moralists, and the like are Characters in this sense.

In certain contexts, two such Characters may confront each other as bluntly as yes and no, thus "negating" one another. But they can do so only insofar as they share some field in common, thus overlapping in a Realm of Maybe.

True, we have subscribed to the principle of "perfection" as an important ingredient in any linguistic motivation. (Its presence in language, as we have said, corresponds to the ubiquity of "God" in theological views of motivation generally.) And the perfect paradigm of definition by an orderly process of narrowing-down is a succession of dichotomies, the splitting of a field into halves, of those halves into quarters, etc. And however positive such order is, we can glimpse the functioning of the negative here, when we think of a systematic attempt to locate a lost object with minimum chances of wasted effort. Instead of searching the entire area at random, we search half of it thoroughly. If the object is *not found* there, we search half of the half we have *not* searched, etc. Each area searched is defined with reference to what we will *not* search, unless the object is *not* found in the area we are searching.

Or, to state it another way: A sentence proceeds somewhat like a conveyer for the sorting of gravel into different sizes by a progressive widening of the mesh through which the gravel mass is sifted.

So, all told, definition is got by the use of terms which are like Characters each having a center of authority but with areas of jurisdiction that it variously shares with other terms or Characters. By appearing in a certain *order*, the terms can contribute *functionally* to a definiteness that they do not possess *individually*. Such order is positive, but it is guided by a feeling for the negative. And though the terms, as Characters, are positive, their adaptation in fixed orders again implies their responsiveness to the genius of negativity.

"Accentuate the positive," the jazz singer exhorts us, obviously trying to undo the nay-saying he spontaneously feels, in suffering the indignities that threaten his songfulness even while they give him a subject for his song.

By all means, accentuate the positive.

But for the limits of this one chapter we would not forget explicitly, as man probably never forgets implicitly, to accentuate the negative, with its genius pervading every language-infested positive.

The Negative. Perhaps the one great motivational principle that man, in his role as the language-using animal, has added to nature.

SECTION FOUR

Postscripts on the Negative

These afterthoughts on the Negative are offered in particular for readers who would rather consider things in more or less self-contained glimpses than follow one protracted exposition. And the notes may bring up points not discussed in the chapter.

Symbol-using demands a feeling for the negative (beginning in the Korzybskian admonition that the word for the thing is *not* that thing). A specifically symbol-using animal will necessarily introduce a symbolic ingredient into every experience. Hence, every experience will be imbued with negativity. Sheer "animality" is not possible to the sensory experiences of a symbol-using animal.

Everything that can be said about "God" has its analogue in something that can be said about *language*. And just as theorizing about God leads to so-called "negative theology," so theorizing about language heads in the all-importance of the Negative.

Thomas Mann (New York *Herald Tribune*, October 27, 1952), in "This I Believe . . ." says: "Deep down I believe that the creation of the universe out of nothingness and that of life out of an inorganic state ultimately aimed at the creation of man. I believe that man is meant as a great experiment whose possible failure by man's own guilt would be paramount to the failure of creation itself. . . . Whether this belief be true or not, man would be well advised if he behaved as though it were." Interesting variant of Pascal's wager, and essentially as nay-minded. For our purposes, the statement would be reducible to this: "All the universe is to be approached in terms of No; even *in*organic nature is to be so understood; and man should not act otherwise than as if it were an undeniable fact that he should strive toward perfection of his Negativity, i.e., toward Ideal Justice."

A child, visiting, had been admonished by his mother not to ask for things, but to wait until they were offered to him. He was standing before a bowl of bananas, looking at them hungrily. The hostess asked him what he was doing. He answered: "I am *not* eating a banana."

When "No" has been generalized: In parts of the world where injustice traditionally prevails, the fear of voicing complaints against specific persons in power can become a Fate-laden fear of voicing any complaints at all. That is, the victim's fear of being punished in case he was caught speaking against some particular authority, becomes a "mysteriously" motivated custom, grounded in a sense of "propriety" or "piety" in general, a feeling that "fate" itself will punish any expressing of complaints, as an undisciplined habit unbecoming to a person of modest rank. There are variants of this motive in the tragic distrust of *hubris*.

One correspondent wrote: "Interesting to observe possible functions of the negative affirmative or affirming negative, i.e., the conjoining of affirmative and negative in a single expression, *Little Big Horn*. Or if this be thought only a linguistic accident, consider *superette*. . . . The grocery business has gone in for supermarkets. The little fellow, eager to get ahead, advertises his *superette*. Is this an enlarging diminutive or a diminishing enlarger?"

Another correspondent wrote: "I have been thinking that one might well envision, each man for himself, an affirmative-negative continuum under the assumption that every 'event' (in the Whitehead sense) contains both affirmative and negative factors. One might thus arrange all of one's own experiences somewhere along the continuum. The most affirmative event in my experience is, I imagine, standing on a mountain top in Hawaii to watch the sun come bursting out of the Pacific ocean. The event that most nearly aproaches complete negativity, I suspect, occurred when as a boy of twelve I witnessed a coroner's jury in a small Missouri town inspect the body of a child strangled by his own mother, herself unwed and the victim (as I recall in after time) of considerable deprivation. Is not a child killed by its own mother at birth as near to complete negation as any event can be, yet to hold any affirmation at all?

"Somewhere along the line between the splendidly affirmative and the stark negative events I have discussed I suspect every other event of my own life could be ranged for its degree of affirmative-negative content."

The binary system in mathematics may be no more or less negatively infused than, say, the decimal system. But this much seems clear: In the application of the binary system to the "electronic brains" of the new calculating devices, the genius of the negative is uppermost as it is in the stop-go signals of traffic regulation. For the binary system lends itself well to technological devices whereby every number is stated as a succession of choices between the closing of an electrical contact and the leaving of the contact open. In effect, then, the number is expressed by a series of yeses and noes, given in one particular order.

Here is a notable reversal of Greek and English usage: The Greek verb meaning "to occupy one's leisure" was *scholazein*. The Greek verb meaning "to be engaged in business activity" was *ascholein*. That is, the word for business activity was formed by the prefixing of an a-privative to the word for the enjoyment of leisure. This is somewhat as though our word for unemployment were grammatically positive, and our word for employment grammatically negative. However, leisure is unemployment in a "good" sense, akin to Latin *otium cum dignitate*, which might be translated "state of being out of work by choice, while enjoying an income which one puts to uses generally deemed admirable." (Following Bentham, we take it that, in monetary economies, "dignity" is likely to imply "money.") But here is the surprise: In Aristotle's *Politics* the "ability to occupy leisure nobly" is called "the first principle of all things," the *arche panton* (*Politics*, 8, 2, 3.) Yet what is such a principle, if not God! Precisely here, in considering these shifts with regard to terms for work and leisure (with the Greeks, in an era of slavery, using a negative where we use a positive, and vice versa), we might glimpse the subtle relation between Aristotle's *Politics* and his Theology (*Metaphysics*), as with the pagan ways of equating social and transcendental lordliness.

A highway, in its sheer materiality, is wholly positive. But the traffic regulations that make it viable are negatively infused. Presumably, the many animals killed on a fast cross-country highway had perceived the road in its positive physicality—that is, they had presumably distinguished the sheer sensation of the pavement from the sensation of the dirt nearby; but they were unaware of its "rules," some of them negatives established by traffic law, some negatives set by men's knowledge of the inconveniences imposed upon a car if it leaves the road. The animals apparently assume that cars, like animals, are likely to go in any direction, not just along the road. . . . The *confinements* of the road are also the conditions of its *freedom*; by its regulations it is made serviceable. . . . Empiricism seeks to approach reality through sheer sensory immediacy, rather than through the stress upon the symbolic element that, like "godhead," inevitably infuses all experience possible to man, the essentially symbol-using animal. In this regard, the empiricist approach to reality would be as close as the empiricist could come to the kind of perception we have attributed to animals just before they get run over.

What of Whitman's "Song of the Open Road"? Historically, it preceded traffic conditions as we now know them in the era of the automobile. But the *principle* of the completely regulated road was already present, in Whitman's time, owing to the fact that the railroad was then the culminative form of travel. Though wrecks were comparatively plentiful, while both safety devices and traffic regulations were comparatively rudimentary, the whole "logic" of railroading was in the direction of more highly developed negatives, as with the elaborate signals and controls on a much-traveled sector of a modern first-class system. So Whitman had had the experience of the *regulated* range; and he could in imagination combine this with the ideal of *free* ranging. The combining of such opposites could be celebrated in a "song" of the "open" road, proclaiming a yea that arose from the mounting tangle of nays. Was it medicine, or hysteria? In any case, it could fuse, or confuse, the obsolescent with the future.

We have repeatedly remarked on the integral relation between the negative and property. There is a similar integral relation between the negative and personality. Recall Aristotle's basic act-agent ratio with regard to ethics: By the practice of virtue a man becomes virtuous (develops a virtuous disposition, *hexis, habitus*). Hence, insofar as a cult of virtue is guided by thou-shalt-not's, personality itself is compounded of negatives. Since personality involves *role*, and since roles necessarily involve enactment through the use of properties set by the given social order, note how personality can turn two ways. It turns in the direction of property, status, material resources, all things that have to do with the *implementing* of an act. And insofar as a given social order contains some measure of injustice, personality turns towards the *ideal transcending* of the social order by negations variously along the line between revolution and gradualist improvement. For "justice" is the logical completion of language, leading one to round the circle by imposing upon oneself the negatives one would impose upon others; and if man is the essentially language-using animal, then it would seem to follow that insofar as a person hopes for special benefits by the doing of unjust acts or through the continuance of unjust conditions, the personality will be in some way "warped" or "thwarted." Thus arise the many and varied kinds of "vindication" that finally become characteristic parts of the personality, each with its subtle variants of victimage that range all the way from genocide to the weeding of a garden, from devoted thoughts of the Crucifixion to mild, apologetic irony, from rabid persecution of others to "psychogenic" illnesses conscientiously willed, against one's will, upon the self.

Addendum to our remarks on Kant: Kant's positivizing of the Negative morality is dialectically completed in his principle of *universalization*. But it could be viewed in another way: The positivizing is contrived through the forming of the Character, or *Personality*. Integrity of action is then derived from the integrity of the agent (agent-act ratio). The line-up, thus, would be: (1) Genius of Language centers in negative; (2) Given social order requires corresponding thou-shalt-not's of property, the negative thus being essential to both linguistic and social pyramids; (3) The principle of universalization whereby one's thou-shalt-not's, addressed to others, circle back upon the self, makes for the equating of justice and conscience—the former "objective," the latter "subjective"; (4) Insofar as one acts through Character, or Personality, one is moved by an "internal," "subjective," "individual" principle of conduct, itself likewise a kind of universalization; (5) Ethical completion arising when one's individual sense of No coincides with the universalization of No, the No is felt as "positive" when it is obeyed through a sense of absolute consistency rather than through fear of punishment. Hegel historicizes this "positive" ethics of personality in his notion of the "world-historical" figure who, in acting sheerly through self-interest, materializes the purposes of the Divine "Idea," or "Spirit." Hegel's invention, for thus bringing the godhead down to earth in terms of purely secular ambitions, moves us farther along the line linking Utilitarianism (in both its theological and secular formulations), Machiavellianism, and Goethe's Great Negator Mephistopheles, "a portion of that power, that always wills the bad and always makes for good."

Perversion is a major aspect of No. Aristotle calls democracy, oligarchy, and tyranny the "perversions" (*parekbaseis*) of timocracy, aristocracy, and monarchy respectively. (See *Nichomachaean Ethics*, VIII, x, for instance). Sexual deviations from the biologic norm would also be classifiable here; and it quite often happens that negations of this sort are characteristic of persons particularly apt at conceits that get things upside down, inside out, and backwards.

Djuna Barnes's *Nightwood* comes to a focus in the formula: "degradation and the night." Degradation is the action (and/or the passion) of an over-stepping No. And night is the scene for such an act. The imagery of highly inventive filth and decay is intensely No-ridden. One member of a criticism class that studied the book, observed with regard to the important character of Nora that there had been a popular song in the Twenties: "No, No, Nora." We wonder: Could it somehow be lurking in her name? . . . He also said: "In this story we see nothing as the devourer, the destroyer, nothing as the maw, the void (taken both ways, as the great emptiness and the great emptying), noun and verb, as the catch-basin or catchall." This is a superb combining of impressionism and analysis. Our only objection would be: We would admonish lest active No get lost in scenic Nothing.

Whether or not Heaven and Hell literally exist, their linguistic function, their nature as terms in language, is this: Both are "positive" or scenic counterparts of the Negative; for both, in their way, provide ultimate kinds of law enforcement—that is, they provide verbal backing for the negative command. But whereas both are terms for "positive" realms, as regards whatever kind of *aesthesis* we are expected to possess in the afterlife, on a higher level hell is related to heaven as is negative to positive. Purgatory is a realm of intermediation between hell's no and heaven's yes, except that it favors the yes side, its yesness being imagined in a climb that, the higher one gets, the easier it becomes, until the rising is rather like a fall. If heaven is yes, and hell is no, then purgatory would be a kind of maybe. But not a maybe that holds one in suspense, as with that ultrafrigid moment in hell where we see Satan undoing himself (Canto XXXIV). Rather, a maybe that is incipiently yes, an arrest emergently active, and thus in essence most gloriously linguistic, too. For whereas, if you condition an animal to yes and no, then jam the two conditionings together, the animal falls into a fit, not knowing which course to choose, precisely at that point humanity blossoms with symbol-using, and atop threatened stoppages erects its meditative systems, that may eventually be studied in appreciation and hypochondriasis, lovingly and clinically, on the chance that we may eventually cease to feel the need to slaughter one another.

Hell is, *to perfection*, a function of the negative. Yes, Hell has its kind of perfection, too. The notion of Hell involves a "scenic" reinforcement of the negative as a principle, the total or ultimate thou-shalt-not. And heaven, linguistically considered, would be so likewise, the scenic Yes dialectically opposed to Hell's scenic No. (Before the world began, it was linguistically decreed that, for every ultimate threat in language, there must be in language an ultimate promise, beginning with the Great Mediator, as absolute Burden-Bearer.

One very relevant correspondent asked: "What of Carlyle, in *Sartor Resartus*?" We had forgotten (and unpardonably, since we had talked about the book in our *Rhetoric*). After reviewing particularly the chapter on Everlasting No, we went back and re-examined the earlier one on Everlasting Yea. It seemed that the chapter on Yea was as Nay-ridden as the chapter on No. Next, we wondered why Yea came so much earlier, and whether No, coming later, might be the breaking-through, and thus the true comment upon everything preceding. That is, in line with our concerns about fulfillments, we wondered whether the flowering Negation should be taken as the mature statement of the burgeoning Yea. Such could be particularly the case with the explosive Carlyle, whose disorders of digestion were so obviously caused by his volcanic ponderings, and the nature of whose magmatic purposes should be revealed in the lava of his expression.

In the *Inferno*, last canto, hell, being the Universal Cesspool, is rife with images of the fecally no-no sort. In his comments on this Canto XXXIV, the editor of the Temple edition borrows Carlyle's formula, "the Everlasting No." As regards fulfillment, observe how No comes to a head in this final canto, in lines 22-27, ablaze with terms for both negation and privation (our italics):

> How icy chill and hoarse I then became, ask *not*, O Reader! for I write it *not*, because all speech would *fail* to tell.
> I did *not* die, and did *not* remain alive; now think, for thyself, if thou hast any grain of ingenuity, what I became, *deprived* of both death and life.

The Canto deals with a kind of Zero Moment. Note how Satan cancels himself, as the batting of his wings but sends forth draughts that freeze him all the more. Here is the ultimate perversion of action, action that blocks its own act. One omission surprises us: Why is there no reference to the near-stopped heart, the Skipped Beat, the pulse so sluggish that one can hardly drag the body forward? If we had the feeling for Italian styles, might we discern such a weight here, perhaps in the sheer rhythm of the lines? The dead center is passed in lines 76-84, when the travelers as it were cross the ridge from one slope to another; climbing to freedom by a grip upon the frozen monster's lewdly problematical hairs.

Then we wondered about the place in the *Odyssey*, where Ulysses out-wits Polyphemus by giving his name as "Noman." Might a closer inspection reveal something notable about the use of the negative here? And, sure enough, we found at least one development quite relevant to our purposes. It has to do with a principle of aesthetic consistency. For the land of the Cyclops, where this incident is to take place, is introduced in strongly nega-tive terms. The Cyclops are lawless; they do not plant nor plow; their land is unsown, untilled; they have neither parliamentary gatherings nor oracles of law; they dwell in hollow caves, and each makes laws for his own family without concern for the others; there is a waste isle stretching outside the harbor; it is neither near nor far away; it has unnumbered wild goats which are frightened by no human paths, for no hunters come there; it has neither flocks nor plowed lands; the soil lies unsown and untilled, desolate of men; the Cyclops have no ships; there are no ship-builders; yet it is not a sorry land; the vines do not decay; there is no need of moorings; Ulysses and his men arrived when there was no light; there was no moon; none of them be-held the island on arriving there. The above is based on an English transla-tion, not checked against the Greek, which might reveal either a few more negatives, or a few less; but surely the tenor of the passage is clear. Here is a wholly negative scene preparing for the negative nature of Ulysses' linguistic act. We can imagine that the lines were originally sung with a meaningful stress upon each of these negatives, so that the audience "got the point," and remembered it when Ulysses rounded out the pattern by giving his name as "Noman."

In Wallace Stevens' "Sunday Morning," when the poet equates the great negative, Death, with something as positive-seeming as Mother, he thereby has a way of bringing efficient and final cause together. Negative end is thus made one with positive beginning; finish as mortality is made inter-changeable with finish as fulfillment or perfection, the poem thus leading up to and away from a "paradise" as so defined. . . . Stevens in "Le Monocle de Mon Oncle":

> There is not nothing, no, no, never nothing,
> Like the clashed edges of two words that kill.

Those who think we are excessive, in approaching "yes" roundabout, as the negating of "no," might well recall that the Greek word for "truth" explicitly employs the a-privative. Truth is *aletheia*, the "non-Lethe," or un-forgotten. Incidentally, might not the thought of this etymology suggest why Plato's theory of "discovery" was also a theory of "remembering," of "being reminded" about things known in a previous ideal existence, and now dimly recalled?

Mohammed allowed the new convert a great initial act of negation, since all previous vows could be canceled. All, that is, except one major quantitative negative: monetary debt.

Also included here should be a note on Hemingway's story, "A Clean, Well-Lighted Place." As one correspondent pointed out, it is an excellent item for our present purposes, since it comes to a focus in a negativized parody of the Lord's Prayer. ("Our nada who art in nada, nada be thy name thy kingdom nada thy will be nada as it is in nada . . ." etc.) Unfortunately, whereas the story is less than 1500 words long, our "note" runs to over 2000; and so we omit it. However, we call attention to it here, as embodying many variants of negation in a very brief space. And we shall reserve for publication elsewhere a detailed account of its motivations.

Private confession (in public). This note might be entitled *Gradus ad Negativum*. Some time back, the author was examining some of his own verses, that he had written over the years. He was distressed to observe much evidence of the "Demonic Trinity," as regards motives he found lurking in his cult of "The Beautiful." That is: Despite his preferences to the contrary, he did not merely keep encountering themes that seemed to him "phallic," a kind of motivation that psychoanalytic sex has made *salonfähig*; he also kept encountering motives that were expressed in images he would class, however remotely or roundabout, as "excremental" or "diuretic." By the "demonic trinity," as discussed in his *Grammar of Motives*, the author refers to the three privy functions, which are as it were a bodily burlesque of heavenly power, wisdom, and love, as with the "three faces" of Satan. Out of such bondage, the author, to his comparative relief, escaped by shifting to an article, "Thanatopsis for Critics: A Brief Thesaurus of Deaths and Dyings," that sought to codify the meanings possible to the imagery of Death, in view of the fact that a poet's imagery is expected to deal with positive experience, yet no poet who has experienced death can return to tell the tale. Next, the author decided that he wanted to know about shadows, as they figure in formal expression. He made an index of Chamisso's story, *Peter Schlemihl*, about a man without a shadow. While he was working on the Chamisso story, he gradually began to decide that he would like to do an article on the Negative. Then he realized that the notes on "Demonic Trinity," Death, and Shadow had all been aspects of an emergent concern with the negative as such.

If language is so greatly Nay-ridden always, think how mighty must be the sway of No in times when persons of influence are beset by exceptional fear for their possessions. Moral indignation is "as prompt as the bee to the blossom," when a man is aroused by threats to whatever dominion, however wide or narrow, he has come to think of as rightfully his. The notion of an irresistible force encountering an immovable body was perhaps in essence not a physicalist principle at all, but the physicalist-seeming prevision of a contest most inhumanely human, in which one vast system of Nays would be inexorably pitted against another. We pray that they may not, in their totality, add up to an Annihilating Nothing. May they contrive rather to build an overall positive order, with negatives of a sort whereby differing suborders, each with its appropriate set of negatives, can accommodate themselves to one another.

Crossing the continent in a car, after having written a long article on the Negative, the fellow mumbled: "Think of all the swamps and deserts, and wasted areas generally, all positively there, and capable of removal or improvement only by a vast extension of the domain of human negativity."

In sum: (1) Property (defined in terms of the particular social pyramid that goes with the particular social order). (2) The Negative (essence of language; it basically reinforces the essence of property, which means "no trespassing"). (3) Mortification (and its variants, self-visited upon those who would exhort themselves not to transgress beyond necessity upon the property of others). (4) No-no imagery (rot, death, offal, associations with such privacy as characterizes the privy parts; generally, the infusion of sensory positives with the genius of moral negatives). (5) Victimage, purification by sacrifice, by *vicarious atonement*, unburdening of guilt within by transference to chosen vessels without. (6) Completion, perfection (linguistic resources whereby local problems of order become translated into grandly Universal replicas—supernatural, metaphysical, or naturalistic—all heading in the Norms of Justice, marked by such fierce sexless love as an ideal father might have for an ideal son). (7) *Da capo.*

"Sensible objects conform to the premonitions of Reason and reflect the conscience. All things are moral; and in their boundless changes have an unceasing reference to spiritual nature. Therefore is nature glorious with form, color, and motion; that every globe in the remotest heaven, every chemical change from the rudest crystal up to the laws of life, every change of vegetation from the first principle of growth in the eye of a leaf, to the tropical forest and antediluvian coal-mine, every animal function from the sponge up to Hercules, shall hint or thunder to man the laws of right and wrong, and echo the Ten Commandments." (Emerson's early essay, "Nature"; Chapter V, "Discipline.") What lines could be more perfect for our purposes? Linguistically, we need but reverse the statement, whereat we find it saying in effect: Start with the spirit of the Decalogue, start with the Compleat Negation, and every material thing encountered along your way will be thus negatively infused.

In their *positive*, material nature as *powers*, our many mighty new technological devices call for a corresponding set of admonitory *controls*, or *negatives*, which are best sanctioned how?

Chapter Eight

Formalist Criticism: Its Principles and Limits

The main steps in my discussion of "Formalist Criticism: Its Principles and Limits" will be these:

First, I shall attempt to isolate the poetic motive along lines indicated by my theory of "symbolic action." Next I shall use as a basis of reference Cleanth Brooks's Formalist "articles of faith." Then I shall consider the problem of locating Mr. Brooks's specific reservations with regard to my position. Fourth, when on the most likely root of our differences, I shall sum up my position. And finally, since Mr. Brooks's recent book on the writings of William Faulkner throws further light on the problems of Formalist criticism, I shall end with some related remarks on Faulkner.

I
The Poetic Motive

Though anyone would grant that there is a critical difference between a material object and its name (we might call it a kind of "Cartesian split" between the *word* "tree" and the *thing* tree), each has its own kind of "reality." A word is as real in its way as a thing; otherwise there could not be the kinds of motion and position that we call words. But however close the correspondence between the nameable and the named (it is as close to total as can be when we call a spade a spade), there is also a world of difference between these two realms. For instance, think how easy it is to turn the *word* "tree" into "five thousand trees," and how different would be the processes required for the similar multiplication of an actual tree—nor should we forget that whereas there are more than fourteen hundred rhymes for the *word* "tree," an actual tree doesn't rhyme with anything.

If we employ the expression "symbolic action" to designate the use of symbol systems generally (in tribal vernaculars, mathematics, philosophic or scientific nomenclatures, dancing, music, painting, architectural styles, etc.), we can safely say that insofar as any symbol system refers to any aspect of the nonsymbolic realm (the realm of sheer motion and position) there is a *qualitative* difference between the symbol and the symbolized. For the symbol is necessarily referring to the symbolized in terms of something that the symbolized is not (in the sense that the *thing* tree is not a *word*).

Besides the many things that are named, the world is full of unnamed things that are potentially nameable. Indeed, being the kind of symbol-using animal we are, we tend to think even of the "ineffable" as the potentially nameable (otherwise, there could be no talk of a possible supernatural realm, or even of discoveries that might still be made within the realm of experience on earth). Also, though one can grasp readily enough the distinction between the *word* "tree" as symbolic and the *thing* tree as nonsymbolic or extrasymbolic, we must also recognize a sense in which a thing itself can become symbolic. For instance, an actual tree, as well as a tree in a poem or a dream, can become a "parent symbol." And by "fetishism" is meant another aspect of such symbolic identifications (as when a garment associated with the beloved can come to stand for the beloved).

Thus, whenever human discourse attempts to consider in terms of symbolic action the entire scope of actual and possible human experience (itself grounded in a realm of sheer motion that would presumably go on somehow were every symbol-using animal and every vestige of his symbols suddenly obliterated from the earth), we need not be surprised that, over the centuries, many different kinds of nomenclature have been enlisted in the task. Each has its peculiar resources, with corresponding limits. Each matches the defects of its qualities with the quality of its defects. Each, to be reflective, must be selective—and in being selective it is to some extent deflective.

But as regards any of such enterprises (ranging from the terminologies of metaphysics and theology, or speculations on human affairs in general, down through homilies, fables, chronicles, histories, to the minutiae of gossip and the day's news), I dare feel that one thing can be said without fear of serious contradiction: All of them (those you agree with as well as those you reject) necessarily involve in some way the use of symbol systems. Also, I dare assume we can agree that however close the correspondence between a thing and its name (be the thing called a *tree*, a *Baum*, or an *arbre*, and so on), in one critical respect we intuitively do and must recognize a qualitative difference between a thing and its name (or, if you will, between a complex *situation* and its name, as with for instance the momentous difference between the particulars of a city and the sheer name that somehow sums them up).

Theologians, metaphysicians, and commonsense usage may employ, in one form or another, the distinction between "spirit" and "matter," or "mind" and "body." The history of philosophy is strewn with doctrines that variously tackled this problem and variously tangled with one another. My point is: Regardless of how you would attempt to solve the many metaphysical paradoxes that subtle thinkers have shown to be implicit in this apparently simple distinction, its analogue in our present realm of discourse presents no difficulties. For in place of "spirit" or "mind" we put the term "symbol-using" (or I would propose for such "symbolic action" the mild neologism "symbolicity"); and for "matter" or "body" we substitute "the realm of the nonsymbolic," or some such term as sheer "motion." As so translated from metaphysics to a critique of language (a theory of "symbolicity" in general), many vexing problems automatically cease to exist. I raise the point because I am here trying to propose an empirical minimum on which I dare hope we could all agree, regardless of our ultimate ontological assumptions.

For instance, metaphysicians may expend incredible ingenuity in the attempt to "explain" how something so diaphanous as "mind" or "spirit" can move brute "matter." But consider a situation of this sort: You are walking along a road. From the distance you hear an approaching rumble. It proves to be a ten-ton truck. It stops ("grinds to a halt"), and the driver asks: "Is this the way to So-and-so?" You answer: "No, you should have taken the road to the left, about a half-mile back." Whereupon, the ten tons of brute matter turn around and go rumbling off, in accordance with your instructions. The sheer diaphanous "essence" or "meaning" of your frail sentence had intervened to turn that mass of brute matter around and send it back in the other direction, with the motor roaring. That is, the symbolic action of the interchange between you and the driver had made this momentous difference in the directing of all the sheer motions involved in the behavior of that stupid, obedient, inanimate, ingeniously manufactured monster.

Your instructions to the truck driver were in the realm of symbolic action ("symbolicity"). They involved sheer matter only in the sense that the vibrations of the air through which they were transmitted and the motions of your brain and his needed a groundwork of matter for their bodily existence. The "meaning" of a sentence is an *essence*; but so far as the realm of empirical symbolicity is concerned, the propounding and interpretation of that meaning involves *existence* in the sense of sheer motion. Though symbolic action is a realm of its own, a realm not reducible to terms of sheer motion, empirically it cannot exist without a grounding in the realm of motion.

But let us consider from another point of view that interchange between the truck driver and the pedestrian whose frail sentence was so effective in altering the behavior of a ten-ton truck. Note that the truck driver had used the resources of symbolicity for a quite practical purpose. And the pedestrian had answered in kind. Had the pedestrian been one of André Gide's ironically idealized hero-villains, then for sheer love of the art, as an *acte gratuit*, he might have deliberately misdirected the truck driver. I fear that we have now made a notable step forward, in the direction of an "aesthetics," though a perverse one. Such a motive would be halfway between two different uses of language, one utilitarian the other nonutilitarian. Yet we could not call it *perfectly* nonutilitarian. Rather, it would be a kind of utility-in-reverse—and the direct antithesis of a motive is not quite free of that motive. To be wholly free of a utilitarian motive, it must belong in a different plane altogether.

In this sense, we do well to question whether it is necessary or proper to think of the "aesthetic" (or "poetic") motive as directly antithetical to the practical, or utilitarian. Before the days of Gidean perversity, the usual dichotomy involved the equating of the aesthetic motive with nonutilitarian "play," in contrast with the utility of work. The clearest evidence of the utilitarian bias that lurks in such a concept of "play" is to be found in the view of play as a "preparation" for more serious activity, or as a mode of "relief" after work. This bias is also evident in the frequent tendency to view such efforts not as "natural" to human *maturity*, but as a survival *from childhood*, a kind of biologic "sport." Yet one may strive many hours a day, year after year, learning how best to "play" an instrument.

The underlying social situation has strange twists. There can be no action without a purpose, an end. People spontaneously feel this to be the case. But society is now so constituted that, for most practical purposes, people do not ask: "Give our lives a meaning, an end, a purpose." Instead they say: "Give us jobs." For now, after many centuries of training, "job," "purpose," and "meaning of life" have become convertible terms. Anxiety enters when the job is not available, or when we are threatened with the loss of it, or when it is of such a nature that it is more like bondage or compulsion than like a purpose in the happy sense of the word. Or a demon of ambition may conceal the quandary from himself and others by such great enterprise and initiative on his part that his self-chosen dedication to his "design" (if we may borrow a key motivational term from Faulkner's *Absalom, Absalom!*) could not properly be called a "compulsion," though some psychologists might call it a "compulsion neurosis."

In any case, to approach the problem in terms of an antithesis between the aesthetic and the practical, between "play" and "work," is still to be constricted by the limits that any utilitarian terminology is bound to impose. Or, if you would retain the term "play," rather than arguing about a word I would simply ask that you add to your concept of play a proviso of this sort:

Although the truck driver who asked for directions was motivated by practical, utilitarian considerations, the pedestrian who corrected his error (we are not now concerned with the Gidean aesthete) need not have done so for correspondingly practical, utilitarian reasons. He might have given the correct information simply because he likes to say how things really are.

That thought (the thought of accurate statement for its own sake) brings us much closer to the poetic motive. For there is a compelling principle of perfection implicit in the nature of language as such, since each language has within it certain "proper" ways of designating things, its own peculiarly proper grammar, syntax, tonal inflections, and the like. In this sense, a love of truth for its own sake has a kind of sheerly technical grounding in the nature of symbolicity as such. And to find that a virtue can be grounded in the technical is almost as reassuring as to find that it can be grounded in vice.

So, all told, we can readily conceive how the pedestrian might answer correctly, not through any particular interest in helping the questioner solve a practical problem, but simply because (other things being equal, as they wouldn't be in the case of our hypothetical perverse Gidean hero-villain) it felt "natural" for him to use his language accurately.

We're now much closer to the poetic motive. Yet not quite close enough. The final step, into "pure symbolicity" as the poetic motive, comes when we add these culminating considerations:

Being a kind of animal that lives by locomotion, the human organism naturally takes delight in freedom of movement. Often we move for specifically practical purposes, to get some things and avoid others. But not all our movements are thus directed by specific utilitarian ends. Also we often move simply because we are the kind of animal that likes to move. Similarly, since we are by nature the typically symbol-using animal, why should we not love symbolic action purely for its own sake? And the greater the range and intenseness of the opportunities for exercising our symbolic prowess, the greater might be our delight in such modes of action.

The range and intenseness of symbolic action here referred to are, of course, supplied for us by such notable instances of symbolic-action-for-its-own-sake as are the prime concern of Poetics. For Poetics inquires into the kind of symbolic action that is undertaken purely through love of the art, to gratify our nature as symbol-using animals.

At first glance, one might think that such a notion of symbolic action for its own sake would not be consistent with doctrines like the Aristotelian view of tragedy as purgative. Yet, just as people who enjoy solving puzzles will prefer hard ones, so the delights of symbolic action can be increased by the imitation of grave and serious conflicts. And while such exercisings are enjoyed for their own sake, they might (as it were by "superabundance") even have practical effects upon one's attitudes toward life, the state, the community. In this way the symbolic purging of unrest could also have figured, for instance, in the role of Greek tragedy as a civic ceremony.

II
Mr. Brooks's Formalist "Articles of Faith"

As a convenient way into our specific subject, I shall next offer some comments on the Formalist critic's "articles of faith," which Cleanth Brooks presented some years ago (1951). Conceivably he might now revise his position in two different directions: He might redefine Formalism itself, or he might state that he no longer advocates Formalistic criticism. In any case, as regards his recent volume on Faulkner, I could subscribe at least in part to this comment by Robert W. Daniel in a recent issue of *Sewanee Review*:

> . . . his method is very little that of the Formalist. Indeed, it is frequently moralistic, greatly concerned with the validity of Faulkner's judgments on his characters. And when this new development on Brooks's part is combined with his critiques of other approaches to Faulkner, some fine theoretical puzzles result.

As we proceed, I think it will become clear why I would not require that the critic hold strictly to his tenets of fifteen years ago. For I contend that "Formalist criticism" is not enough. Indeed, my aim will be a double one: First, to insist upon the strictest possible view of Formalism; and next, to use this very strictness as an argument for further kinds of investigation (among them the kinds I have found necessary inasmuch as the study of Poetics proper does not encompass the entire field of symbolic action; hence, a theory of language in general can treat Poetics as but one aspect of the total subject matter). To take up the ten "articles of faith" in succession:

1) "That literary criticism is a description and evaluation of its object." I agree. But note that this clause would also apply to book reviewing, which gives the prospective customer a description of the book's contents and indicates whether, in the opinion of the reviewer, it is worth reading. A large amount of Mr. Brooks's recent work on Faulkner is an ably managed survey of this sort.

2) "That the primary concern of criticism is with the problem of unity . . . and the kind of whole which the literary work forms or fails to form, and the relation of the various parts to each other in building up this whole." I agree. A work can have identity only by embodying some principle of unity which in turn involves division into interrelated parts. A sentence is so constructed; and a work will somehow, if it is well-formed, maintain this same principle of internal consistency. Such a principle of internal consistency, however, also sets up the possibility that deviations, perversions, alembications of this same principle can be attempted when the time for such contrivances is ripe (some might say "rotten-ripe").

We might note, on the side, that the satisfactions of internal consistency embody at least two, more probably three, principles of form (which I would call progressive, repetitive, and conventional). By "conventional form" is meant any *categorical* expectancy. For instance, Francis Fergusson speaks of "ritual expectation" with regard to Greek tragedy. An Athenian audience presumably expected to find in all tragedies some such ritualized functions as were performed by the recitations and the dance movements of the chorus. Conventional form is harder to detect in the modern experimental theater, where one of the conventions is that the playwright can, within limits, set up his own conventions for the duration of the single work. No such theaters, however, admit the conventions of the Roman circus or the Spanish bullfight, kinds of spectacle involving the expectation of real victimage and not merely imitated victimage. (To consider imitation from this point of view is to be reminded that there is no violence in the novels of Faulkner, quite as there are no bullfights in Hemingway.)

"Progressive" form is ideally the kind of inevitable development from complications to denouement which Aristotle discusses at length in his *Poetics*. There is also a less "syllogistic," purely "qualitative" kind of progressive form (as with the profoundly effective yet not specifically foreshadowed turn from the murder scene to the Porter scene in *Macbeth*). But perhaps the most demanding of all is "repetitive" form, the principle of internal consistency itself (a principle embodied, for instance, in our feeling that characters must act in character and that even when a character undergoes a change of identity, he must do so in ways peculiarly his own). The eighteenth-century preference for the heroic couplet could be called an instance of both repetitive form and conventional form.[1]

Where there is a cast of characters (as in dramas or novels), the interrelationships among them can be viewed *formally* as "derived" from the total situation. For instance, if the work is a tragedy, the situation calls for the simulated sacrifice of an appropriate victim. In this sense, his character

---

[1] In discussing "The Experimental School in American Poetry," Yvor Winters subtitled his essay "An Analytical Survey of Its Structural Methods, Exclusive of Metres." His article did not clearly distinguish between formal principles in my sense and "structural methods" in his. And whereas I would agree that devices such as "pseudoreference," "the alternation of method," and "the double method," are worth isolating and describing, I would point out: All of them embody in one way or another the three principles of form that, in my view, cover the entire field of form, as viewed in terms of expectation.

In answer to an inquiry on my part, however, Mr. Winters wrote me saying that he no longer puts much faith in either my terms or his as regards those early essays of ours. And whereas I still cling to my early "codification" of formal principles, I should admonish that I have found it necessary to introduce one further "dimension" into my speculations. Since circa 1955, I have felt impelled to round out theories of "self-expression" and "communication" with a third term, "consummation." But inasmuch as "consummation" essentially involves matters to do with "tracking down the possibilities implicit in a given terminology," it could be treated as but one further embodiment of the "repetitive" principle.

as a victim is to be treated *formally* as a function of his appointed role in the given work. In a classical tragedy his role requires that he be victimized in a way designed to afford the audience "tragic pleasure." Insofar as he is to be victimized, other characters must be so designed as to contribute characteristically toward his victimage—and in this sense their roles (with corresponding identities) can be *formally* treated, in turn, as functions of the chosen victim's role (or as "deducible" from his role). Insofar as the characters are treated simply as characters, or as representative of the author's general attitude toward life, or as examples of prevailing cultural conditions, though such portraiture on the critic's part may be appealing it does not satisfy the requirements of the strictly formalistic.

3) "That the formal relations in a work of literature may include, but certainly exceed, those of logic." I see no problem here. In Conrad's novel *Victory*, for instance, a good instance of a "scene-act ratio" is utilized for poetic effect when a distant volcano begins erupting simultaneously with a crisis in the action; yet the action is not "logically" related to the crisis (as would be the case if the volcanic eruption set up conditions directly involving the characters in a competitive struggle to escape from its lava or ashes). But in this instance the correlation is like that between "background music" and a movie plot. Analogies linking the human body, what Mr. Ransom has called "world's body," and the body politic readily favor kinds of poetic conformity whereby a motive in one of these realms is sympathetically reinforced by corresponding terms in either or both of the others (as a sense of personal drought may be duplicated by imagery of natural drought or ideas of cultural drought; or as with the equating of rain and tears in Verlaine's lines *"Il pleure dans mon coeur / Comme il pleut sur la ville"*).

And here I might introduce an aside regarding Mr. Ransom's reference to a discussion of whether a poem is "pre-logical" or "post-logical." Might not the salient genius of antithesis sometimes lead us unnecessarily into flat distinctions such as "logical" vs. "illogical," or "rational" vs. "irrational"? And to counter such trends should we not simply say that a poem, like the orderly processes of a healthy body, is neither "rational" nor "irrational," but "methodical"? I have suggested such a compromise in regard to the motives of man in general (*Permanence and Change*, Hermes edition, p. 234); and I still dare to feel that the distinction might be useful when considering the possible "logic" of a work's "formal relations."

4) "That in a successful work, form and content cannot be separated." True. But I have already suggested how content can be treated without formalistic rigor, even in instances where the content is not viewed sheerly as "science," "facts," or "information."

5) "That form is meaning." This clause does not seem to me distinct enough so far as Formalist criticism is concerned. Even the most "factual" of statements has "form" or "meaning." A writer might insert a paragraph

that has no formal function whatever so far as the development of the work is concerned; yet it might still have "form" and "meaning" as a document. For instance, if Mark Antony's famous speech to the mob in *Julius Caesar* had been composed of sections from Aristotle's *Rhetoric* on ways to arouse resentment and tears, the paragraphs would have the form and meaning that they have in Aristotle's treatise. Obviously the equating of "form" and "meaning" from the standpoint of purely Formalist criticism is something else, here left unspecified. I can but offer tentative interpretations. For instance, if "meaning" is equated with "purpose" (as in our previous suggestion that the desire for a "meaning" in life is equatable with the desire for a "purpose"), we can then say that poetic "form" is fully equatable with "meaning" when the "form" (with its "matter") serves some specific poetic "purpose." But such a solution would require the addition of a clause such as is wholly missing from Mr. Brooks's list of Formalistic tenets; namely: That the work be viewed as aiming at some kind of effect (not necessarily the effect of "catharsis" which Aristotle associates with Greek tragedy, but an effect of some sort, with all resources of the work being shaped to this end). I shall later discuss wherein this notion of a "*telos*" differs from what Wimsatt and Beardsley have labeled the "intentional fallacy."

6) "That literature is ultimately metaphorical and symbolic." I am afraid Mr. Brooks would not say I am agreeing with him when I define literature as a form of symbolic action, undertaken for its own sake, and when I note that metaphor rates high among the sources of stylistic appeal. As I tried to show in my volume *Permanence and Change*, metaphor appeals by being always on the edge of "perspective by incongruity"; for it brings together classes of terms that might otherwise be kept in separate compartments of the mind. Thus it enables us to experience strikingly new combinations, thereby letting us see things in a fresh light. (An interesting article by Archibald MacLeish on metaphor, perspective, and incongruity is republished in the paperback volume *Aspects of Poetry: Modern Perspectives*, edited by Mark Linenthal; Little, Brown and Company.) But I do dare to feel that Mr. Brooks would agree with me entirely when in *Counter-Statement*, on the subject of "aesthetic truth," I wrote: "Given the companions of Ulysses in the cave of Polyphemus, it is true that they would escape by clinging to the bellies of the herd let out to pasture."

7) "That the general and the universal are not seized upon by abstraction, but got at through the concrete and the particular." Yes, as per the scholastic formula *universale intelligitur, singulare sentitur*. In the same spirit, I have tried to utilize for purposes of Poetics the Thomistic *principium individuationis*. At the same time, I believe the kind of general outlines discussed in Chapter XVII of Aristotle's *Poetics* makes a neat complement to the stress upon "the concrete and the particular." By reducing a work to the most general statement of its plot or development possible, one is en-

abled to see all the more sharply how the processes of poetic individuation figure. (In my commentary on *Timon of Athens*, pp. 115–117, I try to show systematically how such concerns help point up the function of the play. The same chapter illustrates what I mean when, in connection with the second clause, I refer to characters as "deducible.")

But, with regard to symbolic action in general, we might well recall that no less an authority than Keats referred to the "abstractness" of his work as a poet, despite the exceptionally sensuous concreteness of his diction. For there is a sense in which *all* symbol systems are abstract, as contrasted with the here and now of direct physical contact. A poet builds his particulars out of words, all of which (except proper names) are terms for *classes* of objects—and even proper names readily lend themselves to the resources of classification, as when we speak of "Hamlets" or "Napoleons" or "Madame Bovarys," and as the word "Caesar" itself gave us so many words for ruler, such as "Czar" and "Kaiser."

8) "That literature is not a surrogate for religion." Yes. But the current cult of "myth" is clear evidence of the ways in which dead religions can be embalmed in literature. Also, as I have tried to show in my book *The Rhetoric of Religion: Studies in Logology*, theological doctrines can be profitably studied for the light they shed, by analogy, upon the study of linguistic processes in general. And much poetry can be properly analyzed as a set of devices for finding, in the romantic passion, analogues of the religious passion. (In my *Grammar of Motives* I deal with Keats's "Ode on a Grecian Urn" along these lines.)

9) "That, as Allen Tate says, 'specific moral problems' are the subject matter of literature, but that the purpose of literature is not to point a moral." Yes. Or, as I would state the same issue: Literature transforms moral *problems* into sources of aesthetic *entertainment*. Thus Mr. Ransom quoted Allen Tate as saying that "most of his poems are about something harsh he could do nothing about."

I believe, however, that one can, at times, most clearly indicate the structure of a work by treating it *as if* it were designed to point a moral. Thus, a tragedy may be treated *as if* it were designed to warn us against the evils of "pride," whereas the sheer dramaturgy of the case called for a character who climbed too arrogantly high, since only by such excessiveness could he set up the conditions for a strikingly drastic fall. Or a work may be treated as though designed to warn us about the ever-present imminence of fate, whereas references to the inexorable decrees of fate may be the dramatist's best way of making us forget that his play is but the work of a human artificer.

Today, writers often introduce some "myth" or "archetype" to endow their work with a dimension not otherwise present in the situation with which they are dealing. For instance, consider the resonance of O'Connor's speeches in Djuna Barnes's *Nightwood*, where what would otherwise be a somewhat drab account of an erotic triangle is turned by mythic accents into lamentation. Obviously, one could best point up the functions of the "mythic" in this novel (from the standpoint of its effect) by treating this dimension not as stylistic artifice, but as a document designed to help us meditate on what Eliot, in recommending it, called "the human misery and bondage which is universal."

A related ambiguity seems to plague Mr. Brooks's study of Faulkner. Thus, we find him both lauding "anything calculated to shake the reader's confidence in the accuracy of Faulkner's 'facts,'" and making such comments as: "Thorstein Veblen would have understood Sutpen's relation to traditional culture"; or "Faulkner would have gone along with Tawney's *Religion and the Rise of Capitalism*." The problem arises, I think, because he does not explicitly include among his tenets the poetic thesis that literature aims, or should aim, not at "truth," but at "verisimilitude." I must, however, reserve a fuller discussion of this point until later.

10) "That the principles of criticism define the area relevant to literary criticism; they do not constitute a method for carrying out the criticism." This culminating clause puzzles me because I can't see what it is aiming at. I see the issue thus: I would construct a *philosophy* of language that is based upon a *theory* of language; and this theory of "language as symbolic action" can in turn be shown to imply certain methods of analysis (with appropriate injunctions, or rules of thumb: "What to look for, what to look out for, how, and why?"). I proceed on the assumption that if man is the typical symbol-using animal, and his love of symbolicity for its own sake is grounded in his human nature, then the *method* of "description and evaluation" (if we may revert to clause one) is, or should be, *implied in this definition*.

In any case, the essay also concedes that critical methods other than the Formalistic also contribute to the understanding of literature. And there's no point to my asking that in his book on Faulkner, Mr. Brooks be more Formalistic than he cares to be, or than the nature of his project permits him to be. So far as I can see, it's a simple Formalistic fact that the nature of his project would not permit him to stay within the bounds of Formalist criticism. On that score, I have no objections. But we should make sure that insofar as he is not Formalistic in his own procedures, he abandon Formalistic criteria when criticizing the procedures of other critics.

We are now ready for the next section of this discussion.

III

Problem of Locating Mr. Brooks's Reservations

My problem in locating the precise point at which Mr. Brooks and I diverge is a complex one. First, there was the stage when we seemed in near agreement. That was when, after I had published my analysis of the Keats ode, he published a piece of his own on the same subject, and generously commented:

> I am happy to find that two critics with methods and purposes so different should agree so thoroughly as we do on the poem. I am pleased, for my part, therefore, to acknowledge the amount of duplication which exists between the two essays, counting it as rather important corroboration of a view of the poem which will probably seem to some critics overingenious. In spite of the common elements, however, I feel that the emphasis of my essay is sufficiently different from Burke's to justify my going on with its publication.

"Keats's Sylvan Historian: History without Footnotes" has been generally recognized as a superb essay. And I rejoiced at the opportunity that my piece had to bask a little in its glory, as Mr. Brooks generously retained his comments when reprinting the essay. But in another essay ("The Heresy of Paraphrase"), though I feel sure Mr. Brooks would agree with my thesis (in "*Lexicon Rhetoricae*") that "The 'thoughts' of a writer are the non-paraphrasable aspects of his work, the revelation and the ritual in fusion," he added qualifications of a somewhat problematic nature:

> Two critics for whose work I have high regard have emphasized the dynamic character of poetry. Kenneth Burke argues that if we are to consider a poem as a poem, we must consider it as a "mode of action." R. P. Blackmur asks us to think of it as gesture, "the outward and dramatic play of inward and imagined meaning." I do not mean to commit either of these critics to my own interpretation of dramatic or symbolic action; and I have, on my own part, several rather important reservations with Mr. Burke's position. But there are certainly large areas of agreement among our positions.

As Mr. Brooks did not state what the "important reservations" with regard to my position might be, like a character out of Kafka I must seek to defend myself without being informed of the charge against me. At the time, noting that he referred only to reservations with regard to my theory of language as symbolic action and not to Richard Blackmur's theory of language as gesture, I thought of approximating a defense by making some comments about Richard Blackmur's theory.

But before the public delivery of this paper, I heard the dismal news of Richard Blackmur's death—and since I had always admired him greatly both as a person and a critic, I felt gloomy and embarrassed at the thought of bringing his name into the controversy. Above all, how could I at such a time stress what I took to be the somewhat comic nature of our sparring? So, as I had to curtail my remarks anyhow, I did so mostly in this area.

I had had in mind an argumentative procedure of this sort. When referring to both the Blackmur essay on "language as gesture" and my view of "language as symbolic action," Mr. Brooks had indicated that his "several rather important reservations" applied to my position only. But I felt it could be shown that in the only important critical point likely to be at issue here, both formulas were marked by the same kind of vulnerability, if it was vulnerability. To establish the point, I would first refer to a passage in an essay of mine on proverbs, "Literature as Equipment for Living":

> In his exceptionally discerning essay "A Critic's Job of Work," R. P. Blackmur says, "I think on the whole his [Burke's] method could be applied with equal fruitfulness to Shakespeare, Dashiell Hammett, or Marie Corelli." When I got through wincing, I had to admit that Blackmur was right. This article is an attempt to say for the method what can be said. As a matter of fact, I'll go a step further and maintain: You can't properly put Marie Corelli and Shakespeare apart until you have first put them together. First genus, then differentia. The strategy in common is the genus. The *range* or *scale* or *spectrum* of particularizations is the differentia.

Then I would clinch things by noting that in the brilliant essay on "Language as Gesture" (and it is exceptionally brilliant), illustrations of the thesis range from the poetry of Yeats to a "largish" woman who, by her sheer gestures, indicates her attitudes while being tossed about in a jerky "orange-yellow" bus. I thought that certain possible "important reservations" could be blocked by my showing that there is no essential difference in principle between terms that group Shakespeare with Marie Corelli and terms that group the finest poetry of Yeats with a big woman being tossed about in a bus. Thus in showing that the metaphorical concept of "language as gesture" admits as wide a range of cases as the literal concept of "language as symbolic action," I thought I had an observation that could free us to look elsewhere for the most likely source of our difficulties.

Incidentally, there seems to be some misunderstanding about the nature of critical terminology. Though critics have sometimes objected that my theories of form apply to bad works as well as good, I have never heard anyone object that books on prosody apply equally well to both bad and good poems. And though Mr. Brooks was right in stressing the importance of unity in a work, it is obvious that poor works as well as good can embody such a principle. Two observations are relevant here: (1) An inferior work may even happen to be better unified than a superior one, simply because it did not encounter such great problems of control; and (2) Insofar as a bad work exemplifies good formal principles, to that extent it *is* a good work.

One embarrassment forever besetting the critic is the fact that a work is a combination of many elements. The marvel of the individual poem resides in precisely its particular combination of ingredients, in precisely those proportions. But no *one* such ingredient is enough to assure that a work will be good. Many a dismal play has been written around some variant of the Oedipus complex. *Oedipus Rex* is the instance of a play where it works extremely well. The critic forever confronts the vexing fact that he must talk about one thing at a time, yet no single ingredient in a dish can assure its excellence. The problem is not to be solved by finding a few foolproof titular words. The problem is to be solved pragmatically by adopting a terminology and showing how it can be put to work disclosing the dynamics of poetic structures. Surely there is no better term for literary virtue in general than "propriety" (decorum, *to prepon*). Yet it is but a blanket term that must be applied differently in each case—and besides, it inevitably fluctuates (as we note in the similar concerns of Yvor Winters) between purely internal tests of fitness and social criteria (of morality or politeness).

Also, it is worthwhile remembering that not a single word in the critic's vocabulary of poetic excellence belongs etymologically to the realm of poetics or aesthetics alone. All such terms necessarily have bridges that carry us away from the specific realm of artistic excellence. Nothing more clearly illustrates this point than the terministic antics to which Coleridge subjected himself when setting up the term "imagination" as the special mark of poetic genius. He split things two ways: first, he "desynonymized" by distinguishing between imagination and fancy (one from a Latin root, the other from the Greek); and next he distinguished between a primary and a secondary imagination, the "primary" kind being the faculty that we *all* employ when experiencing images (in the process of seeing, hearing, and so on, and of remembering such), and the "secondary" being reserved for the special faculty that in current cant would probably be called artistic "creativity." (See "The Unburned Bridges of Poetics; or How Keep Poetry Pure?" in *Centennial Review*, Fall, 1964.)

Perhaps an article by René Wellek on "The Main Trends of Twentieth-Century Criticism" (it was published a few years ago in *Yale Review*) best supplies the answer to my question. True, this article departs far from the friendly manner in which Blackmur and Brooks had referred to possible divergencies. Except for one sentence, I got worked over quite roughly; and since that one sentence runs "The early Burke was a good literary critic," I could not help wondering whether I had been let in only that I might be thrown out. In any case, though there was not the slightest hint as to what kind of things the early Burke might have written, I did find some solace in the thought that if only on a hook, the early Burke caught the worm.

The later work, we are told, is "a baffling phantasmagoria of bloodless categories, 'strategies,' 'charts,' and 'situations.'" Apparently my fall had even preceded the publication of the Keats essay to which Mr. Brooks had referred so generously when publishing his. For now the reader is told only that my item interprets the ode "in terms of the identity of love and death, or capitalist individualism and Keats's tubercular fever, in almost complete disregard of the text." There is not the slightest hint of Mr. Brooks's remarks regarding the "insights" in Burke's "brilliant essay," and "the amount of duplication which exists between the two essays." On the score of the "bloodless categories," I cannot defend myself, since none is mentioned specifically (though Formalistic considerations may make it worth pointing out that many of them, such as the pentad and "ratios" of my *Grammar*, are concerned with the sheer *forms* of linguistic action). And if "situations" and "strategies" are heinous terms, at least I'm sinning in good company—for Mr. Brooks uses them both in *The Well Wrought Urn*. The only place I recall using "chart" is as a metaphor, in connection with three terms, explicitly defined thus: "dream (the unconscious or subconscious factors in a poem) . . . prayer (the communicative functions of a poem, involving the many considerations of form) . . . chart (the realistic sizing-up of situations which is sometimes explicit, sometimes implicit, in poetic strategies)." I confess I can't see what's wrong there, even after being warned by Mr. Wellek's wrath.

I wrote a letter to the editor, giving but a partial list of articles I had published (mainly in the 1950's), and picking only literary magazines (*Sewanee Review, Hudson Review, Kenyon Review, Accent,* and *Poetry*) to indicate that I had by no means abandoned literary criticism. But nothing came of it. Mr. Wellek showed a willingness to debate the matter with me in correspondence; but naturally I did not feel that an error made by a historian in public should be rectified entirely in private. Among the items I listed, by the way, was one favorably reviewing the Brooks-Wimsatt history of literary criticism (in *Poetry*, February, 1958), though the reviewer secretly grieved that, except for an undiscussed quotation, not even the early Burke got in.

Be that as it may, Mr. Wellek did make one point that, though it was not stated without animosity, I do agree has a measure of justification. And I speak of it because I think this is the center of our trouble. I have in mind his remark that I would now "devise a system of human behavior and motivation which uses literature only as a document or illustration." *With regard to certain portions of my project* this observation is correct. As I tried to make clear in the Hermes edition of *Counter-Statement* ("*Curriculum Criticum*"), while my "analysis of language and of human motives at some points overlaps upon literary criticism in the strict sense of the term, at many other points it leads into inquiries not central to literary criticism—and sometimes literary critics have quarreled with the author for neglecting the problems of literary criticism proper, whereas no other course was open to him, insofar as he also wanted to discuss symbolic motivations and linguistic action in general."

But while it is true that my project as a whole does often take me outside the realm of literary criticism proper, and that at such times I use literature merely as splendid illustrations of my theories, *it is just as true that Poetics is one of the four categories* ("bloodless"?) *into which I divide my project* (the others being Grammar, Rhetoric, and Ethics). I have written and published much in that dimension, and Deo volente I shall write and publish more. Since scattered articles are hard to keep up with, I cannot object if Mr. Wellek fell into a factual error. I can but ask that he correct it.

Also, I should note that much of my writings on literary criticism have to do with the sheer *theory* of criticism. These portions of my work would not meet the tests required of explications de texte. But certainly Mr. Wellek's "historical" report on *my* criticism couldn't meet such tests either. Obviously, a survey such as he furnished in the article now under discussion could not possibly dig into details, except in the selective sense in which I too am involved, at those places where I must cite texts as illustrations of one critical question or another rather than dealing with them in their total developments (as when Mr. Brooks takes up one of Faulkner's stories after another and talks about its parts). As everywhere I turn I have been assured that Mr. Wellek is an exceptionally amiable person, I 'gin wonder whether the reason he got so vexed with me is because to him my project in its overall dimensions represents ab extra a problem that he in his own way as historian confronts ab intra. For if historians worked on the level of specific analysis that distinguishes a literary critic writing high-class book reviews, they'd be run ragged. As judged by such tests, they can be called either "superficial" or "bloodless," *quite as all literary criticism could be called superficial, or even "bloodless," when viewed from the standpoint of the original text itself.* For by the very nature of the case, unless you happen to love criticism for its own sake, *you can view every comment on a text as little more than a departure from that text.* Could he have been so vexed with me because in a *methodological* way, I confront a problem that he confronts *historiographically*? Maybe yes, maybe no. But if it is true, maybe we need each other as victims. (I speak as one who has given much thought to the ways of victimage.) As compared with the poem itself, every critical comment is "bloodless." And all criticism of criticism or history of criticism and its criticism would be still more bloodless (except for whatever blood may be involved in the personality of all such issues). And alas! if *blood* is to be the test, then as compared with blood even the original poem itself is "bloodless." And so it goes.

In any case, even in the realm of Poetics, when dealing with one particular text, I have often at the same time stressed matters concerning *questions of method* involved in the analysis (in this sense, perhaps, taking a "Formalistic" view of criticism itself).

We are now ready for our next step in this inquiry.

IV

Likely Source of Mr. Brooks's Unstated Reservations
— and Corresponding Statement of My Position

In our essays on the Keats ode, my "dramatistic" view of form coincided
with Mr. Brooks's concept of "dramatic analogues" at those points where
we were treating the Urn as a character that made utterances in accordance
with its character and the character of the situation in which the "fair Attitude" was addressed. Thus, above all, when the Urn vatically announces
that "Beauty is truth, truth beauty," we agreed in viewing this as a statement properly prepared for *within the conditions of the poem*, and not to be
read simply as a "scientific" or "philosophic" proposition equally valid outside its context.

Our differences arise, I think, from our different ways of interpreting
the implications of Mr. Brooks's own remarks in "The Heresy of Paraphrase" when he says: "Where is the dictionary which contains the terms of
a poem? It is a truism that the poet is continually forced to remake language."
I take this just observation to imply that a poet is naturally closer to his
own particular idiom than his readers can ever hope to be, but that by comparing all available contexts (both poetic and extrapoetic) in which the
poet employs a given term, we can get deeper glimpses than were otherwise
possible into the functioning of his particular nomenclature. And these possibilities seem to me worth trying to disclose with regard to the nature of
symbolic action in general, though many of such speculations may not contribute to Poetics in particular. There is a good civilized sense in which we
should be philologists all, when looking at the utterances of one another
(and thereby, poignantly roundabout, philologists even of ourselves).

Underlying my discussion of the Keats ode (and of "The Ancient
Mariner" in *The Philosophy of Literary Form*) there is a procedure of this
sort: First, say what can be said of the work if you had nothing but it,
and didn't even know who wrote it. Here, necessarily, your analysis would
be internal, wholly in the realm of Poetics. Next, if you can place its authorship, and you have other poems written by the same author, examine these
on the assumption that the recurrence of the same terms elsewhere may
throw additional light upon their nature as a special nomenclature (the
meaning of a given term in a "Keats Dictionary" as distinct from its meaning in a "Shelley Dictionary," and so on). Finally, in the attempt *wholly*
outside the realm of Poetics proper to study the ways of symbolic action in
general, introduce any kind of available evidence (such as letters, diaries,
notebooks, biographical data) that might indicate how the terms *within*
the poem link up with problematical situations (personal or social) *outside*
the poem. And surely, at this point, you see why I would not at all object
if Mr. Brooks chooses in his book on Faulkner to touch upon the prob-

lematical personal or social situations Faulkner may have encountered, and which may be embedded in his works. I would object only if his undefined "reservations" about my theories of "symbolic action" would by their indefiniteness keep me out and let him in, whereas if he had but defined them, either we'd both be in or we'd both be out. That's what we have to track down, at least as regards my attempts to help him and myself and all of us figure out as clearly as possible just what all is involved here.

Hence, as a major step along our way, I think I can now state precisely what my tactics are with regard to Poetics in particular. I would propose to make the rules in that dimension as strict as possible. Absolutely no biographical reference would be admissible. History itself would be admissible only in the sense that the meaning (and allusiveness) of a term will change through the centuries, and I'd subscribe to Croce's admonition that unless such changes are taken into account, the critic's analysis of an ancient text will be an unintended "palimpsest." For the later meaning of a term may cover up its meaning at the time when the poem was written; and a critic's failure to make the appropriate discount (there's "propriety" again!) is in effect the imposing of a new text upon an old one. (However, a member of the English department at the University of California, Santa Barbara—I have forgotten exactly which member!—admonished in turn that a given poet may happen to have privately anticipated meanings not current in his day, or the usage may be a throwback. So contemporary tests are not wholly final, even if you are sure of the dates.)[2]

---

[2] In taking notes on a text, one should be free to cross these barriers at random. See in *Hopkins Review*, Winter, 1952, my article " 'Ethan Brand': A Preparatory Investigation." This piece is offered purely as a sample of undigested speculations and observations, a mere "working paper." I find among my pages a letter from Malcolm Cowley, saying among other things that Hawthorne "didn't write the story so much as he put it together out of his notebook—and until one has read the notebook one can't talk with authority about the story." I both agree and disagree with this statement. I agree, in the sense that when one is discussing the story with relation to Hawthorne personally, *all* such data as Mr. Cowley refers to should be included. I disagree, in the sense that when considering the work as an instance of sheer poetic action in and for itself, one should leave such matters out of account. Here the material must stand or fall by reason of its role in the story, regardless of whether it arose in the course of the writing, or was lifted from a notebook, or was even stolen or borrowed from someone else.

I see, however, no absolute reason why, in any given case, the critic should always keep the three stages in separate bins (first considering the poem purely in itself, then along with other poems by the same author, and then in terms of the author's personal susceptibilities as citizen and taxpayer). All that is necessary is to keep it clear to which order a given observation about the work belongs. I make this point because my essay on the Keats ode *specifically* and *methodically* makes clear the distinction between the kind of things one can say about the poem viewed purely as a completed act (its parts analyzable without any reference to authorship) and the kind of things one can say about it once related expressions in Keats's letters are brought to bear upon the study of its nomenclature. A similar structure underlies my treatment of "The Ancient Mariner" in *The Philosophy of Literary Form*.

The work would be judged not by tests of "truth," "scientific" or "factual" accuracy, but on the basis of "verisimilitude." The truth of the "data" in a literary production by no means guarantees its artistic appeal. But to appeal it *must* have some kind of verisimilitude. Thus, only verisimilitude, not truth, can engage a reader who does not believe in hell, but who derives aesthetic pleasure from Dante's Inferno. Truth enters in a secondary sense, for often accuracy of sheerly factual detail can contribute to our sense of a work's verisimilitude. And regardless of whether or not we believe in the ontological reality of hell, to go along with Dante's poem we must believe beyond all doubt that such unending sufferings really would be hellish.

In analyzing a work strictly in terms of Poetics, one would analyze it solely as a form, without any reference to the personality of the author. Thus, I do think it a notable oversight in Mr. Brooks's list of tenets for Formalist criticism that he does not require the ideal Formalist to define works in terms of their *kind*. But in the actual working out of his book on Faulkner, he does propose an overall definition of Faulkner's writing, which in the large he categorizes as a kind of comedy.

But the main point is this: Regardless of what an author may or may not have personally intended, the Formalist critic fulfills his "proper" task by imputing to the work whatever design, or intention, he thinks is best able to account for the nature of the work.

Thus, the question of an "intentional fallacy" becomes quite irrelevant. The *test* of the design is pragmatic. The critic proceeds to substantiate his thesis casuistically, by showing in detail how much the imputed design might account for. If a rival critic can propose different postulates that will account for more aspects of the work, or for more important aspects of it, his job is to offer a different postulate, and to demonstrate pragmatically how much can be accounted for on the basis of his thesis.

A character, let us say, has traits not directly explainable in terms of the intention that a given critic has postulated. A competing critic might propose a postulate that did directly account for these traits. But other possibilities suggest themselves. The problematic traits might be treated as designed to

---

I cannot grumble at Mr. Wellek for not noting that this procedure is embedded in my discussion of the Coleridge poem, since I had not there so explicitly stated my method as I did in the case of the Keats poem. But I can legitimately complain about his failure, even as a mere reporter, to inform his readers about my explicit discussion of my procedures in connection with the ode; and when he cites *only* my treatment of Coleridge's poem as a "ritual for the redemption of his drug," I can't help wondering what a reader would think of Mr. Wellek's accuracy in the light of pp. 78-86 of *The Philosophy of Literary Form* (Vintage edition), where I sum up by warning against "reduction to one 'cause,'" and by discussing the poem in terms of "the aesthetic problem, the marital problem, the political problem, the drug problem, and the metaphysical problem" (the last being the one Robert Penn Warren subsequently treated, after his different but expert fashion, in terms of "sacramentalism").

serve some secondary aspect of the plot. Or the critic might argue that though not directly functional so far as the furthering of the plot is concerned, these traits keep the character from being functional in too simple a sense (as with sheer allegory in case the work is not intended as allegory, or with an overly simplified problem play or *Tendenz-roman*). Another way of putting such a case would be for the critic to show why, in order to make a given character seem "real," the author must endow him with more traits than those most directly needed to account for his actions strictly in terms of his role, as determined by the particular needs of the plot. For the ends of verisimilitude may be shown to require that a character should not be too perfectly adapted to his specific function in furthering the plot, just as one could not design even so simple a tool as a carpenter's hammer that could be used only for the purpose of driving nails.

In any case, as regards strictly Formalist criticism the issue could never lead to such remarks as these by Mr. Brooks, when denying that Faulkner regards Gavin Stevens (in *Intruder in the Dust*) "as a kind of projected image of himself, and means to use him as his mouthpiece": "Doubtless what he says often represents what many Southerners think and what Faulkner himself—at one time or another—may have thought." Or above all, it would not involve such a "sociological" remark as: "His arguments do reflect a very real cultural situation, and the reader could learn from them a great deal about the problem of the South."

Let me make myself clear on this point. I am not discussing the truth or falsity of Mr. Brooks's comments here. I am merely noting that they are not "Formalistic." They could be called "sociological," and maybe even "Marxist," in their relation to a book as reflecting a social situation. The first three chapters ("Faulkner, the Provincial"; "The Plain People: Yeoman Farmers, Sharecroppers, and White Trash"; and "As Nature Poet") have many valuable things to say about the extrapoetic *situations* from which Faulkner is writing, and which his work takes into account. Despite Mr. Wellek's dislike of the term, one might call them "strategies" for the encompassing of such "situations." In any case, one does not convert them into full-blown Formalist criticism simply by an occasional slighting reference to sociology. They *are* sociological, for they are dealing with "the Yoknapatawpha Country" *in terms of Mississippi in particular and the South in general.*

True, they also go *beyond* the strictly sociological, quite as in my discussion of "situations" and "strategies" in *The Philosophy of Literary Form*, I point out that "insofar as situations overlap from individual to individual, or from one historical period to another, the strategies possess universal relevance." But note how readily we slip from the sociological scene to the literary reflection in a passage such as this: "The South as a whole was wretchedly poor, upper classes as well as lower classes, right on from the

Civil War period until the Second World War. The economy of the whole region was basically a colonial economy, manipulated from the outside. Even the so-called aristocracy, as Faulkner depicts them, had little wealth. The Compsons, for example, in 1909 had to sell land in order to send Quentin to Harvard, etc." Is it not a sheerly *sociological* procedure to show how Faulkner's version of the South reflects an aspect of what the Marxists would call the "objective situation"? Again let me repeat, to avoid all possibility of misunderstanding: I am not complaining about such "situational" discussion as such. I am merely asking us to bear in mind that, whatever terms you use, we are here discussing literary *strategies* for confronting *situations*. Indeed, when discussing Charles Mallison's development in *Intruder in the Dust*, Mr. Brooks says (italics mine) that the boy's "vision is not an argument put forward by the author. *It is simply a fact, part of a cultural situation that has to be taken into account.*" Or consider this comment: "To call this passage 'literary, flamboyant, historically ridiculous in terms of America today' is simply beside the point. As a matter of fact there were plenty of Southern boys in the 1940's who felt this way— and there are still some in the Mississippi of 1963." Here he is saying in effect: "The passage has verisimilitude. It sounds plausible and convincing to me. And well it might, since it reflects the actual state of affairs in the social situation itself." In effect, Mr. Brooks here completes tendencies that showed as early as *The Well Wrought Urn* when he referred to "the 'syllogistic' strategies of Donne," and said that poetry "involves a coming to terms with situations."

But before I end this section I should add another admonition. I do not mean to imply that in his work on Faulkner Mr. Brooks has simply abandoned Formalist criticism. On the contrary, his book explicitly contains a great deal of excellent Formalist analysis; and there is much more that, with but slight revision, could be so stated as to bring out the Formalist element now partially obscured by accidents of emphasis. For one thing, Faulkner's own practice of using the same characters in various books can lead a critic to speak of them in a general way rather than with emphasis upon their specific formal function in the development of some particular plot. But whereas Mr. Brooks's view of *Absalom, Absalom!* as "a wonderful detective story" helps bring out the functional element in "the very special way in which the story of Sutpen is mediated to us through a series of partial disclosures, informed guesses, and constantly revised deductions and hypotheses," he fails to note the *liberties* that the method permits the author. Any stage of Sutpen's life that the author himself can't account for (a stage that Balzac, for instance, would have accounted for in detail but to which Faulkner's imagination was an "outsider") can merely be presented as confused unsubstantiated conjectures on the part of Shreve or Quentin.

To treat so many lacunae and ellipses as an example of the detective-story technique is to owe a profound apology to the spirit of Edgar Allen Poe. Actually, it is but one more variant of Faulkner's characteristic narrative device (the obtaining of progressive form not by first acquainting the audience with a situation and then letting them watch the unfolding of its implications, but by a gradual releasing of the information necessary for the audience to know what the situation actually is). Perhaps the device was used most functionally in *The Sound and the Fury*; for here the nature of the characters themselves through whom the story is disclosed helps account for the changing nature of the disclosures. A related device Faulkner employs to give a work progressive form is by telling the story through the developing insights of a person who is growing up.

But when Mr. Brooks writes of *Absalom, Absalom!* that the novel "has to do not merely with the meaning of Sutpen's career but with the nature of historical truth and with the problem of how we can 'know' the past," he comes pretty close to treating the work as an object lesson (a procedure that would require the admonitions I mentioned when on the subject of "pointing a moral").

My main point in this section, however, is to indicate Mr. Brooks's departures from Formalist canons, not as an objection to his methods, but simply to show how "reservations" that he applies to other critics might also apply to himself.

V
Related Remarks on Faulkner

Originally I had no intention of dealing with Faulkner in this discussion. I had thought only of worrying, in a secondary way, over the question of the Keats ode, as well as making a frank admission that whereas I thought I had given an ample internal analysis of the poem, I had also added a speculative dimension extrinsic to the demands of Formalist criticism. (Similarly, in the case of "The Ancient Mariner," along with my purely internal analysis of the poem considered as an act in and for itself, I had gone outside the field to discuss certain "perturbations" in this symbolic act which do not seem to me explainable in terms of Poetics alone, but which can be shown to have an explanation in terms of Coleridge's personal burdens.) But it turns out that some of the problems involved in Mr. Brooks's valuable study of Faulkner, and in Faulkner's own relation to his public, throw further light upon the whole question of Formalist criticism, particularly as regards its limitations. So I shall end on that subject, not in an argumentative mood, but purely in the attempt to see if I can bring out some diagnostic observations that I ran into along the way.

At the start let it be said: In my opinion, one should wholly agree with Mr. Brooks when he protests that no one particular character's speech in favor of the South and no one character's diatribe against the South can safely be taken to stand for Faulkner's personal position. If the issue as Faulkner saw it was not highly complex, he would never have written about it very interestingly in the first place. His "strategy" for handling that "situation" would have been no better than a piece of special pleading, either a sales talk or its flat opposite. Obviously, he wrote as complexly as he did because, to him, the situation seemed to call for so complicated a strategy. In this respect, his novels might best be viewed as narrative equivalents of a Platonic dialogue, to which even the crudest of the voices makes an indispensable contribution, regardless of objections raised by other voices. For when you add things up, all the voices are still there, in various ways needing one another if the author is to get the whole thing said—and they all go on being there, as long as the dialogue exists.

Above all, let's recognize it as a simple fact of literary life: Regardless of what a given regional situation might be, an author who uses it as material for a fiction might seek to entertain us by depicting characters some of whom act in that situation outrageously (if I may borrow a favorite Faulknerian term that he would have had a hard time doing without). The appeal of such a work will depend, among other things, upon the writer's ability to make us feel that the story rings true. That is, it will depend upon the work's *verisimilitude*, regardless of the degree to which such verisimilitude may correspond with the "actualities" of the given situation (when tested as a "reflection" of conditions prevailing outside the work).

Accordingly, the ironic fact is: The greater the verisimilitude in a novel that stresses its affinity with an actual region outside the confines of the book, the greater the "indictment" of that region might seem to be if the work happens to entertain by the depicting of corruption, violence, and similar disorders. Formalistically, we can sympathize with Mr. Brooks when he writes, "Faulkner is writing fiction, not sociology or history, and he has employed all the devices for heightening, special focus, and in some instances, distortion that fiction demands and justifies." But think what is implied in the very next sentence: "Still, the picture of the yeoman farmer and the poor white that emerges is perfectly consonant with the findings recorded in Owsley's history." The "distortions" are justified Formalistically, as resources natural to fiction; but insofar as some aspects of the work reflect what the writer who is here being cited with approval takes to correspond with an actual social or regional (or "provincial") situation outside the work (the sociological facts to which the work imaginatively alludes), a wholly non-Formalist criterion is introduced. Similarly, as regards the grotesque and savage comedy of Erskine Caldwell's *Tobacco Road* and *God's Little Acre*, one might conceivably employ as Formalist justification for such distortions the arguments we just saw Mr. Brooks proffering for distortion in Faulkner. Instead Mr. Brooks treats such resources in Caldwell as "gross oversimplification" of the extra literary situation. (Mr. Brooks applies the expression "grotesque and savage comedy" not to Caldwell but to Faulkner.)

Mr. Brooks once laid great stress upon the paradoxes of irony. Here is an ironic paradox involving the difference between a Formalist and a Regionalist approach to the novels of William Faulkner. An approach from the standpoint of "situations" and "strategies" in general (or, to employ synonyms I developed later, "actions" by "agents" in "scenes") allows for the introduction of further deviations from the strictly Formalistic, though as I have tried to show, such an approach lends itself well to treatment in terms of the strictest Poetics, as one dimension of a concern with the work's "symbolic action." As for the paradox of the Formalist-Regionalist pair (one stressing *form* for its own sake, the other stressing the independent validity of the nonpoetic *matter* the Regionalist adapts for poetic purposes), many examples could be offered. But let us consider one that can serve as a paradigm for the lot.

From the sheerly Formalistic point of view, we readily recognize that the theme of violence serves well as a narrator's device for bringing things to a point of crisis. Hence, imagery of violence is of great assistance in furthering the "entelechial" (or culminative) aspects of a plot.

Viewed psychologically (in terms of an "agent-act ratio," in the sense that the work is viewed as the symbolic act of its creator), a preference for the theme of violence might be analyzed in quite different ways (either as consistent with the personality of the author, in case he were known to be a violent man, or as compensatory to his nature as a private person, in case he were known to be personally either timid or peace-loving).

With regard to the "scene-act ratio" (which is to say, when the work is viewed as a response, in some form or other, to the conditions presented by life itself), the images of violence may properly be interpreted as either directly or indirectly reflecting the cultural situation from which the work arose, and to which it imaginatively or allusively may refer, beyond the confines of the page. Here, once again, we confront possible interpretations in terms of either the consistent or the compensatory. The violence may directly reflect conditions in the author's circumstances, or it may be in contrast with a daily life of great orderliness and quietude, or it may represent an imaginatively magnified replica of minor tantrums, or it may be a literary equivalent of gossip and the news (forms of expression which are untiring in the search for ways to season "human interest" stories), and so on.

Or the work may represent a convergence of many such motives—personal, cultural, and purely formal. But this much is certain: If you want to eliminate psychological and sociological kinds of speculation, you must not introduce *any* reference to the relation between the author and his work, or between his work and its possible reflection of his cultural situation. In brief, you must not relinquish in the slightest a wholly Formalist approach to your material. To adapt a title of Mr. Ransom's, the work must be treated not as "nearly anonymous" but "wholly anonymous." Otherwise, you have opened the floodgates, and have set up conditions that would allow people to ask, "Is there an 'aesthetic of alcohol' in Faulkner's style?" —or to see in the rhetoric of violence a compensation of some sort, or to ask whether he was unconsciously homosexual, or whatever. And, above all, you can't both talk about his books as a reflection of his society and ask that any extreme aspects of his representations be discounted purely on Formalist grounds. The implications of your own procedures will have undermined the supports for such categorical exclusions.

It is perfectly reasonable, on non-Formalist grounds, to introduce such considerations as Faulkner's statement that he considered himself a Christian. But Formalistically the only proper question is not whether or not he thought himself a Christian, but exactly how his books used religion for their particular poetic effects, regardless of what Faulkner said about his beliefs. Mr. Brooks does include many observations that would meet the specifically Formalist test here. (Obviously, for instance, the intenseness of which religion is capable makes it serve as readily as does violence or hubris in the building of characters that contribute vigorously to the dynamics of a plot.) But Mr. Brooks also touches upon Faulkner as a character and upon his books as a reflection of his relation to his religion. Whereas these are wholly legitimate things for critics to speculate about, they fall in the area that I would call not "Poetics in particular" but "Language in general." And if they are allowed in at all, then by the same token a critic cannot be said to have abandoned literary criticism simply because he has been *systematic* in attempting to confront the entire terministic situation involved in such problems. Certainly the issue is not resolved by Mr. Brooks when he is being sociological in the name of No Sociology. High among the ironies that turn up at such times is the fact that when Mr. Brooks stresses the importance of the "community" as a motivating factor in Faulkner's novels, he has hit upon the sociological motive par excellence.

However, though Faulkner is highly adept at transforming social *problems* into modes of aesthetic entertainment, he does not offer sociologically-minded *solutions*, but what we might rather call "mythic" or "archetypal" *resolutions*. Consider *Light in August*, for instance: The ritual emasculation of Joe Christmas (whose initials, despite Mr. Brooks's dislike of "symbol-mongering," do seem to fit the norms of "grotesque and savage comedy"); the twisted head of Joanna Burden; and in contrast, Lena's placid pilgrimage, or quest.

In Faulkner's case, might we be confronting a situation that almost inevitably involves (at least at this time in history) an invasion of Poetics by a problem in Rhetoric? For instance, whatever relevance Shakespeare's

Coriolanus may have had to conditions of his times in London, the play on its face was about factionalism in ancient Rome. Similarly, indications are that in *The Trojan Women* Euripides was alluding to a contemporary incident, the "outrageous" sack of Melos which the war party of Athens had engineered about six months before the production of the play; but the work itself got a kind of "distance" by treating of such issues in terms of "primal" Greek tradition, the sack of Troy.

Regionalist literature proceeds in a quite different manner. Its kind of "verisimilitude" is strongly influenced by modern, scientific concepts of realism, which have dispensed with much of the ritual in older forms (though some of Faulkner's stylistic mannerisms might be novelistic attempts to provide a substitute for such ritual—and let me note that here would be a purely *Formalist* explanation for the stylistics of violence I said might be studied in terms of *psychology*, with quite different results). Fiction is often made to look not just like an artistic "imitation," but rather as having the quality of a documentary "record." In contrast with Shakespeare's play about "Rome," or Euripides' play about "Troy," Regionalist literature is written as by someone who "was there"; hence, it has a suggestion of expert "field work."

Accordingly, if the author would entertain his public by trying to make his work seem *representative* of some region, and if at the same time—if only for formal reasons—he interweaves into his background some tales of violence, corruption, "outrage," he will necessarily confront a dilemma. For if his readers take his books at face value, and are outsiders ("outlanders"), they may irritate him by interpreting his books simply as an indictment. Yet, though he would like the "outlanders" to read his work and be persuaded by it, he must feel that they are like intruders in the dust of his homeland. For the true Regionalist does not write like an exile who has fled from his country and is appealing to the world against a regime that has it in bondage. Rather, the Regionalist is one who, at least in principle and in Faulkner's case in actuality, remains at home. Though he tries to make his plots look "real," he naturally resents it if critics of Marxist cast, or the sociologically-minded in general, look upon them simply as the "evidence" that (in a purely *poetic* sense) he strives to make them resemble. For many of his readers approach the work from the outside, whereas he had written it from the inside, with corresponding differences of attitude. Thus the books are like what Mr. Brooks aptly calls Charles Mallison's "lover's quarrel" with his neighbors; yet the nature of publication has in effect invited all the world to listen in.

When confronting reviews like the one by Edmund Wilson on *Intruder in the Dust*, Mr. Brooks incidentally reveals how the complications that beset Faulkner as an author were also reflected in the problem of an audience. The issue is worth dwelling on, because once again it helps indicate points at which the sheerly Formalistic approach to the books would, by

FURTHER ESSAYS ON SYMBOLISM IN GENERAL

fiat, rule out too much that needs close analysis on another plane. And Mr. Brooks's apparent attempt to persuade himself that his work is much more Formalistic than it is makes the discussion of all such issues unwieldy, if they are considered only in his terms.

Thus when he writes, "The author reconstructs for us what has gone on in the minds of the typical white man in this community," he is saying in effect that Faulkner has given us excellent sociological data, such as would be the envy of an expert field worker. And all such material should be recognized for what it is. Some of the uncertainty in Mr. Brooks's exposition is probably due to the fact that all of the works discussed in his earlier volume *The Well Wrought Urn* are poems, written under local conditions to which the critic was a comparative stranger. Here he is dealing with narrative prose that uses as its active background an extraliterary scene known to the critic intimately. The difference is so great, one can readily understand why Formalist criticism should fly out the window when Regionalist love comes in the door.[3]

---

[3] On p. 124 of *Intruder in the Dust* (paperback edition promising "Murder and Violence in a small Southern town") there is a passage that runs: "no grief to be remembered nor pity nor even awareness of shame, no vindication of the deathless aspiration of man by man to man through the catharsis of pity and shame. . . ." (In the Modern Library edition it is on pp. 192-93.) I was so struck by this, I keep gnawing at the thought: Just what is implied in the fact that "fear" in the famous Aristotelian formula here gets replaced by "shame"? If I but had the time, or could persuade someone to take the time! I know exactly what I'd do. Along the lines of my design in *The Rhetoric of Religion* (my "Cycle of Terms Implicit in the Idea of 'Order'"), I'd go to work on the *nomenclature* that obviously clusters around that moment. Pity, shame, rage, outrage, fury, anguish, vengeance, revenge, degradation, defiance, expiation, injustice, dishonor, ridicule, conscience, compassion, repudiation—thence into related thing-words: dust, blood, outlanders, black abyss, "black vault of his anguish," money—and so on, outwards to the way in which the genius of the terministic cycle manifests itself in dramatis personae and plot and style. The cycle of terms would be a directionless "chart" (with apologies to Mr. Wellek), but the note-taking would be done throughout while having in mind ultimate tests of novelistic form.

And perhaps, along with such confronting of an author's nomenclature, we might consider another possibility. In keeping with my speculations on "perspective by incongruity" (in the middle section of *Permanence and Change*), I keep wondering whether, as regards Coleridge's distinction between "imagination" and "fancy," we might view the "fancy" side of the pair as steadily on the rise from his day through Baudelaire, Rimbaud, French Symbolism, Futurism, Cubism, Surrealism, and various contemporary tinkerings with abstract art, anti-drama, anti-poem, anti-novel, etc. The ultimate paradox of such a thought would be the likelihood that Coleridge's own dream-poem "Kubla Khan" might better be viewed not just along Lowes' lines as an instance of "imagination," but also as a momentous step forward toward the rise in the embodiment of "fancy," if not the explicit recognition of a rise in its prestige. (An earlier form had perhaps been operating in the literature of "wit.") I had such speculations in the back of my mind when I wrote the previously mentioned review of the Brooks-Wimsatt volume, *Literary Criticism: A Short History* along with Northrop Frye's *Anatomy of Criticism*. (See "The Encyclopaedic, Two Kinds of," in *Poetry*, February, 1958.)

Index